Sixth Edition

S. A. Hummelbrunner
K. Suzanne Coombs
Kwantlen University College

**Contributing Author**
Bruce Coombs Kwantlen University College

# Mathematics of Finance
## with Canadian Applications

D1450322

PEARSON

Prentice
Hall

Toronto

**Library and Archives Canada Cataloguing in Publication**

Hummelbrunner, S. A. (Siegfried August)
 Mathematics of finance with Canadian applications /
S. A. Hummelbrunner, K. Suzanne Coombs. — 6th ed.

Includes index.
ISBN-13: 978-0-13-206895-6
ISBN-10:    0-13-206895-8

1. Business mathematics—Textbooks.    I. Coombs, Suzanne    II. Title.

HF5691.H86 2008        650.01'513        C2007-902869-1

BAII PLUS is a trademark of Texas Instruments Incorporated.
EL-733A is a trademark of Sharp Corporation.
HP-10B Business Calculator is a trademark of Hewlett-Packard Company.

ISBN-13: 978-0-13-206895-6
ISBN-10:    0-13-206895-8

Editor-in-Chief: Gary Bennett
Executive Editor: Samantha Scully
Executive Marketing Manager: Cas Shields
Developmental Editor: Madhu Ranadive
Production Editor: Cheryl Jackson
Copy Editor: Rodney Rawlings
Proofreader: Betty Robinson
Production Coordinator: Avinash Chandra
Compositor: Integra
Permissions Researcher: Lisa Brant
Art Director: Julia Hall
Cover and Interior Design: Anthony Leung
Cover Image: Masterfile

1  2  3  4  5      11  10  09  08  07

Printed and bound in the United States.

# NOTE TO USERS OF *MATHEMATICS OF FINANCE*, SIXTH EDITION

The pagination in *Mathematics of Finance*, Sixth Edition, remains unchanged from *Contemporary Business Mathematics*, Eighth Edition, by S. A. Hummelbrunner and K. Suzanne Coombs. For this reason, this book begins on page 177, Chapter 5 (Trade Discount, Cash Discount, Markup, and Markdown). There is also a break in the chapter sequence between chapters 5 and 7. The new numbering sequence for this edition makes it easier for users of *Math of Finance* to draw on all the supplements offered with *Contemporary Business Mathematics*, Eighth Edition. Most significantly, it will give *Math of Finance* users easy reference to the MyMathLab online tool created for *Contemporary Business Mathematics with Canadian Applications*, Eighth Edition.

# BRIEF CONTENTS

**Spreadsheet Template Disk**
* Introduction to Excel Functions and Templates
* Self-contained tutorials that show how to use one of Excel's special
  spreadsheet functions to solve business problems
* Excel Functions Spreadsheet Templates
* Excel Templates for Examples from the Text
* Appendix: Finding the Rate of Interest ($i$) without Preprogramming

# CONTENTS

**Spreadsheet Template Disk**
- Introduction to Excel Functions and Templates
- Self-contained tutorials that show how to use one of Excel's special spreadsheet functions to solve business problems
- Excel Functions Spreadsheet Templates
- Excel Templates for Examples from the Text
- Appendix: Finding the Rate of Interest (*i*) without Preprogramming

# PREFACE

## INTRODUCTION

*Mathematics of Finance* is intended for use in introductory mathematics of finance courses in business administration and accounting programs. In a more general application it also provides a comprehensive basis for those who wish to review and extend their understanding of basic business mathematics.

The primary objective of the text is to increase the student's knowledge and skill in the solution of practical financial and mathematical problems encountered in the business community. It also provides a supportive base for mathematical topics in finance, accounting, and marketing.

## ORGANIZATION

*Mathematics of Finance* is a teaching text using the objectives approach. The systematic and sequential development of the material is supported by carefully selected and worked examples. These detailed step-by-step solutions presented in a clear and colourful layout are particularly helpful in allowing students, in either independent studies or in the traditional classroom setting, to carefully monitor their own progress.

Each topic in each chapter is followed by an Exercise containing numerous drill questions and application problems. The Review Exercises, Self-Tests, and the Case Studies at the end of each chapter integrate the material studied.

The text is based on Canadian practice and reflects current trends using available technology—specifically the availability of reasonably priced electronic pocket calculators. Students using this book should have access to electronic calculators having a power function and a natural logarithm function. The use of such calculators eliminates the arithmetic constraints often associated with financial problems and frees the student from reliance on financial tables.

The power function and the natural logarithm function are often needed to determine values that will be used for further computation. Such values should not be rounded and all available digits should be retained. The student is encouraged to use the memory functions of the calculator to retain such values.

When using the memory the student needs to be aware that the number of digits retained in the registers of the calculator is greater than the number of digits displayed. Depending on whether the memory or the displayed digits are used, slight differences may occur. Such differences will undoubtedly be encountered when working through the examples presented in the text. However, they are insignificant and should not be of concern. In most cases the final answers will agree, whichever method is used.

Students are encouraged to use preprogrammed financial calculators, though this is not essential. The use of preprogrammed calculators facilitates the solving of most financial problems and is demonstrated extensively in Chapters 9 to 16.

## NEW TO THIS EDITION

In this sixth edition, revisions and updates have been made to the text to reflect current practices in Canada and to better suit the needs of users of this book. Examples and exercises have been updated, rewritten, and expanded. To expand the building-block approach, exercises have been reordered to represent a link with the solved examples. Example references have been added to link selected exercises to solved examples.

In Chapter 5 (Trade Discount, Cash Discount, Markup, and Markdown), coverage of partial payments and integrated problems has been expanded using the building-block process to explain. Many new exercises have been added in both chapters.

In Chapter 7 (Simple Interest), the section on finding the principal has been clarified and simplified. Again, using the building-block approach, the coverage of equivalent values now includes more simplified solved examples, and many new exercises have been added.

In Chapter 8 (Simple Interest Applications), coverage of promissory notes has been simplified. Additional coverage of home equity lines of credit has been included.

In Chapter 9 (Compound Interest—Future Value and Present Value) and Chapter 10 (Compound Interest—Further Topics), solved examples have been clarified using a step-by-step approach. Updated examples and exercises and comparison questions have been added.

In Chapters 11, 12, and 13, examples and exercises have been updated, and comparison questions and exercises have been added. A new section on Constant-Growth Annuities has been added to Chapter 12.

In Chapter 13, coverage of deferred ordinary annuities and deferred annuities due has been separated with stand-alone sections. Further explanation for perpetuities has been included. Many new exercise questions have been added in all three chapters, as well as additional calculator solutions.

Chapter 14 includes updated information on CMHC mortgage insurance.

In Chapter 15, bond terminology and calculations have been updated and simplified. Bond interest rates in examples and exercises have been updated.

In general, interest rates used reflect the current economic climate in Canada. Calculator tips and solutions have been updated or clarified. Spreadsheet instructions and Internet site references have been updated. *Pitfalls and Pointers* have been included to assist in performing tasks and interpreting word problems, and sections have been rewritten to clarify the explanations. Many more word problems have been added and references to solved examples have been added. All *Business Math News Boxes* are new or revised and the Case Studies have been updated. Examples involving both business and personal situations are included. Where appropriate, the use of six decimal places has been standardized. The pedagogical elements of the previous edition have been retained. In response to requests and suggestions by users of the book, a number of new features for this edition have been included. They are described below.

## CHAPTER NUMBERING IN *MATHEMATICS OF FINANCE*, SIXTH EDITION

*Mathematics of Finance,* Sixth Edition, is based on Chapters 5 and 7 to 16 of *Contemporary Business Mathematics with Canadian Applications,* Eighth Edition, by S. A. Hummelbrunner and K. Suzanne Coombs. In order to make the powerful MyMathLab online tool available to students and instructors of both texts, chapter numbers and pagination have not been changed between the two books. For this reason, this book begins on page 177, Chapter 5 (Trade Discount, Cash Discount, Markup, and Markdown). There is also a break in the chapter number sequence between Chapters 5 and 7. The new numbering for this edition allows users of *Mathematics of Finance* to easily access all the supplements available for *Contemporary Business Mathematics,* Eighth Edition.

## FEATURES

- A colourful and student-friendly design has been created for the book, making it more accessible and less intimidating to learners at all levels.
- Any preprogrammed financial calculator may be used, but this edition includes extensive instructions for using the Texas Instruments BA II Plus financial calculator. Equivalent instructions are given in Appendix II for the Sharp EL-733A and the Hewlett Packard 10B financial calculators.

- To reduce the amount of "translation" required to go from the formulas in the text to the keystrokes on the preprogrammed financial calculator, the compounding and annuity formulas in Chapters 9 to 16 have been restated in this edition. From the beginning of Chapter 9, the P has been replaced with PV, S has been replaced with FV, and A has been replaced with PMT in these formulas. In addition, the compounding interval, C/Y, has been identified within the calculator solutions.

- An updated Spreadsheet Template Disk has been developed by Bruce Coombs. It is a CD-ROM that accompanies the text and contains Word files and Excel spreadsheet files. It requires Windows XP or newer versions of Windows to run. The disk contains 24 self-contained tutorials that show how to use one of Excel's special spreadsheet functions to solve business problems. Each tutorial gives a brief description of the function, a general example showing how the function might be used, directions for creating a spreadsheet template to use the function, and a list of questions from the text that can be answered using the spreadsheet function. In addition, an Excel file containing ready-to-use examples of each function is included. The student can use these spreadsheets to enter values and obtain immediate results. The Spreadsheet Template Disk also contains spreadsheet templates for the spreadsheet applications described in the text: loan repayment schedules (Chapter 8), accumulation of principal schedules (Chapter 9), amortization schedules (Chapter 14), and sinking fund schedules (Chapter 15). An Excel icon in the text highlights information on the use of Excel to solve problems and the Excel spreadsheet applications, directing students to the spreadsheet template disk.

• A spreadsheet icon in the text highlights the questions in the text that can be solved using an Excel spreadsheet function. An appendix, *Finding the Rate of Interest* (i) *Without Preprogramming,* is also included on the Spreadsheet Template Disk.

• A set of learning objectives is listed at the beginning of each chapter.

• Each chapter opens with a description of a situation familiar to students to emphasize the practical applications of the material to follow.

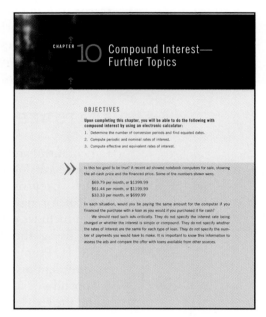

• A *Business Math News Box* is presented in every chapter. This element consists of short excerpts based on material appearing in newspapers, magazines, or websites, followed by a set of questions. These boxes demonstrate how widespread business math applications are in the real world. All of the *Business Math News Boxes* are new or completely revised in this sixth edition.

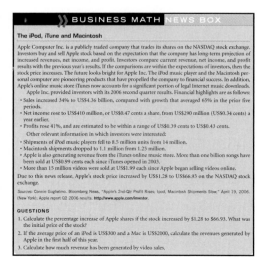

- The *Pointers and Pitfalls* boxes emphasize good practices, highlight ways to avoid common errors, show how to use a financial calculator efficiently, or give hints for tackling business math situations to reduce math anxiety.

- Numerous Examples with worked-out Solutions are provided throughout the book, offering easy-to-follow, step-by-step instructions.

- Programmed solutions using the Texas Instruments BA II Plus calculator are offered for all examples in Chapters 9 to 16. Since this calculator display can be pre-set, it is suggested that the learner set the display to show six decimal places to match the mathematical calculations in the body of the text. Both mathematical and calculator solutions for all Exercises, Review Exercises, and Self-Tests are included in the Instructor's Solutions Manual. An icon highlights information on the use of the BA II Plus calculator.

- Key Terms are introduced in the text in boldface type. A Glossary at the end of each chapter lists each term with its definition and a page reference to where the term was first defined in the chapter.

- Main Equations are highlighted in the chapters and repeated in a Summary of Formulas at the ends of the chapters. Each main formula is presented in colour and labelled numerically (with the letter A suffix if equivalent forms of the formula are presented later). By contrast, equivalent formulae are presented in black and labelled with the number of the related main formula followed by the letter B or C.

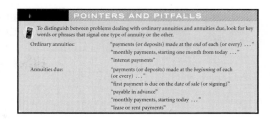

**POINTERS AND PITFALLS**

To distinguish between problems dealing with ordinary annuities and annuities due, look for key words or phrases that signal one type of annuity or the other.

| Ordinary annuities: | "payments (or deposits) made at the *end* of each (or every) ..." |
| | "monthly payments, starting one month from today ..." |
| | "interest payments" |
| Annuities due: | "payments (or deposits) made at the *beginning* of each (or every) ..." |
| | "first payment is due on the date of sale (or signing)" |
| | "payable in advance" |
| | "monthly payments, starting today ..." |
| | "lease or rent payments" |

---

**EXAMPLE 5.1C**  Find the rate of discount for

(i) skis listed at $280 less a discount of $67.20;

(ii) ski gloves listed at $36.80 whose net price is $23.92;

(iii) ski sweaters whose net price is $55.68 after a discount of $40.32.

**SOLUTION**

(i) Rate of discount = $\dfrac{\text{Amount of discount}}{\text{List price}} = \dfrac{67.20}{280.00} = 0.24 = 24\%$

(ii) Since Net price = List price − Amount of discount (Formula 5.2),
   Amount of discount = List price − Net price = 36.80 − 23.92 = $12.88
   Rate of discount = $\dfrac{\text{Amount of discount}}{\text{List price}} = \dfrac{12.88}{36.80} = 0.35 = 35\%$

(iii) Since Net price = List price − Amount of discount (Formula 5.2),
   List price = Net price + Amount of discount = 55.68 + 40.32 = $96.00
   Rate of discount = $\dfrac{\text{Amount of discount}}{\text{List price}} = \dfrac{40.32}{96.00} = 0.42 = 42\%$

---

## 11.1 INTRODUCTION TO ANNUITIES

### A. Basic concepts

An **annuity** is a series of payments, usually of equal size, made at periodic intervals. The length of time between the successive payments is called the **payment interval** or **payment period**. The length of time from the beginning of the first payment interval to the end of the last payment interval is called the **term of an annuity**. The size of each of the regular payments is the **periodic rent**, and the sum of the periodic payments in one year is the **annual rent**.

---

### GLOSSARY

**Blended payments** equal periodic payments that include payment of interest and repayment of principal, usually paid by individuals to financial institutions (p. 283)

**Dated value** the value of a sum of money at a specific time relative to its due date, including interest (p. 273)

**Equation of values** the equation obtained when matching the dated values of the original payments at an agreed focal date to the dated values of the replacement payments at the same focal date (p. 279)

**Equivalent value** see **Dated value**

**Focal date** a specific time chosen to compare the time value of one or more dated sums of money (p. 274)

**Future value of a sum of money** the value obtained when the amount of interest is added to the original principal (p. 266)

**Interest** rent paid for the use of money (p. 257)

**Interest period** the time period for which interest is charged (p. 257)

**Maturity value** see **Future value of a sum of money**

**Nominal rate** the yearly or annual rate of interest charged on the principal of a loan (p. 257)

**Present value** the principal that grows to a given future value (maturity value) over a given period of time at a given rate of interest (p. 269)

**Simple interest** interest calculated on the original principal by the formula I = Prr, and paid only when the principal is repaid (p. 257)

**Time value of money** a concept of money value that allows for a change in the value of a sum of money over time if the sum of money is subject to a rate of interest (p. 269)

---

$$\dfrac{\text{NET PRICE}}{\text{FACTOR (NPF)}} = 100\% - \% \text{ DISCOUNT} \qquad \text{Formula 5.3A}$$

The resulting relationship between net price and list price may be stated generally.

$$\text{NET PRICE} = \dfrac{\text{NET PRICE}}{\text{FACTOR (NPF)}} \times \text{LIST PRICE} \qquad \text{Formula 5.4A}$$

The two relationships represented by Formulas 5.3A and 5.4A can be restated in algebraic terms:

Convert the % discount into its decimal equivalent represented by $d$ and express 100% by its decimal equivalent 1.

$$\text{NET PRICE FACTOR} = 1 - d \qquad \text{Formula 5.3B}$$

Let the list price be represented by L and let the net price be represented by N.

$$N = (1 - d)L \quad \text{or} \quad N = L(1 - d) \qquad \text{Formula 5.4B}$$

- A list of the Main Formulas can be found on the study card bound into this text.

- An Exercise set is provided at the end of each section in every chapter. If students choose, they can use the suggested Excel spreadsheet functions to answer those questions marked with the spreadsheet logo. In addition, each chapter contains a Review Exercise set and a Self-Test. If students choose, they can use an Excel spreadsheet function to answer those questions marked with a spreadsheet logo, but they must decide which function to use. Answers to all the odd-numbered Exercises, Review Exercises, and Self-Tests are given at the back of the book. Solutions for questions answered using Excel spreadsheet functions are given in the Instructor's area of the Hummelbrunner/Coombs Companion Website.

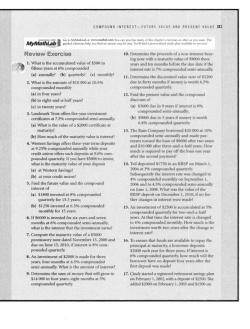

- New to this edition are references to solved Examples from the chapter, which are included at the end of key exercises. Students are directed to specific examples so they can check their work and review fundamental problem types.

- A set of Challenge Problems is provided in each chapter. These problems give users the opportunity to apply the skills learned in the chapter to questions that are pitched at a higher level than the Exercises.

- Thirty-two Case Studies are included in the book, two near the end of each chapter. They present comprehensive realistic

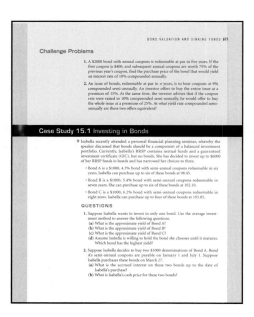

scenarios followed by a set of questions and illustrate some of the important types of practical applications of the chapter material. All of the Case Studies are new or revised in this sixth edition.

- An updated set of Useful Internet Sites is provided at the end of each chapter, with the URL and a brief description provided for each site. These sites are related to the chapter topic or to companies mentioned in the chapter, or they show how business math is important to the day-to-day operations of companies and industries.

| USEFUL INTERNET SITES | |
|---|---|
| | **www.electronicaccountant.com** |
| **Electronic Accountant** | Free access to news and critical accounting industry information. This site includes Newswire, links and commentary, discussion groups, feature articles, and accounting/tax software exhibit halls. |
| | **www.ibc.ca** |
| **Insurance Bureau of Canada** | This site offers an overview of the industry and of recent legal and consumer-related developments and provides significant links to both business and government sites. |

## SUPPLEMENTS

The following supplements have been carefully prepared to accompany this sixth edition.

- An **Instructor's Solutions Manual** provides complete mathematical and calculator solutions to all the Exercises, Review Exercises, Self-Tests, Business Math News Box questions, Challenge Problems, and Case Studies in the textbook. The Instructor's Solutions Manual can be downloaded from the Pearson Education Canada password-protected online catalogue.
- A **Companion Website** provides students with self-test questions that include Case Studies, Multiple Choice, Fill-in-the-Blank, True/False, and Internet-based Exercises. Hints are included for most of the questions, and immediate feedback is available to assist students to study and test themselves. Did You Know? boxes are available for each chapter and offer interesting practical and mathematical facts. Links to other websites of interest and an Internet search of key business math terms have been updated for the eighth edition. Visit the Hummelbrunner/Coombs website at **www.pearsoned.ca/hummelbrunner** and then click on the *Mathematics of Finance with Canadian Applications*, Sixth Edition, cover.

   Also available to instructors who adopt *Mathematics of Finance,* Sixth Edition, is the Instructor's Resource CD-ROM that accompanies *Contemporary Business Mathematics,* Eighth Edition. It includes the Instructor's Solutions Manual in PDF format, Instructor's Resource Manual, PowerPoint® Lecture Slides, Test Generator, and Personal Response System questions. Instructions for accessing each item are available on the CD-ROM.

## MYMATHLAB

MyMathLab is a powerful online homework, tutorial, and assessment system tied directly to *Contemporary Business Mathematics*, Eighth Edition. Students using *Mathematics of Finance* can also access the chapters related to their text in MyMathLab. Ideal for use in a lecture, self-paced, or distance-learning course, MyMathLab

- Diagnoses students' weaknesses and creates a personalized study plan based on their test results.
- Provides students with unlimited practice using a database of algorithmically generated exercises correlated to the exercises in the textbook.
- Offers an interactive guided solution and a sample problem with each tutorial exercise, to help students improve their skills independently.
- Includes an interactive eBook that links directly to supplemental multimedia resources such as Excel spreadsheet templates.
- Provides narrated, animated PowerPoints to reinforce core concepts.

Instructors can use MyMathLab to create online homework assignments, quizzes, and tests that are automatically graded and tracked. Instructors can view and manage all students' homework and test results, study plans, and tutorial work in MyMathLab's flexible online Gradebook.

To learn more about how MyMathLab can enhance the use of *Mathematics of Finance* and to learn how instructors and students can access this material, please contact your Pearson Education Canada Sales and Editorial Representative.

## ACKNOWLEDGMENTS

Special thanks must be given to Bruce M. Coombs of Kwantlen University College for his help in creating and updating the Spreadsheet Template Disk and the Companion Website. His encouraging contribution was invaluable. Also, great thanks go to a new author, Sepand Jazzi, also of Kwantlen University College, who contributed the Business Math News Boxes and Case Studies.

We would like to express our thanks to the many people who offered thoughtful suggestions and recommendations for updating and improving the book. We would particularly like to thank the following instructors for providing formal reviews:

Peter Au, George Brown College
Helen Catania, Centennial College
Hoshiar Gosal, Langara College
Chris Kellman, British Columbia Institute of Technology
Lisa MacKay, Southern Alberta Institute of Technology
Judith I. Palm, Malaspina University-College
Raina Rudko-Buac, Grant MacEwan College
Don St. Jean, George Brown College
Brian Tozer, Conestoga College

We would also like to thank the many people at Pearson Education Canada who helped with the development and production of this book, especially to the production editor, Cheryl Jackson; the production coordinator, Avinash Chandra; the copy editor, Rodney Rawlings; the proofreader, Betty Robinson; and to Dorothy Kubsch, who completed a technical check of the entire manuscript. Special thanks to editors Samantha Scully and Madhu Ranadive for their supportive directions.

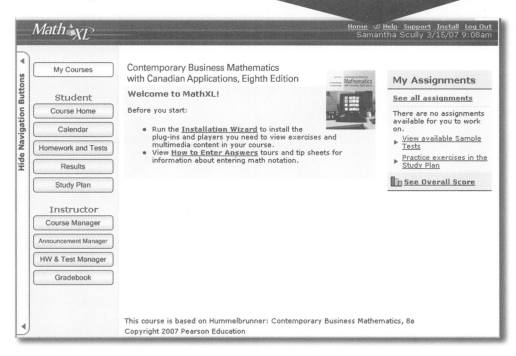

*powered by CourseCompass™ and MathXL®*

# MyMathLab

Access to MyMathLab is packaged at no extra cost with every new copy of *Mathematics of Finance* and *Contemporary Business Mathematics with Canadian Applications*. MyMathLab is a powerful new tool that

- lets you identify your strengths and weaknesses using a diagnostic test and develops a personalized study plan for you that's keyed to your text

- provides you with exercises and problems, using an algorithmic engine that allows you to practise problems over and over again using different examples

- includes a brief animated video about the concepts explained in each chapter

- and more

MyMathLab, *Contemporary Business Mathematics*, Eighth Edition, is also easy to use for students of *Mathematics of Finance*, Sixth Edition.

You'll feel like you're back in class when you're doing your homework!

MyMathLab is powered by MathXL — go to **www.mathxl.com** to log in and get started!

# Trade Discount, Cash Discount, Markup, and Markdown

## OBJECTIVES

**Upon completing this chapter, you will be able to do the following:**

1. Solve problems involving trade discounts.
2. Calculate equivalent single rates of discount for discount series and solve problems involving discount series.
3. Apply the three most commonly used methods of cash discount.
4. Solve problems involving markup based on either cost or selling price.
5. Solve problems involving markdown.
6. Solve integrated problems involving discounts, markup, and markdown.

Suppose you are the owner of a bicycle manufacturing company. You purchase your raw materials from suppliers, who offer their goods to you at a list, or catalogue, price. You might receive a trade discount if you pay for the materials promptly or if you purchase the materials in bulk. When you sell your bicycles to bicycle retailers, you offer your bicycles at a list, or catalogue, price, and you might offer a discount for prompt payment or bulk purchases. As you can see, we need to be careful, since the same terms are used by different companies to represent different dollar amounts.

# INTRODUCTION

A product typically passes through a number of stages of the *merchandising chain* on its way from being a raw material to a finished product purchased by the consumer.

A simple merchandising chain may include manufacturers, wholesalers, and retailers, all of whom must make a profit on the product to remain in business. As the product is purchased and resold along the chain, each merchandiser adds a *markup* above their cost to buy the merchandise, which increases the price of the product. Sometimes a merchandiser sets a *list price*, and then offers a discount from that price in order to sell more of their product or to encourage prompt payment for the product. When the product is sold to the consumer, the regular selling price may be *marked down* to a sale price in response to competitors' prices or other economic conditions.

This chapter deals with trade discount, cash discount, markup, and markdown. These may apply to any of the stages within the merchandising chain.

As you make your way through the merchandising chain, you will find many of the same terms used to represent different things, depending on where you are in the chain. As shown in Figure 5.1, the terms *markup*, *list price*, and *trade discount* are used throughout the merchandising chain.

If you are a manufacturer or supplier, you might mark up an item to create a list, or catalogue, price. If you want to sell the item to a wholesaler for less than that list price, you might offer a trade discount or a series of trade discounts. The wholesaler would add a markup to create a list price at which it offers the item to the retailer. The wholesaler might offer the retailer a trade discount to sell the item for less than the list price. The retailer would then add a markup and offer the item

---

**FIGURE 5.1** **Terminology Used in the Merchandising Chain**

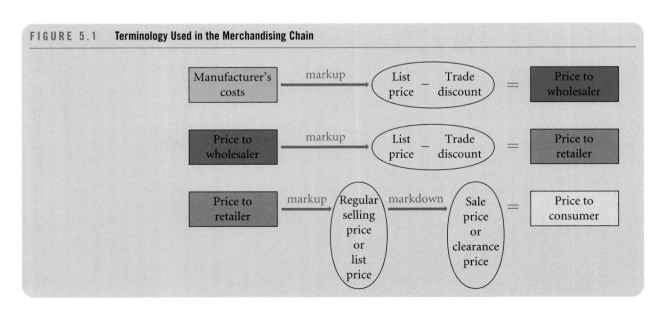

to the consumer at a regular selling price, or list price. The retailer might then offer a markdown on the item to sell the item for less than the regular selling price.

For any particular situation, first identify where you are in the merchandising chain. You will then be able to understand and apply these terms correctly.

# 5.1 TRADE DISCOUNTS

## A. Computing discount amount, discount rate, net price, and list price

The merchandising chain is made up of manufacturers, distributors, wholesalers, and retailers. Merchandise is usually bought and sold among these members of the chain on credit terms. The prices quoted to other members often involve *trade discounts*. A **trade discount** is a reduction of a catalogue or **list price** or **manufacturer's suggested retail price (MSRP)** and is usually stated as a percent of the list price or MSRP. For example, an item with a list price of $35 may be sold at a trade discount of 40%.

Trade discounts are used by manufacturers, wholesalers, and distributors as pricing tools for a number of reasons. The most important reasons are

**(a)** to facilitate the establishment of price differentials for different groups of customers;.
**(b)** to facilitate the communication of changes in prices;
**(c)** to reduce the cost of making changes in prices in published catalogues.

When computing trade discounts, keep in mind that the **rate of discount** is based on the list price.

$$\text{AMOUNT OF DISCOUNT} = \text{RATE OF DISCOUNT} \times \text{LIST PRICE} \quad \text{------ Formula 5.1A}$$

The amount of discount is then subtracted from the list price. The remainder is the **net price**.

$$\text{NET PRICE} = \text{LIST PRICE} - \text{AMOUNT OF DISCOUNT} \quad \text{------ Formula 5.2}$$

To compute the amount of the discount and the net price when the list price and discount rate are known, apply Formula 5.1A to determine the amount of the trade discount, then apply Formula 5.2 to calculate the net price.

**EXAMPLE 5.1A**   An item listed at $80 is subject to a trade discount of 25%.
Compute

(i) the amount of discount;

(ii) the net price.

**SOLUTION**

(i) Amount of trade discount = Rate of discount × List price
$$= (0.25)(80.00) = \$20.00$$

(ii) Net price = List price − Trade discount
$$= 80.00 - 20.00 = \$60.00$$

To compute the list price and net price when the discount rate and discount amount are known, rearrange Formula 5.1A to determine the list price, then rearrange Formula 5.2 to determine the net price.

$$\text{LIST PRICE} = \frac{\text{AMOUNT OF DISCOUNT}}{\text{RATE OF DISCOUNT}}$$ ——————— Formula 5.1B

**EXAMPLE 5.1B**

The 30% discount on a tennis racket amounts to $28.98.
Compute

(i) the list price;

(ii) the net price.

**SOLUTION**

(i) List price = $\dfrac{\text{Amount of discount}}{\text{Rate of discount}} = \dfrac{28.98}{0.30} = \$96.60$

(ii) Net price = List price − Amount of discount
$$= 96.60 - 28.98 = \$67.62$$

Since the rate of trade discount is based on a list price, computing a rate of discount involves comparing the amount of discount to the list price.

$$\text{RATE OF TRADE DISCOUNT} = \frac{\text{AMOUNT OF DISCOUNT}}{\text{LIST PRICE}}$$ ——————— Formula 5.1C

**EXAMPLE 5.1C**

Find the rate of discount for

(i) skis listed at $280 less a discount of $67.20;

(ii) ski gloves listed at $36.80 whose net price is $23.92;

(iii) ski sweaters whose net price is $55.68 after a discount of $40.32.

**SOLUTION**

(i) Rate of discount = $\dfrac{\text{Amount of discount}}{\text{List price}} = \dfrac{67.20}{280.00} = 0.24 = 24\%$

(ii) Since Net price = List price − Amount of discount (Formula 5.2),
Amount of discount = List price − Net price = 36.80 − 23.92 = $12.88

Rate of discount = $\dfrac{\text{Amount of discount}}{\text{List price}} = \dfrac{12.88}{36.80} = 0.35 = 35\%$

(iii) Since Net price = List price − Amount of discount (Formula 5.2),
List price = Net price + Amount of discount = 55.68 + 40.32 = $96.00

Rate of discount = $\dfrac{\text{Amount of discount}}{\text{List price}} = \dfrac{40.32}{96.00} = 0.42 = 42\%$

# B. The net price factor approach

Instead of computing the amount of discount and then deducting this amount from the list price, the net price can be found by using the more efficient net factor approach developed in the following illustration.

Referring back to Example 5.1A, the solution can be restated as follows:

| | |
|---|---:|
| List price | $80.00 |
| Less trade discount 25% of 80.00 | 20.00 |
| Net price | $60.00 |

Since the discount is given as a percent of the list price, the three dollar values may be stated as percents of list price:

| | | |
|---|---|---|
| List price | $80.00 ⟶ | 100% of list price |
| Less trade discount | 20.00 ⟶ | 25% of list price |
| Net price | $60.00 ⟶ | 75% of list price |

*Note:* The resulting "75%" is called the **net price factor** or **net factor** (in abbreviated form **NPF**) and is obtained by deducting the 25% discount from 100%.

$$\boxed{\text{NET PRICE FACTOR (NPF)} = 100\% - \% \text{ DISCOUNT}} \qquad \text{——————— Formula 5.3A}$$

The resulting relationship between net price and list price may be stated generally.

$$\boxed{\text{NET PRICE} = \text{NET PRICE FACTOR (NPF)} \times \text{LIST PRICE}} \qquad \text{——————— Formula 5.4A}$$

The two relationships represented by Formulas 5.3A and 5.4A can be restated in algebraic terms:

Convert the % discount into its decimal equivalent represented by $d$ and express 100% by its decimal equivalent 1.

$$\boxed{\text{NET PRICE FACTOR} = 1 - d} \qquad \text{——————— Formula 5.3B}$$

Let the list price be represented by L and let the net price be represented by N.

$$\boxed{N = (1 - d)L \quad \text{or} \quad N = L(1 - d)} \qquad \text{——————— Formula 5.4B}$$

**EXAMPLE 5.1D**

Find the net price for

(i) list price $36.00 less 15%;

(ii) list price $86.85 less $33\frac{1}{3}$%.

**SOLUTION**

(i) Net price = Net price factor × List price —— using Formula 5.4A
$= (100\% - 15\%)(36.00)$ ——————— using Formula 5.3A
$= (85\%)(36)$ ——————————— subtract
$= (0.85)(36)$ ——————————— convert the percent into a decimal
$= \$30.60$

$$\begin{aligned}
\text{(ii) Net price} &= (100\% - 33\tfrac{1}{3}\%)(86.85) \quad\text{——— using Formula 5.3A} \\
&= (66\tfrac{2}{3}\%)(86.85) \\
&= (0.666667)(86.85) \quad\text{——————— use a sufficient number of decimals} \\
&= \$57.90
\end{aligned}$$

**EXAMPLE 5.1E**

A manufacturer can cover its cost and make a reasonable profit if it sells an article for $63.70. At what price should the article be listed so that a discount of 30% can be allowed?

**SOLUTION**

Let the list price be represented by $L. The net price factor is
$1 - d = 100\% - 30\% = 70\% = 0.70$ and the net price is $63.70.
$63.70 = 0.70L$ ————————————————————— using Formula 5.4A

$$L = \frac{63.70}{0.70} = \$91.00$$

The article should be listed at $91.

## C. Discount series

A manufacturer may offer two or more **discounts** to different members of the merchandising chain. If a list price is subject to two or more discounts, these discounts are called a **discount series**. For example, a chain member closest to the consumer might be offered additional discounts, if there are fewer chain members who must make a profit on an item. If the manufacturer wants to encourage large-volume orders or early orders of seasonal items, it may offer additional discounts. For example, a manufacturer might offer a store a 5% discount on orders over 1000 items and an additional discount of 6% for ordering Christmas items in April. It may also offer additional discounts to compensate for advertising, promotion, and service costs handled by merchandising chain members.

When computing the net price, the discounts making up the discount series are applied to the list price successively. The net price resulting from the first discount becomes the list price for the second discount; the net price resulting from the second discount becomes the list price for the third discount; and so on. In fact, finding the net price when a list price is subject to a discount series consists of solving as many discount problems as there are discounts in the discount series.

**EXAMPLE 5.1F**

An item listed at $150 is subject to the discount series 20%, 10%, 5%. Determine the net price.

**SOLUTION**

| | | |
|---|---:|---|
| List price | $150.00 | ⎫ Problem 1 |
| Less first discount 20% of 150.00 | 30.00 | ⎭ |
| Net price after first discount | $120.00 | ⎫ Problem 2 |
| Less second discount 10% of 120.00 | 12.00 | ⎭ |
| Net price after second discount | $108.00 | ⎫ Problem 3 |
| Less third discount 5% of 108.00 | 5.40 | ⎭ |
| Net price | $102.60 | |

Because the solution to Example 5.1F consists of three problems involving a simple discount, the net price factor approach can be used to solve it or any problem involving a series of discounts.

*Problem 1* Net price after the first discount

$$= \text{NPF for 20\% discount} \times \text{Original list price}$$
$$= (1 - 0.20)(150.00)$$
$$= (0.80)(150.00)$$
$$= \$120.00$$

*Problem 2* Net price after the second discount

$$= \text{NPF for 10\% discount} \times \text{Net price after the first discount}$$
$$= (1 - 0.10)(120.00)$$
$$= (0.90)(120.00)$$
$$= (0.90)(0.80)(150.00)$$
$$= \$108.00$$

*Problem 3* Net price after the third discount

$$= (1 - 0.05)(108.00)$$
$$= (0.95)(108.00)$$
$$= (0.95)(0.90)(0.80)(150.00)$$
$$= \$102.60$$

The final net price of $102.60 is obtained from
$(0.95)(0.90)(0.80)(150.00)$
$= (0.80)(0.90)(0.95)(150.00)$ ——— the order of the factors may be rearranged
$= \text{NPF for 20\%} \times \text{NPF for 10\%} \times \text{NPF for 5\%} \times \text{Original list price}$
$= \text{Product of the NPFs for the discounts in the discount series} \times \text{Original list price}$
$= \text{Net price factor for the discount series} \times \text{Original list price}$

This result may be generalized to find the net price for a list price subject to a discount series.

$$
\begin{array}{c}
\text{NPF FOR THE} \\
\text{DISCOUNT SERIES}
\end{array} = 
\begin{array}{c}
\text{NPF FOR THE} \\
\text{FIRST DISCOUNT}
\end{array} \times 
\begin{array}{c}
\text{NPF FOR THE} \\
\text{SECOND DISCOUNT}
\end{array}
$$
$$
\times \ldots \times \begin{array}{c}
\text{NPF FOR THE} \\
\text{LAST DISCOUNT}
\end{array}
$$

——— **Formula 5.5A**

$$
\text{NET PRICE} = \begin{array}{c}
\text{NPF FOR THE} \\
\text{DISCOUNT SERIES}
\end{array} \times \text{LIST PRICE}
$$

——— **Formula 5.6A**

The two relationships represented by Formulas 5.5A and 5.6A can be restated in algebraic terms:

Let the net price be represented by N,
the original list price by L,
the first rate of discount by $d_1$,
the second rate of discount by $d_2$,
the third rate of discount by $d_3$, and
the last rate of discount by $d_n$.

Then Formula 5.5A can be shown as

$$\boxed{\begin{array}{l} \text{NPF FOR A} \\ \text{DISCOUNT SERIES} \end{array} = (1 - d_1)(1 - d_2)(1 - d_3) \ldots (1 - d_n)} \quad\text{------- Formula 5.5B}$$

and Formula 5.6A can be shown as

$$\boxed{\text{NET PRICE} = (1 - d_1)(1 - d_2)(1 - d_3) \ldots (1 - d_n)\text{L}} \quad\text{------- Formula 5.6B}$$

## D. Single equivalent rates of discount

For every discount series, a **single equivalent rate of discount** exists.

$$\boxed{\begin{array}{l} \text{SINGLE EQUIVALENT RATE OF DISCOUNT FOR A DISCOUNT SERIES} \\ = 1 - \text{NPF FOR THE DISCOUNT SERIES} \\ = 1 - [(1 - d_1)(1 - d_2)(1 - d_3) \ldots (1 - d_n)] \end{array}} \quad\text{------ Formula 5.7}$$

**EXAMPLE 5.1G**

A manufacturer sells skidoos to dealers at a list price of $2100 less 40%, 10%, 5%. Determine

(i) the amount of discount;

(ii) the single rate of discount.

**SOLUTION**

(i) Net price = NPF × List price
$$= (1 - 0.40)(1 - 0.10)(1 - 0.05)(2100.00)$$
$$= (0.60)(0.90)(0.95)(2100.00)$$
$$= \$1077.30$$

Amount of discount = List price − Net price
$$= 2100.00 - 1077.30 = \$1022.70$$

(ii) $\dfrac{\text{Single equivalent}}{\text{rate of discount}} = \dfrac{\text{Amount of discount}}{\text{List price}} = \dfrac{1022.70}{2100.00} = 0.487 = 48.7\%$

**Note:** Taking off a single discount of 48.7% has the *same* effect as using the discount series 40%, 10%, 5%. That is, the single discount of 48.7% is equivalent to the discount series 40%, 10%, 5%. Caution: The sum of the discounts in the series, 40% + 10% + 5% or 55%, is *not* equivalent to the single discount.

You can find the single equivalent rate of discount by choosing a suitable list price and computing first the amount of discount and then the rate of discount.

**EXAMPLE 5.1H**

Find the single equivalent rate of discount for the discount series 30%, 8%, 2%.

**SOLUTION**

Assume a list price of $1000.
Net price = NPF for the series × List price
$$= (0.70)(0.92)(0.98)(1000.00)$$
$$= (0.63112)(1000.00)$$
$$= \$631.12$$

Amount of discount = 1000.00 − 631.12 = $368.88

Single equivalent rate of discount $= \dfrac{368.88}{1000.00} = 0.36888 = 36.888\%$

*Note:* The net price factor for the series = (0.70)(0.92)(0.98) = 0.63112, and 1 − 0.63112 = 0.36888. Therefore, you can find the single equivalent rate of discount by subtracting the net price factor for the series from 1.

*Note:* When computing or using single equivalent rates of discount, use a sufficient number of decimals to ensure an acceptable degree of accuracy.

**EXAMPLE 5.1I**

Determine the amount of discount for a $625 list price subject to the discount series 40%, 12.5%, 8⅓%, 2%.

**SOLUTION**

Single equivalent rate of discount
$= 1 − (1 − 0.40)(1 − 0.125)(1 − 0.08\dot{3})(1 − 0.02)$———using Formula 5.7
$= 1 − (0.60)(0.875)(0.91\dot{6})(0.98)$
$= 1 − 0.471625$
$= 0.528375$
$= 52.8375\%$
Amount of discount = Rate of discount × List price
$= (0.528375)(625.00)$
$= \$330.23$

## POINTERS AND PITFALLS

The single equivalent rate of discount is not simply the sum of the individual discounts. Proper application of Formula 5.7 will always result in a single equivalent discount rate that is less than the sum of the individual discounts. You can use this fact to check whether the single equivalent discount rate you calculate is reasonable.

**EXAMPLE 5.1J**

The local hardware store has listed a power saw for $136 less 30%. A department store in a nearby shopping mall lists the same model for $126 less 20%, less an additional 15%. What additional rate of discount must the hardware store give to meet the department store price?

**SOLUTION**

| | |
|---|---|
| Hardware store net price = 136.00(0.70) | $95.20 |
| Department store price = 126.00(0.80)(0.85) | 85.68 |
| Additional discount needed | $ 9.52 |

Additional rate of discount needed $= \dfrac{9.52}{95.20} = 0.10 = 10\%$

**EXAMPLE 5.1K**

Redden Distributors bought a shipment of camcorders at a net price of $477.36 each, after discounts of 15%, 10%, 4%. What is the list price?

**SOLUTION**

Let the list price be $L.
The net price factor is (0.85)(0.90)(0.96) ———using Formula 5.5A

The net price is $477.36.

$$477.36 = L(0.85)(0.90)(0.96)$$

$$L = \frac{477.36}{(0.85)(0.90)(0.96)} = \$650.00$$

The camcorders were listed at $650.

## EXERCISE 5.1

**A.** Find the missing values (represented by question marks) for each of the following questions.

|  | Rate of Discount | List Price | Amount of Discount | Net Price |
|---|---|---|---|---|
| 1. | 45% | $ 24.60 | ? | ? |
| 2. | $16\frac{2}{3}\%$ | $184.98 | ? | ? |
| 3. | ? | $ 76.95 | ? | $ 51.30 |
| 4. | ? | $724.80 | ? | $616.08 |
| 5. | ? | ? | $37.89 | $214.71 |
| 6. | ? | ? | $19.93 | $976.57 |
| 7. | 62.5% | ? | $83.35 | ? |
| 8. | 1.5% | ? | $13.53 | ? |
| 9. | 37.5% | ? | ? | $ 84.35 |
| 10. | 22.5% | ? | ? | $121.29 |

**B.** Find the missing values (represented by question marks) for each of the following questions.

|  | Rate of Discount | List Price | Net Price | Single Equivalent Rate of Discount |
|---|---|---|---|---|
| 1. | 25%, 10% | $ 44.80 | ? | ? |
| 2. | $33\frac{1}{3}\%$, 5% | $126.90 | ? | ? |
| 3. | 40%, 12.5%, 2% | $268.00 | ? | ? |
| 4. | 20%, $16\frac{2}{3}\%$, 3% | $ 72.78 | ? | ? |
| 5. | 35%, $33\frac{1}{3}\%$, 10% | ? | $617.50 | ? |
| 6. | 20%, 20%, 10% | ? | $ 53.28 | ? |

**C.** Answer each of the following questions.

1. An item with a list price of $125.64 is offered at a discount of 37.5%. What is the net price?

2. An item with a list price of $49.98 is offered at a discount of $16\frac{2}{3}\%$. What is the net price?

3. A mountain bike listed for $975 is sold for $820. What rate of discount was allowed?

4. A washer-dryer combination listed at $1136 has a net price of $760. What is the rate of discount?

5. A 17.5% discount on a flat-screen TV amounts to $560. What is the list price?

6. Golf World sells a set of golf clubs for $762.50 below suggested retail price. Golf World claims that this represents a 62.5% discount. What is the suggested retail price (or list price)?

7. A $16\frac{2}{3}$% discount allowed on a silk shirt amounted to $14.82. What was the net price?

8. A store advertises a discount of $44.75 on a screwdriver set. If the discount is 25%, for how much were the sets of screwdrivers sold?

9. The net price of a freezer after a discount of $16\frac{2}{3}$% is $355. What is the list price?

10. The net price of an article is $63.31. What is the suggested retail price (the list price) if a discount of 35% was allowed?

11. Compute the equivalent single rate of discount for each of the following discount series.
   (a) 30%, 12.5%
   (b) $33\frac{1}{3}$%, 20%, 3%

12. Determine the equivalent single rate of discount for each of the following series of discounts.
   (a) $16\frac{2}{3}$%, 7.5%
   (b) 25%, $8\frac{1}{3}$%, 2%

13. An outdoor furniture set is listed for $599 less 30%, 20%, 5%.
   (a) What is the net price?
   (b) What is the total amount of discount allowed?
   (c) What is the exact single rate of discount that was allowed?

14. A power saw is listed for $174 less $16\frac{2}{3}$%, 10%, 8%.
   (a) What is the net price?
   (b) What is the total amount of discount allowed?
   (c) What is the exact single rate of discount that was allowed?

15. A compressor is listed for $786.20 less 36%, 10%, 2%.
   (a) What is the net price?
   (b) What is the total amount of discount allowed?
   (c) What is the exact single rate of discount that was allowed?

16. A tractor is listed for $1293.44 less $18\frac{1}{3}$%, $9\frac{1}{9}$%, 3%.
   (a) What is the net price?
   (b) What is the total amount of discount allowed?
   (c) What is the exact single rate of discount that was allowed?

17. An item listed by a wholesaler for $750 less 20%, 5%, 2% is reduced at a clearance sale to $474.81. What additional rate of discount was offered?

18. An office desk listed at $440 less 25%, 15% is offered at a further reduced price of $274.89. What additional rate of discount was offered?

19. An electronic game listed at $180 less 30%, 12.5%, 5% is offered at a further reduced price of $99.50. What additional rate of discount was offered?

20. A computer listed at $1260 less $33\frac{1}{3}$%, $16\frac{2}{3}$% is offered at a clearance price of $682.50. What additional rate of discount was offered?

21. Arrow Manufacturing offers discounts of 25%, 12.5%, 4% on a line of products. For how much should an item be listed if it is to be sold for $113.40?

22. What is the list price of an article that is subject to discounts of $33\frac{1}{3}$%, 10%, 2% if the net price is $564.48?

23. A distributor lists an item for $85 less 20%. To improve lagging sales, the net price of the item is reduced to $57.80. What additional rate of discount does the distributor offer?

24. A hat is listed for $66 less 40%. The net price of the hat is further reduced to $35.64. What additional rate of discount is offered?

25. Galaxy Jewellers sells diamond necklaces for $299 less 25%. Brilliants Jewellers offers the same necklace for $350 less 35%, 10%. What additional rate of discount must Galaxy offer to meet the competitor's price?

26. Polar Bay Wines advertises California Juice listed at $125 per bucket at a discount of 24%. A nearby competitor offers the same type of juice for $87.40 per bucket. What additional rate of discount must Polar Bay Wines give to meet the competitor's price?

# 5.2 PAYMENT TERMS AND CASH DISCOUNTS

## A. Basic concepts

Manufacturers, wholesalers, distributors, and retailers usually sell amongst each other goods on credit rather than for cash. An invoice for the goods is sent, and the seller specifies **payment terms** on the invoice. These payment terms indicate when the invoice amount is due for payment and how much is to be paid. The business selling the goods can offer a **cash discount** to encourage prompt payment. This discount reduces the amount to be paid, and is based on the original amount of the invoice, the discount rate, and the timing of the payment or payments.

All payment terms have three things in common:

1. The **rate of discount** is stated as a percent of the net amount of the invoice. The net amount of the invoice is the amount after trade discounts are deducted.
2. The **discount period** is stated, indicating the time period when the cash discount can be applied.
3. The **credit period** is stated, indicating the time period when the invoice must be paid.

If payment is not made during the stated discount period, the net amount of the invoice is to be paid by the end of the credit period. The end of the credit period is called the *due date*, and is either stipulated by the payment terms or implied by the prevailing business practice. If payment is not made by the due date, the account is considered to be overdue and may be subject to a late payment fee or interest charges.

Cash discounts are offered in a variety of ways. The three most commonly used methods are

1. ordinary dating;
2. end-of-the-month dating;
3. receipt-of-goods dating.

The mathematics of working with cash discounts is similar to that used in working with trade discounts.

## B. Ordinary dating

The most frequently used method of offering a cash discount is **ordinary dating**, and the most commonly used payment terms are *2/10, n/30* (read "two ten, net thirty").

This payment term means that if payment is made *within* ten days of the date of the invoice, a discount of 2% may be deducted from the net amount of the invoice. Otherwise, payment of the net amount of the invoice is due within 30 days. (See Figure 5.2.)

**FIGURE 5.2    Interpretation of Payment Terms**

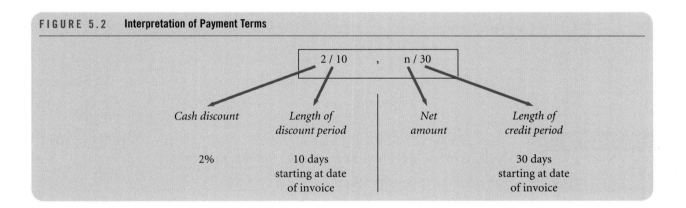

**EXAMPLE 5.2A**    Determine the payment needed to settle an invoice with a net amount of $950 dated September 22, terms 2/10, n/30, if the invoice is paid

(i) on October 10;

(ii) on October 1.

**SOLUTION**    The terms of the invoice indicate a credit period of 30 days and state that a 2% discount may be deducted from the invoice net amount of $950 if the invoice is paid within ten days of the invoice date of September 22. The applicable time periods and dates are shown in Figure 5.3.

FIGURE 5.3    **Discount and Credit Periods—Example 5.3A, Ordinary Dating**

Ten days after September 22 is October 2. The discount period ends October 2.

(i) Payment on October 10 is beyond the last day for taking the discount. The discount cannot be taken. The full amount of the invoice of $950 must be paid.

(ii) October 1 is within the discount period; the 2% discount can be taken.

$$\text{Amount paid} = \text{Net amount} - 2\% \text{ of the net amount}$$
$$= 950.00 - 0.02(950.00)$$
$$= 950.00 - 19.00$$
$$= \$931.00$$

**Alternatively:** Using the net price factor approach,

$$\text{Amount paid} = \text{NPF for a 2\% discount} \times \text{Net amount}$$
$$= (1 - 0.02)\,(950.00)$$
$$= 0.98(950.00)$$
$$= \$931.00$$

---

**EXAMPLE 5.2B**

An invoice for $752.84 dated March 25, terms 5/10, 2/30, n/60, is paid in full on April 20. What is the total amount paid to settle the account?

**SOLUTION**

The payment terms state that

(i) a 5% discount may be taken within ten days of the invoice date (up to April 4); or

(ii) a 2% discount may be taken within 30 days of the invoice date (after April 4 but no later than April 24); or

(iii) the net amount is due within 60 days of the invoice date if advantage is not taken of the cash discounts offered.

The 5% cash discount is *not* allowed; payment on April 20 is after the end of the discount period for the 5% discount. However, the 2% discount *is* allowed, since payment on April 20 is within the 30 day period for the 2% discount.

$$\text{Amount paid} = 0.98(752.84) = \$737.78 \text{ (See Figure 5.4.)}$$

**FIGURE 5.4**    **Discount and Credit Periods—Example 5.2B, Ordinary Dating**

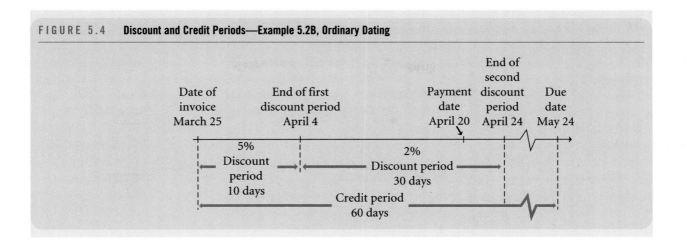

| EXAMPLE 5.2C |
| --- |

Three invoices with terms 5/10, 3/20, and n/60 are paid on November 15. The invoices are for $645 dated September 30, $706 dated October 26, and $586 dated November 7. What is the total amount paid?

| SOLUTION |
| --- |

| Invoice Dated | End of Discount Period | | Discount Allowed | Amount Paid |
| --- | --- | --- | --- | --- |
| | For 5% | For 3% | | |
| Sept. 30 | Oct. 10 | Oct. 20 | None | $ 645.00 |
| Oct. 26 | Nov. 5 | Nov. 15 | 3% | 0.97(706.00)   684.82 |
| Nov. 7 | Nov. 17 | Nov. 27 | 5% | 0.95(586.00)   556.70 |
| | | | Amount paid | $1886.52 |

## C. End-of-the-month dating

**End-of-the-month dating** is shown in the terms of payment by the abbreviation E.O.M. (*end of month*), as in "2/10, n/30 E.O.M." The abbreviation means that the discount may be taken within the stipulated number of days following the end of the month shown in the invoice date. It has the effect of shifting the invoice date to the last day of the month.

Commonly, in end-of-the-month dating, the credit period (such as n/30) is not stated. In our example, "2/10, n/30 E.O.M." would be written "2/10 E.O.M." In this case, it is understood that the end of the credit period (the due date) is *twenty* days after the last day for taking the discount.

| EXAMPLE 5.2D |
| --- |

An invoice for $1233.95 dated July 16, terms 2/10 E.O.M., is paid on August 10. What is the amount paid?

| SOLUTION |
| --- |

The abbreviation E.O.M. means that the invoice is to be treated as if the invoice date were July 31. Therefore, the last day for taking the discount is August 10.

Amount paid = 0.98(1233.95) = $1209.27 (See Figure 5.5.)

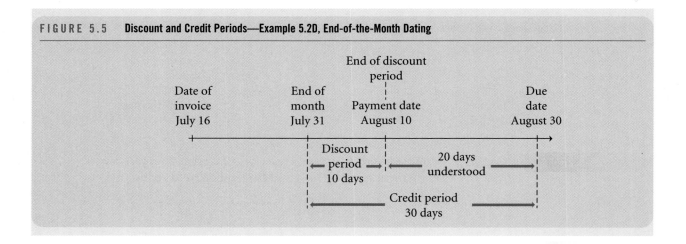

FIGURE 5.5    Discount and Credit Periods—Example 5.2D, End-of-the-Month Dating

## D. Receipt-of-goods dating

When the abbreviation R.O.G. (*receipt of goods*) appears in the terms of payment, as in "2/10, n/30 R.O.G.," the last day for taking the discount is the stipulated number of days after the date the merchandise is received rather than the invoice date. This method, known as **receipt-of-goods dating**, of offering a cash discount is used when the transportation of the goods takes a long time, as in the case of long-distance overland shipments by rail or truck, or shipments by boat.

**EXAMPLE 5.2E**    Hansa Import Distributors has received an invoice of $8465 dated May 10, terms 3/10, n/30 R.O.G., for a shipment of cuckoo clocks that arrived on July 15. What is the last day for taking the cash discount and how much is to be paid if the discount is taken?

**SOLUTION**    The last day for taking the discount is ten days after receipt of the shipment, that is, July 25.

Amount paid = 0.97(8465.00) = $8211.05 (See Figure 5.6.)

FIGURE 5.6    Discount and Credit Periods—Example 5.2E, Receipt-of-Goods Dating

# E. Partial payments and additional problems

The problem of a cash discount for a **partial payment** arises when a business pays *part* of an invoice within the discount period. In such cases, the purchaser is entitled to the cash discount on the partial amount paid. Each time a partial payment is made, separate the invoice into different parts, then determine whether the discount applies to each individual part.

**EXAMPLE 5.2F**

George Brown Inc. has received an invoice of $2780 dated August 18, terms 2/10 E.O.M. What payment must be made on September 10 to reduce the debt

(i) by $1000?

(ii) to $1000?

**SOLUTION**

Since the terms of payment involve end-of-month dating, the last day for taking the cash discount is September 10. The discount of 2% may be taken off the partial payment.

(i) Reducing the debt by $1000 requires paying $1000 less the discount.

Amount paid = 1000(0.98) = $980

Even though less than $1000 has been paid, the debt still owing has been reduced by $1000. This amount must be subtracted from the balance before the payment to determine the amount owing after the payment. The balance of the debt still owing is now $2780.00 − $1000.00 = $1780.00.

(ii) Reducing the debt to $1000 requires separating the debt into two parts, the first debt being $2780 − $1000, that is, $1780. Then, determine whether or not the $1780 is eligible for the discount. Since the first payment is made within the discount period, the discount is to be applied.

Amount paid = 1780.00(0.98) = $1744.40

The balance of the debt still owing in this case is now $2780 − $1780 = $1000.

**EXAMPLE 5.2G**

Applewood Supplies received a payment of $807.50 from Main Street Service on October 10 on an invoice of $2231.75 dated September 15, terms 5/10 E.O.M.

(i) For how much should Applewood credit Main Street Service's account for the payment?

(ii) How much does Main Street Service still owe on the invoice?

**SOLUTION**

Since the payment terms involve end-of-month dating, the payment is within the discount period. Main Street Service is entitled to the 5% discount on the partial payment. The amount of $807.50 represents a partial payment already reduced by 5%.

Let the credit allowed be $x$.

Amount paid = NPF × Credit allowed

$$807.50 = 0.95x$$

$$x = \frac{807.50}{0.95} = \$850.00$$

(i) Applewood should credit the account of Main Street Service with $850.

(ii) Main Street Service still owes ($2231.75 − 850.00) = $1381.75.

---

**EXAMPLE 5.2H**

Thrifty Furniture sells family room furniture consisting of a couch, loveseat, and two tables for a package price of $2495 if the purchase is financed. The company also advertises "no interest for one year." Diana buys the furniture and pays $2395.20 in cash at the time of the purchase.

(i) How much was the discount for paying cash?

(ii) What was the rate of discount on the cash purchase?

**SOLUTION**

Since the payment was in cash at the time of purchase, Thrifty Furniture did allow a discount. The question then arises, "Is this actually no interest for one year?"

List price − Amount paid = Discount

$$\$2495.00 − 2395.20 = \$99.80$$

(i) Thrifty Furniture allowed a discount of $99.80.

$$\text{Discount rate} = \frac{99.80}{2495.00} = 4\%$$

(ii) Thrifty Furniture allowed a 4% discount rate for this cash payment.

## EXERCISE 5.2

**A.** Determine the amount paid to settle each of the following eight invoices on the date indicated.

| | Invoice Amount | Payment Terms | Date of Invoice | Date Goods Received | Date Paid |
|---|---|---|---|---|---|
| 1. | $ 640.00 | 2/10, n/30 | Aug. 10 | Aug. 11 | Sept. 9 |
| 2. | $1520.00 | 3/15, n/60 | Sept. 24 | Sept. 27 | Oct. 8 |
| 3. | $ 783.95 | 3/10, 1/20, n/60 | May 18 | May 20 | June 5 |
| 4. | $1486.25 | 5/10, 2/30, n/60 | June 28 | June 30 | July 8 |
| 5. | $1160.00 | 2/10 E.O.M. | Mar. 22 | Mar. 29 | April 10 |
| 6. | $ 920.00 | 3/15 E.O.M. | Oct. 20 | Oct. 30 | Nov. 12 |
| 7. | $4675.00 | 2/10 R.O.G. | April 15 | May 28 | June 5 |
| 8. | $2899.65 | 4/20 R.O.G. | July 17 | Sept. 21 | Oct. 10 |

 **B.** Determine the missing values for each of the following six invoices. Assume that a partial payment was made on each of the invoices by the last day for taking the cash discount.

|  | Invoice Amount | Payment Terms | Amount of Credit for Payment | Net Payment Received | Invoice Balance Due |
|---|---|---|---|---|---|
| 1. | $1450.00 | 3/10, n/30 | $ 600.00 | ? | ? |
| 2. | $3126.54 | 2/10 E.O.M. | $2000.00 | ? | ? |
| 3. | $ 964.50 | 5/20 R.O.G. | ? | ? | $400.00 |
| 4. | $1789.95 | 4/15, n/60 | ? | ? | $789.95 |
| 5. | $1620.00 | 3/20 E.O.M. | ? | $ 785.70 | ? |
| 6. | $2338.36 | 2/10 R.O.G. | ? | $1311.59 | ? |

**C.** Answer the following questions.

1. Canadian Wheel received an invoice dated May 13 with terms 2/10, n/30. The amount stated on the invoice was $2499.
   (a) What is the last day for taking the cash discount?
   (b) What is the amount due if the invoice is paid on the last day for taking the discount?

2. An invoice was received for $6200 dated June 21 with terms 2/10, n/30.
   (a) What is the last day for taking the cash discount?
   (b) What is the amount due if the invoice is paid on the last day for taking the discount?

3. Triton Company received an invoice for $842 dated March 9 with terms 5/10, 2/20, n/60.
   (a) If the invoice is paid on March 19, how much is to be paid?
   (b) If the invoice is paid on March 27, how much is to be paid?
   (c) If the invoice is paid on April 3, how much is to be paid?

4. Manual Company received an invoice for $2412 dated January 22 with terms 3/15, 1/30, n/60.
   (a) If the invoice is paid on January 31, how much is to be paid?
   (b) If the invoice is paid on February 20, how much is to be paid?
   (c) If the invoice is paid on March 22, how much is to be paid?

5. What amount must be remitted if invoices dated July 25 for $929, August 10 for $763, and August 29 for $864, all with terms 3/15 E.O.M., are paid together on September 12?

6. The following invoices, all with terms 5/10, 2/30, n/60, were paid together on May 15. Invoice No. 234 dated March 30 is for $394.45; Invoice No. 356 dated April 15 is for $595.50; and Invoice No. 788 dated May 10 is for $865.20. What amount was remitted?

7. An invoice for $5275 dated November 12, terms 4/10 E.O.M., was received on November 14. What payment must be made on December 10 to reduce the debt to $3000?

8. What amount will reduce the amount due on an invoice of $1940 by $740 if the terms of the invoice are 5/10, n/30 and the payment was made during the discount period?

9. Santucci Appliances received an invoice dated August 12 with terms 3/10 E.O.M. for the items listed below:

   5 GE refrigerators at $980 each less 25%, 5%;

   4 Inglis dishwashers at $696 each less $16\frac{2}{3}$%, 12.5%, 4%.

   (a) What is the last day for taking the cash discount?
   (b) What is the amount due if the invoice is paid on the last day for taking the discount?
   (c) What is the amount of the cash discount if a partial payment is made such that a balance of $2000 remains outstanding on the invoice?

10. Import Exclusives Ltd. received an invoice dated May 20 from Dansk Specialties of Copenhagen with terms 5/20 R.O.G. for:

   100 teak trays at $34.30 each;
   25 teak icebuckets at $63.60 each;
   40 teak salad bowls at $54.50 each.

   All items are subject to trade discounts of $33\frac{1}{3}$%, $7\frac{1}{2}$%, 5%.

   (a) If the shipment was received on June 28, what is the last day of the discount period?
   (b) What is the amount due if the invoice is paid in full on July 15?
   (c) If a partial payment only is made on the last day of the discount period, what amount is due to reduce the outstanding balance to $2500?

11. Sheridan Service received an invoice dated September 25 from Wolfedale Automotive. The invoice amount was $2540.95, and the payment terms were 3/10, 1/20, n/30. Sheridan Service made a payment on October 5 to reduce the balance due by $1200, made a second payment on October 15 to reduce the balance to $600, and paid the remaining balance on October 25.
   (a) How much did Sheridan Service pay on October 5?
   (b) How much did it pay on October 15?
   (c) What was the amount of the final payment on October 25?

12. The Ski Shop received an invoice for $9600 dated August 11, terms 5/10, 2/30, n/90, for a shipment of skis. The Ski Shop made two partial payments.
   (a) How much was paid on August 20 to reduce the unpaid balance to $7000?
   (b) How much was paid on September 10 to reduce the outstanding balance by $3000?
   (c) What is the remaining balance on September 10?

13. Jelinek Sports received a cheque for $1867.25 in partial payment of an invoice owed by The Ski Shop. The invoice was for $5325 with terms 3/20 E.O.M. dated September 15, and the cheque was received on October 18.
   (a) By how much should Jelinek Sports credit the account of The Ski Shop?
   (b) How much does The Ski Shop still owe Jelinek?

14. Darrigo Grape received an invoice for $13 780 dated September 28, terms 5/20 R.O.G., from Nappa Vineyards for a carload of grape juice received October 20. Darrigo made a partial payment of $5966 on November 8.
   (a) By how much did Darrigo reduce the amount due on the invoice?
   (b) How much does Darrigo still owe?

15. Highway One Gas sells gas for vehicles at $1.12 per litre. Louis purchases 50 litres of gas for his car. He pays for the purchase in cash, paying a total of $54.04.
    (a) How much did he save by paying cash?
    (b) What was the rate of discount on the cash purchase?

16. Deals on Wheels advertises a vehicle at $26 465. Marina buys the vehicle, paying $24 877.10 in cash.
    (a) How much did she save by paying cash?
    (b) What was the rate of discount on the cash purchase?

# 5.3 MARKUP

## A. Basic concepts and calculations

The primary purpose of operating a business is to generate profits. Businesses engaged in merchandising generate profits through their buying and selling activities. The amount of profit depends on many factors, one of which is the pricing of goods. The selling price must cover

1. the cost of buying the goods;
2. the operating expenses (or overhead) of the business;
3. the profit required by the owner to stay in business.

| SELLING PRICE = COST OF BUYING + EXPENSES + PROFIT |
|---|

$$S = C + E + P$$ ———————————————— Formula 5.8A

**EXAMPLE 5.3A**

Main Street Service buys a certain type of battery at a cost of $84 each. Operating expenses of the business are 25% of cost and the owner requires a profit of 10% of cost. For how much should Main Street sell this type of battery?

**SOLUTION**

Selling price = Cost of buying + Expenses + Profit
= 84.00 + 25% of 84.00 + 10% of 84.00
= 84.00 + 0.25(84.00) + 0.10(84.00)
= 84.00 + 21.00 + 8.40
= $113.40

Main Street should sell the batteries for $113.40 to cover the cost of buying, the operating expenses, and the required profit.

In Example 5.3A, the selling price is $113.40 while the cost is $84. The difference between selling price and cost = 113.40 − 84.00 = $29.40. This difference covers operating expenses of $21 and a profit of $8.40 and is known as the **markup, margin,** or **gross profit.**

$$\boxed{\text{MARKUP} = \text{EXPENSES} + \text{PROFIT}}$$

$$\boxed{M = E + P}$$ ——————————————————Formula 5.9

Using this relationship between markup, expenses, and profit, the relationship stated in Formula 5.8A becomes

$$\boxed{\text{SELLING PRICE} = \text{COST OF BUYING} + \text{MARKUP}}$$

$$\boxed{S = C + M}$$ ——————————————————Formula 5.8B

Figure 5.7 illustrates the relationships among cost of buying (C), markup (M), operating expenses (E), profit (P), and selling price (S) established in Formulas 5.8A, 5.8B, and 5.9.

**FIGURE 5.7**

**EXAMPLE 5.3B**

Frisson Business Machines bought two types of electronic calculators for resale. Model A costs $42 and sells for $56.50. Model B costs $78 and sells for $95. Business overhead is 24% of cost. For each model, determine

(i) the markup (or gross profit);

(ii) the operating expenses (or overhead);

(iii) the profit.

**SOLUTION**

| **Model A** | **Model B** |
|---|---|
| (i)    $C + M = S$ | $C + M = S$ ———— using Formula 5.8B |
| $42.00 + M = 56.50$ | $78.00 + M = 95.00$ |
| $M = 56.50 - 42.00$ | $M = 95.00 - 78.00$ |
| $M = 14.50$ | $M = 17.00$ |
| The markup on Model A is $14.50. | The markup on Model B is $17 |

(ii) Expenses (or overhead)  Expenses (or overhead)
    $= 24\%$ of 42.00            $= 24\%$ of 78.00
    $= 0.24(42.00)$             $= 0.24(78.00)$
    $= 10.08$                    $= 18.72$
    Overhead for Model A is $10.08.  Overhead for Model B is $18.72.

(iii)      $E + P = M$          $E + P = M$ ——— Formula 5.9
        $10.08 + P = 14.50$      $18.72 + P = 17.00$
              $P = 14.50 - 10.08$      $P = 17.00 - 18.72$
              $P = 4.42$          $P = -1.72$
        Profit on Model A is $4.42.      Profit on Model B is $-$1.72,
                          that is, a loss of $1.72.

**EXAMPLE 5.3C**

A ski shop bought 100 pairs of skis for $105 per pair and sold 60 pairs for the regular selling price of $295 per pair. The remaining skis were sold during a clearance sale for $180 per pair. Overhead is 40% of the regular selling price. Determine

(i) the markup, the overhead, and the profit per pair of skis sold at the regular selling price;

(ii) the markup, the overhead, and the profit per pair of skis sold during the clearance sale;

(iii) the total profit realized.

**SOLUTION**

(i) *At regular selling price*          (ii) *At clearance price*

**Markup**                  **Markup**
$C + M = S$                  $C + M = S$
$105.00 + M = 295.00$              $105.00 + M = 180.00$
        $M = \$190.00$                  $M = \$75.00$

**Overhead**                  **Overhead**
$E = 40\%$ of regular selling price      $E = 40\%$ of regular selling price
    $= 0.40(295.00)$              $= 0.40(295.00)$
    $= \$118.00$                  $= \$118.00$

**Profit**                  **Profit**
$E + P = M$                  $E + P = M$
$118.00 + P = 190.00$              $118.00 + P = 75.00$
        $P = \$72.00$                  $P = -\$43.00$

(iii) Profit from sale of 60 pairs
        at regular selling price $= 60(72.00)$      $4320.00
    Profit from sale of 40 pairs
        during clearance sale $= 40(-43.00)$      $-1720.00
                    Total profit      $\underline{\$2600.00}$

## B. Rate of markup

A markup may be stated in one of two ways:

**1.** As a percent of cost; or
**2.** As a percent of selling price.

The method used is usually determined by the way in which a business keeps its records. Since most manufacturers keep their records in terms of cost, they usually calculate markup as a percent of cost. Since most department stores and other retailers keep their records in terms of selling price, they usually calculate markup as a percent of selling price.

Computing the rate of markup involves comparing the amount of markup to a base amount. Depending on the method used, the base amount is either the cost or the selling price. Since the two methods produce different results, great care must be taken to note whether the markup is based on the cost or on the selling price.

$$\text{RATE OF MARKUP BASED ON COST} = \frac{\text{MARKUP}}{\text{COST}} = \frac{M}{C} \qquad \text{Formula 5.10}$$

$$\frac{\text{RATE OF MARKUP BASED}}{\text{ON SELLING PRICE}} = \frac{\text{MARKUP}}{\text{SELLING PRICE}} = \frac{M}{S} \qquad \text{Formula 5.11}$$

| EXAMPLE 5.3D |
|---|

Compute (a) the missing value (cost, selling price, or markup), (b) the rate of markup based on cost, and (c) the rate of markup based on selling price for each of the following:

(i) cost, $60; selling price, $75

(ii) cost, $48; markup, $16

(iii) selling price, $88; markup, $33

(iv) cost, $8; markup, $8

(v) selling price, $24; markup, $18

| SOLUTION |
|---|

|  | (a)<br>Missing Value | (b)<br>Rate of Markup<br>Based on Cost | (c)<br>Rate of Markup<br>Based on Selling Price |
|---|---|---|---|
| (i) | Markup<br>= 75.00 − 60.00<br>= $15.00 | $\dfrac{15}{60} = 0.25 = 25\%$ | $\dfrac{15}{75} = 0.20 = 20\%$ |
| (ii) | Selling price<br>= 48.00 + 16.00<br>= $64.00 | $\dfrac{16}{48} = \dfrac{1}{3} = 33\dfrac{1}{3}\%$ | $\dfrac{16}{64} = 0.25 = 25\%$ |

TRADE DISCOUNT, CASH DISCOUNT, MARKUP, AND MARKDOWN **201**

| | | | |
|---|---|---|---|
| (iii) | Cost | $\dfrac{33}{55} = 0.60 = 60\%$ | $\dfrac{33}{88} = 0.375 = 37.5\%$ |
| | = 88.00 − 33.00 | | |
| | = $55.00 | | |
| (iv) | Selling price | $\dfrac{8}{8} = 1.00 = 100\%$ | $\dfrac{8}{16} = 0.50 = 50\%$ |
| | = 8.00 + 8.00 | | |
| | = $16.00 | | |
| (v) | Cost | $\dfrac{18}{6} = 3.00 = 300\%$ | $\dfrac{18}{24} = 0.75 = 75\%$ |
| | = 24.00 − 18.00 | | |
| | = $6.00 | | |

## C. Finding the cost or the selling price

When the rate of markup is given and either the cost or the selling price is known, the missing value can be found using Formula 5.8B.

$$\boxed{\text{COST} + \text{MARKUP} = \text{SELLING PRICE}} \qquad \boxed{C + M = S}$$

When using this formula, pay special attention to the base of the markup, that is, whether it is based on cost or based on selling price.

**EXAMPLE 5.3E**

What is the selling price of an article costing $72 if the markup is

(i) 40% of cost?

(ii) 40% of the selling price?

**SOLUTION**

(i)
$$C + M = S \qquad\qquad \text{using Formula 5.8B}$$
$$C + 40\% \text{ of } C = S \qquad \text{replacing M by 40\% of C is the crucial}$$
$$72.00 + 0.40(72.00) = S \qquad\quad \text{step in the solution}$$
$$72.00 + 28.80 = S$$
$$S = 100.80$$

When the markup is 40% based on cost, the selling price is $100.80.

(ii)
$$C + M = S$$
$$C + 40\% \text{ of } S = S$$
$$72.00 + 0.40S = S$$
$$72.00 = S - 0.40S$$
$$72.00 = 0.60S$$
$$S = \frac{72.00}{0.60}$$
$$S = 120.00$$

When the markup is 40% based on selling price, the selling price is $120.00.

*Note:* In problems of this type, replace M by $X\%$ of C or $X\%$ of S before using specific numbers. This approach is used in the preceding problem and in the following worked examples.

**EXAMPLE 5.3F**

What is the cost of an article selling for $65 if the markup is

(i) 30% of selling price?

(ii) 30% of cost?

**SOLUTION**

(i)
$$C + M = S$$
$$C + 30\% \text{ of } S = S \quad \text{------------ replace M by 30\% of S}$$
$$C + 0.30(65.00) = 65.00$$
$$C + 19.50 = 65.00$$
$$C = 65.00 - 19.50$$
$$C = 45.50$$

When the markup is 30% based on selling price, the cost is $45.50.

(ii)
$$C + M = S$$
$$C + 30\% \text{ of } C = S \quad \text{------------ replace M by 30\% of C}$$
$$C + 0.30C = 65.00$$
$$1.30C = 65.00$$
$$C = \frac{65.00}{1.30}$$
$$C = 50.00$$

If the markup is 30% based on cost, the cost is $50.

**EXAMPLE 5.3G**

The Beaver Ski Shop sells ski vests for $98. The markup based on cost is 75%.

(i) What did the Beaver Ski Shop pay for each vest?

(ii) What is the rate of markup based on the selling price?

**SOLUTION**

(i)
$$C + M = S$$
$$C + 75\% \text{ of } C = S$$
$$C + 0.75C = 98.00$$
$$1.75C = 98.00$$
$$C = 56.00$$

The Beaver Ski Shop paid $56 for each vest.

(ii) Rate of markup based on selling price $= \dfrac{\text{Markup}}{\text{Selling price}}$

$$= \frac{98.00 - 56.00}{98.00}$$

$$= \frac{42.00}{98.00} = 0.428571 = 42.86\%$$

**EXAMPLE 5.3H**

Main Street Service bought four Michelin tires from a wholesaler for $343 and sold the tires at a markup of 30% of the selling price.

(i) For how much were the tires sold?

(ii) What is the rate of markup based on cost?

**SOLUTION**

(i)
$$C + M = S$$
$$C + 30\% \text{ of } S = S$$
$$343.00 + 0.30S = S$$
$$343.00 = 0.70S$$
$$S = 490.00$$

Main Street Service sold the tires for $490.

(ii) Rate of markup based on cost $= \dfrac{\text{Markup}}{\text{Cost}}$

$$= \frac{490.00 - 343.00}{343.00}$$

$$= \frac{147.00}{343.00} = 0.428571 = 42.86\%$$

**EXAMPLE 5.31**

The markup, or gross profit, on each of two separate articles is $25.80. If the rate of markup for Article A is 40% of cost while the rate of markup for Article B is 40% of the selling price, determine the cost and the selling price of each.

**SOLUTION**

*For Article A*
Markup (or gross profit) = 40% of cost
$$25.80 = 0.40C$$
$$C = 64.50$$

The cost of Article A is $64.50.
The selling price is 64.50 + 25.80 = $90.30.

*For Article B*
Markup (or gross profit) = 40% of selling price
$$25.80 = 0.40S$$
$$S = 64.50$$

The selling price of Article B is $64.50.
The cost = 64.50 − 25.80 = $38.70.

# EXERCISE 5.3

  For each of the following six questions, determine
(a) the amount of markup;
(b) the amount of overhead;
(c) the profit or loss realized on the sale;
(d) the rate of markup based on cost;
(e) the rate of markup based on selling price.

| | Cost | Selling Price | Overhead |
|---|---|---|---|
| 1. | $24.00 | $30.00 | 16% of cost |
| 2. | $72.00 | $96.00 | 15% of selling price |
| 3. | $52.50 | $87.50 | 36% of selling price |
| 4. | $42.45 | $67.92 | 60% of cost |
| 5. | $27.00 | $37.50 | 34% of selling price |
| 6. | $36.00 | $42.30 | 21% of cost |

**B.** For each of the following twelve questions, compute the missing values represented by the question marks.

| | Cost | Selling Price | Markup | Rate of Markup Based On: Cost | Selling Price |
|---|---|---|---|---|---|
| 1. | $25.00 | $ 31.25 | ? | ? | ? |
| 2. | $63.00 | $ 84.00 | ? | ? | ? |
| 3. | $64.00 | ? | $38.40 | ? | ? |
| 4. | ? | $162.00 | $27.00 | ? | ? |
| 5. | $54.25 | ? | ? | 40% | ? |
| 6. | ? | $ 94.50 | ? | ? | 30% |
| 7. | ? | $ 66.36 | ? | 50% | ? |
| 8. | ? | $133.25 | ? | $66\frac{2}{3}$% | ? |
| 9. | $31.24 | ? | ? | ? | 60% |
| 10. | $87.74 | ? | ? | ? | $33\frac{1}{3}$% |
| 11. | ? | ? | $22.26 | ? | $16\frac{2}{3}$% |
| 12. | ? | ? | $90.75 | 125% | ? |

**C.** Answer each of the following questions.

1. Giuseppe's buys supplies to make pizzas for $4. Operating expenses of the business are 110% of the cost and the profit made is 130% of cost. What is the regular selling price of each pizza?

2. Neptune Dive Shop sells snorkelling equipment for $50. Their cost is $25 and their operation expenses are 30% of regular selling price. How much profit will they make on each sale?

3. Mi Casa imports pottery from Mexico. Their operation expenses are 260% of the cost of buying and the profit is 110% of the cost of buying. They sell a vase for $14.10. What is their cost for each piece?

4. Windsor Hardware buys outdoor lights for $5 per dozen less 20%, 20%. The store's overhead is 45% of cost and the required profit is 15% of cost. For how much per dozen should the lights be sold?

5. A merchant buys an item listed at $96 less $33\frac{1}{3}$% from a distributor. Overhead is 32% of cost and profit is 27.5% of cost. For how much should the item be retailed?

6. Tennis racquets were purchased for $55 less 40% (for purchasing more than 100 items), and less a further 25% (for purchasing the racquets in October). They were sold for $54.45.

   (a) What is the markup as a percent of cost?
   (b) What is the markup as a percent of selling price?

7. A dealer bought personal computers for $1240 less 50%, 10%. They were sold for $1395.
   (a) What was the markup as a percent of cost?
   (b) What was the markup as a percent of selling price?

8. The Bargain Bookstore marks up textbooks by $3.42 per textbook. The store's markup is 15% of cost.
   (a) For how much did the bookstore buy each textbook?
   (b) What is the selling price of each textbook?
   (c) What is the rate of markup based on the selling price?

9. An appliance store sells electric kettles at a markup of 18% of the selling price. The store's margin on a particular model is $6.57.
   (a) For how much does the store sell the kettles?
   (b) What was the cost of the kettles to the store?
   (c) What is the rate of markup based on cost?

10. The markup on an item selling for $74.55 is 40% of cost.
   (a) What is the cost of the item?
   (b) What is the rate of markup based on the selling price?

11. Sheridan Service sells oil at a markup of 40% of the selling price. If Sheridan paid $0.99 per litre of oil,
   (a) what is the selling price per litre?
   (b) what is the rate of markup based on cost?

12. The Ski Shop purchased ski poles for $12.80 per pair. The poles are marked up 60% of the selling price.
   (a) For how much does The Ski Shop sell a pair of ski poles?
   (b) What is the rate of markup based on cost?

13. Neal's Photographic Supplies sells a Pentax camera for $444.98. The markup is 90% of cost.
   (a) How much does the store pay for this camera?
   (b) What is the rate of markup based on selling price?

14. The Cookery buys sets of cookware for $45 and marks them up at $33\frac{1}{3}\%$ of cost.
   (a) What is the selling price of the cookware sets?
   (b) What is the rate of markup based on selling price?

15. The Leather Factory buys bags for $84 and marks them up at 40% of selling price.
   (a) What is the selling price of the bags?
   (b) What is the rate of markup based on cost?

16. Boxes of candles are sold for $3.24. The store's markup based on selling price is $16\frac{2}{3}\%$.
   (a) What is the cost of the boxes of candles?
   (b) What is the rate of markup based on cost?

17. It's About Time sells clocks for $23.10. The store's markup based on cost is 37.5%.
    (a) What is the cost of the clocks?
    (b) What is the rate of markup based on selling price?

18. A car accessory is sold for $42.90. The store's markup based on cost is 50%.
    (a) What is the cost of the car accessory?
    (b) What is the rate of markup based on selling price?

# 5.4 MARKDOWN

## A. Pricing strategies

The pricing relationship, Selling price = Cost + Expense + Profit, or (S = C + E + P), plays an important role in pricing. It describes how large a markup is needed to cover overhead and a reasonable profit, and how large a markdown can be tolerated. One pricing strategy is to set a selling price based on the business' "internal" factors—actual costs and expenses, and a desired profit level. However, pricing decisions must often be based on "external" market factors—competitors' prices, consumers' sensitivity to a high price, economic conditions that affect interest rates and income available for purchases, and so on. Often, selling prices must be marked down more than anticipated in response to market conditions, leading to less-than-desired profit levels. Use the pricing relationship S = C + E + P as a guide to determine the effect of markdown decisions on the operations of a business.

The cost of buying an article plus the overhead represents the **total cost**, or handling cost, of the article.

$$\boxed{\text{TOTAL COST} = \text{COST OF BUYING} + \text{EXPENSES}}$$

If an article is sold at a price that *equals* the total cost, the business makes no profit nor does it suffer a loss. This price is called the break-even point. Any business, of course, prefers to sell at a price that is at least the break-even price. If the price is insufficient to recover the total cost, the business will suffer an operating loss. If the price does not even cover the cost of buying the item, the business suffers an absolute loss. To determine the profit or loss, the following accounting relationship is used.

$$\boxed{\text{PROFIT} = \text{SELLING PRICE} - \text{TOTAL COST}}$$

$$\boxed{\text{PROFIT} = \text{REVENUE} - \text{TOTAL COST}}$$

## B. Basic concepts and calculations

A **markdown** is a reduction in the price of an article sold to the consumer. Markdowns are used for a variety of purposes, such as sales promotions, meeting competitors' prices, reducing excess inventories, clearing out seasonal merchandise, and selling off discontinued items. A markdown, unlike a markup, is always stated as a percent of the price to be reduced and is computed as if it were a discount.

FIGURE 5.8

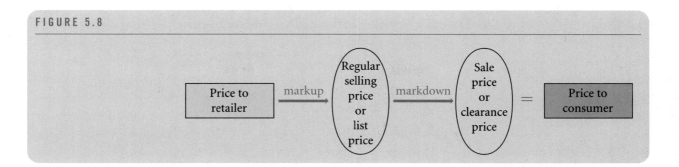

While markdowns are simple to calculate, the rather wide variety of terms used to identify both the price to be reduced (such as *regular selling price, selling price, list price, marked price, price tag*) and the reduced price (such as *sale price* or *clearance price*) introduces an element of confusion. In this text, we use **regular selling price** to describe the price to be reduced and **sale price** to describe the reduced price.

In general,

> SALE PRICE = REGULAR SELLING PRICE − MARKDOWN

However, since the markdown is a percent of the regular selling price, the net price factor approach used with discounts is applicable (see Formula 5.4A).

> SALE PRICE = NPF × REGULAR SELLING PRICE
> where NPF = 100% − % markdown

**EXAMPLE 5.4A**

The Cook Nook paid $115.24 for a set of dishes. Expenses are 18% of selling price and the required profit is 15% of selling price. During an inventory sale, the set of dishes was marked down 30%.

(i) What was the regular selling price?

(ii) What was the sale price?

(iii) What was the operating profit or loss?

**SOLUTION**

(i) Selling price = Cost + Expenses + Profit

$$S = C + 18\% \text{ of } S + 15\% \text{ of } S$$
$$S = C + 0.18S + 0.15S$$
$$S = 115.24 + 0.33S$$
$$0.67S = 115.24$$
$$S = \frac{115.24}{0.67} = \$172.00$$

The regular selling price is $172.

(ii) Sale price = Regular selling price − Markdown

$$= S - 30\% \text{ of } S$$
$$= S - 0.30S$$
$$= 0.70S$$
$$= 0.70(172.00)$$
$$= \$120.40$$

The sale price is $120.40.

(iii) Total cost = Cost of buying + Expenses

$$= C + 18\% \text{ of } S$$
$$= 115.24 + 0.18(172.00)$$
$$= 115.24 + 30.96$$
$$= \$146.20$$

Profit = Revenue − Total cost

$$= 120.40 - 146.20$$
$$= -\$25.80$$

The dishes were sold at an operating loss of $25.80.

---

**EXAMPLE 5.4B**

Lund Sporting Goods sold a bicycle regularly priced at $195 for $144.30.

(i) What is the amount of markdown?

(ii) What is the rate of markdown?

**SOLUTION**

(i) Markdown = Regular selling price − Sale price

$$= 195.00 - 144.30$$
$$= \$50.70$$

(ii) Rate of markdown $= \dfrac{\text{Markdown}}{\text{Regular selling price}}$

$$= \frac{50.70}{195.00} = 0.26 = 26\%$$

---

**EXAMPLE 5.4C**

During its annual Midnight Madness Sale, The Ski Shop sold a pair of ski boots, regularly priced at $245, at a discount of 40%. The boots cost $96 and expenses are 26% of the regular selling price.

(i) For how much were the ski boots sold?

(ii) What was the total cost of the ski boots?

(iii) What operating profit or loss was made on the sale?

**SOLUTION**

(i) Sale price = 0.60(245.00) = $147.00

(ii) Total cost = Cost of buying + Expenses

$$= 96.00 + 0.26(245.00)$$
$$= 96.00 + 63.70$$
$$= \$159.70$$

(iii) Profit = Revenue − Total cost
= 147.00 − 159.70
= −$12.70 (a loss)

Since the total cost was higher than the revenue received from the sale of the ski boots, The Ski Shop had an operating loss of $12.70.

**EXAMPLE 5.4D**

The Winemaker sells Okanagan concentrate for $22.50. The store's overhead expenses are 50% of cost and the owners require a profit of 30% of cost.

(i) For how much does The Winemaker buy the concentrate?

(ii) What is the price needed to cover all of the costs and expenses?

(iii) What is the highest rate of markdown at which the store will still break even?

(iv) What is the highest rate of discount that can be advertised without incurring an absolute loss?

**SOLUTION**

(i)  $S = C + E + P$
$S = C + 50\% \text{ of } C + 30\% \text{ of } C$
$S = C + 0.50C + 0.30C$
$22.50 = 1.80C$
$C = \dfrac{22.50}{1.80} = \$12.50$

The Winemaker buys the concentrate for $12.50.

(ii) Total cost = C + 50% of C
= 1.50C
= 1.50(12.50)
= $18.75

The price needed to cover costs and expenses is $18.75.

(iii) To break even, the maximum markdown is 22.50 − 18.75 = $3.75.

Rate of markdown $= \dfrac{3.75}{22.50} = 0.166667 = 16\frac{2}{3}\%$

The highest rate of markdown to break even is $16\frac{2}{3}\%$.

(iv) The lowest price at which the concentrate can be offered for sale without incurring an absolute loss is the cost at which the concentrate was purchased, that is, $12.50. The maximum amount of discount is 22.50 − 12.50 = $10.00.

Rate of discount $= \dfrac{10.00}{22.50} = 0.444444 = 44\frac{4}{9}\%$

The maximum rate of discount that can be advertised without incurring an absolute loss is $44\frac{4}{9}\%$.

# EXERCISE 5.4

**A.** Compute the values represented by question marks for each of the following six questions.

| | Regular Selling Price | Markdown | Sale Price | Cost (C) | Overhead | Total Cost | Operating Profit (Loss) |
|---|---|---|---|---|---|---|---|
| 1. | $85.00 | 40% | ? | $ 42.00 | 20% of S | ? | ? |
| 2. | ? | $33\frac{1}{3}$% | $ 42.00 | $ 34.44 | 12% of S | ? | ? |
| 3. | ? | 35% | $ 62.66 | ? | 25% of S | $54.75 | ? |
| 4. | $72.80 | $12\frac{1}{2}$% | ? | $ 54.75 | 20% of C | ? | ? |
| 5. | ? | 25% | $120.00 | $105.00 | ?  of S | ? | ($4.20) |
| 6. | $92.40 | $16\frac{2}{3}$% | ? | ? | 15% of C | ? | $8.46 |

**B.**  1. The Music Store paid $14.95 for a DVD. Expenses are 21% of selling price and the required profit is 11% of selling price. During an inventory sale, the DVD was marked down 20%.
   (a) What was the regular selling price?
   (b) What was the sale price?
   (c) What was the operating profit or loss?    Reference Example 5.4A

  2. A retail store paid $44 for a microwave oven. Expenses are 27% of selling price and the required profit is 18% of selling price. During an inventory sale, the microwave was marked down 40%.
   (a) What was the regular selling price?
   (b) What was the sale price?
   (c) What was the operating profit or loss?

  3. A sports drink was offered for sale at $1.99 at West Store. At East Store, the regular selling price of a similar sports drink was $2.49. What rate of mark-down would East Store have to offer to sell the drink at the same price as West Store?    Reference Example 5.4B

  4. An eyeglass company sells frames for $279. If they wanted to offer the lower price of $239, what rate of markdown would they have to offer?

  5. A seminar was advertised at a price of $125 per person. If the tickets were purchased at least two weeks in advance, the price would be lowered to $105 per person. What rate of markdown has been offered?

  6. A seven-day Mexican cruise was advertised at a price of $1299 per person based on double occupancy. If the cruise was booked two months in advance, the price would be lowered to $935 per person. What rate of markdown has been offered?

  7. Luigi's Restaurant offered a "buy one get one half off" sale for the midweek period. The "one half off" referred to the lesser-priced dinner. A customer ordered a steak dinner, with a regular price of $19, and a chicken dinner, with a regular price of $14.
   (a) What was the overall markdown at which the dinners were sold?
   (b) What was the overall rate of markdown at which the dinners were sold?

**8.** A lakeside resort offered a midweek package at $199 per night for two people. The package included accommodation in a one-bedroom suite, which regularly sold for $225, breakfast for two, regularly priced at $12 per person, and a 25% discount on spa services, a value of $20 per person.
   **(a)** What was the overall markdown at which the packages were sold?
   **(b)** What was the overall rate of markdown at which the packages were sold?

**9.** Par Putters Company sells golf balls for $29 per dozen. The store's overhead expenses are 43% of cost and the owners require a profit of 20% of cost.
   **(a)** For how much does Par Putters Company buy the golf balls?
   **(b)** What is the price needed to cover all of the costs and expenses?
   **(c)** What is the highest rate of markdown at which the store will still break even?
   **(d)** What is the highest rate of discount that can be advertised without incurring an absolute loss?      Reference Example 5.4D

**10.** Get-Aways Company sells sightseeing tours for the Ottawa valley for C$3849 per person. Overhead expenses for the company are 31% of cost and the target profit is 17% of cost.
   **(a)** How much does Get-Aways Company pay for the tours?
   **(b)** What is the lowest price they can offer while still covering all of the costs and expenses?
   **(c)** What is the highest rate of markdown at which the company will still break even?

# 5.5 INTEGRATED PROBLEMS

Many businesses encounter complex situations where discounts, markups, and markdowns are involved. In order to determine desired profits, prices must be set carefully. To determine the appropriate price, each complex situation must be separated into the different steps and calculations needed, and a solution determined for each part before an overall solution can be determined.

**EXAMPLE 5.5A**

Solomon ski bindings purchased for $57.75 were marked up 45% of the selling price. When the binding was discontinued, it was marked down 40%. What was the sale price of the binding?

**SOLUTION**

Consider the given information step by step. The following computations are necessary to determine the sale price.

**STEP 1**

First determine the regular selling price S.
$$C + M = S$$
$$C + 45\% \text{ of } S = S$$
$$57.75 + 0.45S = S$$
$$57.75 = 0.55S$$
$$S = \$105.00$$

The regular selling price is $105.

**STEP 2**   Next, determine the sale price.

Sale price = Regular selling price − Markdown
   = 105.00 − 40% of 105.00
   = 105.00 − 42.00
   = $63.00

*Alternatively:*

Sale price = NPF × Regular selling price
   = 0.60 × 105.00
   = $63.00

The sale price is $63.

**EXAMPLE 5.5B**   Canadian Car Company has just introduced its latest model, the Cheetah, marketed as fast, quiet, and efficient. Andretti's Cars, the local dealer, purchased one of the cars for $27 685 less 30%. Andretti's marks all vehicles at a list or sticker price that allows them to offer a discount of 20% and maintain a markup based on cost of 25%. During its annual midsummer sale, the car was advertised at $27 995. Determine the cost, the regular price, the normal selling price, and the midsummer sale markdown rate.

**SOLUTION**   To solve this problem, start with a step-by-step approach. The following computations are necessary to determine the profit.

**STEP 1**   The cost C (or purchase price) to the store;

**STEP 2**   The selling price S required to maintain the markup based on cost;

**STEP 3**   The list price L from which the 20% discount is offered;

**STEP 4**   The midsummer sale markdown rate.

**Step-by-Step Computations**

**STEP 1**   Cost = NPF × Manufacturer's list price

Cost = (0.70)(27 685.00) = $19 379.50

**STEP 2**   Let the normal selling price be S.

S = C + Markup
S = C + 25% of C
S = C + 0.25C
S = 1.25(19 379.50)
S = $24 224.38

The normal selling price is $24 224.38.

**STEP 3**  List price − Discount = Normal selling price
Let the regular price be L.

$$L - 20\% \text{ of } L = 24\,224.38$$
$$L - 0.20L = 24\,224.38$$
$$0.80L = 24\,224.38$$
$$L = \frac{24\,224.38}{0.80} = \$30\,280.48$$

The list price was \$30 280.48.

**STEP 4**  Markdown = List price − Midsummer sale price

$$= 30\,280.48 - 27\,995.00$$
$$= 2285.48$$
$$\text{Markdown rate} = \frac{2285.48}{30\,280.48} = 7.55\%$$

The markdown rate was 7.55%.

---

**EXAMPLE 5.5C**

Big Sound Electronics bought stereo equipment at a cost of \$960 less 30%, 15%. Big Sound marks all merchandise at a list price that allows the store to offer a discount of 20% while still making its usual profit of 15% of regular selling price. Overhead is 25% of regular selling price. During its annual Boxing Week sale, the usual discount of 20% was replaced by a markdown of 45%. What operating profit or loss was made when the equipment was sold?

**SOLUTION**

Complex problems of this type are best solved by a systematic approach. Consider the given information step by step. The following computations are necessary to determine the profit.

**STEP 1**  The cost C (or purchase price) to the store;

**STEP 2**  The regular selling price S required to cover cost, expenses, and the usual profit;

**STEP 3**  The list price L from which the 20% discount is offered;

**STEP 4**  The Boxing Week sale price;

**STEP 5**  The total cost (cost and expenses);

**STEP 6**  The resulting operating profit or loss.

**Step-by-Step Computations**

**STEP 1**  Cost = NPF × List price = (0.70)(0.85)(960.00) = \$571.20

**STEP 2**  Let the regular selling price be S.

$$S = C + E + P$$
$$S = C + 25\% \text{ of } S + 15\% \text{ of } S$$
$$S = C + 0.25S + 0.15S$$
$$S = 571.20 + 0.40S$$
$$0.60S = 571.20$$
$$S = \frac{571.20}{0.60} = \$952.00$$

The regular selling price is \$952.

**STEP 3**    List price − Discount = Regular selling price
Let the List price be L.
$$L - 20\% \text{ of } L = 952.00$$
$$L - 0.20L = 952.00$$
$$0.80L = 952.00$$
$$L = \frac{952.00}{0.80} = \$1190.00$$

The list price was $1190.

**STEP 4**    Boxing Week sale price = List price − Markdown
$$= 1190.00 - 45\% \text{ of } 1190.00$$
$$= 1190.00 - 0.45(1190.00)$$
$$= 1190.00 - 535.50$$
$$= \$654.50$$

**STEP 5**    Total cost = Cost of buying + Expenses
$$= C + 25\% \text{ of } S$$
$$= 571.20 + 0.25(952.00)$$
$$= 571.20 + 238.00$$
$$= \$809.20$$

**STEP 6**    Profit = Sale price − Total cost
$$= 654.50 - 809.20$$
$$= -\$154.70$$

The equipment was sold at an operating loss of $154.70.

---

**EXAMPLE 5.5D**    Magder's Furniture Emporium bought a dining room suite that must be retailed for $5250 to cover the cost, overhead expenses of 50% of the cost, and a normal net profit of 25% of the cost. The suite is marked at a list price so that the store can allow a 20% discount and still receive the required regular selling price.

When the suite remained unsold, the store owner decided to mark the suite down for an inventory clearance sale. To arrive at the rate of markdown, the owner decided that the store's profit would have to be no less than 10% of the normal net profit and that part of the markdown would be covered by reducing the commission paid to the salesperson. The normal commission (which accounts for 40% of the overhead) was reduced by $33\frac{1}{3}\%$.

What is the maximum rate of markdown that can be advertised instead of the usual 20%?

**SOLUTION**

**STEP 1**    Determine the cost C.
Let the regular selling price be S.
$$S = C + E + P$$
$$S = C + 50\% \text{ of } C + 25\% \text{ of } C$$
$$S = C + 0.50C + 0.25C$$
$$5250.00 = 1.75C$$
$$C = \frac{5250.00}{1.75} = \$3000.00$$

**STEP 2** Determine the list price L.
Let the list price be $L.

$$\text{List price} - \text{Discount} = \text{Regular selling price}$$
$$L - 20\% \text{ of } L = 5250.00$$
$$L - 0.20L = 5250.00$$
$$0.80L = 5250.00$$
$$L = \frac{5250.00}{0.80} = \$6562.50$$

**STEP 3** Determine the required profit.
$$\text{Normal net profit} = 25\% \text{ of cost}$$
$$= 0.25(3000.00)$$
$$= \$750.00$$
$$\text{Required net profit} = 10\% \text{ of normal net profit}$$
$$= 0.10(750.00)$$
$$= \$75.00$$

**STEP 4** Determine the amount of overhead expense to be recovered.
$$\text{Normal overhead expense} = 50\% \text{ of cost}$$
$$= 0.50(3000.00)$$
$$= \$1500.00$$
$$\text{Normal commission} = 40\% \text{ of normal overhead expense}$$
$$= 0.40(1500.00)$$
$$= \$600.00$$
$$\text{Reduction in commission} = 33\tfrac{1}{3}\% \text{ of normal commission}$$
$$= 33\tfrac{1}{3}\%(600.00)$$
$$= \$200.00$$
$$\text{Overhead expense to be recovered} = 1500.00 - 200.00 = \$1300.00$$

**STEP 5** Determine the inventory clearance price.
$$\text{Inventory clearance price} = \text{Cost} + \text{Overhead} + \text{Profit}$$
$$= 3000.00 + 1300.00 + 75.00$$
$$= \$4375.00$$

**STEP 6** Determine the amount of markdown.
$$\text{Markdown} = \text{List price} - \text{Inventory clearance price}$$
$$= 6562.50 - 4375.00$$
$$= \$2187.50$$

**STEP 7** Determine the rate of markdown.

$$\text{Rate of markdown} = \frac{\text{Amount of markdown}}{\text{List price}}$$
$$= \frac{2187.50}{6562.50}$$
$$= 0.333333$$
$$= 33\tfrac{1}{3}\%$$

Instead of the usual 20%, the store can advertise a markdown of $33\tfrac{1}{3}\%$.

# EXERCISE 5.5

  **A.** Answer each of the following questions.

1. A cookware set that cost a dealer $440 less 55%, 25% is marked up 180% of cost. For quick sale, the cookware was reduced 45%.
   (a) What is the sale price?
   (b) What rate of markup based on cost was realized?  Reference Example 5.5A

2. A gas barbecue cost a retailer $420 less $33\frac{1}{3}$%, 20%, 5%. It carries a regular selling price on its price tag at a markup of 60% of the regular selling price. During the end-of-season sale, the barbecue is marked down 45%.
   (a) What is the end-of-season sale price?
   (b) What rate of markup based on cost will be realized during the sale?

3. The Stereo Shop sold a radio regularly priced at $125 for $75. The cost of the radio was $120 less $33\frac{1}{3}$%, 15%. The store's overhead expense is 12% of the regular selling price.
   (a) What was the rate of markdown at which the radio was sold?
   (b) What was the operating profit or loss?
   (c) What rate of markup based on cost was realized?
   (d) What was the rate of markup based on the sale price?

4. An automatic dishwasher cost a dealer $620 less $37\frac{1}{2}$%, 4%. It is regularly priced at $558. The dealer's overhead expense is 15% of the regular selling price and the dishwasher was cleared out for $432.45.
   (a) What was the rate of markdown at which the dishwasher was sold?
   (b) What is the regular markup based on selling price?
   (c) What was the operating profit or loss?
   (d) What rate of markup based on cost was realized?

5. A hardware store paid $33.45 for a set of cookware. Overhead expense is 15% of the regular selling price and profit is 10% of the regular selling price. During a clearance sale, the set was sold at a markdown of 15%. What was the operating profit or loss on the sale?

6. Aldo's Shoes bought a shipment of 200 pairs of women's shoes for $42 per pair. The store sold 120 pairs at the regular selling price of $125 per pair, 60 pairs at a clearance sale at a discount of 40%, and the remaining pairs during an inventory sale at a price that equals cost plus overhead (i.e., a break-even price). The store's overhead is 50% of cost.
   (a) What was the price at which the shoes were sold during the clearance sale?
   (b) What was the selling price during the inventory sale?
   (c) What was the total profit realized on the shipment?
   (d) What was the average rate of markup based on cost that was realized on the shipment?  Reference Example 5.5B

7. The Pottery bought 600 pans auctioned off en bloc for $4950. This means that each pan has the same cost. On inspection, the pans were classified as normal quality, seconds, or substandard. The 360 normal-quality pans

were sold at a markup of 80% of cost, the 190 pans classified as seconds were sold at a markup of 20% of cost, and the remaining pans classified as substandard were sold at 80% of their cost.

(a) What was the unit price at which each of the three classifications was sold?

(b) If overhead is $33\frac{1}{3}$% of cost, what was the amount of profit realized on the purchase?

(c) What was the average rate of markup based on the selling price at which the pans were sold?

8. A clothing store buys shorts for $24 less 40% for buying over 50 pairs, and less a further $16\frac{2}{3}$% for buying last season's style. The shorts are marked up to cover overhead expenses of 25% of cost and a profit of $33\frac{1}{3}$% of cost.

(a) What is the regular selling price of the shorts?

(b) What is the maximum amount of markdown to break even?

(c) What is the rate of markdown if the shorts are sold at the break-even price?

9. Furniture City bought chairs for $75 less $33\frac{1}{3}$%, 20%, 10%. The store's overhead is 75% of cost and net profit is 25% of cost.

(a) What is the regular selling price of the chairs?

(b) At what price can the chairs be put on sale so that the store incurs an operating loss of no more than $33\frac{1}{3}$% of the overhead?

(c) What is the maximum rate of markdown at which the chairs can be offered for sale in part (b)?

10. Bargain City clothing store purchased raincoats for $36.75. The store requires a markup of 30% of the sale price. What regular selling price should be marked on the raincoats if the store wants to offer a 25% discount without reducing its markup?

11. A jewellery store paid $36.40 for a watch. Store expenses are 24% of regular selling price and the normal net profit is 20% of regular selling price. During a Special Bargain Day Sale, the watch was sold at a discount of 30%. What operating profit or loss was realized on the sale?

12. The Outdoor Shop buys tents for $264 less 25% for buying more than 20 tents. The store operates on a markup of $33\frac{1}{3}$% of the sale price and advertises that all merchandise is sold at a discount of 20% of the regular selling price. What is the regular selling price of the tents?

13. The Blast bought stereo equipment listed at $900 less 60%, $16\frac{2}{3}$%. Expenses are 45% of the regular selling price and net profit is 15% of the regular selling price. The store decided to change the regular selling price so that it could advertise a 37.5% discount while still maintaining its usual markup. During the annual inventory sale, the unsold equipment was marked down 55% of the new regular selling price. What operating profit or loss was realized on the equipment sold during the sale?

14. Lund's Pro Shop purchased sets of golf clubs for $500 less 40%, $16\frac{2}{3}$%. Expenses are 20% of the regular selling price and the required profit is

17.5% of the regular selling price. The store decided to change the regular selling price so that it could offer a 36% discount without affecting its margin. At the end of the season, the unsold sets were advertised at a discount of 54% of the new regular selling price. What operating profit or loss was realized on the sets sold at the end of the season?

15. Big Boy Appliances bought self-cleaning ovens for $900 less 33⅓%, 5%. Expenses are 15% of the regular selling price and profit is 9% of the regular selling price. For competitive reasons, the store marks all merchandise with a new regular selling price so that a discount of 25% can be advertised without affecting the margin. To promote sales, the ovens were marked down 40%. What operating profit or loss did the store make on the ovens sold during the sales promotion?

16. Blue Lake Marina sells a make of cruiser for $16 800. This regular selling price covers overhead of 15% of cost and a normal net profit of 10% of cost. The cruisers were marked with a new regular selling price so that the marina can offer a 20% discount while still maintaining its regular gross profit. At the end of the boating season, the cruiser was marked down. The marina made 25% of its usual profit and reduced the usual commission paid to the sales personnel by 33⅓%. The normal commission accounts for 50% of the normal overhead. What was the rate of markdown?

## BUSINESS MATH NEWS BOX

### The 2006 National Hockey League Salary Cap

From coast to coast, Canada loves its hockey. Millions of fans flock to arenas every season to cheer on their favorite team, dreaming of the day when their team will hoist the Stanley Cup.

There are currently six Canadian teams in the 30-team National Hockey League (NHL); Toronto Maple Leafs, Montreal Canadiens, Ottawa Senators, Edmonton Oilers, Calgary Flames, and Vancouver Canucks.

However, during the 2004/2005 season, NHL owners locked out the players for the first time in league history. The major cause for the lockout was a disagreement between team owners and players regarding player contracts and salaries.

The players felt that the owners were greedy, believing that owners did not want to share in league profits. On the other hand, the owners felt they could no longer afford the spiraling players' salaries. Owners believed that if a salary limit were not put into action, unprofitable franchises would be in financial ruins within a few years.

After a full season of no hockey, owners and players came to a settlement. It was decided that all teams in the NHL would have a salary cap to limit the escalating salaries. Under the salary cap agreement, it was established that no team could spend more than US$39 million for players' salaries. The $39 million NHL salary cap was based on estimated total league revenues of US$1.8 billion.

Recently, the NHL Commissioner, Gary Bettman, announced that the NHL's salary cap could rise as much as 12% to US$44 million in the 2006/2007 season because total league revenues had increased.

*Sources:* National Hockey League Fans' Association website. "Salary-Cap views prompted impasse." Downloaded February 9, 2007. David Pollack, *San Jose Mercury News*, September 16, 2004. **www.nhlfa.com/news/nr09_16_04.asp;** CBC website. "NHL Salary Cap expected to rise." Downloaded February 9, 2007. *CBC Sports.* December 20, 2005. **www.cbc.ca/sports/story/2005/12/15/ nhl051215.html#skip300x250;** USA Today website. *Salaries Database.* Downloaded February 9, 2007. **http://asp.usatoday.com/ sports/hockey/nhl/salaries/teamdetail.aspx?year=2003-04&team=28;** Larry DiTore and Sophie Caronello. Bloomberg News, "NHL's Salary Cap May Rise 12 Percent on Higher League Revenue," June 6, 2006. (New York).

## QUESTIONS

1. What is total payroll for all 30 teams during the 2005/2006 season?

2. If league revenues remain at $1.8 billion, yet each team increases its salary cap to $44 million, how much profit is earned by the NHL? What is the value of profit as a percentage of league revenues?

3. The Toronto Maple Leafs have a 22-man roster. Ten of their high profile players have been signed. Based on a league cap of $44 million, calculate the average salary for the remaining 12 players.

| Player | Annual Salary (in $ Millions) |
|---|---|
| Mats Sundin | $7.60 |
| Bryan McCabe | $7.15 |
| Pavel Kubina | $5.00 |
| Tomas Kaberle | $4.25 |
| Mike Peca | $2.50 |
| Hal Gill | $2.05 |
| Andrew Raycroft | $1.80 |
| Darcy Tucker | $1.60 |
| Jeff O'Neill | $1.50 |
| Chad Kilger | $1.20 |

Go to MyMathLab at www.mathxl.com. You can practise many of this chapter's exercises as often as you want. The guided solutions help you find an answer step by step. You'll find a personalized study plan available to you too!

## Review Exercise

1. A toolbox is listed for $56 less 25%, 20%, 5%.

   (a) What is the net price of the toolbox?

   (b) What is the amount of discount?

   (c) What is the single rate of discount that was allowed?

2. Compute the rate of discount allowed on a lawn-mower that lists for $168 and is sold for $105.

3. Determine the single rate of discount equivalent to the discount series 35%, 12%, 5%.

4. A 40% discount allowed on an article amounts to $1.44. What is the net price?

5. Baton Construction Supplies has been selling wheelbarrows for $112 less 15%. What additional discount percent must the company offer to meet a competitor's price of $80.92?

6. A freezer was sold during a clearance sale for $387.50. If the freezer was sold at a discount of $16\frac{2}{3}$%, what was the list price?

7. The net price of a snow shovel is $20.40 after discounts of 20%, 15%. What is the list price?

8. On May 18, an invoice dated May 17 for $4000 less 20%, 15%, terms 5/10 E.O.M., was received by Aldo Distributors.

   (a) What is the last day of the discount period?

   (b) What is the amount due if the invoice is paid within the discount period?

9. Air Yukon received a shipment of plastic trays on September 2. The invoice amounting to $25 630 was dated August 15, terms 2/10, n/30 R.O.G. What is the last day for taking the cash discount and how much is to be paid if the discount is taken?

10. What amount must be remitted if the following invoices, all with terms 5/10, 2/30, n/60, are paid together on December 8?
    Invoice No. 312 dated November 2 for $923.00
    Invoice No. 429 dated November 14 for $784.00
    Invoice No. 563 dated November 30 for $873.00

11. Delta Furnishings received an invoice dated May 10 for a shipment of goods received June 21. The invoice was for $8400.00 less $33\frac{1}{3}$%, $12\frac{1}{2}$% with terms 3/20 R.O.G. How much must Delta pay on July 9 to reduce its debt

    (a) by $2000?

    (b) to $2000?

12. The Peel Trading Company received an invoice dated September 20 for $16 000 less 25%, 20%, terms 5/10, 2/30, n/60. Peel made a payment on September 30 to reduce the debt to $5000 and a payment on October 20 to reduce the debt by $3000.

    (a) What amount must Peel remit to pay the balance of the debt at the end of the credit period?

    (b) What is the total amount paid by Peel?

13. Emco Ltd. received an invoice dated May 5 for $4000 less 15%, $7\frac{1}{2}$%, terms 3/15 E.O.M. A cheque for $1595.65 was mailed by Emco on June 15 as part payment of the invoice.

    (a) By how much did Emco reduce the amount due on the invoice?

    (b) How much does Emco still owe?

14. Homeward Hardware buys cat litter for $6 less 20% per bag. The store's overhead is 45% of cost and the owner requires a profit of 20% of cost.

    (a) For how much should the bags be sold?

    (b) What is the amount of markup included in the selling price?

    (c) What is the rate of markup based on selling price?

    (d) What is the rate of markup based on cost?

    (e) What is the break-even price?

    (f) What operating profit or loss is made if a bag is sold for $6?

15. A retail store realizes a markup of $31.50 if it sells an article at a markup of 35% of the selling price.

    (a) What is the regular selling price?

    (b) What is the cost?

(c) What is the rate of markup based on cost?

(d) If overhead expense is 28% of cost, what is the break-even price?

(e) If the article is sold at a markdown of 24%, what is the operating profit or loss?

**16.** Using a markup of 35% of cost, a store priced a book at $8.91.

(a) What was the cost of the book?

(b) What is the markup as a percent of selling price?

**17.** A bicycle helmet costing $54.25 was marked up to realize a markup of 30% of the regular selling price.

(a) What was the regular selling price?

(b) What was the markup as a percent of cost?

**18.** A bedroom suite that cost a dealer $1800 less 37.5%, 18% carries a price tag with a regular selling price at a markup of 120% of cost. For quick sale, the bedroom suite was marked down 40%.

(a) What was the sale price?

(b) What rate of markup based on cost was realized?

**19.** Gino's purchased men's suits for $195 less $33\frac{1}{3}$%. The store operates at a normal markup of 35% of regular selling price. The owner marks all merchandise with new regular selling prices so that the store can offer a $16\frac{2}{3}$% discount while maintaining the same gross profit. What is the new regular selling price?

**20.** An appliance store sold GE coffeemakers for $22.95 during a promotional sale. The store bought the coffeemakers for $36 less 40%, 15%. Overhead is 25% of the regular selling price.

(a) If the store's markup is 40% of the regular selling price, what was the rate of markdown?

(b) What operating profit or loss was made during the sale?

(c) What rate of markup based on cost was realized?

**21.** Billington's buys shirts for $21 less 25%, 20%. The shirts are priced at a regular selling price to cover expenses of 20% of regular selling price and a profit of 17% of regular selling price. For a special weekend sale, shirts were marked down 20%.

(a) What was the operating profit or loss on the shirts sold during the weekend sale?

(b) What rate of markup was realized based on cost?

**22.** A jewellery store paid a unit price of $250 less 40%, $16\frac{2}{3}$%, 8% for a shipment of designer watches. The store's overhead is 65% of cost and the normal profit is 55% of cost.

(a) What is the regular selling price of the watches?

(b) What must the sale price be for the store to break even?

(c) What is the rate of markdown to sell the watches at the break-even price?

**23.** Sight and Sound bought large-screen colour TV sets for $1080.00 less $33\frac{1}{3}$%, $8\frac{1}{3}$%. Overhead is 18% of regular selling price and required profit is $15\frac{1}{3}$% of regular selling price. The TV sets were marked at a new regular selling price so that the store was able to advertise a discount of 25% while still maintaining its margin. To clear the inventory, the remaining TV sets were marked down $37\frac{1}{2}$%.

(a) What operating profit or loss is realized at the clearance price?

(b) What is the realized rate of markup based on cost?

**24.** Ward Machinery lists a log splitter at $1860 less $33\frac{1}{3}$%, 15%. To meet competition, Ward wants to reduce its net price to $922.25. What additional percent discount must Ward allow?

**25.** West End Appliances bought bread makers for $180 less 40%, $16\frac{2}{3}$%, 10%. The store's overhead is 45% of regular selling price and the profit required is $21\frac{1}{4}$% of regular selling price.

(a) What is the break-even price?

(b) What is the maximum rate of markdown that the store can offer to break even?

(c) What is the realized rate of markup based on cost if the bread makers are sold at the break-even price?

26. A merchant realizes a markup of $42 by selling an item at a markup of 37.5% of cost.

(a) What is the regular selling price?

(b) What is the rate of markup based on the regular selling price?

(c) If the merchant's overhead expenses are 17.5% of the regular selling price, what is the break-even price?

(d) If the article is reduced for sale to $121.66, what is the rate of markdown?

27. The Knit Shoppe bought 250 sweaters for $3100; 50 sweaters were sold at a markup of 150% of cost and 120 sweaters at a markup of 75% of cost; 60 of the sweaters were sold during a clearance sale for $15 each and the remaining sweaters were disposed of at 20% below cost. Assume all sweaters had the same cost.

(a) What was the amount of markup realized on the purchase?

(b) What was the percent markup realized based on cost?

(c) What was the gross profit realized based on selling price?

## Self-Test

1. Determine the net price of an article listed at $590 less 37.5%, 12.5%, $8\frac{1}{3}$%.

2. What rate of discount has been allowed if an item that lists for $270 is sold for $168.75?

3. Compute the single discount percent equivalent to the discount series 40%, 10%, $8\frac{1}{3}$%.

4. Discount Electronics lists an article for $1020 less 25% and 15%. A competitor carries the same article for $927 less 25%. What further discount (correct to the nearest $\frac{1}{10}$ of 1%) must the competitor allow so that its net price is the same as Discount's?

5. What amount must be remitted if the following invoices, all with terms 4/10, 2/30, n/60, are paid on May 10?
   $850 less 20%, 10% dated March 21
   $960 less 30%, $16\frac{2}{3}$% dated April 10
   $1040 less $33\frac{1}{3}$%, 25%, 5% dated April 30

6. An invoice for $3200, dated March 20, terms 3/10 E.O.M., was received March 23. What payment must be made on April 10 to reduce the debt to $1200?

7. On January 15, Sheridan Service received an invoice dated January 14, terms 4/10 E.O.M., for $2592. On February 9, Sheridan Service mailed a cheque for $1392 in partial payment of the invoice. By how much did Sheridan Service reduce its debt?

8. What is the regular selling price of an item purchased for $1270 if the markup is 20% of the regular selling price?

9. The regular selling price of merchandise sold in a store includes a markup of 40% based on the regular selling price. During a sale, an item that cost the store $180 was marked down 20%. For how much was the item sold?

10. The net price of an article is $727.20 after discounts of 20% and 10% have been allowed. What was the list price?

11. An item that cost the dealer $350 less 35%, 12.5% carries a regular selling price on the tag at a markup of 150% of cost. For quick sale, the item was reduced 30%. What was the sale price?

12. Find the cost of an item sold for $1904 to realize a markup of 40% based on cost.

13. An article cost $900 and sold for $2520. What was the percent markup based on cost?

14. A markup of $90 is made on a sale. If the markup was 45% based on selling price, what was the cost?

15. An appliance shop reduces the price of an appliance for quick sale from $1560 to $1195. Compute the markdown correct to the nearest $\frac{1}{100}$ of 1%.

16. An invoice shows a net price of $552.44 after discounts of $33\frac{1}{3}$%, 20%, $8\frac{1}{3}$%. What was the list price?

17. A retailer buys an appliance for $1480 less 25%, 15%. The store marks the merchandise at a regular selling price to cover expenses of 40% of the regular selling price and a net profit of 10% of the regular selling price. During a clearance sale, the appliance was sold at a markdown of 45%. What was the operating profit or loss?

18. Discount Electronics buys stereos for $830 less 37.5%, 12.5%. Expenses are 20% of the regular selling price and the required profit is 15% of the regular selling price. All merchandise is marked with a new regular selling price so that the store can advertise a discount of 30% while still maintaining its regular markup. During the annual clearance sale, the new regular selling price of unsold items is marked down 50%. What operating profit or loss does the store make on items sold during the sale?

## Challenge Problems

1. Rose Bowl Florists buys and sells roses only by the complete dozen. The owner buys 12 dozen fresh roses daily for $117. He knows that 10% of the roses will wilt before they can be sold. What price per dozen must Rose Bowl Florists charge for its saleable roses to realize a 55% markup based on selling price?

2. A merchant bought some goods at a discount of 25% of the list price. She wants to mark them at a regular selling price so that she can give a discount of 20% of the regular selling price and still make a markup of 25% of the sale price.
   (a) At what percent of the list price should she mark the regular selling price of the goods?
   (b) Suppose the merchant decides she must make a markup of 25% of the cost price. At what percent of the list price should she mark the regular selling price of the goods?

3. On April 13, a stereo store received a new sound system with a list price of $2500 from the manufacturer. The stereo store received a trade discount of 25%. The invoice, with terms 2/10, n/30, arrived on the same day as the sound system. The owner of the store marked up the sound system by 60% of the invoice amount (before cash discount) to cover overhead and profits. The owner paid the invoice on April 20. How much extra profit will be made on the sale, as a percent of the regular selling price, due to the early payment of the invoice?

# Case Study 5.1 Planning for Production

» Ethan Baxter has decided to expand his garden supply manufacturing business. He has an available factory site that is presently costing him $65 000 per year in taxes and maintenance. Ethan has made a deal with Stellar Supply Company to provide him with the necessary material to produce 1400 garden sprinklers. Stellar has agreed to supply the material for $7200 less 2% for quantity discount. Ethan's shop steward has informed him that labour costs will amount to $11 500 to make the sprinklers.

## QUESTIONS

1. Ethan expects that it will take three months to produce the garden sprinklers, and he intends to market them at $35.99 per sprinkler. How many sprinklers must Ethan sell to break even?

2. What is the break-even point as a percent of capacity?

3. If Ethan sells all 1400 sprinklers, how much profit can he expect to make assuming the costs listed above?

4. Ethan has been informed that the union has negotiated a 3.5% wage increase.
   (a) What effect will the wage increase have on the break-even point?
   (b) What effect will the wage increase have on Ethan's profit if 1400 units are sold?

# Case Study 5.2 Calculating Car Costs

» Abraham is concerned about the high-cost gasoline that his current car consumes. He is considering purchasing a new car. He realizes that he must take into account the purchase price of the new car as well as the savings in gasoline costs to determine when he would be saving money by having a new car.

Abraham has designed a mathematical formula to calculate the number of years he must drive the new car. He uses the following variables in his formula:

$y$ = the number of years Abraham must own the new car

$m$ = the gasoline used by the current car, measured in kilometres per litre

$n$ = the gasoline used by the new car, measured in kilometres per litre

$c$ = the net cost of the new car (purchase price of the new car minus trade-in value of the old car)

$d$ = the average number of kilometres driven per year

$p$ = the price of gasoline per litre

$x$ = the number of years to break even

Abraham has decided the "current car–new car" relationship might be expressed as follows:

Cost of gasoline for current car during break-even period = Cost of gasoline for new car during break-even period + Net cost of new car

## QUESTIONS

1. Using the variables defined by Abraham, what is the expression for each side of the "current car–new car" relationship?

2. What is the general formula for the break-even period for the "current car–new car" relationship?

3. What is the break-even period if Abraham's current car has a trade-in value of $6500 and gets 9 km/L? Gasoline prices in Abraham's neighbourhood average $0.95/L. Assume Abraham drives an average of 35 000 kilometres per year.

4. Assume that the price of gasoline can vary by 25% from the price of $0.95/L.
   (a) How does the break-even period change when the price of gasoline declines by 25%?
   (b) How does the break-even period change when the price of gasoline increases by 25%?

5. What is the expected break-even period if Abraham buys a car costing $23 000 with an expected gas consumption of 18 km/L if the average price is
   (a) $0.95/L?
   (b) $1.05/L?
   (c) $1.10/L?

6. What assumptions did you make when you solved these problems? What cost factors have not been considered?

## SUMMARY OF FORMULAS

**Formula 5.1A**

$$\text{AMOUNT OF DISCOUNT} = \text{RATE OF DISCOUNT} \times \text{LIST PRICE}$$

Finding the amount of discount when the list price is known

**Formula 5.1B**

$$\text{LIST PRICE} = \frac{\text{AMOUNT OF DISCOUNT}}{\text{RATE OF DISCOUNT}}$$

Finding the list price when the amount of discount is known

**Formula 5.1C**

$$\frac{\text{RATE OF}}{\text{DISCOUNT}} = \frac{\text{AMOUNT OF DISCOUNT}}{\text{LIST PRICE}}$$

**Finding the rate of discount when the amount of discount is known**

**Formula 5.2**

NET PRICE = LIST PRICE − AMOUNT OF DISCOUNT

**Finding the net amount when the amount of discount is known**

**Formula 5.3A**

$$\frac{\text{NET PRICE}}{\text{FACTOR (NPF)}} = 100\% - \%\ \text{DISCOUNT}$$

**Finding the net price factor (NPF)**

**Formula 5.3B**

NET PRICE FACTOR (NPF) $= (1 - d)$
where $d$ = rate of discount in decimal form

**Restatement of Formula 5.3A in algebraic terms**

**Formula 5.4A**

$$\text{NET PRICE} = \frac{\text{NET PRICE}}{\text{FACTOR (NPF)}} \times \text{LIST PRICE}$$

**Finding the net amount directly without computing the amount of discount**

**Formula 5.4B**

$N = (1 - d)L$ or $N = L(1 - d)$

**Restatement of Formula 5.4A in algebraic terms**

**Formula 5.5A**

$$\frac{\text{NET PRICE FACTOR}}{\text{(NPF) FOR}}_{\text{THE DISCOUNT SERIES}} = \frac{\text{NPF FOR THE}}{\text{FIRST DISCOUNT}} \times \frac{\text{NPF FOR THE}}{\text{SECOND DISCOUNT}} \times \ldots \times \frac{\text{NPF FOR THE}}{\text{LAST DISCOUNT}}$$

**Formula 5.5B**

NPF FOR A DISCOUNT SERIES $= (1 - d_1)(1 - d_2)(1 - d_3) \ldots (1 - d_n)$     **Restatement of Formula 5.5A in algebraic terms**

**Formula 5.6A**

$$\text{NET PRICE} = \frac{\text{NET PRICE FACTOR FOR}}{\text{THE DISCOUNT SERIES}} \times \text{LIST PRICE}$$

**Finding the net amount directly when a list price is subject to a series of discounts**

**Formula 5.6B**

$$\frac{\text{NET}}{\text{PRICE}} = (1 - d_1)(1 - d_2)(1 - d_3) \ldots (1 - d_n)L$$

**Restatement of Formula 5.6A in algebraic terms**

**Formula 5.7**

SINGLE EQUIVALENT RATE OF DISCOUNT
FOR A DISCOUNT SERIES
$= 1 - $ NPF FOR THE DISCOUNT SERIES
$= 1 - [(1 - d_1)(1 - d_2)(1 - d_3) \ldots (1 - d_n)]$

**Finding the single rate of discount that has the same effect as a given series of discounts**

**Formula 5.8A**

$$\text{SELLING PRICE} = \text{COST OF BUYING} + \text{EXPENSES} + \text{PROFIT}$$

or

$$S = C + E + P$$

Basic relationship between selling price, cost of buying, operating expenses (or overhead), and profit

**Formula 5.8B**

$$\text{SELLING PRICE} = \text{COST OF BUYING} + \text{MARKUP}$$

or

$$S = C + M$$

**Formula 5.9**

$$\text{MARKUP} = \text{EXPENSES} + \text{PROFIT}$$

or

$$M = E + P$$

Basic relationship between markup, cost of buying, operating expenses (or overhead), and profit

**Formula 5.10**

$$\text{RATE OF MARKUP BASED ON COST} = \frac{\text{MARKUP}}{\text{COST}} = \frac{M}{C}$$

Finding the rate of markup as a percent of cost

**Formula 5.11**

$$\text{RATE OF MARKUP BASED ON SELLING PRICE} = \frac{\text{MARKUP}}{\text{SELLING PRICE}} = \frac{M}{S}$$

Finding the rate of markup as a percent of selling price

## GLOSSARY

**Cash discount** a reduction in the amount of an invoice, usually to encourage prompt payment of the invoice (*p. 188*)

**Credit period** the time period at the end of which an invoice has to be paid (*p. 188*)

**Discount** a reduction from the original price (*p. 182*)

**Discount period** the time period during which a cash discount applies (*p. 188*)

**Discount series** two or more discounts taken off a list price in succession (*p. 182*)

**End-of-month dating** payment terms based on the last day of the month in which the invoice is dated (*p. 191*)

**Gross profit** *see* **Markup**

**List price** price printed in a catalogue or in a list of prices (*p. 179*)

**Manufacturer's suggested retail price (MSRP)** catalogue or list price that is reduced by a trade discount (*p. 179*)

**Margin** *see* **Markup**

**Markdown** a reduction in the price of an article sold to the consumer (*p. 206*)

**Markup** the difference between the cost of merchandise and the selling price (*p. 197*)

**Net factor** *see* **Net price factor (NPF)**

**Net price** the difference between a list price and the amount of discount (*p. 179*)

**Net price factor (NPF)** the difference between 100% and a percent discount—the net price expressed as a fraction of the list price (*p. 181*)

**Ordinary dating** payment terms based on the date of an invoice (*p. 189*)

**Partial payment** part payment of an invoice (*p. 193*)

**Payment terms**   a statement of the conditions under which a cash discount may be taken *(p. 188)*

**Rate of discount**   a reduction in price expressed as a percent of the original price *(p. 179, 188)*

**Receipt-of-goods dating**   payment terms based on the date the merchandise is received *(p. 192)*

**Regular selling price**   the price of an article sold to the consumer before any markdown is applied *(p. 207)*

**Sale price**   the price of an article sold to the consumer after a markdown has been applied *(p. 207)*

**Single equivalent rate of discount**   the single rate of discount that has the same effect as a specific series of discounts *(p. 184)*

**Total cost**   the cost at which merchandise is purchased plus the overhead *(p. 206)*

**Trade discount**   a reduction of a catalogue or list price *(p. 179)*

## USEFUL INTERNET SITES

**www.electronicaccountant.com**

**Electronic Accountant**   Free access to news and critical accounting industry information. This site includes Newswire, links and commentary, discussion groups, feature articles, and accounting/tax software exhibit halls.

**www.ibc.ca**

**Insurance Bureau of Canada**   This site offers an overview of the industry and of recent legal and consumer-related developments and provides significant links to both business and government sites.

# Simple Interest

## OBJECTIVES

**Upon completing this chapter, you will be able to do the following:**

1. Compute the amount of simple interest using the formula $I = Prt$.

2. Compute the principal, interest rate, or time using variations of the formula $I = Prt$.

3. Compute the maturity value (future value) using the formula $S = P(1 + rt)$.

4. Compute the principal (present value) using the formula $P = \dfrac{S}{1 + rt}$

5. Compute equivalent or dated values for specified focal dates.

Every day in business, money is borrowed for short periods of time. Businesses lend money when they extend credit to customers or clients, or when they make short-term investments. Businesses borrow money when they purchase on credit from vendors, use a line of credit from a financial institution, or utilize credit cards to make a purchase. With these loans, interest must be considered.

## INTRODUCTION

Transactions in business often involve the daily borrowing or loaning of money. To compensate the lenders for the use of their money, interest is paid. The amount of interest paid is based on three factors: the amount of money borrowed, the rate of interest at which it is borrowed, and the time period for which it is borrowed.

# 7.1 FINDING THE AMOUNT OF SIMPLE INTEREST

## A. Basic concepts and formula

**Interest** is the rent charged for the use of money. The amount of **simple interest** is determined by the relationship

Interest = Principal $\times$ Rate $\times$ Time

$$I = Prt$$ —————— Formula 7.1A

where    I is the amount of interest earned, measured in dollars and cents;
P is the principal sum of money earning the interest, measured in dollars and cents;
$r$ is the simple annual (yearly or **nominal**) **rate** of interest, expressed as a percent, which can be converted into a decimal;
$t$ is the **interest period** in years.

Simple interest is often used in business, through short-term loans to and from financial institutions, vendors, and customers.

---

## POINTERS AND PITFALLS

To use the TI BA II Plus financial calculator to determine the number of days between two dates, choose the DATE worksheet by pressing [2nd] [DATE]. The first date, DT1, is usually the earlier date. The date format can be set to show the U.S. format, mm/dd/yy, or the European format, dd/mm/yy. When the U.S. format is used, enter the date by choosing the one- or two-digit number representing the month, followed by a period, and then enter two digits for the day and the last two digits for the year. Only one period is entered between the month and the day. Press [Enter] to save the data. To move to the next label, press the down arrow. The second date, DT2, is usually the later date. Enter the second date in the same manner as the first date, with one or two digits for the number of the month, a period, two digits for the day, and two digits for the year. Following the second date is the "days between dates" calculation. Press the down arrow to access this part of the worksheet. To show the exact days, press [CPT] (Compute) to instruct the calculator to perform the calculation. When the first date precedes the second date, the days between dates will appear as a positive number. If the second date is entered as the earlier date, the days between dates will appear as a negative number. The fourth label within the worksheet sets the calculator to show the actual number of days between the dates indicated, including adjustments for leap years. Set this label to ACT by pressing [2nd] [SET].

For example, to determine the number of days between April 23, 2009, and July 21, 2009, press

| 2nd | DATE | DT1 | 04.2309 | Enter | ↓ |
| | | DT2 | 07.2109 | Enter | ↓ |
| CPT | | DBD | | | Result is 89 |

Note that the month is entered first, with one or two digits, followed by a period; the day is entered using two digits; and then the year is entered using two digits.

If only one of the dates and the desired days between the dates are entered, it is possible to determine the second date.

 If you choose, you can use Excel's Coupon Days, or days between dates (COUPDAYSNC) function, to find the number of days between two dates. Refer to COUPDAYSNC on the Spreadsheet Template Disk to learn how.

You can also use Excel's Accrued Interest (ACCRINT) function to compute the amount of interest when the time is given in days. Refer to ACCRINT on the Spreadsheet Template Disk to learn how.

## B. Matching *r* and *t*

While the time may be stated in days, months, or years, the rate of interest is generally stated as a yearly charge, often followed by "per annum" or "p.a." In using the simple interest formula, it is imperative that the time *t* correspond to the interest rate *r*. Time expressed in months or days often needs to be converted into years. The number of days between two dates can be determined manually or by using the DATE function on a business calculator. Manual techniques are outlined in a section on the CD accompanying the text.

**EXAMPLE 7.1A**

State *r* and *t* for each of the following:

(i) rate 4%; time 3 years;

(ii) rate 6.5% p.a. (per annum); time 18 months;

(iii) rate 5.25% p.a.; time 243 days.

**SOLUTION**

(i) The annual rate $r = 4\% = 0.04$
The time in years $t = 3$

(ii) The annual rate $r = 6.5\% = 0.065$
The time in years $t = \dfrac{18}{12}$

*Note:* To convert months into years, divide by 12.

(iii) The annual rate $r = 5.25\% = 0.0525$
The time in years $t = \dfrac{243}{365}$

*Note:* To convert days into years, divide by 365.

## C. Computing the amount of interest

When the principal, rate, and time are known, the amount of interest can be determined by the formula $I = Prt$.

**EXAMPLE 7.1B**

Compute the amount of interest for

   (i) $3600 at 6.25% p.a. (per annum) for 3 years;

  (ii) $5240 at 4.5% p.a. for 16 months;

 (iii) $1923.60 at 3% p.a. for 215 days.

**SOLUTION**

   (i) $P = \$3600.00; \quad r = 6.25\% = 0.0625; \quad t = 3$
$I = Prt = (3600.00)(0.0625)(3) = \$675.00$

  (ii) $P = \$5240.00; \quad r = 4.5\% = 0.045; \quad t = 16 \text{ months} = \dfrac{16}{12}$

$I = Prt = (5240.00)(0.045)\left(\dfrac{16}{12}\right) = \$314.40$

 (iii) $P = \$1923.60; \quad r = 3\% = 0.03; \quad t = 215 \text{ days} = \dfrac{215}{365}$

$I = Prt = (1923.60)(0.03)\left(\dfrac{215}{365}\right) = \$33.99$

**EXAMPLE 7.1C**

Compute the amount of interest on $785.95 borrowed at 18% p.a. from January 30, 2009, until March 21, 2009.

**SOLUTION**

Number of days = 50

$$P = 785.95; \quad r = 18\% = 0.18; \quad t = \dfrac{50}{365}$$

$$I = (785.95)(0.18)\left(\dfrac{50}{365}\right) = \$19.38$$

**EXAMPLE 7.1D**

Compute the amount of interest on $1240 earning 6% p.a. from September 30, 2009, to May 16, 2010.

**SOLUTION**

The starting date is September 30, 2009 (DT1). The ending date is May 16, 2010 (DT2).

Days between dates (DBD) = 228

$$P = 1240.00; \quad r = 6\% = 0.06; \quad t = \dfrac{228}{365}$$

$$I = (1240.00)(0.06)\left(\dfrac{228}{365}\right) = \$46.47$$

## EXERCISE 7.1

**A.** State *r* and *t* for each of the following:
1. rate is 3½%; time is 1¼ years
2. rate is 9¾%; time is 21 months
3. rate is 8.25%; time is 183 days
4. rate is 5½%; time is 332 days

**B.** Compute the amount of interest for each of the following:
1. $5000 at 9¾% for 2¼ years
2. $645 at 6¼% for 1¾ years
3. $1755 at 4.65% for 14 months
4. $1651.43 at 4.9% for 9 months
5. $980 at 11.5% for 244 days
6. $1697.23 at 3.4% for 163 days
7. $275 at 9.25% from November 30, 2009 to May 5, 2010
8. $1090.60 at 7.8% from October 12, 2011 to April 24, 2012
9. $424.23 at 8¾% from April 4, 2010 to November 4, 2010
10. $1713.09 at 4.4% from August 30, 2010 to March 30, 2011
11. $629.99 at 6.9% from June 16, 2009 to January 24, 2010
12. $17 000 at 15.6% from November 12, 2008 to July 31, 2009

**C.**
1. On April 1, 2009, Faircloud Variety Company deposited $24 000 into a savings account earning simple interest of 1.5%. Interest is paid to the account at the end of every calendar quarter. How much interest was paid to Faircloud's account on June 30, 2009?

2. Leah deposited $1500 into a savings account that earned simple interest of 2.25% on July 17, 2009. How much interest was earned and paid into Leah's account on December 1, 2009?

3. Kenneth borrowed $6100 to buy a car. If interest was charged on the loan at 9.7%, how much interest would he have to pay in 30 days?

4. Lin Yan borrowed $1800 from her parents to finance a vacation. If interest was charged on the loan at 7.2%, how much interest would she have to pay in 100 days?

# 7.2 FINDING THE PRINCIPAL, RATE, OR TIME

## A. Formulas derived from the simple interest formula

The simple interest formula $I = Prt$ contains the four variables I, P, $r$, and $t$. If any three of the four are given, the value of the unknown variable can be computed by substituting the known values in the formula or by solving for the unknown variable first and then substituting in the resulting derived formula.

The three derived formulas are

(i) To find the principal P,

$$P = \frac{I}{rt}$$ ————————— Formula 7.1B

(ii) To find the rate of interest $r$,

$$r = \frac{I}{Pt}$$ ————————— Formula 7.1C

(iii) To find the time period $t$,

$$t = \frac{I}{Pr}$$ ————————— Formula 7.1D

***Note:***
(a) In Formula 7.1C, if the time period $t$ is expressed in years, the value of $r$ represents an annual rate of interest in decimal form.
(b) In Formula 7.1D, if the rate of interest $r$ is an annual rate, the value of $t$ represents years in decimal form.

## POINTERS AND PITFALLS

This diagram is a useful aid in remembering the various forms of the simple interest formula $I = Prt$.

## B. Finding the principal

When the amount of interest, the rate of interest, and the time period are known, the principal can be determined.

**EXAMPLE 7.2A**     What principal will earn interest of $18.20 at 3.25% in 8 months?

**SOLUTION**     $I = 18.20; \quad r = 3.25\%; \quad t = \dfrac{8}{12}$

(i) Using the formula $I = Prt$,

$$18.20 = (P)(0.0325)\left(\frac{8}{12}\right)$$ ———————— by substitution

$$18.20 = (P)(0.021667) \quad\text{————————}\quad (0.0325)\left(\frac{8}{12}\right)$$

$$P = \frac{18.20}{0.021667} \quad\text{————————}\quad \text{divide 18.20 by the coefficient of P}$$

$$= \$840.00$$

(ii) Using the derived formula $P = \dfrac{I}{rt}$,

$$P = \frac{18.20}{(0.0325)\left(\frac{8}{12}\right)} \quad\text{————————}\quad \text{by substitution}$$

$$= \frac{18.20}{0.021667} = \$840.00$$

**EXAMPLE 7.2B**   Determine the amount of money that must be invested for 245 days at 5.75% to earn $42.46.

**SOLUTION**   $I = 42.46; \quad r = 5.75\% = 0.0575; \quad t = \dfrac{245}{365}$

(i) Using the formula $I = Prt$,

$$42.46 = (P)(0.0575)\left(\frac{245}{365}\right)$$

$$42.46 = (P)(0.038596)$$

$$P = \frac{42.46}{0.038596} = \$1100.11$$

(ii) Using the derived formula $P = \dfrac{I}{rt}$,

$$P = \frac{42.46}{(0.0575)\left(\frac{245}{365}\right)} = \$1100.11$$

## C. Finding the rate

When the amount of interest, the principal, and the time period are known, the rate of interest can be determined.

**EXAMPLE 7.2C**   Find the annual rate of interest required for $744 to earn $75.95 in 14 months.

**SOLUTION**   $I = 75.95; \quad P = 744.00; \quad t = \dfrac{14}{12}$

(i) Using the formula $I = Prt$,

$$75.95 = (744)(r)\left(\frac{14}{12}\right)$$

$$75.95 = (868)(r)$$

$$r = \frac{75.95}{868} = 0.0875 = 8.75\% \quad\text{————————}\quad \text{convert to a percent}$$

(ii) Using the derived formula $r = \dfrac{I}{Pt}$,

$$r = \frac{75.95}{(744.00)\left(\frac{14}{12}\right)}$$

$$= \frac{75.95}{868.00} = 0.0875 = 8.75\%$$

## D. Finding the time

When the amount of interest, the principal, and the rate of interest are known, the time period can be determined.

**EXAMPLE 7.2D**

Find the number of years required for $745 to earn $178.80 simple interest at 8% p.a.

**SOLUTION**

$I = 178.80$;   $P = 745.00$;   $r = 8\% = 0.08$

(i) Using the formula I $= Prt$,

$178.80 = (745.00)(0.08)(t)$

$178.80 = (59.60)(t)$

$$t = \frac{178.80}{59.60}$$

$$= 3.00 \text{ (years)}$$

(ii) Using the derived formula $t = \dfrac{I}{Pr}$,

$$t = \frac{178.80}{(745.00)(0.08)}$$

$$= 3.00 \text{ (years)}$$

***Note:*** The value of $t$ in the formula I $= Prt$ will be in years. If the time period is to be stated in months or in days, it is necessary to multiply the initial value of $t$ by 12 for months or 365 for days.

**EXAMPLE 7.2E**

Determine the number of months required for a deposit of $1320 to earn $16.50 interest at 3.75%.

**SOLUTION**

$I = 16.50$;   $P = 1320.00$;   $r = 3.75\% = 0.0375$

(i) Using the formula I $= Prt$,

$16.50 = (1320.00)(0.0375)(t)$

$16.50 = (49.50)(t)$

$$t = \frac{16.50}{49.50}$$

$$= 0.333333 \text{ years}$$

$$= (0.333333)(12) \text{ months}$$

$$= 4 \text{ months}$$

**B.** Find the value indicated for each of the following:

1. Find the principal that will earn $148.32 at 6.75% in 8 months.

2. Determine the deposit that must be made to earn $39.27 in 225 days at 2.75%.

3. A loan of $880 can be repaid in 15 months by paying the principal sum borrowed plus $104.50 interest. What was the rate of interest charged?

4. Joan borrowed $650 and is to repay the balance plus interest of $23.70 in seven months. What was the rate of interest charged?

5. At what rate of interest will $1387 earn $63.84 in 200 days?

6. A deposit of $2400 will earn $22.74 in 91 days at what rate of interest?

7. In how many months will $1290 earn $100.51 interest at $8\frac{1}{2}$%?

8. Interest of $20.95 is earned at 3.15% on a deposit of $2660 in how many months?

9. Determine the number of days it will take $564 to earn $15.09 at $7\frac{3}{4}$%.

10. How many days will it take $1200 to earn $12.22 interest at 16.9%?

11. What principal will earn $39.96 from June 18, 2009 to December 15, 2009 at 9.25%?

12. What rate of interest is required for $740.48 to earn $42.49 interest from September 10, 2011 to March 4, 2012?

13. Philip wants to supplement his pension by $2000 per month with income from his investments. His investments pay him monthly and earn 6% p.a. What value of investments must Philip have in his portfolio to generate enough interest to give him his desired income?

14. Bunny's Antiques received $88.47 interest on a 120-day term deposit of $7800. At what rate of interest was the term deposit invested?

15. Anne's Dress Shop borrowed $3200 to buy material. The loan was paid off seven months later by a lump-sum payment that included $168 of interest. What was the simple rate of interest at which the money was borrowed?

16. Mac's credit card statement included $360 in cash advances and $3.20 in interest charges. The interest rate on the statement was 13.5%. For how many days was Mac charged interest?

17. Bill filed his income tax return with the Canada Revenue Agency (CRA) after the April 30 deadline. He calculated that he owed the CRA $3448, but did not include a payment for this amount when he sent in his tax return. The CRA's Notice of Assessment indicated agreement with Bill's tax calculation. It also showed that the balance due was $3827.66, which included a 10% late-filing penalty and interest at 9% p.a. For how many days was Bill charged interest?

18. On August 15, 2010, Low Rider Automotive established a line of credit at its bank, with interest at 8.75% p.a. This line of credit was used to purchase

$5000 of inventory and supplies. Low Rider paid $5113.87 to satisfy the incurred debt. On what date did Low Rider Automotive honour the line of credit?

# 7.3 COMPUTING FUTURE VALUE (MATURITY VALUE)

## A. Basic concept

When you borrow money, you are obligated to repay both the sum borrowed (the principal) and any interest due. Therefore, the **future value of a sum of money** (or **maturity value**) is the value obtained by adding the original principal and the interest due.

$$\text{FUTURE VALUE (OR MATURITY VALUE)} = \text{PRINCIPAL} + \text{INTEREST}$$
$$S = P + I$$

———— Formula 7.2

**EXAMPLE 7.3A**    Determine the future value (maturity value), principal, or interest as indicated.

(i) The principal is $2200 and the interest is $240. Find the future value (maturity value).

**SOLUTION**
$$P = 2200.00; \quad I = 240.00$$
$$S = P + I$$
$$= 2200.00 + 240.00$$
$$= \$2440.00$$

The future value is $2440.

(ii) The principal is $850 and the future value (maturity value) is $920. Compute the amount of interest.

**SOLUTION**
$$P = 850.00; \quad S = 920.00$$
$$S = P + I$$
$$I = S - P$$
$$I = 920.00 - 850.00$$
$$I = \$70.00$$

The amount of interest is $70.

(iii) The future value (maturity value) is $430 and the interest is $40. Compute the principal.

**SOLUTION**
$$S = 430.00; \quad I = 40.00$$
$$S = P + I$$
$$P = S - I$$
$$P = 430.00 - 40.00$$
$$P = \$390.00$$

The principal is $390.

# B. The future value formula S = P(1 + *rt*)

To obtain the future value (maturity value) formula for simple interest, the formulas I = P*rt* and S = P + I are combined.

S = P + I

S = P + P*rt* ———————————————————————— substitute P*rt* for I

S = P(1 + *rt*) ———————————————————————— take out the common factor P

$$\boxed{S = P(1 + rt)}$$ ———————————————————————— Formula 7.3A

---

**EXAMPLE 7.3B**

Find the future value (maturity value) of an investment of $720 earning 4% p.a. for 146 days.

**SOLUTION**

$P = 720.00; \quad r = 4\% = 0.04; \quad t = \dfrac{146}{365}$

$S = P(1 + rt)$

$= (720.00)\left[1 + (0.04)\left(\dfrac{146}{365}\right)\right]$

$= (720.00)(1 + 0.016)$

$= (720.00)(1.016)$

$= \$731.52$

The future value of the investment is $731.52.

---

**EXAMPLE 7.3C**

Find the maturity value of a deposit of $1250 invested at 2.75% p.a. from October 15, 2009 to May 1, 2010.

**SOLUTION**

The time period in days = 198

$P = 1250.00; \quad r = 2.75\% = 0.0275; \quad t = \dfrac{198}{365}$

$S = P(1 + rt)$

$= (1250.00)\left[1 + (0.0275)\left(\dfrac{198}{365}\right)\right]$

$= (1250.00)(1 + 0.014918)$

$= (1250.00)(1.014918)$

$= \$1268.65$

The maturity value of the deposit is $1268.65.

## EXERCISE 7.3

**A.** Use the future value (maturity value) formula to answer each of the following.

1. Find the future value of $480 at 3½% for 220 days.

2. Find the future value of $1100 invested at 6.75% for 360 days.

3. Find the maturity value of $732 invested at 9.8% from May 20, 2010 to November 23, 2010.

4. Find the maturity value of $775 invested at 6.25% from March 1, 2009 to October 20, 2009.

5. Compute the future value of $820 over nine months at 4¾%.

6. Compute the future value of $570 over seven months at 5½%.

7. What payment is required to pay off a loan of $1200 at 7% fourteen months later?

8. What payment is required to pay off a loan of $2000 at 6% eighteen months later?

**B.**

1. Paul invested $2500 in a 180-day term deposit at 3.45% p.a. What is the maturity value of the deposit?

2. Suzette invested $800 in a 210-day term deposit at 2.75% p.a. What is the maturity value of the deposit?

3. Jack signed a two-year loan of $12 000 at 7.5% p.a. How much will he owe at maturity?

4. Hao Lin borrowed $8000 at 8.55% p.a. for fifteen months. How much will he owe at maturity?

5. On September 30, 2010, Red Flag Inn invested $26 750 in a short-term investment of 215 days. An investment of this length earns 1.3% p.a. How much will the investment be worth at maturity?

6. Jo-Mar Consulting invested $17 200 on July 18, 2009 into a short-term investment of 150 days. The investment would earn 1.85% p.a. How much will the investment be worth at maturity?

7. Speedy Courier invested $13 500 in a 270-day term deposit. What is the maturity value if the rate of interest is 3.65%?

8. Diamond Drilling invested $40 000 in a 240-day term deposit earning interest at 2.43%. What is the maturity value of the investment?

9. Mishu wants to invest an inheritance of $50 000 for one year. His credit union offers 3.95% for a one-year term or 3.85% for a six-month term.

   (a) How much will Mishu receive after one year if he invests at the one-year rate?
   (b) How much will Mishu receive after one year if he invested for six months at a time at 3.85% each time?
   (c) What would the one-year rate have to be to yield the same amount of interest as the investment described in part (b)?

10. Prairie Grains Cooperative wants to invest $45 000 in a short-term deposit. The bank offers 1.3% interest for a one-year term and 1.1% for a six-month term.

(a) How much would Prairie Grains receive if the $45 000 is invested for one year?

(b) How much would Prairie Grains receive at the end of one year if the $45 000 is invested for six months and then the principal and interest earned is reinvested for another six months?

(c) What would the one-year rate have to be to yield the same amount of interest as the investment described in part (b)?

# 7.4 FINDING THE PRINCIPAL (PRESENT VALUE)

## A. Finding the principal when the maturity value (future value) is known

When the maturity value, the rate, and the time are given, calculation of the principal utilizes the formula $S = P(1 + rt)$.

When interest is paid for the use of money, the value of any sum of money subject to interest changes with time. This change is called the **time value of money**. The **present value** of an amount at any given time is the principal needed to grow to that amount at a given rate of interest over a given period of time.

Since the problem of finding the present value is equivalent to finding the principal when the future value, rate, and time are given, the future value formula $S = P(1 + rt)$ applies. However, because the problem of finding the present value of an amount is one of the frequently recurring problems in financial analysis, it is useful to solve the future value formula for P to obtain the present value formula.

$$S = P(1 + rt)$$ ———————— starting with the future value formula

$$\frac{S}{(1 + rt)} = \frac{P(1 + rt)}{(1 + rt)}$$ ———————— divide both sides by $(1 + rt)$

$$\frac{S}{(1 + rt)} = P$$ ———————— reduce the fraction $\frac{(1 + rt)}{(1 + rt)}$ to 1

This is the present value formula for simple interest.

$$P = \frac{S}{(1 + rt)}$$ ———————— Formula 7.3B

**EXAMPLE 7.4A**

Compute the value of an investment eight months before the maturity date that earns interest at 6% p.a. and has a maturity value of $884.

FIGURE 7.1    Time Graph for Example 7.4A

**SOLUTION**

$S = 884.00; \quad r = 6\% = 0.06; \quad t = \dfrac{8}{12}$

$P = \dfrac{S}{(1 + rt)}$ ———————————— use the present value formula when S is known

$P = \dfrac{884.00}{1 + (0.06)\left(\frac{8}{12}\right)}$ ———————— using Formula 7.3B

$P = \dfrac{884.00}{1.04}$

$= \$850.00$

The present value of the investment is $850.00

---

**EXAMPLE 7.4B**

What sum of money must be invested on January 31, 2008 to amount to $7700 on August 18, 2008 at 10% p.a.?

**SOLUTION**

The time period in days = 200.

$P = \dfrac{S}{(1 + rt)}$ ———————————— use the present value formula when S is known

$S = 7700.00; \quad r = 10\% = 0.10; \quad t = \dfrac{200}{365}$

$P = \dfrac{7700.00}{1 + (0.10)\left(\frac{200}{365}\right)}$

$P = \dfrac{7700.00}{1.054795}$

$= \$7300.00$

***Note:***

    **1.** The total interest earned is $7700 − $7300 = $400.

    **2.** The daily amount of interest is $\dfrac{\$400}{200} = \$2$.

To illustrate the concept of the time value of money, Example 7.4B is represented on the time graph shown in Figure 7.2.

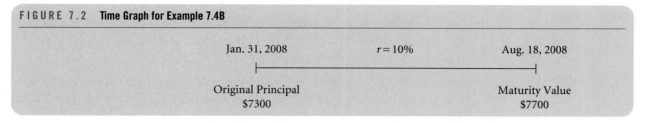

**FIGURE 7.2** **Time Graph for Example 7.4B**

Jan. 31, 2008        $r = 10\%$        Aug. 18, 2008

Original Principal        Maturity Value
$7300        $7700

The original principal of $7300 will grow to $7700 at 10% in 200 days. Interest of $400 will be earned in those 200 days, indicating that the original principal will grow by $2 each day. The value of the investment changes day by day. On January 31, 2008, the $7300 principal is known as the present value of the August 18, 2008 $7700.

## EXERCISE 7.4

 **A.** Find the principal and the missing value in each of the following.

| | Present Value (Principal) | Interest Amount | Future Value (Maturity Value) | Interest Rate | Time |
|---|---|---|---|---|---|
| 1. | ? | ? | $ 279.30 | 4% | 15 months |
| 2. | ? | $117.30 | $ 729.30 | ? | 20 months |
| 3. | ? | $ 29.67 | ? | 8.6% | 8 months |
| 4. | ? | $ 27.11 | ? | 9.5% | 240 days |
| 5. | ? | $ 84.24 | $2109.24 | 5.2% | ? |
| 6. | ? | ? | $1035.38 | 7.5% | 275 days |

 **B.** Solve each of the following.

**1.** What principal will have a future value of $1241.86 at 3.9% in five months?

**2.** What amount of money will accumulate to $480.57 in 93 days at 4.6%?

**3.** Determine the present value of a debt of $1760 due in four months if interest at 9¾% is allowed.

**4.** Compute the present value of a debt of $708.13 eighty days before it is due if money is worth 5.3%.

**5.** Compute the amount of money that, deposited in an account on April 1, 2009, will grow to $657.58 by September 10, 2009 at 4.75% p.a.

**6.** The annual Deerfield Golf Club membership fees of $1750 are due on March 1, 2010. Club management offers a reduction of membership fees of 18.9% p.a. to members who pay the dues by September 1, 2009. How much must a member pay on September 1 if she chooses to take advantage of the club management's offer?

**7.** You are the accountant for Peel Credit Union. The lawyer for a member has sent a cheque for $7345.64 in full settlement of the member's loan balance including interest at 6.25% for 11 months. How much of the payment is interest?

8. On March 15, 2009, Ben bought a government-guaranteed short-term investment maturing on September 12, 2009. How much did Ben pay for the investment if he will receive $10 000 on September 12, 2009 and interest is 5.06%?

9. On October 29, 2009, Toddlers' Toys borrowed money with a promise to pay $23 520.18 on March 5, 2010. This loan included interest at 6.5%. How much money did Toddlers' Toys borrow on October 29?

10. On May 28, 2010, Ling purchased a government-guaranteed short-term investment maturing on August 4, 2010. How much did Ling pay for the investment if $10 000 will be received on August 4, 2010, and interest is 1.35% p.a.?

## »» BUSINESS MATH NEWS BOX

### The iPod, iTune and Macintosh

Apple Computer Inc. is a publicly traded company that trades its shares on the NASDAQ stock exchange. Investors buy and sell Apple stock based on the expectation that the company has long-term projection of increased revenues, net income, and profit. Investors compare current revenue, net income, and profit results with the previous year's results. If the comparisons are within the expectations of investors, then the stock price increases. The future looks bright for Apple Inc. The iPod music player and the Macintosh personal computer are pioneering products that have propelled the company to financial success. In addition, Apple's online music store iTunes now accounts for a significant portion of legal Internet music downloads.

Apple Inc. provided investors with its 2006 second quarter results. Financial highlights are as follows:

• Sales increased 34% to US$4.36 billion, compared with growth that averaged 65% in the prior five periods.
• Net income rose to US$410 million, or US$0.47 cents a share, from US$290 million (US$0.34 cents) a year earlier.
• Profits rose 41%, and are estimated to be within a range of US$0.39 cents to US$0.43 cents.

Other relevant information in which investors were interested:

• Shipments of iPod music players fell to 8.5 million units from 14 million.
• Macintosh shipments dropped to 1.1 million from 1.25 million.
• Apple is also generating revenue from the iTunes online music store. More than one billion songs have been sold at US$0.99 cents each since iTunes opened in 2003.
• More than 15 million videos were sold at US$1.99 each since Apple began selling videos online.

Due to this news release, Apple's stock price increased by US$1.28 to US$66.93 on the NASDAQ stock exchange.

*Sources:* Connie Guglielmo. Bloomberg News, "Apple's 2nd-Qtr Profit Rises; Ipod, Macintosh Shipments Slow," April 19, 2006. (New York); Apple report Q2 2006 results. **http://www.apple.com/investor**.

### QUESTIONS

1. Calculate the percentage increase of Apple shares if the stock increased by $1.28 to $66.93. What was the initial price of the stock?

2. If the average price of an iPod is US$300 and a Mac is US$2000, calculate the revenues generated by Apple in the first half of this year.

3. Calculate how much revenue has been generated by video sales.

# 7.5 COMPUTING EQUIVALENT VALUES

## A. Dated values

If an amount of money is subject to a rate of interest, it will grow over time. Thus, the value of the amount of money changes with time. This change is known as the time value of money. For example, if you invested $1000 today at 4% p.a. simple interest, your investment has a value of $1000 today, $1010 in three months, $1020 in six months, and $1040 in one year.

The value of the original amount at any particular time is a **dated value**, or **equivalent value**, of that amount. The dated value combines the original sum with the interest earned up to the dated value date. Each dated value at a different time is equivalent to the original amount of money. The table below shows four dated values for $1000 invested at 4% p.a. The longer the time is from today, the greater is the dated value. This is so because interest has been earned on the principal over a longer time period.

| Time | Dated Value |
|------|-------------|
| Today | $1000.00 |
| 3 months from today | $1010.00 |
| 6 months from today | $1020.00 |
| 1 year from today | $1040.00 |

Timberwest Company owes Abco Inc. $500 and payment is due today. Timberwest asks for an extension of four months to pay off the obligation. How much should they expect to pay in four months' time if money is worth 6%?

Since Abco could invest the $500 at 6% p.a., Timberwest should be prepared to pay the dated value. This dated value includes interest for the additional four-month time period. It represents the amount to which the $500 will grow in four months (the future value) and is found using Formula 7.3A.

$$S = P(1 + rt)$$

$$= 500.00\left[1 + (0.06)\left(\frac{4}{12}\right)\right]$$

$$= 500.00 \, (1 + 0.02)$$

$$= \$510.00$$

In addition, Red Rock Construction owes Abco Inc. $824, due to be paid six months from now. Suppose Red Rock Construction offers to pay the debt today. How much should Red Rock Construction pay Abco Inc. if money is worth 6%?

Since Abco Inc. could invest the payment at 6%, the payment should be the sum of money that will grow to $824 in six months earning 6% p.a. interest. By definition, this amount of money is the present value of the $824. The present value represents today's dated value of the $824 and is found using Formula 7.3B.

$$P = \frac{S}{1 + rt}$$

$$= \frac{824.00}{1 + (0.06)\left(\frac{6}{12}\right)}$$

$$= \frac{824.00}{1 + 0.03}$$

$$= \$800.00$$

Because of the time value of money, sums of money given at different times are not directly comparable. For example, imagine you are given a choice between $2000 today and $2200 one year from now. It does not automatically follow, from the point of view of investing money, that either the larger amount of money or the chronologically earlier amount of money is preferable.

To make a rational choice, we must allow for the rate of interest money can earn and choose a comparison date or **focal date** to obtain the dated values of the amounts of money at a specific time.

Equivalent values on the same date are directly comparable and may be obtained for simple interest by using either the maturity value (future value) formula, Formula 7.3A, $S = P(1 + rt)$, or the present value formula, Formula 7.3B,

$$P = \frac{S}{1 + rt}$$

## B. Choosing the appropriate formula

The choice of which formula to use for computing dated values depends on the due date of the sum of money relative to the selected focal (or comparison) date.

(a) If the due date falls before the focal date, use the future value (maturity value) formula.

FIGURE 7.3    **When to Use the Future Value (or Maturity Value) Formula**

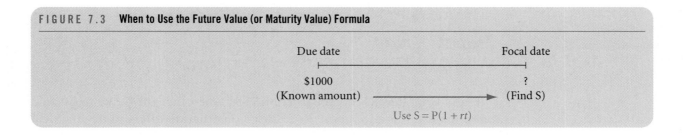

*Explanation of Figure 7.3:* We are looking for a future value relative to the given value. This future value will be higher than the known value by the interest that accumulates on the known value from the due date to the focal date. Because this is a future value problem (note that the arrow points to the right), the future value (or maturity value) formula $S = P(1 + rt)$ applies.

(b) If the due date falls after the focal date, use the present value formula.

**FIGURE 7.4**   **When to Use the Present Value Formula**

*Explanation of Figure 7.4:* We are looking for an earlier value relative to the given value. This earlier value will be less than the given value by the interest that would accumulate on the unknown earlier value from the focal date to the due date. We are, in fact, looking for the principal that will grow to the given value. Because this is a present value problem (note that the arrow points to the left), the present value formula $P = \dfrac{S}{1 + rt}$ is appropriate.

## C. Finding the equivalent single payment

**EXAMPLE 7.5A**

A debt can be paid off by payments of $872 one year from now and $1180 two years from now. Determine the single payment now that would fully repay the debt. Allow for simple interest at 9% p.a.

**SOLUTION**

See Figure 7.5 for the graphic representation of the dated values. Refer to Figures 7.3 and 7.4 to determine which formula is appropriate.

**FIGURE 7.5**   **Graphical Representation of the Dated Values**

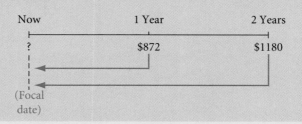

Since the focal date is *earlier* relative to the dates for the given sums of money (the arrows point to the left), the present value formula $P = \dfrac{S}{1 + rt}$ is appropriate.

(i) The dated (present) value of the $872.00 at the focal date:

$$P = \frac{872.00}{1 + (0.09)(1)} = \frac{872.00}{1.09} = \$800.00$$

(ii) The dated (present) value of the $1180.00 at the focal date

$$P = \frac{1180.00}{1 + (0.09)(2)} = \frac{1180.00}{1.18} = \$1000.00$$

(iii) Single payment required now = 800.00 + 1000.00 = $1800.00

---

**EXAMPLE 7.5B**

Two amounts owing from the past were to be paid today. One debt was $620 from one year ago and $925 from six months ago. Determine the single payment today that would fully repay the debts. Allow for simple interest at 12% p.a.

**SOLUTION**

See Figure 7.6 for the graphic representation of the dated values. Refer to Figures 7.3 and 7.4 to determine which formula is appropriate.

FIGURE 7.6   **Graphical Representation of the Dated Values**

Since the focal date is *future* relative to the dates for the given sums of money (the arrows point to the right), the future value formula $S = P(1 + rt)$ is appropriate.

(i) The dated (future) value of the $620 at the focal date:

$$S = 620.00\left[1 + (0.12)\left(\frac{12}{12}\right)\right] = \$694.40$$

(ii) The dated (future) value of the $925 at the focal date:

$$S = 925.00\left[1 + (0.12)\left(\frac{6}{12}\right)\right] = \$980.50$$

(iii) Single payment required now = 694.40 + 980.50 = $1674.90

---

**EXAMPLE 7.5C**

You are owed payments of $400 due today, $500 due in five months, and $618 due in one year. You have been approached to accept a single payment nine months from now with interest allowed at 12% p.a. How much will the single payment be?

**SOLUTION**

**FIGURE 7.7** **Graphical Representation of the Dated Values**

Since the focal date is in the *future* relative to the $400 now and the $500 five months from now (the arrows point to the right), the future value formula $S = P(1 + rt)$ is appropriate for these two amounts. However, since the focal date is *earlier* relative to the $618 one year from now (the arrow points to the left), the present value formula $P = \dfrac{S}{1 + rt}$ is appropriate for this amount.

(i) The dated (future) value of $400 at the focal date:

$$P = 400.00; \quad r = 12\% = 0.12; \quad t = \frac{9}{12}$$

$$S = 400\left[1 + (0.12)\left(\frac{9}{12}\right)\right] = 400(1 + 0.09) = 400(1.09) = \$436.00$$

(ii) The dated (future) value of $500 at the focal date:

$$P = 500.00; \quad r = 12\% = 0.12; \quad t = \frac{4}{12}$$

$$S = 500\left[1 + (0.12)\left(\frac{4}{12}\right)\right] = 500(1 + 0.04) = 500(1.04) = \$520.00$$

(iii) The dated (present) value of $618 at the focal date:

$$S = 618.00; \quad r = 12\% = 0.12; \quad t = \frac{3}{12}$$

$$P = \frac{618.00}{1 + (0.12)\left(\frac{3}{12}\right)}$$

$$= \frac{618.00}{1 + 0.03}$$

$$= \frac{618.00}{1.03} = \$600.00$$

(iv) The single payment to be made nine months from now will be = 436.00 + 520.00 + 600.00 = $1556.00.

**EXAMPLE 7.5D**

Scheduled payments of $400 due now and $700 due in five months are to be settled by a payment of $500 in three months and a final payment in eight months. Determine the amount of the final payment at 6% p.a., using eight months from now as the focal date.

**SOLUTION**

Let the value of the final payment be $x.

(i) Use a time diagram to represent the given data.

**FIGURE 7.8**   **Graphical Representation of Data**

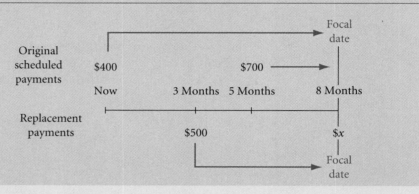

(ii) Dated value of the original scheduled payments:
  (a) The value at the focal date of the $400 payment due eight months before the focal date is found by using the future value formula.

$$S = 400\left[1 + (0.06)\left(\frac{8}{12}\right)\right] = 400(1 + 0.04) = 400(1.04) = \$416.00$$

  (b) The value at the focal date of the $700 payment due three months before the focal date is found by using the future value formula.

$$S = 700\left[1 + (0.06)\left(\frac{3}{12}\right)\right]$$

$$= 700(1 + 0.015)$$

$$= 700(1.015)$$

$$= \$710.50$$

(iii) Dated value of the replacement payments:
  (a) The value at the focal date of the $500 payment made five months before the focal date is found by using the future value formula.

$$S = 500\left[1 + (0.06)\left(\frac{5}{12}\right)\right]$$

$$= 500(1 + 0.025)$$

$$= 500(1.025)$$

$$= \$512.50$$

(b) The value at the focal date of the final payment is $x (no adjustment for interest is necessary for an amount of money located at the focal date).

(iv) The **equation of values** at the focal date is now set up by matching the dated values of the original debts to the dated values of the replacement payments.

$$500\left[1 + (0.06)\left(\frac{5}{12}\right)\right] + x = 400\left[1 + (0.06)\left(\frac{8}{12}\right)\right] + 700\left[1 + (0.06)\left(\frac{3}{12}\right)\right]$$

$$512.50 + x = 416.00 + 710.50$$

$$512.50 + x = 1126.50$$

$$x = 1126.50 - 512.50$$

$$x = 614.00$$

The final payment to be made in eight months is $614.

## D. Finding the value of two or more equivalent payments

The equivalent values (the dated value of the original scheduled payments) obtained when using simple interest formulas are influenced by the choice of focal date. Choose a focal date on the basis of the date when an equivalent value must be calculated. When two or more equivalent values must be calculated, choose one of the dates for which an equivalent value must be calculated.

**EXAMPLE 7.5E**

Jeremy had two equal outstanding loans, one from 63 days ago and one from 105 days ago. He repaid both loans today with the single amount of $3700. If interest is 9% on the loans, what was the size of the equal amounts borrowed?

**SOLUTION**

Let the value of each of the equal loans be $x.

(i) Use a time diagram to represent the given data.

**FIGURE 7.9** **Graphical Representation of Data**

(ii) Dated value of the original scheduled payments:
   (a) The value at the focal date of the first $x payment due 105 days before the focal date is found by using the future value formula.

$$S = x\left[1 + (0.09)\left(\frac{105}{365}\right)\right] = x(1 + 0.025890) = 1.025890x$$

   (b) The value at the focal date of the second $x payment due 63 days before the focal date is found by using the future value formula.

$$S = x\left[1 + (0.09)\left(\frac{63}{365}\right)\right] = x(1 + 0.015534) = 1.015534x$$

(iii) Dated value of the replacement payments:
   (a) The value at the focal date of the repayment is $3700 on the focal date.
   (b) The value at the focal date of the two equal payments is

$$1.025890x + 1.015534x = 2.041424x$$

(iv) The equation of values at the focal date is now set up by matching the dated values of the original debts to the dated values of the replacement payments.

> THE SUM OF THE DATED VALUES OF THE REPLACEMENT PAYMENTS =
> THE SUM OF THE DATED VALUES OF THE ORIGINAL SCHEDULED PAYMENTS

$$3700 = 2.041424x$$

$$x = \frac{3700.00}{2.041424}$$

$$x = 1812.46$$

Each of the two equal loans had been $1812.46.

**EXAMPLE 7.5F**

Clarkson Developments was supposed to pay Majestic Flooring $2000 sixty days ago and $1800 in thirty days. Majestic Flooring agreed to accept three equal payments due today, 60 days from today, and 120 days from today. Compute the size of the equal payments at 10% p.a. Use today as the focal date.

**SOLUTION**

Let the size of the equal payments be $x.

   (i) Graphical representation of data:

**FIGURE 7.10**   **Graphical Representation of Data**

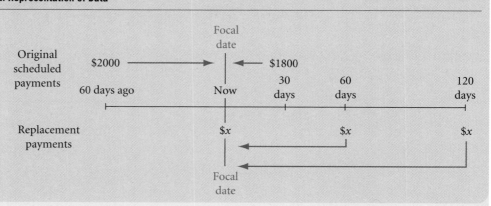

(ii) Dated value of the original scheduled payments at the focal date:

(a) Because the $2000 payment is due 60 days before the focal date, the future value formula is appropriate.

$$S = 2000\left[1 + (0.10)\left(\frac{60}{365}\right)\right] = 2000(1 + 0.016438) = \$2032.88$$

(b) Because the $1800 payment is due 30 days after the focal date, the present value formula is appropriate.

$$P = \frac{1800.00}{1 + (0.10)\left(\frac{30}{365}\right)} = \frac{1800.00}{1 + 0.008219} = \$1785.33$$

(iii) Dated value of the replacement payments at the focal date:

(a) Since the first payment is to be made at the focal date, its value is $x.
(b) Because the second payment is to be made 60 days after the focal date, the present value formula is appropriate.

$$P = \frac{x}{1 + (0.10)\left(\frac{60}{365}\right)} = \frac{x}{1 + 0.016438} = \frac{1(x)}{1.016438} = \$0.983828x$$

(c) Because the third payment is to be made 120 days after the focal date, the present value formula is appropriate.

$$P = \frac{x}{1 + (0.10)\left(\frac{120}{365}\right)} = \frac{x}{1 + 0.032877}$$

$$= \frac{1(x)}{1.0032877} = \$0.968170x$$

(iv) The equation of values (dated value of the replacement payments = dated value of the original scheduled payments):

$$x + 0.983828x + 0.968170x = 2032.88 + 1785.33$$

$$2.951998x = 3818.21$$

$$x = \frac{3818.21}{2.951998}$$

$$x = \$1293.43$$

The size of each of the three equal payments is $1293.43.

---

**EXAMPLE 7.5G**

Two debts, one of $4000 due in three months with interest at 8% and the other of $3000 due in eighteen months with interest at 10%, are to be discharged by making two equal payments. What is the size of the equal payments if the first is due one year from now, the second two years from now, money is worth 12%, and the chosen focal date is one year from now?

**SOLUTION**

Let the size of the equal payments be $x.

(i) Graphical representation of data:

FIGURE 7.11   **Graphical Representation of Data**

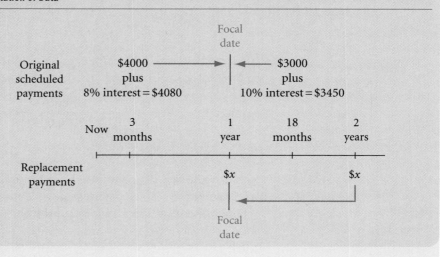

(ii) Maturity value of the original debts:
Since the two original debts are interest-bearing, their maturity values need to be determined first so that the principal and interest of these original debts are discharged by the two equal payments.

(a) For the $4000 debt: $P = 4000$;   $r = 8\% = 0.08$;   $t = \dfrac{3}{12}$

$$\text{Maturity value, } S = 4000\left[1 + (0.08)\left(\frac{3}{12}\right)\right] = 4000(1.02) = \$4080$$

(b) For the $3000 debt: $P = 3000$;   $r = 10\% = 0.10$;   $t = \dfrac{18}{12}$

$$\text{Maturity value, } S = 3000\left[1 + (0.10)\left(\frac{18}{12}\right)\right] = 3000(1.15) = \$3450$$

(iii) Dated value of the money value of the original payments at 12%:
(a) Because the maturity value of $4080 is due nine months before the focal date, the future value formula is appropriate.

$$S = 4080\left[1 + (0.12)\left(\frac{9}{12}\right)\right] = 4080(1.09) = \$4447.20$$

(b) Because the maturity value of $3450 is due six months after the focal date, the present value formula is appropriate.

$$P = \frac{3450}{1 + (0.12)\left(\frac{6}{12}\right)} = \frac{3450}{1.06} = \$3254.72$$

(iv) Dated value of the replacement payments:
(a) Since the first replacement payment is made at the focal date, its value is $x.

(b) Because the second replacement payment is made 12 months after the focal date, the present value formula is appropriate.

$$P = \frac{x}{1 + (0.12)\left(\frac{12}{12}\right)} = \frac{x}{1.12} = 0.892857x$$

(v) The equation of values:

$$x + 0.892857x = 4447.20 + 3254.72$$

$$1.892857x = 7701.92$$

$$x = \frac{7701.92}{1.892857}$$

$$x = \$4068.94$$

The size of the equal payments is $4068.94.

## E. Loan repayments

Loans by financial institutions to individuals are usually repaid by **blended payments**, which are equal periodic payments that include payment of interest and repayment of principal. To repay the loan, the sum of the present values of the periodic payments must equal the original principal. The concept of equivalent values is used to determine the size of the blended payments.

**EXAMPLE 7.5H**

A loan of $2000 made at 8.5% p.a. is to be repaid in four equal payments due at the end of the next four quarters respectively. Determine the size of the quarterly payments if the agreed focal date is the date of the loan.

**SOLUTION**

Let the size of the equal quarterly payments be represented by $x.

(i) Graphical representation of data:

**FIGURE 7.12**   **Graphical Representation of Data**

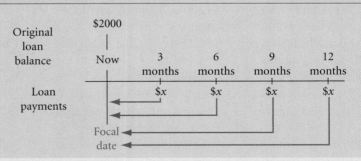

(ii) Dated value of the loan balance at the focal date is $2000.

(iii) Dated value of the loan payments at the focal date:
The payments are due three, six, nine, and twelve months after the focal date respectively. Their values are

(a) $P_1 = \dfrac{x}{1 + (0.085)\left(\frac{3}{12}\right)} = \dfrac{x}{1 + 0.02125} = \dfrac{1(x)}{1.02125} = 0.979192x$

(b) $P_2 = \dfrac{x}{1 + (0.085)\left(\frac{6}{12}\right)} = \dfrac{x}{1 + 0.0425} = \dfrac{1(x)}{1.0425} = 0.959233x$

(c) $P_3 = \dfrac{x}{1 + (0.085)\left(\frac{9}{12}\right)} = \dfrac{x}{1 + 0.06375} = \dfrac{1(x)}{1.06375} = 0.940071x$

(d) $P_4 = \dfrac{x}{1 + (0.085)\left(\frac{12}{12}\right)} = \dfrac{x}{1 + 0.085} = \dfrac{1(x)}{1.085} = 0.921659x$

(iv) $0.979192x + 0.959233x + 0.940071x + 0.921659x = 2000.00$

$$3.800155x = 2000.00$$
$$x = 526.29$$

The size of the quarterly payment is $526.29.

## EXERCISE 7.5

  **A.** Find the equivalent replacement payments indicated for each of the following scheduled payments.

| Original Scheduled Payments | Replacement Payments | Focal Date | Rate |
|---|---|---|---|
| 1. $800 due today | In full | 4 months from today | 11% |
| 2. $1200 due 4 months ago | In full | Today | 6% |
| 3. $600 due in 2 months | In full | 7 months from today | 7% |
| 4. $1000 due in 8 months | In full | 2 months from today | 10% |
| 5. $500 due 4 months ago, $600 due in 2 months | In full | Today | 5% |
| 6. $800 due today, $700 due in 2 months | In full | 4 months from today | 9% |
| 7. $2000 due today | $1200 in 4 months and the balance in 8 months | Today | 6% |
| 8. $400 due 1 month ago, $600 due in 3 months | $500 today and the balance in 6 months | Today | 8% |
| 9. $1500 due today | Two equal payments due in 2 and 7 months | Today | 10% |
| 10. $1800 due 30 days ago | Three equal payments due today, in 30 days, and in 60 days | Today | 9% |
| 11. $1500 due 4 months ago, $1200 due in 8 months with 10% interest | $700 due now and two equal payments due in 6 months and in 12 months | Today | 5% |
| 12. $2000 due in 6 months with interest at 8%, $1600 due in 2 years with interest at 7% | Three equal payments due in 6, 12, and 18 months respectively | 1 year from today | 11% |

**B.**  Solve each of the following problems.

1. Scheduled debt payments of $600 each are due three months and six months from now respectively. If interest at 10% is allowed, what single payment today is required to settle the two scheduled payments?  <small>Reference Example 7.5A</small>

2. Debt payments are due of $700 in two months and $800 in five months. If interest at 8.3% is allowed, what single payment today is required to settle the two scheduled payments?

3. A loan payment of $1000 was due 60 days ago and another payment of $1200 is due 30 days from now. What single payment 90 days from now will pay off the two obligations if interest is to be 8% and the agreed focal date is 90 days from now?  <small>Reference Example 7.5B</small>

4. A loan payment of $2200 was due 91 days ago and another payment of $1800 is due 45 days from now. What single payment 75 days from now will pay off the two obligations if interest is to be 9% and the agreed focal date is 75 days from now?

5. Jay was due to make loan payments of $500 four months ago, $800 today, and $400 in three months. He has agreed instead to make a single payment one month from today. If money is worth 10.5% and the agreed focal date is one month from today, what is the size of the replacement payment?  <small>Reference Example 7.5C</small>

6. Jane was due to make loan payments of $1200 six months ago, $1500 one month ago, and $700 in two months. Instead, she is to make a single payment today. If money is worth 9.8% and the agreed focal date is today, what is the size of the replacement payment?

7. Loan payments of $400 due 95 days ago and $700 due today are to be repaid by a payment of $600 30 days from today and the balance in 125 days. If money is worth 6% and the agreed focal date is 125 days from today, what is the size of the final payment?  <small>Reference Example 7.5D</small>

8. Loan payments of $4000 due 200 days ago and $6000 due 63 days ago are to be replaced by a payment of $5000 today and the balance 92 days from today. If money is worth 8.3% and the agreed focal date is 92 days from today, what is the size of the final payment?

9. Dan borrowed $1100 today and is to repay the loan in two equal payments, one in four months and one in six months. If interest is 8.5% on the loan, what is the size of the equal payments if a focal date of today is used?  <small>Reference Example 7.5E</small>

10. When Ruby borrowed $2300, she agreed to repay the loan in two equal payments, to be made 90 days and 135 days from the day the money was borrowed. If interest is 9.25% on the loan, what is the size of the equal payments if a focal date of today is used?

11. Ruben repaid $800, paying back two equal outstanding loans from seven months ago and five months ago. If interest is 11% on the loans, and the agreed focal date is today, what was the size of the equal amount borrowed?

12. Judy received a payment of $2950 and paid back two equal outstanding loans from 45 days ago and 190 days ago. If interest is 12.5% on the loans, and the agreed focal date is today, what was the size of the equal amounts borrowed?

13. Jessica should have made two payments of $800 each. The first was due 60 days ago and the second payment was due 30 days ago. The two original scheduled payments are to be settled by two equal payments to be made today and 60 days from now respectively. If interest allowed is 7.25% and the agreed focal date is today, what is the size of the equal payments?

14. Krista borrowed $14 000. The loan is to be repaid by three equal payments due in 120, 240, and 260 days from now respectively. Determine the size of the equal payments at 7% with a focal date of today.    Reference Example 7.5F

15. Jerry borrowed $4000. The loan is to be repaid by three equal payments due in four, eight, and twelve months from now respectively. Determine the size of the equal payments at 8.5% with a focal date of today.

16. On March 1, Bear Mountain Tours borrowed $1500. Three equal payments are required, on April 30, June 20, and August 10, and a final payment of $400 on September 30 of the same year. If the focal date is September 30, what is the amount of the equal payments at 6.75%?

17. Two debt payments, of $1900 due today and $1200 due with interest at 9% nine months from now, are to be settled by two equal payments due in three and six months respectively. Determine the amount of the equal payments if money is worth 7% and the focal date is today.    Reference Example 7.5G

18. Wayne's Windows should have made a payment of $1200 to Shane's Woodcraft one year ago. They are also scheduled to pay $1500 due with interest of 8% in nine months. Shane's Woodcraft agreed to accept three equal payments due today, six months from now, and one year from now at 9.5%. Determine the amount of the equal payments if the focal date is one year from today.

## Review Exercise

1. Determine the number of days from
   (a) April 25, 2009 to October 14, 2009;
   (b) July 30, 2011 to February 29, 2012.

2. Compute the amount of interest for
   (a) $1975.00 at 5.5% for 215 days;
   (b) $844.65 at 8.25% from May 30, 2009 to January 4, 2010.

3. What principal will earn
   (a) $34.80 interest at 5% in 219 days?
   (b) $34.40 interest at 9.75% from October 30, 2009 to June 1, 2010?

4. Answer each of the following.
   (a) What was the rate of interest if the interest on a loan of $675 for 284 days was $39.39?
   (b) How many days will it take for $2075 to earn $124.29 interest at $8\frac{1}{4}$% p.a.?
   (c) If $680 is worth $698.70 after three months, what interest rate was charged?
   (d) How many months will it take $750 to grow to $795.00 at 7.2% p.a.?

5. Solve each of the following.
   (a) What principal will have a maturity value of $785.96 at 10% in 175 days?
   (b) What is the present value of $6300.00 due in 16 months at 7.75%?

6. What principal will earn $24.87 at 4.75% in 156 days?

7. What sum of money will earn $148.57 from September 1, 2009 to April 30, 2010 at 7.5%?

8. At what rate of interest must a principal of $1545 be invested to earn interest of $58.93 in 150 days?

9. At what rate of interest will $1500 grow to $1562.04 from June 1, 2009 to December 1, 2009?

10. In how many months will $2500 earn $51.04 interest at 3.5%?

11. In how many days will $3100 grow to $3195.72 at 5.75%?

12. Compute the accumulated value of $4200 at 4.5% after 11 months.

13. What is the amount to which $1550 will grow from June 10, 2009 to December 15, 2009 at 6.5%?

14. What amount of money will accumulate to $1516.80 in eight months at 8%?

15. What principal will amount to $3367.28 if invested at 9% from November 1, 2011 to May 31, 2012?

16. What is the present value of $3780 due in nine months if interest is 5%?

17. Compute the present value on June 1, 2009 of $1785 due on October 15, 2009 if interest is 7.5%.

18. Payments of $1750 and $1600 are due four months from now and nine months from now respectively. What single payment is required to pay off the two scheduled payments today if interest is 9% and the focal date is today?

19. A loan payment of $1450 was due 45 days ago and a payment of $1200 is due in 60 days. What single payment made 30 days from now is required to settle the two payments if interest is 7% and the focal date is 30 days from now?

20. Scheduled payments of $800 due two months ago and $1200 due in one month are to be repaid by a payment of $1000 today and the balance in three months. What is the amount of the final payment if interest is 7.75% and the focal date is one month from now?

21. An obligation of $10 000 is to be repaid by equal payments due in 60 days, 120 days, and 180 days. What is the amount of the equal payments if money is worth 6.5% and the focal date is today?

22. Payments of $4000 each due in four, nine, and eleven months from now are to be settled by three equal payments due today, six months

from now, and twelve months from now. What is the amount of the equal payments if interest is 7.35% and the agreed focal date is today?

**23.** A loan of $5000 due in one year is to be repaid by three equal payments due today, six months from now, and one year from now. What is the amount of the equal payments if interest is 6.5% and the focal date is today?

**24.** Three debts, the first for $1000 due two months ago, the second for $1200 due in two months, and the third for $1400 due in four months, are to be paid by a single payment today. How much is the single payment if money is worth 8.25% p.a. and the focal date is today?

**25.** Loan payments of $700 due three months ago and of $1000 due today are to be paid by a payment of $800 in two months and a final payment in five months. If 9% interest is allowed, and the focal date is five months from now, what is the amount of the final payment?

**26.** A loan of $5000 is to be repaid in three equal installments due 60, 120, and 180 days after the date of the loan. If the focal date is the date of the loan and interest is 6.9% p.a., compute the amount of the installments.

**27.** Three loan payments, the first for $2000 due three months ago, the second for $1400 with interest of 7.5% due in nine months, and the third for $1200 with interest of 5.75% due in sixteen months, are to be paid in three equal installments due today, four months from now, and one year from now. If money is worth 8.5% and the focal date is today, determine the amount of the equal payments. (Compute the maturity values of the original debts first.)

**28.** A loan of $7000 is to be settled by four equal payments due today, and one year, two years, and three years from now. Determine the amount of the equal payments if money is worth 5.75% and the focal date is today.

##  Self-Test

**1.** Compute the amount of interest earned by $1290 at 3.5% p.a. in 173 days.

**2.** In how many months will $8500 grow to $8818.75 at 5% p.a.?

**3.** What interest rate is paid if the interest on a loan of $2500 for six months is $81.25?

**4.** What principal will have a maturity value of $10 000 at 8.25% p.a. in three months?

**5.** What is the amount to which $6000 will grow at 3.75% p.a. in ten months?

**6.** What principal will earn $67.14 interest at 6.25% for 82 days?

**7.** What is the present value of $4400 due at 3.25% p.a. in 243 days?

**8.** What rate of interest is paid if the interest on a loan of $2500 is $96.06 from November 14, 2009 to May 20, 2010?

**9.** How many days will it take for $8500 to earn $689.72 at 8.25% p.a.?

**10.** What principal will earn $55.99 interest at 9.75% p.a. from February 4, 2008 to July 6, 2008?

**11.** What amount invested will accumulate to $7500 at 3.75% p.a. in 88 days?

**12.** Compute the amount of interest on $835 at 7.5% p.a. from October 8, 2011 to August 4, 2012.

13. A loan of $3320 is to be repaid by three equal payments due in 92 days, 235 days, and 326 days. Determine the amount of the equal payments at 8.75% p.a. with a focal date of today.

14. Loan payments of $1725 due today, $510 due in 75 days, and $655 due in 323 days are to be combined into a single payment to be made 115 days from now. What is that single payment if money is worth 8.5% p.a. and the focal date is 115 days from now?

15. Scheduled payments of $1010 due five months ago and $1280 due today are to be repaid by a payment of $615 in four months and the balance in seven months. If money is worth 7.75% p.a. and the focal date is in seven months, what is the amount of the final payment?

16. A payment of $1310 due five months ago and a second payment of $1225 with interest at 12% p.a. due in three months are to be settled by two equal payments due now and seven months from now. Compute the amount of the equal payments at 6.5%, with the focal date now.

## Challenge Problems

1. Nora borrows $37 500 on September 28, 2011 at 7% p.a. simple interest, to be repaid on October 31, 2012. She has the option of making payments toward the loan before the due date. Nora pays $6350 on February 17, 2012, $8250 on July 2, 2012, and $7500 on October 1, 2012. Compute the payment required to pay off the debt on the focal date of October 31, 2012.

2. A supplier will give Shark Unibase Company a discount of 2% if an invoice is paid 60 days before its due date. Suppose Shark wants to take advantage of this discount but needs to borrow the money. It plans to pay back the loan in 60 days. What is the highest annual simple interest rate at which Shark Unibase can borrow the money and still save by paying the invoice 60 days before its due date?

# Case Study 7.1 Short-Term Loans

» Skyline Sports stocked and sold seasonal sporting equipment for hiking and skiing. Due to a spell of warm weather during the ski season, sales of skiing and snowboarding equipment had not been as high as expected. Since Skyline Sports had already purchased the equipment from their suppliers, payment was due. Aaron Baxter, the manager, was trying to borrow the cash to make the payment of $14 600. At the company's bank, he would be able to obtain a one-month loan for the full amount, at 6.95% per annum simple interest. At a second bank, he would have three months to pay, with interest at 7.3%.

Later that same day, in talking with his suppliers, Aaron learned that they were willing to finance the purchases at 8.15% per annum if he signed a promissory note. Three equal payments would then be due, two months, four months, and six months from now.

### QUESTIONS

1. What are the maturity values of the two different bank loans?

2. What equal payments would have to be made to the supplier?

3. As of today's date, compute the equivalent values of each of the three options. Which option should Aaron choose?

---

# Case Study 7.2 Cost of Financing Pay Now or Pay Later

» Along with licensing, the purchase of auto insurance for vehicles is required in Canada. Benefits of auto insurance are as follows:

• Safeguards the investment in the automobile.

• Pays for medical expenses in case of an accident.

• Covers losses caused by uninsured or underinsured drivers.

• Compensates for damage due to theft, vandalism, or natural disasters.

Quick Courier Service is about to purchase insurance on its new delivery van. Taylor, the manager, has the company's insurance agent outline three payment plans to provide coverage for the next 12 months.

Plan One requires that the full year's premium of $4000 be paid at the beginning of the year.

Plan Two allows payment of the annual premium in two installments. The first installment would have to be paid immediately and would amount to one-half of the annual premium, plus a $60 service charge. The second installment would be paid in six months' time, and would amount to the remaining half of the premium.

Plan Three allows for twelve equal monthly payments of $355 each. These payments would be made on the same date within each month, starting immediately.

Quick Courier Service pays its insurance using Plan One. However, the company realizes that it is missing out on interest it could have earned on this money when it pays the full year's premium at the beginning of the policy term. Taylor considers this to be the "cost" of paying its bill in one lump sum. Taylor is interested in knowing the cost of its insurance payment options.

### QUESTIONS

1. Suppose Quick Courier Service could earn 4% p.a. simple interest on its money over the next year. Assume the first premium payment is due today (the first day of the insurance policy term) and the focal date is today. Ignoring all taxes, compute the cost to Quick Courier Service of paying the insurance using each of the three payment plans.

**2.** Suppose Quick Courier Service expects to earn 2.5% p.a. simple interest on any money it invests in the first three months of this year, and 1.8% p.a. simple interest on any money it invests during the rest of this year. Assume the focal date is today. Which option—Plan One, Plan Two, or Plan Three—will have the least cost for the company?

**3.** Examine a vehicle insurance policy of your own or of a family member. Calculate what you could earn on your money at today's rates of interest. What is the cost of this insurance policy if you pay the annual premium at the beginning of the policy term? Make the focal date the first day of the policy term.

## SUMMARY OF FORMULAS

Formula 7.1A

$$I = Prt$$

Finding the amount of interest when the principal, the rate, and the time are known

Formula 7.1B

$$P = \frac{I}{rt}$$

Finding the principal directly when the amount of interest, the rate of interest, and the time are known

Formula 7.1C

$$r = \frac{I}{Pt}$$

Finding the rate of interest directly when the amount of interest, the principal, and the time are known

Formula 7.1D

$$t = \frac{I}{Pr}$$

Finding the time directly when the amount of interest, the principal, and the rate of interest are known

Formula 7.2

$$S = P + I$$

Finding the future value (maturity value) when the principal and the amount of interest are known

Formula 7.3A

$$S = P(1 + rt)$$

Finding the future value (maturity value) at simple interest directly when the principal, rate of interest, and time are known

Formula 7.3B

$$P = \frac{S}{1 + rt}$$

Finding the present value at simple interest when the future value (maturity value), the rate of interest, and the time are known

## GLOSSARY

**Blended payments**    equal periodic payments that include payment of interest and repayment of principal, usually paid by individuals to financial institutions *(p. 283)*

**Dated value**    the value of a sum of money at a specific time relative to its due date, including interest *(p. 273)*

**Equation of values**    the equation obtained when matching the dated values of the original payments at an agreed focal date to the dated values of the replacement payments at the same focal date *(p. 279)*

**Equivalent value**    see **Dated value**

**Focal date**    a specific time chosen to compare the time value of one or more dated sums of money *(p. 274)*

**Future value of a sum of money**    the value obtained when the amount of interest is added to the original principal *(p. 266)*

**Interest**    rent paid for the use of money *(p. 257)*

**Interest period**    the time period for which interest is charged *(p. 257)*

**Maturity value**    see **Future value of a sum of money**

**Nominal rate**    the yearly or annual rate of interest charged on the principal of a loan *(p. 257)*

**Present value**    the principal that grows to a given future value (maturity value) over a given period of time at a given rate of interest *(p. 269)*

**Simple interest**    interest calculated on the original principal by the formula $I = Prt$, and paid only when the principal is repaid *(p. 257)*

**Time value of money**    a concept of money value that allows for a change in the value of a sum of money over time if the sum of money is subject to a rate of interest *(p. 269)*

## USEFUL INTERNET SITES

**www.cis-pec.gc.ca**
**Canada Investment and Savings (CIS)**    CIS is a special operating agency of the Department of Finance that markets and manages savings and investment products for Canadians. Their site provides information on products, including Canada Savings Bonds, as well as rates, savings programs, and publications.

**www.tsx.com**
**Toronto Stock Exchange (TSX)**    Visit this site to see the latest market trends, get quotes, and read about the market data services offered.

**www.m-x.ca/accueil_en.php**
**Montreal Stock Exchange**    Visit this site to see companies traded on the exchange, its history, mission, operations, and FAQs.

**www.standardandpoors.com**
**Standard and Poor's**    Standard and Poor's research services provide data, analysis, and economic forecasts, and analyze economic events and trends in business and government around the globe to help people make informed business decisions.

# 8 Simple Interest Applications

## OBJECTIVES

**Upon completing this chapter, you will be able to do the following:**

1. Identify and define promissory notes and their related terms.

2. Compute the maturity value of interest-bearing promissory notes.

3. Compute the present value of promissory notes and treasury bills.

4. Compute interest and balances for demand loans.

5. Compute interest and balances for lines of credit and credit card loans.

6. Construct repayment schedules for loans using blended payments.

A business often needs to borrow money for periods of less than one year. It may need to pay for products purchased or for work done by employees now, but will not collect the money owed to it until some time in the future. A business may need to replace higher-interest-rate loans, such as credit card debts, with lower-interest-rate loans, such as a bank loan or line of credit. Financial institutions are making it easier for businesses and individuals to borrow money, and are making it more convenient to repay what is borrowed. In addition to the traditional promissory notes, demand loans and lines of credit are being made available for use.

# INTRODUCTION

Businesses often encounter situations that involve the application of simple interest. Simple interest calculation is usually restricted to financial instruments subject to time periods of less than one year. In this chapter we apply simple interest to short-term promissory notes, treasury bills, lines of credit, credit card loans, and demand loans.

# 8.1 PROMISSORY NOTES—BASIC CONCEPTS AND COMPUTATIONS

## A. Nature of promissory notes and illustration

A **promissory note** is a written promise by one party to pay a certain sum of money, with or without interest, at a specific date or on demand, to another party. (See Figure 8.1.)

---

**FIGURE 8.1**    **Promissory Note**

$650.00      MISSISSAUGA, ONTARIO      OCTOBER 30, 2010

FOUR MONTHS    after date    I    promise to pay to the order of

CREDIT VALLEY NURSERY

SIX-HUNDRED-FIFTY and 00/100 ·································· Dollars

at      SHERIDAN CREDIT UNION LIMITED      for value received

with interest at    7.25%    per annum.

Signed    *D. Peel*

---

This is an **interest-bearing promissory note** because it is a note subject to the rate of interest stated on the face of the note.

## B. Related terms explained

The following information is directly available in the promissory note (see items a, b, c, d, e, f below) or can be determined (see items g, h, i, j).

**(a)** The **maker** of the note is the party making the promise to pay. —— **(D. Peel)**

**(b)** The **payee** of the note is the party to whom the promise to pay is made. ———————————————— **(Credit Valley Nursery)**

**(c)** The **face value** of the note is the sum of money (principal) specified. ———————————————— **($650.00)**

**(d)** The **rate of interest** is stated as a simple annual rate based on the face value. ———————————————— **(7.25%)**

SIMPLE INTEREST APPLICATIONS

**(e)** The **date of issue** or **issue date** is the date on which the note was made. ——————————————————————— (October 30, 2010)

**(f)** The **term** of the promissory note is the length of time before the note matures (becomes payable). ——————————— (four months)

**(g)** The **due date** or **date of maturity** is the date on which the note is to be paid. ————————————————— (See Subsection C)

**(h)** The **interest period** is the time period from the date of issue to the legal due date. ——————————————————— (See Subsection C)

**(i)** The **amount of interest** is payable together with the face value on the legal due date. ———————————— (See Subsection C)

**(j)** The **maturity value** is the amount payable on the due date (face value plus interest). ——————————— (See Subsection C)

The Canadian law relating to promissory notes adds **three days of grace** to the term of the note to obtain the **legal due date** (Bills of Exchange Act, Section 41). This is to allow for the situation of the repayment date falling on a statutory holiday. In this case, without three days of grace, you would either have to pay the note early, or take a penalty for paying three days late. Therefore, three days are added to the due date of a promissory note. Interest must be paid for those three days of grace, but there is no late payment penalty and your credit rating remains good. Today, with electronic banking, you can arrange to pay your note at any time, even on the weekend, so you may not need the three days of grace. If you decide not to include the three days of grace, write "No Grace Days" on the note when you negotiate the loan.

## C. Computed values

**EXAMPLE 8.1A**

For the promissory note illustrated in Figure 8.1, determine
   (i) the due date;
  (ii) the interest period;
 (iii) the amount of interest;
 (iv) the maturity value.

**SOLUTION**

(i) *Finding the due date*

Add three days of grace to the term of the note to obtain the legal due date. Since calendar months vary in length, the month in which the term ends does not necessarily have a date that corresponds to the date of issue. In such cases, the last day of the month is used as the end of the term of the note. Three days of grace are added to that date to determine the legal due date. (Throughout this chapter, we have included three days of grace in the exercises. However, as we pointed out earlier, electronic banking has reduced the need for three days of grace.)

With reference to the promissory note in Figure 8.1,
   • the date of issue is October 30, 2010;
   • the term of the note is four months;
   • the month in which the term ends is February 2011;

- the end of the term is February 28 (since February has no day corresponding to day 30, the last day of the month is used to establish the end of the term of the note);
- the legal due date (adding 3 days) is March 3.

(ii) *Determining the interest period*
If the note bears interest, the interest period covers the number of days from the date of issue of the note to the legal due date.

October 30 to March 3 = 124 days

(iii) *Computing the amount of interest*
The interest payable on the note is the simple interest based on the face value of the note for the interest period at the stated rate. It is found using the simple interest formula:

$$\boxed{I = Prt} \text{———————————— Formula 7.1A}$$

$$I = (650.00)(0.0725)\left(\frac{124}{365}\right) = \$16.01$$

(iv) *Finding the maturity value of the note*
The maturity value of the promissory note is the total amount payable at the legal due date.
Face value + Interest = 650.00 + 16.01 = \$666.01

In Excel, use the following functions to do these calculations:

| | |
|---|---|
| COUPDAYSNC | Days between dates |
| ACCRINTM | Accrued interest |
| YIELDDISC | Simple interest yields |
| ACCRINTM | Accrued interest to maturity |

## EXERCISE 8.1

 **A.** Determine each of the items listed from the information provided in the promissory note below.

---

$530.00        OAKVILLE, ONTARIO        DECEMBER 30, 2010

FIVE MONTHS    after date   I   promise to pay

to the order of            JANE WELTON

FIVE-HUNDRED-THIRTY and 00/100 ⋯⋯⋯⋯⋯⋯⋯ Dollars

at            SHERIDAN CENTRAL BANK            for value received

with interest at    6.5%    per annum.

Signed    *E. Salt*

---

**1.** Date issued         **2.** Legal due date

**3.** Face value         **4.** Interest rate

**5.** Interest period (days)     **6.** Amount of interest

**7.** Maturity value

**B.** For each of the following notes, determine

(a) the legal due date;         (b) the interest period (in days);

(c) the amount of interest;     (d) the maturity value.

1. The face value of a five-month, 6% note dated September 30, 2011 is $840.

2. A note for $760 dated March 20, 2010, with interest at 5% per annum, is issued for 120 days.

3. A 60-day, 6.5% note for $1250 is issued January 31, 2008.

4. A four-month, 5.25% note for $2000 is issued July 31, 2009.

# 8.2 MATURITY VALUE OF INTEREST-BEARING PROMISSORY NOTES

## A. Using the formula S = P(1 + *rt*)

Since the maturity value of a promissory note is the principal (face value) plus the interest accumulated to the legal due date, the future value formula for simple interest will determine the maturity value directly.

$$\boxed{S = P(1 + rt)} \text{──────── Formula 7.3A}$$

$S =$ maturity value of the promissory note;
$P =$ the face value of the note;
$r =$ the rate of interest on the note;
$t =$ the interest period (the number of days between the *date of issue* and the *legal due date*).

## B. Worked examples

**EXAMPLE 8.2A**

Find the maturity value of an $800, six-month note with interest at 7.5% dated May 31, 2010.

**SOLUTION**

The date of issue is May 31, 2010;
the term of the note is six months;
the term ends November 30, 2010;
the legal due date is December 3, 2010;
the interest period (May 31 to December 3) has 186 days.

$$P = 800.00; \quad r = 0.075; \quad t = \frac{186}{365}$$

$$S = 800.00\left[1 + (0.075)\left(\frac{186}{365}\right)\right] = 800.00(1 + 0.038219) = \$830.58$$

**EXAMPLE 8.2B**

Determine the maturity value of a 90-day, $750 note dated December 15, 2011, with interest at 8%.

**SOLUTION**

The date of issue is December 15, 2011;
the term is 90 days;
the term ends March 14, 2012 (from 90 days take away 17 days remaining in December, 31 days for January, 29 days for February, 2012 being a leap year, which leaves 13 days for March);
the legal due date (adding the three days of grace) is March 17;
the interest period (December 15 to March 17) has 93 days.

$$P = 750.00; \quad r = 0.08; \quad t = \frac{93}{365}$$

$$S = 750.00\left[1 + (0.08)\left(\frac{93}{365}\right)\right] = 750.00(1 + 0.020384) = \$765.29$$

## EXERCISE 8.2

**A.** Use the future value formula to compute the maturity value of each of the following promissory notes.

    **1.** A four-month, 5.25% note for $620 is issued May 25, 2009.

    **2.** A $350 note is issued on October 30, 2011 at 4.5% for 90 days.

    **3.** A 150-day note for $820 with interest at 5% is dated June 28, 2010.

    **4.** A seven-month, $575 note dated November 1, 2011 earns interest at 7.5%.

    **5.** A five-month, 6.18% note for $835 is issued January 24, 2010.

    **6.** A $230 note is issued on July 18, 2011 at 7.5% for 101 days.

    **7.** A 92-day note for $10 200 with interest at 8.05% is dated August 22, 2010.

    **8.** A ten-month, $5650 note dated September 1, 2011 earns interest at 3.8%.

# 8.3 PRESENT VALUE OF PROMISSORY NOTES

## A. Finding the face value

The face value (or principal) of promissory notes can be obtained by solving the future value formula $S = P(1 + rt)$ for P, that is, by using the present value formula

$$P = \frac{S}{1 + rt}$$ ———— Formula 7.3B

P = the face value (or present value) of the note at the date of issue;
S = the maturity value;
r = the rate of interest;
t = the interest period.

**EXAMPLE 8.3A**

A five-month note dated January 31, 2011 and bearing interest at 8% p.a. (per annum, i.e., per year) has a maturity value of $558.11. Find the face value of the note.

**SOLUTION**

FIGURE 8.2    **Graphical Representation of Data**

The term of the note ends June 30;
the legal due date is July 3;
the interest period (January 31 to July 3) has 153 days.

$$S = 558.11; \quad r = 0.08; \quad t = \frac{153}{365}$$

$$P = \frac{558.11}{1 + (0.08)\left(\dfrac{153}{365}\right)} = \frac{558.11}{1 + 0.033534} = \$540.00$$

## B. Present value of promissory notes

The present value of a promissory note is its value any time before the due date, allowing for the rate money is worth, the time between the present date and its date of maturity, and its maturity value.

The first step in determining the present value is to ascertain whether the note is an interest-bearing or a non-interest-bearing note.

If the rate of interest is stated, the promissory note is an interest-bearing note. The face value of the note is the principal amount borrowed. To determine the present value of an interest-bearing note, two steps are required:

1. First, the maturity value of the note must be calculated, using the stated interest rate.
2. Next, the present value of the note must be calculated, using the **rate money is worth.**

If there is no rate of interest stated, the promissory note is a non-interest-bearing note. Interest on money borrowed may be implied, but is not stated. The face value of the note is the amount to be repaid at maturity. To determine the present value of a non-interest-bearing note, use the rate at which money is worth. The present value can be computed in one step.

Because the two rates are likely to be *different*, take care in using them.

**EXAMPLE 8.3B**

A seven-month note for $1500 is issued on March 31, 2010, bearing interest at 9%. Compute the present value of the note on the date of issue if money is worth 7%.

**SOLUTION**

(i) First, determine the *maturity value* of the note. Use the date of issue as the focal date.
The term of the note ends October 31;
the legal due date is November 3;
the interest period (March 31 to November 3) has 217 days;
the interest rate to be used is 9%.

**FIGURE 8.3**   **Graphical Representation of Data**

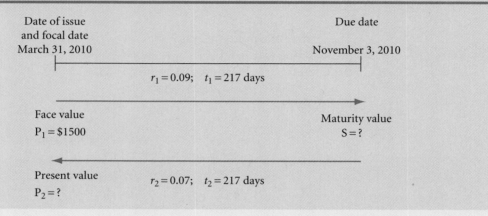

$$P_1 = 1500.00; \quad r_1 = 0.09; \quad t_1 = \frac{217}{365}$$

$$S = 1500\left[1 + (0.09)\left(\frac{217}{365}\right)\right] = 1500(1 + 0.053507) = \$1580.26$$

(ii) Second, use the maturity value found in part (i) to determine the *present value* at the specified date.
The focal date (date of issue) is March 31;
the legal due date is November 3;
the interest period (March 31 to November 3) has 217 days;
the interest rate to be used is 7%.

$$S = 1580.26; \quad r_2 = 0.07; \quad t_2 = \frac{217}{365}$$

$$P_2 = \frac{1580.26}{1 + (0.07)\left(\dfrac{217}{365}\right)} = \frac{1580.26}{1 + 0.041616} = \$1517.12$$

**Note:** The present value at the date of issue is more than the face value of the note, because the interest rate on the note (9%) is more than the rate money is worth (7%).

**EXAMPLE 8.3C**     A 180-day note for $2000 with interest at 7% is dated September 18, 2010. Compute the value of the note on December 1, 2010 if money is worth 5%.

**SOLUTION**

FIGURE 8.4    **Graphical Representation of Data**

(i) *Compute the maturity value of the note.*
The term of the note is 180 days plus 3 days of grace; therefore, the term ends March 20, 2011; the interest rate to be used is 7%.

$$P_1 = 2000; \quad r_1 = 0.07; \quad t_1 = \frac{183}{365}$$

$$S = 2000\left[1 + (0.07)\left(\frac{183}{365}\right)\right] = 2000(1 + 0.035096) = \$2070.19$$

(ii) *Compute the present value.*
The focal date is December 1, 2010; the interest period (December 1, 2010 to March 20, 2011) has 109 days: the interest rate to be used is 5%.

$$S = 2070.19; \quad r_2 = 0.05; \quad t_2 = \frac{109}{365}$$

$$P_2 = \frac{2070.19}{\left[1 + (0.05)\left(\dfrac{109}{365}\right)\right]} = \frac{2070.19}{(1 + 0.014932)} = \$2039.73$$

**EXAMPLE 8.3D**     Compute the present value on the date of issue of a non-interest-bearing $950, three-month promissory note dated April 30, 2010 if money is worth 6.5%.

**SOLUTION**

**FIGURE 8.5**    **Graphical Representation of Data**

Date of issue
and focal date
April 30, 2010

Due date
August 2, 2010

Maturity value
S = $950

Present value          $r = 0.065$;   $t = 94$ days
$P_2 = ?$

(i) Since this is a non-interest-bearing note, the maturity value of the note is the face value, $950.
The term of the note ends July 30, 2010, plus 3 days of grace; therefore, the legal due date is August 2, 2010; the interest period (April 30 to August 2) has 94 days; the interest rate to be used is 6.5%.

$$S = 950; \quad r = 0.065; \quad t = \frac{94}{365}$$

$$P = \frac{950}{\left[1 + (0.065)\left(\dfrac{94}{365}\right)\right]} = \frac{950}{(1 + 0.016740)} = \$934.36$$

**EXAMPLE 8.3E**    Henry purchased a large-screen TV at a local store that had advertised, "No payment until 2009." He signed the contract on March 14, 2008, agreeing to pay $1995 on January 2, 2009. If money is worth 11%, what is the value of the note on the day of signing?

**SOLUTION**    Between March 14, 2008 and January 2, 2009 are 294 days; the maturity value of the contract is its face value, $1995.00.

**FIGURE 8.6**    **Graphical Representation of Data**

March 14, 2008                                    January 2, 2009

$1832.62      $t = 294$ days      $1995

Focal date

$$S = 1995.00; \quad r = 0.11; \quad t = \frac{294}{365}$$

$$P = \frac{1995.00}{\left[1 + (0.11)\left(\dfrac{294}{365}\right)\right]} = \frac{1995.00}{(1 + 0.088603)} = \$1832.62$$

## C. Present value of treasury bills

**Treasury bills** (or **T-bills**) are promissory notes issued by the federal government and most provincial governments to meet short-term financing requirements.

Government of Canada T-bills are for terms of 91 days, 182 days, and 364 days. There are no days of grace with T-bills. T-bills are auctioned by the Bank of Canada on behalf of the federal government. They are available in denominations of $1000, $5000, $25 000, $100 000, and $1 000 000. T-bills are bought at the auction mainly by chartered banks and investment dealers for resale to other investors, such as smaller financial institutions, corporations, mutual funds, and individuals.

T-bills are promissory notes that do not carry an interest rate. The issuing government guarantees payment of the face value at maturity. The investor purchases T-bills at a discounted price reflecting a rate of return that is determined by current market conditions. The discounted price is determined by computing the present value of the T-bills.

**EXAMPLE 8.3F**

An investment dealer bought a 91-day Canada T-bill to yield an annual rate of return of 4.21%.

(i) What was the price paid by the investment dealer for a T-bill with a face value of $100 000?

(ii) The investment dealer resold the $100 000 T-bill the same day to an investor to yield 4.06%. What was the investment dealer's profit on the transaction?

**SOLUTION**

(i) *Find the purchase price, $P_1$.*

The maturity value is the face value of the T-bill, $100 000.00; the discount period has 91 days (no days of grace are allowed on T-bills).

$$S = 100\ 000.00; \quad r_1 = 0.0421; \quad t_1 = \frac{91}{365}$$

$$P_1 = \frac{S}{1 + r_1 t_1} = \frac{100\ 000.00}{1 + 0.0421\left(\dfrac{91}{365}\right)} = \frac{100\ 000.00}{1 + 0.010496} = \$98\ 961.29$$

The investment dealer paid $98 961.29 for a $100 000 T-bill.

(ii) *Find the resale price, $P_2$.*

$$S = 100\ 000.00; \quad r_2 = 0.0406; \quad t_2 = \frac{91}{365}$$

$$P_2 = \frac{100\ 000.00}{1 + 0.0406\left(\dfrac{91}{365}\right)} = \frac{100\ 000.00}{1 + 0.010122} = \$98\ 997.92$$

Investment dealer's profit = Resale price – Price paid by dealer
$$= P_2 - P_1$$
$$= 98\ 997.92 - 98\ 961.29 = \$36.63$$

The investment dealer's profit on the transaction was $36.63.

**EXAMPLE 8.3G**

An investor purchased $250 000 in 364-day T-bills 315 days before maturity to yield 3.38%. He sold the T-bills 120 days later to yield 3.72%.
  (i) How much did the investor pay for the T-bills?
  (ii) For how much did the investor sell the T-bills?
  (iii) What rate of return did the investor realize on the investment?

**SOLUTION**

(i) *Find the purchase price of the T-bills, $P_1$.*

$$S = 250\ 000.00; \quad r_1 = 0.0338; \quad t_1 = \frac{315}{365}$$

$$P_1 = \frac{250\ 000.00}{1 + 0.0338\left(\dfrac{315}{365}\right)} = \frac{250\ 000.00}{1 + 0.029170} = \$242\ 914.23$$

The investor sold the T-bills for $242 914.23.

(ii) *Find the selling price of the T-bills, $P_2$.*
The time to maturity at the date of sale is 195 days (315−120).

$$S = 250\ 000.00; \quad r_2 = 0.0372; \quad t_2 = \frac{195}{365}$$

$$P_2 = \frac{250\ 000.00}{1 + 0.0372\left(\dfrac{195}{365}\right)} = \frac{250\ 000.00}{1 + 0.019874} = \$245\ 128.33$$

The investor sold the T-bills for $245 128.33.

(iii) The investment of $242 914.23 grew to $245 128.33 in 120 days.
To compute the rate of return, use the future value formula (Formula 7.3A).

$$P = 242\ 914.23; \quad S = 245\ 128.33; \quad t = \frac{120}{365}$$

$$S = P(1 + rt)$$

$$245\ 128.33 = 242\ 914.23\left[1 + r\left(\frac{120}{365}\right)\right]$$

$$\frac{245\ 128.33}{242\ 914.23} = 1 + \left(\frac{120}{365}\right)r$$

$$1.009115 = 1 + 0.328767r$$

$$0.009115 = 0.328767r$$

$$\frac{0.009115}{0.328767} = r$$

$$r = 0.027724 = 2.77\%$$

The investor realized a rate of return of about 2.77%.

***Alternatively:***
The gain realized represents the interest.

$$I = 245\ 128.33 - 242\ 914.23 = \$2214.10$$

Using the formula $r = \dfrac{I}{Pt}$,

$$r = \frac{2214.10}{242\,914.23\left(\dfrac{120}{365}\right)} = \frac{2214.10}{79\,862.21} = 0.027724 = 2.77\%.$$

## EXERCISE 8.3

   **A.** Compute the face value of each of the following promissory notes.

1. A six-month note dated April 9, 2009, with interest at 4% has a maturity value of $510.19.

2. The maturity value of a 150-day, 5% note dated March 25, 2010 is $1531.44.

  **B.** Find the present value, on the date indicated, of each of the following promissory notes.

1. A non-interest-bearing note for $1500 issued August 10, 2010 for three months if money is worth 7.5%, on the date of issue;

2. A non-interest-bearing note for $750 issued February 2, 2012 for 180 days if money is worth 6.25%, on June 1, 2012;

3. A 60-day, 9% note for $1600 issued October 28 if money is worth 7%, on November 30;

4. A four-month note for $930 dated April 1 with interest at 6.5% if money is worth 8%, on June 20.

  **C.** Answer each of the following questions.

1. What is the price of a 91-day, $100 000 Government of Canada treasury bill that yields 3.83% per annum?

2. An investment dealer bought a 182-day Government of Canada treasury bill at the price required to yield an annual rate of return of 4.02%.
   (a) What was the price paid by the investment dealer if the T-bill has a face value of $1 000 000?
   (b) Later the same day, the investment dealer sold this T-bill to a large corporation to yield 3.88%. What was the investment dealer's profit on this transaction?

3. An investment dealer acquired a $5000, 91-day Province of Alberta treasury bill on its date of issue at a price of $4966.20. What was the annual rate of return?

4. On June 2 you bought for $24 767.75 a $25 000 Province of New Brunswick treasury bill maturing October 7. What was the discount rate at which you bought the treasury bill?

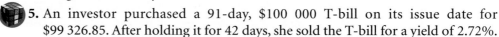 5. An investor purchased a 91-day, $100 000 T-bill on its issue date for $99 326.85. After holding it for 42 days, she sold the T-bill for a yield of 2.72%.
   (a) What was the original yield of the T-bill?
   (b) For what price was the T-bill sold?
   (c) What rate of return (per annum) did the investor realize while holding this T-bill?

**6.** On April 1, $25 000 364-day treasury bills were auctioned off to yield 2.92%.

(a) What is the price of each $25 000 T-bill on April 1?

(b) What is the yield rate on August 15 if the market price is $24 377.64?

(c) Calculate the market value of each $25 000 T-bill on October 1 if the rate of return on that date is 4.545%.

(d) What is the rate of return realized if a $25 000 T-bill purchased on April 1 is sold on November 20 at a market rate of 4.625%?

# 8.4 DEMAND LOANS

## A. Nature of demand loans

A **demand loan** is a loan for which repayment, in full or in part, may be required at any time, or made at any time. The financial instrument representing a demand loan is called a **demand note**.

When borrowing on a demand note, the borrower receives the full face value of the note. The lender may demand payment of the loan in full or in part at any time. Conversely, the borrower may repay all of the loan or any part at any time without notice and without interest penalty. Interest, based on the unpaid balance, is usually payable monthly. The interest rate on such loans is normally not fixed for the duration of the loan but fluctuates with market conditions. Thus the total interest cost cannot be predicted with certainty. Note that the method of counting days is to count the first day but not the last.

## B. Examples

**EXAMPLE 8.4A**

Rose 'n' Blooms borrowed $1200 from the Royal Bank on a demand note. It agreed to repay the loan in six equal monthly installments (each payment is made at the end of the month) and also authorized the bank to collect interest monthly from its bank account at 6% p.a. calculated on the unpaid balance. What will the loan cost?

**SOLUTION**

$$\text{Monthly payment of principal} = \frac{1200.00}{6} = \$200.00$$

$$\text{Monthly rate of interest} = \frac{6\%}{12} = 0.5\% = 0.005$$

| Month | Loan Amount Owing During Month | | Interest Collected for Month | |
|-------|-------------|------------|-------------|------------|
| 1 | $1200.00 | Original | $ 6.00 | (1200)(0.005) |
| 2 | $1000.00 | 1200 – 200 | $ 5.00 | (1000)(0.005) |
| 3 | $ 800.00 | 1000 – 200 | $ 4.00 | (800)(0.005) |
| 4 | $ 600.00 | 800 – 200 | $ 3.00 | (600)(0.005) |
| 5 | $ 400.00 | 600 – 200 | $ 2.00 | (400)(0.005) |
| 6 | $ 200.00 | 400 – 200 | $ 1.00 | (200)(0.005) |
| | Total interest cost | | $21.00 | |

**EXAMPLE 8.4B**

On August 17, 2010 Sheridan Toy Company borrowed $30 000 from Peel Credit Union on a demand note to finance its inventory. Interest on the loan, calculated on the daily balance, is charged against the borrower's current account on the 17th of each month while the loan is in force. The company makes a payment of $5000 on September 24, makes a further payment of $10 000 on October 20, and pays the balance on December 10. The interest on demand loans on August 17 was 6% p.a. The rate was changed to 7% effective October 1, to 8.5% effective November 1, and to 8% effective December 1. Determine the cost of financing the loan.

**SOLUTION**

| Date | Interest Period | Principal | Rate | Interest Due | |
|------|----------------|-----------|------|--------------|---|
| Sept. 17 | Aug. 17–Sept. 17 | $30 000.00 | 6.0% | $152.88 | — $(30\ 000)(0.06)\left(\frac{31}{365}\right)$ |
| Oct. 17 | Sept. 17–Sept. 24 | $30 000.00 | 6.0% | 34.52 | — $(30\ 000)(0.06)\left(\frac{7}{365}\right)$ |
| | Sept. 24–Sept. 30* | $25 000.00 | 6.0% | 28.77 | — $(25\ 000)(0.06)\left(\frac{7}{365}\right)$ |
| | Oct. 1–Oct. 17 | $25 000.00 | 7.0% | 76.71 | — $(25\ 000)(0.07)\left(\frac{16}{365}\right)$ |
| | | | | $292.88 | |
| Nov. 17 | Oct. 17–Oct. 20 | $25 000.00 | 7.0% | $ 14.38 | — $(25\ 000)(0.07)\left(\frac{3}{365}\right)$ |
| | Oct. 20–Oct. 31* | $15 000.00 | 7.0% | 34.52 | — $(15\ 000)(0.07)\left(\frac{12}{365}\right)$ |
| | Nov. 1–Nov. 17 | $15 000.00 | 8.5% | 55.89 | — $(15\ 000)(0.85)\left(\frac{16}{365}\right)$ |
| | | | | $104.79 | |
| Dec. 10 | Nov. 17–Nov. 30* | $15 000.00 | 8.5% | $ 48.90 | — $(15\ 000)(0.85)\left(\frac{14}{365}\right)$ |
| | Dec. 1–Dec. 10 | $15 000.00 | 8.0% | 29.59 | — $(15\ 000)(0.8)\left(\frac{9}{365}\right)$ |
| | | | | $ 78.49 | |
| *Inclusive | Total cost of financing | | ⟶ | $476.16 | |

## C. Partial payments

Demand loans and similar debts are sometimes paid off by a series of **partial payments**. The commonly used approach to dealing with this type of loan repayment is the **declining balance approach**, requiring that each partial payment be applied first to the accumulated interest. Any remainder is then used to reduce the outstanding principal. Thus, interest is always calculated on the unpaid balance and the new unpaid balance is determined after each partial payment.

The following step-by-step procedure is useful in dealing with such problems:
(a) Compute the interest due to the date of the partial payment.
(b) Compare the interest due computed in part (a) with the partial payment received, and do part (c) if the partial payment is *greater than* the interest due or do part (d) if the partial payment is *less than* the interest due.
(c) *Partial payment greater than interest due:*
  (i) Deduct the interest due from the partial payment.
  (ii) Deduct the remainder in part (i) from the principal balance to obtain the new unpaid balance.
(d) *Partial payment less than interest due:*
  In this case, the partial payment is not large enough to cover the interest due.
  (i) Deduct the partial payment from the interest due to determine the unpaid interest due at the date of the principal payment.
  (ii) Keep a record of this balance and apply any future partial payments to this unpaid interest first.

---

**EXAMPLE 8.4C**

On April 20, 2011, Bruce borrowed $4000 at 5% on a note requiring payment of principal and interest on demand. Bruce paid $600 on May 10 and $1200 on July 15. What payment is required on September 30 to pay the note in full?

**SOLUTION**

**April 20**
  Original loan balance ⟶ $4000.00

**May 10**
  Deduct
  First partial payment ⟶ $ 600.00
  Less interest
    April 20–May 10 ⟶ 10.96 ———— $(4000)(0.05)\left(\frac{20}{365}\right)$
                                  589.04
  Unpaid balance ⟶ $3410.96

**July 15**
  Deduct
  Second partial payment ⟶ $1200.00
  Less interest
    May 10–July 15 ⟶ 30.84 ———— $(3410.96)(0.05)\left(\frac{66}{365}\right)$

                                  1169.16
  Unpaid balance ⟶ $2241.80

**September 30**
  Add
  Interest
    July 15–Sept. 30 ⟶ 23.65 — $(2241.80)(0.05)\left(\frac{77}{365}\right)$
    Payment required
    to pay the note in full ⟶ $2265.45

## POINTERS AND PITFALLS

When determining the number of days in any given time period between interest rate changes or between two partial payments, remember to always count the first day and omit the last day. As well, keep in mind that

(a) The date on which there is a change in the interest rate is counted as the first day at the new interest rate.

(b) The date on which a partial payment is made is counted as the first day at the new outstanding principal balance.

---

**EXAMPLE 8.4D**

The Provincial Bank lent $20 000 to the owner of the Purple Pelican on April 1, 2010 for commercial improvements. The loan was secured by a demand note subject to a variable rate of interest. This rate was 7% on April 1. The rate of interest was raised to 9% effective August 1 and reduced to 8% effective November 1. Partial payments, applied to the loan by the declining balance method, were made as follows: June 10, $1000; September 20, $400; November 15, $1200. How much interest is due to the Provincial Bank on December 31?

**SOLUTION**

**April 1**
  Original loan balance ⟶ $20 000.00

**June 10**
  Deduct
  First partial payment ⟶ $1000.00
  Less interest
    April 1–June 10 ⟶ 268.49 ———— $(20\ 000)(0.07)\left(\frac{70}{365}\right)$
                                       731.51
    Unpaid loan balance ⟶ $19 268.49

**September 20**
  Deduct
  Second partial payment              $ 400.00
  Less interest
    June 10–Sept. 20:
    June 10–July 31      $192.16       ———— $(19\ 268.49)(0.07)\left(\frac{52}{365}\right)$
      (inclusive)
    Aug. 1–Sept. 20       237.56   429.72 ———— $(19\ 268.49)(0.09)\left(\frac{50}{365}\right)$

  Unpaid interest to
    Sept. 20 ⟶ $ 29.72
  Unpaid loan balance ⟶ $19 268.49

**November 15**
  Deduct
  Third partial payment ⟶ $1200.00

Less interest
Unpaid interest to
Sept. 20 ⟶ $ 29.72 ——————— (see above)

Sept. 20–Oct. 31 ⟶ 199.55 ——————— $(19\,268.49)(0.09)\left(\frac{42}{365}\right)$
(inclusive)

Nov. 1–Nov. 15 ⟶ 59.13 ——————— $(19\,268.49)(0.08)\left(\frac{42}{365}\right)$

288.40

911.60

Unpaid loan balance ⟶ $18 356.89

**December 31**
Interest due
Nov. 15–Dec. 31 ⟶ $ 185.08 $-(18\,356.89)(0.08)\left(\frac{42}{365}\right)$

## EXERCISE 8.4

**A.** Determine the total interest cost for each of the following loans.

**1.** On June 15, 2009, Jean-Luc borrowed $2500 from his bank secured by a demand note. He agreed to repay the loan in five equal monthly installments and authorized the bank to collect the interest monthly from his bank account at 6.0% per annum calculated on the unpaid balance.

**2.** James TV & Stereo borrowed $1800 from the Teachers' Credit Union. The loan was to be repaid in six equal monthly payments, plus interest of 7.5% per annum calculated on the unpaid balance.

**3.** Jamie borrowed $900 from the Essex District Credit Union. The loan agreement provided for repayment of the loan in four equal monthly payments plus interest at 12% per annum calculated on the unpaid balance.

**4.** Erindale Automotive borrowed $8000 from the Bank of Montreal on a demand note on May 10. Interest on the loan, calculated on the daily balance, is charged to Erindale's current account on the 10th of each month. Erindale made a payment of $2000 on July 20, a payment of $3000 on October 1, and repaid the balance on December 1. The rate of interest on the loan on May 10 was 8% per annum. The rate was changed to 9.5% on August 1 and to 8.5% on October 1.

**5.** The Tomac Swim Club arranged short-term financing of $12 500 on July 20 with the Bank of Commerce and secured the loan with a demand note. The club repaid the loan by payments of $6000 on September 15, $3000 on November 10, and the balance on December 30. Interest, calculated on the daily balance and charged to the club's current account on the last day of each month, was at 9.5% per annum on July 20. The rate was changed to 8.5% effective September 1 and to 9% effective December 1.

**B.** Answer each of the following.

1. On March 10, Fat Tires Ltd. borrowed $10 000 with an interest rate of 5.5%. The loan was repaid in full on November 15, with payments of $2500 on June 30 and $4000 on September 4. What was the final payment?

2. Automotive Excellence Inc. borrowed $20 000 on August 12 with an interest rate of 6.75% per annum. On November 1 $7500 was repaid, and on December 15 $9000 was repaid. Automotive Excellence paid the balance of the loan on February 20. What was the final payment?

3. A loan of $6000 made at 11% per annum on March 10 is repaid in full on November 15. Payments were made of $2000 on June 30 and $2500 on September 5. What was the final payment?

4. D. Slipp borrowed $15 000 on August 12. She paid $6000 on November 1, $5000 on December 15, and the balance on February 20. The rate of interest on the loan was 10.5%. How much did she pay on February 20?

5. The Continental Bank made a loan of $20 000 on March 25 to Dr. Hirsch to purchase equipment for her office. The loan was secured by a demand loan subject to a variable rate of interest that was 7% on March 25. The rate of interest was raised to 8.5% effective July 1 and to 9.5% effective September 1. Dr. Hirsch made partial payments on the loan as follows: $600 on May 15; $800 on June 30; and $400 on October 10. The terms of the note require payment of any accrued interest on October 31. How much must Dr. Hirsch pay on October 31?

6. Dirk Ward borrowed $12 000 for investment purposes on May 10 on a demand note providing for a variable rate of interest and payment of any accrued interest on December 31. He paid $300 on June 25, $150 on September 20, and $200 on November 5. How much is the accrued interest on December 31 if the rate of interest was 7.5% on May 10, 6% effective August 1, and 5% effective November 1?

# 8.5 LINES OF CREDIT AND CREDIT CARD LOANS

A **line of credit** is a pre-approved loan agreement between a financial institution and a borrower. The borrower may withdraw money, up to an agreed maximum, at any time. Interest is charged only on the amount withdrawn from the line of credit. A minimum repayment may be required each month. The borrower may repay any additional amount at any time without further penalty. The rate of interest charged for money borrowed on a line of credit is often lower than the rate of interest charged on most credit cards. The interest rate can change over time.

A **credit card** is a plastic card entitling the bearer to a revolving line of credit with a pre-established credit limit. Interest rates are set by the credit card issuers, vary considerably, and can be changed at any time. Generally, interest rates charged on credit cards are higher than rates charged on loans made by financial institutions. Some credit card issuers require an annual fee to be paid by the user. When the bearer withdraws cash by presenting the credit card, a cash advance fee is usually charged. Depending on the issuer of the credit card, the cash advance fee may be deducted directly from the cash advance at the time the money is received or it may be posted to the account on the day the cash is received. Interest on the cash advance is calculated starting from the day the money is withdrawn. The bearer of the credit card, with an authorizing signature, may make purchases instead of using cash to pay.

An **unsecured line of credit** is a line of credit with no assets promised to the lender to cover non-payment of the loan. Since no security is offered to the lender, the limit of an unsecured line of credit depends on the individual's credit rating and past relationship with the lender.

A **secured line of credit** is a line of credit with assets promised to the lender to cover non-payment of the loan. For example, homeowners might pledge the value of their home, that is, their home equity, to secure a line of credit. In general, the limit of a secured line of credit is higher than the limit of an unsecured one. Furthermore, the interest rate of a secured line of credit is lower than the interest rate of an unsecured one.

Lines of credit secured by home equity are becoming quite popular and are used by some borrowers as an alternative to mortgages. Home equity lines of credit (HELOC) provide access to larger credit limits.

---

**EXAMPLE 8.5A**

Suppose your business has secured a line of credit and receives the following statement of account for the month of February.

| Date | Transaction Description | Deposit | Withdrawal | Balance |
|------|------------------------|---------|------------|---------|
| Feb. 01 | Balance | | | −600.00 |
| 04 | Cheque 262 | | 500.00 | −1100.00 |
| 10 | Deposit | 2050.00 | | 950.00 |
| 16 | Cheque 263 | | 240.00 | 710.00 |
| 20 | Cheque 264 | | 1000.00 | −290.00 |
| 22 | Cheque 265 | | 80.00 | −370.00 |
| 27 | Cheque 266 | | 150.00 | −520.00 |
| 28 | Interest earned | ? | | |
| | Line of credit interest | | ? | |
| | Overdraft interest | | ? | |
| | Service charge | | ? | |

**Note:** "−" indicates a negative balance.

The limit on your line of credit is $1000. You receive daily interest of 1.5% p.a. on positive balances and pay daily interest of 7% p.a. on *negative (line of credit) balances*. Overdraft interest is 18% p.a. on the daily amount exceeding your line of credit limit. There is a service charge of $5 for each transaction causing an overdraft or adding to an overdraft.

Determine
  (i) the amount of interest earned;
 (ii) the amount of interest charged on the line of credit;
(iii) the amount of interest charged on overdrafts;

(iv) the amount of the service charge;

(v) the account balance on February 28.

**SOLUTION**

(i) Interest earned (on positive balances):

February 10 to February 15 inclusive: 6 days at 1.5% on $950.00

$$I = 950.00(0.015)\left(\frac{6}{365}\right) = \$0.23$$

February 16 to February 19 inclusive: 4 days at 1.5% on $710.00

$$I = 710.00(0.015)\left(\frac{4}{365}\right) = \$0.12$$

Total interest earned = 0.23 + 0.12 = $0.35

(ii) Line of credit interest charged (on negative balances up to $1000.00):

February 1 to February 3 inclusive: 3 days at 7% on $600.00

$$I = 600.00(0.07)\left(\frac{3}{365}\right) = \$0.35$$

February 4 to February 9 inclusive: 6 days at 7% on $1000.00

$$I = 1100.00(0.07)\left(\frac{6}{365}\right) = \$1.27$$

February 20 to February 21 inclusive: 2 days at 7% on $290.00

$$I = 290.00(0.07)\left(\frac{2}{365}\right) = \$0.11$$

February 22 to February 26 inclusive: 5 days at 7% on $370.00

$$I = 370.00(0.07)\left(\frac{5}{365}\right) = \$0.35$$

February 27 to February 28 inclusive: 2 days at 7% on $520.00

$$I = 520.00(0.07)\left(\frac{2}{365}\right) = \$0.20$$

Total line of credit interest charged
= 0.35 + 1.27 + 0.11 + 0.35 + 0.20 = $2.28

(iii) Since your line of credit limit is $1000.00, overdraft interest is charged on the amount in excess of a negative balance of $1000.00. You were in overdraft from February 4 to February 9 inclusive in the amount of $100.00.

$$\text{Overdraft interest} = 100.00\,(0.18)\left(\frac{6}{365}\right) = \$0.30$$

(iv) You had one transaction causing an overdraft or adding to an overdraft.
Service charge = 1(5.00) = $5.00

(v) The account balance on February 28
= −520.00 + 0.35 − 2.28 − 0.30 − 5.00 = −$527.23

**EXAMPLE 8.5B**

You have applied for and received a credit card. The interest rate charged is 18.9% per annum. You note the following transactions for the month of September.

September 6    Purchased textbooks and supplies for a total of $250.
September 10   Withdrew $100 as a cash advance through your credit card.
September 30   Received the credit card statement, showing a minimum balance owing of $25. A payment date of October 10 is stated on the statement.

(i) Compute the amount of interest charged on the cash advance from September 10 until September 30.
(ii) You decide to pay the amount owing, in full, on October 1. How much must you pay?
(iii) Instead of paying the full amount, you decide to pay the minimum, $25, on October 1. What would be the balance owing after the payment?
(iv) If there are no further transactions during October, how much is owing at the end of October?

**SOLUTION**

(i) Interest charged (on cash advance):
September 10 to September 30 inclusive: $100 at 18.9% for 21 days.

$$I = 100.00(0.189)\left(\frac{21}{365}\right) = \$1.09$$

(ii) $250.00 + 100.00 + 1.09 = \$351.09$

(iii) $351.09 - 25.00 = \$326.09$

(iv)
$$I = 326.09(0.189)\left(\frac{31}{365}\right) = \$5.23$$

$326.09 + 5.23 = \$331.32$
At the end of October $331.32 is owing.

# EXERCISE 8.5

**A.**  Determine the missing information for each of the following lines of credit.

**1.** Suppose you have a line of credit and receive the following statement for the month of March.

| Date | Transaction Description | Deposit | Withdrawal | Balance |
|---|---|---|---|---|
| Feb. 28 | Balance | | | −527.71 |
| Mar. 02 | Cheque 264 | | 600.00 | −1127.71 |
| 05 | Cheque 265 | | 300.00 | −1427.71 |
| 10 | Deposit | 2000.00 | | 572.29 |
| 16 | Cheque 266 | | 265.00 | 307.29 |

| 20 | Cheque 267 | | 1000.00 | −692.71 |
|----|------------|----|---------|---------|
| 22 | Cheque 268 | | 83.50 | −776.21 |
| 27 | Cheque 269 | | 165.00 | −941.21 |
| 31 | Interest earned | ? | | |
| | Line of credit interest | | ? | |
| | Overdraft interest | | ? | |
| | Service charge | | ? | ? |

***Note:*** " −" indicates a negative balance.

The limit on the line of credit is $1000. Daily interest of 1.25% p.a. is received on positive balances and daily interest of 8% p.a. is paid on negative (line of credit) balances. Overdraft interest is 18% p.a. on the daily amount exceeding the line of credit limit. There is a service charge of $5 for each transaction causing an overdraft or adding to an overdraft.

(**a**) Calculate the amount of interest earned.
(**b**) Calculate the amount of interest charged on the line of credit.
(**c**) Calculate the amount of interest charged on overdrafts.
(**d**) Calculate the amount of the service charge.
(**e**) What is the account balance on March 31?

2. Exotic Furnishings Ltd. has a line of credit secured by the equity in the business. The limit on the line of credit is $45 000. Transactions for the period April 1 to September 30 are shown below. Exotic owed $25 960.06 on its line of credit on April 1.

| Date | Principal Withdrawal | Principal Payment | Interest Payment | Balance |
|------|---------------------|-------------------|------------------|---------|
| Apr. 01 | | | | −25 960.06 |
| 30 | | 200.00 | ? | |
| May 23 | 5 000.00 | | | |
| 31 | | 200.00 | ? | |
| June 30 | | 200.00 | ? | |
| July 19 | 5 000.00 | | | |
| 31 | | 200.00 | ? | |
| Aug. 05 | 10 500.00 | | | |
| 31 | | 200.00 | ? | |
| Sept. 30 | | 200.00 | ? | |

***Note:*** " −" indicates a negative balance.

The line of credit agreement requires a regular payment of $200 on the principal plus interest (including overdraft interest) by electronic transfer after closing on the last day of each month. Overdraft interest is 17% p.a. The line of credit interest is variable. It was 6.00% on April 1, 5.50% effective June 20, and 5.00% effective September 10.

(**a**) Calculate the interest payments on April 30, May 31, June 30, July 31, August 31, and September 30.
(**b**) What is the account balance on September 30?

# 8.6 LOAN REPAYMENT SCHEDULES

## A. Purpose

In the case of loans repaid in fixed installments (often called a **blended payment**), the constant periodic payment is first applied to pay the accumulated interest. The remainder of the payment is then used to reduce the unpaid balance of the principal.

While lenders are obliged to disclose to the borrower the total cost of borrowing as well as the interest rate (see Figure 8.7), a detailed statement of the cost of borrowing as well as the effect of the periodic payments on the principal may be obtained by constructing a **loan repayment schedule**, or an **amortization schedule**.

FIGURE 8.7    Statement of Disclosure

The information usually contained in such a schedule includes
(**a**) the payment number or payment date;
(**b**) the amount paid at each payment date;
(**c**) the interest paid by each payment;
(**d**) the principal repaid by each payment;
(**e**) the unpaid loan balance after each payment.

Figure 8.8 provides a possible design for such schedules and the same design is used in the Solution to Example 8.6A.

FIGURE 8.8    Basic Design of a Loan Repayment Schedule

| ① Payment Number | ② Balance Before Payment | ③ Amount Paid | ④ Interest Paid | ⑤ Principal Repaid | ⑥ Payment After Balance |
|---|---|---|---|---|---|

# B. Construction of loan repayment schedules illustrated

**EXAMPLE 8.6A**

Great Lakes Marina borrowed $1600 from Sheridan Credit Union at 9% p.a. and agreed to repay the loan in monthly installments of $300 each, such payments to cover interest due and repayment of principal. Use the design shown in Figure 8.8 to construct a complete repayment schedule including the totalling of columns ③, ④, and ⑤ ("Amount Paid," "Interest Paid," and "Principal Repaid").

**SOLUTION**

See Figure 8.9 and the explanatory notes that follow.

**FIGURE 8.9**  **Loan Repayment Schedule for Example 8.6A**

| ① Payment Number | ② Balance Before Payment | ③ Amount Paid (1) | ④ Interest Paid (2) | | ⑤ Principal Repaid (3) | | ⑥ Payment After Balance (4) | |
|---|---|---|---|---|---|---|---|---|
| 0 | | | | | | | 1600.00 | (5) |
| 1 | 1600.00 | 300.00 | 12.00 | (6) | 288.00 | (7) | 1312.00 | (8) |
| 2 | 1312.00 | 300.00 | 9.84 | (9) | 290.16 | (10) | 1021.84 | (11) |
| 3 | 1021.84 | 300.00 | 7.66 | | 292.34 | | 729.50 | |
| 4 | 729.50 | 300.00 | 5.47 | | 294.53 | | 434.97 | |
| 5 | 434.97 | 300.00 | 3.26 | | 296.74 | | 138.23 | (12) |
| 6 | 138.23 | 139.27 (15) | 1.04 | (14) | 138.23 | (13) | 0.00 | |
| Totals (16) | | 1639.27 (18) | 39.27 | (19) | 1600.00 | (17) | | |

*Notes:*

(1) The Amount Paid shown in column ③ is the agreed-upon monthly payment of $300.

(2) The Interest Paid shown in column ④ is at 9% per annum. This figure is converted into a periodic (monthly) rate of $\frac{9\%}{12}$ (0.75% per month) to facilitate the computation of the monthly amount of interest paid. (See notes (6) and (9).)

(3) The amount of Principal Repaid each month shown in column ⑤ is found by subtracting the Interest Paid for the month (column ④) from the Amount Paid for the month (column ③). (See notes (7) and (10).)

(4) The Balance After Payment for a month shown in column ⑥ is found by subtracting the Principal Repaid for the month (column ⑤) from the Balance Before Payment for the month (column ②) *or* from the previous Balance After Payment figure (column ⑥). (See notes (8) and (11).)

(5) The original loan balance of $1600 is introduced as the starting amount for the schedule and is the only amount shown in Line 0.

(6) Interest paid in Payment Number 1
  = 0.75% of 1600.00 = (0.0075)(1600.00) = $12.00

(7) Principal repaid by Payment Number 1
  = 300.00 − 12.00 = $288.00

(8) Balance after Payment Number 1
= 1600.00 − 288.00 = $1312.00

(9) Interest paid in Payment Number 2
= 0.75% of 1312.00 = (0.0075)(1312.00) = $9.84

(10) Principal repaid by Payment Number 2
= 300.00 − 9.84 = $290.16

(11) Balance after Payment Number 2
= 1312.00 − 290.16 = $1021.84

(12) The Balance after Payment Number 5 of $138.23 is smaller than the regular monthly payment of $300. The next payment need only be sufficient to pay the outstanding balance of $138.23 plus the interest due. (See notes (13), (14), and (15).)

(13) Principal repaid in Payment Number 6 must be $138.23 to pay off the outstanding loan balance.

(14) Interest paid in Payment Number 6 is the interest due on $138.23
= 0.75% of 138.23 = (0.0075)(138.23) = $1.04.

(15) Amount paid in Payment Number 6
= 138.23 + 1.04 = $139.27.

(16) The Totals of columns ③, ④, and ⑤ serve as a check of the arithmetic accuracy of the payment schedule. (See notes (17), (18), and (19).)

(17) Principal Repaid, the total of column 5, must equal the original loan balance of $1600.

(18) Amount Paid, the total of column ③, must equal the total of all the payments made (five payments of $300 each plus the final payment of $139.27).

(19) Interest paid, the total of column ④, must be the difference between the totals of columns ④ and ⑤ = 1639.27 − 1600.00 = $39.27.

## C. Computer application—loan repayment schedule

This exercise assumes a basic understanding of spreadsheet applications; however, an individual who has no previous experience with spreadsheets can complete this task.

Microsoft Excel and other spreadsheet programs allow the user to easily create a flexible loan repayment schedule. The finished repayment schedule will reflect any changes made to the loan amount, the interest rate, or the schedule of payments. (The following example was created in Excel, but most programs work similarly.)

The following Excel application is based on Example 8.6A, which uses six months to repay the loan. An additional row of formulas similar to row 3 would be added for each additional month required to repay the loan.

**STEP 1** Enter the labels shown in Figure 8.10 in row 1 and in column A.

**STEP 2** Enter the numbers shown in row 2.

**STEP 3** Enter only the formulas shown in row 3 and row 9. Make sure that the entry includes the dollar sign ($) as shown in the figure.

FIGURE 8.10

| | A | B | C | D | E | F | G |
|---|---|---|---|---|---|---|---|
| | | | Workbook 1 | | | | |
| 1 | Payment | Balance before payment | Amount paid | Interest paid | Principal repaid | Balance | |
| 2 | 0 | | | | | 1600.00 | 300.00 |
| 3 | 1 | = F2 | = $G$2 | = $G$4*B3 | = C3–D3 | = B3–E3 | |
| 4 | 2 | = F3 | = $G$2 | = $G$4*B4 | = C4–D4 | = B4–E4 | = 0.09/12 |
| 5 | 3 | = F4 | = $G$2 | = $G$4*B5 | = C5–D5 | = B5–E5 | |
| 6 | 4 | = F5 | = $G$2 | = $G$4*B6 | = C6–D6 | = B6–E6 | |
| 7 | 5 | = F6 | = $G$2 | = $G$4*B7 | = C7–D7 | = B7–E7 | |
| 8 | 6 | = F7 | = D8+E8 | = $G$4*B8 | = B8 | = B8–E8 | |
| 9 | Totals | | = SUM(C3:C8) | = SUM(D3:D8) | = SUM(E3:E8) | | |

**STEP 4** The formulas that are entered in row 3 can be copied through the remaining rows.
(a) Select and copy the formulas in row 3.
(b) Select cells C4 to C8, and select Paste.
(c) The formulas are now active in all the cells.

**STEP 5** To ensure readability of the spreadsheet, format the numbers to display as two decimal places, and widen the columns to display the full labels.

This spreadsheet can now be used to reflect changes in aspects of the loan and display the effects quickly. Put a new principal amount in cell F2 and a new interest rate in cell G4. The interest rate must be divided by 12 to convert the annual interest rate to a monthly rate. For example, new annual interest rate of 5% would be entered as $\dfrac{0.05}{12}$.

A copy of this spreadsheet, called Template 2, appears on the Spreadsheet Template Disk.

## EXERCISE 8.6

A. Use the design shown in Figure 8.8 to construct a complete repayment schedule including the totalling of the Amount Paid, Interest Paid, and Principal Repaid columns for each of the following loans.

1. Carla borrowed $1200 from the Royal Bank at 8.5% per annum calculated on the monthly unpaid balance. She agreed to repay the loan in blended payments of $180 per month.

2. Blended payments on a $3400 loan were $800 per month. Interest was charged at 7.75% per annum calculated on the monthly unpaid balance.

3. On March 15, Julio borrowed $900 from Sheridan Credit Union at 7.5% per annum calculated on the daily balance. He gave the Credit Union six cheques

for $135 dated the 15th of each of the next six months starting April 15 and a cheque dated October 15 for the remaining balance to cover payment of interest and repayment of principal.

4. On February 8, Manuel borrowed $700 from his uncle at 6% per annum calculated on the daily balance. He gave his uncle seven cheques for $100 dated the 8th of each of the next seven months starting March 8 and a cheque dated September 8 for the remaining balance to cover payment of interest and repayment of principal.

## BUSINESS MATH NEWS BOX

### It Keeps Getting Easier to Fall into the Debt Trap

Canadians' love affair with debt continues unabated. The ratio of consumer credit and mortgage debt to personal disposable income rose to a new high of 100.1% in the second quarter of this year, Statistics Canada reported last week. This means we owe more than $1 in debt for every dollar of income we earn. As long as interest rates stay low, most people seem to be handling the higher debt loads in relative comfort. However, there are some casualties. The number of consumer bankruptcies in Canada rose 8% to 49 730 in the first seven months of 2003. Canadians' personal debt loads—which now average $22 697 for every man, woman, and child in the country—will keep escalating. Stanley Kershman is a bankruptcy lawyer in Ottawa who's spent 25 years helping people and companies get back on their feet. He just finished acting for the bankrupt Ottawa Senators hockey team. "Marketers will find more innovative ways to lend people money," he says. "Furniture stores such as Leon's and The Brick used to advertise buying on store credit and paying no interest for six months. "The interest-free period grew to 12 months and now it's 16 months. They're spreading out the payments longer and longer to make it more attractive for people to buy." In a similar trend, Visa and MasterCard issuers once required payments of 3% of the balance owing to keep an account in good standing. Now the minimum payment is slipping to 2%.

*Source:* Ellen Roseman, "It Keeps Getting Easier to Fall into the Debt Trap," *Toronto Star*, October 1, 2003, p. C.03. Reprinted with Permission of Torstar Syndication Services.

### QUESTIONS

1. Estimate the value of Canadian consumer credit card debt in Canada, given that the Canadian population is approximately 32 million.

2. Given the information above, calculate the number of bankruptcies at the beginning of 2003.

3. A credit card has a $3000 balance with an interest rate of 18.9% per annum compounded monthly. If the credit card holder pays $100 per month toward the debt, calculate how long it will take to pay off this debt.

4. Calculate the interest paid on a $3000 credit card balance given monthly payments made over seven years. Assume interest is at 18.9% per annum compounded monthly.

Go to MyMathLab at www.mathxl.com. You can practise many of this chapter's exercises as often as you want. The guided solutions help you find an answer step by step. You'll find a personalized study plan available to you too!

## Review Exercise

1. A four-month promissory note for $1600 dated June 30 bears interest at 6.5%.

   (a) What is the due date of the note?

   (b) What is the amount of interest payable at the due date?

   (c) What is the maturity value of the note?

2. Determine the maturity value of a 120-day note for $1250 dated May 23 and bearing interest at 5.75%.

3. Compute the face value of a 120-day note dated September 10 bearing interest at 6.75% whose maturity value is $1534.12.

4. The maturity value of a seven-month promissory note issued July 31, 2009 is $3275. What is the present value of the note on the date of issue if interest is 7.75%?

5. Compute the maturity value of a 150-day, 6% promissory note with a face value of $5000 dated August 5.

6. What is the face value of a three-month promissory note dated November 30, 2011, with interest at 4.5 percent if its maturity value is $950.89?

7. A 90-day, $800 promissory note was issued July 31 with interest at 8%. What is the value of the note on October 20?

8. On June 1, 2010, a four-month promissory note for $1850 with interest at 5% was issued. Compute the proceeds of the note on August 28, 2010, if money is worth 6.5%.

9. Determine the value of a $1300 non-interest-bearing note four months before its maturity date of July 13, 2010, if money is worth 7%.

10. Compute the proceeds of a five-month, $7000 promissory note dated September 6, 2009, with interest at 5.5% if the note is paid on November 28, 2009, when money is worth 6.5%.

11. An investment dealer paid $24 256.25 to acquire a $25 000, 182-day Government of Canada treasury bill at the weekly auction. What was the rate of return on this T-bill?

12. Government of Alberta 364-day T-bills with a face value of $1 000 000 were purchased on April 7 for $971 578. The T-bills were sold on May 16 for $983 500.

    (a) What was the market yield rate on April 7?

    (b) What was the yield rate on May 16?

    (c) What was the rate of return realized?

13. Mel's Photography borrowed $15 000 on March 10 on a demand note. The loan was repaid by payments of $4000 on June 20, $3000 on September 1, and the balance on November 15. Interest, calculated on the daily balance and charged to Mel's Photography current account on the last day of each month, was at 5.5% on March 10 but was changed to 6.25% effective June 1 and to 6% effective October 1. How much did the loan cost?

14. Quick Print Press borrowed $20 000 from the Provincial Bank on May 25 at 7.5% and secured the loan by signing a promissory note subject to a variable rate of interest. Quick Print made partial payments of $5000 on July 10 and $8000 on September 15. The rate of interest was increased to 8% effective August 1 and to 8.5% effective October 1. What payment must Quick Print make on October 31 if, under the terms of the loan agreement, any interest accrued as of October 31 is to be paid on October 31?

15. Muriel has a line of credit with a limit of $10 000. She owed $8195 on July 1. Principal withdrawals for the period July 1 to November 30 were $3000 on August 20 and $600 on October 25. The line of credit agreement requires regular payments of $300 on the 15th day of each month. Muriel has made all required payments. Interest (including overdraft interest) is charged to the account on the last day of each month. The interest rate was 8% on July 1, but was changed to 7.5% effective

September 15. Overdraft interest is 16% for any balance in excess of $10 000.

**(a)** Calculate the interest charges on July 31, August 31, September 30, October 31, and November 30.

**(b)** Calculate the account balance on November 30.

**16.** You borrowed $3000 at 9% per annum calculated on the unpaid monthly balance and agreed to repay the principal together with interest in monthly payments of $500 each. Construct a complete repayment schedule.

 Self-Test

**1.** For the following promissory note, determine the amount of interest due at maturity.

| $565.00 | TORONTO, ONTARIO | JANUARY 10, 2008 |
| --- | --- | --- |

___FIVE MONTHS___  after date  __we__  promise to pay to the order of

__WILSON LUMBER COMPANY__

EXACTLY  FIVE-HUNDRED-SIXTY-FIVE and 00/100 --------------- Dollars

at _____WILSON LUMBER COMPANY_____  for value received

with interest at  __8.25%__  per annum.

Due _____                                  (seal) _____

                                                      (seal) _____

**2.** Find the maturity value of a $1140, 7.75%, 120-day note dated February 19, 2010.

**3.** Determine the face value of a four-month promissory note dated May 20, 2011, with interest at 7.5% p.a. if the maturity value of the note is $1190.03.

**4.** Find the present value of a non-interest-bearing seven-month promissory note for $1800 dated August 7, 2011, on December 20, 2011, if money is then worth 6%.

**5.** A 180-day note dated September 14, 2010 is made at 5.25% for $1665. What is the present value of the note on October 18, 2010, if money is worth 6.5%?

**6.** What is the price of a 91-day, $25 000 Government of Canada treasury bill that yields 3.28% per annum?

**7.** An investor purchased a 182-day, $100 000 T-bill on its issue date. It yielded 3.85%. The investor held the T-bill for 67 days, then sold it for $98 853.84.

**(a)** What was the original price of the T-bill?

**(b)** When the T-bill was sold, what was its yield?

 **8.** The owner of Jane's Boutique borrowed $6000 from Halton Community Credit Union on June 5, 2010. The loan was secured by a demand note with interest calculated on the daily balance and charged to the store's account on the 5th day of each month. The loan was repaid by payments of $1500 on July 15, $2000 on October 10, and $2500 on December 30. The rate of interest charged by the credit union was 8.5% on June 5. The rate was changed to 9.5% effective July 1 and to 10% effective October 1. Determine the total interest cost on the loan.

9. Herb's Restaurant borrowed $24 000 on March 1, 2009 on a demand note providing for a variable rate of interest. While repayment of principal is open, any accrued interest is to be paid on November 30. Payments on the loan were made as follows: $600 on April 15, $400 on July 20, and $400 on October 10. The rate of interest was 7% on March 1 but was changed to 8.5% effective August 1 and to 7.5% effective November 1. Using the declining balance method to record the partial payments, determine the accrued interest on November 30.

10. Jing has a line of credit from her local bank with a limit of $10 000. On March 1, 2010, she owed $7265. From March 1 to June 30, she withdrew principal amounts of $3000 on April 10 and $500 on June 20. According to the line of credit agreement, Jing must make a regular payment of $200 on the 15th of each month. She has made these payments. Interest (including overdraft interest) is charged to the account on the last day of each month. On March 1, the interest rate was 9%, but it was changed to 8.5% effective May 15. Overdraft interest is 18% for any balance in excess of $10 000.

    (a) Calculate the interest charges on March 31, April 30, May 31, and June 30.

    (b) What is the account balance on June 30?

11. Use the design shown in Figure 8.8 to construct a complete repayment schedule, including the totalling of the "Amount Paid," "Interest Paid," and "Principal Repaid" columns, for a loan of $4000 repaid in monthly installments of $750 each including interest of 6.5% per annum calculated on the unpaid balance.

## Challenge Problems

1. Mike Kornas signed a 12-month, 11% p.a. simple interest promissory note for $12 000 with MacDonald's Furniture. After 100 days, MacDonald's Furniture sold the note to the Royal Bank at a rate of 13% p.a. Royal Bank resold the note to Friendly Finance Company 25 days later at a rate of 9% p.a. Find the gain or loss on this note for each company and bank involved.

2. A father wanted to show his son what it might be like to borrow money from a financial institution. When his son asked if he could borrow $120, the father lent him the money and set up the following arrangements. He charged his son $6 for the loan of $120. The son therefore received $114 and agreed to pay his father 12 installments of $10 a month, beginning one month from today, until the loan was repaid. Find the approximate rate of simple interest the father charged on this loan.

# Case Study 8.1 The Business of Borrowing

》 Bits and Bytes Computer Store agrees to purchase some new computer monitors costing $3500 plus 6% GST. Farid Kamlani, the store's owner, was informed that if he paid cash on receipt of the goods he could take a cash discount of 4.5% of the invoice price before GST. GST would then be added to the new invoice price. Farid would like to take advantage of this discount, but his store is short of cash right now. A number of customers are expected to pay their invoices in the next 30 to 60 days.

Farid went to his bank manager to negotiate a short-term loan to pay for the monitors when they arrive and take advantage of the cash discount. The bank manager suggested a 60-day promissory note bearing interest at 6.5%. Farid agreed to the note and suggested that the three days of grace should be added to provide him more repayment flexibility.

## QUESTIONS

1. What is the maturity value of the 60-day promissory note using three days of grace for the goods including GST?

2. Suppose Farid decides he does not need the three days of grace. What effect would this have on the maturity value of the note?

3. Farid later discussed his situation with a friend, who suggested that Farid could have negotiated a short-term loan for 60 days instead of using a promissory note. What is the highest annual simple interest rate at which Farid could have borrowed the money and still saved by taking the cash discount?

# Case Study 8.2 Debt Consolidation

》 Shannon and Duncan Fisher were concerned about their level of debt. They had borrowed from their bank to purchase their house, car, and computer. For these three loans, the Fishers must make regular monthly payments. The couple also owe $6000 to MasterCard and $2500 to Visa. Shannon and Duncan decided to meet with a consumer credit counsellor to gain control of their debts.

The counsellor explained to them the details of their loans and credit card debts. Shannon and Duncan were shocked to discover that whereas their computer and car loans had an interest rate of 10.5% p.a., their credit cards had an interest rate of 19.5% p.a. The counsellor pointed out that the interest rate on their three loans was reasonable. However, because the interest rate on the credit cards was so high, she advised Shannon and Duncan to borrow money at a lower interest rate and pay off the credit card debts.

The credit counsellor suggested that they should consider obtaining a line of credit. She explained that the rate of interest on the line of credit would likely be a few percentage points higher than the prime rate, but much lower than the rate of interest charged on credit card balances. Shannon and Duncan would have to make a minimum payment every month, similar to that of a credit card. The payment would then be applied to pay all the interest and a portion of the principal balance owing on the line of credit. The line of credit would allow them to make monthly payments higher than the minimum so that they could pay as much toward the principal balance as they could afford. Due to the much lower interest rate on a line of credit as compared to a typical credit card, the money they would save on interest each month could be paid toward the principal. A line of credit appealed to Shannon and Duncan, as it helped them feel more in control of their finances and gave them the resolve to pay off their credit card debts.

Shannon and Duncan then met with their bank manager and were approved for a $15 000 line of credit. Immediately, they paid off the $6000 owed to MasterCard and the $2500 owed to Visa with money from the line of credit. They then decided to pay off the line of credit over the next ten months by making monthly payments equal to one-tenth of the original line of credit balance plus the simple interest owed on the remaining line of credit balance. The simple interest rate on the line of credit is expected to be 6.25% over the next ten months. Shannon and Duncan agreed to cut up their credit cards and not charge any more purchases until they had paid off their line of credit.

## QUESTIONS

1. Suppose Shannon and Duncan pay off their credit cards with their line of credit on April 20. They will make their monthly payments on the 20th of each month, beginning in May. Create a schedule showing their monthly payments for the next ten months. How much interest will they pay using this repayment plan?

2. Suppose Shannon and Duncan had not gotten a line of credit but kept their credit cards. They decided not to make any more credit card purchases. Instead, they made monthly payments equal to one-tenth of the original credit card balance plus the simple interest owed on the remaining credit card balance. They will make their monthly payments on the 20th of each month, beginning in May. Create a schedule showing their monthly payments for the next ten months. How much interest would they have paid using this repayment plan?

3. How much money did Shannon and Duncan save on interest by getting the line of credit?

4. What are the requirements for obtaining a line of credit from your financial institution?

## SUMMARY OF FORMULAS

Formula 7.1A
$$I = Prt$$
**Finding the amount of interest on promissory notes**

Formula 7.3A
$$S = P(1 + rt)$$
**Finding the maturity value of promissory notes directly**

Formula 7.3B
$$P = \frac{S}{1 + rt}$$
**Finding the present value of promissory notes or treasury bills given the maturity value**

## GLOSSARY

**Amortization schedule**    see **Loan repayment schedule**

**Amount of interest**    interest, in dollars and cents, payable to the payee on the legal due date *(p. 295)*

**Blended payment**    the usual method of repaying a personal consumer loan by a fixed periodic (monthly) payment that covers payment of interest and repayment of principal *(p. 316)*

**Credit card**    a card entitling the bearer to a revolving line of credit with a pre-approved credit limit *(p. 311)*

**Date of issue**    the date on which a promissory note is made *(p. 295)*

**Date of maturity**    see **Legal due date**

**Declining balance approach**    the commonly used approach to applying partial payments to demand loans whereby each partial payment is first applied to pay the interest due and then applied to the outstanding principal *(p. 307)*

**Demand loan**    a loan for which repayment in full or in part may be required at any time or made at any time *(p. 306)*

**Demand note**    the financial instrument representing a demand loan *(p. 306)*

**Due date**    see **Legal due date**

**Face value**    the sum of money specified on the promissory note *(p. 294)*

**Interest-bearing promissory note**    a note subject to the rate of interest stated on the note *(p. 294)*

**Interest period**    the time, in days, from the date of issue to the legal due date for promissory notes *(p. 295)*

**Issue date**    see **Date of issue**

**Legal due date**    the date on which the promissory note is to be paid; it includes three days of grace unless "No Grace Days" is written on the promissory note *(p. 295)*

**Line of credit**    a pre-approved loan amount issued by a financial institution for use by an individual or business at any time for any purpose; interest is charged only for the time money is borrowed on the line of credit; a minimum monthly payment is required (similar to a credit card); the interest rate can change over time *(p. 311)*

**Loan repayment schedule**    a detailed statement of installment payments, interest cost, repayment of principal, and outstanding balance of principal for an installment plan *(p. 316)*

**Maker**    the party making the promise to pay by signing the promissory note *(p. 294)*

**Maturity value**    the amount (face value plus interest) that must be paid on the legal due date to honour the note *(p. 295)*

**Partial payments**    a series of payments on a debt *(p. 307)*

**Payee**    the party to whom the promise to pay is made *(p. 294)*

**Promissory note**    a written promise to pay a specified sum of money after a specified period of time or on demand, with or without interest as specified *(p. 294)*

**Rate money is worth**    the prevailing rate of interest *(p. 299)*

**Rate of interest**    the simple annual rate of interest based on the face value *(p. 294)*

**Secured line of credit**   a line of credit with assets pledged as security *(p. 312)*

**T-bills**   *see* Treasury bills

**Term (of a promissory note)**   the time period for which the note was written (in days or months) *(p. 295)*

**Three days of grace**   the number of days added to the term of a note in Canada to determine its legal due date *(p. 295)*

**Treasury bills**   promissory notes issued at a discount from their face values by the federal government and most provincial governments to meet short-term financing requirements (the maturity value of treasury bills is the same as their face value) *(p. 303)*

**Unsecured line of credit**   a line of credit in which no assets are pledged by the borrower to the lender to cover non-payment of the line of credit *(p. 312)*

## USEFUL INTERNET SITES

**www.royalbank.com**

**Royal Bank**   Visit the "Daily Numbers" area of this site for current interest rates on investment products. This site also provides links to detailed rate schedules for mortgages, T-bills, personal accounts, and RRSPs.

**www.bankofcanada.ca/en/rates/exchange.html**

**Bank of Canada**   Current T-bill rates are posted on this section of the Bank of Canada site. A link to selected historical interest rates is also provided.

**www.bankrate.com**

**Bankrate.com**   Go to "Calculators" and select "Credit Cards" to determine what it really costs to pay the minimum payment on your credit card. (This is a U.S. site. Some of the interest rates displayed will not be applicable in Canada.)

CHAPTER 9

# Compound Interest—
# Future Value and
# Present Value

## OBJECTIVES

**Upon completing this chapter, you will be able to do the following:**

1. Calculate interest rates and the number of compounding periods.

2. Compute future (maturity) values of investments.

3. Compute present values of future sums of money.

4. Discount long-term promissory notes.

5. Solve problems involving equivalent values.

The world of computerized banking and investing uses compound interest extensively. With compound interest, you earn interest on a principal, and the interest is then added to form a new principal. You then earn interest on this new higher principal. This is what is meant by the expression "earning interest on interest."

To calculate compound interest, and to decide which interest terms are best for you, you need to understand how compound interest works. When you need to calculate compound interest amounts for all sorts of interest rates and time periods, calculators and computers make the job easy. To calculate compound interest amounts using formulas, an understanding of exponents is required.

# INTRODUCTION

Under the compound interest method, interest is added periodically to the principal. As we did with simple interest, we use compound interest calculations to determine future values and present values. The compound interest formulas contain the compounding factor $(1 + i)^n$. The calculations are not difficult if you use electronic calculators equipped with an exponential function, especially if they are financial calculators preprogrammed with the ability to calculate future value and present value for compound interest.

# 9.1 BASIC CONCEPTS AND COMPUTATIONS

## A. Basic procedure for computing compound interest

The term **compound interest** refers to a procedure for computing interest whereby the interest for a specified time period is added to the original principal. The resulting amount becomes the new principal for the next time period. The interest earned in earlier periods earns interest in future periods.

The compound interest method is generally used to calculate interest for long-term investments. The amount of compound interest for the first interest period is the same as the amount of simple interest, but for further interest periods the amount of compound interest becomes increasingly greater than the amount of simple interest.

The basic procedure for computing compound interest and the effect of compounding is illustrated in Table 9.1. The table also provides a comparison of

| Table 9.1 | Compound Interest versus Simple Interest for a Principal of $10 000 Invested at 10% per Annum for 6 Years | | | | |
|---|---|---|---|---|---|
| | | **At Compound Interest** | | **At Simple Interest** | |
| **Year** | | Interest Computation | Amount | Interest Computation | Amount |
| | Original principal | | $10 000.00 | | $10 000.00 |
| 1 | Add interest | (0.10)(10 000.00) | 1 000.00 | (0.10)(10 000.00) | 1 000.00 |
| | Amount end Year 1 | | 11 000.00 | | 11 000.00 |
| 2 | Add interest | (0.10)(11 000.00) | 1 100.00 | (0.10)(10 000.00) | 1 000.00 |
| | Amount end Year 2 | | 12 100.00 | | 12 000.00 |
| 3 | Add interest | (0.10)(12 100.00) | 1 210.00 | (0.10)(10 000.00) | 1 000.00 |
| | Amount end Year 3 | | 13 310.00 | | 13 000.00 |
| 4 | Add interest | (0.10)(13 310.00) | 1 331.00 | (0.10)(10 000.00) | 1 000.00 |
| | Amount end Year 4 | | 14 641.00 | | 14 000.00 |
| 5 | Add interest | (0.10)(14 641.00) | 1 464.10 | (0.10)(10 000.00) | 1 000.00 |
| | Amount end Year 5 | | 16 105.10 | | 15 000.00 |
| 6 | Add interest | (0.10)(16 105.10) | 1 610.51 | (0.10)(10 000.00) | 1 000.00 |
| | Amount end Year 6 | | $17 715.61 | | $16 000.00 |

compound interest and simple interest for an original principal of $10 000 invested at 10% per annum for six years.

The method of computation used in Table 9.1 represents the step-by-step approach used in maintaining a compound interest record, such as a savings account. Note that the amount of interest is determined for each interest period on the basis of the previous balance and is then added to that balance.

Note the following about the end results after six years:

|  | At compound interest | At simple interest |
|---|---|---|
| Amount after six years | $17 715.61 | $16 000.00 |
| Less original principal | 10 000.00 | 10 000.00 |
| Amount of interest | $ 7 715.61 | $ 6 000.00 |

In this case, the compound interest exceeds the simple interest by $1715.61. This difference represents the amount of interest earned by interest added to the principal at the end of each compounding period.

## B. Computer application—accumulation of principal using a spreadsheet

Table 9.1 displays the manual calculations for the accumulation of a principal of $10 000 earning compound interest at 10% per annum for six years. Microsoft Excel and other spreadsheet programs can be used to create a file that will immediately display the results of a change in the principal, interest rate, or number of years of accumulation.

The following steps are general instructions for creating a file to calculate the compound interest data in Table 9.1. The formulas in the spreadsheet file were created using Excel; however, most spreadsheet programs work similarly.

Although this exercise assumes a basic understanding of spreadsheet applications, someone without previous spreadsheet experience will be able to complete this task.

**STEP 1**   Enter the labels shown in Figure 9.1 in row 1.

**STEP 2**   Enter the principal in cell B2. Do not type in the dollar sign or a comma.

**STEP 3**   Enter only the formulas shown in cells C2, D2, and B3. Make sure that the formula entry includes the dollar ($) sign as shown in Figure 9.1. Use Copy and Paste to enter the remainder of the formulas shown.

**STEP 4**   The formulas that were entered in Step 3 can be copied through the remaining cells.
(a) Select and Copy the formulas in cells C2 and D2.
(b) Select cells C3 to C7, and Paste.

**FIGURE 9.1**

| | A | B | C | D | E |
|---|---|---|---|---|---|
| **1** | Year | Amount, beginning of year | Interest | Amount, end of year | 0.10 |
| **2** | 1 | 10000 | = B2*$E$1 | = B2+C2 | |
| **3** | 2 | = D2 | = B3*$E$1 | = B3+C3 | |
| **4** | 3 | = D3 | = B4*$E$1 | = B4+C4 | |
| **5** | 4 | = D4 | = B5*$E$1 | = B5+C5 | |
| **6** | 5 | = D5 | = B6*$E$1 | = B6+C6 | |
| **7** | 6 | = D6 | = B7*$E$1 | = B7+C7 | |

Workbook 1

(c) Select and Copy the formula in cell B3.

(d) Select cells B4 to B7, and Paste.

(e) The formulas are now active in all the cells.

**STEP 5** To ensure readability of the spreadsheet, format the numbers to display as two decimal places, and widen the columns to display the full labels.

This spreadsheet can now be used to reflect changes in aspects of the investment. You will be able to input the changes and see the effects quickly. Use cell B2 for a new principal amount and cell E1 for a new interest rate.

## C. The future value formula for compound interest

Creating a compound interest table is useful, and serves many purposes, but can be time-consuming. As in calculating simple interest, the **future value**, **maturity value**, or **amount** of a loan or investment can be found by using the future value formula.

For *simple interest*, the future value formula is $S = P(1 + rt)$, Formula 7.3A.

For *compound interest*, the formula for the future value is

$$S = P(1 + i)^n$$ restated as:

$$FV = PV(1 + i)^n$$ ——————————————— Formula 9.1A

S or FV = the future or maturity value;

P or PV = the original principal;

$i$ = the periodic rate of interest;

$n$ = the number of compounding periods for the term of the loan or investment.

The results of Table 9.1 could have been obtained by using the two future value formulas.

*For simple interest*: P = 10 000.00;   $r = 0.10$;   $t = 6$

$$S = P(1 + rt) = 10\ 000.00[1 + (0.10)(6)]$$
$$= 10\ 000.00(1 + 0.60)$$
$$= 10\ 000.00(1.60)$$
$$= \$16\ 000.00$$

*For compound interest*: PV = 10 000.00;   $i = 0.10$;   $n = 6$

$$FV = PV(1 + i)^n = 10\ 000.00(1 + 0.10)^6$$
$$= 10\ 000.00(1.10)^6$$
$$= 10\ 000.00(1.10)(1.10)(1.10)(1.10)(1.10)(1.10)$$
$$= 10\ 000.00(1.771561)$$
$$= \$17\ 715.61$$

When using the compound interest formula, determining the factor $(1 + i)^n$ is the main computational problem. The value of this factor, called the **compounding factor** or **accumulation factor**, depends on the values of $i$ and $n$.

## D. Determining the periodic rate of interest

The value of $i$, the **periodic rate of interest**, is determined from the stated rate of interest to be used in the compounding situation. The stated rate is called the **nominal rate of interest**. Since the nominal rate of interest is usually stated as an annual rate, the value of $i$ depends on the **compounding (or conversion) frequency** per year. The value of $i$ is obtained by dividing the nominal annual rate by the number of **compounding (or conversion) periods** per year.

The compounding (conversion) periods commonly used in business and finance cover a number of months, usually an exact divisor of 12, and are listed in Table 9.2.

| Table 9.2 | Commonly Used Compounding Frequencies and Conversion Periods | | |
|---|---|---|---|
| | Compounding (Conversion) Frequency | Length of Compounding (Conversion) Period | Number of Compounding (Conversion) Periods per Year |
| | Annual | 12 months (1 year) | 1 |
| | Semi-annual | 6 months | 2 |
| | Quarterly | 3 months | 4 |
| | Monthly | 1 month | 12 |

The relationship between the periodic rate of interest and the nominal annual rate of interest can be stated in the form of a formula.

$$\text{PERIODIC RATE OF INTEREST, } i = \frac{\text{NOMINAL (ANNUAL) RATE}}{\text{NUMBER OF COMPOUNDING (CONVERSION) PERIODS PER YEAR}}$$

Therefore,

$$i = \frac{j}{m}$$ ————————————————————— Formula 9.2

where $i$ = periodic rate of interest
$\quad\quad j$ = nominal annual rate of interest
$\quad\quad m$ = number of compounding (conversion) periods per year

---

**EXAMPLE 9.1A**

Determine the periodic rate of interest $i$ for
(i) 5% p.a. compounded annually;
(ii) 7% p.a. compounded semi-annually;
(iii) 12% p.a. compounded quarterly;
(iv) 10.5% p.a. compounded monthly.

**SOLUTION**

|  | (i) | (ii) | (iii) | (iv) |
|---|---|---|---|---|
| The nominal annual rate $j$ | 5% | 7% | 12% | 10.5% |
| The compounding (conversion) frequency | annually | semi-annually | quarterly | monthly |
| The length of the compounding (conversion) period | 12 months | 6 months | 3 months | 1 month |
| The number of compounding (conversion) periods per year $m$ | 1 | 2 | 4 | 12 |
| The periodic rate of interest $i = \dfrac{j}{m}$ | $\dfrac{5\%}{1}$ | $\dfrac{7\%}{2}$ | $\dfrac{12\%}{4}$ | $\dfrac{10.5\%}{12}$ |
|  | = 5.0% | = 3.5% | = 3.0% | = 0.875% |

# E. Determining the number of compounding (conversion) periods in the term of an investment or loan

To find the number of compounding (conversion) periods in the term of an investment or a loan, multiply the number of years in the term by the number of compounding periods per year.

**EXAMPLE 9.1B**

Determine the number of compounding periods when
   (i) compounding annually for 14 years;
  (ii) compounding semi-annually for 15 years;
 (iii) compounding quarterly for 12.5 years;
 (iv) compounding monthly for 10.75 years;
  (v) compounding quarterly for 30 months;
 (vi) compounding semi-annually for 42 months.

**SOLUTION**

| | Term (in years) | Compounding Frequency | Number of Compounding Periods per Year, $m$ | Number of Compounding Periods in Term, $n$ |
|---|---|---|---|---|
| (i) | 14 | annually | 1 | $14(1) = 14$ |
| (ii) | 15 | semi-annually | 2 | $15(2) = 30$ |
| (iii) | 12.5 | quarterly | 4 | $12.5(4) = 50$ |
| (iv) | 10.75 | monthly | 12 | $10.75(12) = 129$ |
| (v) | $\dfrac{30}{12} = 2.5$ | quarterly | 4 | $2.5(4) = 10$ |
| (vi) | $\dfrac{42}{12} = 3.5$ | semi-annually | 2 | $3.5(2) = 7$ |

## POINTERS AND PITFALLS

Many students have difficulty determining the value of $m$ when compounding is stated as "quarterly." This term means that interest is compounded every quarter of a year. Since there are four quarters in a year, $m$ then becomes 4, each quarter of a year being 3 months in length. The value of $m$ is never 3.

## F. Setting up the compounding factor $(1 + i)^n$

The *compounding (accumulation) factor* $(1 + i)^n$ can be set up by first determining $i$ and $n$ and then substituting $i$ and $n$ in the general form of the factor, $(1 + i)^n$.

**EXAMPLE 9.1C**

Set up the compounding factor $(1 + i)^n$ for
   (i) 5% p.a. compounded annually for 14 years;
  (ii) 7% p.a. compounded semi-annually for 15 years;
 (iii) 12% p.a. compounded quarterly for 12.5 years;
 (iv) 10.5% p.a. compounded monthly for 10.75 years;

(v) 8% p.a. compounded quarterly for 30 months;
(vi) 9.5% p.a. compounded semi-annually for 42 months.

**SOLUTION**

| | $i$ | $m$ | $n$ | $(1 + i)^n$ |
|---|---|---|---|---|
| (i) | 5% = 0.05 | 1 | 14(1) = 14 | $(1 + 0.05)^{14} = 1.05^{14}$ |
| (ii) | 3.5% = 0.035 | 2 | 15(2) = 30 | $(1 + 0.035)^{30} = 1.035^{30}$ |
| (iii) | 3.0% = 0.03 | 4 | 12.5(4) = 50 | $(1 + 0.03)^{50} = 1.03^{50}$ |
| (iv) | 0.875% = 0.00875 | 12 | 10.75(12) = 129 | $(1 + 0.00875)^{129} = 1.00875^{129}$ |
| (v) | 2% = 0.02 | 4 | 30/12 = 10 | $(1 + 0.02)^{10} = 1.02^{10}$ |
| (vi) | 4.75% = 0.0475 | 2 | 42/12 = 7 | $(1 + 0.0475)^{7} = 1.0475^{7}$ |

## G. Computing the numerical value of the compounding factor $(1 + i)^n$

The numerical value of the compounding factor can now be computed using an electronic calculator. For calculators equipped with the exponential function feature $\boxed{y^x}$, the numerical value of the compounding factor can be computed directly.

**STEP 1** Enter the numerical value of $(1 + i)$ in the keyboard.

**STEP 2** Press the exponential function key $\boxed{y^x}$.

**STEP 3** Enter the numerical value of $n$ in the keyboard.

**STEP 4** Press $\boxed{=}$.

**STEP 5** Read the answer in the display.

The numerical value of the compounding factors in Example 9.1C are obtained as follows.

| | | (i) | (ii) | (iii) | (iv) | (v) | (vi) |
|---|---|---|---|---|---|---|---|
| **STEP 1** | Enter | 1.05 | 1.035 | 1.03 | 1.00875 | 1.02 | 1.0475 |
| **STEP 2** | Press | $\boxed{y^x}$ | $\boxed{y^x}$ | $\boxed{y^x}$ | $\boxed{y^x}$ | $\boxed{y^x}$ | $\boxed{y^x}$ |
| **STEP 3** | Enter | 14 | 30 | 50 | 129 | 10 | 7 |
| **STEP 4** | Press | $\boxed{=}$ | $\boxed{=}$ | $\boxed{=}$ | $\boxed{=}$ | $\boxed{=}$ | $\boxed{=}$ |
| **STEP 5** | Read | 1.979932 | 2.806794 | 4.383906 | 3.076647 | 1.218994 | 1.383816 |

*Note:* Do not be concerned if your calculator shows a difference in the last decimal. There is no error. It reflects the precision of the calculator and the number of decimal places formatted to show on the display of the calculator.

With the increasing availability of inexpensive electronic calculators, the two traditional methods of determining the compounding factor $(1 + i)^n$—logarithms and tables—are rapidly falling into disuse. Neither method is used in this text.

## EXERCISE 9.1

**A.** Determine $m$, $i$, and $n$ for each of the following.

**1.** 12% compounded annually for 5 years

**2.** 7.4% compounded semi-annually for 8 years

**3.** 5.5% compounded quarterly for 9 years

**4.** 7% compounded monthly for 4 years

**5.** 11.5% compounded semi-annually for 13.5 years

**6.** 4.8% compounded quarterly for $5\frac{3}{4}$ years

**7.** 8% compounded monthly for 12.5 years

**8.** 10.75% compounded quarterly for 3 years, 9 months

**9.** 12.25% compounded semi-annually for 54 months

**10.** 8.1% compounded monthly for 15.5 years

**B.** Set up and compute the compounding factor $(1 + i)^n$ for each of the questions in part A.

**C.** Answer each of the following questions.

**1.** For a sum of money invested at 10% compounded quarterly for 12 years, state
   **(a)** the number of compounding periods;
   **(b)** the periodic rate of interest;
   **(c)** the compounding factor $(1 + i)^n$;
   **(d)** the numerical value of the compounding factor.

**2.** For each of the following periodic rates of interest, determine the nominal annual compounding rate.
   **(a)** $i = 2\%$; compounding is quarterly
   **(b)** $i = 0.75\%$; compounding is monthly
   **(c)** $i = 5.5\%$; compounding is semi-annually
   **(d)** $i = 9.75\%$; compounding is annually

# 9.2 USING THE FORMULA FOR THE FUTURE VALUE OF A COMPOUND AMOUNT FV = PV $(1 + i)^n$

## A. Finding the future value (maturity value) of an investment

**EXAMPLE 9.2A**

Find the amount to which $6000 will grow if invested at 10% per annum compounded quarterly for five years.

**SOLUTION**

The original principal PV = 6000.00;
the nominal annual rate $j$ = 10%;
the number of compounding periods per year $m$ = 4;
the quarterly rate of interest $i = \dfrac{10\%}{4}$ = 2.5% = 0.025;
the number of compounding periods (quarters) $n$ = (5)(4) = 20.

$$FV = PV(1 + i)^n \qquad \text{——————— using Formula 9.1A}$$
$$= 6000.00(1 + 0.025)^{20} \text{——————— substituting for P, } i, n$$
$$= 6000.00(1.025)^{20} \text{——————— exponential form of factor}$$
$$= 6000.00(1.638616) \text{——————— using a calculator}$$
$$= \$9831.70$$

**EXAMPLE 9.2B**

What is the future value after 78 months of $2500 invested at 5.25% p.a. compounded semi-annually?

**SOLUTION**

The original principal PV = 2500.00;
the nominal annual rate $j$ = 5.25;
the number of compounding periods per year $m$ = 2;
the semi-annual rate of interest $i = \dfrac{5.25\%}{2}$ = 2.625% = 0.02625;

the number of compounding periods (each period is six months)
$$n = \left(\frac{78}{12}\right)(2) = (6.5)(2) = 13.$$

$$FV = PV(1 + i)^n$$
$$= 2500.00(1 + 0.02625)^{13}$$
$$= 2500.00(1.02625)^{13}$$
$$= 2500.00(1.400526)$$
$$= \$3501.32$$

**EXAMPLE 9.2C**

Accumulate a deposit of $1750 made into a registered retirement savings plan from March 1, 1995 to December 1, 2010 at 4.4% p.a. compounded quarterly.

**SOLUTION**

The original principal PV = 1750.00; $j$ = 4.4%; $m$ = 4;
the quarterly rate of interest $i = \dfrac{4.4\%}{4}$ = 1.1% = 0.011;

the time period from March 1, 1995 to December 1, 2010 contains 15 years and 9 months, or 15.75 years: $n = (15.75)(4) = 63$.

$$\begin{aligned} FV &= PV(1 + i)^n \\ &= 1750.00(1 + 0.011)^{63} \\ &= 1750.00(1.011)^{63} \\ &= 1750.00(1.992154) \\ &= \$3486.27 \end{aligned}$$

## B. Using preprogrammed financial calculators

Compound interest calculations, which can become complex, are performed frequently and repeatedly. Doing the calculations algebraically can enhance your understanding and appreciation of the theory, but it can also be time-consuming, laborious, and subject to mechanical errors. Using preprogrammed financial calculators can save time and reduce or eliminate mechanical errors, assuming they are set up properly and numerical sign conventions are observed when entering data and interpreting results.

Different models of financial calculators vary in their operation and labelling of the function keys and faceplate. Appendix II, entitled "Instructions and Tips for Three Preprogrammed Financial Calculator Models," highlights the relevant variations for students using Texas Instruments' BAII Plus, Sharp's EL-733A, and Hewlett-Packard's 10B calculators. (Note that Appendix II is intended to help you use one of these three calculators, and merely supplements the instruction booklet that came with your calculator. Refer to the instruction booklet for your particular model to become familiar with your calculator.)

Specific function keys on preprogrammed financial calculators correspond to the five variables used in compound interest calculations. Function keys used for the calculator models presented in Appendix II are shown in Table 9.3.

The function keys are used to enter the numerical values of the known variables into the appropriate preprogrammed calculator registers. The data may be entered in any order. The answer is then displayed by using a computation key or by depressing the key representing the unknown variable, depending on the calculator model.

Before entering the numerical data to complete compound interest calculations, it is important to verify that your calculator has been set up correctly to ensure error-free operation. There are a number of items to check during this "pre-calculation" phase. Specifically, does the calculator require a mode change within a register to match the text presentation? Does the calculator have to be in the financial mode? Are the decimal places set to the correct number to ensure the required accuracy?

Further checks must be made when entering data during the "calculation" phase. For example, have the function key registers been cleared? What numerical data require a minus sign to avoid errors in operation and incorrect answers? How can the data entered be confirmed? Responses to these queries in the "pre-calculation" and "calculation" phases for three preprogrammed financial calculators are given in Appendix II, along with general information.

| Table 9.3 | Financial Calculator Function Keys that Correspond to Variables Used in Compound Interest Calculations | | | |
|---|---|---|---|---|
| | | Function Key | | |
| Variable | Algebraic Symbol | TI BAII+ | Sharp EL-733A | HP 10B |
| The number of compounding periods | $n$ | N | n | N |
| The rate of interest[1] | $i$ | I/Y  C/Y | i | I/YR |
| The periodic annuity payment[2] | R | PMT | PMT | PMT |
| The present value or principal | P | PV | PV | PV |
| The future value or maturity value | S | FV | FV | FV |

*Notes:* 1. The periodic rate of interest is entered as a percent and not as a decimal equivalent (as it is when using the algebraic method to solve compound interest problems). For example, 8% is entered as "8" not ".08". With some calculators, the rate of interest is the periodic rate. In the case of the BAII Plus, the rate of interest entered is the rate per year (nominal rate).

2. The periodic annuity payment function key PMT is used only for annuity calculations, which are introduced in Chapter 11.

Instructions in this text are given for the Texas Instruments BAII Plus calculator. Refer to Appendix II for instructions for setting up and using the Sharp EL-733A and Hewlett-Packard 10B calculators.

### Using the Texas Instruments BAII Plus to Solve Compound Interest Problems

Follow the steps below to compute the future value of a sum of money using the formula $FV = PV(1 + i)^n$ and a Texas Instruments BAII Plus calculator. Compare your result with Example 9.2A.

### Pre-calculation Phase (Initial Setup)

**STEP 1**
The P/Y register, and behind it the C/Y register, must be set to match the calculator's performance to the text presentation. The P/Y register is used to represent the number of regular payments per year. If the text of the question does not discuss regular payments per year, this should be set to equal the C/Y in the calculator. The C/Y register is used to represent the number of compounding periods per year, that is, the compounding frequency. The description of the compounding frequency is usually contained within the phrase that describes the nominal interest rate. An example would be "8% p.a. compounded quarterly." This means that the nominal, or annual, interest rate of 8% is compounded four times each year at 8%/4, or 2%, each period. The compounding frequency of 4 is entered into the C/Y register within the calculator.

| Key in | Press | Display shows |
|---|---|---|
| | 2nd (P/Y) | P/Y = 12 —— checks the P/Y register |
| 4 | ENTER | P/Y = 4 —— changes the value to "4" |
| | ↓ | C/Y = 4 —— changed automatically to match the P/Y |
| | 2nd (QUIT) | 0 —————— returns to the standard calculation mode |

**STEP 2**

Verify that the decimal format is set to the number you require. A setting of "9" represents a floating decimal point format. The default setting is "2."

| Key in | Press | Display shows |
|---|---|---|
| | 2nd (Format) | DEC = 2 — checks the decimal format |
| 6 | ENTER | DEC = 6 — changes to "6" |
| | 2nd (QUIT) | 0 —————— returns to the standard calculation mode |

This calculator is ready for financial calculations in its standard mode.

**Calculation Phase**

**STEP 3**

Always clear the function key registers before beginning compound interest calculations.

| Key in | Press | Display shows |
|---|---|---|
| | 2nd (CLR TVM) | 0 —————— clears the function key registers |

**STEP 4**

To solve Example 9.2A in which P = 6000, $i$ = 2.5%, and $n$ = 20, use the following procedure. Remember that $i$ represents the interest rate per compounding period, and $n$ represents the number of times that interest is compounded. To enter the accurate information into the calculator, you must determine the nominal interest rate for the year, and enter this information into the I/Y register. In this example, the interest rate per year is 10%. The compounding frequency, denoted by the phrase "compounded quarterly," is four times per year. This must be entered into the C/Y register. Also, notice that 6000 is entered as a negative number since it is cash paid out for an investment. This "cash flow sign convention" is explained below.

If you follow this convention, your calculation will be error-free, and the answer will be accurate and interpreted consistently.

| Key in | Press | | Display shows | |
|--------|-------|--|---------------|--|
| | 2nd (P/Y) | | P/Y = 12 | ———— checks the P/Y register |
| 4 | ENTER | | P/Y = 4 | ———— changes the value to "4" |
| | ↓ | | C/Y = 4 | ———— changed automatically to match the P/Y |
| | 2nd (QUIT) | | 0 | ———— returns to the standard calculation mode |
| 6000 | ± | PV | PV = −6000 | ———— this enters the present value P (principal) with the correct sign convention |
| 10 | I/Y | | I/Y = 10 | ———— this enters the nominal interest rate as a percent |
| 20 | N | | N = 20 | this enters the number of compounding periods $n$ |
| | CPT | FV | FV = 9831.698642 | ——— this computes and displays the unknown future value S |

The future value is $9831.70.

### Cash Flow Sign Convention for Entering Numerical Data

The Texas Instruments BAII Plus calculator follows the established convention of treating cash inflows (cash received) as positive numbers and cash outflows (cash paid out) as negative numbers. In the calculation above, the present value was considered to be cash paid out for an investment and so the present value of 6000 was entered as a negative number. The resulting future value was considered to be cash received from the investment and so had a positive value. Note that if the present value had been entered as a positive value, then the future value would have been displayed as a negative number. The *numerical* value would have been correct but the result would have been a negative number. "Error 5" is displayed when calculating $i$ or $n$ if both the present value and future value are entered using the same sign. Therefore, to avoid errors, always enter the present value as a negative number for compound interest calculations. Enter all other values as positive numbers. This topic is discussed further in Appendix II and throughout this text as required.

Excel has a ***Future Value (FV)*** function you can use to calculate the future value of an investment subject to compound interest. Refer to **FV** on the Spreadsheet Template Disk to learn how to use this Excel function.

## C. Finding the future value when $n$ is a fractional value

The value of $n$ in the compounding factor $(1 + i)^n$ is not restricted to integral values; $n$ may take any fractional value. The future value can be determined by means of the formula $FV = PV(1 + i)^n$ whether the time period contains an integral number of conversion periods or not.

**EXAMPLE 9.2D**

Find the accumulated value of $1000 invested for two years and nine months at 10% p.a. compounded annually.

**SOLUTION**

The entire time period is 2 years and 9 months; the number of whole conversion periods is 2; the fractional conversion period is $\frac{9}{12}$ of a year.

$$PV = 1000.00; I/Y = 10; C/Y = 1; i = 10\% = 0.10; n = 2\frac{9}{12} = 2.75$$

$$FV = 1000.00(1.10)^{2.75} = 1000.00(1.299660) = \$1299.66$$

**Programmed Solution**

(Set P/Y, C/Y = 1) [2nd] (CLR TVM) 1000 [±] [PV] 10 [I/Y]

2.75 [N] [CPT] [FV] [1299.660393]

**EXAMPLE 9.2E**

Determine the compound amount of $400 invested at 6% p.a. compounded quarterly for three years and five months.

**SOLUTION**

$$PV = 400.00; \quad i = 1.5\% = 0.015$$

$$n = \left(3\frac{5}{12}\right)(4) = \left(\frac{41}{12}\right)(4) = \frac{41}{3} = 13\frac{2}{3} = 13.666667$$

$$FV = 400.00(1.015)^{13.666667} = 400.00(1.225658) = \$490.26$$

**Programmed Solution**

(Set P/Y, C/Y = 4) [2nd] (CLR TVM) 400 [±] [PV] 6 [I/Y]

13.666667 [N] [CPT] [FV] [490.263134]

**EXAMPLE 9.2F**

A debt of $3500 dated August 31, 2009 is payable together with interest at 9% p.a. compounded quarterly on June 30, 2012. Determine the amount to be paid.

**SOLUTION**

$$PV = 3500.00; I/Y = 9; C/Y = 4; i = \frac{9\%}{4} = 2.25\% = 0.0225; \text{ the time period}$$

August 31, 2009 to June 30, 2012 contains 2 years and 10 months; the number of quarters $n = 11.333333$.

$$FV = 3500.00(1.0225)^{11.333333}$$
$$= 3500.00(1.286819)$$
$$= \$4503.87$$

**Programmed Solution**

(Set P/Y, C/Y = 4) [2nd] (CLR TVM) 3500 [±] [PV] 9 [I/Y]

11.333333 [N] [CPT] [FV] [4503.867756]

# D. Applications involving changes in interest rate or principal

**EXAMPLE 9.2G**

A deposit of $2000 earns interest at 6% p.a. compounded monthly for four years. At that time, the interest rate changes to 7% p.a. compounded quarterly. What is the value of the deposit three years after the change in the rate of interest?

**SOLUTION**

The data given can be represented on a time diagram as shown in Figure 9.2.

**FIGURE 9.2**    **Graphical Representation of Data**

Separate the entire problem into the time periods where different interest rates apply.

**STEP 1**

Determine the accumulated value of the original deposit at the time the interest rate changes, that is, after four years.

$$PV = 2000.00; \; I/Y = 6; \; C/Y = 12; \; i = \frac{6\%}{12} = 0.5\% = 0.005; \; n = 48$$

$$FV_1 = 2000.00\,(1 + 0.005)^{48} = 2000.00(1.270489) = \$2540.98$$

**STEP 2**

Use the accumulated value after four years as the new principal and calculate its accumulated value three years later using the new rate of interest.

$$PV = 2540.98; \; I/Y = 7; \; C/Y = 4; \; i = \frac{7\%}{4} = 1.75\% = 0.0175; \; n = 12$$

$$FV_2 = 2540.98\,(1 + 0.0175)^{12} = 2540.98(1.231439) = \$3129.06$$

**Solution By Preprogrammed Calculator**
Keys are applicable to the Texas Instruments BAII Plus calculator (this is the case throughout the rest of this chapter).

| STEP 1 | Key in | Press | | Display shows |
|---|---|---|---|---|
| | | 2nd (P/Y) | | |
| | 12 | ENTER | | P/Y = 12 |
| | | ↓ | | C/Y = 12 |
| | | 2nd (QUIT) | | 0 |
| | | 2nd (CLR TVM) | | 0 |
| | 2000 | ± PV | | −2000 |
| | 6 | I/Y | | 6 |
| | 48 | N | | 48 |
| | | CPT FV | | 2540.978322 ——answer to Step 1 (FV₁ = 2540.978322) |

Do *not* clear your display. Proceed to Step 2.

| STEP 2 | Key in | Press | | Display shows |
|---|---|---|---|---|
| | | ± PV | | −2540.978322 – this step enters the new principal and the proper sign convention, since this amount is reinvested (a cash outflow) |
| | | 2nd (P/Y) | | P/Y = 12 |
| | 4 | ENTER | | P/Y = 4 |
| | | ↓ | | C/Y = 4 |
| | | 2nd (QUIT) | | 0 |
| | 7 | I/Y | | 7 |
| | 12 | N | | 12 |
| | | CPT FV | | 3129.060604 — final answer (FV₂ = $3129.06) |

---

**EXAMPLE 9.2H**

A debt of $500 accumulates interest at 8% p.a. compounded quarterly from April 1, 2008 to July 1, 2009, and 9% p.a. compounded monthly thereafter. Determine the accumulated value of the debt on December 1, 2010.

**SOLUTION**

**STEP 1** Determine the accumulated value of the debt on July 1, 2009.

$PV = 500.00;\ I/Y = 8;\ C/Y = 4;\ i = \dfrac{8\%}{4} = 2\% = 0.02;$

the period April 1, 2008 to July 1, 2009 contains 15 months: $n = 5$

$FV_1 = 500.00(1.02)^5 = 500.00(1.104081) = \$552.04$

**STEP 2** Use the result of Step 1 as new principal and find its accumulated value on December 1, 2010.

$$PV = 552.04; \ I/Y = 9; P/Y = 12; i = \frac{9\%}{12} = 0.75\% = 0.0075;$$

the period July 1, 2009 to December 1, 2010 contains 17 months: $n = 17$
$$FV_2 = 552.04(1.0075)^{17} = 552.04(1.135445) = \$626.81$$

**Programmed Solution**

**STEP 1** (Set P/Y, C/Y = 4) | 2nd | (CLR TVM) 500 | ± | | PV | 8 | I/Y | 5 | N | | CPT | | FV |

Result: | 552.040402 |

**STEP 2** 552.040402 | ± | | PV | (Set P/Y, C/Y = 12) 9 | I/Y | 17 | N | | CPT | | FV |

Result: | 626.811268 |

---

**EXAMPLE 9.21**

Jay opened a registered retirement savings plan with his credit union on February 1, 2007, with a deposit of $2000. He added $1900 on February 1, 2008 and another $1700 on February 1, 2011. What will his account amount to on August 1, 2017, if the plan earns a fixed rate of interest of 7% p.a. compounded semi-annually?

**SOLUTION**

**FIGURE 9.3** **Graphical Representation of Data**

**STEP 1** Determine the future value, $FV_1$, of the initial deposit on February 1, 2008.

$$PV = 2000.00; I/Y = 7; C/Y = 2; i = \frac{7\%}{2} = 3.5\% = 0.035;$$

the period February 1, 2007 to February 1, 2008 contains 1 year: $n = 2$
$$FV_1 = 2000.00(1.035)^2 = 2000.00(1.071225) = \$2142.45$$

**STEP 2**   Add the deposit of $1900 to the amount of $2142.45 to obtain the new principal as of February 1, 2008, and determine its future value, $FV_2$, on February 1, 2011.

$PV = 2142.45 + 1900.00 = 4042.45$; $i = 0.035$;
the period February 1, 2008 to February 1, 2011 contains 3 years: $n = 6$
$FV_2 = 4042.45(1.035)^6 = 4042.45(1.229255) = \$4969.20$

**STEP 3**   Add the deposit of $1700 to the amount of $4969.20 to obtain the new principal as of February 1, 2011, and determine its future value, $FV_3$, on August 1, 2017.

$PV = 4969.20 + 1700.00 = 6669.20$; $i = 0.035$;
the period February 1, 2011 to August 1, 2017 contains 6.5 years: $n = 13$
$FV_3 = 6669.20(1.035)^{13} = 6669.20(1.563956) = \$10\,430.34$

**Programmed Solution**

**STEP 1**   (Set P/Y, C/Y=2) [2nd] (CLRTVM) 2000 [±] [PV] 7 [I/Y] 2 [N] [CPT] [FV]

Result: [ 2142.45 ]

**STEP 2**   [+] 1900 [=] [ 4042.65 ] [±] [PV] 6 [N] [CPT] [FV]

Result: [ 4969.203194 ]

**STEP 3**   [+] 1700 [=] [ 6669.20 ] [±] [PV] 13 [N] [CPT] [FV]

Result: [ 10430.34075 ]

*Note:* There is no need to key in the interest rate in Steps 2 and 3—it is already programmed from Step 1.

---

**EXAMPLE 9.2J**   A demand loan of $10 000 is repaid by payments of $5000 in one year, $6000 in four years, and a final payment in six years. Interest on the loan is 10% p.a. compounded quarterly during the first year, 8% p.a. compounded semi-annually for the next three years, and 7.5% p.a. compounded annually for the remaining years. Determine the final payment.

**SOLUTION**

**STEP 1**   Determine the accumulated value of the debt at the time of the first payment.
$PV = 10\,000.00$; $I/Y = 10$; $C/Y = 4$; $i = \dfrac{10\%}{4} = 2.5\% = 0.025$; $n = 4$
$FV_1 = 10\,000.00(1.025)^4 = 10\,000.00(1.103813) = \$11\,038.13$

**STEP 2**   Subtract the payment of $5000 from the accumulated value of $11 038.13 to obtain the debt balance. Now determine its accumulated value at the time of the second payment three years later.

**FIGURE 9.4** **Graphical Representation of Data**

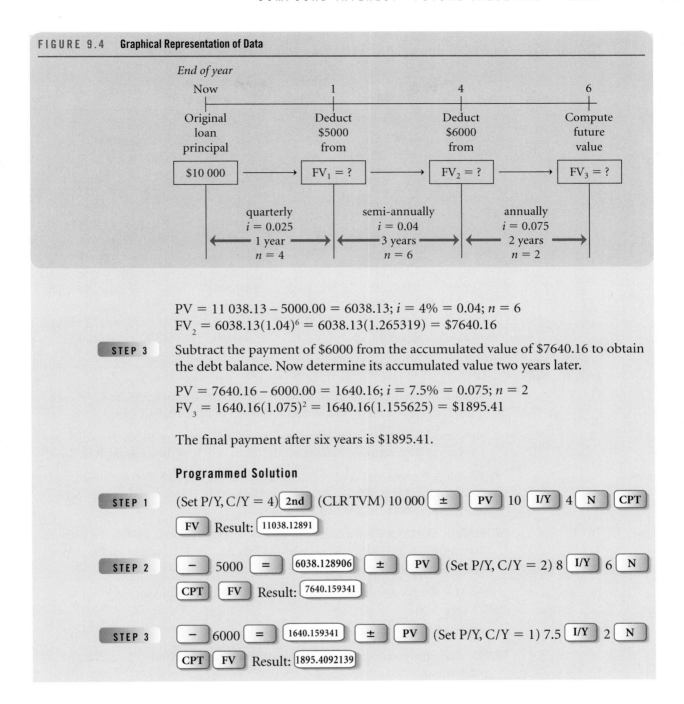

$PV = 11\,038.13 - 5000.00 = 6038.13;\ i = 4\% = 0.04;\ n = 6$
$FV_2 = 6038.13(1.04)^6 = 6038.13(1.265319) = \$7640.16$

**STEP 3** Subtract the payment of $6000 from the accumulated value of $7640.16 to obtain the debt balance. Now determine its accumulated value two years later.

$PV = 7640.16 - 6000.00 = 1640.16;\ i = 7.5\% = 0.075;\ n = 2$
$FV_3 = 1640.16(1.075)^2 = 1640.16(1.155625) = \$1895.41$

The final payment after six years is $1895.41.

**Programmed Solution**

**STEP 1** (Set P/Y, C/Y = 4) 2nd (CLR TVM) 10 000 $\pm$ PV 10 I/Y 4 N CPT FV Result: 11038.12891

**STEP 2** $-$ 5000 $=$ 6038.128906 $\pm$ PV (Set P/Y, C/Y = 2) 8 I/Y 6 N CPT FV Result: 7640.159341

**STEP 3** $-$ 6000 $=$ 1640.159341 $\pm$ PV (Set P/Y, C/Y = 1) 7.5 I/Y 2 N CPT FV Result: 1895.4092139

# EXERCISE 9.2

If you choose, you can use Excel's *Future Value (FV)* function to calculate the future value of an investment subject to compound interest. Refer to **FV** on the Spreadsheet Template Disk to learn how to use this Excel function.

**A.** Find the future value for each of the investments in the table below.

| | Principal | Nominal Rate | Frequency of Conversion | Time |
|---|---|---|---|---|
| 1. | $ 400.00 | 7.5% | annually | 8 years |
| 2. | 1000.00 | 3.5 | semi-annually | 12 years |
| 3. | 1250.00 | 6.5 | quarterly | 9 years |
| 4. | 500.00 | 12 | monthly | 3 years |
| 5. | 1700.00 | 8 | quarterly | 14.75 years |
| 6. | 840.00 | 5.5 | semi-annually | 8.5 years |
| 7. | 2500.00 | 8 | monthly | 12.25 years |
| 8. | 150.00 | 10.8 | quarterly | 27 months |
| 9. | 480.00 | 9.4 | semi-annually | 42 months |
| 10. | 1400.00 | 4.8 | monthly | 18.75 years |
| 11. | 2500.00 | 7 | annually | 7 years, 6 months |
| 12. | 400.00 | 9 | quarterly | 3 years, 8 months |
| 13. | 1300.00 | 5 | semi-annually | 9 years, 3 months |
| 14. | 4500.00 | 3.5 | monthly | 7.5 months |

**B.** Answer each of the following questions.

1. What is the maturity value of a five-year term deposit of $5000 at 6.5% compounded semi-annually? How much interest did the deposit earn?

2. How much will a registered retirement savings deposit of $1500 be worth in 15 years at 8% compounded quarterly? How much of the amount is interest?

3. You made a registered retirement savings plan deposit of $1000 on December 1, 2008 at a fixed rate of 5.5% compounded monthly. If you withdraw the deposit on August 1, 2015, how much will you receive?

4. Ray's parents made a trust deposit of $500 on October 31, 1990 to be withdrawn on Ray's eighteenth birthday on July 31, 2008. To what will the deposit amount on that date at 7% compounded quarterly?

5. What is the accumulated value of $100 invested for eight years at 9% p.a. compounded

   **(a)** annually?    **(b)** semi-annually?    **(c)** quarterly?    **(d)** monthly?

6. To what future value will a principal of $500.00 amount in five years at 7.5% p.a. compounded

   **(a)** annually?    **(b)** semi-annually?    **(c)** quarterly?    **(d)** monthly?

7. What is the future value of and the amount of compound interest for $100 invested at 8% compounded quarterly for

   **(a)** 5 years?    **(b)** 10 years?    **(c)** 20 years?

8. Find the future value of and the compound interest on $500 invested at 4.5% compounded monthly for

   **(a)** 3.5 years;    **(b)** 6 years;    **(c)** 11.5 years.

9. A demand loan for $5000 with interest at 9.75% compounded semi-annually is repaid after five years, ten months. What is the amount of interest paid?

10. Suppose $4000 is invested for four years, eight months at 8.5% compounded annually. What is the compounded amount?

11. Determine the maturity value of a $600 promissory note dated August 1, 2004 and due on June 1, 2009, if interest is 5% p.a. compounded semi-annually.

12. Find the maturity value of a promissory note for $3200 dated March 31, 2006 and due on August 31, 2012, if interest is 7% compounded quarterly.

13. A debt of $8000 is payable in seven years, five months. Determine the accumulated value of the debt at 10.8% p.a. compounded annually.

14. A $6000 investment matures in three years, eleven months. Find the maturity value if interest is 9% p.a. compounded quarterly.

15. The Canadian Consumer Price Index was approximately 98.5 (base year 1992) at the beginning of 1991. If inflation continued at an average annual rate of 3%, what would the index have been at the beginning of 2008?

16. Peel Credit Union expects an average annual growth rate of 20% for the next five years. If the assets of the credit union currently amount to $2.5 million, what will the forecasted assets be in five years?

17. A local bank offers $5000 five-year certificates at 6.75% compounded semi-annually. Your credit union makes the same type of deposit available at 6.5% compounded monthly.

    (a) Which investment gives more interest over the five years?
    (b) What is the difference in the amount of interest?

18. The Continental Bank advertises capital savings at 4.25% compounded semi-annually while TD Canada Trust offers premium savings at 4% compounded monthly. Suppose you have $1000 to invest for two years.

    (a) Which deposit will earn more interest?
    (b) What is the difference in the amount of interest?

 **C.** Answer each of the following questions.

1. A deposit of $2000 earns interest at 3% p.a. compounded quarterly. After two-and-a-half years, the interest rate is changed to 2.75% compounded monthly. How much is the account worth after six years?

2. An investment of $2500 earns interest at 4.5% p.a. compounded monthly for three years. At that time the interest rate is changed to 5% compounded quarterly. How much will the accumulated value be one-and-a-half years after the change?

3. A debt of $800 accumulates interest at 10% compounded semi-annually from February 1, 2008 to August 1, 2010, and 11% compounded quarterly thereafter. Determine the accumulated value of the debt on November 1, 2013.

**4.** Accumulate $1300 at 8.5% p.a. compounded monthly from March 1, 2006 to July 1, 2008, and thereafter at 8% p.a. compounded quarterly. What is the amount on April 1, 2011?

**5.** Patrice opened an RRSP deposit account on December 1, 2002, with a deposit of $1000. He added $1000 on July 1, 2004 and $1000 on November 1, 2006. How much is in his account on January 1, 2010, if the deposit earns 6% p.a. compounded monthly?

**6.** Terri started an RRSP on March 1, 2000, with a deposit of $2000. She added $1800 on December 1, 2002 and $1700 on September 1, 2004. What is the accumulated value of her account on December 1, 2011, if interest is 7.5% compounded quarterly?

**7.** A debt of $4000 is repaid by payments of $1500 in nine months, $2000 in 18 months, and a final payment in 27 months. If interest was 10% compounded quarterly, what was the amount of the final payment?

**8.** Sheridan Service has a line of credit loan with the bank. The initial loan balance was $6000. Payments of $2000 and $3000 were made after four months and nine months respectively. At the end of one year, Sheridan Service borrowed an additional $4000. Six months later, the line of credit loan was converted into a collateral mortgage loan. What was the amount of the mortgage loan if the line of credit interest was 9% compounded monthly?

**9.** A demand loan of $3000 is repaid by payments of $1500 after two years, $1500 after four years, and a final payment after seven years. Interest is 9% compounded quarterly for the first year, 10% compounded semi-annually for the next three years, and 10% compounded monthly thereafter. What is the size of the final payment?

**10.** A variable rate demand loan showed an initial balance of $12 000, payments of $5000 after eighteen months, $4000 after thirty months, and a final payment after five years. Interest was 11% compounded semi-annually for the first two years and 12% compounded monthly for the remaining time. What was the size of the final payment?

**11.** Joan borrowed $15 000 to buy a car. She repaid $2000 two months later and $5000 seven months later. After twelve months, she borrowed an additional $4000, and repaid $3000 after 16 months. She paid the entire balance, including the interest, after 24 months. Interest was 7% compounded monthly for the first year and 7.5% compounded monthly for the remaining time. What was the size of the final payment?

**12.** A variable rate demand loan showed an initial balance of $9000, payments of $2500 after six months, $2500 after 21 months, and a final payment after four years. Interest was 8% compounded quarterly for the first 21 months and 7.75% compounded monthly for the remaining time. What was the size of the final payment?

# 9.3 PRESENT VALUE AND COMPOUND DISCOUNT

## A. The present value concept and related terms

**EXAMPLE 9.3A**  Find the principal that will amount in six years to $17 715.61 at 10% p.a. compounded annually.

**SOLUTION**  The problem may be graphically represented as shown in Figure 9.5.

**FIGURE 9.5**  **Graphical Representation of Data**

This problem is the inverse of the problem used to illustrate the meaning of compound interest. Instead of knowing the value of the principal and finding its future value, we know that the future value is $17 715.61. What we want to determine is the value of the principal.

To solve the problem, we use the future value formula $FV = PV(1 + i)^n$ and substitute the known values.

$FV = 17\ 715.61; I/Y = 10; C/Y = 1; i = \dfrac{10\%}{1} = 10\% = 0.10; n = 6$

$17\ 715.61 = PV(1.10)^6$ —————— by substituting in $FV = PV(1 + i)^n$

$17\ 715.61 = PV(1.771561)$ ————— computing $(1.10)^6$

$PV = \dfrac{17\ 715.61}{1.771561}$ ————— solve for PV by dividing both sides by 1.771561

$PV = \$10\ 000.00$

The principal that will grow to $17 715.61 in six years at 10% p.a. compounded annually is $10 000.

This principal is called the **present value** or **discounted value** or **proceeds** of the known future amount.

The difference between the known future amount of $17 715.61 and the computed present value (principal) of $10 000 is the **compound discount** and represents the compound interest accumulating on the computed present value.

The process of computing the present value or discounted value or proceeds is called **discounting**.

# B. The present value formula

With compound interest, the present value of an amount at a given time is defined as the principal that will grow to the given amount if compounded at a given periodic rate of interest over a given number of conversion periods.

Since the problem of finding the present value is equivalent to finding the principal when the future value, the periodic rate of interest, and the number of conversion periods are given, the formula for the future value formula, $FV = PV(1 + i)^n$, applies.

However, because the problem of finding the present value of an amount is frequently encountered in financial analysis, it is useful to solve the future value formula for PV to obtain the present value formula.

$$FV = PV(1 + i)^n$$ —————— start with the future value formula, Formula 9.1A

$$\frac{FV}{(1 + i)^n} = \frac{PV(1 + i)^n}{(1 + i)^n}$$ —————— divide both sides by the compounding factor $(1 + i)^n$

$$\frac{FV}{(1 + i)^n} = PV$$ —————— reduce the fraction $\frac{(1 + i)^n}{(1 + i)^n}$ to 1

The present value formula for compound interest is:

$$\boxed{PV = \frac{FV}{(1 + i)^n}}$$ —————— Formula 9.1B

---

**EXAMPLE 9.3B**  Find the present value of $6836.56 due in nine years at 6% p.a. compounded quarterly.

**SOLUTION**  $FV = 6836.56$; $I/Y = 6$; $P/Y = 4$; $i = \dfrac{6\%}{4} = 1.5\% = 0.015$; $n = 36$

$$PV = \frac{FV}{(1 + i)^n}$$ —————— using the present value formula

$$= \frac{6836.56}{(1 + 0.015)^{36}}$$ —————— by substitution

$$= \frac{6836.56}{1.709140}$$

$$= \$4000.00$$

**Note:** The division of 6836.56 by 1.709140, like any division, may be changed to a multiplication by using the reciprocal of the divisor.

$$\frac{6836.56}{1.709140}$$ —————— the division to be changed into a multiplication

$$= 6836.56 \left( \frac{1}{1.709140} \right)$$ —————— the reciprocal of the divisor 1.709140 is found by dividing 1 by 1.709140

$$= 6836.56(0.585090)$$ —————— computed value of the reciprocal

$$= \$4000.00$$

For calculators equipped with the reciprocal function key $\boxed{1/x}$, converting the division into a multiplication is easily accomplished by first computing the compounding factor and then using the $\boxed{1/x}$ key to obtain the reciprocal.

**EXAMPLE 9.3C**

What principal will amount to $5000 seven years from today if interest is 9% p.a. compounded monthly?

**SOLUTION**

Finding the principal that amounts to a future sum of money is equivalent to finding the present value.

$$FV = 5000.00; \ I/Y = 9; \ C/Y = 12; \ i = \frac{9\%}{12} = 0.75\% = 0.0075; \quad n = 84$$

$$\begin{aligned}
PV &= \frac{5000.00}{(1.0075)^{84}} && \text{using Formula 9.1B} \\[6pt]
&= \frac{5000.00}{1.873202} && \text{computing the factor } (1.0075)^{84} \\[6pt]
&= 5000.00(0.533845) && \text{using the reciprocal function key} \\[6pt]
&= \$2669.23
\end{aligned}$$

Using the reciprocal of the divisor to change division into multiplication is reflected in the practice of stating the present value formula with a negative exponent.

$$\frac{1}{a^n} = a^{-n} \qquad\qquad \text{negative exponent rule}$$

$$\frac{1}{(1 + i)^n} = (1 + i)^{-n}$$

$$\frac{FV}{(1 + i)^n} = FV(1 + i)^{-n}$$

Formula 9.1B, the present value formula, can be restated in multiplication form using a negative exponent.

$$\boxed{PV = FV(1 + i)^{-n}} \qquad\qquad \text{Formula 9.1C}$$

The factor $(1 + i)^{-n}$ is called the **discount factor** and is the reciprocal of the compounding factor $(1 + i)^n$.

## C. Using preprogrammed financial calculators to find present value

As explained in Section 9.2B, preprogrammed calculators provide quick solutions to compound interest calculations. Three of the four variables are entered and the value of the fourth variable is retrieved.

To solve Example 9.3C, in which FV = 5000, $i$ = 0.75%, $n$ = 84, and PV is to be determined, use the following procedure. (Remember that the interest rate for the year, 9%, must be entered into the calculator as I/Y.)

| Key in | Press | Display shows | |
|--------|-------|---------------|--|
| | 2nd (CLR TVM) | 0 | clears the function key registers |
| | 2nd (P/Y) | 0 | checks the P/Y register |
| 12 | ENTER | P/Y = 12 | changes the value to "12" |
| | ↓ | C/Y = 12 | changed automatically to match the P/Y |
| | 2nd (QUIT) | 0 | returns to the standard calculation mode |
| 5000 | FV | 5000 | enters the future value amount FV |
| 9 | I/Y | 9 | enters the nominal interest rate |
| 84 | N | 84 | enters the number of compounding periods $n$ |
| | CPT PV | −2669.226329 | retrieves the unknown principal (present value) PV, an investment or cash outflow as indicated by the negative sign |

The principal is $2669.23.

 Excel has a ***Present Value (PV)*** function you can use to calculate the present value of an investment subject to compound interest. Refer to **PV** on the Spreadsheet Template Disk to learn how to use this Excel function.

## D. Finding the present value when $n$ is a fractional value

When PV is to be determined, use Formula 9.1A, FV = PV$(1 + i)^n$, or Formula 9.1B, PV = $\dfrac{FV}{(1 + i)^n}$, or Formula 9.1C, PV = FV$(1 + i)^{-n}$, where $n$ is a fractional value representing the *entire* time period and FV is a known value.

**EXAMPLE 9.3D**

Find the present value of $2000 due in three years and eight months if money is worth 8% p.a. compounded quarterly.

**SOLUTION**

FV = 2000.00;  I/Y = 8; P/Y = 4; $i = \dfrac{8\%}{4} = 2\% = 0.02$;

$n = \left(3\dfrac{8}{12}\right)(4) = 14\dfrac{2}{3} = 14.666667$

$PV = \dfrac{FV}{(1 + i)^n}$ ———————————————— using Formula 9.1B

$= \dfrac{2000.00}{(1 + 0.02)^{14.666667}}$ ———————— use as many decimals as are available in your calculator

$= 2000.00(0.747936)$ ———————— multiply by the reciprocal

$= \$1495.87$

**Programmed Solution**

(Set P/Y, C/Y = 4) [ 2nd ] (CLR TVM) 2000 [ FV ] 8 [ I/Y ]

14.666667 [ N ] [ CPT ] [ PV ] [ −1495.871001 ]

---

**EXAMPLE 9.3E**

Determine the principal that will accumulate to $2387.18 from September 1, 2008 to April 1, 2012 at 5% p.a. compounded semi-annually.

**SOLUTION**

Finding the principal that will grow to the given amount of $2387.18 is equivalent to finding the present value or discounted value of this amount.

The time period September 1, 2008 to April 1, 2012 contains three years and seven months; that is, it consists of seven whole conversion periods of six months each and a fractional conversion period of one month.

Use $PV = \dfrac{FV}{(1 + i)^n}$

FV = 2387.18;  I/Y = 5; P/Y = 2; $i = \dfrac{5\%}{2} = 2.5\% = 0.025$;

$n = \left(3\dfrac{7}{12}\right)(2) = 7\dfrac{1}{6} = 7.166667$

$PV = \dfrac{2387.18}{(1.025)^{7.166667}}$

$= \dfrac{2387.18}{1.193588}$

$= 2387.18(0.837810)$

$= \$2000.00$

**Programmed Solution**

(Set P/Y = 2) [ 2nd ] (CLR TVM) 2387.18 [ FV ] 5 [ I/Y ]

7.166667 [ N ] [ CPT ] [ PV ] [ −2000.003696 ]

## EXERCISE 9.3

If you choose, you can use Excel's *Present Value (PV)* function to calculate the present value of an investment subject to compound interest. Refer to **PV** on the Spreadsheet Template Disk to learn how to use this Excel function.

  **A.** Find the present value of each of the following amounts.

|  | Amount | Nominal Rate | Frequency of Conversion | Time |
|---|---|---|---|---|
| 1. | $1000.00 | 8% | quarterly | 7 years |
| 2. | 1500.00 | 6.5 | semi-annually | 10 years |
| 3. | 600.00 | 8 | monthly | 6 years |
| 4. | 350.00 | 7.5 | annually | 8 years |
| 5. | 1200.00 | 9 | monthly | 12 years |
| 6. | 3000.00 | 12.25 | semi-annually | 5 years, 6 months |
| 7. | 900.00 | 6.4 | quarterly | 9 years, 3 months |
| 8. | 500.00 | 8.4 | monthly | 15 years |
| 9. | 1500.00 | 4.5 | annually | 15 years, 9 months |
| 10. | 900.00 | 5.5 | semi-annually | 8 years, 10 months |
| 11. | 6400.00 | 7 | quarterly | 5 years, 7 months |
| 12. | 7200.00 | 6 | monthly | 21.5 months |

**B.** Answer each of the following questions.

1. Find the present value and the compound discount of $1600 due four-and-a-half years from now if money is worth 4% compounded semi-annually.

2. Find the present value and the compound discount of $2500 due in six years, three months, if interest is 6% compounded quarterly.

3. Find the principal that will amount to $1250 in five years at 10% p.a. compounded quarterly.

4. What sum of money will grow to $2000 in seven years at 9% compounded monthly?

5. A debt of $5000 is due November 1, 2015. What is the value of the obligation on February 1, 2009, if money is worth 7% compounded quarterly?

6. How much would you have to deposit in an account today to have $3000 in a five-year term deposit at maturity if interest is 7.75% compounded annually?

7. What is the principal that will grow to $3000 in eight years, eight months at 9% compounded semi-annually?

8. Find the sum of money that accumulates to $1600 at 5% compounded quarterly in six years, four months.

9. You have the choice of receiving $100 000 now or $60 000 now and another $60 000 five years from now. In terms of today's dollar, which choice is better and by how much? Money is worth 6% compounded annually.

10. In winning the lottery you have the choice of receiving $50 000 now or $20 000 now and $35 000 two years from now. In terms of today's dollar, which choice is better and by how much? Money is worth 4.25% compounded annually.

11. Joe is negotiating the purchase of a sound system. He can either pay $2000 now or pay $100 now and $2200 in eighteen months. Which option is better if money is worth 8% compounded monthly?

12. Jane is purchasing a membership in a fitness centre. She can pay either $350 now or pay $130 now, $150 in twelve months, and $170 in fifteen months. Which option is better if money is worth 7.5% compounded monthly?

# 9.4 APPLICATION—DISCOUNTING NEGOTIABLE FINANCIAL INSTRUMENTS AT COMPOUND INTEREST

## A. Discounting long-term promissory notes

Long-term promissory notes (written for a term longer than one year) are usually subject to compound interest. Long-term promissory notes are negotiable and can be bought and sold (*discounted*) at any time before maturity. The principles involved in discounting long-term promissory notes are similar to those used in discounting short-term promissory notes by the simple discount method *except* that no requirement exists to add three days of grace in determining the legal due date of a long-term promissory note.

The discounted value (or proceeds) of a long-term promissory note is the present value at the date of discount of the maturity value of the note. It is found using the present value formula $PV = \dfrac{FV}{(1 + i)^n}$ or $PV = FV(1 + i)^{-n}$.

For non-interest-bearing notes, the maturity value is the face value. However, for interest-bearing promissory notes, the maturity value must be determined first by using the future value formula $FV = PV(1 + i)^n$.

Like promissory notes, long-term bonds promise to pay a specific face value at a specified future point in time. In addition, there is a promise to periodically pay a specified amount of interest. Long-term bonds will be covered in detail in Chapter 15.

## B. Discounting non-interest-bearing promissory notes

Since the face value of a non-interest-bearing note is also its maturity value, the proceeds of a non-interest-bearing note are the present value of its face value at the date of discount.

**EXAMPLE 9.4A**

Determine the proceeds of a non-interest-bearing note for $1500 discounted two-and-a-quarter years before its due date at 9% p.a. compounded monthly.

**SOLUTION**

The maturity value FV = 1500.00;

the rate of discount $I/Y = 9$; P/Y, C/Y = 12; $i = \dfrac{9\%}{12} = 0.75\% = 0.0075$;

the number of conversion periods $n = (2.25)(12) = 27$.

$$PV = FV(1 + i)^{-n} \text{ —————————————— using restated Formula 9.1C}$$
$$= 1500.00(1 + 0.0075)^{-27}$$
$$= 1500.00\left(\frac{1}{1.223535}\right)$$
$$= 1500.00(0.817304)$$
$$= \$1225.96$$

**Programmed Solution**

(Set P/Y, C/Y = 12) [2nd] (CLR TVM) 1500 [FV] 9 [I/Y] 27 [N] [CPT] [PV]

[−1225.955705]

---

**EXAMPLE 9.4B**

A four-year, non-interest-bearing promissory note for $6000 dated August 31, 2008 was discounted on October 31, 2009 at 6% p.a. compounded quarterly. Determine the proceeds of the note.

**SOLUTION**

The due date of the note is August 31, 2012; the discount period October 31, 2009 to August 31, 2012 contains 2 years and 10 months.

$$FV = 6000.00; I/Y = 6; C/Y = 4; i = \frac{6\%}{4} = 1.5\% = 0.015;$$
$$n = \left(2\frac{10}{12}\right)(4) = 11\frac{1}{3} = 11.333333$$
$$PV = FV(1 + i)^{-n}$$
$$= 6000.00(1 + 0.015)^{-11.333333}$$
$$= 6000.00(0.844731)$$
$$= \$5068.38$$

**Programmed Solution**

(Set P/Y, C/Y = 4) [2nd] (CLR TVM) 6000 [FV] 6 [I/Y] 11.333333 [N] [CPT]

[PV] [−5068.383148]

## C. Discounting interest-bearing promissory notes

The proceeds of an interest-bearing note are equal to the present value at the date of discount of the value of the note at maturity. Therefore, the maturity value of an interest-bearing promissory note must be determined before finding the discounted value.

**EXAMPLE 9.4C**

Determine the proceeds of a promissory note for $3600 with interest at 6% p.a. compounded quarterly, issued September 1, 2008, due on June 1, 2014, and discounted on December 1, 2010 at 8% p.a. compounded semi-annually.

**SOLUTION**

**STEP 1** Find the maturity value of the note using Formula 9.1A, FV 5 PV(1 1 i)n.

$PV = 3600.00; I/Y = 6; P/Y, C/Y = 4; i = \dfrac{6\%}{4} = 1.5\% = 0.015$; the interest period,

September 1, 2008 to June 1, 2014, contains 5 years and 9 months:
$n = (5\frac{9}{12})(4) = 23.$

$FV = 3600.00(1 + 0.015)^{23}$

$= 3600.00(1.408377)$

$= \$5070.16$

**STEP 2** Find the present value at the date of discount of the maturity value found in Step 1 using $PV = FV(1 + i)^{-n}$.

$FV = 5070.16; I/Y = 8; P/Y, C/Y = 2; i = \dfrac{8\%}{2} = 4\% = 0.04;$

the discount period, December 1, 2010 to June 1, 2014, contains 3 years and 6 months: $n = (3\frac{6}{12})(2) = 7.$

$PV = 5070.16(1 + 0.04)^{-7}$
$= 5070.16(0.759918)$
$= \$3852.90$

The proceeds of the note on December 1, 2010 are $3852.90. The method and the data are represented graphically in Figure 9.6.

FIGURE 9.6    **Graphical Representation of Method and Data**

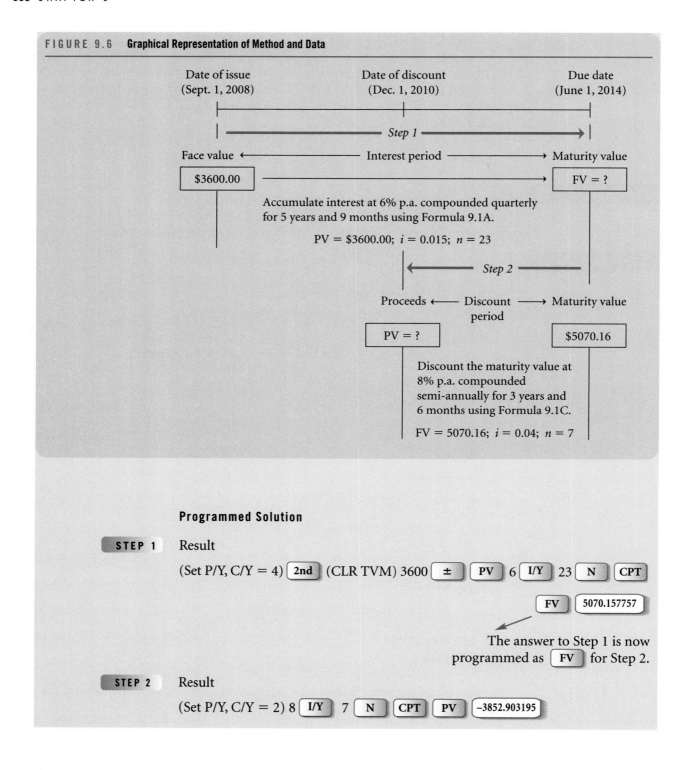

**Programmed Solution**

**STEP 1**    Result

(Set P/Y, C/Y = 4) [2nd] (CLR TVM) 3600 [±] [PV] 6 [I/Y] 23 [N] [CPT]

[FV] [5070.157757]

The answer to Step 1 is now programmed as [FV] for Step 2.

**STEP 2**    Result

(Set P/Y, C/Y = 2) 8 [I/Y] 7 [N] [CPT] [PV] [−3852.903195]

**EXAMPLE 9.4D**    A five-year note for $8000 bearing interest at 6% p.a. compounded monthly is discounted two years and five months before the due date at 5% p.a. compounded semi-annually. Determine the proceeds of the note.

**SOLUTION**

**STEP 1**    Find the maturity value using $FV = PV(1 + i)^n$.

$PV = 8000.00$; $I/Y = 6$; $P/Y, C/Y = 12$; $i = \dfrac{6\%}{12} = 0.5\% = 0.005$; $n = 60$

$FV = 8000.00(1.005)^{60}$

$\quad = 8000.00(1.348850)$

$\quad = \$10\ 790.80$

**STEP 2**    Find the present value of the maturity value found in Step 1 using

$PV = FV(1 + i)^{-n}$.

$FV = 10\ 790.80$; $I/Y = 5$; $P/Y = 2$; $i = \dfrac{5\%}{2} = 2.5\% = 0.025$;

$n = \left(\dfrac{29}{12}\right)(2) = 4.833333$

$PV = 10\ 790.80(1.025)^{-4.833333}$

$\quad = 10\ 790.80(0.887499)$

$\quad = \$9576.83$

**Programmed Solution**

**STEP 1**    (Set P/Y, C/Y = 12) [ 2nd ] (CLR TVM) 8000 [ ± ] [ PV ] 6 [ I/Y ] 60 [ N ] [ CPT ]

[ FV ] [ 10790.80122 ]

**STEP 2**    (Set P/Y, C/Y = 2) 5 [ I/Y ] 4.833333 [ N ] [ CPT ] [ PV ]

[ −9576.82776 ]

# EXERCISE 9.4

If you choose, you can use Excel's *Future Value (FV)* or *Present Value (PV)* functions to answer the questions below. Refer to **FV** and **PV** on the Spreadsheet Template Disk to learn how to use these Excel functions.

**A.**    Find the proceeds and the compound discount for each of the long-term promissory notes shown in the table below. Note that the first six are non-interest-bearing promissory notes.

| | Face Value | Date of Issue | Term | Int. Rate | Frequency of Conversion | Date of Discount | Discount Rate | Frequency of Conversion |
|---|---|---|---|---|---|---|---|---|
| 1. | $2000.00 | 30-06-2010 | 5 years | — | — | 31-12-2012 | 5% | semi-annually |
| 2. | 700.00 | 01-04-2008 | 10 years | — | — | 01-07-2013 | 10 | quarterly |
| 3. | 5000.00 | 01-04-2008 | 10 years | — | — | 01-08-2013 | 5 | annually |
| 4. | 900.00 | 31-08-2009 | 8 years | — | — | 30-06-2014 | 4 | quarterly |
| 5. | 3200.00 | 31-03-2010 | 6 years | — | — | 31-10-2013 | 8 | quarterly |
| 6. | 1450.00 | 01-10-2007 | 9 years | — | — | 01-12-2012 | 6 | semi-annually |
| 7. | 780.00 | 30-09-2007 | 10 years | 8% | annually | 30-04-2011 | 8 | quarterly |
| 8. | 2100.00 | 01-02-2006 | 12 years | 6 | monthly | 01-07-2013 | 7 | semi-annually |
| 9. | 1850.00 | 01-11-2012 | 5 years | 10 | quarterly | 01-10-2014 | 9 | semi-annually |
| 10. | 3400.00 | 31-01-2009 | 7 years | 9 | monthly | 31-12-2013 | 7.5 | quarterly |
| 11. | 1500.00 | 31-05-2009 | 8 years | 7 | annually | 31-05-2014 | 8 | semi-annually |
| 12. | 4000.00 | 30-09-2011 | 4 years | 5 | semi-annually | 31-03-2013 | 4 | quarterly |
| 13. | 800.00 | 01-02-2010 | 7.75 years | 9 | quarterly | 01-11-2015 | 9 | monthly |
| 14. | 2200.00 | 31-10-2009 | 8.25 years | 6 | monthly | 31-01-2012 | 7 | quarterly |

 **B.** Find the proceeds of each of the following promissory notes.

1. A non-interest-bearing promissory note for $6000, discounted 54 months before its due date at 6% compounded quarterly.

2. A $4200, non-interest-bearing note due August 1, 2014 discounted on March 1, 2010 at 7.5% compounded monthly.

3. A promissory note with a maturity value of $1800 due on September 30, 2011 discounted at 8.5% compounded semi-annually on March 31, 2008.

4. A fifteen-year promissory note discounted after six years at 9% compounded quarterly with a maturity value of $7500.

5. A five-year promissory note for $3000 with interest at 8% compounded semi-annually, discounted 21 months before maturity at 9% compounded quarterly.

6. A $5000, seven-year note bearing interest at 8.0% compounded quarterly, discounted two-and-a-half years after the date of issue at 6.0% compounded monthly.

7. A six-year, $900 note bearing interest at 10% compounded quarterly, issued June 1, 2007, discounted on December 1, 2012 to yield 8.5% compounded semi-annually.

8. A ten-year promissory note dated April 1, 2003, with a face value of $1300 bearing interest at 7% compounded semi-annually, discounted seven years later when money was worth 9% compounded quarterly.

 **C.** Solve each of the following problems.

1. Determine the proceeds of an investment with a maturity value of $10 000 if discounted at 9% compounded monthly 22.5 months before the date of maturity.

2. Compute the discounted value of $7000 due in three years, five months if money is worth 8% compounded quarterly.

3. Find the discounted value of $3800 due in six years, eight months if interest is 7.5% compounded annually.

4. Calculate the proceeds of $5500 due in seven years, eight months discounted at 4.5% compounded semi-annually.

5. A four-year non-interest-bearing promissory note for $3750 is discounted 32 months after the date of issue at 5.5% compounded semi-annually. Find the proceeds of the note.

6. A seven-year non-interest-bearing note for $5200 is discounted three years, eight months before its due date at 9% compounded quarterly. Find the proceeds of the note.

7. A non-interest-bearing eight-year note for $4500 issued August 1, 2006 is discounted April 1, 2010 at 6.5% compounded annually. Find the compound discount.

8. A $2800 promissory note issued without interest for five years on September 30, 2008 is discounted on July 31, 2011 at 8% compounded quarterly. Find the compound discount.

9. A six-year note for $1750 issued on December 1, 2009, with interest at 6.5% compounded annually, is discounted on March 1, 2012 at 7% compounded semi-annually. What are the proceeds of the note?

10. A ten-year note for $1200 bearing interest at 6% compounded monthly is discounted at 8% compounded quarterly three years, ten months after the date of issue. Find the proceeds of the note.

11. Four years, seven months before its due date, a seven-year note for $2650 bearing interest at 9% compounded quarterly is discounted at 8% compounded semi-annually. Find the compound discount.

12. On April 15, 2014, a ten-year note dated June 15, 2009 is discounted at 10% compounded quarterly. If the face value of the note is $4000 and interest is 8% compounded quarterly, find the compound discount.

## >> BUSINESS MATH NEWS BOX

### Payday Loan Firm Charged "Criminal" Rates

A B.C. Supreme Court judge says a B.C. payday loan company was charging "criminal" rates of interest to clients borrowing to make it through to their next paycheque.

In the first class-action civil ruling of its kind in Canada, the multimillion-dollar decision is expected to create a ripple effect for payday loan companies across the country.

Justice Brenda Brown has ruled the processing fees and late fees charged by the A OK Payday Loans Inc. were interest.

The court heard during the trial in April that A OK charges a 21% interest rate and a processing fee of $9.50 for every $50 borrowed.

There is a $75 fee if a cheque is returned and if the borrower wants to put off a loan payment, A OK charges $25 for every $100 deferred.

"I accept the plaintiff's submission that if processing fees and late fees are interest, and their payment results in payments at a criminal rate, then A OK has necessarily received interest at a criminal rate," Brown said in a written ruling released Monday.

An expert testified that with fees added in, the interest rate was well above the 60% annual rate allowed under the Criminal Code.

Paul Bennett, the lawyer for the representative plaintiff Doris Kilroy, said they're very pleased with the ruling.

"This is the first decision in Canada that has been rendered in a class proceeding with respect to the fees charged to payday loan companies," he said.

*Source:* "Payday Loan Firm Charged 'Criminal' Rates, Judge Says," *Times-Colonist*, August 15, 2006, p. B.9 Copyright by the *Canadian Press.*

**QUESTIONS**

1. Suppose $1000 is borrowed for six months, and all processing fees are deducted when the cash is borrowed. Calculate the monthly payments required to pay back this amount. Assume a 60% rate of interest compounded monthly.

2. If $500 is borrowed for three months and payment is due at the end of this period and includes all processing fees, calculate the rate of interest if compounding is assumed to be monthly.

3. Assuming that the rate of interest is 60% per annum compounded quarterly, calculate the lump-sum final payment required in one month to pay off a $700 loan. Assume all processing fees are deducted when the transaction occurs.

# 9.5 EQUIVALENT VALUES

## A. Equations of value

Because of the time value of money, amounts of money have different values at different times, as explained in Chapter 7. When sums of money fall due or are payable at different times, they are not directly comparable. To make such sums of money comparable, a point in time—the **comparison date** or **focal date**—must be chosen. Allowance must be made for interest from the due dates of the sums of money to the selected focal date; that is, the dated values of the sums of money must be determined.

Any point in time may be chosen as the focal date; the choice does not affect the final answers. It is advisable, however, to choose a date on which an amount is unknown. The choice of date determines which formula is to be used. For compound interest, equations of value need to be set up.

Which formula is appropriate depends on the position of the due dates relative to the focal date. The following rules apply:

(a) If an amount in the future of, or after, the focal date is to be determined, use the future value formula, $FV = PV(1 + i)^n$ (see Figure 9.7).

(b) If an amount in the past of, or before, the focal date is to be determined, use the present value formula, $PV = FV(1 + i)^{-n}$ (see Figure 9.8).

## B. Finding the equivalent single payment

**Equivalent values** are the dated values of an original sum of money.

**EXAMPLE 9.5A**

$4000 is due for payment three years from now. If money is worth 9% p.a. compounded semi-annually, determine the equivalent value

(i) seven years from now;                    (ii) now.

**SOLUTION**

(i) Using "seven years from now" as the focal date, the method and the data can be represented graphically as shown in Figure 9.7.

**FIGURE 9.7**    Graphical Representation of Method and Data

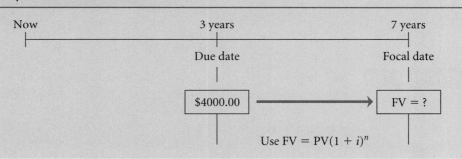

Since the due date falls *before* the focal date, use the future value formula.

$$PV = 4000.00;\ I/Y = 9;\ P/Y, C/Y = 2;\ i = \frac{9\%}{2} = 0.045;\ n = 4(2) = 8$$

$FV = 4000.00(1 + 0.045)^8 = 4000.00(1.422101) = \$5688.40$

The equivalent value of the $4000 seven years from now is $5688.40.

(ii) Using "now" as the focal date, the method and the data can be represented graphically as shown in Figure 9.8.

FIGURE 9.8    **Graphical Representation of Method and Data**

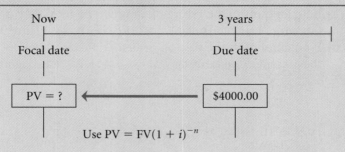

Since the due date falls *after* the focal date, use the present value formula.

$FV = 4000.00;\ i = \dfrac{9\%}{2} = 0.045;\ n = 3(2) = 6$

$PV = 4000.00(1 + 0.045)^{-6} = 4000.00(0.767896) = \$3071.58$

The equivalent value of the $4000.00 now is $3017.58.

**Programmed Solution**

(i)  (Set P/Y, C/Y = 2) [ 2nd ] (CLR TVM) 4000 [ ± ] [ PV ] 9 [ I/Y ]

8 [ N ] [ CPT ] [ FV ] [ 5688.402451 ]

(ii)  [ 2nd ] (CLR TVM) 4000 [ FV ] 9 [ I/Y ] 6 [ N ] [ CPT ] [ PV ] [ −3071.582953 ]

---

**EXAMPLE 9.5B**

Joanna plans to pay off a debt by payments of $1600 one year from now, $1800 eighteen months from now, and $2000 thirty months from now. Determine the single payment now that would settle the debt if money is worth 8% p.a. compounded quarterly.

**SOLUTION**

While any date may be selected as the focal date, a logical choice for the focal date is the time designated "now," since the single payment "now" is wanted. As is shown in Figure 9.9, the due dates of the three scheduled payments are after the focal date. Therefore, the present value formula $PV = FV(1 + i)^{-n}$ is appropriate for finding the equivalent values of each of the three scheduled payments.

The equivalents of the three scheduled payments at the selected focal date are

$PV_1 = 1600.00(1 + 0.02)^{-4} = 1600.00(0.923845) = \$1478.15$
$PV_2 = 1800.00(1 + 0.02)^{-6} = 1800.00(0.887971) = \$1598.35$
$PV_3 = 2000.00(1 + 0.02)^{-10} = 2000.00(0.820348) = \$1640.70$

The equivalent single payment to settle the debt now is $4717.20.

FIGURE 9.9 **Graphical Representation of Method and Data**

$$i = \frac{8\%}{4} = 0.02$$

| Now | 1 year | 18 months | 30 months |
|---|---|---|---|

Focal date

PV$_1$ = ?  ←  $n = 4$  $1600.00

PV$_2$ = ?  ←  $n = 6$  $1800.00

PV$_3$ = ?  ←  $n = 10$  $2000.00

**Programmed Solution**

PV$_1$ (Set P/Y, C/Y = 4) [2nd] (CLR TVM) 1600 [FV] 8 [I/Y] 4 [N] [CPT] [PV]

[−1478.152682] [±] [STO] 1

PV$_2$ [2nd] (CLR TVM) 1800 [FV] 8 [I/Y] 6 [N] [CPT] [PV] [−1598.348488]

[±] [STO] 2

PV$_3$ [2nd] (CLR TVM) 2000 [FV] 8 [I/Y] 10 [N] [CPT] [PV] [−1640.6966]

[±] [STO] 3

*Note:* Remember that the negative sign indicates a cash payment or outflow. Disregard the negative signs when finding equivalent single payments.

Since you know you will need these numbers later, store them in memory. Use your [RCL] key to bring them back when needed as follows:

[RCL] 1 + [RCL] 2 + [RCL] 3 =

1478.152682 + 1598.348488 + 1640.6966 = 4717.19777 = $4717.20

**EXAMPLE 9.5C**

Debt payments of $400 due five months ago, $600 due today, and $800 due in nine months are to be combined into one payment due three months from today at 12% p.a. compounded monthly.

**SOLUTION**

The logical choice for the focal date is "3 months from now," the date when the equivalent single payment is to be made.

As shown in Figure 9.10, the first two scheduled payments are due before the focal date; the future value formula FV = PV$(1 + i)^n$ should be used. However, the third scheduled payment is due *after* the focal date, which means that, for it, the present value formula $PV = FV(1 + i)^{-n}$ applies.

The equivalent values (designated $E_1$, $E_2$, $E_3$) of the scheduled debt payments at the selected focal date are

$$E_1 = 400.00(1 + 0.01)^8 = 400.00(1.082857) = \$\ 433.14$$
$$E_2 = 600.00(1 + 0.01)^3 = 600.00(1.030301) = \ 618.18$$
$$E_3 = 800.00(1 + 0.01)^{-6} = 800.00(0.942045) = \underline{\ 753.64}$$

The equivalent single payment to settle the debt three months from now is $\underline{\$1804.96}$

**FIGURE 9.10**    **Graphical Representation of Method and Data**

**Programmed Solution**

$E_1$ (Set P/Y, C/Y = 12) [2nd] (CLR TVM) 400 [±] [PV] 12 [I/Y] 8 [N] [CPT]

[FV] [433.142682] [STO] 1

$E_2$ [2nd] (CLR TVM) 600 [±] [PV] 12 [I/Y] 3 [N] [CPT] [FV]

[618.1806] [STO] 2

$E_3$ [2nd] (CLR TVM) 800 [FV] 12 [I/Y] 6 [N] [CPT] [PV]

[−753.636188] [±] [STO] 3

Remember to treat this payment as a positive amount.

[RCL] 1 + [RCL] 2 + [RCL] 3

$433.142682 + 618.1806 + 753.636188 = 1804.959470 = \$1804.96$

**EXAMPLE 9.5D**

Payments of $500 are due at the end of each of the next five years. Determine the equivalent single payment five years from now (just after the last scheduled payment is due) if money is worth 10% p.a. compounded annually.

**SOLUTION**

Select as the focal date "five years from now."

Let the equivalent single payment be represented by E and the dated values of the first four scheduled payments be represented by $E_1$, $E_2$, $E_3$, $E_4$ as indicated in Figure 9.11. Then the following equation of values can be set up.

$$
\begin{aligned}
E &= 500.00 + E_4 + E_3 + E_2 + E_1 \\
&= 500.00 + 500.00(1.1) + 500.00(1.1)^2 + 500.00(1.1)^3 + 500.00(1.1)^4 \\
&= 500.00[1 + (1.1) + (1.1)^2 + (1.1)^3 + (1.1)^4] \\
&= 500.00(1 + 1.1 + 1.21 + 1.331 + 1.4641) \\
&= 500.00(6.1051) \\
&= \$3052.55
\end{aligned}
$$

The equivalent single payment after five years is $3052.55.

**FIGURE 9.11**    **Graphical Representation of Method and Data**

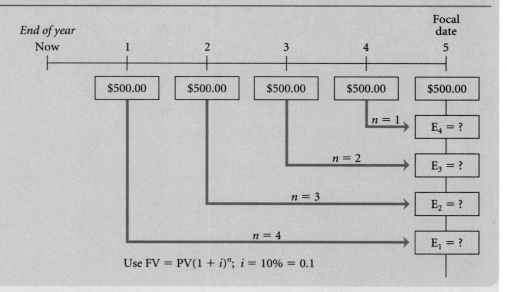

Use $FV = PV(1 + i)^n$; $i = 10\% = 0.1$

**Programmed Solution**

(Set P/Y, C/Y =1) $E_1$ [2nd] (CLR TVM) 500 [±] [PV] 10 [I/Y] 4 [N]

[CPT] [FV] ⟨732.05⟩ [STO] 1

$E_2$ [2nd] (CLR TVM) 500 [±] [PV] 10 [I/Y] 3 [N]

[CPT] [FV] ⟨665.50⟩ [STO] 2

$E_3$ [2nd] (CLR TVM) 500 [±] [PV] 10 [I/Y] 2 [N]

[CPT] [FV] ⟨605.00⟩ [STO] 3

$E_4$ 2nd (CLR TVM) 500 ± PV 10 I/Y 1 N

CPT FV 550.00 STO 4

RCL 1 + RCL 2 + RCL 3 + RCL 4 + 500 =

or

$732.05 + 665.50 + 605.00 + 550.00 + 500.00 = \$3052.55$

**EXAMPLE 9.5E**

Payments of $200 are due at the end of each of the next five quarters. Determine the equivalent single payment that will settle the debt now if interest is 9% p.a. compounded quarterly.

**SOLUTION**

Select as the focal date "now."

Let the equivalent single payment be represented by E and the dated values of the five scheduled payments by $E_1$, $E_2$, $E_3$, $E_4$, $E_5$ respectively as shown in Figure 9.12.

Then the following equation of values can be set up.

$$
\begin{aligned}
E &= E_1 + E_2 + E_3 + E_4 + E_5 \\
&= 200.00(1.0225)^{-1} + 200.00(1.0225)^{-2} + 200.00(1.0225)^{-3} \\
&\quad + 200.00(1.0225)^{-4} + 200.00(1.0225)^{-5} \\
&= 200.00[(1.0225)^{-1} + (1.0225)^{-2} + (1.0225)^{-3} + (1.0225)^{-4} + (1.0225)^{-5}] \\
&= 200.00(0.977995 + 0.956474 + 0.935427 + 0.914843 + 0.894712) \\
&= 200.00(4.679452) \\
&= \$935.89
\end{aligned}
$$

The equivalent single payment now is $935.89.

**FIGURE 9.12** **Graphical Representation of Method and Data**

*End of quarter*

Use $PV = FV(1 + i)^{-n}$; $i = \dfrac{9\%}{4} = 0.0225$

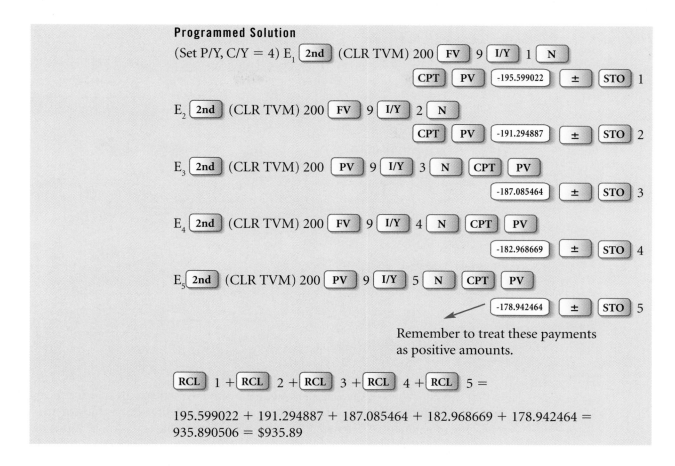

**Programmed Solution**

(Set P/Y, C/Y = 4) $E_1$ [2nd] (CLR TVM) 200 [FV] 9 [I/Y] 1 [N]

[CPT] [PV] -195.599022 [±] [STO] 1

$E_2$ [2nd] (CLR TVM) 200 [FV] 9 [I/Y] 2 [N]

[CPT] [PV] -191.294887 [±] [STO] 2

$E_3$ [2nd] (CLR TVM) 200 [PV] 9 [I/Y] 3 [N] [CPT] [PV]

-187.085464 [±] [STO] 3

$E_4$ [2nd] (CLR TVM) 200 [FV] 9 [I/Y] 4 [N] [CPT] [PV]

-182.968669 [±] [STO] 4

$E_5$ [2nd] (CLR TVM) 200 [PV] 9 [I/Y] 5 [N] [CPT] [PV]

-178.942464 [±] [STO] 5

Remember to treat these payments as positive amounts.

[RCL] 1 + [RCL] 2 + [RCL] 3 + [RCL] 4 + [RCL] 5 =

195.599022 + 191.294887 + 187.085464 + 182.968669 + 178.942464 =
935.890506 = $935.89

## C. Finding the value of two or more equivalent replacement payments

When two or more equivalent replacement payments are needed, an equation of values matching the dated values of the original scheduled payments against the dated values of the proposed replacement payments on a selected focal date should be set up. This procedure is similar to the one used for simple interest in Chapter 7.

**EXAMPLE 9.5F**

Scheduled debt payments of $1000 due today and $2000 due one year from now are to be settled by a payment of $1500 three months from now and a final payment eighteen months from now. Determine the size of the final payment if interest is 10% p.a. compounded quarterly.

**SOLUTION**

Let the size of the final payment be $x. The logical focal date is the date of the final payment.

As shown in Figure 9.13, the two original scheduled debt payments and the first replacement payment are due before the selected focal date. The future value formula $FV = PV(1 + i)^n$ applies. Because the final payment is dated on the focal date, its dated value is $x.

FIGURE 9.13    **Graphical Representation of Method and Data**

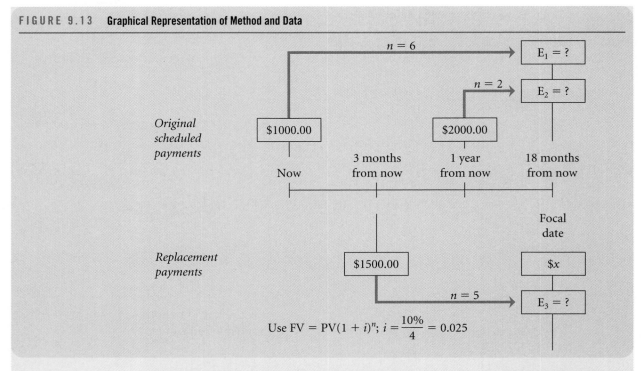

The equivalent values of the original scheduled debt payments at the selected focal date, designated $E_1$ and $E_2$, are matched against the equivalent values of the replacement payments, designated $E_3$ and $x$, giving rise to the equation of values.

$$E_1 + E_2 = x + E_3$$
$$1000.00(1.025)^6 + 2000.00(1.025)^2 = x + 1500.00(1.025)^5$$
$$1000.00(1.159693) + 2000.00(1.050625) = x + 1500.00(1.131408)$$
$$1159.69 + 2101.25 = x + 1697.11$$
$$x = 1563.83$$

The final payment is $1563.83.

**Programmed Solution**

$E_1$ (Set P/Y, C/Y = 4) [2nd] (CLR TVM) 1000 [±] [PV] 10 [I/Y] 6 [N] [CPT]
[FV] [1159.693418] [STO] 1

$E_2$ [2nd] (CLR TVM) 2000 [±] [PV] 10 [I/Y] 2 [N] [CPT] [FV]
[2101.25] [STO] 2

$E_3$ [2nd] (CLR TVM) 1500 [±] [PV] 10 [I/Y] 5 [N] [CPT] [FV]
[1697.11239] [STO] 3

[RCL] 1 + [RCL] 2 − [RCL] 3 = x

$$1159.693418 + 2101.25 = x + 1697.112319$$
$$x = 1563.831099$$

**EXAMPLE 9.5G**

What is the size of the equal payments that must be made at the end of each of the next five years to settle a debt of $5000 due in five years if money is worth 9% p.a. compounded annually?

**SOLUTION**

Select as the focal date "five years from now." Let the equal payments be represented by $x$ and let the dated values of the first four payments be represented by $E_1$, $E_2$, $E_3$, and $E_4$ respectively as shown in Figure 9.14.

Then the equation of values may be set up.

$$5000.00 = x + E_4 + E_3 + E_2 + E_1$$
$$5000.00 = x + x(1.09) + x(1.09)^2 + x(1.09)^3 + x(1.09)^4$$
$$5000.00 = x[1 + (1.09) + (1.09)^2 + (1.09)^3 + (1.09)^4]$$
$$5000.00 = x(1 + 1.09 + 1.1881 + 1.295029 + 1.411582)$$
$$5000.00 = 5.984711x$$
$$x = \$835.46$$

The size of the equal payments is $835.46.

**FIGURE 9.14**    **Graphical Representation of Method and Data**

Use $FV = PV(1 + i)^n$; $i = 9\% = 0.09$

**Programmed Solution**

(Set P/Y, C/Y = 1) E₁ [2nd] (CLR TVM) 1 [±] [PV] 9 [I/Y] 4 [N] [CPT]

[FV] [1.411582] [STO] 1

E₂ [2nd] (CLR TVM) 1 [±] [PV] 9 [I/Y] 3 [N] [CPT] [FV]

[1.295029] [STO] 2

E$_3$ [2nd] (CLR TVM) 1 [±] [PV] 9 [I/Y] 2 [N] [CPT] [FV]

[1.1881] [STO] 3

E$_4$ [2nd] (CLR TVM) 1 [±] [PV] 9 [I/Y] 1 [N] [CPT] [FV]

[1.09] [STO] 4

[RCL] 1 + [RCL] 2 + [RCL] 3 + [RCL] 4 + 1 = 5.984711 [STO] 5
or
$$1.411582x + 1.295029x + 1.1881x + 1.09x + x = \$5000.00$$
$$5.984711x = \$5000.00$$
$$x = \$835.46 \quad (5000 \div [RCL]\ 5 =)$$

**EXAMPLE 9.5H**

What is the size of the equal payments that must be made at the end of each of the next five quarters to settle a debt of $3000 due now if money is worth 12% p.a. compounded quarterly?

**SOLUTION**

Select as the focal date "now." Let the size of the equal payments be represented by $x$ and let the dated values of the five payments be represented by E$_1$, E$_2$, E$_3$, E$_4$, and E$_5$ respectively as shown in Figure 9.15.

**FIGURE 9.15** **Graphical Representation of Method and Data**

Use PV = FV$(1 + i)^{-n}$; $i = \dfrac{12\%}{4} = 0.03$

Then the equation of values may be set up.

$3000.00 = E_1 + E_2 + E_3 + E_4 + E_5$

$3000.00 = x(1.03)^{-1} + x(1.03)^{-2} + x(1.03)^{-3} + x(1.03)^{-4} + x(1.03)^{-5}$

$3000.00 = x[(1.03)^{-1} + (1.03)^{-2} + (1.03)^{-3} + (1.03)^{-4} + (1.03)^{-5}]$

$3000.00 = x(0.970874 + 0.942596 + 0.915142 + 0.888487 + 0.862609)$

$3000.00 = 4.579707x$

$$x = \frac{3000.00}{4.579707}$$

$$x = \$655.06$$

The size of the equal payments is $655.06.

**Programmed Solution**

(Set P/Y = 4) $E_1$ | 2nd | (CLR TVM) 1 | FV | 12 | I/Y | 1 | N | CPT | PV |

-0.970874 | ± | STO | 1

$E_2$ | 2nd | (CLR TVM) 1 | FV | 12 | I/Y | 2 | N | CPT | PV |

-0.942596 | ± | STO | 2

$E_3$ | 2nd | (CLR TVM) 1 | FV | 12 | I/Y | 3 | N | CPT | PV |

-0.915142 | ± | STO | 3

$E_4$ | 2nd | (CLR TVM) 1 | FV | 12 | I/Y | 4 | N | CPT | PV |

-0.888487 | ± | STO | 4

$E_5$ | 2nd | (CLR TVM) 1 | FV | 12 | I/Y | 5 | N | CPT | PV |

-0.862609 | ± | STO | 5

Remember to treat these payments as positive amounts.

| RCL | 1 + | RCL | 2 + | RCL | 3 + | RCL | 4 + | RCL | 5 = 4.594707 | STO | 6

$0.970874x + 0.942596x + 0.915142x + 0.888487x + 0.862609x = \$3000.00$

$4.579707x = \$3000.00$

$x = \$655.06$ (3000 ÷ | RCL | 6 =)

---

**EXAMPLE 9.51**

Scheduled debt payments of $750 due seven months ago, $600 due two months ago, and $900 due in five months are to be settled by two equal replacement payments due now and three months from now respectively. Determine the size of the equal replacement payments at 9% p.a. compounded monthly.

**SOLUTION**

Let the size of the equal replacement payments be represented by $x and choose "now" as the focal date.

$$I/Y = 9; \text{P/Y, C/Y} = 12; i = \frac{9\%}{12} = 0.0075$$

Figure 9.16 shows the method and data.

FIGURE 9.16    **Graphical Representation of Method and Data**

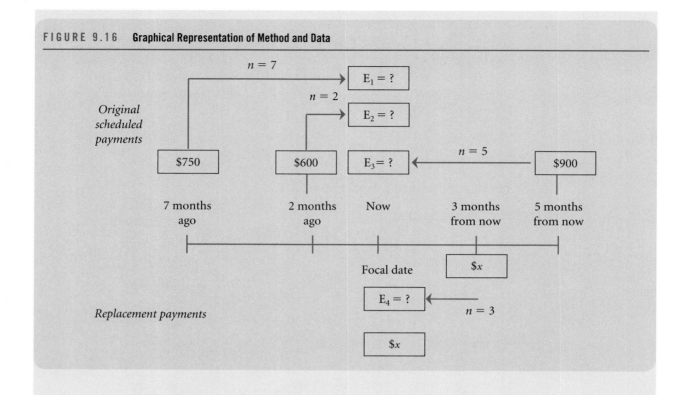

STEP 1    DATED VALUES OF SCHEDULED PAYMENTS
First, consider the dated values of the original scheduled debt payments at the chosen focal date.

The due dates of the debt payments of $750 and $600 are seven months and two months respectively before the focal date. Their dated values at the focal date are $750.00(1.0075)^7$ and $600.00(1.0075)^2$, represented by $E_1$ and $E_2$ respectively.

The due date of the scheduled payment of $900 is five months after the focal date. Its dated value is $900.00(1.0075)^{-5}$, shown as $E_3$.

STEP 2    DATED VALUES OF REPLACEMENT PAYMENTS
Second, consider the dated values of the replacement payments at the selected focal date.

The first replacement payment due at the focal date is $x. The second replacement payment is due three months after the focal date. Its dated value is $x(1.0075)^{-3}$, shown as $E_4$.

STEP 3    EQUATION OF DATED VALUES
Now equate the dated values of the replacement payments with the dated values of the original scheduled debt payments to set up the equation of values.

$$x + x(1.0075)^{-3} = 750.00(1.0075)^7 + 600.00(1.0075)^2 + 900.00(1.0075)^{-5}$$
$$x + 0.977833x = 750.00(1.053696) + 600.00(1.015056) + 900.00(0.963329)$$
$$1.977833x = 790.27 + 609.03 + 867.00$$

$1.977833x = 2266.30$

$$x = \frac{2266.30}{1.9778333}$$

$$x = \$1145.85$$

The size of the two equal payments is $1145.85.

For $E_1$ and $E_2$, use $FV = PV(1 + i)^n$; $i = \dfrac{9\%}{12} = 0.0075$

For $E_3$ and $E_4$, use or $PV = FV(1 + i)^{-n}$; $i = \dfrac{9\%}{12} = 0.0075$

**Programmed Solution**

$x + x(1.0075)^{-3}$

(Set P/Y, C/Y = 12) [ 2nd ] (CLR TVM) 1 [ FV ] 9 [ I/Y ] 3 [ N ] [ CPT ] [ PV ]

[ -0.977833 ] [ ± ] [ STO ] 1 ($E_4$)

$x + 0.977833x$

$750(1.0075)^7$

[ 2nd ] (CLR TVM) 750 [ ± ] [ PV ] 9 [ I/Y ] 7 [ N ] [ CPT ] [ FV ]

[ 790.272095 ] [ STO ] 2 ($E_1$)

$600(1.0075)^2$

[ 2nd ] (CLR TVM) 600 [ ± ] [ PV ] 9 [ I/Y ] 2 [ N ] [ CPT ] [ FV ]

[ 609.03375 ] [ STO ] 3 ($E_2$)

$900(1.0075)^{-5}$

[ 2nd ] (CLR TVM) 900 [ FV ] 9 [ I/Y ] 5 [ N ] [ CPT ] [ PV ]

[ −866.996283 ] [ ± ] [ STO ] 4 ($E_3$)

1 + [ RCL ] 1 = [ STO ] 5 [ RCL ] 2 + [ RCL ] 3 + [ RCL ] 4 = [ STO ] 6

or $x + (E_4) = (E_1) + (E_2) + (E_3)$
$x + 0.977833x = 790.272095 + 609.03375 + 866.996283$
$\quad 1.977833x = 2266.302128$
$\qquad\qquad x = 1145.85$  $\left( \boxed{RCL}\ 6 \div \boxed{RCL}\ 5 = \right)$

***Note:*** In $x(1.0075)^{-3}$, [ FV ] is not known. To obtain the factor $(1.0075)^{-3}$, use

[ FV ] $= 1$.

**EXAMPLE 9.5J**

Two scheduled payments, one of $4000 due in three months with interest at 9% compounded quarterly and the other of $3000 due in eighteen months with interest at 8.5% compounded semi-annually, are to be discharged by making two equal replacement payments. What is the size of the equal replacement payments if the first is due one year from now, the second two years from now, and money is now worth 10% compounded monthly?

**SOLUTION**

Let the size of the equal replacement payments be represented by $x. Choose "one year from now" as the focal date.

Figure 9.17 illustrates the problem.

FIGURE 9.17    **Graphical Representation of Method and Data**

**STEP 1**    MATURITY VALUES OF SCHEDULED PAYMENTS

Since the two scheduled payments are interest-bearing, first determine their maturity value.

The maturity value of $4000 due in three months at 9% compounded quarterly = $4000(1.0225)^1 = \$4090.00$, shown as $E_1$.

The maturity value of $3000 due in eighteen months at 8.5% compounded semi-annually = $3000(1.0425)^3 = 3000(1.1329955) = \$3398.99$, shown as $E_3$.

**STEP 2**    DATED VALUES OF SCHEDULED PAYMENTS

Now determine the dated values of the two maturity values at the selected focal date subject to 10% compounded monthly.

The first scheduled payment matures nine months *before* the selected focal date. Its dated value = $4090.00(1.008333)^9 = 4090.00(1.077549) = \$4407.18$, shown as $E_2$.

     The second scheduled payment matures six months *after* the selected focal date. Its dated value $= 3398.99(1.008333)^{-6} = 3398.99(0.951427) = \$3233.89$, shown as $E_4$.

STEP 3    DATED VALUES OF REPLACEMENTS PAYMENTS

The dated values of the two replacement payments at the selected focal date are $\$x$ and $\$x(1.008333)^{-12}$, shown as $E_5$.

STEP 4    EQUATION OF VALUES

Therefore, the equation of values is

$$x + x(1.008333)^{-12} = 4407.18 + 3233.89$$

$$x + 0.905212x = 7641.07$$

$$x = \frac{7641.07}{1.905212}$$

$$x = \$4010.61$$

The size of the two equal replacement payments is $4010.61.

For $E_1$ use $FV = PV(1 + i)^n$; $\; i = \dfrac{9\%}{4} = 0.0225$

For $E_3$ use $FV = PV(1 + i)^n$; $\; i = \dfrac{8.5\%}{2} = 0.0425$

For $E_2$ use $FV = PV(1 + i)^n$; $\; i = \dfrac{10\%}{12} = 0.008333$

For $E_4$ and $E_5$, use $PV = \dfrac{FV}{(1 + i)^n}$ or $PV = FV(1 + i)^{-n}$; $\; i = \dfrac{10\%}{12} = 0.008333$

**Programmed Solution**

*Maturity value of $4000*

(Set P/Y, C/Y = 4) [ 2nd ] (CLR TVM) 4000 [ ± ] [ PV ] 9 [ I/Y ] 1 [ N ] [ CPT ]

[ FV ] [ 4090 ] [ STO ] 1

*Maturity value of $3000*

(Set P/Y, C/Y = 2) [ 2nd ] (CLR TVM)3000 [ ± ] [ PV ] 8.5 [ I/Y ] 3 [ N ] [ CPT ]

[ FV ] [ 3398.98656 ] [ STO ] 2

$x + x(1.008333)^{-12}$

(Set P/Y, C/Y = 12) [ 2nd ] (CLR TVM) 1 [ FV ] 10 [ I/Y ] 12 [ N ] [ CPT ] [ PV ]

[ −0.9052124 ] [ ± ] [ STO ] 3

This gives $x + 0.905212x$.

[ 2nd ] (CLR TVM) 4090 [ ± ] [ PV ] 10 [ I/Y ] 9 [ N ] [ CPT ] [ FV ]

[ 4407.176326 ] [ STO ] 4

$$x + 0.905212x = 4407.176326 + 3233.885594$$
$$1.905212x = 7641.062280$$
$$x = 4010.61 \;(\boxed{\text{RCL}}\; 7 \div \boxed{\text{RCL}}\; 6 =)$$

## EXERCISE 9.5

EXCEL NOTES

If you choose, you can use Excel's **Future Value (FV)** or **Present Value (PV)** functions to answer the questions below. Refer to **FV** and **PV** on the Spreadsheet Template Disk to learn how to use these Excel functions.

**A.** Find the equivalent single replacement payment on the given focal date for each of the following eight situations.

| | Scheduled Payments | Int. Rate | Frequency of Conversion | Focal Date |
|---|---|---|---|---|
| 1. | $5000.00 due in 2 years | 6% | monthly | 5 years from now |
| 2. | $1600.00 due in 18 months | 8% | quarterly | 42 months from now |
| 3. | $3400.00 due in 4 years | 10% | semi-annually | 1 year from now |
| 4. | $2700.00 due in 60 months | 7% | quarterly | 6 months from now |
| 5. | $800.00 due in 6 months and $700.00 due in 15 months | 9.5% | monthly | 2 years from now |
| 6. | $1000.00 due in 9 months and $1200.00 due in 18 months | 8.8% | quarterly | 3 years from now |
| 7. | $400.00 due in 3 years and $600.00 due in 5 years | 11% | semi-annually | now |
| 8. | $2000.00 due in 20 months and $1500.00 due in 40 months | 10.5% | monthly | 9 months from now |

**B.** Solve each of the following problems.

**1.** A loan of $4000 is due in five years. If money is worth 7% compounded annually, find the equivalent payment that would settle the debt
(a) now;  (b) in 2 years;  (c) in 5 years;  (d) in 10 years.

**2.** A debt payment of $5500 is due in 27 months. If money is worth 8.4% p.a. compounded quarterly, what is the equivalent payment
(a) now?  (b) 15 months from now?
(c) 27 months from now?  (d) 36 months from now?

3. A debt can be paid by payments of $2000 scheduled today, $2000 scheduled in three years, and $2000 scheduled in six years. What single payment would settle the debt four years from now if money is worth 10% compounded semi-annually?                                                      Reference Example 9.5A

4. Scheduled payments of $600, $800, and $1200 are due in one year, three years, and six years respectively. What is the equivalent single replacement payment two-and-a-half years from now if interest is 7.5% compounded monthly?

5. Scheduled payments of $400 due today and $700 due with interest at 4.5% compounded monthly in eight months are to be settled by a payment of $500 six months from now and a final payment in fifteen months. Determine the size of the final payment if money is worth 6% compounded monthly.

6. Scheduled payments of $1200 due one year ago and $1000 due six months ago are to be replaced by a payment of $800 now, a second payment of $1000 nine months from now, and a final payment eighteen months from now. What is the size of the final payment if interest is 10.8% compounded quarterly?

7. Two debts—the first of $800 due six months ago and the second of $1400 borrowed one year ago for a term of three years at 6.5% compounded annually—are to be replaced by a single payment one year from now. Determine the size of the replacement payment if interest is 7.5% compounded quarterly and the focal date is one year from now.

8. Scheduled payments of $2000 due now and $2000 due in four years are to be replaced by a payment of $2000 due in two years and a second payment due in seven years. Determine the size of the second payment if interest is 10.5% compounded annually and the focal date is seven years from now.

9. Scheduled loan payments of $1500 due in six months and $1900 due in 21 months are rescheduled as a payment of $2000 due in three years and a second payment due in 45 months. Determine the size of the second payment if interest is 7% compounded quarterly and the focal date is 45 months from now.      Reference Example 9.5C

10. An obligation of $8000 due one year ago is to be settled by four equal payments due at the beginning of each year, with the first payment now. What is the size of the equal payments if interest is 8% compounded semi-annually?
                                                                    Reference Example 9.5D

11. A loan of $3000 borrowed today is to be repaid in three equal installments due in one year, three years, and five years respectively. What is the size of the equal installments if money is worth 7.2% compounded monthly?

12. Scheduled payments of $500 each are due at the end of each of the next five years. If money is worth 11% compounded annually, what is the single equivalent replacement payment
    (a) five years from now?            (b) now?

13. What is the size of the equal payments that must be made at the end of each of the next four years to settle a debt of $3000 subject to interest at 10% p.a. compounded annually
    (a) due four years from now?         (b) due now?                Reference Example 9.5E

14. Scheduled payments of $800 due two years ago and $1000 due in five years are to be replaced by two equal payments. The first replacement payment is due in four years and the second payment is due in eight years. Determine the size of the two replacement payments if interest is 12% compounded semi-annually and the focal date is four years from now.

15. Loan payments of $3000 due one year ago and $2500 due in four years are to be rescheduled by two equal payments. The first replacement payment is due now and the second payment is due in six years. Determine the size of the two replacement payments if interest is 6.9% compounded monthly and the focal date is now. Reference Example 9.5I

16. A payment of $500 is due in six months with interest at 12% compounded quarterly. A second payment of $800 is due in 18 months with interest at 10% compounded semi-annually. These two payments are to be replaced by a single payment nine months from now. Determine the size of the replacement payment if interest is 9% compounded monthly and the focal date is nine months from now.

17. Scheduled payments of $900 due in three months with interest at 11% compounded quarterly and $800 due in thirty months with interest at 11% compounded quarterly are to be replaced by two equal payments. The first replacement payment is due today and the second payment is due in three years. Determine the size of the two replacement payments if interest is 9% compounded monthly and the focal date is today. Reference Example 9.5J

18. Scheduled payments of $1400 due today and $1600 due with interest at 11.5% compounded annually in five years are to be replaced by two equal payments. The first replacement payment is due in 18 months and the second payment is due in four years. Determine the size of the two replacement payments if interest is 11% compounded quarterly and the focal date is 18 months from now.

**MyMathLab** Go to MyMathLab at www.mathxl.com. You can practise many of this chapter's exercises as often as you want. The guided solutions help you find an answer step by step. You'll find a personalized study plan available to you too!

# Review Exercise

1. What is the accumulated value of $500 in fifteen years at 6% compounded

   (a) annually?  (b) quarterly?  (c) monthly?

2. What is the amount of $10 000 at 10.5% compounded monthly

   (a) in four years?

   (b) in eight-and-a-half years?

   (c) in twenty years?

3. Landmark Trust offers five-year investment certificates at 7.5% compounded semi-annually.

   (a) What is the value of a $2000 certificate at maturity?

   (b) How much of the maturity value is interest?

4. Western Savings offers three-year term deposits at 9.25% compounded annually while your credit union offers such deposits at 9.0% compounded quarterly. If you have $5000 to invest, what is the maturity value of your deposit

   (a) at Western Savings?

   (b) at your credit union?

5. Find the future value and the compound interest of

   (a) $1800 invested at 8% compounded quarterly for 15.5 years;

   (b) $1250 invested at 6.5% compounded monthly for 15 years.

6. If $6000 is invested for six years and seven months at 6% compounded semi-annually, what is the interest that the investment earns?

7. Compute the maturity value of a $5000 promissory note dated November 15, 2000 and due on June 15, 2010, if interest is 8% compounded quarterly.

8. An investment of $2000 is made for three years, four months at 4.5% compounded semi-annually. What is the amount of interest?

9. Determine the sum of money that will grow to $14 000 in four years, eight months at 5% compounded quarterly.

10. Determine the proceeds of a non-interest-bearing note with a maturity value of $9000 three years and ten months before the due date if the interest rate is 7% compounded semi-annually.

11. Determine the discounted value now of $5200 due in forty months if money is worth 6.5% compounded quarterly.

12. Find the present value and the compound discount of

    (a) $3600 due in 9 years if interest is 8% compounded semi-annually;

    (b) $9000 due in 5 years if money is worth 6.8% compounded quarterly.

13. The Ram Company borrowed $20 000 at 10% compounded semi-annually and made payments toward the loan of $8000 after two years and $10 000 after three-and-a-half years. How much is required to pay off the loan one year after the second payment?

14. Ted deposited $1750 in an RRSP on March 1, 2004 at 3% compounded quarterly. Subsequently the interest rate was changed to 4% compounded monthly on September 1, 2006 and to 4.5% compounded semi-annually on June 1, 2008. What was the value of the RRSP deposit on December 1, 2010, if no further changes in interest were made?

15. An investment of $2500 is accumulated at 5% compounded quarterly for two-and-a-half years. At that time the interest rate is changed to 6% compounded monthly. How much is the investment worth two years after the change in interest rate?

16. To ensure that funds are available to repay the principal at maturity, a borrower deposits $2000 each year for three years. If interest is 6% compounded quarterly, how much will the borrower have on deposit four years after the first deposit was made?

17. Cindy started a registered retirement savings plan on February 1, 2002, with a deposit of $2500. She added $2000 on February 1, 2003 and $1500 on

February 1, 2008. What is the accumulated value of her RRSP account on August 1, 2012, if interest is 5% compounded quarterly?

18. A demand loan of $8000 is repaid by payments of $3000 after fifteen months, $4000 after thirty months, and a final payment after four years. If interest was 8% for the first two years and 9% for the remaining time, and compounding is quarterly, what is the size of the final payment?

19. A non-interest-bearing note for $1500 is due on June 30, 2012. The note is discounted at 10% compounded quarterly on September 30, 2008. What are the proceeds of the note?

20. Find the present value and the compound discount of $4000 due in seven years and six months if interest is 8.8% compounded quarterly.

21. Find the principal that will accumulate to $6000 in fifteen years at 5% compounded monthly.

22. Find the proceeds of a non-interest-bearing promissory note for $75 000 discounted 42 months before maturity at 6.5% compounded semi-annually.

23. A ten-year promissory note for $1750 dated May 1, 2003 bearing interest at 4% compounded semi-annually is discounted on August 1, 2009 to yield 6% compounded quarterly. Determine the proceeds of the note.

24. A seven-year, $10 000 promissory note bearing interest at 8% compounded quarterly is discounted four years after the date of issue at 7% compounded semi-annually. What are the proceeds of the note?

25. A $40 000, 15-year promissory note dated June 1, 2000, bearing interest at 12% compounded semi-annually is discounted on September 1, 2008 at 11% compounded quarterly. What are the proceeds of the note?

26. A fifteen-year promissory note for $16 500 bearing interest at 12% compounded semi-annually is discounted at 9% compounded monthly three years and four months after the date of issue. Compute the proceeds of the note.

27. An eight-year promissory note for $20 000 dated May 2, 2007, bearing interest at 10% compounded quarterly, is discounted on September 2, 2009 at 9.5% compounded semi-annually. Determine the proceeds of the note.

28. Three years and five months after its date of issue, a six-year promissory note for $3300 bearing interest at 7.5% compounded monthly is discounted at 7% compounded semi-annually. Find the proceeds of the note.

29. A sum of money has a value of $3000 eighteen months from now. If money is worth 6% compounded monthly, what is its equivalent value
    (a) now?          (b) one year from now?
    (c) three years from now?

30. Payments of $1000, $1200, and $1500 are due in six months, eighteen months, and thirty months from now, respectively. What is the equivalent single payment two years from now if money is worth 9.6% compounded quarterly?

31. An obligation of $10 000 is due one year from now with interest at 10% compounded semi-annually. The obligation is to be settled by a payment of $6000 in six months and a final payment in fifteen months. What is the size of the second payment if interest is now 9% compounded monthly?

32. Waldon Toys owes $3000 due in two years with interest at 11% compounded semi-annually and $2500 due in fifteen months at 9% compounded quarterly. If the company wants to discharge these debts by making two equal payments, the first one now and the second eighteen months from now, what is the size of the two payments if money is now worth 8.4% compounded monthly?

33. Debt payments of $400 due today, $500 due in eighteen months, and $900 due in three years are to be combined into a single payment due two years from now. What is the size of the single payment if interest is 8% p.a. compounded quarterly?

**34.** Debt payments of $2600 due one year ago and $2400 due two years from now are to be replaced by two equal payments due one year from now and four years from now respectively. What is the size of the equal payments if money is worth 9.6% p.a. compounded semi-annually?

**35.** A loan of $7000 taken out two years ago is to be repaid by three equal installments due now, two years from now, and three years from now, respectively. What is the size of the equal installments if interest on the debt is 12% p.a. compounded monthly?

 ## Self-Test

**1.** What sum of money invested at 4% compounded quarterly will grow to $3300 in 11 years?

**2.** Find the compound interest earned by $1300 invested at 7.5% compounded monthly for seven years.

**3.** Determine the compounding factor for a sum of money invested for 14.5 years at 7% compounded semi-annually.

**4.** Determine the maturity value of $1400 due in 71 months compounded annually at 7.75%.

**5.** Five years after Anne deposited $3600 in a savings account that earned interest at 4.8% compounded monthly, the rate of interest was changed to 6% compounded semi-annually. How much was in the account twelve years after the deposit was made?

**6.** A debt can be repaid by payments of $4000 today, $4000 in five years, and $3000 in six years. What single payment would settle the debt one year from now if money is worth 7% compounded semi-annually?

**7.** A $10 200 debt will accumulate for five years at 11.6% compounded semi-annually. For how much will the debt sell three years after it was incurred if the buyer of the debt charges 10% compounded quarterly?

**8.** What is the present value of $5900 payable in 15 years if the current interest rate is 7.5% compounded semi-annually?

**9.** Determine the compound discount on $8800 due in 7.5 years if interest is 9.6% compounded monthly.

**10.** Two debt payments, the first for $800 due today and the second for $600 due in nine months with interest at 10.5% compounded monthly, are to be settled by a payment of $800 six months from now and a final payment in 24 months. Determine the size of the final payment if money is now worth 9.5% compounded quarterly.

**11.** A note dated July 1, 1998 promises to pay $8000 with interest at 7% compounded quarterly on January 1, 2007. Find the proceeds from the sale of the note on July 1, 2002 if money is then worth 8% compounded semi-annually.

**12.** Adam borrowed $5000 at 10% compounded semi-annually. He repaid $2000 after two years and $2500 after three years. How much will he owe after five years?

13. A debt of $7000 due today is to be settled by three equal payments due three months from now, 15 months from now, and 27 months from now, respectively. What is the size of the equal payments at 11% compounded quarterly?

14. Seven years and two months after its date of issue, an eleven-year promissory note for $8200 bearing interest at 13.5% compounded monthly is discounted at 10.5% compounded semi-annually. Find the proceeds of the note.

15. Compute the proceeds of a non-interest-bearing note for $1100 three years and seven months before the due date if money is worth 7.5% compounded annually.

## Challenge Problems

1. Jean-Guy Renoir wanted to leave some money to his grandchildren in his will. He decided that they should each receive the same amount of money when they each turn 21. When he died, his grandchildren were 19, 16, and 13, respectively. How much will they each receive when they turn 21 if Jean-Guy left a lump sum of $50 000 to be shared among them equally? Assume the interest rate will remain at 7.75% p.a. compounded semi-annually from the time of Jean-Guy's death until the youngest grandchild turns 21.

2. Miranda has $1000 to invest. She has narrowed her options to two four-year certificates, A and B. Certificate A pays interest at 8% p.a. compounded semi-annually the first year, 8% p.a. compounded quarterly the second year, 8% p.a. compounded monthly the third year, and 8% p.a. compounded daily the fourth year. Certificate B pays 8% p.a. compounded daily the first year, 8% p.a. compounded monthly the second year, 8% p.a. compounded quarterly the third year, and 8% p.a. compounded semi-annually the fourth year.
   (a) What is the value of each certificate at the end of the four years?
   (b) How do the values of certificates A and B compare with the value of a third certificate that pays interest at 7% compounded daily for the full four-year term?

# Case Study 9.1 Your Best Interest

» Regan received a bonus from her employer and decided to deposit the bonus into a savings account at her bank. Her personal banking representative explained to her that there were four different savings accounts that she should consider. All of them pay compound interest.

The Daily Interest Savings Account has an interest rate of 1.50%; compound interest is calculated on the minimum balance in the account each day and is paid monthly. The Monthly Interest Savings Account has an interest rate of 2.00%; compound interest is calculated on the minimum balance in the account during the month and is paid monthly. The Investment Savings Account has an interest rate of 2.50%; compound interest is calculated on the minimum monthly balance and paid monthly, but only when the balance remains above $10 000 for the whole month. If the balance drops below $5000 at any time during the month, no interest is paid for that month. Compound interest on the Basic Savings Account is calculated on the minimum balance in the account during the six-month periods ending April 30 and October 31, and is paid on those dates. The Basic Savings Account has an interest rate of 2.80%.

The personal banking representative advised Regan that she should also consider the number of transactions made in the account each month or year when choosing an account. She thanked the representative and went home to consider her options.

## QUESTIONS

1. Suppose Regan's bonus was $9000 and she planned to invest the money immediately in a bank account for one year. Assume that the bank's interest rates will remain the same throughout the year.
   (a) For each of the bank's four savings accounts, how much interest would Regan earn in one year's time?
   (b) Which savings account would pay the most interest?

2. Suppose Regan's bonus was $12 000 and she planned to leave the money in a savings account for one year. Assume that the bank's interest rates will remain the same throughout the year.
   (a) For each of the bank's four savings accounts, how much interest would Regan earn in one year's time if she left the money in the account for one year?
   (b) Which savings account would pay the most interest?
   (c) Suppose Regan knew she would have to withdraw $3500 after ten months. Which savings account would pay the most interest?

3. Suppose Regan had $12 000 to put into a savings account. She planned to leave the money in the account for one year, then withdraw $5000. She would then leave the remaining balance in the account for one more year. Which savings account would pay the most interest over the two-year period? Assume that the bank's interest rates will stay the same over the next two years.

4. For the savings accounts at your bank, credit union, or trust company, find the features and interest rates offered for each. If you had $3500 to deposit for one year, which account would you choose?

# Case Study 9.2 Planning Ahead

» Precision Machining Corporation has been growing steadily over the past decade. Demand for the company's products continues to rise, so management has decided to expand their production facility; $2 800 000 has been set aside for this over the next four years.

Management has developed two different plans for expanding over the next four years, Plan A and Plan B. Plan A would require equal amounts of $750 000 one year from now, two years from now, three years from now, and four years from now. Plan B would require $300 000 now, $700 000 one year from now, $900 000 two years from now, and $975 000 four years from now.

The company has decided to fund the expansion with only the $2 800 000 and any interest it can earn on it. Before deciding which plan to use, the company asks its treasurer to predict the rates of interest it can earn on the $2 800 000. The treasurer expects that Precision Machining Corporation can invest the $2 800 000 and earn interest at a rate of 4.5% p.a. compounded semi-annually during Year 1, 5.0% p.a. compounded semi-annually during Years 2 and 3, and 5.5% p.a. compounded semi-annually during Year 4. The company can withdraw part of the money from this investment at any time without penalty.

## QUESTIONS

1. (a) Could Precision Machining Corporation meet the cash requirement of Plan A by investing the $2 800 000 as described above? (Use "now" as the focal date.)

   (b) What is the exact difference between the cash required and the cash available from the investment?

2. (a) Could Precision Machining Corporation meet the cash requirements of Plan B by investing the $2 800 000 as described above? (Use "now" as the focal date.)

   (b) What is the difference between the cash required and the cash available from the investment?

3. (a) Suppose Plan A was changed so that it required equal amounts of $750 000 now, one year from now, two years from now, and four years from now. Could Precision Machining Corporation meet the cash requirements of the new Plan A by investing the $2 800 000 as described above? (Use "now" as the focal date.)

   (b) What is the difference between the cash required and the cash available from the investment?

4. Suppose the treasurer found another way to invest the $2 800 000 that earned interest at a rate of 4.9% compounded quarterly for the next five years.
   (a) Could the company meet the cash requirements of the original Plan A with this new investment? (Show all your calculations.)
   (b) Could the company meet the cash requirements of Plan B with this new investment? (Show all your calculations.)
   (c) If the company could meet the cash requirements of both plans, which plan would the treasurer recommend? In other words, which plan would have the lower present value?

## SUMMARY OF FORMULAS

**Formula 9.1A**

$$S = P(1 + i)^n$$

Finding the future value (or maturity value) when the original principal, the rate of interest, and the time period are known

restated as

$$FV = PV(1 + i)^n$$

**Formula 9.1B**

$$P = \frac{S}{(1 + i)^n}$$

Finding the present value (or principal or proceeds or discounted value) when the future value, the rate of interest, and the time period are known

restated as

$$PV = \frac{FV}{(1 + i)^n}$$

**Formula 9.1C**

$$P = S(1 + i)^{-n}$$

Finding the present value by means of the discount factor (the reciprocal of the compounding factor)

restated as

$$PV = FV(1 + i)^{-n}$$

**Formula 9.2**

$$i = \frac{j}{m}$$

Finding the periodic rate of interest

## GLOSSARY

**Accumulation factor**   *see* **Compounding factor**

**Amount**   *see* **Future value**

**Comparison date**   *see* **Focal date**

**Compound discount**   the difference between a given future amount and its present value (or proceeds or discounted value) at a specified time *(p. 351)*

**Compound interest**   a procedure for computing interest whereby interest earned during an interest period is added onto the principal at the end of the interest period *(p. 329)*

**Compounding factor**   the factor $(1 + i)^n$ found in compound interest formulas *(p. 332)*

**Compounding frequency**   the number of times interest is compounded during a given time period (usually one year) *(p. 332)*

**Compounding period**   the time between two successive interest dates *(p. 332)*

**Conversion frequency**   *see* **Compounding frequency**

**Conversion period**   *see* **Compounding period**

**Discount factor**   the factor $(1 + i)^{-n}$; the reciprocal of the compounding factor *(p. 353)*

**Discounted value**   *see* **Present value**

**Discounting**   the process of computing the present value (or proceeds or discounted value) of a future sum of money *(p. 351)*

**Equivalent values**   the dated values of an original sum of money *(p. 365)*

**Focal date**   a specific date chosen to compare the time values of one or more dated sums of money *(p. 364)*

**Future value**   the sum of money to which a principal will grow at compound interest in a specific number of compounding or conversion periods at a specified periodic rate of interest *(p. 331)*

**Maturity value**   *see* **Future value**

**Nominal rate of interest** the stated rate at which the compounding is done one or more times per year; usually stated as an annual rate *(p. 332)*

**Periodic rate of interest** value of interest is obtained by dividing the nominal annual rate by the number of compounding periods per year *(p. 332)*

**Present value** the principal at any time that will grow at compound interest to a given future value over a given number of compounding periods at a given rate of interest *(p. 351)*

**Proceeds** *see* **Present value**

## USEFUL INTERNET SITES

**www.globefund.com**

**Globefund.com** This popular site for mutual fund information and analysis is hosted by the *Globe and Mail* Website.

**www.fin.gc.ca/fin-eng.html**

**Department of Finance** This site has information on the preparation of the federal government's budget that shows what is happening to taxes, as well as information related to interest rates and the economy.

**www.cannex.com**

**CANNEX** This site has a large list of comparative interest rates for GICs and term deposits offered by financial institutions in Canada, the United States, Australia, and New Zealand.

# Compound Interest— Further Topics

## OBJECTIVES

**Upon completing this chapter, you will be able to do the following with compound interest by using an electronic calculator:**

1. Determine the number of conversion periods and find equated dates.

2. Compute periodic and nominal rates of interest.

3. Compute effective and equivalent rates of interest.

Is this too good to be true? A recent ad showed notebook computers for sale, showing the all-cash price and the financed price. Some of the numbers shown were:

$69.79 per month, or $1399.99

$61.44 per month, or $1199.99

$33.33 per month, or $699.99

In each situation, would you be paying the same amount for the computer if you financed the purchase with a loan as you would if you purchased it for cash?

We should read such ads critically. They do not specify the interest rate being charged or whether the interest is simple or compound. They do not specify whether the rates of interest are the same for each type of loan. They do not specify the number of payments you would have to make. It is important to know this information to assess the ads and compare the offer with loans available from other sources.

## INTRODUCTION

In the previous chapter, we considered future value and present value when using compound interest. In this chapter, we will look at other aspects of compound interest, including finding the number of conversion periods, and computing equated dates and equivalent and effective rates of interest.

For these calculations we can either manipulate the formulas or use electronic calculators. In this and the following chapters, we will use calculators.

We can save time on our calculations by using the memory of the calculator when working with these functions. Of course, we might get slightly different results if we use memory rather than rekeying the displayed digits, because the number of digits retained in memory is almost always greater than the number of digits displayed. However, the differences are so small that we can ignore them. For the worked examples in this text, we have used the memory whenever it was convenient to do so.

# 10.1 FINDING *n* AND RELATED PROBLEMS

## A. Finding the number of conversion periods

If the principal PV, the future value FV, and the periodic rate of interest $i$ are known, the number of conversion periods $n$ can be determined by substituting the known values in Formula 9.1A and solving for $n$.

$$FV = PV(1 + i)^n \text{\underline{\hspace{5cm}}} \text{ Formula 9.1A}$$

 You can use Excel's **Number of Compounding Periods (NPER)** function to find the number of conversion periods. Refer to **NPER** on the Spreadsheet Template Disk to learn how to use this Excel function.

---

**EXAMPLE 10.1A**  In how many years will $2000.00 grow to $2440.38 at 4% compounded quarterly?

**SOLUTION**

$$PV = 2000.00; \ FV = 2440.38; \ I/Y = 4; \ P/Y = 4; \ i = \frac{4\%}{4} = 1\% = 0.01$$

$$2440.38 = 2000.00(1.01)^n \text{\hspace{0.5cm}} \longrightarrow \text{ substituting in Formula 9.1A}$$
$$(1.01)^n = 1.22019$$
$$n \ln 1.01 = \ln 1.22019 \longrightarrow \text{ solve for } n \text{ using the natural logarithm}$$
$$0.009950n = 0.199007 \longrightarrow \text{ obtain the numerical values using the}$$

$$\boxed{\text{LN}} \ \text{key}$$

$$n = \frac{0.199007}{0.009950}$$
$$= 19.999998 = 20 \text{ (quarters)}$$
$$\text{Number of years} = \frac{20}{4} = 5$$

**Programmed Solution**

You can use preprogrammed financial calculators to find $n$ by the same procedure previously used to find FV, PV.

(Set P/Y, C/Y = 4) [ **2nd** ] (CLR TVM) 2000 [ ± ] [ PV ]

2440.38 [ FV ] 4 [ I/Y ] [ CPT ] [ N ] [ 19.999997 ]

At 10% compounded quarterly, $2000 will grow to $2440.38 in 20 quarters or five years.

**Note:** Another way to solve Example 10.1A is first to rearrange Formula 9.1A to solve for $n$:

$$FV = PV(1 + i)^n$$

$$(1 + i)^n = \frac{FV}{PV}$$

$$n \ln(1 + i) = \ln\left(\frac{FV}{PV}\right)$$

$$n = \frac{\ln\left(\dfrac{FV}{PV}\right)}{\ln(1 + i)}$$

Recall that the total number of conversion periods is $n$. To convert to years if compounding semi-annually, divide $n$ by 2; if compounding quarterly, divide by 4; if compounding monthly, divide by 12; and if compounding daily, divide by 365. Remember, you do not have to memorize this equation if you understand the principles of formula rearrangement.

**EXAMPLE 10.1B**

How long does it take for money to double
 (i) at 5% p.a.?
 (ii) at 10% p.a.?

**SOLUTION**

While neither PV nor FV is given, any sum of money may be used as principal. For this calculation, a convenient value for the principal is $1.00.

PV = 1.00;  FV = 2.00;  I/Y = 5;  P/Y = 1

 (i) At 5% p.a., $i = 5\% = 0.05$

$$2 = 1(1.05)^n$$
$$1.05^n = 2$$
$$n \ln 1.05 = \ln 2$$
$$0.048790n = 0.693147$$
$$n = 14.206699 \text{ (years)}$$

**Programmed Solution**

(Set P/Y, C/Y = 1) [ **2nd** ] (CLR TVM) 1 [ ± ] [ PV ] 2 [ FV ] 5 [ I/Y ]

[ CPT ] [ N ] [ 14.206699 ] (years)

At 5% p.a., money doubles in approximately 14 years and 3 months.

(ii) At 10% p.a., I/Y = 10;  P/Y = 1;  $i = 10\% = 0.10$
$$2 = 1(1 + 0.10)^n$$
$$1.10^n = 2$$
$$n \ln 1.10 = \ln 2$$
$$0.095310n = 0.693147$$
$$n = 7.272541 \text{ (years)}$$

**Programmed Solution**

[2nd] (CLR TVM)1 [±] [PV] 2 [FV]

10 [I/Y] [CPT] [N] 7.272541 (years)

At 10% p.a., money doubles in approximately 7 years and 4 months.

## POINTERS AND PITFALLS

 ### The Rule of 70

Did you know that there is a quick way to estimate the number of conversion periods needed to double an amount of money? It is known as the *Rule of 70*. According to this rule, the number of conversion periods required to double money is 70 divided by the periodic rate of interest $i$.

Suppose we want to estimate how long it will take to double money if the interest rate is 10% compounded semi-annually. Applying the Rule of 70, we find it will take about 7 years (that is 70/5 half-year conversion periods). By comparison, if we calculate the time using the standard formulas, we get a result of about 7.103 years (i.e., about 14.207 half-year conversion periods).

**EXAMPLE 10.1C**

How long will it take for money to triple at 6% compounded monthly?

**SOLUTION**

Let PV = 1;   then FV = 3;  I/Y = 6;  P/Y = 12;  $i = \dfrac{6\%}{12} = 0.5\% = 0.005$

$$3 = 1(1.005)^n$$
$$1.005^n = 3$$
$$n \ln 1.005 = \ln 3$$
$$0.004988n = 1.098612$$
$$n = 220.271 \text{ (months)}$$

**Programmed Solution**

(Set P/Y, C/Y = 12) [2nd] (CLR TVM) 1 [±] [PV] 3 [FV]

6 [I/Y] [CPT] [N] 220.271307 (months)

At 6% compounded monthly, money triples in approximately 18 years and 4 months.

# B. Equated date

In Chapter 9, Section 9.5, we considered the concept of *equivalence* of values when using the compound interest method. In solving problems of equivalence, the unknown value was the size of a payment at the selected focal date. While we often need to find the size of the payment, occasionally we need to find the focal date or the interest rate instead.

The **equated date** is the date on which a single sum of money is equal to the sum of two or more dated sums of money. To find an equated date, an equation of values can be set up by the same technique used in Section 9.5. However, solving the equation for $n$ requires the same technique as used in Section 10.1A. Since this method involves the use of logarithms, you can solve the problem using an electronic calculator as long as the calculator is equipped with the natural logarithm function ( LN  key).

You may also use a financial calculator that is preprogrammed with the time value of money (TVM) worksheet. After entering all of the relevant data into the calculator, press CPT  N . Note that the units of N calculated are in the compounding period. For example, if you are compounding quarterly, your answer for N is in quarters. If you wish to determine a specific date to solve your problem, use the DATE worksheet within the calculator. An explanation of how to use this worksheet is included on the CD attached to this text.

**EXAMPLE 10.1D**

A financial obligation requires the payment of $2000 in 6 months, $3000 in 15 months, and $5000 in 24 months. When can the obligation be discharged by the single payment equal to the sum of the required payments if money is worth 9% p.a. compounded monthly?

**SOLUTION**

The single payment equal to the sum of the required payments is $2000 plus $3000 plus $5000, or $10 000. Select as the focal date "now." Let the number of compounding periods from the focal date to the equated date be represented by $n$. Since the compounding is done monthly, $n$ will be a number of months, I/Y = 9, P/Y = 12, and $i + \dfrac{9}{12} \% = 0.75\% = 0.0075$. The method and data are shown graphically in Figure 10.1.

Let $E_1$, $E_2$, and $E_3$ represent the equivalent values of the original payments at the focal date as shown in Figure 10.1.

Let $E_4$ represent the equivalent value of the single payment of $10 000 at the focal date.

The equation of values can now be set up.

$$E_4 = E_1 + E_2 + E_3$$

$$10\,000.00(1.0075)^{-n} = 2000.00(1.0075)^{-6} + 3000.00(1.0075)^{-15}$$
$$+ 5000.00(1.0075)^{-24}$$

$$10\,000.00(1.0075)^{-n} = 2000.00(0.956158) + 3000.00(0.893973)$$
$$+ 5000.00(0.835831)$$

$$10\,000.00(1.0075)^{-n} = 1912.32 + 2681.92 + 4179.16$$

$$10\,000.00(1.0075)^{-n} = 8773.40$$

$$(1.0075)^{-n} = \frac{8773.40}{10\,000.00}$$

$$(1.0075)^{-n} = 0.87734$$

$$-n(\ln 1.0075)^{-n} = \ln 0.87734$$

$$-n(0.007472)^{-n} = -0.130861$$

$$n = \frac{0.130861}{0.007472}$$

$$n = 17.513477$$

The equated date is about 17.5 months from now.

---

**FIGURE 10.1**  **Graphical Representation of Method and Data**

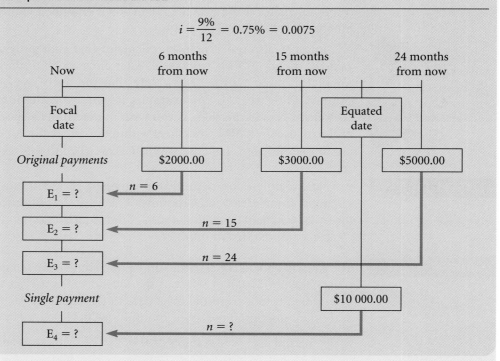

$$i = \frac{9\%}{12} = 0.75\% = 0.0075$$

### Programmed Solution

First simplify the equation $E_4 = E_1 + E_2 + E_3$.

$$10\,000(1.0075)^{-n} = 2000.00(1.0075)^{-6} + 3000(1.0075)^{-15} + 5000(1.0075)^{-24}$$

$2000(1.0075)^{-6}$

(Set P/Y, C/Y = 12) [2nd] (CLR TVM) 2000 [FV]

9 [I/Y] 6 [N] [CPT] [PV] [-1912.316036] [±] [STO] 1

$3000(1.0075)^{-15}$

[2nd] (CLR TVM) 3000 [FV] 9 [I/Y] 15 [N]

[CPT] [PV] [-2681.917614] [±] [STO] 2

$5000(1.0075)^{-24}$

or

$10\ 000(1.0075)^{-n} = 1912.316036 + 2681.917614 + 4179.15702$

**Remember to remove the negative (cash outflow) signs.**

$10\ 000(1.0075)^{-n} = 8773.39067$

Now solve the simplified equation:

$10\ 000(1.0075)^{-n} = 8773.39067$

in which FV = 10 000;  PV = 8773.39067;  $i = 0.75\%$

The equated date is approximately 17.5 months from now.

While the definition of equated date requires that the single sum of money be equal to the sum of the dated sums of money considered, the method used in solving the problem can be applied to problems in which the single sum of money does not equal the sum of the dated sums of money considered.

**EXAMPLE 10.1E**

A loan is to be repaid by three equal payments of $1500 due now, two years from now, and four years from now, respectively. When can the obligation be paid off by a single payment of $5010 if interest is 10% compounded annually?

**SOLUTION**

Select as the focal date "now." Let the number of compounding periods from the focal date to the equated date be represented by $n$. Since the compounding is done annually, $n$ will be a number of years, I/Y = 10, P/Y = 1, and $i = 10\% = 0.10$.

Let $E_1$, $E_2$, and $E_3$ represent the equivalent values of the original payments at the focal date.

$$E_1 = 1500.00 = 1500.00$$
$$E_2 = 1500.00(1.10)^{-2} = 1500.00(0.826446) = 1239.67$$
$$E_3 = 1500.00(1.10)^{-4} = 1500.00(0.683014) = \underline{1024.52}$$
$$E_1 + E_2 + E_3 = \underline{\underline{3764.19}}$$

Let $E_4$ represent the equivalent value of the single payment of $5010 at the focal date.

$$E_4 = 5010.00(1.10)^{-n}$$
$$E_4 = E_1 + E_2 + E_3$$
$$5010.00(1.10)^{-n} = 3764.19$$
$$(1.10)^{-n} = 0.751335$$
$$-n(\ln 1.10) = \ln 0.751335$$
$$-0.095310n = -0.285903$$
$$n = 3$$

**Programmed Solution**

$E_4 = E_1 + E_2 + E_3$
$5010.00(1.10)^{-n} = 1500.00 + 1500(1.10)^{-2} + 1500(1.10)^{-4}$
$1500(1.10)^{-2}$
(Set P/Y, C/Y = 1) 2nd (CLR TVM) 1500 FV 10 I/Y

2 N CPT PV -1239.669421 ± STO 1

$1500(1.10)^{-4}$
2nd (CLR TVM)1500 FV 10 I/Y 4 N

CPT PV -1024.520183 ± STO 2

RCL 1 + RCL 2 =

$5010.00(1.10)^{-n} = 1500.00 + 1239.67 + 1024.52$
$5010.00(1.10)^{-n} = 3764.19$
2nd (CLR TVM) 5010 FV 3764.19 ± PV

10 I/Y CPT N 2.999713

The single payment should be made three years from now.

**EXAMPLE 10.1F**

A loan of $2000 taken out today is to be repaid by a payment of $1200 in six months and a final payment of $1000.00. If interest is 12% compounded monthly, when should the final payment be made?

**SOLUTION**

Let the focal point be "now"; I/Y = 12; P/Y = 12; $i = \dfrac{12\%}{12} = 1.0\% = 0.01$.

$$2000.00 = 1200.00(1.01)^{-6} + 1000.00(1.01)^{-n}$$
$$2000.00 = 1200.00(0.942045) + 1000.00(1.01)^{-n}$$
$$2000.00 = 1130.45 + 1000.00(1.01)^{-n}$$
$$869.55 = 1000.00(1.01)^{-n}$$
$$(1.01)^{-n} = 0.86955$$
$$-n(\ln 1.01) = \ln 0.86955$$
$$-0.009950n = -0.139779$$
$$n = 14.0478 \text{ (months)}$$

**Programmed Solution**

$2000.00 = 1200.00(1.01)^{-6} + 1000(1.01)^{-n}$
$1200.00(1.01)^{-6}$
(Set P/Y, C/Y = 12) 2nd (CLR TVM) 1200 FV 12 I/Y

6 N CPT PV -1130.454282

$2000.00 = 1130.454282 + 1000(1.01)^{-n}$
$869.545717 = 1000(1.01)^{-n}$
869.545717 ± PV 1000 FV 12 I/Y

CPT N 14.048213 (months)

$$n = 427 \ days \qquad \underline{\phantom{xxxxxxxxxxxxxxxxxxxxxxxxx}} \left(\dfrac{14.048213}{12}\right)(365)$$

The final payment should be made in 427 days.

## EXERCISE 10.1

 **EXCEL NOTES**  If you choose, you can use Excel's ***Number of Compounding Periods (NPER)*** function to answer the questions indicated below. Refer to **NPER** on the Spreadsheet Template Disk to learn how to use this Excel function.

**A.**

1. Determine the number of compounding periods for each of the following six investments.

|  | Principal | Future Value | Interest Rate | Frequency of Conversion |
|---|---|---|---|---|
| **(a)** | $2600.00 | $6437.50 | 7% | annually |
| **(b)** | 1240.00 | 1638.40 | 4 | quarterly |
| **(c)** | 560.00 | 1350.00 | 9 | monthly |
| **(d)** | 3480.00 | 4762.60 | 8 | semi-annually |
| **(e)** | 950.00 | 1900.00 | 7.5 | quarterly |
| **(f)** | 1300.00 | 3900.00 | 6 | semi-annually |

2. Find the equated date at which the original payments are equivalent to the single payment for each of the following four sets of payments.

|  | Original Payments | Interest Rate | Frequency of Conversion | Single Payment |
|---|---|---|---|---|
| **(a)** | $400 due in 9 months and $700 due in 21 months | 12% | quarterly | $1256.86 |
| **(b)** | $1200 due today and $2000 due in 5 years | 8 | semi-annually | 3808.70 |
| **(c)** | $1000 due 8 months ago, $1200 due in 6 months, and $1500 due in 16 months | 9 | monthly | 3600.00 |
| **(d)** | $600 due in 2 years, $800 due in 3.5 years, and $900 due in 5 years | 10 | quarterly | 1800.00 |

**B.**

Answer each of the following questions.

1. How long will it take $400 to accumulate to $760 at 7% p.a. compounded semi-annually?

2. In how many days will $580 grow to $600 at 4.5% p.a. compounded monthly?

3. In how many years will money quadruple at 8% compounded quarterly?

4. In how many months will money triple at 9% compounded semi-annually?

5. If an investment of $800 earned interest of $320 at 6% compounded monthly, for how many years was the money invested?

6. A loan of $2000 was repaid together with interest of $604.35. If interest was 8% compounded quarterly, for how many months was the loan taken out?

7. If you borrowed $1000 on May 1, 2009, at 10% compounded semi-annually and interest on the loan amounts to $157.63, on what date is the loan due?

8. A promissory note for $600 dated May 15, 2008 requires an interest payment of $150 at maturity. If interest is at 9% compounded monthly, determine the due date of the note.

9. A non-interest-bearing promissory note for $1500 was discounted at 5% p.a. compounded quarterly. If the proceeds of the note were $1375.07, how many months before the due date was the note discounted?

10. A five-year, $1000 note bearing interest at 9% compounded annually was discounted at 12% compounded semi-annually yielding proceeds of $1416.56. How many months before the due date was the discount date?

11. A contract requires payments of $4000 today, $5000 in three years, and $6000 in five years. When can the contract be fulfilled by a single payment equal to the sum of the required payments if money is worth 9% p.a. compounded monthly?

12. A financial obligation requires the payment of $500 in nine months, $700 in fifteen months, and $600 in 27 months. When can the obligation be discharged by a single payment of $1600 if interest is 10% compounded quarterly?

13. When Brenda bought Sheridan Service from Ken, she agreed to make three payments of $6000 each in one year, three years, and five years respectively. Because of initial cash flow difficulties, Brenda offered to pay $8000 in two years and a second payment of $10 000 at a later date. When should she make the second payment if interest is 9.75% compounded semi-annually?

14. Leo sold a property and is to receive $3000 in six months, $4000 in 24 months, and $5000 in 36 months. The deal was renegotiated after nine months at which time Leo received a payment of $7000; he was to receive a further payment of $6000 later. When should Leo receive the second payment if money is worth 11% compounded quarterly?

# 10.2 FINDING *i* AND RELATED PROBLEMS

## A. Finding the periodic rate *i* and the nominal annual rate of interest *j*

If the original principal PV, the future value FV, and the number of conversion periods *n* are known, the periodic rate of interest (conversion rate) *i* can be determined by substituting in Formula 9.1A, $FV = PV(1 + i)^n$, and solving for *i*. The nominal annual rate of interest *j* can then be found by multiplying *i* by the number of conversion periods per year *m*.

**EXAMPLE 10.2A**

What is the annual compounding rate if $200 accumulates to $318.77 in eight years?

**SOLUTION**

PV = 200.00;  FV = 318.77;  C/Y($m$) = 1;  $n = 8$

$318.77 = 200.00(1 + i)^8$ ——————— $i$ is an *annual* rate
$(1 + i)^8_1 = 1.59385$
$[(1 + i)^8]^{\frac{1}{8}} = 1.59385^{0.125}$ ——————— raise each side to the power $\frac{1}{8}$
$1 + i = 1.59385^{0.125}$
$1 + i = 1.060000$
$i = 0.06000$
$i = 6.0\%$ ——————— the desired annual rate

The annual compounding rate is 6.0%.

**Programmed Solution**

You can use preprogrammed financial calculators to find $i$ by the same procedure used previously to determine FV or PV. That is, select the compound interest mode, enter the given variables FV, PV, and N, and retrieve the fourth variable I/Y.

(Set P/Y, C/Y = 1) ⎡2nd⎤ (CLR TVM) 200 ⎡±⎤ ⎡PV⎤ 318.77 ⎡FV⎤

8 ⎡N⎤ ⎡CPT⎤ ⎡I/Y⎤ ⎡6.000016⎤ (annual)

***Note:*** It is important to know how to rearrange the terms of an equation. For instance, another way to solve Example 10.2A is first to rearrange Formula 9.1A to solve for $i$:

$$FV = PV(1 + i)^n$$

$$(1 + i)^n = \frac{FV}{PV}$$

$$1 + i = \left(\frac{FV}{PV}\right)^{\frac{1}{n}}$$

$$i = \left(\frac{FV}{PV}\right)^{\frac{1}{n}} - 1$$

Recall that $i$ is the periodic rate of interest. If interest is calculated $m$ times per year, then the nominal annual rate of interest $j = m(i)$.

Remember, you do not have to memorize this equation if you understand the principles of formula rearrangement.

***Note:*** In the financial calculator that you use, you must determine whether the interest rate to be entered represents $i$, the periodic rate of interest, or $j$, the nominal rate of interest. In the BAII Plus calculator the ⎡I/Y⎤ to be used equates to $j$ in the formula. Thus, the variables in the formula $i = j/m$ can be translated into $i = $ ⎡I/Y⎤ / ⎡C/Y⎤ for use in the calculator. The value of I/Y obtained from the calculator is to be expressed as the nominal rate. For example, if C/Y = 4, or quarterly, and the calculator determines that I/Y = 8.5, then the rate is expressed as 8.5% p.a. compounded quarterly.

| EXAMPLE 10.2B | Find the nominal annual rate of interest compounded quarterly if $1200 accumulates to $2064.51 in five years. |

| SOLUTION | PV = 1200.00   FV = 2064.51;   C/Y($m$) = 4;   $n = 20$;   $m = 4$ |

$2064.51 = 1200.00(1+i)^{20}$ ——————— $i$ is a *quarterly* rate
$(1+i)^{20} = 1.720425$
$\quad 1 + i = 1.720425^{0.05}$ ——————— raise both side to the power $\frac{1}{20}$, that is, 0.05
$\quad 1 + i = 1.027500$
$\quad\quad\quad i = 0.027500$
$\quad\quad\quad i = 2.75\%$

The quarterly compounding rate is 2.75%.

Nominal rate = 2.75% × 4 = 11% compounded quarterly.

### Programmed Solution

(Set P/Y, C/Y = 4) [2nd] (CLR TVM) 1200 [±] [PV]

2064.51 [FV] 20 [N] [CPT] [I/Y] [11.00]

The nominal annual rate of interest is 11.0% per annum compounded quarterly. The periodic rate of interest would be $i = j/m = 11.0\%/4 = 2.75\%$ per quarter.

| EXAMPLE 10.2C | At what nominal rate of interest compounded quarterly will money double in four years? |

| SOLUTION | While neither PV nor FV are given, any sum of money may be used as principal. For this calculation, a convenient value for the principal is $1.00. |

PV = 1;   FV = 2;   C/Y($m$) = 4;   $n = 16$;   $m = 4$
$\quad\quad\quad 2 = 1(1 + i)^{16}$ ——————— $i$ is a *quarterly* rate
$(1+i)^{16} = 2$
$\quad 1 + i = 2^{\frac{1}{16}}$
$\quad 1 + i = 2^{0.0625}$
$\quad 1 + i = 1.044274$
$\quad\quad\quad i = 0.044274$
$\quad\quad\quad i = 4.4274\%$

Nominal rate = 4.4274% × 4 = 17.71% compounded quarterly.

### Programmed Solution

(Set P/Y, C/Y= 4) [2nd] (CLR TVM) 1 [±] [PV] 2 [FV] 16 [N]

[CPT] [I/Y] [17.709513]

The nominal annual rate is 17.709513% per annum compounded quarterly. The quarterly rate is 17.709513%/4 = 4.427%.

**EXAMPLE 10.2D**

Suppose $1000 earns interest of $93.81 in one year.

  (i) What is the nominal annual rate of interest compounded annually?

  (ii) What is the nominal annual rate of interest compounded monthly?

**SOLUTION**

(i) PV = 1000.00;  I = 93.81;  FV = PV + I = 1093.81;  C/Y($m$) = 1;  $n = 1$

$$1093.81 = 1000.00(1 + i)^1 \text{——————} \text{\textit{i} is an \textit{annual} rate (\textit{m} = 1)}$$
$$1 + i = 1.09381$$
$$i = 0.09381$$
$$i = 9.381\%$$

**Programmed Solution**

(Set P/Y, C/Y = 1) [ **2nd** ] (CLR TVM) 1000 [ ± ] [ PV ]

                     1093.81 [ FV ] 1 [ N ] [ CPT ] [ I/Y ]    9.381

The annual rate of interest is 9.381%.

Notice that both the nominal rate and the periodic rate of interest are 9.381%, since interest is compounded annually.

(ii)         P/Y = 12

$$1093.81 = 1000.00 (1 + i)^{12} \text{——————} \text{\textit{i} is a \textit{monthly} rate (\textit{m} = 12)}$$
$$(1 + i)^{12} = 1.09381$$
$$1 + i = 1.09381^{\frac{1}{12}}$$
$$1 + i = 1.09381^{0.083333}$$
$$1 + i = 1.007500$$
$$i = 0.007500$$
$$i = 0.75\%$$

Nominal rate = 0.75% × 12 = 9.0% compounded quarterly

**Programmed Solution**

(Set P/Y, C/Y = 12) [ **2nd** ] (CLR TVM) 1000 [ ± ] [ PV ]

                     1093.81 [ FV ] 12 [ N ] [ CPT ] [ I/Y ]   9.000286

The nominal annual rate of interest compounded monthly is 9% p.a. The periodic rate of interest is 9%/12 = 0.75% per month.

You can use Excel's **Compound Interest Rate per Period (RATE)** function to find the periodic rate of interest $i$. Refer to **RATE** on the Spreadsheet Template Disk to learn how to use this Excel function.

## EXERCISE 10.2

**A.** Answer each of the following.

Find the nominal annual rate of interest for each of the following investments.

| | Principal | Future Value | Time Due | Frequency of Conversion |
|---|---|---|---|---|
| 1. | $1400.00 | $1905.21 | 7 years | annually |
| 2. | 2350.00 | 3850.00 | 5 years | quarterly |
| 3. | 690.00 | 1225.00 | 6 years | monthly |
| 4. | 1240.00 | 2595.12 | 12 years | semi-annually |
| 5. | 3160.00 | 5000.00 | 4 years, 9 months | quarterly |
| 6. | 900.00 | 1200.00 | 3 years, 8 months | monthly |

**B.** Solve each of the following.

1. What is the nominal annual rate of interest compounded quarterly at which $420 will accumulate to $1000 in nine years and six months?

2. A principal of $2000 compounded monthly amounts to $2800 in 7.25 years. What is the nominal annual rate of interest?

3. At what nominal annual rate of interest will money double itself in
   (a) six years, nine months if compounded quarterly?
   (b) nine years, two months if compounded monthly?

4. What is the nominal annual rate of interest at which money will triple itself in 12 years
   (a) if compounded annually?
   (b) if compounded semi-annually?

5. Yin Li deposited $800 into a savings account that compounded interest monthly. What nominal annual rate compounded monthly was earned on the investment if the balance was $952.75 in five years?

6. An investment of $4000 earned interest semi-annually. If the balance after $6\frac{1}{2}$ years was $6000, what nominal annual rate compounded semi-annually was charged?

7. Surinder borrowed $1200 and agreed to pay $1400 in settlement of the debt in three years, three months. What annual nominal rate compounded quarterly was charged on the debt?

8. A debt of $600 was to be repaid in 15 months. If $750.14 was repaid, what was the nominal rate compounded monthly that was charged?

# 10.3 EFFECTIVE AND EQUIVALENT INTEREST RATES

## A. Effective rate of interest

In Example 10.2D, compounding at an annual rate of interest of 9.381% has the same effect as compounding at 9.0% p.a. compounded monthly since, in both cases, the interest amounts to $93.81.

The annually compounded rate of 9.381% is called the **effective rate of interest.** This rate is defined as the rate of interest compounded annually that yields the same amount of interest as a nominal annual rate of interest compounded a number of times per year other than one.

Converting nominal rates of interest to effective rates is the method used for comparing nominal rates of interest. Since the effective rates of interest are the equivalent rates of interest compounded annually, they may be obtained for any set of nominal rates by computing the accumulated value of $1 after one year for each of the nominal rates under consideration.

### Effective Rates Using the BAII Plus

The BAII Plus is programmed in the [ **2nd** ] function to quickly and efficiently calculate effective interest rates by inputting the nominal rate and the number of compounds. You can also calculate the nominal rate if you know the effective rate.

To go from nominal to effective the process is:

1. [ **2nd** ] (ICONV) (2-key).

2. Enter the nominal rate, NOM =

3. Arrow down to C/Y= and enter the number of times interest compounds in a year.

4. Arrow up to EFF= and press [ **CPT** ] .

To go from effective to nominal the process is:

1. [ **2nd** ] (ICONV).

2. Arrow down to EFF= and enter the effective rate.

3. Arrow down to C/Y= and enter the compounding number relating to the nominal rate you are converting to.

4. Arrow down to NOM= and press [ **CPT** ] .

### Equivalent Rates Using the BAII Plus

The BAII Plus can be used to calculate equivalent interest rates by using the effective rate as a constant to make equivalent calculations.

The process is:

1. [ **2nd** ] (ICONV).

2. Enter any nominal rate, NOM =

3. Arrow down to C/Y= and enter the compounds relating to the nominal rate entered in Step 2.

4. Arrow up to EFF= and press [ **CPT** ] .

5. Arrow down and change C/Y= to the compounds you want to convert to.

6. Arrow down to NOM= and press [ **CPT** ] .

7. Repeat the process as many times as required to calculate all equivalent rates you are interested in.

**EXAMPLE 10.3A**

Assume you are given a choice of a term deposit paying 7.2% compounded monthly or an investment certificate paying 7.25% compounded semi-annually. Which rate offers the higher rate of return?

**SOLUTION**

The investment certificate offers the higher nominal rate of return while the term deposit offers the higher compounding frequency. Because of the different compounding frequencies, the two nominal rates are not directly comparable. To determine which nominal rate offers the higher rate of return, we need to determine the effective rates for the two given rates.

*For the term deposit*

I/Y = 7.2; P/Y = 12; $i = 0.6\% = 0.006$; $m = 12$;
the accumulated value of $1 after one year,
FV = $1(1.006)^{12} = 1.074424$

The decimal fraction 0.074424 is the interest earned in one year and represents the effective rate of interest = 7.44242%.

*For the investment certificate*

I/Y = 7.25; P/Y = 2; $i = 3.625\% = 0.03625$; $m = 2$;

the accumulated value of $1 after one year,
FV = $1(1.03625)^2 = 1.073814$

The decimal fraction 0.073814 represents the effective rate of interest = 7.3814%.

Since the term deposit has the higher effective rate, it offers the higher rate of return.

**Programmed Solution**

*For the term deposit*

$(1 + i)^{12} = (1.0006)^{12} = 1.0744242$

(Set P/Y, C/Y = 12) **2nd** (CLR TVM) 1 **±** **PV** 7.2 **I/Y**

12 **N** **CPT** **FV** 1.074424

*Alternatively:*

**2nd** (IConv) Nom = 7.2; C/Y = 12; Eff = **CPT** 7.4424

*For the investment certificate*

$(1 + i)^2 = (1.03625)^2 = 1.073814$

(Set P/Y, C/Y = 2) **2nd** (CLR TVM) 1 **±** **PV** 7.25 **I/Y**

2 **N** **CPT** **FV** 1.073814

*Alternatively:*

**2nd** (IConv) Nom = 7.25; C/Y = 2; Eff = **CPT** 7.3814

The nominal annual rate is 7.4424% for the term deposit and 7.3814% for the investment certificate.

**EXAMPLE 10.3B**

How much better is a rate of 8.4% compounded monthly than 8.4% compounded quarterly?

**SOLUTION**

*For 8.4% compounded monthly*

I/Y = 8.4;  P/Y = 12;  $i = 0.7\% = 0.007$;  $m = 12$;
the accumulated value of $1 after one year,
FV $= 1(1.007)^{12} = 1.087311$

The decimal fraction 0.087311 is the interest earned in one year and represents the effective rate of interest = 8.7311%.

*For 8.4% compounded quarterly*

I/Y = 8.4;  P/Y = 4;  $i = 2.1\% = 0.021$;  $m = 4$;
the accumulated value of $1 after one year,
FV $= 1(1.021)^{4} = 1.086683$

The decimal fraction 0.086683 represents the effective rate of interest = 8.6683%.
Difference = 8.7311% − 8.6683% = 0.0628%.

**Programmed Solution**

*For 8.4% compounded monthly*

$(1 + i)^{12} = (1.007)^{12} = 1.087311$
(Set P/Y, C/Y = 12) | **2nd** | (CLR TVM) 1 | **±** | | **PV** | 8.4

| **I/Y** | 12 | **N** | | **CPT** | | **FV** | | 1.087311 |

*Alternatively:*

| **2nd** | (IConv) Nom = 8.4;  C/Y = 12;  Eff = | **CPT** | 8.7311

*For 8.4% compounded quarterly*

$(1 + i)^{4} = (1.021)^{4} = 1.086683$
(Set P/Y, C/Y = 4) | **2nd** | (CLR TVM) 1 | **±** | | **PV** | 8.4 | **I/Y** |

4 | **N** | | **CPT** | | **FV** | | 1.086683 |

*Alternatively:*

| **2nd** | (IConv) Nom = 8.4;  C/Y = 4;  Eff = | **CPT** | 8.6683

The effective rate is 8.7311% with 8.4% compounded monthly and 8.6683% for 8.4% compounded quarterly.

The effective rates of interest can also be determined by using Formula 10.1 obtained from the method of calculation used in Examples 10.3A and 10.3B.

The formula is obtained as follows:

Let the nominal annual rate of interest be compounded $m$ times per year and let the interest rate per conversion period be $i$.

Then the accumulated amount after one year is $FV_1 = PV(1 + i)^m$.

Let the corresponding effective annual rate of interest be $f$.

Then the accumulated amount after one year is $FV_1 = PV(1 + f)^1$.

$PV(1 + f)^1 = PV(1 + i)^m$ —————— the amounts are equal by definition

$1 + f = (1 + i)^m$ ———————— divide both sides by PV

$$\boxed{f = (1 + i)^m - 1}$$ ———————— Formula 10.1

---

**EXAMPLE 10.3C**

Determine the effective rate of interest corresponding to 9% p.a. compounded

(i) monthly;
(ii) quarterly;
(iii) semi-annually;
(iv) annually;
(v) daily.

**SOLUTION**

(i) $i = \left(\dfrac{9\%}{12}\right) = 0.0075; \quad m = 12$

$f = (1 + i)^m - 1$ ————————————— using Formula 10.1

$= (1 + 0.0075)^{12} - 1$

$= 1.093807 - 1$

$= 0.093807$

$= 9.381\%$

(ii) $i = \left(\dfrac{9\%}{4}\right) = 0.0225; \quad m = 4$

$f = (1.0225)^4 - 1$

$= 1.093083 - 1$

$= 0.093083$

$= 9.308\%$

(iii) $i = \left(\dfrac{9\%}{2}\right) = 0.045; \quad m = 2$

$f = (1.045)^2 - 1$

$= 1.092025 - 1$

$= 9.2025\%$

(iv) $i = 9\% = 0.09; \quad m = 1$

$f = (1.09)^1 - 1$

$= 9.000\%$

(v) $i = \left(\dfrac{9\%}{365}\right) = 0.000246; \quad m = 365$

$f = (1.000246)^{365} - 1$

$= 1.094162 - 1$

$= 9.416\%$

*Summary of Results*

For a nominal annual rate of 9% p.a., effective rates are

| | |
|---|---|
| when compounding annually ($m = 1$) | $f = 9.000\%$ |
| when compounding semi-annually ($m = 2$) | $f = 9.2025\%$ |
| when compounding quarterly ($m = 4$) | $f = 9.308\%$ |
| when compounding monthly ($m = 12$) | $f = 9.381\%$ |
| when compounding daily ($m = 365$) | $f = 9.416\%$ |

## Programmed Solution

*For 9% compounded monthly*

$$(1 + i)^{12} = (1.0075)^{12} = 1.093807$$

(Set P/Y, C/Y = 12) [ **2nd** ] (CLR TVM) 1 [ **±** ] [ **PV** ] 9 [ **I/Y** ]

12 [ **N** ] [ **CPT** ] [ **FV** ] [ 1.093807 ]

*Alternatively:*

[ **2nd** ] (IConv) Nom = 9; C/Y = 12; Eff = [ **CPT** ] 9.3807

*For 9% compounded quarterly*

$$(1 + i)^4 = (1.0225)^4 = 1.093083$$

(Set P/Y, C/Y = 4) [ **2nd** ] (CLR TVM) 1 [ **±** ] [ **PV** ] 9 [ **I/Y** ]

4 [ **N** ] [ **CPT** ] [ **FV** ] [ 1.093083 ]

*Alternatively:*

[ **2nd** ] (IConv) Nom = 9; C/Y = 4; Eff = [ **CPT** ] 9.3083

*For 9% compounded semi-annually*

$$(1 + i)^2 = (1.045)^2 = 1.092025$$

(Set P/Y, C/Y = 2) [ **2nd** ] (CLR TVM) 1 [ **±** ] [ **PV** ] 9 [ **I/Y** ]

2 [ **N** ] [ **CPT** ] [ **FV** ] [ 1.092025 ]

*Alternatively:*

[ **2nd** ] (IConv) Nom = 9; C/Y = 2; Eff = [ **CPT** ] 9.2025

*For 9% compounded annually*

$$(1 + i)^1 = (1.09)^1 = 1.09$$

(Set P/Y, C/Y = 1) [ **2nd** ] (CLR TVM) 1 [ **±** ] [ **PV** ] 9 [ **I/Y** ]

1 [ **N** ] [ **CPT** ] [ **FV** ] [ 1.09 ]

*Alternatively:*

[2nd] (IConv) Nom = 9;  C/Y = 1;  Eff = [CPT] 9

*For 9% compounded daily*

$(1 + i)^{365} = (1.000246)^{365} = 1.094162$

(Set P/Y, C/Y = 365) [2nd] (CLR TVM) 1 [±] [PV] 9 [I/Y]

365 [N] [CPT] [FV]  1.094162

*Alternatively:*

[2nd] (IConv) Nom = 9; C/Y = 365; Eff = [CPT] 9.4162

## POINTERS AND PITFALLS

For nominal annual interest rates and effective rates, the following two points are always true:

1. The nominal annual rate is the effective rate of interest *only* if the number of conversion periods per year is 1, that is, if compounding annually.
2. For a given nominal annual rate, the effective rate of interest increases as the number of conversion periods per year increases.

**EXAMPLE 10.3D**

You have money to invest in interest-earning deposits. You have determined that suitable deposits are available at your bank paying 6.5% p.a. compounded semi-annually, at a local trust company paying 6.625% compounded annually, and at your credit union paying 6.45% p.a. compounded monthly. What institution offers the best rate of interest?

**SOLUTION**

Since the methods of conversion differ, the interest rates are not directly comparable. To make the rates comparable, determine the effective rates of interest corresponding to the nominal annual rates.

*For the bank:*

$i = \left(\dfrac{6.5\%}{2}\right) = 0.0325; \quad m = 2$

$f = (1 + 0.0325)^2 - 1 = 1.066056 - 1 = 0.066056 = 6.606\%$

*For the trust company:*

$i = 6.625 = 0.06625; \quad m = 1$

$f = i = 6.625\%$

*For the credit union:*

$i = \left(\dfrac{6.45\%}{12}\right) = 0.005375; \quad m = 12$

$f = (1.005375)^{12} - 1 = 1.066441 - 1 = 0.066441 = 6.644\%$

While the nominal rate offered by the credit union is lowest, the corresponding effective rate of interest is highest due to the higher frequency of conversion. The rate offered by the credit union is best.

**Programmed Solution**

*For the bank:*

6.5% compounded semi-annually:

$(1 + i)^2 = (1.032500)^2 = 1.066056$

(Set P/Y, C/Y = 2) [2nd] (CLR TVM) 1 [±] [PV] 6.5 [I/Y]

2 [N] [CPT] [FV] [1.066056]

*Alternatively:*

[2nd] (IConv) Nom = 6.5; C/Y = 2; Eff = [CPT] 6.6056

*For the trust company:*

6.625% compounded annually:

$(1 + i)^1 = (1.06625)^1 = 1.06625$

(Set P/Y, C/Y = 1) [2nd] (CLR TVM) 1 [±] [PV] 6.625 [I/Y]

1 [N] [CPT] [FV] [1.06625]

*Alternatively:*

[2nd] (IConv) Nom = 6.625; C/Y = 1; Eff = [CPT] 6.625

*For the credit union:*

6.45% compounded monthly:

$(1 + i)^{12} = (1.005375)^{12} = 1.066441$

(Set P/Y, C/Y = 12) [2nd] (CLR TVM) 1 [±] [PV] 6.45 [I/Y]

12 [N] [CPT] [FV] [1.066441]

*Alternatively:*

[2nd] (IConv) Nom = 6.45; C/Y = 12; Eff = [CPT] 6.6441

## B. Equivalent rates

Notice that in Example 10.2D, two different nominal annual rates of interest (9.381% compounded annually and 9% compounded monthly) produced the same future value ($1093.81) for a given principal ($1000.00) after one year. Interest rates that increase a given principal to the same future value over the same period of time are called **equivalent rates**—9.381% compounded annually and 9% compounded monthly are equivalent rates.

**EXAMPLE 10.3E**    Find the future value after one year of $100 accumulated at

   (i) 12.55% compounded annually;
  (ii) 12.18% compounded semi-annually;
 (iii) 12.00% compounded quarterly;
 (iv) 11.88% compounded monthly.

**SOLUTION**

|  | (i) | (ii) | (iii) | (iv) |
|---|---|---|---|---|
| Principal (PV) | 100.00 | 100.00 | 100.00 | 100.00 |
| Nominal rate | 12.55% | 12.18% | 12.00% | 11.88% |
| $i$ | 0.1255 | 0.0609 | 0.03 | 0.0099 |
| $n$ | 1 | 2 | 4 | 12 |
| Future value (FV) | $100.00(1.1255)^1$ $= 100.00(1.1255)$ $= \$112.55$ | $100.00(1.0609)^2$ $= 100.00(1.125509)$ $= \$112.55$ | $100.00(1.03)^4$ $= 100.00(1.125509)$ $= \$112.55$ | $100.00(1.0099)^{12}$ $= 100.00(1.125487)$ $= \$112.55$ |

*Note:* The four different nominal annual rates produce the same future value of $112.55 for the same principal of $100 over the same time period of one year. By definition, the four nominal rates are equivalent rates.

We can find equivalent rates by equating the accumulated values of $1 for the rates under consideration based on a selected time period, usually one year.

**EXAMPLE 10.3F**

Find the nominal annual rate compounded semi-annually that is equivalent to an annual rate of 6% compounded annually.

**SOLUTION**

Let the semi-annual rate of interest be represented by $i$; P/Y = 2.
For PV = 1, $n = 2$, the accumulated value $FV_1 = (1 + i)^2$.
For the given nominal rate compounded annually the accumulated value $FV_2 = (1 + 0.06)^1$.
By definition, to be equivalent, $FV_1 = FV_2$.

$$(1 + i)^2 = 1.06$$
$$1 + i = 1.06^{0.5}$$
$$1 + i = 1.029563$$
$$i = 0.029563 \text{ ——————— semi-annual rate}$$

Nominal rate $= 2.9563\% \times 2 = 5.9126\%$ compounded semi-annually.

**Programmed Solution**

$$1\ (1 + i)^2 = 1.06$$

PV ↓      FV ↓

(Set P/Y, C/Y = 2) [2nd] (CLR TVM) 1 [±] [PV] 1.06 [FV]

2 [N] [CPT] [I/Y] [5.912603]

*Alternatively:*

[2nd] (IConv) Eff = 6.0; C/Y = 2; Nom = [CPT] 5.912603

The nominal annual rate compounded semi-annually is 5.91%.
The periodic rate is 5.912603%/2 = 2.956301% per semi-annual period.

**EXAMPLE 10.3G**

What nominal annual rate compounded quarterly is equivalent to 8.4% p.a. compounded monthly?

**SOLUTION**

Let the quarterly rate be $i$; PV = 1; $n = 4$.
The accumulated value of $1 after one year $FV_1 = (1 + i)^4$.

For the given rate I/Y = 8.4; P/Y = 12; $i = \dfrac{8.4\%}{12} = 0.7\% = 0.007$; $n = 12$.

The accumulated value of $1 after one year $FV_2 = (1.007)^{12}$.
To be equivalent, $FV_1 = FV_2$.

$$(1 + i)^4 = (1.007)^{12}$$
$$1 + i = (1.007)^3$$
$$1 + i = 1.021147$$
$$i = 0.021147 \text{ ———————— quarterly rate}$$

**Programmed Solution**

(Set P/Y, C/Y = 12) [2nd] (CLR TVM) 1 [±] [PV] 8.4 [I/Y]

12 [N] [CPT] [FV] [1.087311]

(Set P/Y, C/Y = 4) [2nd] (CLR TVM) 1 [±] [PV] 1.087311 [FV]

4 [N] [CPT] [I/Y] 8.458937%

*Alternatively:*

[2nd] (IConv) Nom = 8.4; C/Y = 12; Eff = [CPT] 8.7311

C/Y = 4; Nom = [CPT] 8.458937

The nominal annual rate compounded quarterly is 8.46%. The periodic rate is 2.11473% per quarterly period.

**EXAMPLE 10.3H**

Peel Credit Union offers premium savings deposits at 8% interest paid semi-annually. The board of directors wants to change to monthly payment of interest. What nominal annual rate compounded monthly should the board set to maintain the same yield?

**SOLUTION**

Let the monthly rate be $i$; P/Y = 12; $n = 12$; PV = 1.
The accumulated value of $1 after one year $FV_1 = (1 + i)^{12}$.
For the existing rate, P/Y = 2; $n = 2$, $i = 0.04$.
The accumulated value of $1 in one year $FV_2 = (1.04)^2$.
To maintain the same yield the two rates must be equivalent.

$$(1 + i)^{12} = (1.04)^2$$
$$1 + i = (1.04)^{\frac{1}{6}}$$
$$1 + i = 1.006558$$
$$i = 0.006558 \text{ ——————————— monthly rate}$$

Nominal rate = 0.6558% × 12 = 7.87% compounded monthly.

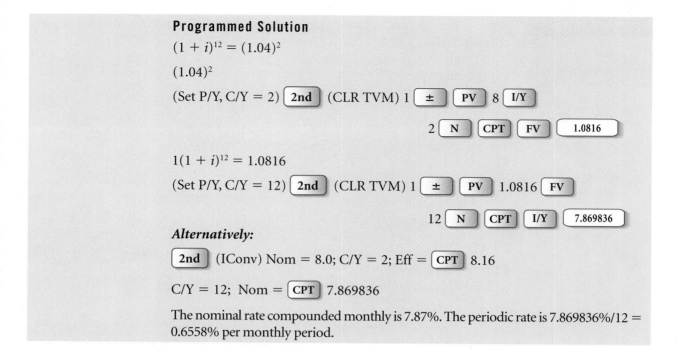

**Programmed Solution**

$(1 + i)^{12} = (1.04)^2$

$(1.04)^2$

(Set P/Y, C/Y = 2) [**2nd**] (CLR TVM) 1 [ ± ] [ PV ] 8 [ I/Y ]

2 [ N ] [ CPT ] [ FV ] [ 1.0816 ]

$1(1 + i)^{12} = 1.0816$

(Set P/Y, C/Y = 12) [**2nd**] (CLR TVM) 1 [ ± ] [ PV ] 1.0816 [ FV ]

12 [ N ] [ CPT ] [ I/Y ] [ 7.869836 ]

*Alternatively:*

[**2nd**] (IConv) Nom = 8.0; C/Y = 2; Eff = [ CPT ] 8.16

C/Y = 12; Nom = [ CPT ] 7.869836

The nominal rate compounded monthly is 7.87%. The periodic rate is 7.869836%/12 = 0.6558% per monthly period.

# EXERCISE 10.3

If you choose, you can use Excel's *Effective Annual Interest Rate (EFFECT)* or *RATE* functions to answer the questions indicated below. Refer to **EFFECT** or **RATE** on the Spreadsheet Template Disk to learn how to use these functions.

**A.** Answer each of the following.

**1.** Find the nominal rate of interest compounded annually equivalent to each of the following.
   **(a)** 12.5% compounded semi-annually
   **(b)** 6% compounded monthly
   **(c)** 7.2% compounded quarterly
   **(d)** 10.2% compounded monthly

**2.** Compute the effective annual rate of interest for each of the following.
   **(a)** 9.5% compounded semi-annually
   **(b)** 10.5% compounded quarterly
   **(c)** 5.0% compounded monthly
   **(d)** 7.2% compounded monthly
   **(e)** 3.6% compounded quarterly
   **(f)** 8.2% compounded semi-annually

**3.** Find the nominal annual rate compounded
   **(a)** quarterly that is equivalent to 9% compounded semi-annually
   **(b)** monthly that is equivalent to 6.5% compounded quarterly
   **(c)** monthly that is equivalent to 7.5% compounded semi-annually
   **(d)** semi-annually that is equivalent to 4.25% compounded quarterly

**B.** Solve each of the following.

1. What is the effective annual rate of interest if $100 grows to $150 in six years compounded quarterly?

2. What is the effective annual rate of interest if $450 grows to $750 in three years, five months compounded monthly?

3. If $1100 accumulates to $1350 in four years, six months compounded semi-annually, what is the effective annual rate of interest?

4. An amount of $2300 earns $500 interest in three years, two months. What is the effective annual rate if interest compounds monthly?

5. Find the nominal annual rate of interest compounded quarterly that is equal to an effective rate of 9.25%.

6. What nominal annual rate of interest compounded semi-annually is equivalent to an effective rate of 6.37%?

7. If the effective rate of interest on an investment is 6.4%, what is the nominal rate of interest compounded monthly?

8. What is the nominal rate of interest compounded quarterly if the effective rate of interest on an investment is 5.3%?

9. The Central Bank pays 7.5% compounded semi-annually on certain types of deposits. If interest is compounded monthly, what nominal rate of interest will maintain the same effective rate of interest?

10. The treasurer of National Credit Union proposes changing the method of compounding interest on premium savings accounts to daily compounding. If the current rate is 6% compounded quarterly, what nominal rate should the treasurer suggest to the board of directors to maintain the same effective rate of interest?

11. Sofia made a deposit of $600 into a bank account that earns interest at 3.5% compounded monthly. The deposit earns interest at that rate for five years.
    (a) Find the balance of the account at the end of the period.
    (b) How much interest is earned?
    (c) What is the effective rate of interest?

12. Ying invested $5000 into an account earning 2.75% interest compounding daily for two years.
    (a) Find the balance of the account at the end of the period.
    (b) How much interest is earned?
    (c) What is the effective rate of interest?

13. An RRSP earns interest at 4.25% compounded quarterly. An amount of $1200 is invested into the RRSP and earned interest for ten years.
    (a) Find the balance of the account at the end of the period.
    (b) How much interest is earned?
    (c) What is the effective rate of interest?

**14.** Josef invested $1750 into an RRSP that earned interest at 5% compounded semi-annually for eight years.

   **(a)** Find the balance of the account at the end of the period.
   **(b)** How much interest is earned?
   **(c)** What is the effective rate of interest?

---

## ≫ BUSINESS MATH NEWS BOX

### How to Maximize Savings for a Child's Education

You can tell when school has started when the nights are cooler and parents' wallets are emptier.

Looking longer term toward college funding, there are two main ways to save. The first is the Registered Education Savings Plan, or RESP. The other way is simply to put money away, either in your name or in an account in your name "in-trust" for your child or grandchild.

The advantage to the RESP is that the government will put in one dollar for every five dollars you put in, up to a maximum government grant (CESG) of $400 per year per child. That's based on a $2000 contribution from you, although you are allowed to put in up to $4000 per year.

The money invested inside an RESP grows tax deferred. The original capital can be withdrawn tax free at any time, but the investment income and the grant are taxable to the student beneficiary, when withdrawn. This assumes that the beneficiary enrolls in some form of post-secondary education. This could be technical or community college, university, or a number of other full-time courses of study.

If the beneficiary (or any of the beneficiaries, in a family plan RESP) does not attend a qualifying course of study, then the income and grant become taxable to the subscriber (the adult who set up the plan). There is also a 20% surcharge, above the regular income taxes, which really just makes up for the grant money and the time all of the money was allowed to grow tax-deferred.

The bottom line is that the RESP is likely the best means of accumulating money for post-secondary education, at least to the extent of $2000 a year per child.

*Source:* "How to Maximize Savings for a Child's Education" by David Christianson. *Winnipeg Free Press*, August 25, 2006, p. B.4. Edited excerpt reprinted with permission.

### QUESTIONS

**1.** Assume the Wong family contributes $2000 per year over a 16-year period to an RESP plan earning 4.85% interest compounded semi-annually.
   **a.** Calculate the value the plan would have at the start of the 17th year.
   **b.** Calculate the value of annual contributions of $2000 into a non-RESP plan over a 16-year period at 4.85% interest compounded semi-annually.
   **c.** Determine the difference in plan values of the RESP plan from those of the non-RESP plan.

**2.** Assume that $1000 was contributed at the beginning of each year into an RESP plan for 10 years.
   **a.** If the rate of interest was 4% per annum compounded annually for the first 5 years, and 5.2% compounded quarterly for the last 5 years, calculate the amount of the plan.
   **b.** If the tax rate is 40% and the student uses this amount for a four-year degree, calculate the monthly value that can be used by the student.

## Review Exercise

1. At what nominal rate of interest compounded monthly will $400 earn $100 interest in four years?

2. At what nominal rate of interest compounded quarterly will $300 earn $80 interest in six years?

3. Find the equated date at which payments of $500 due six months ago and $600 due today could be settled by a payment of $1300 if interest is 9% compounded monthly.

4. Find the equated date at which two payments of $600 due four months ago and $400 due today could be settled by a payment of $1100 if interest is 7.25% compounded semi-annually.

5. In what period of time will money triple at 10% compounded semi-annually?

6. In how many years will money double at 8% compounded monthly?

7. What nominal rate of interest compounded monthly is equivalent to an effective rate of 6.2%?

8. What nominal rate of interest compounded quarterly is equivalent to an effective rate of 5.99%?

9. Find the nominal annual rate of interest
   (a) at which $2500 will grow to $4000 in eight years compounded quarterly;
   (b) at which money will double in five years compounded semi-annually;
   (c) if the effective annual rate of interest is 9.2% and compounding is done monthly;
   (d) that is equivalent to 8% compounded quarterly.

10. Find the nominal annual rate of interest
   (a) at which $1500 will grow to $1800 in four years compounded monthly;
   (b) at which money will double in seven years compounded quarterly;
   (c) if the effective annual rate of interest is 7.75% and compounding is done monthly;
   (d) that is equivalent to 6% compounded quarterly.

11. Compute the effective annual rate of interest
   (a) for 4.5% compounded monthly;
   (b) at which $2000 will grow to $3000 in seven years compounded quarterly.

12. Compute the effective annual rate of interest
   (a) for 6% compounded monthly;
   (b) at which $1100 will grow to $2000 in seven years compounded monthly.

13. What is the nominal annual rate of interest compounded monthly that is equivalent to 8.5% compounded quarterly?

14. What is the nominal annual rate of interest compounded quarterly that is equivalent to an effective annual rate of 5%?

15. Patrick had $2000 to invest. Which of the following options should he choose?
   (a) 4% compounded annually
   (b) 3.75% compounded semi-annually
   (c) 3.5% compounded quarterly
   (d) 3.25% compounded monthly

16. (a) How many years will it take for $7500 to accumulate to $9517.39 at 3% compounded semi-annually?
   (b) Over what period of time will money triple at 9% compounded quarterly?
   (c) How many years will it take for a loan of $10 000 to amount to $13 684 at 10.5% compounded monthly?

17. Matt had agreed to make two payments—a payment of $2000 due in nine months and a payment of $1500 in a year. If Matt makes a payment of $1800 now, when should he make a second payment of $1700 if money is worth 8% compounded quarterly?

**18.** A four-year, $3200 promissory note with interest at 7% compounded monthly was discounted at 9% compounded quarterly yielding proceeds of $3870.31. How many months before the due date was the discount date?

**19.** A financial obligation requires the payment of $2000 now, $2500 in six months, and $4000 in one year. When will a single payment of $9000 discharge the obligation if interest is 6% compounded monthly?

**20.** Girard owes two debt payments—a payment of $5000 due in six months and a payment of $6000 due in fifteen months. If Girard makes a payment of $5000 now, when should he make a second payment of $6000 if money is worth 11% compounded semi-annually?

**21.** Payment of a debt of $10 000 incurred on December 1, 2008, with interest at 9.5% compounded semi-annually is due on December 1, 2011. If a payment of $7500 is made on December 1, 2010, on what date should a second payment of $7500 be made if money is worth 12% compounded quarterly?

**22.** A seven-year, $1500 promissory note with interest at 10.5% compounded semi-annually was discounted at 12% compounded quarterly yielding proceeds of $2150. How many months before the due date was the discount date?

## Self-Test

**1.** A ten-year, $9200 promissory note with interest at 6% compounded monthly is discounted at 5% compounded semi-annually yielding proceeds of $12 915.60. How many months before the due date was the date of discount?

**2.** An amount of $1400 was invested for 71 months, maturing to $2177.36. What annually compounded rate was earned?

**3.** Determine the effective annual rate of interest equivalent to 5.4% compounded monthly.

**4.** How many months from now can a payment of $1000 due twelve months ago and a payment of $400 due six months from now be settled by a payment of $1746.56 if interest is 10.2% compounded monthly?

**5.** At what nominal rate of interest compounded semi-annually will $6900 earn $3000 interest in five years?

**6.** In how many years will money double at 7.2% compounded quarterly?

**7.** What is the nominal rate of interest compounded semi-annually that is equivalent to an effective rate of 10.25%?

**8.** Seven years and two months after its date of issue, an eleven-year promissory note for $8200 bearing interest at 13.5% compounded monthly is discounted to yield $24 253.31. What semi-annually compounded nominal discount rate was used?

**9.** A non-interest-bearing note for $1100 is discounted three years and seven months before the due date. What annually compounded rate of interest yields proceeds of $848.88?

## Challenge Problems

1. Olga deposited $800 in an investment certificate paying 9% compounded semi-annually. On the same day, her sister Ursula deposited $600 in an account paying 7% compounded semi-annually. To the nearest day, when will the future value of Olga's investment be equal to twice the future value of Ursula's investment?

2. A financial institution is advertising a new three-year investment certificate. The interest rate is 7.5% compounded quarterly the first year, 6.5% compounded monthly the second year, and 6% compounded daily the third year. What nominal rate of interest compounded semi-annually for three years would a competing institution have to offer to match the interest produced by this investment certificate?

# Case Study 10.1 Choosing a Credit Card

» Jane Zhao is deciding which credit card to apply for. She has just received advertising from several large credit card companies, some of which feature low introductory rates. She has estimated that, based on her good credit rating, she could apply for any of the credit cards being offered.

Credit card A has a $33 annual fee and advertises the relatively low interest rate of 9.5%. A $5 fee is charged for each cash advance, plus the applicable interest charges.

Credit card B has no annual fee and advertises a 17.5% interest rate on purchases and cash advances.

Credit card C advertises an introductory promotional interest rate of 3.9% on cash advances and balance transfers for the first six months, if you make your minimum monthly payments on time. The regular annual interest rate is 18.50% on purchases and cash advances.

For all three credit cards, interest will not be assessed if the monthly statement amount is paid in full by the payment due date and no cash advances have been taken during the billing period. If the new balance is not paid in full, interest will be charged (1) on the outstanding balance from the statement closing date and (2) on future purchases from the day the purchases are posted to the account. On cash advance transactions, interest is always charged from the date the cash advance is taken.

Currently, Jane has a credit card with a major Canadian department store. For this card, D, there is an outstanding balance of $1000. Its annual interest rate is 27.5%. If she receives one of the other three cards, she would transfer the department store credit card balance to the new card.

### QUESTIONS

1. Jane maintains an average daily balance of $1500 for the first year, based solely on purchases and balance transfers. For each of the four credit cards,

   (a) calculate the interest charge and fees that she would have to pay over a twelve-month period;
   (b) determine the effective annual rate of interest over the first twelve-month period; and
   (c) decide which credit card she should choose.

**2.** If the introductory interest rate fell to 2.5% for credit card C, and the regular annual interest rate rose to 19.50% on purchases, what would be the effective annual rate of interest over the twelve-month period?

**3.** If you have a credit card, how do its rates and conditions compare with those of the cards described above?

# Case Study 10.2 Comparing Car Loans

» After reading consumer car guides and receiving advice from family and friends, Aysha has chosen the new car she wants to purchase. She now wants to research her financing options to choose the best way to pay for the car.

Aysha knows that with taxes, licence, delivery, and dealer preparation fees, her car will cost $17 850. She has saved $7500 toward the purchase price but must borrow the rest. She has narrowed her financing choices to three options: dealer financing, credit union financing, and bank financing.

(i) The car dealer has offered 48-month financing at 8.5% compounded monthly.

(ii) The credit union has offered 36-month financing at 9.0% compounded quarterly. It has also offered 48-month financing at 9.3% compounded quarterly.

(iii) The bank has offered 36-month financing at 8.8% compounded semi-annually. It has also offered 48-month financing at 9.1% compounded semi-annually.

Aysha desires the financing option that offers the best interest rate. However, she also wants to explore the financing options that allow her to pay off her car loan more quickly.

## QUESTIONS

**1.** Aysha wants to compare the 48-month car loan options offered by the car dealer, the credit union, and the bank.

**(a)** What is the effective annual rate of interest for each 48-month option?
**(b)** How much interest will Aysha save by choosing the best option as against the worst option?

**2.** Suppose Aysha wants to try to pay off her car loan within three years.

**(a)** What is the effective annual rate of interest for both of the 36-month options?
**(b)** How much interest will Aysha save by choosing the better option?

**3.** If you wanted to get a car loan today, what are the rates of interest for 36-month and 48-month terms? Are car dealers currently offering better interest rates than the banks or credit unions? If so, why?

## SUMMARY OF FORMULAS

**Formula 9.1A**
$$FV = PV(1 + i)^n$$
**Finding the future value of a sum of money when *n* is a fractional value using the exact method**

**Formula 9.1B**
$$PV = \frac{FV}{(1 + i)^n}$$
**Finding the present value (discounted value or proceeds) when *n* is a fractional value using the exact method**

**Formula 9.1C**
$$PV = FV(1 + i)^{-n}$$

**Formula 10.1**
$$f = (1 + i)^m - 1$$
**Finding the effective rate of interest *f* for a nominal annual rate compounded *m* times per year**

## GLOSSARY

**Effective rate of interest**   the annual rate of interest that yields the same amount of interest per year as a nominal rate compounded a number of times per year *(p. 405)*

**Equated date**   the date on which a single sum of money is equal to the sum of two or more dated sums of money *(p. 395)*

**Equivalent rates**   interest rates that accumulate a given principal to the same future value over the same period of time *(p. 411)*

## USEFUL INTERNET SITES

**mathforum.org/dr.math**
**The Rule of 70**   Visit the "Ask Dr. Math" site to read about how to use the Rule of 70 or ask other math-related questions.

**www.rate.net**
**Rate.net**   Rate.net tracks over 11 000 financial institutions in 175 markets nationwide. The site analyzes interest rate performance and financial stability.

**www.money.canoe.ca**
**Credit Card Rates**   To compare credit card rates and terms for major Canadian financial institutions and department stores, visit this (independent) Website and click on "Rates," then "Credit Cards."

## OBJECTIVES

**Upon completing this chapter, you will be able to do the following:**

1. Distinguish between types of annuities based on term, payment date, and conversion period.

2. Compute the future value (or accumulated value) FV for ordinary simple annuities.

3. Compute the present value (or discounted value) PV for ordinary simple annuities.

4. Compute the payment PMT for ordinary simple annuities.

5. Compute the number of periods N for ordinary simple annuities.

6. Compute the interest rate I/Y for ordinary simple annuities.

In many business situations, we have seen the use of simple and compound interest and their calculations involving present value and future value. In other situations, we pay or receive regular, equal amounts of money, possibly for payment of rent, insurance, car loans, student loans, and mortgages. We may also receive regular, equal amounts of money, such as wages, salaries, and pensions. These are all examples of annuities. The same principles apply to all of the examples above. Annuity formulas and calculations enable us to answer questions such as "How much money will I have in five years if I deposit $100 per month into a savings account?" and "If I make regular payments toward the purchase of a car, how much am I really paying for it?"

## INTRODUCTION

An annuity is a series of payments, usually of equal size, made at periodic time intervals. The word *annuity* implies yearly payments but the term applies to all periodic payment plans, the most frequent of which require annual, semi-annual, quarterly, or monthly payments. Practical applications of annuities are widely encountered in the finances of both businesses and individuals. Various types of annuities are identified based on the term of an annuity, the date of payment, and the length of the conversion period. In this chapter, we will deal with ordinary simple annuities, and calculate the future value, present value, payment amount, number of periods, or the interest rate.

# 11.1 INTRODUCTION TO ANNUITIES

## A. Basic concepts

An **annuity** is a series of payments, usually of equal size, made at periodic intervals. The length of time between the successive payments is called the **payment interval** or **payment period**. The length of time from the beginning of the first payment interval to the end of the last payment interval is called the **term of an annuity**. The size of each of the regular payments is the **periodic rent,** and the sum of the periodic payments in one year is the **annual rent**.

## B. Types of annuities

Several time variables affect annuities, and annuities are classified according to the time variable considered. The term of the annuity can be fixed or can be indefinite. Annuities are classified based on this differentiation.

**Annuities certain** are annuities for which the term is fixed, that is, for which both the beginning date and ending date are known. Typical examples of annuities certain include rental payments for real estate, lease payments on equipment, installment payments on loans, mortgage payments, and interest payments on bonds and debentures.

**Contingent annuities** are annuities for which the beginning date or the ending date or both are uncertain. Life insurance premiums and pension payments or payments from an RRSP converted into a life annuity are typical examples of contingent annuities. The ending date is unknown for these annuities since they terminate with the death of the recipient. Some contingent annuities are the result of clauses in wills, where the beginning date of periodic payments to a beneficiary is unknown, or of payments from a trust fund for the remaining life of a surviving spouse, since neither the beginning date nor the ending date is known.

A special type of annuity is the **perpetuity**, an annuity for which the payments continue forever. Perpetuities result when the size of the period rent is equal to or less than the periodic interest earned by a fund, such as a scholarship fund or an endowment fund to a university.

Variations in the date of payment are another way to classify annuities certain. If payments are made at the end of each payment period, we are dealing with an **ordinary annuity**. If, on the other hand, payments are made at the beginning of each payment period, we are dealing with an **annuity due**.

Typical examples of ordinary annuities are installment payments on loans, mortgage payments, and interest payments on bonds and debentures. Rent payments on real estate and lease payments on equipment rentals are examples of annuities due.

Deferring the first payment for a specified period of time gives rise to a **deferred annuity**. This type may be either an ordinary annuity or an annuity due, depending on whether the future payments are at the beginning or at the end of each payment interval.

A third time variable used to classify annuities is the length of the conversion period relative to the payment period. We distinguish between simple annuities and general annuities, depending on whether the conversion period coincides with the payment interval.

A **simple annuity** is an annuity in which the conversion period coincides with the payment interval. An example is when there are monthly payments on a loan for which the interest is compounded monthly. Since the compound interest period is the same as the payment period, this is a simple annuity, and P/Y and C/Y are equal.

A **general annuity** is an annuity in which the conversion period and the payment interval do not coincide. Typically, mortgages on homes are compounded semi-annually but repaid by monthly payments. Often, lending institutions offer the borrower the option of making weekly or bi-weekly payments. This is an example of a general annuity, since the conversion period is different from the payment period.

We will introduce ordinary simple annuities in this chapter. In Chapter 12, we will introduce ordinary general annuities. Other annuities, such as annuities due, deferred annuities, and perpetuities, will be introduced in Chapter 13.

**EXAMPLE 11.1A**

Classify each of the following annuities by

  (i) term;          (ii) date of payment;          (iii) conversion period.

  (a) Deposits of $150 earning interest at 12% compounded quarterly are made at the beginning of each quarter for four years.

**SOLUTION**

  (i) annuity certain (the term is fixed: four years)

  (ii) annuity due (payments are made at the beginning of each quarter)

  (iii) simple annuity (the quarterly conversion period equals the quarterly payment period)

  (b) Payments of $200 are made at the end of each month for five years. Interest is 9% compounded semi-annually.

**SOLUTION**

  (i) annuity certain (the term is fixed: five years)

  (ii) ordinary annuity (payments are made at the end of each month)

  (iii) general annuity (semi-annual conversion period does not match the monthly payment period)

(c) A fund of $10 000 is deposited in a trust account earning interest compounded annually. Starting five years from the date of deposit, the interest earned for the year is to be paid out as a scholarship.

**SOLUTION**

(i) perpetuity (the payments can go on forever)

(ii) deferred annuity (the first payment is deferred for five years)

(iii) simple annuity (the annual conversion period equals the annual interest period)

(d) In his will, Dr. Chu directed that part of his estate be invested in a trust fund earning interest compounded quarterly. His surviving wife was to be paid, for the remainder of her life, $2000 at the end of every three months starting three months after his death.

**SOLUTION**

(i) contingent annuity (both the starting date and the ending date are uncertain)

(ii) ordinary annuity (payments at the end of every three months)

(iii) simple annuity (the quarterly conversion period equals the quarterly payment period)

## EXERCISE 11.1

**A.** Classify each of the following by (a) term; (b) date of payment; (c) conversion period.

**1.** Payments of $50 are made at the beginning of each month for five years at 5% compounded semi-annually.

**2.** Deposits of $500 are made at the end of each quarter for nine years earning interest at 7% compounded quarterly.

**3.** A fund with an initial deposit of $50 000 is set up to provide annual scholarships to eligible business students in an amount not exceeding the annual interest earned by the fund. Scholarship payments are to begin three years from the date of deposit. Interest earned by the fund is compounded semi-annually.

**4.** The Saskatoon Board of Education introduced a long-term disability plan for its employees. The plan provides for monthly payments equal to 90% of regular salary starting one month after the beginning of the disability. Assume that the plan is subject to monthly compounding.

**5.** Gary invested $10 000 in an account paying interest compounded monthly with the provision that equal monthly payments be made to him from the account for fifteen years at the beginning of each month starting ten years from the date of deposit.

**6.** Ms. Baka set up a trust fund earning interest compounded semi-annually to provide equal monthly support payments for her surviving husband starting one month after her death.

# 11.2 ORDINARY SIMPLE ANNUITY—FINDING FUTURE VALUE FV

## A. Future value of a series of payments—basic computation

**EXAMPLE 11.2A**

Deposits of $2000, $4000, $5000, $1000, and $3000 were made at the end of each of five consecutive years respectively at 6% compounded annually. Find the future value just after the last deposit was made.

**SOLUTION**

The series of deposits can be represented on a time graph as shown:

To find the future value of the series of deposits, we need to determine the combined value of the five deposits, including interest, at the focal point five years from now. This can be done using Formula 9.1A, $FV = PV(1 + i)^n$. A graphical representation of the method and data is shown in Figure 11.1 below.

**FIGURE 11.1**    **Graphical Representation of Method and Data**

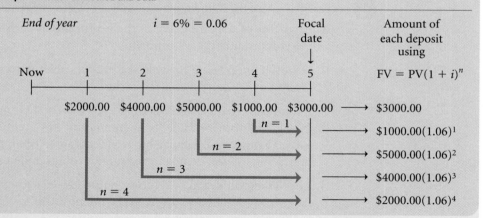

*Explanations regarding the amount of each deposit:*
The deposit of $3000 has just been made and has a value of $3000 at the focal date. The deposit of $1000 has been in for one year ($n = 1$) and has earned interest for one year at the focal date. Similarly, the deposit of $5000 has been in for two years ($n = 2$), the deposit of $4000 for three years ($n = 3$), and the deposit of $2000.00 for four years ($n = 4$).

The problem can now be solved by computing the future value of the individual deposits and adding.

| | | | | |
|---|---|---|---|---|
| *Deposit 5* | 3000.00 | | = | $3 000.00 |
| *Deposit 4* | $1000.00(1.06)^1 = 1000.00(1.06)$ | | = | 1 060.00 |
| *Deposit 3* | $5000.00(1.06)^2 = 5000.00(1.1236)$ | | = | 5 618.00 |
| *Deposit 2* | $4000.00(1.06)^3 = 4000.00(1.191016)$ | | = | 4 764.06 |
| *Deposit 1* | $2000.00(1.06)^4 = 2000.00(1.262477)$ | | = | 2 524.95 |
| | | TOTAL | = | $16 967.01 |

**EXAMPLE 11.2B**

Find the future value of five deposits of $3000 each made at the end of each of five consecutive years respectively at 6% compounded annually, just after the last deposit has been made.

**SOLUTION**

This example is basically the same as Example 11.2A except that all deposits are equal in size. The problem can be solved in the same way.

While the approach to solving the problem is fundamentally the same as in Example 11.2A, the fact that the deposits are *equal in size* permits a useful mathematical simplification. The equal deposit of $3000 can be taken out as a common factor and the individual compounding factors can be added. This method avoids computing the amount of each individual deposit. In other words, it avoids computing separately $3000.00(1)$, $3000.00(1.06)^1$, $3000.00(1.06)^2$, and so on.

**FIGURE 11.2**   **Graphical Representation of Method and Data**

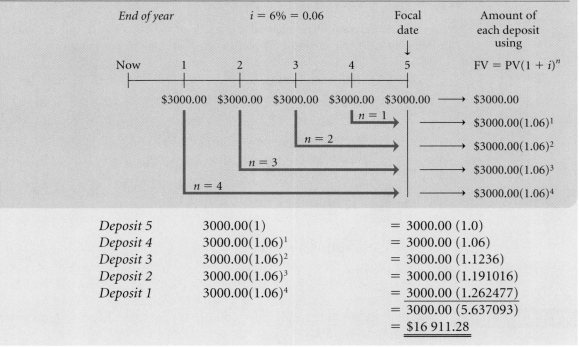

| | | | |
|---|---|---|---|
| *Deposit 5* | 3000.00(1) | | = 3000.00 (1.0) |
| *Deposit 4* | $3000.00(1.06)^1$ | | = 3000.00 (1.06) |
| *Deposit 3* | $3000.00(1.06)^2$ | | = 3000.00 (1.1236) |
| *Deposit 2* | $3000.00(1.06)^3$ | | = 3000.00 (1.191016) |
| *Deposit 1* | $3000.00(1.06)^4$ | | = 3000.00 (1.262477) |
| | | | = 3000.00 (5.637093) |
| | | | = $16 911.28 |

Since the deposits in Example 11.2B are equal in size and are made at the end of each period and the payment interval is the same as the compounding period (one year), the problem is an ordinary simple annuity. Finding the sum of the accumulated values of the individual payments at the end of the term of the annuity is defined as finding the **future value of an annuity**.

## B. Formula for finding the future value of an ordinary simple annuity

Because annuities are geometric progressions, the following formula has been developed for finding the accumulated value of this type of series of payments.

$$S_n = R\left[\frac{(1 + i)^n - 1}{i}\right]$$ ——— Formula 11.1 ——— future value of an ordinary simple annuity

where  $S_n$ = the future value (accumulated value) of an ordinary simple annuity;
  $R$ = the size of the periodic payment (rent);
   $i$ = the interest rate per conversion period;
   $n$ = the number of periodic payments (which for simple annuities is also the number of conversion periods).

The factor $\dfrac{(1 + i)^n - 1}{i}$ is called the **compounding** or **accumulation factor for annuities** or the **accumulated value of one dollar per period.**

---

**EXAMPLE 11.2C**

Find the accumulated value of quarterly payments of $50 made at the end of each quarter for ten years just after the last payment has been made if interest is 8% compounded quarterly.

**SOLUTION**

Since the payments are of equal size made at the end of each quarter and compounding is quarterly, the problem is an ordinary simple annuity.

$R = 50.00$; $I/Y = 8$; $P/Y, C/Y = 4$; $i = \dfrac{8\%}{4} = 2\% = 0.02$; $n = 10(4) = 40$

$S_n = 50.00\left[\dfrac{(1 + 0.02)^{40} - 1}{0.02}\right]$ ——————— substituting in Formula 11.1

$= 50.00\left(\dfrac{2.208040 - 1}{0.02}\right)$

$= 50.00\left(\dfrac{1.208040}{0.02}\right)$

$= 50.00(60.401983)$

$= \$3020.10$

---

**EXAMPLE 11.2D**

You deposit $10 at the end of each month for five years in an account paying 6% compounded monthly.

  (i) What will be the balance in your account at the end of the five-year term?

 (ii) How much of the balance will you have contributed?

(iii) How much is interest?

**SOLUTION**

(i) R = 10.00;  I/Y = 6;  P/Y = 12;  $i = \dfrac{6\%}{12} = 0.5\% = 0.005$;  $n = 60$

$$S_n = 10.00\left[\frac{(1 + i)^n - 1}{i}\right]$$

$$= 10.00\left[\frac{1.005^{60} - 1}{0.005}\right]$$

$$= 10.00\left[\frac{(1.348850 - 1)}{0.005}\right]$$

$$= 10.00(69.770031)$$

$$= \$697.70$$

(ii) Your contribution is $10 per month for 60 months, or 10.00(60) = $600.

(iii) Since your contribution is $600, the interest earned is 697.70 − 600.00 = $97.70.

## C. Restatement of the ordinary simple annuity formula

The algebraic symbols used in the ordinary simple annuity formula correspond to the calculator keys of four preprogrammed financial calculators. To make it easier to relate annuity formulas directly to the symbols used on financial calculator keys and in spreadsheet software such as Excel, we will make the following changes to restate this and upcoming annuity formulas:

**1.** Replace $A_n$ with $PV_n$ as the symbol for Present Value;

**2.** Replace $S_n$ with $FV_n$ as the symbol for Future Value;

**3.** Replace R with PMT as the symbol for Periodic Payment.

From now on

Formula 11.1, $S_n = R\left[\dfrac{(1 + i)^n - 1}{i}\right]$ will be presented as $FV_n = PMT\left[\dfrac{(1 + i)^n - 1}{i}\right]$

## D. Using preprogrammed financial calculators

In the same way that you can for compound interest calculations, you can use pre-programmed financial calculators to solve annuity problems efficiently by entering given values and retrieving the answer.

Specific function keys on preprogrammed financial calculators correspond to the five variables used in ordinary simple annuity calculations. Different models of financial calculators vary in their operation and labelling of the function keys. Appendix II, "Instructions and Tips for Three Preprogrammed Financial

Calculator Models," highlights the relevant variations for students using Texas Instruments' BAII Plus, Sharp's EL-733A, and Hewlett-Packard's 10BII calculators. The function keys used for the calculator models presented in Appendix II are shown in Table 11.1.

**Table 11.1 Financial Calculator Function Keys That Correspond to Variables Used in Ordinary Simple Annuity Calculations**

| Variable | Algebraic Symbol | Function Key | | |
|---|---|---|---|---|
| | | TI BAII+ | Sharp EL-733A | HP 10BII |
| The number of compounding periods | $n$ | N | $n$ | N |
| The periodic rate of interest[1] | $i$ | I/Y + C/Y | $i$ | I/YR + P/YR |
| The periodic annuity payment | PMT or R | PMT | PMT | PMT |
| The present value or principal | PV or $A_n$ | PV | PV | PV |
| The future value or maturity value | FV or $S_n$ | FV | FV | FV |

**Note:** The periodic rate of interest is entered as a percent and not as a decimal equivalent. For example, 8% is entered as "8" not ".08."

Instructions in this text are given for the Texas Instruments BAII Plus calculator. Refer to Appendix II for instructions for using the Sharp EL-733A and Hewlett-Packard 10BII calculators.

To begin an ordinary simple annuity calculation, previous data must be cleared. The following key sequence resets all entries to the defaults for each field: 2nd CLR TVM .

The number of payments per year must be determined. Enter this number as the P/Y . If the number of payments per year is specified as "monthly," follow the sequence 2nd P/Y 12 Enter 2nd QUIT . Substitute the number for the appropriate number of payments per year in each case. The most common frequencies are monthly, quarterly, semi-annually, or annually. Enter the given values in any order. Pressing CPT followed by the key representing the unknown variable then retrieves the value of the unknown variable.

**Note:** This assumes that the calculator is in the "END" mode. This is the default. To check, look at the upper right corner of the display screen. If no letters are shown in that corner, you are in the END mode. If the letters BGN are there, you must switch modes:

**2nd** **BGN** (**PMT** key)

**2nd** **SET** (END will now appear.)

**2nd** **QUIT** (Back to standard calculator—upper-right corner now blank.)

When performing an annuity calculation, usually only one of either the present value PV *or* the future value FV is involved. To avoid incorrect answers, the present value **PV** should be set to zero when determining the future value **FV** and vice versa. In addition, recall that the Texas Instruments BAII Plus calculator follows the established convention of treating cash inflows (cash received) as positive numbers and cash outflows (cash paid out) as negative numbers. Since periodic annuity payments are considered to be cash outflows, always enter the periodic payment as a negative number. Also, continue to always enter the present value as a negative number (if the present value is other than 0) to ensure your result has a positive value.

To solve Example 11.2D, in which PMT = 10.00, I/Y = 6; P/Y = 12, and $n$ = 60, use the following procedure.

| | Key in | Press | Display shows | |
|---|---|---|---|---|
| (Set P/Y, C/Y = 12) | 0 | PV | 0 | a precaution to avoid incorrect answers |
| | 10 | ± PMT | 10 | this enters the periodic payment PMT |
| | 6.0 | I/Y | 6.0 | this enters the interest rate per year |
| | 60 | N | 60 | this enters the number of payments $n$ |
| | CPT | FV | 697.700305 | this retrieves the wanted amount FV |

The future value is $697.70.

## E. Applications

**EXAMPLE 11.2E**

Jim set up a savings plan with Interior Trust whereby he deposits $300 at the end of each quarter for eight years. The amount in his account at that time will become a term deposit withdrawable after a further five years. Interest throughout the total time period is 5% compounded quarterly.

(i) How much will be in Jim's account just after he makes his last deposit?
(ii) What will be the balance of his account when he can withdraw the deposit?
(iii) How much of the total at the time of withdrawal did Jim contribute?
(iv) How much is the interest earned?

**SOLUTION**

As Figure 11.3 shows, problems of this type may be solved in stages. The first stage involves finding the future value of an *ordinary annuity*. This amount becomes the principal for the second stage, which involves finding the future value of a *single* sum of money invested for five years.

(i) $\text{PMT} = 300.00$; $\text{I/Y} = 5$; $\text{P/Y, C/Y} = 4$; $i = \dfrac{5\%}{4} = 1.25\% = 0.0125$;
$n = 8(4) = 32$

$$\text{FV}_1 = 300.00\left[\frac{(1.0125^{32} - 1)}{0.0125}\right] \quad \text{———— Formula 11.1}$$

$$= 300.00\left[\frac{(1.488131 - 1)}{0.0125}\right]$$

$$= 300.00(39.050441)$$

$$= \$11\ 715.13$$

(ii) $\text{PV} = \text{FV}_1 = 11\ 715.13$; $i = 0.0125$; $n = 5(4) = 20$
$$\text{FV}_2 = 11\ 715.13(1.0125)^{20} \quad \text{———————— Formula 9.1A}$$
$$= 11\ 715.13(1.282037)$$
$$= \$15\ 019.23$$

---

**FIGURE 11.3**    **Graphical Representation of Method and Data**

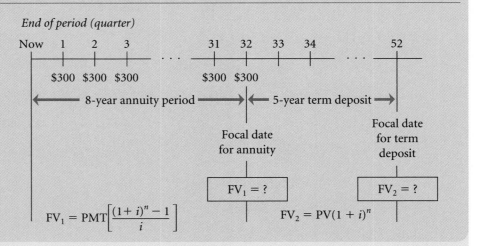

(iii) Jim's contribution $= 32(300.00) = \$9600.00$.

(iv) The amount of interest earned $= 15\ 019.23 - 9600.00 = \$5419.23$.

### Programmed Solution for Parts (i) and (ii)

(i) (Set P/Y, C/Y = 4) 0 [ PV ] 300 [ ± ] [ PMT ]

                              5.0 [ I/Y ] 32 [ N ] [ CPT ] [ FV ] [ 11715.13221 ]

(ii) 11 715.13221 [ ± ] [ PV ] 0 [ PMT ]

                              5.0 [ I/Y ] 20 [ N ] [ CPT ] [ FV ] [ 15019.23566 ]

**EXAMPLE 11.2F**

The Gordons saved for the purchase of their dream home by making deposits of $1000 per year for ten consecutive years in an account with Cooperative Trust in Saskatoon. The account earned interest at 5.75% compounded annually. At the end of the ten-year contribution period, the deposit was left for a further six years earning interest at 5.5% compounded semi-annually.

(i) What down payment were the Gordons able to make on their house?

(ii) How much of the down payment was interest?

**SOLUTION**

**STEP 1**

(i) Find the amount in the account at the end of the term of the ordinary annuity formed by the yearly deposits.

PMT $= 1000.00$; I/Y $= 5.75$; P/Y $= 1$; $i = 5.75\% = 0.0575$; $n = 10$

$$FV_1 = 1000.00\left[\frac{(1.0575^{10} - 1)}{0.0575}\right]$$

$$= 1000.00\left[\frac{1.749056 - 1}{0.0575}\right]$$

$$= 1000.00(13.027064)$$

$$= \$13\ 027.06$$

**STEP 2**

Then compute the accumulated value of $FV_1$ in six years.

PV $= FV_1 = 13\ 027.06$; I/Y $= 5.5$; P/Y $= 2$; $i = \dfrac{5.5\%}{2} = 2.75\% = 0.0275$; $n = 12$

$$FV_2 = 13\ 027.06(1.0275)^{12}$$

$$= 13\ 027.06(1.384784)$$

$$= \$18\ 039.66$$

The Gordons made a down payment of $18 039.66.

(ii) Since the Gordons contributed $(1000.00)(10) = \$10\ 000.00$, the amount of interest in the down payment is $8039.66.

**Programmed Solution for Part (i)**

(Set P/Y, C/Y = 1) 0 [PV] 1000 [±] [PMT]

5.75 [I/Y] 10 [N] [CPT] [FV] [13027.06408]

(Set P/Y, C/Y = 2) 13 027.06408 [±] [PV]

0 [PMT] 5.5 [I/Y] 12 [N] [CPT] [FV] [18039.66698]

**EXAMPLE 11.2G**

Marisa has contributed $1500 per year for the last twelve years into an RRSP deposit account with her bank in Windsor. Interest earned by these deposits was 4.5% compounded annually for the first eight years and 5.5% compounded annually for the last four years. Five years after the last deposit, she converted her

RRSP into a registered retirement income fund (RRIF). How much was the beginning balance in the RRIF if interest for those five years remained at 5.5%?

**SOLUTION**

As Figure 11.4 shows, the problem may be divided into two simple annuities. The first simple annuity covers the deposits for the first eight years; the second simple annuity covers the next four payments.

**STEP 1**

The focal date for the first annuity is at the end of Year 8 (focal date 1). The accumulated value (future value) of this simple annuity is computed using Formula 11.1.

$$FV_1 = 1500.00\left[\frac{(1.045^8 - 1)}{0.045}\right]$$
$$= 1500.00\left[\frac{1.422101 - 1}{0.045}\right]$$
$$= 1500.00(9.380014)$$
$$= \$14070.02$$

**STEP 2**

$FV_1$ then accumulates for nine years (to the end of Year 17) at 5.5% to obtain $FV_4$ at the focal date for the beginning balance in the RRIF (focal date 3).

$$FV_4 = 14\,070.02(1.055)^9$$
$$= 14\,070.02(1.619094)$$
$$= \$22\,780.69$$

---

**FIGURE 11.4**    **Graphical Representation of Method and Data**

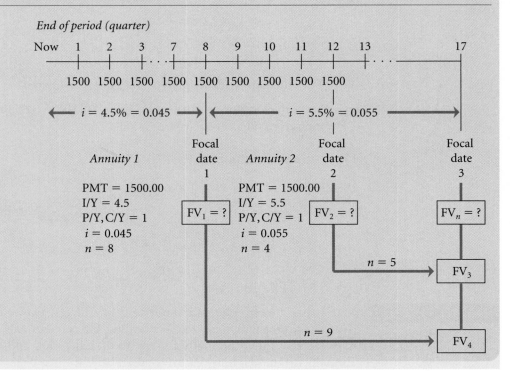

**STEP 3**  The focal date for the second simple annuity is at the end of Year 12 (focal date 2).

$$FV_2 = 1500.00\left[\frac{(1.055^4 - 1)}{0.055}\right]$$

$$= 1500.00\left[\frac{1.238825 - 1}{0.055}\right]$$

$$= 1500.00(4.342266)$$

$$= \$6513.40$$

**STEP 4**  $FV_2$ then accumulates for five years (to the end of Year 17) to obtain $FV_3$ at focal date 3.

$$FV_3 = 6513.40(1.055)^5$$

$$= 6513.40(1.306960)$$

$$= \$8512.75$$

**STEP 5**  The beginning balance $FV_n$ in the RRIF is then obtained by adding $FV_3$ and $FV_4$.

$$FV_n = 8512.75 + 22\,780.69$$

$$= \$31\,293.44$$

### Programmed Solution

$FV_1$
(Set P/Y, C/Y = 1) 0 [ PV ] 1500 [ ± ] [ PMT ]

4.5 [ I/Y ] 8 [ N ] [ CPT ] [ FV ] [ 14070.02043 ]

$FV_4$
14 070.02043 [ ± ] [ PV ] 0 [ PMT ]

5.5 [ I/Y ] 9 [ N ] [ CPT ] [ FV ] [ 22780.6895 ] [ STO1 ]

$FV_2$
0 [ PV ] 1500 [ ± ] [ PMT ] 5.5 [ I/Y ] 4 [ N ] [ CPT ] [ FV ] [ 6513.399563 ]

$FV_3$
6513.399563 [ ± ] [ PV ] 0 [ PMT ]

5.5 [ I/Y ] 5 [ N ] [ CPT ] [ FV ] [ 8512.752734 ] [ STO2 ]

[ RCL ] 1 + [ RCL ] 2 = 31 293.44

$$FV_n = FV_3 + FV_4 = 8512.75 + 22\,780.69 = \$31\,293.44$$

## EXERCISE 11.2

If you choose, you can use Excel's *Future Value (FV)* function to answer the questions indicated below. Refer to **FV** on the Spreadsheet Template Disk to learn how to use this Excel function.

**A.** Find the future value of the ordinary simple annuity for each of the following six series of payments.

|  | Periodic Payment | Payment Interval | Term | Interest Rate | Conversion Period |
|---|---|---|---|---|---|
| 1. | $1500 | 1 quarter | $7\frac{1}{2}$ years | 5% | quarterly |
| 2. | 20 | 1 month | 6.75 years | 6 | monthly |
| 3. | 700 | 6 months | 20 years | 7 | semi-annually |
| 4. | 10 | 1 month | 15 years | 9 | monthly |
| 5. | 320 | 3 months | 8 years, 9 months | 10.4 | quarterly |
| 6. | 2000 | $\frac{1}{2}$ year | 11 years, 6 months | 8.8 | semi-annually |

**B.** Answer each of the following questions.

1. Find the accumulated value of payments of $200 made at the end of every three months for twelve years if money is worth 5% compounded quarterly.

Reference Example 11.2C

2. What will deposits of $60 made at the end of each month amount to after six years if interest is 4.8% compounded monthly?

3. How much interest is included in the future value of an ordinary simple annuity of $1500 paid every six months at 7% compounded semi-annually if the term of the annuity is fifteen years?

4. Jane Allison made ordinary annuity payments of $15 per month for sixteen years earning 9% compounded monthly. How much interest is included in the future value of the annuity?

5. Saving for his retirement 25 years from now, Jimmy Olsen set up a savings plan whereby he will deposit $25 at the end of each month for the next 15 years. Interest is 3.6% compounded monthly.
   (a) How much money will be in Mr. Olsen's account on the date of his retirement?
   (b) How much will Mr. Olsen contribute?
   (c) How much is interest?     Reference Example 11.2E

6. Mr. and Mrs. Wolf have each contributed $1000 per year for the last ten years into RRSP accounts earning 6% compounded annually. Suppose they leave their accumulated contributions for another five years in the RRSP at the same rate of interest.
   (a) How much will Mr. and Mrs. Wolf have in total in their RRSP accounts?
   (b) How much did the Wolfs contribute?
   (c) How much will be interest?

7. Cam saved $250 each month for the last five years while he was working. Since he has now gone back to school, his income is lower and he cannot

continue to save this amount during the time he is studying. He plans to continue with his studies for four years and not withdraw any money from his savings account. Money is worth 4.5% compounded monthly.

(a) How much will Cam have in total in his savings account?

(b) How much did he contribute?

(c) How much will be interest?

8. Scott has saved $560 per quarter for the last three years in a savings account earning 5.20% compounded quarterly. He plans to leave the accumulated savings for seven years in the savings account at the same rate of interest.

(a) How much will Scott have in total in his savings account?

(b) How much did he contribute?

(c) How much will be interest?

9. Ms. Pitt has made quarterly payments of $1375 at the end of each quarter into an RRSP for the last seven years earning interest at 7% compounded quarterly. If she leaves the accumulated money in the RRSP for another three years at 8% compounded semi-annually, how much will she be able to transfer at the end of the three years into a registered retirement income fund?

*Reference Example 11.2G*

10. For the last six years Joe Borelli has made deposits of $300 at the end of every six months earning interest at 5% compounded semi-annually. If he leaves the accumulated balance in an account earning 6% compounded quarterly, what will the balance be in Joe's account at the end of another ten years?

# 11.3 ORDINARY SIMPLE ANNUITY—FINDING PRESENT VALUE PV

## A. Present value of series of payments—basic computation

**EXAMPLE 11.3A**  Find the single sum of money whose value now is equivalent to payments of $2000, $4000, $5000, $1000, and $3000 made at the end of each of five consecutive years respectively at 6% compounded annually.

**SOLUTION**  The series of payments can be represented on a time graph.

*End of period (year)*                                    $i = 6\% = 0.06$

| Now | 1 | 2 | 3 | 4 | 5 |
|---|---|---|---|---|---|
| | $2000.00 | $4000.00 | $5000.00 | $1000.00 | $3000.00 |

To find the present value of the series of payments, we need to determine the combined present value of the five payments at the focal point "now." This can be done using Formula 9.1C, $PV = FV(1 + i)^{-n}$. A graphical representation of the method and data is shown in Figure 11.5.

The solution to the problem can be completed by computing the present value of the individual payments and adding.

FIGURE 11.5    **Graphical Representation of Method and Data**

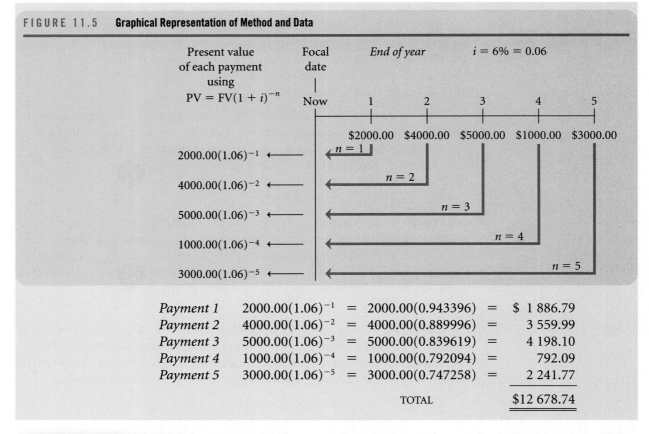

| | | | | |
|---|---|---|---|---|
| *Payment 1* | $2000.00(1.06)^{-1}$ | $= 2000.00(0.943396)$ | $=$ | $\$ 1\ 886.79$ |
| *Payment 2* | $4000.00(1.06)^{-2}$ | $= 4000.00(0.889996)$ | $=$ | $3\ 559.99$ |
| *Payment 3* | $5000.00(1.06)^{-3}$ | $= 5000.00(0.839619)$ | $=$ | $4\ 198.10$ |
| *Payment 4* | $1000.00(1.06)^{-4}$ | $= 1000.00(0.792094)$ | $=$ | $792.09$ |
| *Payment 5* | $3000.00(1.06)^{-5}$ | $= 3000.00(0.747258)$ | $=$ | $2\ 241.77$ |
| | | | TOTAL | $\underline{\underline{\$12\ 678.74}}$ |

**EXAMPLE 11.3B**    Find the present value of five payments of $3000 made at the end of each of five consecutive years respectively if money is worth 6% compounded annually.

**SOLUTION**    This example is basically the same as Example 11.3A except that all payments are equal in size.

FIGURE 11.6    **Graphical Representation of Method and Data**

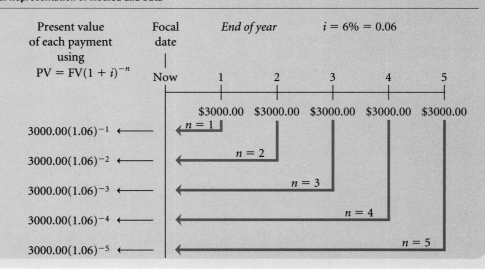

While the approach to solving the problem is fundamentally the same as in Example 11.3A, the fact that the payments are equal in size permits the same mathematical simplification used for Example 11.2B. The equal payment of $3000 can be taken out as a common factor and the individual discount factors can be added.

*Payment 1*    $3000.00(1.06)^{-1}$ = $3000.00 (0.943396)$

*Payment 2*    $3000.00(1.06)^{-2}$ = $3000.00 (0.889996)$

*Payment 3*    $3000.00(1.06)^{-3}$ = $3000.00 (0.839619)$

*Payment 4*    $3000.00(1.06)^{-4}$ = $3000.00 (0.792094)$

*Payment 5*    $3000.00(1.06)^{-5}$ = $3000.00 (0.747258)$

                                           = $3000.00 (4.212363)$

                                           = $\$12\ 637.09$

Since the payments in Example 11.3B are equal in size and are made at the end of each period, and the payment period is the same as the compounding period (one year), the problem is an ordinary simple annuity. Finding the sum of the present values of the individual payments at the beginning of the term of an annuity is defined as finding the present value of an annuity. It is useful to carry the mathematical simplification beyond simply taking out the common factor 3000.00.

## B. Formula for finding the present value of an ordinary simple annuity

Because annuities are geometric progressions, the following formula for finding the present value of an ordinary simple annuity has been developed.

$$A_n = R\left[\frac{1 - (1 + i)^{-n}}{i}\right]$$ ——— Formula 11.2 ——— present value of an ordinary simple annuity

where    $A_n$ = the present value (discounted value) of an ordinary simple annuity;

        $R$ = the size of the periodic payment (rent);

        $i$ = the interest rate per conversion period;

       $n$ = the number of periodic payments (which for simple annuities equals the number of conversion periods).

The factor $\dfrac{1 - (1 + i)^{-n}}{i}$ is called the present value factor or discount factor for annuities or the discounted value of one dollar per period.

**EXAMPLE 11.3C**

Find the present value at the beginning of the first payment period of payments of $50 made at the end of each quarter for ten years, if interest is 8% compounded quarterly.

**SOLUTION**

Because the payments are of equal size made at the end of each quarter and compounding is quarterly, the problem is an ordinary simple annuity. Since the focal date is the beginning of the term of the annuity, the formula for finding the present value of an ordinary simple annuity applies.

$$R = 50.00; \quad I/Y = 8; \quad P/Y, C/Y = 4; \quad i = \frac{8\%}{4} = 0.02; \quad n = 10(4) = 40$$

$$A_n = 50.00\left[\frac{1 - (1 + 0.02)^{-40}}{0.02}\right] \quad\text{——— substituting in Formula 11.2}$$

$$= 50.00\left[\frac{1 - 0.452890}{0.02}\right]$$

$$= 50.00\left[\frac{0.547110}{0.02}\right]$$

$$= 50.00(27.355480)$$

$$= \$1367.77$$

**EXAMPLE 11.3D**

Suppose you want to withdraw $100 at the end of each month for five years from an account paying 4.5% compounded monthly.

   (i) How much must you have on deposit at the beginning of the month in which the first withdrawal is made at the end of the month?

   (ii) How much will you receive in total?

   (iii) How much of what you will receive is interest?

**SOLUTION**

(i) $R = 100.00; \quad I/Y = 4.5; \quad P/Y, C/Y = 12; \quad i = \frac{4.5\%}{12} = 0.375\% = 0.00375; \quad n = 60$

$$A_n = R\left[\frac{1 - (1 + i)^{-n}}{i}\right]$$

$$= 100.00\left[\frac{1 - (1.00375)^{-60}}{0.00375}\right]$$

$$= 100.00\left[\frac{(1 - 0.798852)}{0.00375}\right]$$

$$= 100.00\left(\frac{0.201148}{0.00375}\right)$$

$$= 100(53.639381)$$

$$= \$5363.94$$

(ii) Total receipts will be $100 per month for 60 months or $6000.

(iii) Since the initial balance must be $5363.94, the interest received will be $6000.00 - 5363.94 = \$636.06$.

## C. Restatement of the ordinary simple annuity formula

To make it easier to relate annuity formulas directly to the symbols used on financial calculator keys and in spreadsheet software such as Excel, we will make the changes noted on page 439 to restate Formula 11.2. From now on

$$\text{Formula 11.2,} \quad A_n = R\left[\frac{1 - (1 + i)^{-n}}{i}\right], \text{ will be presented as}$$

$$PV_n = PMT\left[\frac{1 - (1 + i)^{-n}}{i}\right]$$

## D. Present value using preprogrammed financial calculators

 Refer to Appendix II for instructions for using the Sharp EL-733A and Hewlett-Packard 10B calculators to perform annuity calculations. The instructions given in this text are for the Texas Instruments BAII Plus calculator.

To find the present value of the ordinary simple annuity in Example 11.3D, in which R or PMT = 100.00, I/Y = 4.5, P/Y, C/Y = 12, and $n$ = 60, proceed as follows.

| | Key in | Press | Display shows | |
|---|---|---|---|---|
| (Set P/Y, C/Y = 12) | 0 | FV | 0 | —————— a precaution |
| | 100 | ± PMT | 100 | |
| | 4.5 | I/Y | 4.5 | |
| | 60 | N | 60 | |
| | CPT | PV | 5363.938035 | —— pressing the PV key retrieves the unknown present value $PV_n$ |

You must have $5363.94 on deposit.

## E. Applications

When buying a home or vehicle, most people do not have enough money saved to pay the entire price. However, a small initial payment, called a **down payment**, is often accepted in the meantime. A mortgage loan from a financial institution is needed to supply the balance of the purchase price. The larger the down payment, the lesser the amount that needs to be borrowed. Based on the amount borrowed, the rate of interest, and the time to repay, the payments are determined. The amount of the loan is the *present value of the future periodic payments*.

The *cash value* is the price of the property at the date of purchase and represents the dated value of all payments at that date.

CASH VALUE = DOWN PAYMENT + PRESENT VALUE OF THE PERIODIC PAYMENTS

**EXAMPLE 11.3E**

Mr. and Mrs. Hong bought a vacation property, paying $3000 as a down payment and making further payments of $1000 every six months for twelve years. If interest is 7% compounded semi-annually, what was the cash value of the property?

**SOLUTION**

Since the first ongoing payment is due at the end of the first six-month period and compounding is semi-annual, the present value of the periodic payments is the present value of an ordinary simple annuity.

$$PMT = 1000.00; \ I/Y = 7; \ P/Y, C/Y = 2; \ i = \frac{7\%}{2} = 3.5\% = 0.035; \ n = 12(2) = 24$$

$$
\begin{aligned}
PV_n &= 1000.00\left[\frac{(1 - 1.035^{-24})}{0.035}\right] \\
&= 1000.00\left[\frac{(1 - 0.437957)}{0.035}\right] \\
&= 1000.00\left(\frac{0.562043}{0.035}\right) \\
&= 1000.00(16.058368) \\
&= \$16\ 058.37
\end{aligned}
$$

**Programmed Solution**

(Set P/Y, C/Y = 2) 0 [ FV ] 1000 [ ± ] [ PMT ]

7.0 [ I/Y ] 24 [ N ] [ CPT ] [ PV ] [ 16058.3676 ]

The cash value = 3000.00 + 16 058.37 = $19 058.37.

**EXAMPLE 11.3F**

Armand Rice expects to retire in seven years and would like to receive $500 per month for ten years starting at the end of the first month after his retirement. To achieve this goal, he deposited part of the proceeds of $50 000 from the sale of a property into a fund earning 10.5% compounded monthly.

(i) How much must be in the fund at the date of his retirement?

(ii) How much of the proceeds did he deposit in the fund?

(iii) How much does he expect to receive from the fund?

(iv) How much of what he will receive is interest?

| SOLUTION | As Figure 11.7 shows, problems of this type should be solved in stages. The first step involves finding the present value of an annuity. This sum of money becomes the future amount for the second step, which involves finding the present value of that future amount at the date of deposit. |

FIGURE 11.7    **Graphical Representation of Method and Data**

*End of period (month)* I/Y = 10.5;  P/Y, C/Y= 12;  $i = \dfrac{10.5\%}{12} = 0.875\% = 0.00875$

(i)  PMT = 500.00;  I/Y = 10.5;  P/Y, C/Y = 12;  $i = \dfrac{10.5\%}{12} = 0.875\% = 0.00875$;  $n=120$

$$PV_n = 500.00\left[\frac{(1 - 1.00875^{-120})}{0.00875}\right]$$

$$PV_n = 500.00\left[\frac{(1 - 0.35154)}{0.00875}\right]$$

$$= 500.00(74.109758)$$

$$= \$37\ 054.88$$

(ii)   FV = $PV_n$ = 37 054.88;  $i = 0.00875$;  $n = 84$

$$PV = 37\ 054.88(1.00875)^{-84}$$
$$= 37\ 054.88(0.481041)$$
$$= \$17\ 824.91$$

(iii)  He expects to receive 500.00(120) = \$60 000.00.

(iv)  Interest received will be 60 000.00 − 17 824.91 = \$42 175.09.

**Programmed Solution for Parts (i) and (ii)**

(i) (Set P/Y, C/Y = 12) 0 [ FV ] 500 [ ± ] [ PMT ]

10.5 [ I/Y ] 120 [ N ] [ CPT ] [ PV ] [ 37054.87916 ]

(ii) 37 054.87916 [ FV ] 0 [ PMT ]

10.5 [ I/Y ] 84 [ N ] [ CPT ] [ PV ] [ −17824.9119 ]

---

**EXAMPLE 11.3G**

Sheila Davidson borrowed money from her credit union and agreed to repay the loan in blended monthly payments of $161.75 over a four-year period. Interest on the loan was 9% compounded monthly.

(i) How much did she borrow?

(ii) If she missed the first eleven payments, how much would she have to pay at the end of the first year to bring her payments up to date?

(iii) If the credit union demanded payment in full after one year, how much money would Sheila Davidson need?

(iv) If the loan is paid off after one year, what would have been its total cost?

(v) How much of the total loan cost is additional interest paid on the missed payments?

**SOLUTION**

(i) The amount borrowed is the present value (or discounted value) of the 48 payments, as the time diagram shows.

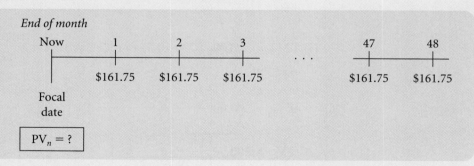

$$\text{PMT} = 161.75; \ \text{I/Y} = 9; \ \text{P/Y, C/Y} = 12; \ i = \frac{9\%}{12} = 0.75\% = 0.0075;$$

$$n = 4(12) = 48$$

$$\text{PV}_n = 161.75\left[\frac{(1 - 1.0075^{-48})}{0.0075}\right] \quad \text{——— using Formula 11.2}$$

$$= 161.75\left[\frac{1 - 0.698614}{0.0075}\right]$$

$$= 161.75(40.184782)$$

$$= \$6499.89$$

**Programmed Solution**

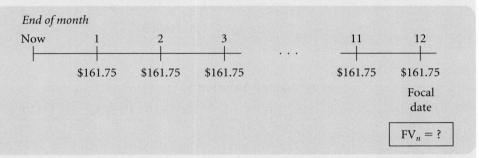

(Set P/Y, C/Y = 12) 0 [ FV ] 161.75 [ ± ] [ PMT ]

9.0 [ I/Y ] 48 [ N ] [ CPT ] [ PV ] [ 6499.88847 ]

(ii) As the diagram below shows, Sheila Davidson must pay the accumulated value of the first twelve payments to bring her payments up to date after one year.

*End of month*

Now    1       2       3        . . .      11      12
├──────┼───────┼───────┼──────────────────┼───────┼
     $161.75  $161.75  $161.75            $161.75  $161.75

                                                   Focal
                                                   date

                                                   $FV_n = ?$

$$PMT = 161.75; \quad i = 0.0075; \quad n = 12$$

$$FV_n = 161.75\left[\frac{(1.0075^{12} - 1)}{0.0075}\right] \quad\text{——— using Formula 11.1}$$

$$= 161.75\left[\frac{1.093807 - 1}{0.0075}\right]$$

$$= 161.75(12.507586)$$

$$= \$2023.10$$

**Programmed Solution**

0 [ PV ] 161.75 [ ± ] [ PMT ] 9.0 [ I/Y ] 12 [ N ] [ CPT ] [ FV ] [ 2023.102093 ]

(iii) The sum of money required to pay off the loan in full is the sum of the accumulated values of the first 12 payments plus the discounted values of the remaining 36 payments.

*End of month*

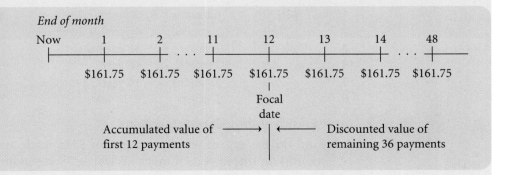

Now    1       2      11      12      13      14       48
├──────┼───────┼── . . . ──┼───────┼───────┼───── . . . ──┤
     $161.75  $161.75  $161.75  $161.75  $161.75  $161.75  $161.75
                                   │
                                 Focal
                                 date

Accumulated value of ──→ │ ←── Discounted value of
first 12 payments                 remaining 36 payments

The accumulated value of the first 12 payments, as computed in part (ii) above, is $2023.10. The discounted value of the remaining payments is found using Formula 11.2.

$$PMT = 161.75; \quad i = 0.0075; \quad n = 36$$

$$PV_n = 161.75\left[\frac{(1 - 1.0075^{-36})}{0.0075}\right]$$

$$= 161.75\left[\frac{1 - 0.764149}{0.0075}\right]$$

$$= 161.75(31.446805)$$

$$= \$5086.52$$

**Programmed Solution**

0 [FV] 161.75 [±] [PMT] 9.0 [I/Y] 36 [N] [CPT] [PV] [5086.520749]

The amount of money needed is 5086.52 + 2023.10 = $7109.62.

(iv) The total cost of the loan if paid off after one year is 7109.62 − 6499.89 = $609.73.

(v) To bring the payments up to date, $2023.10 is needed. Since the normal amount paid during the first year would have been 161.75(12) = $1941.00, the additional interest paid is 2023.10 − 1941.00 = $82.10.

# EXERCISE 11.3

**EXCEL NOTES**

If you choose, you can use **Excel's Present Value (PV)** function to answer the questions indicated below. Refer to **PV** on the Spreadsheet Template Disk to learn how to use this Excel function.

**A.** Determine the present value of the ordinary simple annuity for each of the following series of payments.

|    | Periodic Payment | Payment Interval | Term | Interest Rate | Compounding Period |
|----|------------------|------------------|------|---------------|--------------------|
| 1. | $1600 | 6 months | $3\frac{1}{2}$ years | 8.5% | semi-annually |
| 2. | 700 | 1 quarter | 4 years, 9 months | 5 | quarterly |
| 3. | 4000 | 1 year | 12 years | 7.5 | annually |
| 4. | 45 | 1 month | 18 years | 6.6 | monthly |
| 5. | 250 | 3 months | 14 years, 3 months | 4.4 | quarterly |
| 6. | 80 | 1 month | 9.25 years | 7.2 | monthly |

**B.** Answer each of the following questions.

1. Find the present value of payments of $375 made at the end of every six months for fifteen years if money is worth 7% compounded semi-annually.

2. What is the discounted value of payments of $60 made at the end of each month for nine years if interest is 4.5% compounded monthly?

3. You want to receive $600 at the end of every three months for five years. Interest is 7.6% compounded quarterly.
   (a) How much would you have to deposit at the beginning of the five-year period?
   (b) How much of what you receive is interest?

4. An installment contract for the purchase of a car requires payments of $252.17 at the end of each month for the next three years. Suppose interest is 8.4% p.a. compounded monthly.
   (a) What is the amount financed?
   (b) How much is the interest cost?

5. For home entertainment equipment, Ted paid $400 down and signed an installment contract that required payments of $69.33 at the end of each month for three years. Suppose interest is 10.8% compounded monthly.
   (a) What was the cash price of the equipment?
   (b) How much was the cost of financing?

6. Elynor bought a vacation property for $2500 down and quarterly mortgage payments of $550.41 at the end of each quarter for five years. Interest is 8% compounded quarterly.
   (a) What was the purchase price of the property?
   (b) How much interest will Elynor pay?

7. Ed intends to retire in eight years. To supplement his pension he would like to receive $450 every three months for fifteen years. If he is to receive the first payment three months after his retirement and interest is 5% p.a. compounded quarterly, how much must he invest today to achieve his goal? Reference Example 11.3F

8. Planning for their son's college education, Vivien and Adrian Marsh opened an account paying 6.3% compounded monthly. If ordinary annuity payments of $200 per month are to be paid out of the account for three years starting seven years from now, how much did the Marshes deposit?

9. Joel and Jacquie each have a savings account that they will deposit money into today. From his account, Joel is planning to withdraw $50 at the end of each month for the next five years, starting one month from today. From her account, Jacquie is planning to wait three years, then withdraw $50 per month for the next five years. If the savings accounts pay interest at 3.6% compounded monthly, who needs to deposit more today and by how much?

10. Diane and Mike are planning to purchase a new plasma TV. They are debating whether it is better to pay $150 at the end of each month for eighteen months, starting now, or to take advantage of the store's offer of no payment for one year. They would then pay $180 at the end of each of eighteen months after the first payment. Which option results in the lower cost to purchase the TV if the interest rate on the loan is 13.56% compounded monthly?

11. Kimiko signed a mortgage requiring payments of $234.60 at the end of every month for six years at 7.2% compounded monthly.
    (a) How much was the original mortgage balance?
    (b) If Kimiko missed the first five payments, how much would she have to pay after six months to bring the mortgage payments up to date?
    (c) How much would Kimiko have to pay after six months to pay off the mortgage?
    (d) If the mortgage were paid off after six months, what would the total interest cost be?
    (e) How much of the total interest cost is additional interest because of the missed payments? *Reference Example 11.3G*

12. Field Construction agreed to lease payments of $642.79 on construction equipment to be made at the end of each month for three years. Financing is at 9% compounded monthly.
    (a) What is the value of the original lease contract?
    (b) If, due to delays, the first eight payments were deferred, how much money would be needed after nine months to bring the lease payments up to date?
    (c) How much money would be required to pay off the lease after nine months?
    (d) If the lease were paid off after nine months, what would the total interest be?
    (e) How much of the total interest would be due to deferring the first eight payments?

## » BUSINESS MATH NEWS BOX

### Get Rich, DRIP by DRIP

A lot of investors don't realize it, but if they DRIPped, they could find themselves awash in cash years down the road.

DRIPs—dividend reinvestment plans—enable you to take a particular corporation's dividends and use the money to buy more of its stock. If that wasn't brilliant enough, investors typically don't have to pay a commission on the reinvested dividends, unlike when they make their initial share purchase.

When the company's dividends are paid out, the proceeds are immediately used to buy shares in the company. This eliminates the temptation to try to time the market.

Lou Caci, an investment executive at ScotiaMcLeod in Winnipeg, says some companies will allow you to buy their shares through a DRIP at a discount of between 3% and 5% from the current market price. If, for example, your dividend comes in and the stock is trading at $20, you may be able to purchase shares for as little as $19 each. "It's kind of like a member's privilege. The deal is only available to shareholders," he says.

So if you decide you'd like to dip into a DRIP, just how much money will you have to reinvest in your favourite stocks? Dividends tend to average between 1% and 3% per year of the value of a stock, with blue-chip companies typically sitting at the upper end of the range. It might not seem like much in the short term, but over the long run the financial benefits can be substantial.

*Source:* "Get Rich, DRIP by DRIP: Enjoy Them While They Last," Geoff Kirbyson, *Winnipeg Free Press*, June 26, 2006, p. A.29. Edited excerpt reprinted with permission.

**QUESTIONS**

1. You purchase 1000 shares of a stock each year for five years. Assume that in the first year the stock price is $20 per share and the shares increase in price by 1% per year.

 a. What is the value of your investment in five years?
 b. If the same company provides annual dividends equal to 3% of stock price, calculate the amount of dividends that an investor will attain over this five-year period.
 c. If a company provided a DRIP that allows investors to attain a discount of 5% on the stock price, calculate the value of the investment after five years.

# 11.4 ORDINARY SIMPLE ANNUITIES—FINDING THE PERIODIC PAYMENT PMT

## A. Finding the periodic payment PMT when the future value of an annuity is known

If the future value of an annuity $FV_n$, the number of conversion periods $n$, and the conversion rate $i$ are known, you can find the periodic payment PMT by substituting the given values in the appropriate future value formula.

For ordinary simple annuities, use Formula 11.1.

$$FV_n = PMT \left[ \frac{(1 + i)^n - 1}{i} \right]$$ ———————— **Formula 11.1**

When using a preprogrammed financial calculator, you can find PMT by entering the five known values (FV, N, I/Y, P/Y, and C/Y) and pressing CPT PMT.

Recall that the PMT amount will be negative since payments are considered to be cash outflows.

**EXAMPLE 11.4A**

What deposit made at the end of each quarter will accumulate to $10 000 in four years at 4% compounded quarterly?

**SOLUTION**

$FV_n = 10\ 000.00$; $I/Y = 4$; $P/Y, C/Y = 4$; $i = \dfrac{4\%}{4} = 1.0\% = 0.01$; $n = 16$

$10\ 000.00 = PMT \left( \dfrac{1.01^{16} - 1}{0.01} \right)$ ———————— substituting in Formula 11.1

$10\ 000.00 = PMT \left( \dfrac{1.172579 - 1}{0.01} \right)$

$10\ 000.00 = PMT(17.25786)$

$PMT = \dfrac{10\ 000.00}{17.25786}$

$PMT = \$579.45$

As we have emphasized throughout this book, understanding how to rearrange terms in a formula is a very important skill. By knowing how to do this, you avoid having to memorize equivalent forms of the same formula.

When using a scientific calculator, you can find PMT by first rearranging the terms of the future value formulas as shown below. Then substitute the three known values (FV, $n$, and $i$) into the rearranged formula and use the calculator to solve for PMT.

$$FV_n = PMT \left[ \frac{(1 + i)^n - 1}{i} \right]$$ ———— Formula 11.1

$$PMT = \frac{FV_n}{\left[ \dfrac{(1 + i)^n - 1}{i} \right]}$$ ———— divide both sides by $\left[ \dfrac{(1 + i)^n - 1}{i} \right]$

$$PMT = \frac{FV_n \, i}{(1 + i)^n - 1}$$ ———— dividing by a fraction is the same as inverting the fraction and multiplying

$$FV_n = 10\,000.00; \quad i = 0.01; \quad n = 16$$

$$PMT = \frac{10\,000.00(0.01)}{1.01^{16} - 1}$$ ———— substituting in rearranged Formula 11.1

$$PMT = \$579.45$$

---

**EXAMPLE 11.4B**

If you want to have $5000 on deposit in your bank account in three years, how much must you deposit at the end of each month if interest is 4.5% compounded monthly?

**SOLUTION**

$$FV_n = 5000.00; \quad I/Y = 4.5; \quad P/Y, C/Y = 12; \quad i = 0.375\%; \quad n = 36$$

(Set P/Y = 12) | 2nd | (CLR TVM) 0 | PV | 5000 | FV |

4.5 | I/Y | 36 | N | | CPT | | PMT | −129.984622

The monthly deposit required is $129.98.

---

## B. Finding the periodic payment PMT when the present value of an annuity is known

If the present value of an annuity $PV_n$, the number of conversion periods $n$, and the conversion rate $i$ are known, you can find the periodic payment PMT by substituting the given values in the appropriate present value formula.

For ordinary simple annuities, use Formula 11.2.

$$PV_n = PMT \left[ \frac{1 - (1 + i)^{-n}}{i} \right]$$ ———— Formula 11.2

When using a scientific calculator, you can find PMT by first rearranging the terms of the present value formulas above. Then substitute the three known values (PV, *n*, and *i*) into the rearranged formula and solve for PMT.

When using a preprogrammed financial calculator, you can find PMT by entering the five known values (PV, N, P/Y, C/Y, and I/Y) and pressing CPT PMT .

---

**EXAMPLE 11.4C**

What semi-annual payment at the end of each six-month period is required to pay off a loan of $8000 in ten years if interest is 10% compounded semi-annually?

**SOLUTION**

$$PV_n = 8000.00; \ I/Y = 10; \ P/Y, C/Y = 2; \ i = \frac{10\%}{2} = 5\% = 0.05; \ n = 10(2) = 20$$

$$8000.00 = PMT\left(\frac{1 - 1.05^{-20}}{0.05}\right) \quad\text{— substituting in Formula 11.2}$$

$$8000.00 = PMT\left(\frac{1 - 0.376889}{0.05}\right)$$

$$8000.00 = PMT(12.462210)$$

$$PMT = \frac{8000.00}{12.462210}$$

$$PMT = \$641.94$$

*Alternatively:*

You can first rearrange the terms of Formula 11.2 to solve for PMT.

$$PV_n = PMT\left[\frac{1 - (1 + i)^{-n}}{i}\right] \quad\text{— Formula 11.2}$$

$$PMT = \frac{PV_n}{\left[\dfrac{1 - (1 + i)^{-n}}{i}\right]} \quad\text{— divide both sides by } \left[\frac{1 - (1 + i)^{-n}}{i}\right]$$

$$PMT = \frac{PV_n \, i}{1 - (1 + i)^{-n}} \quad\begin{array}{l}\text{— divide by a fraction is the same}\\\text{as inverting the fraction and}\\\text{multiplying}\end{array}$$

$$PV_n = 8000.00; \quad i = 0.05; \quad n = 20$$

$$PMT = \frac{8000.00(0.05)}{1 - 1.05^{-20}}$$

$$PMT = \$641.94$$

**EXAMPLE 11.4D**

Derek bought a new car valued at $9500.00. He paid $2000 down and financed the remainder over five years at 9% compounded monthly. How much must Derek pay at the end of each month?

**SOLUTION**

$PV_n = 9500.00 - 2000.00 = 7500.00$; I/Y = 9; P/Y, C/Y = 12; $i = \dfrac{9\%}{12} = 0.75\%$; $n = 60$

(Set P/Y = 12) 0 [ FV ] 7500 [ ± ] [ PV ]

9 [ I/Y ] 60 [ N ] [ CPT ] [ PMT ]   155.687664

Derek's monthly payment is $155.69.

## C. Applications

**EXAMPLE 11.4E**

Taylor Marche, now age 37, expects to retire at age 62. To plan for her retirement, she intends to deposit $1500.00 at the end of each of the next 25 years in a registered retirement savings plan. After her last contribution, she intends to convert the existing balance into a registered retirement income fund from which she expects to make 20 equal annual withdrawals. If she makes the first withdrawal one year after her last contribution and interest is 6.5% compounded annually, how much is the size of the annual retirement withdrawal?

**SOLUTION**

As the following time diagram shows, the problem can be broken down into two steps.

**STEP 1**

Compute the *accumulated* value $FV_n$ of the 25 annual deposits of $1500.00 into the RRSP.

PMT = 1500.00; I/Y = 6.5; P/Y = 1; $i = 6.5\% = 0.065$; $n = 25$

$$FV_n = 1500.00\left(\frac{1.065^{25} - 1}{0.065}\right)$$ —————— substituting in Formula 11.1

$$= 1500.00(58.887679)$$
$$= \$88\,331.52$$

**STEP 2** Compute the annual payment that can be withdrawn from the RRIF that has an initial balance of $88 331.52.

$$PV_n = 88\ 331.52; \quad i = 0.065; \quad n = 20$$

$$88\ 331.52 = PMT\left(\frac{1 - 1.065^{-20}}{0.065}\right) \quad\text{——— using Formula 11.2}$$

$$88\ 331.52 = PMT\ (11.018507)$$
$$PMT = \$8016.65$$

**Programmed Solution**

**STEP 1** (Set P/Y, C/Y = 1) 0 [PV] 1500 [±] [PMT] 6.5 [I/Y]

25 [N] [CPT] [FV] [88331.51788]

**STEP 2** 88 331.518 [±] [PV] 0 [FV] 6.5 [I/Y] 20 [N] [CPT] [PMT] [8016.650159]

The sum of money that Taylor can withdraw each year is $8016.65.

## EXERCISE 11.4

If you choose, you can use Excel's **Payment (PMT)** function to answer all of the questions below. Refer to **PMT** on the Spreadsheet Template Disk to learn how to use this Excel function.

**A.** For each of the following ten ordinary annuities, determine the size of the periodic rent.

|  | Future Value | Present Value | Payment Period | Term of Annuity | Interest Rate | Conversion Period |
|---|---|---|---|---|---|---|
| 1. | $15 000 | | 6 months | 7 years, 6 mos. | 5.5% | semi-annually |
| 2. | 6 000 | | 1 quarter | 9 years, 9 mos. | 8 | quarterly |
| 3. | | $12 000 | 12 months | 15 years | 4.5 | annually |
| 4. | | 7 000 | 6 months | 12.5 years | 7.5 | semi-annually |
| 5. | 8 000 | | 3 months | 6 years | 6.8 | quarterly |
| 6. | | 20 000 | 1 month | 20 years | 12 | monthly |
| 7. | 45 000 | | 1 month | 10 years | 9 | monthly |
| 8. | | 35 000 | 1 quarter | 15 years | 4 | quarterly |
| 9. | | 20 000 | 6 months | 8 years | 7 | semi-annually |
| 10. | 16 500 | | 3 months | 15 years | 5.75 | quarterly |

**B.** Answer each of the following questions.

1. What deposit made at the end of each quarter for fifteen years will accumulate to $20 000 at 6% compounded quarterly? *Reference Example 11.4B*

2. What payment is required at the end of each month for five years to repay a loan of $8000 at 8.4% compounded monthly?

3. A contract can be fulfilled by making an immediate payment of $7500 or equal payments at the end of every six months for ten years. What is the size of the semi-annual payments at 9.6% compounded semi-annually?

4. What payment made at the end of each month for eighteen years will amount to $16 000 at 9.6% compounded monthly?

5. What payment is required at the end of each month for twelve years to repay a $32 000 mortgage if interest is 6.5% compounded monthly?

6. How much must be deposited at the end of each quarter for nine years to accumulate to $11 000 at 4% compounded quarterly?

7. What payment made at the end of every six months for fifteen years will accumulate to $18 000 at 5% compounded semi-annually?

8. How much does a depositor have to save at the end of every three months for seven years to accumulate $3500 if interest is 3.75% compounded quarterly?

9. How much would you have to pay into an account at the end of every six months to accumulate $10 000 in eight years if interest is 3% compounded semi-annually?

10. Ontario Credit Union entered a lease contract valued at $7200. The contract provides for payments at the end of each quarter for three years. If interest is 6.5% compounded quarterly, what is the size of the quarterly payment?

11. Hunan bought a car priced at $15 300 for 15% down and equal monthly payments for four years. If interest is 8% compounded monthly, what is the size of the monthly payment? 

    Reference Example 11.4D

12. Ruben bought a boat valued at $16 500 on the installment plan requiring a $2000 down payment and equal monthly payments for five years. If the first payment is due one month after the date of purchase and interest is 7.5% compounded monthly, what is the size of the monthly payment?

13. Olivia bought a car priced at $10 600 for 10% down and the balance in equal monthly payments over four years at 7.2% compounded monthly. How much does Olivia have to pay at the end of each month?

14. The Watsons bought a rental property valued at $50 000 by paying 20% down and mortgaging the balance over twenty-five years through equal payments at the end of each quarter at 10% compounded quarterly. What was the size of the quarterly payments?

15. Jie purchased a computer priced at $949.99, financing it by paying $75.12 on the date of purchase, and signing a contract to pay equal monthly payments over the next fifteen months. If the terms of the contract state that interest is calculated at 10.4% compounded monthly, how much does Jie have to pay at the end of each month?

16. George plans to deposit $1200 at the end of every six months for fifteen years into an RRSP account. After the last deposit, he intends to convert the

existing balance into an RRIF and withdraw equal amounts at the end of every six months for twenty years. If interest is expected to be 7.5% compounded semi-annually, how much will George be able to collect every six months?

Reference Example 11.4E

**17.** Starting three months after her grandson Robin's birth, Mrs. Devine made deposits of $60 into a trust fund every three months until Robin was twenty-one years old. The trust fund provides for equal withdrawals at the end of each quarter for four years, beginning three months after the last deposit. If interest is 4.75% compounded quarterly, how much will Robin receive every three months?

**18.** On the day of his daughter's birth, Mr. Dodd deposited $2000 in a trust fund with his credit union at 5% compounded quarterly. Following her eighteenth birthday, the daughter is to receive equal payments at the end of each month for four years while she is at college. If interest is to be 6% compounded monthly after the daughter's eighteenth birthday, how much will she receive every month?

**19.** Equal payments are to be made into a fund at the end of each month for fifteen years with interest at 9% compounded monthly. After the last payment, the fund is to be invested for seven years at 10% compounded quarterly and have a maturity value of $20 000. What is the size of the monthly payment?

**20.** Mr. Talbot received a retirement bonus of $18 000, which he deposited in an RRSP. He intends to leave the money for fourteen years, then transfer the balance into an RRIF and make equal withdrawals at the end of every six months for twenty years. If interest is 6.5% compounded semi-annually, what will be the size of each withdrawal?

**21.** When his aunt died, Ariel inherited $30 000. The terms of the will stated that he was to place the money into a savings account for eight years, and then withdraw equal amounts at the end of each month for ten years. If interest is 4.37% compounded monthly, what will be the size of each withdrawal?

# 11.5 FINDING THE TERM *n* OF AN ANNUITY

## A. Finding the term *n* when the future value of an annuity is known

If the future value of an annuity $FV_n$, the periodic payment PMT, and the conversion rate $i$ are known, you can find the term of the annuity $n$ by substituting the given values in the appropriate future value formula.

For ordinary simple annuities, use Formula 11.1.

$$FV_n = PMT\left[\frac{(1 + i)^n - 1}{i}\right]$$ ——————— **Formula 11.1**

**EXAMPLE 11.5A**

How long will it take for $200 deposited at the end of each quarter to amount to $5726.70 at 6% compounded quarterly?

**SOLUTION**

$FV_n = 5726.70$; $I/Y = 6$; $P/Y, C/Y = 4$; $i = \dfrac{6\%}{4} = 1.5\% = 0.015$; $PMT = 200.00$

$$5726.70 = 200.00\left(\frac{1.015^n - 1}{0.015}\right) \quad\text{—— substituting in Formula 11.1}$$

$$28.6335 = \frac{1.015^n - 1}{0.015} \quad\text{——— divide both sides by 200.00}$$

$$0.429503 = 1.015^n - 1 \quad\text{——— multiply both sides by 0.015}$$
$$1.015^n = 1.429503 \quad\text{——— add 1 to both sides}$$

$$n\ln 1.015 = \ln 1.429503 \quad\text{——— solve for }n\text{ using natural logarithms}$$

$$0.014889n = 0.357327$$

$$n = \frac{0.357327}{0.014889}$$

$$n = 24 \text{ (quarters)}$$

It will take 24 quarters or six years for $200 per quarter to grow to $5726.70.

*Alternatively:*

You can first rearrange the terms of Formula 11.1 to solve for $n$.

$$FV_n = PMT\left[\frac{(1 + i)^n - 1}{i}\right] \quad\text{——— Formula 11.1}$$

$$\frac{FV_n}{PMT} = \frac{(1 + i)^n - 1}{i} \quad\text{——— divide both sides by PMT}$$

$$(1 + i)^n = \left(\frac{FV_n\,i}{PMT}\right) + 1 \quad\text{——— multiply both sides by }i \text{ and add 1 to both sides}$$

$$n\ln(1 + i) = \ln[(FV_n i/PMT) + 1] \quad\text{——— solve for }n\text{ using natural logarithms}$$

$$n = \frac{\ln[(FV_n i/PMT) + 1]}{\ln(1 + i)} \quad\text{——— divide both sides by }\ln(1 + i)$$

$FV_n = 5726.70$; $i = 0.015$; $PMT = 200.00$

$$n = \frac{\ln[5726.70 \times 0.015/200.00 + 1]}{\ln 1.015}$$

$$n = \frac{0.357327}{0.014889}$$

$$n = 24 \text{ (quarters)}$$

## POINTERS AND PITFALLS

For annuity problems in which the period of investment or loan repayment must be determined, once $n$ has been calculated, simply divide $n$ by $m$ to calculate the period of investment or loan repayment in years. To illustrate, the solution in Example 11.5A is $n = 24$. Since $m = 4$ (the question states "at the end of each quarter"), the period of investment is $n / m$, or $24 / 4 = 6$ years.

---

**EXAMPLE 11.5B**

In how many months will your bank account grow to $3000 if you deposit $150 at the end of each month and the account earns 9% compounded monthly?

**SOLUTION**

$FV_n = 3000.00;$   $PMT = 150.00;$   $I/Y = 9;$   $P/Y, C/Y = 12;$   $i = \dfrac{9\%}{12} = 0.75\%$

(Set P/Y, C/Y = 12) 0 [ PV ] 3000 [ FV ]

150 [ ± ] [ PMT ] 9 [ I/Y ] [ CPT ] [ N ] [ 18.7047 ]

It will take about 19 months to accumulate $3000.00.

### Interpretation of Result

When $FV_n$, PMT, and $i$ are known, it is unlikely that $n$ will be a whole number. The fractional time period of 0.7 month indicates that the accumulated value of 18 deposits of $150 will be less than $3000, while the accumulated value of 19 deposits will be more than $3000. This point can be verified by computing $FV_{18}$ and $FV_{19}$.

$$FV_{18} = 150.00\left(\frac{1.0075^{18} - 1}{0.0075}\right) = 150.00(19.194718) = \$2879.21$$

$$FV_{19} = 150.00\left(\frac{1.0075^{19} - 1}{0.0075}\right) = 150.00(20.338679) = \$3050.80$$

The definition of an annuity does not provide for making payments at unequal time intervals. The appropriate answer to problems in which $n$ is a fractional value is a whole number. The usual approach is to round upward so that in this case $n = 19$.

Rounding upward implies that the deposit made at the end of the nineteenth month is smaller than the usual deposit of $150.00. The method of computing the size of the final deposit or payment when the term of the annuity is a fractional value rounded upward is considered in Chapter 14.

## B. Finding the term *n* when the present value of an annuity is known

If the present value $PV_n$, the periodic payment PMT, and the conversion rate $i$ are known, you can find the term of the annuity $n$ by substituting the given values in the present value formula.

$$\boxed{PV_n = PMT\left[\frac{1 + (1 + i)^{-n}}{i}\right]} \quad \text{——— Formula 11.2}$$

When using a scientific calculator, you can find $n$ by first rearranging the terms of the present value formulas above. Then substitute the three known values (PV, PMT, and $i$) into the rearranged formula and solve for $n$.

When using a preprogrammed financial calculator, you can find $n$ by entering the five known values (PV, PMT, P/Y, C/Y, and I/Y) and pressing [CPT] [N].

*Note:* When using the Texas Instruments BAII Plus financial calculator, you *must* enter *either* the PV or PMT as a negative amount, *but not both*. Due to the sign conventions used by this calculator, entering *both* PV and PMT as negative amounts or as positive amounts will lead to an *incorrect* final answer. The calculator does *not* indicate that the answer is incorrect or that an entry error was made. (This has not been an issue until now because either PV or PMT was 0 in all the examples we discussed.) To avoid incorrect answers, *always* enter the PV amount as a negative number and the PMT amount as a positive number when FV = 0 and you are calculating $n$. However, if PV = 0, enter PMT as a negative number and FV as a positive number. The examples in this text follow these rules. Refer to Appendix II to check whether this step is necessary if you use the Sharp EL-733A or the Hewlett-Packard 10B calculator.

**EXAMPLE 11.5C**

How many quarterly payments of $600 are required to repay a loan of $5400 at 6% compounded quarterly?

**SOLUTION**

$PV_n = 5400.00$; $PMT = 600.00$; $I/Y = 6$; $P/Y, C/Y = 4$; $i = \dfrac{6\%}{4} = 1.5\% = 0.015$

$5400.00 = 600.00\left(\dfrac{1 - 1.015^{-n}}{0.015}\right)$ ——— substituting in Formula 11.2

$9.00 = \dfrac{1 - 1.015^{-n}}{0.015}$ ——— divide both sides by 600.00

$0.135 = 1 - 1.015^{-n}$ ——— multiply both sides by 0.015

$1.015^{-n} = 0.865$

$-n \ln 1.015 = \ln 0.865$ ——— solve for $n$ using natural logarithms

$-0.014889n = -0.145026$

$n = \dfrac{-0.145026}{-0.014889}$

$n = 9.740726$

$n = 10$ quarters

To repay the loan, 10 quarterly payments are required.

***Alternatively:***

You can first rearrange the terms of Formula 11.2 to solve for $n$.

$$PV_n = PMT\left[\frac{1 - (1 + i)^{-n}}{i}\right] \quad \text{——— Formula 11.2}$$

$$\frac{PV_n}{PMT} = \frac{1 - (1 + i)^{-n}}{i}$$ ——————— divide both sides by PMT

$$\left(\frac{PV_n i}{PMT}\right) - 1 = -(1 + i)^{-n}$$ ——————— multiply both sides by $i$ and subtract 1 from both sides

$$(1 + i)^{-n} = 1 - \left(\frac{PV_n i}{PMT}\right)$$ ——————— multiply both sides by $-1$

$$-n \ln(1 + i) = \ln\left[1 - \left(\frac{PV_n i}{PMT}\right)\right]$$ ——————— solve for $n$ using natural logarithms

$$n = \frac{\ln\left[1 - \left(\frac{PV_n i}{PMT}\right)\right]}{-\ln(1 + i)}$$ ——————— divide both sides by $-\ln(1+i)$

$$PV_n = 5400.00; \quad PMT = 600.00; \quad i = 0.015$$

$$n = \frac{\ln\left[1 - \dfrac{(5400.00)(0.015)}{600.00}\right]}{-\ln(1.015)}$$ ——————— substituting in rearranged Formula 11.2

$$n = \frac{-0.145026}{-0.014889}$$

$$n = 9.740718$$

$$n = 10 \text{ quarters}$$

---

**EXAMPLE 11.5D**

On his retirement, Art received a bonus of $8000 from his employer. Taking advantage of the existing tax legislation, he invested the money in an annuity that provides for semi-annual payments of $1200 at the end of every six months. If interest is 6.25% compounded semi-annually, how long will the annuity exist?

**SOLUTION**

$$PV_n = 8000.00; PMT = 1200.00; I/Y = 6.25; P/Y, C/Y = 2; i = \frac{6.25\%}{2} = 3.125\%$$

(Set P/Y, C/Y = 2) 0 | FV | 8000 | ± | PV |

1200 | PMT | 6.25 | I/Y | CPT | N | 7.59188 |

↑

half-year periods

The annuity will be in existence for four years. Art will receive seven half-yearly payments of $1200 and a final payment that will be less than $1200.

## EXERCISE 11.5

If you choose, you can use Excel's **Number of Compounding Periods (NPER)** function to answer all of the questions below. Refer to **NPER** on the Spreadsheet Template Disk to learn how to use this Excel function.

  **A.** Find the term of each of the following ten ordinary annuities. (State your answer in years and months.)

|  | Future Value | Present Value | Periodic Rent | Payment Interval | Interest Rate | Conversion Period |
|---|---|---|---|---|---|---|
| **1.** | $20 000 |  | $ 800 | 1 year | 7.5% | annually |
| **2.** | 17 000 |  | 35 | 1 month | 9 | monthly |
| **3.** |  | $14 500 | 190 | 1 month | 5.25 | monthly |
| **4.** |  | 5 000 | 300 | 3 months | 4 | quarterly |
| **5.** | 3 600 |  | 175 | 6 months | 7.4 | semi-annually |
| **6.** |  | 9 500 | 740 | 1 quarter | 5.2 | quarterly |
| **7.** |  | 21 400 | 1660 | 6 months | 4.5 | semi-annually |
| **8.** | 13 600 |  | 140 | 3 months | 8 | quarterly |
| **9.** | 7 200 |  | 90 | 1 month | 3.75 | monthly |
| **10.** |  | 9 700 | 315 | 3 months | 11 | quarterly |

**B.** Answer each of the following questions.

1. How long would it take you to save $4500 by making deposits of $50 at the end of every month into a savings account earning 6% compounded monthly? Reference Example 11.5A

2. How long will it take to save $5000 by making deposits of $60 at the end of every month into an account earning interest at 6% monthly?

3. Suppose $646.56 is deposited at the end of every six months into an account earning 6.5% compounded semi-annually. If the balance in the account four years after the last deposit is to be $20 000, how many deposits are needed?

4. For how long can $1000 be withdrawn at the end of each month from an account containing $36 000 if interest is 6.4% compounded monthly?

5. In what period of time could you pay back a loan of $3600 by making payments of $96 at the end of each month if interest is 10.5% compounded monthly? Reference Example 11.5C

6. For how long will Amir have to make payments of $300 at the end of every three months to repay a loan of $5000 if interest is 7% compounded quarterly?

7. Josie borrowed $8000 compounded monthly to help finance her education. She contracted to repay the loan in monthly payments of

$300 each. If the payments are due at the end of each month and interest is 4% compounded monthly, how long will Josie have to make monthly payments?

8. A mortgage of $26 500 is to be repaid by making payments of $1560 at the end of every six months. If interest is 7% compounded semi-annually, what is the term of the mortgage?

9. A car loan of $12 000 is to be repaid with end-of-month payments of $292.96. If interest is 8% compounded monthly, how long is the term of the loan?

10. A deposit of $4000 is made today. For how long can $500 be withdrawn from the account at the end of every three months starting three months from now if interest is 4% compounded quarterly? Reference Example 11.5D

11. Lauren deposited $12 000 today. He plans to withdraw $1100 every six months. For how long can he withdraw from the account starting six months from now if interest is 3.9% compounded semi-annually?

12. Cathy placed $7000 into a savings account. For how long can $800 be withdrawn from the account at the end of every month starting one month from now if interest is 4.58% compounded monthly?

13. Rae deposited $5741, the earnings from her part-time job, into a savings account. If she withdraws $650 at the end of each month, how long will the money last if interest is 5.15% compounded monthly?

14. Kaye deposited $6000 into a savings account today. For how long can $730 be withdrawn from the account at the end of every three months starting three months from now if interest is 3.9% compounded quarterly?

# 11.6 FINDING THE PERIODIC RATE OF INTEREST $i$ USING PREPROGRAMMED FINANCIAL CALCULATORS

## A. Finding the periodic rate of interest $i$ for simple annuities

Preprogrammed financial calculators are especially helpful when solving for the conversion rate $i$. Determining $i$ without a financial calculator is extremely time-consuming. However, it *can* be done by hand, as illustrated in Appendix B on the CD-ROM.

When the future value or present value, the periodic payment PMT, and the term $n$ of an annuity are known, the periodic rate of interest $i$ can be found by entering the three known values into a preprogrammed financial calculator. (Remember, if both PV and PMT are non-zero, enter PV only as a negative amount.) For ordinary simple annuities, retrieve the answer by pressing CPT I/Y . This represents the nominal annual rate of interest $j$. By dividing $j$ by the number of compounding periods per year $m$, you can obtain the periodic interest rate $i$.

**EXAMPLE 11.6A**

Compute the nominal annual rate of interest at which $100 deposited at the end of each month for ten years will amount to $15 000.

**SOLUTION**

$FV_n = 15\ 000.00$;    $PMT = 100.00$;    $P/Y, C/Y = 12$;    $n = 120$;    $m = 12$

(Set P/Y, C/Y = 12) 0 | PV | 15 000 | FV | 100 | ± | PMT |

120 | N | CPT | I/Y | 4.350057 |

↑
Allow several seconds
for the computation.

The nominal annual rate of interest is approximately 4.35% compounded monthly. The monthly conversion rate is approximately 4.350057/12 = 0.362505 per month.

**EXAMPLE 11.6B**

A loan of $6000 is paid off over five years by monthly payments of $120.23. What is the nominal annual rate of interest on the loan?

**SOLUTION**

$PV_n = 6000.00$;    $PMT = 120.23$;    $n = 60$;    $P/Y, C/Y = 12$

(Set P/Y, C/Y = 12) 0 | FV | 6000 | ± | PV | 120.23 | PMT |

60 | N | CPT | I/Y | 7.500810 |

↑
Allow several seconds
for the computation.

The nominal annual rate of interest is approximately 7.5% compounded monthly. The monthly compounding rate is approximately 7.500810/12 = 0.625067%.

# EXERCISE 11.6

**A.** Compute the nominal annual rate of interest for each of the following eight ordinary simple annuities.

| | Future Value | Present Value | Periodic Rent | Payment Interval | Term | Conversion Period |
|---|---|---|---|---|---|---|
| **1.** | $ 9 000 | | $ 230.47 | 3 months | 8 years | quarterly |
| **2.** | 4 800 | | 68.36 | 1 month | 5 years | monthly |
| **3.** | | $ 7 400 | 119.06 | 1 month | 7 years | monthly |
| **4.** | | 6 980 | 800.00 | 6 months | 5 years | semi-annually |
| **5.** | 70 000 | | 1014.73 | 1 year | 25 years | annually |
| **6.** | | 42 000 | 528.00 | 1 month | 10 years | monthly |
| **7.** | | 28 700 | 2015.00 | 6 months | 15 years | semi-annually |
| **8.** | 36 000 | | 584.10 | 3 months | 12 years | quarterly |

**B.** Answer each of the following questions.

1. Compute the nominal annual rate of interest at which $350 paid at the end of every three months for six years accumulates to $12 239.76.

   Reference Example 11.6A

2. Katrina contributed $2500 at the end of every year into an RRSP for ten years. What nominal annual rate of interest will the RRSP earn if the balance in Katrina's account just after she made her last contribution was $33 600?

3. What nominal annual rate of interest compounded monthly was paid if contributions of $250 made into an RRSP at the end of every month amounted to $35 000 after ten years?

4. Compute the nominal annual rate of interest compounded monthly at which $400 paid at the end of the month for eight years accumulates to $45 000.

5. What is the nominal annual rate of interest if a four-year loan of $6000 is repaid by end-of-month payments of $144.23?

6. Rita converted an RRSP balance of $119 875.67 into an RRIF that will pay her $1800 at the end of every month for nine years. What is the nominal annual rate of interest?

7. A car valued at $11 400 can be purchased for 10% down and end-of-month payments of $286.21 for three-and-a-half years. What is the effective annual cost of financing?

8. Property worth $50 000 can be purchased for 20% down and mortgage payments of $1000 at the end of each quarter for 25 years. What effective annual rate of interest is charged?

9. What is the nominal annual rate of interest compounded quarterly if a loan of $21 500 is repaid in seven years by payments of $1000 made at the end of every three months?

10. A property worth $35 000 is purchased for 10% down and payments of $2100 at the end of every six months for twelve years. What is the effective annual rate of interest?

Go to MyMathLab at www.mathxl.com. You can practise many of this chapter's exercises as often as you want. The guided solutions help you find an answer step by step. You'll find a personalized study plan available to you too!

## Review Exercise

1. Payments of $360 are made into a fund at the end of every three months for twelve years. The fund earns interest at 7% compounded quarterly.
   (a) What will be the balance in the fund after twelve years?
   (b) How much of the balance is deposits?
   (c) How much of the balance is interest?

2. A trust fund is set up to make payments of $950 at the end of each month for seven-and-a-half years. Interest on the fund is 7.8% compounded monthly.
   (a) How much money must be deposited into the fund?
   (b) How much will be paid out of the fund?
   (c) How much interest is earned by the fund?

3. How much interest is included in the accumulated value of $75.90 paid at the end of each month for four years if interest is 9% compounded monthly?

4. If a loan was repaid by payments of $320 at the end of each quarter in five years at 8% compounded quarterly, how much money had been borrowed?

5. How long will it take to build up a fund of $10 000 by saving $300 at the end of every six months at 4.5% compounded semi-annually?

6. What is the term of a mortgage of $35 000 repaid by end-of-month payments of $475 if interest is 7.5% compounded monthly?

7. Suppose you would like to have $10 000 in your savings account and interest is 8% compounded quarterly. How much must you deposit every three months for five years if the deposits are made at the end of each quarter?

8. Equal sums of money are withdrawn monthly from a fund of $20 000 for fifteen years. If interest is 9% compounded monthly, what is the size of each withdrawal if the withdrawal is made at the end of each month?

9. If you contribute $1500 into an RRSP at the end of every six months for twelve years and interest on the deposits is 8% compounded semi-annually, how much would the balance in the RRSP be seven years after the last contribution?

10. Doris purchased a piano with $300 down and end-of-month payments of $124 for two-and-a-half years at 9% compounded monthly. What was the purchase price of the piano?

11. A contract valued at $11 500 requires payment of $1450 at the end of every six months. If interest is 10.5% compounded semi-annually, what is the term of the contract?

12. What nominal annual rate of interest is paid on RRSP contributions of $1100 made at the end of each quarter for fifteen years if the balance just after the last contribution is $106 000?

13. What nominal annual rate of interest was charged on a loan of $5600 repaid in end-of-month installments of $121.85 in four-and-a-half years?

14. Glenn has made contributions of $250 at the end of every three months into an RRSP for ten years. Interest for the first four years was 4% compounded quarterly. Since then the interest rate has been 5% compounded quarterly. How much will Glenn have in his RRSP three years after the last contribution?

15. Avi expects to retire in twelve years. Beginning one month after his retirement he would like to receive $500 per month for twenty years. How much must he deposit into a fund today to be able to do so if the rate of interest on the deposit is 6% compounded monthly?

16. A contract is signed requiring payments of $750 at the end of every three months for eight years. How much is the cash value of the contract if money is worth 9% compounded quarterly?

17. The amount of $10 000 is put into a five-year term deposit paying 7.5% compounded semi-annually. After five years the deposit is converted

into an ordinary annuity of equal semi-annual payments of $2000 each. If interest remains the same, what is the term of the annuity?

**18.** Mirielle has deposited $125 at the end of each month for 15 years at 7.5% compounded monthly. After her last deposit she converted the balance into an ordinary annuity paying $1200 every three months for twelve years. If interest on the annuity is compounded quarterly, what is the effective annual rate of interest paid by the annuity?

**19.** A contract is signed requiring payments of $750 at the end of every three months for eight years.

How much is the cash value of the contract if money is worth 10.5% compounded quarterly?

**20.** A savings plan requiring deposits of $400 at the end of each quarter for twenty years provides for a lump-sum payment of $92 000 just after the last deposit has been made.

**(a)** What is the effective annual rate of interest on the savings plan?

**(b)** If, instead of the lump sum, monthly ordinary annuity payments of $1350 may be accepted at the same nominal rate of interest (correct to two decimals) but compounded monthly, what is the term of the annuity?

## Self-Test

**1.** You won $100 000 in a lottery and you want to set some of that sum aside for ten years. After ten years, you would like to receive $2400 at the end of every three months for eight years. How much of your winnings must you set aside if interest is 5.5% compounded quarterly?

**2.** A sum of money is deposited at the end of every month for ten years at 7.5% compounded monthly. After the last deposit, interest for the account is to be 6% compounded quarterly and the account is to be paid out by quarterly payments of $4800 over six years. What is the size of the monthly deposit?

**3.** Compute the nominal annual rate of interest compounded semi-annually on a loan of $48 000 repaid in installments of $4000 at the end of every six months in ten years.

**4.** A loan of $14 400 is to be repaid in end-of-the-quarter payments of $600. How many payments are required to repay the loan at 10.5% compounded quarterly?

**5.** The amount of $57 426 is invested at 6% compounded monthly for six years. After the initial six-year period, the balance in the fund is converted into an annuity due paying $3600 at the end of every three months. If interest on the annuity is 5.9% compounded quarterly, what is the term of the annuity in months?

**6.** A loan was repaid in seven years by end-of-month payments of $450. If interest was 12% compounded monthly, how much interest was paid?

**7.** Ms. Simms made deposits of $540 at the end of every three months into a savings account. For the first five years interest was 5% compounded quarterly. Since then the rate of interest has been 5.5% compounded quarterly. How much is the account balance after thirteen years?

**8.** How much interest is included in the accumulated value of $3200 paid at the end of every six months for four years if the interest rate is 6.5% compounded semi-annually?

**9.** What is the size of deposits made at the end of each period that will accumulate to $67 200 after eight years at 6.5% compounded semi-annually?

## Challenge Problems

1. After winning some money at a casino, Tony is considering purchasing an annuity that promises to pay him $300 at the end of each month for 12 months, then $350 at the end of each month for 24 months, and then $375 at the end of each month for 36 months. If the first payment is due at the end of the first month and interest is 7.5% compounded monthly over the life of the annuity, find Tony's purchase price.

2. On March 1, 2008, Yves decided to save for a new truck. He deposited $500 at the end of every three months in a bank account earning interest at 5% compounded quarterly. He made his first deposit on June 1, 2008. On June 1, 2010, Yves decided that he needed the money to go to college, so on September 1, 2010, he stopped making deposits and started withdrawing $300 at the end of each quarter until December 1, 2011. How much is left in his account after the last withdrawal if his bank account interest rate changed to 6.5% compounded quarterly on March 1, 2011?

# Case Study 11.1 Saving for Your Dream

» Andrea Shertov dreams of spending an extended holiday in Thailand. If she can save enough money, she wants to have six months to travel with friends. She has done some research and determined that she would need approximately $1800 in Canadian currency per month to achieve her dream.

At her current salary, she plans to save $150 at the end of each month, investing it at 2.8% interest compounded monthly. She hopes to be able to take this trip three years from now.

### QUESTIONS

1. If Andrea saves $150 per month for three years, will she have enough to pay for her trip?

2. If Andrea saves the $150 per month, and earns an interest rate of 4.6% compounded monthly, will she have enough to pay for her trip?

3. If Andrea saves $300 per month for three years, with interest at 5.5% compounded monthly, how much will she have in her vacation investment account?

# Case Study 11.2 Getting the Picture

» Suzanne had a summer job working in the business office of Blast-It TV and Stereo, a local chain of home electronics stores. When Michael Jacobssen, the owner of the chain, heard she had completed one year of business courses, he asked Suzanne to calculate the profitability of two new large-screen TVs. He plans to offer a special payment plan for the two new models to attract customers to his stores. He wants to heavily promote the more profitable TV.

When Michael gave Suzanne the information about the two TVs, he told her to ignore all taxes when making her calculations. The cost of TV A to the company is $1950 and the cost of TV B to the company is $2160, after all trade discounts have been taken. The company plans to sell TV A for a $500 down payment and $230 per month for twelve months, beginning one month from the date of the purchase. The company plans to sell TV B for a $100 down payment and $260 per month for eighteen months, beginning one month from the date of purchase. The monthly payments for both TVs reflect an interest rate of 15.5% compounded monthly.

Michael wants Suzanne to calculate the profit of TV A and TV B as a percent of the TV's cost to the company. To calculate profit, Michael deducts overhead (which he calculates as 15% of cost) and the cost of the item from the selling price of the item. When he sells items that are paid for at a later time, he calculates the selling price as the *cash value* of the item. (Remember that cash value equals the down payment plus the present value of the periodic payments.)

Suzanne realized that she could calculate the profitability of each TV by using her knowledge of ordinary annuities. She went to work on her assignment to provide Michael with the information he requested.

## QUESTIONS

1. (a) What is the cash value of TV A? Round your answer to the nearest dollar.
   (b) What is the cash value of TV B? Round your answer to the nearest dollar.

2. (a) Given Michael's system of calculations, how much overhead should be assigned to TV A?
   (b) How much overhead should be assigned to TV B?

3. (a) According to Michael's system of calculations, what is the profit of TV A as a percent of its cost?
   (b) What is the profit of TV B as a percent of its cost?
   (c) Which TV should Suzanne recommend be more heavily promoted?

4. Three months later, due to Blast-It's successful sales of TV A and TV B, the suppliers of each model gave the company new volume discounts. For TV A, Blast-It received a discount of 9% off its current cost, and for TV B one of 6%. The special payment plans for TV A and TV B will stay the same. Under these new conditions, which TV should Suzanne recommend be more heavily promoted?

## SUMMARY OF FORMULAS

**Formula 9.1A**

$$FV = PV(1 + i)^n$$

Finding the future value of a compound amount (maturity value) when the original principal, the rate of interest, and the time period are known

**Formula 9.1C**

$$PV = FV(1 + i)^{-n}$$

Finding the present value by means of the discount factor (the reciprocal of the compounding factor)

**Formula 10.1**

$$f = (1 + i)^m - 1$$

Finding the effective rate of interest $f$ for a nominal annual rate compounded $m$ times per year

**Formula 11.1**

$$S_n = R\left[\frac{(1 + i)^n - 1}{i}\right]$$

Finding the future value (accumulated value) of an ordinary simple annuity

restated as

$$FV_n = PMT\left[\frac{(1 + i)^n - 1}{i}\right]$$

**Formula 11.2**

$$A_n = R\left[\frac{1 - (1 + i)^{-n}}{i}\right]$$

Finding the present value (discounted value) of an ordinary simple annuity

restated as

$$PV_n = PMT\left[\frac{1 - (1 + i)^{-n}}{i}\right]$$

## GLOSSARY

**Accumulated value of one dollar per period**
*see* **Accumulation factor for annuities**

**Accumulation factor for annuities**    the factor
$$\frac{(1 + i)^n - 1}{i} \ \text{(p. 428)}$$

**Annual rent**    the sum of the periodic payments in one year *(p. 423)*

**Annuity**    a series of payments, usually equal in size, made at equal periodic time intervals *(p. 423)*

**Annuity certain**    an annuity for which the term is fixed *(p. 423)*

**Annuity due**    an annuity in which the periodic payments are made at the beginning of each payment interval *(p. 424)*

**Compounding factor for annuities**    *see* **Accumulation factor for annuities**

**Contingent annuity**    an annuity in which the term is uncertain; that is, either the beginning date of the term or the ending date of the term or both are unknown *(p. 423)*

**Deferred annuity**    an annuity in which the first payment is delayed for a number of payment periods *(p. 424)*

**Down payment**    the portion of the purchase price that is supplied by the purchaser as an initial payment *(p. 441)*

**Future value of an annuity**    the sum of the accumulated values of the periodic payments at the end of the term of the annuity *(p. 427)*

**General annuity**    an annuity in which the conversion (or compounding) period is different from the payment interval *(p. 424)*

**Ordinary annuity**    an annuity in which the payments are made at the end of each payment interval *(p. 424)*

**Payment interval**   the length of time between successive payments *(p. 423)*

**Payment period**   *see* **Payment interval**

**Periodic rent**   the size of the regular periodic payment *(p. 423)*

**Perpetuity**   an annuity for which the payments continue forever *(p. 423)*

**Simple annuity**   an annuity in which the conversion period is the same as the payment interval *(p. 424)*

**Term of an annuity**   the length of time from the beginning of the first payment interval to the end of the last payment interval *(p. 423)*

## USEFUL INTERNET SITES

**www.gordonpape.com**

**Building Wealth on the Net**   Visit Buildwealth.ca to read Gordon Pape's latest financial advice or subscribe to the Internet Wealth Builder. Pape is one of Canada's best-known and highly regarded investment advisors.

**www.nmfn.com/tn/learnctr--lifeevents--longevity**

**The Longevity Game**   Click on "Learning Centre/The Longevity Game" to predict your life expectancy with this game on Northwestern Mutual Life Insurance Company's site. Life expectancy is used to calculate life insurance rates.

**www.money.msn.ca**

**RRSP**   This Canadian site provides information on advantages and disadvantages of RRSPs, including a calculator to determine tax savings. Some U.S. news is included.

# 12 Ordinary General Annuities

## OBJECTIVES

**Upon completing this chapter, you will be able to do the following:**

1. Compute the future value (or accumulated value) for ordinary general annuities.

2. Compute the present value (or discounted value) for ordinary general annuities.

3. Compute the payment for ordinary general annuities.

4. Compute the number of periods for ordinary general annuities.

5. Compute the interest rate for ordinary general annuities.

We often encounter situations where the frequency of the payment in an annuity is not the same as the frequency of the compounding when interest is applied. In these cases, we are dealing with a general annuity. When the payment is made at the end of the period, we have an ordinary general annuity. It is necessary to understand these annuities so that we can make informed decisions about different payment options. When considering borrowing money to buy a car, or negotiating a mortgage, we must determine when it is best for us to make the payments and how much we can afford. The timing of the payments is crucial in planning our cash flow.

## INTRODUCTION

In Chapter 11, we calculated the present value, future value, payment, term, and interest rate for ordinary simple annuities. In this chapter, we will calculate the present value, future value, payment, term, and interest rate for ordinary general annuities. We will analyze the relationship between the payment interval and the interest conversion period. We will introduce new formulas to calculate the future value and the present value of an ordinary general annuity. We will rearrange these formulas to determine the payment, term, and interest rate for these annuities. We will also use preprogrammed calculators as an alternative to determining the results.

# 12.1 ORDINARY GENERAL ANNUITIES—FINDING THE FUTURE VALUE

## A. Basic concepts and computation

Chapter 11 considered ordinary simple annuities in detail. Simple annuities are a special case in which the payment interval and the interest conversion period are the same length. However, interest is often compounded more or less frequently than payments are made. In Canada, for example, residential mortgages are usually compounded semi-annually while payments are made monthly.

Annuities in which the length of the interest conversion period is different from the length of the payment interval are called *general annuities*.

The basic method of solving problems involving interest uses equivalent sets of financial obligations at a selected focal date. Thus, when dealing with any kind of annuity, including general annuities, the essential tool is an equation of value. This basic approach is used to make the basic computations and develop useful formulas.

| EXAMPLE 12.1A | What is the accumulated value of $100 deposited at the end of every six months for three years if interest is 4% compounded annually? |

| SOLUTION | Since the payments are made semi-annually while the compounding is done annually, this annuity is classified as a general annuity. Furthermore, since the payments are at the end of each payment interval, the annuity is an ordinary general annuity. While the difference in the length of the payment period compared to the length of the compounding period introduces a mathematical complication, the basic approach to finding the amount of the ordinary general annuity is the same as that used in finding the amount of an ordinary simple annuity. |

The basic solution and data for the problem are shown graphically in Figure 12.1. Since deposits are made at the end of every six months for three years, there are six deposits of $100 at the times indicated. Because interest is compounded annually, I/Y = 4%, P/Y = 2, C/Y = 1, $i = 4\% = 0.04$, and there are three conversion periods.

**FIGURE 12.1**   **Graphical Representation of Method and Data**

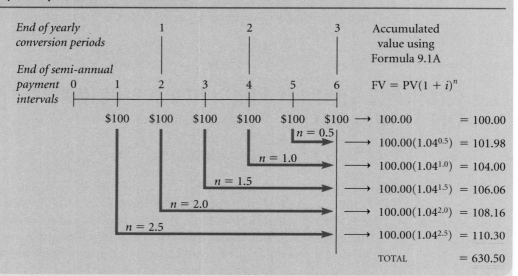

The focal point is at the end of Year 3. The last deposit is made at the focal date and has a value of $100 on that date. The fifth deposit is made after 2.5 years and, in terms of conversion periods, has accumulated for a half conversion period ($n = 0.5$); its accumulated value is $100.00(1.04^{0.5}) = \$101.98$ at the focal date.

The fourth deposit made after two years has accumulated for one conversion period ($n = 1.0$); its accumulated value at the focal date is $100.00(1.04^{1.0}) = \$104.00$. Similarly, the accumulated value of the third deposit is $100.00(1.04^{1.5}) = \$106.06$, while the accumulated value of the second deposit is $100.00(1.04^{2.0}) = \$108.16$. Finally, the accumulated value of the first deposit is $100.00(1.04^{2.5}) = \$110.30$. The total accumulated value after three years is $630.50.

**EXAMPLE 12.1B**

What is the accumulated value of deposits of $100 made at the end of each year for four years if interest is 4% compounded quarterly?

**SOLUTION**

Since the deposits are made at the end of every year for four years, there are four payments of $100.00 at the times shown in Figure 12.2. Since interest is compounded quarterly, I/Y = 4, P/Y, C/Y = 4, $i = \frac{4}{4}\% = 1\% = 0.01\%$, and there are $4(4) = 16$ conversion periods.

FIGURE 12.2     **Graphical Representation of Method and Data**

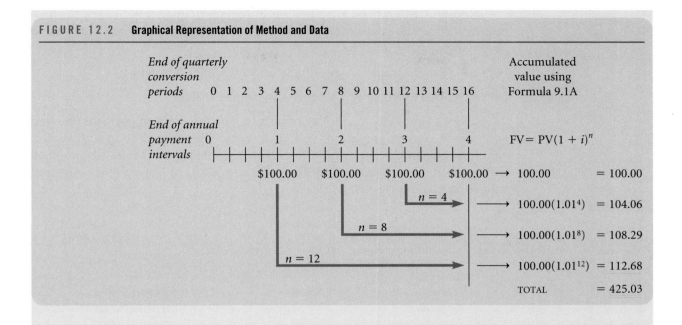

The focal point is the end of Year 4. The last payment is made at the focal point and has a value of $100 at that date. The third payment is made after three years and, in terms of conversion periods, has accumulated for four conversion periods ($n = 4$); its accumulated value is $100.00(1.01^4) = \$104.06$. The second deposit has accumulated for 8 conversion periods ($n = 8$); its accumulated value is $100.00(1.018) = \$108.29$. The first deposit has accumulated for 12 conversion periods ($n = 12$); its accumulated value is $100.00(1.0112) = \$112.68$. The total accumulated value of the deposits after four years is $425.03.

## B. Relationship between payment interval and interest conversion period

Examples 12.1A and 12.1B illustrate the two possible cases of ordinary general annuities.

CASE 1     The interest conversion period is *longer* than the payment period; each payment interval contains only a fraction of one conversion period.

CASE 2     The interest conversion period is *shorter* than the payment period; each payment period contains more than one conversion period.

The number of interest conversion periods per payment interval, designated by the letter $c$, can be determined from the following ratio.

$$c = \frac{\text{THE NUMBER OF INTEREST CONVERSION PERIODS PER YEAR}}{\text{THE NUMBER OF PAYMENT PERIODS PER YEAR}}$$

In dealing with general annuities it is important to understand clearly the relationship between the *payment interval* and the number of *interest conversion periods* per payment interval.

For Case 1 (see Example 12.1A), *c* has a fractional value less than 1.

For Case 2 (see Example 12.1B), *c* has a value greater than 1.

Table 12.1 provides a sampling of possible combinations of payment intervals and interest conversion periods you might encounter when dealing with general annuities. One of the most important is the monthly payment interval combined with semi-annual compounding since this combination is usually encountered with residential mortgages in Canada.

**Table 12.1**   **Some Possible Combinations of Payment Intervals and Interest Conversion Periods**

| Numerator: Interest Conversion Period | Denominator: Payment Interval | Number of Interest Conversion Periods per Payment Interval |
|---|---|---|
| monthly | semi-annually | $c = \dfrac{12}{2} = 6$ |
| monthly | quarterly | $c = \dfrac{12}{4} = 3$ |
| quarterly | annually | $c = \dfrac{4}{1} = 4$ |
| annually | semi-annually | $c = \dfrac{1}{2} = 0.5$ |
| annually | quarterly | $c = \dfrac{1}{4} = 0.25$ |
| semi-annually | monthly | $c = \dfrac{2}{12} = \dfrac{1}{6}$ |
| quarterly | monthly | $c = \dfrac{4}{12} = \dfrac{1}{3}$ |
| annually | monthly | $c = \dfrac{1}{12}$ |

## C. Computing the effective rate of interest per payment period

In Chapter 10 you were introduced to the concept of the effective rate of interest. It was defined as the nominal rate of interest compounded annually and represented by the symbol *f*. It can readily be determined from the periodic rate of interest *i* by means of Formula 10.1, $f = (1 + i)^m - 1$, where *m* is the number of compounding periods per year.

When dealing with general annuities, it is useful to utilize the **equivalent rate of interest per payment period**. Depending on the length of the payment interval, the equivalent interest rate per payment period may be a monthly, quarterly, semi-annual, or annual rate. It can be obtained from the periodic rate of interest $i$ by a formula identical in nature to Formula 10.1.

To avoid confusion, we will distinguish the equivalent rate of interest per payment period from the effective annual rate of interest $f$ by using the symbol $p$ for the equivalent rate of interest per payment period. It can be determined by means of Formula 12.1 that

$$\boxed{p = (1 + i)^c - 1} \qquad\text{———— Formula 12.1}$$

$$\text{where } c = \frac{\text{THE NUMBER OF INTEREST CONVERSION PERIODS PER YEAR}}{\text{THE NUMBER OF PAYMENT PERIODS PER YEAR}}$$

*Note:* Formula 12.1 is the same as Formula 10.1 except that $f$ is replaced by $p$, and $m$ is replaced by $c$. Also note that when the payment interval is one year, $p = f$.

## POINTERS AND PITFALLS

Formula 12.1, which is $p = (1 + i)^c - 1$, is useful in calculating the equivalent interest rate per rent payment period in general annuity problems, while Formula 10.1, which is the effective rate formula $f = (1 + i)^m - 1$, is useful in making conversions between compound rates of interest and corresponding effective rates of interest.

When using an electronic calculator equipped with a universal power key, the given periodic rate of interest $i$ can be easily converted into the equivalent rate of interest per payment period.

**EXAMPLE 12.1C**

Jean receives annuity payments at the end of every six months. If she deposits these payments in an account earning interest at 9% compounded monthly, what is the semi-annually compounded rate of interest?

**SOLUTION**

Since the payments are made at the end of every six months while interest is compounded monthly,

$$c = \frac{\text{THE NUMBER OF INTEREST CONVERSION PERIODS PER YEAR}}{\text{THE NUMBER OF PAYMENT PERIODS PER YEAR}} = \frac{12}{2} = 6$$

$$i = \frac{9\%}{12} = 0.75\% = 0.0075$$

$$p = (1 + i)^c - 1$$

$$p = 1.0075^6 - 1$$

$$p = 1.045852 - 1$$

$$p = 0.045852 = 4.5852\%$$

The rate of interest is 4.5852% per semi-annual period.

**EXAMPLE 12.1D**

Peel Credit Union pays 6% compounded quarterly on its Premium Savings Accounts. If Roland Catchpole deposits $25 in his account at the end of every month, what is the monthly compounded rate of interest?

**SOLUTION**

Since the payments are made at the end of every month while interest is compounded quarterly,

$$c = \frac{4}{12} = \frac{1}{3}; \quad i = \frac{6\%}{4} = 1.5\% = 0.015$$

$$p = 1.015^{\frac{1}{3}} - 1$$

$$p = 1.004975 - 1$$

$$p = 0.004975 = 0.4975\%$$

The rate of interest is 0.4975% per month.

## D. Future value of an ordinary general annuity using the equivalent rate of interest per payment period

Determining the equivalent rate per payment period $p$ allows us to convert the ordinary general annuity problem into an ordinary simple annuity problem. To be consistent with the symbols previously used for developing formulas for ordinary simple annuities, we will use the following notation:

$FV_{nc}$ = the future value (or accumulated value) of an ordinary general annuity;
PMT = the size of the periodic payment;
$\quad n$ = the number of periodic payments;
$\quad c$ = the number of interest conversion periods per payment interval;
$\quad i$ = the interest rate per interest conversion period;
$\quad p$ = the equivalent rate of interest per payment period.

Substituting $p$ for $i$ in Formula 11.1, we obtain

$$FV_{nc} = PMT\left[\frac{(1 + p)^n - 1}{p}\right] \text{ where } p = (1 + i)^c - 1 \quad \text{------- Formula 12.2}$$

**EXAMPLE 12.1E**

Determine the accumulated value after ten years of payments of $2000 made at the end of each year if interest is 6% compounded monthly.

**SOLUTION**

This problem is an ordinary general annuity.

$$PMT = 2000.00; \quad n = 10; \quad c = 12; \quad i = \frac{6\%}{12} = 0.5\% = 0.005$$

The equivalent annual rate

$$p = 1.005^{12} - 1 = 1.061678 - 1 = 0.061678 = 6.1678\%$$

The given ordinary general annuity can be converted into an ordinary simple annuity.

$$PMT = 2000.00; \quad n = 10; \quad p = 0.061678$$

$$FV_{nc} = 2000.00\left(\frac{1.061678^{10} - 1}{0.061678}\right) \text{————— substituting in Formula 12.2}$$

$$= 2000.00(13.285114)$$

$$= \$26\ 570.23$$

The accumulated value after ten years is about $26 570.23.

**EXAMPLE 12.1F**

Crestview Farms set aside $1250 at the end of each month for the purchase of a combine. How much money will be available after five years if interest is 6.0% compounded semi-annually?

**SOLUTION**

This problem involves an ordinary general annuity.

$$PMT = 1250.00; \quad n = 5(12) = 60; \quad c = \frac{2}{12} = \frac{1}{6}; \quad i = \frac{6.0\%}{2} = 3.0\% = 0.03$$

The equivalent monthly rate of interest

$$p = 1.03^{\frac{1}{6}} - 1 = 1.004939 - 1 = 0.004939 = 0.4939\%$$

$$FV_{nc} = 1250.00\left(\frac{1.004939^{60} - 1}{0.004939}\right) \text{————— substituting in Formula 12.2}$$

$$= 1250(69.638936)$$

$$= \$87\ 048.67$$

After five years, the amount available is $87 048.67.

# E. Using preprogrammed calculators to find the future value of an ordinary general annuity

The use of $p$ rather than $i$ as the rate of interest is the only difference in the programmed solution for the general annuity compared to the programmed solution for a simple annuity.

 When using preprogrammed calculators, such as the BAII Plus, the calculator must be set for the number of payment periods per year P/Y and the number of interest compounding periods per year C/Y. To set the calculator for Example 12.1G, follow these steps:

| 2nd | P/Y | 2 | Enter | ↓ | C/Y | 4 | Enter | 2nd | QUIT |

To show the nominal interest rate per year, I/Y needs to be entered. In this example, the number is 6, indicating 6%.

Remember also that $n$ denotes the number of payments made. In this example, there are 20 payments (10 years × P/Y of 2).

*Note:* This assumes the calculator is in the default setting "END."

Note that each time the P/Y is changed, the C/Y automatically changes to match the P/Y. To make the C/Y different from the P/Y, it must be re-entered separately, after the P/Y may have been changed.

---

**EXAMPLE 12.1G**

Find the future value of $2500 deposited at the end of every six months for ten years if interest is 6% compounded quarterly.

**SOLUTION**

$\text{PMT} = 2500.00; \quad n = 2(10) = 20; \quad \text{P/Y} = 2; \quad \text{C/Y} = 4; \quad c = \dfrac{4}{2} = 2;$

$\text{I/Y} = 6; \quad i = \dfrac{6\%}{4} = 1.5\% = 0.015$

To use the formula:

**STEP 1**

Convert $i$ into the equivalent semi-annual rate of interest.
$p = 1.015^2 - 1 = 1.030225 - 1 = 0.030225 = 3.0225\%$

**STEP 2**

Using $p$ as the interest rate per payment period, determine the amount of the ordinary annuity.
To use the calculator:

(Set P/Y = 2; C/Y = 4)

| Key in | Press | Display shows | |
|--------|-------|---------------|---|
| 6 | I/Y | 6 | |
| 0 | PV | 0 | |
| 2500 | ± PMT | −2500 | |
| 20 | N | 20 | ——— the number of payments |
| CPT | FV | 67329.89319 | |

The amount on deposit after ten years will be $67 329.89.

---

**EXAMPLE 12.1H**

Determine the accumulated value of payments of $1250 made at the end of each quarter for eight years if interest is 5.5% compounded annually.

**SOLUTION**

$\text{PMT} = 1250.00; \quad n = 8(4) = 32; \quad \text{P/Y} = 4; \quad \text{C/Y} = 1; \quad c = \dfrac{1}{4} = 0.25;$
$\text{I/Y} = 5.5; \quad i = 5.5\% = 0.055$

To use the formula:

$p = 1.055^{0.25} - 1 = 1.013475 - 1 = 0.013475 = 1.3475\%$

To use the calculator:

(Set P/Y = 4; C/Y = 1) 5.5 ⟨ I/Y ⟩ 0 ⟨ PV ⟩

1250 ⟨ ± ⟩ ⟨ PMT ⟩ 32 ⟨ N ⟩ ⟨ CPT ⟩ ⟨ FV ⟩ ⟨ 49599.22016 ⟩

The accumulated value of the payments is $49 599.22.

## EXERCISE 12.1

If you choose, you can use Excel's *Future Value (FV)* function to answer the questions indicated below. Refer to **FV** on the Spreadsheet Template Disk to learn how to use this Excel function.

**A.** Find the future value of each of the following eight ordinary annuities.

| | Periodic Payment | Payment Interval | Term | Interest Rate | Conversion Period |
|---|---|---|---|---|---|
| **1.** | $2500 | 6 months | 7 years | 8% | quarterly |
| **2.** | 900 | 3 months | 5 years | 6 | monthly |
| **3.** | 72 | 1 month | 15 years | 3 | semi-annually |
| **4.** | 225 | 3 months | 10 years | 5 | annually |
| **5.** | 1750 | 6 months | 12 years | 7 | annually |
| **6.** | 680 | 1 month | 3 years | 9 | annually |
| **7.** | 7500 | 1 year | 4 years | 6 | quarterly |
| **8.** | 143 | 1 month | 9 years | 4 | quarterly |

**B.** Answer each of the following questions.

1. Find the future value of payments of $425 made at the end of every three months for nine years if interest is 9% compounded monthly.

Reference Example 12.1B

2. What is the accumulated value of deposits of $1500 made at the end of every six months for six years if interest is 6% compounded quarterly?

3. How much will deposits of $15 made at the end of each month amount to after ten years if interest is 5% compounded quarterly? Reference Example 12.1D

4. What is the future value of payments of $250 made at the end of every three months in fifteen years if interest is 7.5% compounded annually?

5. Mr. Tomas has contributed $1000 at the end of each year into an RRSP paying 6% compounded quarterly.
   **(a)** How much will Mr. Tomas have in the RRSP after ten years?
   **(b)** After ten years, how much of the amount is interest?

6. Alexa Sanchez saves $5 at the end of each month and deposits the money in an account paying 4% compounded quarterly.
   **(a)** How much will she accumulate in 25 years?
   **(b)** How much of the accumulated amount is interest?

7. Edwin Ng has made deposits of $500 into his savings account at the end of every three months for ten years. If interest is 4.5% compounded semi-annually and if

he leaves the accumulated balance for another five years, what will be the balance in his account then?

8. Mrs. Cook has made deposits of $950 at the end of every six months for fifteen years. If interest is 3% compounded monthly, how much will Mrs. Cook have accumulated ten years after the last deposit?

9. For the last four years, Joely has authorized the payroll department at her work to deduct $30 per week to be placed into an RRSP account. If interest is 5.17% compounded monthly, how much will Joely have accumulated in her RRSP?

10. Clark's younger brother has saved $18 per month from his paper route for the last two years. If interest is 4% compounded quarterly, how much will he have accumulated in his savings account?

# 12.2 ORDINARY GENERAL ANNUITIES—FINDING THE PRESENT VALUE PV

## A. Present value of an ordinary general annuity using the equivalent rate of interest per payment period

As with the future value of an ordinary general annuity, we can convert the given periodic rate of interest $i$ into the effective rate of interest per payment period.

$$p = (1 + i)^c - 1$$

The use of $p$ converts the ordinary general annuity problem into an ordinary simple annuity problem.

Substituting $p$ for $i$ in Formula 11.2, we obtain

$$PV_{nc} = PMT\left[\frac{1 - (1 + p)^{-n}}{p}\right]$$ ——————— Formula 12.3

| EXAMPLE 12.2A | A loan is repaid by making payments of $2000 at the end of every six months for twelve years. If interest on the loan is 8% compounded quarterly, what was the principal of the loan? |

| SOLUTION | |

$PMT = 2000.00; \quad n = 12(2) = 24; \quad P/Y = 2; \quad C/Y = 4; \quad c = \dfrac{4}{2} = 2;$

$I/Y = 8; \quad i = \dfrac{8\%}{4} = 2\% = 0.02$

The equivalent semi-annual rate of interest

$p = 1.02^2 - 1 = 1.0404 - 1 = 0.0404 = 4.04\%$

$PV_{nc} = 2000.00\left(\dfrac{1 - 1.0404^{-24}}{0.0404}\right)$ ——————— substituting in Formula 12.3

$\quad = 2000.00(15.184713)$

$\quad = \$30\ 369.43$

The loan principal was $30 369.43.

**EXAMPLE 12.2B**

A second mortgage requires payments of $370 at the end of each month for fifteen years. If interest is 11% compounded semi-annually, what was the amount borrowed?

**SOLUTION**

PMT = 370.00; $\quad n = 15(12) = 180; \quad$ P/Y = 12; $\quad$ C/Y = 2; $\quad c = \dfrac{2}{12} = \dfrac{1}{6}$;

I/Y = 11; $\quad i = \dfrac{11\%}{2} = 5.5\% = 0.055$

The effective monthly rate of interest

$p = 1.055^{\frac{1}{6}} - 1 = 1.008963 - 1 = 0.008963 = 0.8963\%$

$\text{PV}_{nc} = 370.00\left(\dfrac{1 - 1.008963^{-180}}{0.008963}\right)$ ———————— substituting in Formula 12.3

$= 370.00(89.180057)$

$= \$32\ 996.62$

The amount borrowed was $32 996.62.

## B. Using preprogrammed calculators to find the present value of an ordinary general annuity

**STEP 1** Set P/Y as the number of payment periods per year.

**STEP 2** Set C/Y as the number of compounding periods per year and I/Y as the nominal interest rate.

**STEP 3** Determine the present value of the ordinary general annuity.

**EXAMPLE 12.2C**

A contract is fulfilled by making payments of $8500 at the end of every year for fifteen years. If interest is 7% compounded quarterly, what is the cash price of the contract?

**SOLUTION**

PMT = 8500.00; $\quad n = 15; \quad$ P/Y = 1; $\quad$ C/Y = 4; $\quad c = 4; \quad$ I/Y = 7

$i = \dfrac{7\%}{4} = 1.75\% = 0.0175$

(Set P/Y = 1; C/Y = 4)  7 [ I/Y ]  0 [ FV ]  8500 [ ± ] [ PMT ]

15 [ N ] [ CPT ] [ PV ] [ 76516.37862 ]

The cash price of the contract is $76 516.38.

**EXAMPLE 12.2D**

A 25-year mortgage on a house requires payments of $619.94 at the end of each month. If interest is 9.5% compounded semi-annually, what was the mortgage principal?

**SOLUTION**

PMT = 619.94; $\quad n = 25(12) = 300; \quad$ P/Y = 12; $\quad$ C/Y = 2; $\quad c = \dfrac{2}{12} = \dfrac{1}{6}$;

I/Y = 9.5; $\quad i = \dfrac{9.5\%}{2} = 4.75\% = 0.0475$

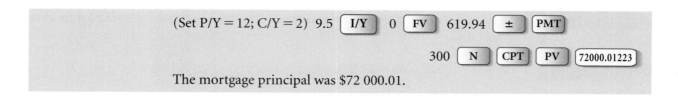

(Set P/Y = 12; C/Y = 2)  9.5 [ I/Y ]  0 [ FV ]  619.94 [ ± ] [ PMT ]

300 [ N ] [ CPT ] [ PV ] [ 72000.01223 ]

The mortgage principal was \$72 000.01.

## EXERCISE 12.2

If you choose, you can use Excel's **_Present Value (PV)_** function to answer the questions indicated below. Refer to **PV** on the Spreadsheet Template Disk to learn how to use this Excel function.

**A.** Find the present value of the following eight ordinary annuities.

| | Periodic Payment | Payment Interval | Term | Interest Rate | Conversion Period |
|---|---|---|---|---|---|
| **1.** | \$1400 | 3 months | 12 years | 6% | monthly |
| **2.** | 6000 | 1 year | 9 years | 10 | quarterly |
| **3.** | 3000 | 3 months | 4 years | 6 | annually |
| **4.** | 200 | 1 month | 2 years | 5 | semi-annually |
| **5.** | 95 | 1 month | 5 years | 4.5 | annually |
| **6.** | 975 | 6 months | 8 years | 8 | annually |
| **7.** | 1890 | 6 months | 15 years | 7 | quarterly |
| **8.** | 155 | 1 month | 10 years | 8 | quarterly |

**B.** Answer each of the following questions.

1. Find the present value of payments of \$250 made at the end of every three months for twelve years if money is worth 3% compounded monthly.

Reference Example 12.2A

2. What is the discounted value of \$1560 paid at the end of each year for nine years if interest is 6% compounded quarterly?

3. What cash payment is equivalent to making payments of \$825 at the end of every three months for 16 years if interest is 7% compounded semi-annually?

Reference Example 12.2B

4. What is the principal from which \$175 can be withdrawn at the end of each month for twenty years if interest is 5% compounded quarterly?

5. A property was purchased for \$5000 down and payments of \$2500 at the end of every six months for six years. Interest is 6% compounded monthly.
   (a) What was the purchase price of the property?
   (b) How much is the cost of financing?

6. A car was purchased for \$1500 down and payments of \$265 at the end of each month for four years. Interest is 9% compounded quarterly.
   (a) What was the purchase price of the car?
   (b) How much interest will be paid?

7. Payments of $715.59 are made at the end of each month to repay a 25-year mortgage. If interest is 10% compounded semi-annually, what is the original mortgage principal?

8. A 15-year mortgage is amortized by making payments of $1031.61 at the end of every three months. If interest is 8.25% compounded annually, what was the original mortgage balance?

9. Mac Dale purchased a retirement annuity paying $1200 every three months for twenty years. If the first payment is due three months after his retirement and interest is 6.6% compounded monthly, how much did Mr. Dale invest in the annuity?

10. For her daughter's education, Georgina Harcourt has invested an inheritance in a fund paying 5.2% compounded quarterly. If ordinary annuity payments of $178 per month are to be made out of the fund for eight years, how much was the inheritance?

11. As a settlement for an insurance claim, Craig was offered one of two choices. He could either accept a lump-sum amount of $5000 now, or accept quarterly payments of $145 for the next ten years. If the money is placed into a trust fund earning 3.95% compounded semi-annually, which is the better option and by how much?

12. Carl Hightop, a popular basketball player, has been offered a two-year salary deal. He can either accept $2 000 000 now or accept monthly amounts of $100 000 payable at the end of each month. If money can be invested at 5.7% compounded quarterly, which option is the better option for Carl and by how much?

# 12.3 ORDINARY GENERAL ANNUITIES—FINDING THE PERIODIC PAYMENT PMT

## A. Finding the periodic payment PMT when the future value of a general annuity is known

If the future value of an annuity $FV_{nc}$, the number of conversion periods $n$, and the conversion rate $i$ are known, you can find the periodic payment PMT by substituting the given values in the future value Formula 12.2.

$$FV_{nc} = PMT\left[\frac{(1 + p)^n - 1}{p}\right] \text{ where } p = (1 + i)^c - 1 \quad\text{—— Formula 12.2}$$

As we have emphasized throughout this book, understanding how to rearrange terms in a formula is a very important skill. By knowing how to do this, you avoid having to memorize equivalent forms of the same formula.

When using a scientific calculator, you can find PMT by first rearranging the terms of the future value formulas as shown below. Then substitute the three known values (FV, $n$, and $i$) into the rearranged formula and use the calculator to solve for PMT.

$$FV_{nc} = PMT\left[\frac{(1 + p)^n - 1}{p}\right] \quad \text{— Formula 12.2}$$

$$PMT = \frac{FV_{nc}}{\left[\dfrac{(1 + p)^n - 1}{p}\right]} \quad \text{— divide both sides by } \left[\frac{(1 + p)^n - 1}{p}\right]$$

$$PMT = \frac{FV_{nc}\,p}{(1 + p)^n - 1} \quad \text{— Formula 12.2A: dividing by a fraction is the same as inverting the fraction and multiplying}$$

When using a preprogrammed financial calculator, you can find PMT by entering the five known values (FV, N, I/Y, P/Y, and C/Y) and pressing $\boxed{\text{CPT}}$ $\boxed{\text{PMT}}$.

Recall that the PMT amount will be negative since payments are considered to be cash outflows.

**EXAMPLE 12.3A** What sum of money must be deposited at the end of every three months into an account paying 6% compounded monthly to accumulate to $25 000 in ten years?

**SOLUTION** $FV_{nc} = 25\,000.00;\quad n = 10(4) = 40;\quad P/Y = 4;\quad C/Y = 12;\quad c = \dfrac{12}{4} = 3;$

$I/Y = 6;\quad i = 0.5\% = 0.005$

The effective quarterly rate of interest

$$p = 1.005^3 - 1 = 1.015075 - 1 = 0.015075 = 1.5075\%$$

$$25\,000.00 = PMT\left(\frac{1.015075^{40} - 1}{0.015075}\right) \quad \text{— substituting in Formula 12.2}$$

$$25\,000.00 = PMT(54.354225)$$

$$PMT = \frac{25\,000.00}{54.354225}$$

$$PMT = \$459.95$$

Using Formula 12.2A, which is Formula 12.2 rearranged,

$$PMT = \frac{FV_{nc}\,p}{(1 + p)^n - 1}$$

$$PMT = \frac{25\,000.000(0.015075)}{1.015075^{40} - 1} \quad \text{— substituting in Formula 12.2A}$$

$$PMT = \$459.95$$

**Programmed Solution**

(Set P/Y = 4; C/Y = 12) $\boxed{\text{2nd}}$ (CLR TVM) 6 $\boxed{\text{I/Y}}$ 0 $\boxed{\text{PV}}$

25 000 $\boxed{\text{FV}}$ 40 $\boxed{\text{N}}$ $\boxed{\text{CPT}}$ $\boxed{\text{PMT}}$ $\boxed{-459.945847}$

The required quarterly deposit is $459.95.

# B. Finding the periodic payment PMT when the present value of a general annuity is known

If the present value of a general annuity $PV_{nc}$, the number of conversion periods $n$, and the conversion rate $i$ are known, you can find the periodic payment PMT by substituting the given values in the present value Formula 12.3.

$$PV_{nc} = PMT\left[\frac{1 - (1 + p)^{-n}}{p}\right]$$ ——— **Formula 12.3**

When using a scientific calculator, you can find PMT by first rearranging the terms of the present value formulas. Then substitute the three known values (PV, $n$, and $i$) into the rearranged formula and solve for PMT.

$$PV_{nc} = PMT\left[\frac{1 - (1 + p)^{-n}}{p}\right]$$ ——— **Formula 12.3**

$$PMT = \frac{PV_{nc}}{\left[\dfrac{1 - (1 + p)^{-n}}{p}\right]}$$ ——— divide both sides by $\left[\dfrac{1-(1 + p)^{-n}}{p}\right]$

$$PMT = \frac{PV_{nc}\,p}{1 - (1 + p)^{-n}}$$ ——— **Formula 12.3A:** dividing by a fraction is the same as inverting the fraction and multiplying

When using a preprogrammed financial calculator, you can find PMT by entering the five known values (PV, N, I/Y, P/Y, and C/Y) and pressing CPT PMT .

**EXAMPLE 12.3B**

Mr. and Mrs. White applied to their credit union for a first mortgage of $60 000 to buy a house. The mortgage is to be amortized over 25 years and interest on the mortgage is 8.5% compounded semi-annually. What is the size of the monthly payment if payments are made at the end of each month?

**SOLUTION**

$PV_{nc} = 60\ 000.00$;   $n = 25(12) = 300$;   $P/Y = 12$;   $C/Y = 2$;   $c = \dfrac{2}{12} = \dfrac{1}{6}$;

$I/Y = 8.5$;   $i = \dfrac{8.5\%}{2} = 4.25\% = 0.0425$

The effective monthly rate of interest

$p = 1.0425^{\frac{1}{6}} - 1 = 1.006961 - 1 = 0.006961 = 0.6961\%$

$60\ 000.00 = PMT\left(\dfrac{1 - 1.006961^{-300}}{0.006961}\right)$ ——— substituting in Formula 12.3

$60\ 000.00 = PMT(125.72819)$

$PMT = \dfrac{60\ 000.00}{125.72819}$

$PMT = \$477.22$

**Programmed Solution**

(Set P/Y = 12; C/Y = 2) 8.5 [ I/Y ]  0 [ FV ]  60 000 [ ± ] [ PV ]

300 [ N ] [ CPT ] [ PMT ] [ 477.218111 ]

The monthly payment due at the end of each month is $477.22.

## EXERCISE 12.3

 If you choose, you can use Excel's **Payment (PMT)** function to answer all of the questions below. Refer to **PMT** on the Spreadsheet Template Disk to learn how to use this Excel function.

**A.** For each of the following ten ordinary general annuities, determine the size of the periodic rent.

| | Future Value | Present Value | Payment Period | Term of Annuity | Interest Rate | Conversion Period |
|---|---|---|---|---|---|---|
| 1. | $15 000 | | 6 months | 7 years, 6 mos | 5.5% | annually |
| 2. | 6 000 | | 1 quarter | 9 years, 9 mos | 8 | monthly |
| 3. | | $12 000 | 12 months | 15 years | 4.5 | semi-annually |
| 4. | | 7 000 | 6 months | 12.5 years | 7.5 | quarterly |
| 5. | 8 000 | | 3 months | 6 years | 6.8 | semi-annually |
| 6. | | 20 000 | 3 months | 20 years | 12 | monthly |
| 7. | 45 000 | | 6 months | 10 years | 9 | quarterly |
| 8. | 35 000 | | 1 year | 15 years | 4 | quarterly |
| 9. | 20 000 | | 1 month | 8 years | 7 | semi-annually |
| 10. | 16 500 | | 3 months | 15 years | 5.75 | annually |

**B.** Answer each of the following questions.

1. What payment made at the end of each quarter for fifteen years will accumulate to $12 000 at 6% compounded monthly?   *Reference Example 12.3A*

2. What payment is required at the end of each month for five years to repay a loan of $6000 at 7% compounded semi-annually?

3. A contract can be fulfilled by making an immediate payment of $9500 or equal payments at the end of every six months for eight years. What is the size of the semi-annual payments at 7.4% compounded quarterly?

4. What payment made at the end of each year for eighteen years will amount to $16 000 at 4.2% compounded monthly?

5. What payment is required at the end of each month for fifteen years to amortize a $32 000 mortgage if interest is 9.5% compounded semi-annually?

*Reference Example 12.3B*

6. How much must be deposited at the end of each quarter for ten years to accumulate to $12 000 at 6% compounded monthly?

7. What payment made at the end of every three months for twenty years will accumulate to $20 000 at 7% compounded semi-annually?

8. Derrick bought a car priced at $9300 for 15% down and equal monthly payments for four years. If interest is 8% compounded semi-annually, what is the size of the monthly payment?

9. Equal payments are to be made at the end of each month for fifteen years with interest at 9% compounded quarterly. After the last payment, the fund is to be invested for seven years at 10% compounded quarterly and have a maturity value of $20 000. What is the size of the monthly payment?

10. To finance the development of a new product, a company borrowed $30 000 at 7% compounded monthly. If the loan is to be repaid in equal quarterly payments over seven years and the first payment is due three months after the date of the loan, what is the size of the quarterly payment?

# 12.4 ORDINARY GENERAL ANNUITIES—FINDING THE TERM $n$

## A. Finding the term $n$ when the future value of a general annuity is known

If the future value of an annuity $FV_{nc}$, the periodic payment PMT, and the conversion rate $i$ are known, you can find the term of the annuity $n$ by substituting the given values in the future value Formula 12.2.

$$\boxed{FV_{nc} = PMT\left[\frac{(1 + p)^n - 1}{p}\right] \text{ where } p = (1 + i)^c - 1} \quad\text{——— Formula 12.2}$$

When using a scientific calculator, you can find $n$ by first rearranging the terms of the future value Formula 12.2. Then substitute the three known values (FV, PMT, and $p$) into the rearranged formula and solve for $n$.

$$FV_{nc} = PMT\left[\frac{(1 + p)^n - 1}{p}\right] \quad\text{——— Formula 12.2}$$

$$\frac{FV_{nc}}{PMT} = \frac{(1 + p)^n - 1}{p} \quad\text{——————— divide both sides by PMT}$$

$$(1 + p)^n = \left(\frac{FV_{nc}\,p}{PMT}\right) + 1 \quad\text{——————— multiply both sides by } p \text{ and add 1 to both sides}$$

$$n \ln(1 + p) = \ln[(FV_{nc}\,p/PMT) + 1] \quad\text{——— solve for } n \text{ using natural logarithms}$$

$$n = \frac{\ln[FV_{nc}\,p/PMT + 1]}{\ln(1 + p)} \quad\text{——— Formula 12.2B: divide both sides by } \ln(1 + p)$$

When using a preprogrammed financial calculator, you can find $n$ by entering the five known values (FV, PMT, I/Y, P/Y, and C/Y) and pressing CPT N .

**EXAMPLE 12.4A**

What period of time is required for $125 deposited at the end of each month at 11% compounded quarterly to grow to $15 000?

**SOLUTION**

$FV_{nc} = 15\,000.00$; $PMT = 125.00$; $P/Y = 12$; $C/Y = 4$;

$c = \dfrac{4}{12} = \dfrac{1}{3}$; $I/Y = 11$; $i = \dfrac{11\%}{4} = 2.75\% = 0.0275$

The effective monthly rate of interest

$p = 1.0275^{\frac{1}{3}} - 1 = 1.009084 - 1 = 0.009084 = 0.9084\%$

$15\,000.00 = 125.00\left(\dfrac{1.009084^n - 1}{0.009084}\right)$ ———— using Formula 12.2

$120.00 = \dfrac{(1.009084^n - 1)}{0.009084}$

$1.090068 = 1.009084^n - 1$

$1.009084^n = 2.090068$

$n \ln 1.009084 = \ln 2.090068$

$n(0.009043) = 0.737197$

$n = \dfrac{0.737197}{0.009043}$

$n = 81.522227$

$n = 82$ months approximately

With a preprogrammed calculator, the procedure is

(Set P/Y = 12; C/Y = 4) 11 [ I/Y ] 0 [ PV ] 15 000 [ FV ]

125 [ ± ] [ PMT ] [ CPT ] [ N ] [ 81.522240 ]

It will take about 82 months to accumulate $15 000.

## B. Finding the term *n* when the present value of a general annuity is known

If the present value $PV_{nc}$, the periodic payment PMT, and the conversion rate $i$ are known, you can find the term of the annuity $n$ by substituting the given values in the present value Formula 12.3.

$$PV_{nc} = PMT\left[\dfrac{1 - (1 + p)^{-n}}{p}\right]$$ ———— Formula 12.3

Alternatively, you can first rearrange the terms of Formula 12.3 to solve for *n*.

$\dfrac{PV_{nc}}{PMT} = \dfrac{1 - (1 + p)^{-n}}{p}$ ———— divide both sides by PMT

$\left(\dfrac{PV_{nc}p}{PMT}\right) = 1 - (1 + p)^{-n}$ ———— multiply both sides by *i* and subtract 1 from both sides

$$(1 + p)^{-n} = 1 - \left( \frac{PV_{nc}p}{PMT} \right) \text{————————} \text{multiply both sides by } -1$$

$$-n \ln(1 + p) = \ln\left[ 1 - \left( \frac{PV_{nc}p}{PMT} \right) \right] \text{————————} \text{solve for } n \text{ using natural logarithms}$$

$$n = \frac{\ln\left[ 1 - \left( \frac{PV_{nc}p}{PMT} \right) \right]}{-\ln (1 + p)} \text{————————} \text{Formula 12.3B: divide both sides by } -\ln(1 + p)$$

When using a scientific calculator, you can find $n$ by first rearranging the terms of the present value formulas above. Then substitute the three known values (PV, PMT, and $i$) into the rearranged formula and solve for $n$.

When using a preprogrammed financial calculator, you can find $n$ by entering the five known values (PV, PMT, I/Y, P/Y, and C/Y) and pressing [CPT] [N].

*Note:* When using the Texas Instruments BAII Plus financial calculator, you *must* enter *either* the PV or PMT as a negative amount, *but not both*. Due to the sign conventions used by this calculator, entering *both* PV and PMT as negative amounts or as positive amounts will lead to an *incorrect* final answer. The calculator does *not* indicate that the answer is incorrect or that an entry error was made. (This has not been an issue until now because either PV or PMT was 0 in all the examples we discussed.) To avoid incorrect answers, *always* enter the PV amount as a negative number and the PMT amount as a positive number when FV = 0 and you are calculating N. However, if PV = 0, enter PMT as a negative number and FV as a positive number. The examples in this text follow these rules. Refer to Appendix II to check whether this step is necessary if you use the Sharp EL-733A or the Hewlett-Packard 10BII calculator.

---

**EXAMPLE 12.4B**

A business valued at $96 000 is bought for a down payment of 25% and payments of $4000 at the end of every three months. If interest is 9% compounded monthly, for how long will payments have to be made?

**SOLUTION**

$PV_{nc} = 96\ 000.00(0.75) = 72\ 000.00;$ $\quad$ PMT $= 4000.00;$

$P/Y = 4;$ $\quad$ $C/Y = 12;$ $\quad$ $c = \dfrac{12}{4} = 3;$ $\quad$ $I/Y = 9;$ $\quad$ $i = \dfrac{9\%}{12} = 0.75\% = 0.0075$

The effective quarterly rate of interest

$p = 1.0075^3 - 1 = 1.022669 - 1 = 0.022669 = 2.2669\%$

$$72\ 000.00 = 4000.00\left( \frac{1 - 1.022669^{-n}}{0.022669} \right) \text{————————} \text{using Formula 12.3}$$

$$0.408046 = 1 - 1.022669^{-n}$$
$$1.022669^{-n} = 0.591954$$
$$-n \ln 1.022669 = \ln 0.591954$$
$$-n(0.022416) = -0.524326$$
$$n = 23.390585 \text{ (quarters)}$$

**Programmed Solution**

(Set P/Y = 4; C/Y = 12) 9 [ I/Y ] 0 [ FV ] 72 000

[ ± ] [ PV ] 4000 [ PMT ] [ CPT ] [ N ] [ 23.390604 ]

Payments will have to be made for 24 quarters or six years.

## EXERCISE 12.4

If you choose, you can use Excel's *Number of Compounding Periods (NPER)* function to answer all of the questions below. Refer to **NPER** on the Spreadsheet Template Disk to learn how to use this Excel function.

 **A.** Find the term of each of the following ten ordinary general annuities. (State your answer in years and months.)

|  | Future Value | Present Value | Periodic Rent | Payment Interval | Interest Rate | Compounding Period |
|---|---|---|---|---|---|---|
| 1. | $20 000 |  | $ 800 | 1 year | 7.5% | semi-annually |
| 2. | 17 000 |  | 35 | 3 months | 9 | monthly |
| 3. |  | $14 500 | 190 | 1 month | 5.25 | quarterly |
| 4. |  | 5 000 | 300 | 3 months | 4 | semi-annually |
| 5. | 36 000 |  | 175 | 6 months | 7.4 | annually |
| 6. |  | 9 500 | 740 | 1 quarter | 5.2 | monthly |
| 7. |  | 21 400 | 1660 | 6 months | 4.5 | monthly |
| 8. | 13 600 |  | 140 | 6 months | 8 | quarterly |
| 9. | 72 000 |  | 90 | 1 month | 3.75 | semi-annually |
| 10. |  | 11 700 | 315 | 3 months | 11 | annually |

 **B.** Answer each of the following questions.

1. How long would it take you to save $5000 by making deposits of $100 at the end of every month into a savings account earning 6% compounded quarterly?

Reference Example 12.4A

2. How long will it take to save $15 000 by making deposits of $90 at the end of every month into an account earning interest at 4% compounded quarterly?

3. In what period of time could you pay back a loan of $3000 by making monthly payments of $90 if interest is 10.5% compounded semi-annually?

Reference Example 12.4B

4. For how long will Jack have to make payments of $350 at the end of every three months to repay a loan of $6000 if interest is 9% compounded monthly?

5. Mirsad is saving $500 at the end of each month. How soon can he retire if he wants to have a retirement fund of $120 000 and interest is 5.4% compounded quarterly?

6. For how long must contributions of $2000 be made at the end of each year to accumulate to $100 000 at 6% compounded quarterly?

7. For how long can $800 be withdrawn at the end of each month from an account originally containing $16 000, if interest is 6.8% compounded semi-annually?

8. A mortgage of $120 000 is to be repaid by making payments of $750 at the end of each month. If interest is 5.75% compounded semi-annually, what is the term of the mortgage?

9. Suppose $370.37 is deposited at the end of every three months into an account earning 6.5% compounded semi-annually. If the balance in the account is to be $20 000, how many deposits are needed?

10. Mr. Deneau accumulated $100 000 in an RRSP. He converted the RRSP into an RRIF and started to withdraw $4500 at the end of every three months from the fund. If interest is 6.75% compounded monthly, for how long can Mr. Deneau make withdrawals?

# 12.5 ORDINARY GENERAL ANNUITIES—FINDING THE PERIODIC INTEREST RATE *i*

## A. Finding the periodic rate of interest *i* using preprogrammed financial calculators

Preprogrammed financial calculators are especially helpful when solving for the conversion rate *i*. Determining *i* without a financial calculator is extremely time-consuming. However, it *can* be done by hand, as illustrated in Appendix B on the CD-ROM.

## »» BUSINESS MATH NEWS BOX

### University of Windsor Enters Bond Market

The University of Windsor took a first-time trip to the financial markets and issued $108.3 million in bonds to fund major construction projects—creating the largest debenture in its 43-year history as a public institution.

The first project to benefit from the infusion of cash will be a new school of engineering worth $53 million. The university expects to pay for the new digs for aspiring engineers with government funding, fundraising dollars, and some of the borrowed money.

The university will pay an interest rate of 5.37% to the bond's investors over 40 years. Of the $108.3 million, $29 million will be used to pay off the school's existing debt. Another $14 million will be placed in a sinking fund that will be used to help pay off the bond's principal in 2046.

The balance will be invested and interest will be earned on the money until it is needed for capital projects, Paul said.

The decision to issue bonds came earlier this year as the school's board of governors considered its options to raise the cash for capital projects. A bond is essentially a loan. The purchaser of a bond is lending money to the issuer—in this case the university. The purchaser is paid a certain rate of interest at fixed intervals, plus the original investment when the bond matures.

*Source:* "University of Windsor enters bond market: $108M to help finance projects," by Roseann Danese, *The Windsor Star,* June 29, 2006. Material reprinted with the express permission of: "Windsor Star Group Inc.," a CanWest Partnership.

**QUESTIONS**

1. Calculate the interest provided to investors if the coupon rate is 5.37% paid semi-annually.

2. Calculate the amount remaining after all plans for the $108 million bond have been satisfied.

3. **a.** If a sinking fund is created with this remaining amount, earning 4.2% p.a. compounded quarterly, calculate the future value after 40 years.

   **b.** What amount is required to add to this sinking fund on a quarterly basis in order to satisfy the loan repayment?

When the future value or present value, the periodic payment PMT, and the term $n$ of a general annuity are known, retrieve the value of I/Y by pressing CPT I/Y.

---

**EXAMPLE 12.5A**

Irina deposited $150 in a savings account at the end of each month for 60 months. If the accumulated value of the deposits was $10 000 and interest was compounded semi-annually, what was the nominal annual rate of interest?

**SOLUTION**

FV = 10 000.00; PMT = 150.00; $n = 60$; P/Y = 12; C/Y = 2; $c = \dfrac{2}{12} = \dfrac{1}{6}$

(Set P/Y = 12; C/Y = 2) 0 [ PV ] 10 000 [ FV ]

150 [ ± ] [ PMT ] 60 [ N ] [ CPT ] [ I/Y ] [ 4.255410 ]

The nominal annual rate of interest is 4.26% p.a. compounded semi-annually.

---

**EXAMPLE 12.5B**

Compute the nominal annual rate of interest compounded monthly at which $500 paid at the end of every three months for ten years will eliminate a debt of $16 000.

**SOLUTION**

PV = 16 000.00; PMT = 500.00; $n = 40$; P/Y = 4; C/Y = 12; $c = \dfrac{12}{4} = 3$

(Set P/Y = 4; C/Y = 12) 0 [ FV ] 16 000 [ PV ]

500 [ ± ] [ PMT ] 40 [ N ] [ CPT ] [ I/Y ] [ 4.528237 ]

The nominal annual rate is 4.53% p.a. compounded monthly.

# EXERCISE 12.5

**A.** For each of the following eight ordinary general annuities, determine the nominal annual rate of interest.

| | Future Value | Present Value | Periodic Payment | Payment Interval | Term | Conversion Period |
|---|---|---|---|---|---|---|
| 1. | $39 200 | | $2 300 | 1 year | 12 years | monthly |
| 2. | | $ 9 600 | 1 220 | 6 months | 5 years | monthly |
| 3. | | 62 400 | 2 600 | 6 months | 25 years | annually |
| 4. | 55 500 | | 75 | 1 month | 20 years | semi-annually |
| 5. | 6 400 | | 200 | 6 months | 9 years | monthly |
| 6. | 25 000 | | 790 | 1 year | 15 years | quarterly |
| 7. | | 7 500 | 420 | 3 months | 5 years | monthly |
| 8. | | 60 000 | 450 | 1 month | 25 years | semi-annually |

**B.** Answer each of the following questions.

1. What is the nominal annual rate of interest compounded quarterly if deposits of $253 made each month for 3½ years accumulate to $11 600?

    Reference Example 12.5A

2. Victoria saved $416 every six months for eight years. What nominal rate of interest compounded annually is earned if the savings account amounts to $7720 in eight years?

3. What is the nominal annual rate of interest compounded semi-annually if a four-year loan of $6000 is repaid by monthly payments of $144.23?

    Reference Example 12.5B

4. A car valued at $11 400 can be purchased for 10% down and monthly payments of $286.21 for three-and-a-half years. What is the nominal rate of interest compounded annually?

5. A property worth $50 000 can be purchased for 20% down and quarterly mortgage payments of $1000 for 25 years. What nominal rate of interest compounded monthly is charged?

6. A vacation property valued at $25 000 was bought for fifteen payments of $2200 due at the end of every six months. What nominal annual rate of interest compounded annually was charged?

7. Compute the nominal annual rate of interest compounded monthly at which $400 paid at the end of every three months for eight years accumulates to $20 000.

8. What is the nominal annual rate of interest compounded quarterly if a loan of $21 500 is repaid in seven years by payments of $2000 made at the end of every six months?

9. If Paige has accumulated $4850 by saving $120 every month for 3 years, what nominal annual rate of interest compounded quarterly has been earned?

10. Deanna wants to save $3500 in two years by depositing $420 every three months into a savings account. What nominal rate of interest compounded annually does her savings have to earn?

11. A mortgage of $27 500 is repaid by making payments of $280 at the end of each month for fifteen years. What is the nominal annual rate of interest compounded semi-annually?

12. A property worth $35 000 is purchased for 10% down and semi-annual payments of $2100 for twelve years. What is the effective annual rate of interest if interest is compounded quarterly?

# 12.6 CONSTANT-GROWTH ANNUITIES

The annuities we have considered so far have the common feature of periodic payments that are equal in size. **Constant-growth annuities** differ from these fixed-payment-size annuities in that the periodic payments change (usually grow) at a constant rate. The assumption of constant growth is often used in sales forecasting and long-term financial planning. It is consistent with the indexing of pensions and is also present in federal tax policies.

The types of constant-growth annuities parallel the types of fixed payment annuities considered in Chapter 11 and the previous sections of Chapter 12. However, we will deal only with ordinary simple constant-growth annuities.

With ordinary simple constant-growth annuities, the computations may involve determining the size of any periodic payment, the total amount of the periodic payments, the future value and present value of the stream of periodic payments, the amount of interest earned by the periodic payments, and the size of the first payment if either the present value or the future value is known. We will also consider in this section the special case when the constant growth rate equals the periodic rate of interest.

## A. Future value of an ordinary simple constant-growth annuity

To compute the future value of a series of payments growing at a constant rate, the approach is similar to that used in Example 11.2B.

In general, if the first payment is represented by PMT and the constant rate of growth by $k$, the constant growth factor for the annuity payments is $(1 + k)$ and the size of the successive payments is as follows:

| | |
|---|---|
| 1st payment | $= \text{PMT}$ |
| 2nd payment | $= \text{PMT}(1 + k)$ |
| 3rd payment | $= \text{PMT}(1 + k)^2$ |
| 4th payment | $= \text{PMT}(1 + k)^3$ |
| $\downarrow$ | $\downarrow$ |
| $\downarrow$ | $\downarrow$ |
| 10th payment | $= \text{PMT}(1 + k)^9$ |

$$\boxed{\text{SIZE OF THE } n\text{TH PAYMENT} = \text{PMT}(1 + k)^{n-1}} \quad \text{———— Formula 12.4}$$

The periodic constant-growth payments form an ordinary simple annuity in which PMT is the size of the first payment, $k$ is the periodic compounding rate, and $n$ is the number of payments.

> SUM OF THE PERIODIC CONSTANT-GROWTH PAYMENTS $= \text{PMT}\dfrac{(1 + k)^n - 1}{k}$  —— Formula 12.5

*Note:* Formula 12.5 is the same as Formula 11.1 except that $i$ has been replaced by $k$.

The formula for finding the future value of an ordinary simple constant-growth annuity is similar in structure to future value Formula 11.1.

> $$\text{FV} = \text{PMT}\frac{(1 + i)^n - (1 + k)^n}{i - k}$$  —————————————— Formula 12.6

where FV = the future (accumulated) value of an ordinary simple constant-growth annuity;

PMT = the size of the first annuity payment;
$\quad i$ = the interest rate per conversion period;
$\quad k$ = the constant growth rate of the annuity payments;
$\quad n$ = the number of conversion periods.

The factor $\dfrac{(1 + i)^n - (1 + k)^n}{i - k}$ is the compounding factor for constant-growth annuities. If $k = 0$, which means there is no growth in the periodic payments, the factor becomes the compounding factor used in Formula 11.1. Formula 11.1 is, in fact, a special case of Formula 12.6—the "zero-growth case."

---

**EXAMPLE 12.6A**

Five deposits increasing at a constant rate of 2% are made at the end of each of four successive years respectively. The size of the first deposit is $3000 and the fund earns interest at 6% compounded annually.

  (i) What is the size of the last deposit?

 (ii) How much was deposited in total?

(iii) What is the accumulated value of the deposits?

(iv) What is the interest earned by the deposits?

**SOLUTION**

The situation is pictured in Figure 12.3.

FIGURE 12.3    **End of period (year) $i = 6\% = 0.06$**

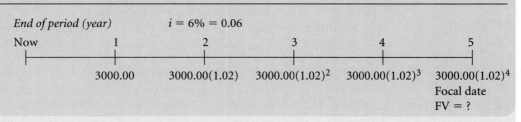

(i) $\text{PMT} = 3000.00; \quad k = 2\% = 0.02; \quad n = 5$

Size of the 5th payment

$= \text{PMT}(1+k)^{n-1}$ ———————————— using Formula 12.4

$= 3000.00(1.02)^4$

$= 3000.00(1.082432)$

$= \$3247.30$

(ii) $\text{PMT} = 3000.00; \quad k = 2\% = 0.02; \quad n = 5$

Sum of the constant-growth deposits

$= \text{PMT}\left[\dfrac{(1+k)^n - 1}{k}\right]$ ———————— using Formula 12.5

$= 3000.00\left[\dfrac{(1.02)^5 - 1}{0.02}\right]$

$= 3000.00\left[\dfrac{1.010408 - 1}{0.02}\right]$

$= 3000.00(5.20404)$

$= \$15\,612.12$

(iii) $\text{PMT} = 3000.00; \quad k = 2\% = 0.02; \quad n = 5; \quad i = 6\% = 0.06$

Sum of the constant-growth deposits

$\text{FV} = \text{PMT}\left[\dfrac{(1+i)^n - (1+k)^n}{i-k}\right]$ ———————— using Formula 12.6

$= 3000.00\left[\dfrac{(1.06)^5 - (1.02)^5}{0.06 - 0.02}\right]$

$= 3000.00\left[\dfrac{1.338226 - 1.104081}{0.02}\right]$

$= 3000.00(5.853620)$

$= \$17\,560.86$

(iv) The interest earned by the deposits

$= 17\,560.86 - 15\,612.12 = \$1948.74.$

## B. Present value of an ordinary simple constant-growth annuity

The approach to determining the present value of a series of payments forming a constant-growth annuity is the same as for finding the future value of the series of payments except that each payment must be discounted using Formula 9.1C, $\text{PV} = \text{FV}(1+i)^{-n}$.

$$\text{PV} = \text{PMT}\left[\dfrac{1 - (1+k)^n(1+i)^{-n}}{i-k}\right] \qquad \text{Formula 12.7}$$

where PV = the present (discounted) value of an ordinary simple constant-growth annuity;

PMT = the size of the first annuity payment;
$i$ = the interest rate per conversion period;
$k$ = the constant growth rate of the annuity payments;
$n$ = the number of conversion periods.

The factor $\left[\dfrac{1 - (1 + k)^n(1 + i)^{-n}}{i - k}\right]$ is the discount factor for constant-growth annuities. If $k = 0$, which means there is no growth in the periodic payments, the factor becomes the discount factor used in Formula 11.2. Formula 11.2 is, in fact, a special case of formula 12.7—the "zero-growth case."

Constant-growth annuity formulas are not part of the programming of most financial calculators. Problems involving constant-growth annuities can be solved by substituting in the appropriate formulas as shown in Examples 12.6A and 12.6B.

**EXAMPLE 12.6B**

Use Formula 12.7 to calculate the present value of the deposits in Example 12.6A.

**SOLUTION**

PMT = 3000.00; $k = 2\% = 0.02$; $n = 5$; $i = 6\% = 0.06$;

$$PV = 3000.00\left[\frac{1 - (1.02)^5(1.06)^{-5}}{0.06 - 0.02}\right] \text{ —— using Formula 12.7}$$

$$PV = 3000.00\left[\frac{1 - (1.104081)(0.747258)}{0.04}\right]$$

$$PV = 3000.00(4.374165)$$

$$PV = \$13\ 122.50$$

When the constant-growth rate of the annuity payments and the number of conversion periods are the same, Formula 12.8 is used to calculate future value of an ordinary simple constant-growth annuity.

$$FV = n(PMT)(1 + i)^{n-1} \text{ —— Formula 12.8}$$

When the constant-growth rate of the annuity payments and the number of conversion periods are the same, Formula 12.9 is used to calculate present value of an ordinary simple constant-growth annuity.

$$PV = n(PMT)(1 + i)^{-1} \text{ —— Formula 12.9}$$

## EXERCISE 12.6

 **A.** Answer each of the following questions.

1. You plan to make twenty-five periodic deposits into your RRSP starting with $500 and increasing thereafter by 3%.
   (a) What will be the size of the twenty-fifth deposit?
   (b) What will be the total amount deposited?

2. Sally has accumulated a sizeable balance in her investment fund. She wants to make annual withdrawals for fifteen years starting with $5000 and decreasing (negative growth) by 5% thereafter.
   (a) What will be the size of the fifteenth withdrawal? (*Hint:* Let $k = -5\%$.)
   (b) What will be the total amount withdrawn?

3. Twenty semi-annual deposits are made earning interest of 5% compounded semi-annually. The size of the first deposit is $1200 and the deposits increase at 1.5% thereafter.
   (a) Determine the total amount deposited.
   (b) How much was the accumulated value of the deposits just after the last deposit was made?
   (c) What is the size of the twelfth deposit?
   (d) What is the amount of interest included in the accumulated value?

4. Withdrawals increasing at a constant rate of 4% are made quarterly for six years from an account earning 6% compounded quarterly.
   (a) What must be the balance in the account to permit the withdrawals if the first withdrawal is $1500?
   (b) What is the size of the last withdrawal?
   (c) What is the total amount withdrawn?
   (d) How much interest is included in the withdrawals?

**B.** Solve each of the following.

1. Lucy won a large sum in the lottery. She invested part of her winnings into a fund earning 6% compounded monthly. She has arranged a systematic withdrawal plan that provides for 120 monthly payments increasing at a constant rate of 0.5% per payment. The first payment of $400 is due one month after she set up the fund. How much interest is included in the payments?

Reference Example 12.6A

2. Trent has opened an RRSP account by making an initial deposit of $1500. He intends to make semi-annual deposits for 30 years increasing at a constant rate of 3.5%. How much of the accumulated value just after the last deposit was made is interest if interest is 7% compounded semi-annually?

Reference Example 12.6B

3. Shelby paid $150 000 for a 10-year indexed annuity in which the monthly payments received at the end of each month diminish by 0.6% per payment. What is the total amount received by Shelby if interest is 7.2% compounded monthly?

4. Cecile intends to make end-of-the-year payments growing by 8% per payment for 12 years. If the payments earn 7% compounded annually, what is the size of the last payment if the accumulated value of the payments is $250 000?

# Review Exercise

1. Payments of $375 made every three months are accumulated at 3% compounded monthly. What is their future value after eight years if the payments are made at the end of every three months?

2. What is the accumulated value after twelve years of monthly deposits of $145 earning interest at 5% compounded semi-annually if the deposits are made at the end of each month?

3. What single cash payment is equivalent to payments of $3500 every six months at 7% compounded quarterly if the payments are made at the end of every six months for fifteen years?

4. What is the principal invested at 6.5% compounded semi-annually from which monthly withdrawals of $240 can be made at the end of each month for twenty-five years?

5. Contributions of $500 are made at the end of every three months into an RRSP. What is the accumulated balance after twenty years if interest is 6% compounded semi-annually?

6. A 25-year mortgage is amortized by payments of $761.50 made at the end of each month. If interest is 9.5% compounded semi-annually, what is the mortgage principal?

7. Kristan wants to accumulate $18 000 into an account earning 7.5% compounded semi-annually. How much must she deposit
   (a) at the end of each month for ten years?
   (b) at the end of each year for eight years?

8. What sum of money can be withdrawn from a fund of $15 750 invested at 4.25% compounded semi-annually
   (a) at the end of every month for twelve years?
   (b) at the end of each year for fifteen years?

9. How long will it take for payments of $350 to accumulate to $12 000 at 3% compounded monthly if made

(a) at the end of every three months?
(b) at the end of every six months?

10. A $92 000 mortgage with a 25-year term is repaid by making payments at the end of each month. If interest is 5.8% compounded semi-annually, how much are the payments?

11. A debt of $14 000 is repaid by making payments of $1500. If interest is 9% compounded monthly, for how long will payments have to be made
    (a) at the end of every six months?
    (b) at the end of each year?

12. What is the nominal rate of interest compounded monthly at which payments of $200 made at the end of every three months accumulate to $9200 in eight years?

13. A debt of $2290 is repaid by making payments of $198. If interest is 16.95% compounded monthly, for how long will quarterly payments have to be made?

14. A $60 000 mortgage with a 25-year term is repaid by making monthly payments of $480. What is the nominal annual rate of interest compounded semi-annually on the mortgage?

15. Marc invested a bonus of $6000 in an RRSP earning 4.9% compounded semi-annually for twenty years. At the end of the twenty years, he rolled the RRSP balance over into an RRIF paying $2000 at the end of each quarter starting three months after the date of rollover. If interest on the RRIF is 4.3% compounded monthly, for how long will Marc receive quarterly payments?

16. Satwinder deposited $145 at the end of each month for fifteen years at 7.5% compounded monthly. After her last deposit she converted the balance into an ordinary annuity paying $1200 every three months for twelve years. If interest on the annuity is compounded semi-annually, what is the nominal rate of interest paid by the annuity?

**17.** Mrs. Jolly contributes $222 at the end of every three months to an RRSP. Interest on the account is 6% compounded monthly.

  (**a**) What will the balance in the account be after eleven years?

  (**b**) How much of the balance will be interest?

  (**c**) If Mrs. Jolly converts the balance after eleven years into an RRIF paying 5% compounded monthly and makes equal quarterly withdrawals for twelve years starting three months after the conversion into her RRIF, what is the size of the quarterly withdrawal?

  (**d**) What is the combined interest earned by the RRSP and the RRIF?

**18.** How much must be contributed into an RRSP at the end of each year for twenty-five years to accumulate to $100 000 if interest is 8% compounded quarterly?

**19.** For how long must $75 be deposited at the end of each month to accumulate to $9500 at 6.5% compounded quarterly?

**20.** A $70 000 mortgage is amortized by making monthly payments of $534.95. If interest is 7.2% compounded semi-annually, what is the term of the mortgage?

**21.** Toby has opened an RRSP account by making an initial deposit of $1200. She intends to make quarterly deposits for twenty years increasing at a constant rate of 1.5%. How much of the accumulated value just after the last deposit was made is interest if interest is 7% compounded quarterly?

**22.** Harry paid $250 000 for a fifteen-year indexed annuity in which the monthly payments received at the end of each month increase by 0.7% per payment. What is the total amount received by Harry if interest is 8.4% compounded monthly?

## Self-Test

**1.** Monthly deposits of $480 were made at the end of each month for eight years. If interest is 4.5% compounded semi-annually, what amount can be withdrawn immediately after the last deposit?

**2.** A loan was repaid in five years by end-of-quarter payments of $1200 at 9.5% compounded semi-annually. How much interest was paid?

**3.** A loan of $6000 was repaid by quarterly payments of $450. If interest was 12% compounded monthly, how long did it take to pay back the loan?

**4.** A mortgage of $95 000 is to be amortized by monthly payments over twenty-five years. If the payments are made at the end of each month and interest is 8.5% compounded semi-annually, what is the size of the monthly payments?

**5.** The amount of $46 200 is invested at 9.5% compounded quarterly for four years. After four years the balance in the fund is converted into an annuity. If interest on the annuity is 6.5% compounded semi-annually and payments are made at the end of every three months for seven years, what is the size of the payments?

6. A $45 000 mortgage is repaid in twenty years by making monthly payments of $387.72. What is the nominal annual rate of interest compounded semi-annually?

7. For how long would you have to deposit $491 at the end of every three months to accumulate $20 000 at 6.0% compounded monthly?

8. What is the size of monthly deposits that will accumulate to $67 200 after eight years at 6.5% compounded semi-annually?

9. Eva contributed $200 every month for five years into an RRSP earning 4.3% compounded quarterly. Six years after the last contribution, she converted the RRSP into an annuity that is to pay her monthly for thirty years. If the first payment is due one month after the conversion into the annuity and interest on the annuity is 5.4% compounded semi-annually, how much will Eva receive every month?

10. Joy would like to receive $6000 at the end of every three months for ten years after her retirement. If she retires now and interest is 6.5% compounded semi-annually, how much must she deposit into an account?

11. Mira has opened a registered retirement income fund (RRIF) with a starting balance of $250 000. Beginning six months later, she plans to make semi-annual withdrawals from the RRIF for twenty years. The withdrawals will increase at a constant rate of 1.75%. If the RRIF earns 8% compounded semi-annually, how much is the amount of interest included in the total withdrawals?

## Challenge Problems

1. After winning some money at a casino, Tony is considering purchasing an annuity that promises to pay him $300 at the end of each month for 12 months, then $350 at the end of each month for 24 months, and then $375 at the end of each month for 36 months. If the first payment is due at the end of the first month and interest is 7.5% compounded annually over the life of the annuity, find Tony's purchase price.

2. A loan of $5600 is to be repaid at 9% compounded annually by making ten payments at the end of each quarter. Each of the last six payments is two times the amount of each of the first four payments. What is the size of each payment?

# Case Study 12.1 Vehicle Cash-Back Incentives

» Karim Soltan is shopping for a new vehicle, and has noticed that many vehicle manufacturers are offering special deals to sell off the current year's vehicles before the new models arrive. Karim's local Ford dealership is advertising 3.9% financing for a full 48 months (i.e., 3.9% compounded monthly) or up to $4000 cash back on selected vehicles.

The vehicle that Karim wants to purchase costs $24 600 including taxes, delivery, licence, and dealer preparation. This vehicle qualifies for $1800 cash back if Karim pays cash for the vehicle. Karim has a good credit rating and knows that he could arrange a vehicle loan at his bank for the full price of any vehicle he chooses. His other option is to take the dealer financing offered at 3.9% for 48 months.

Karim wants to know which option requires the lower monthly payment. He knows he can use annuity formulas to calculate the monthly payments.

## QUESTIONS

1. Suppose Karim buys the vehicle on July 1. What monthly payment must Karim make if he chooses the dealer's 3.9% financing option and pays off the loan over 48 months? (Assume he makes each monthly payment at the end of the month and his first payment is due on July 31.)

2. Suppose the bank offers Karim a 48-month loan with the interest compounded monthly and the payments due at the end of each month. If Karim accepts the bank loan, he can get $1800 cash back on this vehicle.

   Karim works out a method to calculate the bank rate of interest required to make bank financing the same cost as dealer financing. First, calculate the monthly rate of interest that would make the monthly bank payments equal to the monthly dealer payments. Then calculate the effective rate of interest represented by the monthly compounded rate. If the financing from the bank is at a lower rate of interest compounded monthly, choose the bank financing. The reason is that the monthly payments for the bank's financing would be lower than the monthly payments for the dealer's 3.9% financing.

   (a) How much money would Karim have to borrow from the bank to pay cash for this vehicle?

   (b) Using the method above, calculate the effective annual rate of interest and the nominal annual rate of interest required to make the monthly payments for bank financing exactly the same as for dealer financing.

3. Suppose Karim decides to explore the costs of financing a more expensive vehicle. The more expensive vehicle costs $34 900 in total and qualifies for the 3.9% dealer financing for 48 months or $2500 cash back. What is the highest effective annual rate of interest at which Karim should borrow from the bank instead of using the dealer's 3.9% financing?

## Case Study 12.2 Fiscal Fitness

» Rosalinda is planning to open Fitness Quest, a new health and fitness club. She must decide what to charge for each type of membership and what payment options to offer.

Rosalinda plans to offer two types of memberships. General membership allows members to use all facilities, and it provides a simple locker room. Premium membership allows members to use all facilities, and it provides towels, shower supplies, and a sauna. When members pay for their annual membership when they join, the fee is $550 for the General membership and $700 for the Premium membership.

### QUESTIONS

1. Rosalinda wants to offer members the option of paying their annual membership fees in twelve equal monthly installments. The first installment would be due on the day of joining.
   (a) To the nearest dollar, how much should Rosalinda charge General members monthly if she wants to make interest of 17.5% compounded monthly?
   (b) To the nearest dollar, how much should she charge Fitness Quest members monthly if she wants to make interest of 21% compounded monthly?

2. Rosalinda knows that many of the Fitness Quest members will be executives whose companies will pay for their memberships. Many companies prefer to make quarterly payments for annual memberships. For this reason, Rosalinda decides to offer a quarterly payment option. The first installment would be due on the day of joining. To the nearest dollar, how much should Rosalinda charge Fitness Quest members quarterly if she wants to make interest of 21% compounded monthly?

3. As an opening special, Rosalinda wants to offer all members who join during the opening week three free months of membership. To calculate the nominal rate of interest she would earn on these opening special memberships, Rosalinda will add the payments made for the year for a membership, then spread the total payments equally over fifteen months as if the payment period were fifteen months. She would then calculate the nominal rate of interest earned on these new monthly payments over the fifteen-month membership period.
   (a) What is the nominal rate of interest earned on the opening special for the General membership with the monthly payment option?
   (b) What is the nominal rate of interest earned on the opening special for the Premium membership with the monthly payment option?
   (c) What is the nominal rate of interest earned on the opening special for the Premium membership with the quarterly payment option?

## SUMMARY OF FORMULAS

**Formula 12.1**

$$p = (1 + i)^c - 1$$

Finding the equivalent rate of interest per payment period $p$ for a nominal annual rate of interest compounded $c$ times per payment interval

**Formula 12.2**

$$FV_{nc} = PMT \left[ \frac{(1 + p)^n - 1}{p} \right]$$

Finding the future value of an ordinary general annuity using the effective rate of interest per payment period

where $p = (1 + i)^c - 1$

**Formula 12.2A**

$$PMT = \frac{FV_{nc}\, p}{(1 + p)^n - 1}$$

Finding the payment of an ordinary general annuity using the effective rate of interest per payment period when the future value is known

**Formula 12.2B**

$$n = \frac{\ln[FV_n p/PMT + 1]}{\ln(1 + p)}$$

Finding the number of payments of an ordinary general annuity using the effective rate of interest per payment period when the future value is known

**Formula 12.3**

$$PV_{nc} = PMT \left[ \frac{1 - (1 + p)^{-n}}{p} \right]$$

Finding the present value of an ordinary general annuity using the effective rate of interest per payment period

**Formula 12.3A**

$$PMT = \frac{PV_{nc}\, p}{1 - (1 + p)^{-n}}$$

Finding the payment of an ordinary general annuity using the effective rate of interest per payment period when the present value is known

**Formula 12.3B**

$$n = \frac{\ln[1 - (PV_n\, p/PMT)]}{-\ln(1 + p)}$$

Finding the number of payments of an ordinary general annuity using the effective rate of interest per payment period when the present value is known

**Formula 12.4**

$$\text{SIZE OF THE } n\text{TH PAYMENT} = PMT(1 + k)^{n-1}$$

Finding the size of the $n$th payment of a constant-growth annuity

**Formula 12.5**

$$\text{SUM OF THE PERIODIC CONSTANT-GROWTH PAYMENTS} = \frac{PMT\,(1 + k)^{n-1}}{k}$$

Finding the sum of the periodic payments of a constant-growth annuity.

Formula 12.6

$$FV = PMT \frac{(1 + i)^n - (1 + k)^n}{i - k}$$

**Finding the future value of an ordinary simple constant-growth annuity**

Formula 12.7

$$PV = PMT \left[ \frac{1 - (1 + k)^n (1 + i)^{-n}}{i - k} \right]$$

**Finding the present value of a series of payments forming a constant-growth annuity**

Formula 12.8

$$FV = n (PMT)(1 + i)^{n-1}$$

**Finding the future value of an ordinary simple constant-growth annuity when the constant-growth rate and the number of conversion periods are the same**

Formula 12.9

$$PV = n (PMT)(1 + i)^{-1}$$

**Finding the present value of an ordinary simple constant-growth annuity when the constant-growth rate and the number of conversion periods are the same**

## GLOSSARY

**Constant-growth annuity**   an annuity in which the payments change by the same percentage from one period to the next *(p. 494)*

**Equivalent rate of interest per payment period**   the rate of interest earned during the payment period that yields the same amount of interest as a nominal annual rate compounded $c$ times per year, where $c$ is the number of payment periods per year *(p. 475)*

## USEFUL INTERNET SITES

**www.money.canoe.ca**
**RRIF: Savings**   Find current information and rates of return on RRIFs from several financial institutions and financial services providers on the Canoe Money site.

**www.fidelity.ca**
**Growth Calculator**   Click on "Investor Centre," "Education/Planning," "Calculators," and then "Growth Calculator." This interactive chart on the Fidelity Investments site allows you to calculate both simple and compound earnings on investment capital by entering values for a series of variables.

**www.butterworths.ca**
**The Bottom Line**   A monthly Canadian magazine for finance professionals. Click on "The Bottom Line."

# Annuities Due, Deferred Annuities, and Perpetuities

## OBJECTIVES

**Upon completing this chapter, you will be able to do the following:**

1. Compute the future value, present value, periodic payment, term, and interest rate for simple annuities due.

2. Compute the future value, present value, periodic payment, term, and interest rate for general annuities due.

3. Compute the future value, present value, periodic payment, term, and interest rate for ordinary deferred annuities.

4. Compute the future value, present value, periodic payment, term, and interest rate for deferred annuities due.

5. Compute the present value, periodic payment, and interest rate for ordinary perpetuities, perpetuities due, and deferred perpetuities.

When you pay rent on an apartment, a house or a commercial space, your rent is due at the beginning of the month. This series of regular, equal payments paid at the beginning of the period represents a type of annuity called an annuity due. The payment schedule for an annuity due differs from that of an ordinary annuity (which we discussed in Chapters 11 and 12) where payments were due at the end of each period.

In some situations, a series of regular, equal payments may not begin until some future time. These payment situations are known as deferred annuities. For example, if you won a large amount of money today and you wanted a series of regular, equal payments to begin five years from now, you would set up a deferred annuity. Both ordinary annuities and annuities due can be deferred.

## INTRODUCTION

In the previous chapters, we considered ordinary annuities, both simple and general, in which the payments are made at the end of each payment period.

In this chapter we will consider other annuities resulting from variations in the payment dates and the length of time that the payments continue. These include annuities due (in which payments are made at the beginning of the period), deferred annuities (in which the first payment is made after the first or several payment intervals have been completed), and perpetuities (in which payments continue indefinitely).

# 13.1 SIMPLE ANNUITIES DUE

## A. Future value of a simple annuity due

An **annuity due** is an annuity in which the periodic payments are made at the beginning of each payment interval. The future value of an annuity due is closely related to the future value of an ordinary annuity. This same close relationship also holds for the present value.

**EXAMPLE 13.1A**
Find the accumulated value (future value) at the end date of the last payment period of deposits of $3000 each made at the beginning of five consecutive years respectively with interest at 6% compounded annually.

**SOLUTION**
As for any problem involving a series of payments, the method of solution and the data can be shown on a time diagram.

**FIGURE 13.1**  **Graphical Representation of Method and Data**

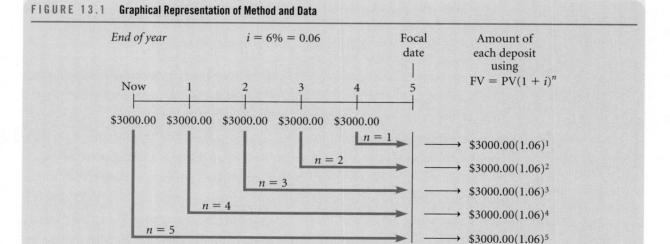

As shown in Figure 13.1, the first deposit is located at the beginning of Year 1, which is the same as "now"; the second deposit is located at the beginning of Year 2, which is the same as the end of Year 1; the third at the beginning of Year 3; the fourth at the beginning of Year 4; and the fifth and last deposit at the beginning of Year 5, which is also the beginning of the last payment period. The focal date, however, is located at the *end* of the last payment period.

The accumulated values of the individual deposits are obtained by using Formula 9.1A, $FV = PV(1 + i)^n$. Finding the combined total of the five accumulated values is made easier by taking out the common factors 3000.00 and 1.06 as follows:

$$
\begin{array}{l}
\textit{Deposit 5}\ \ 3000.00(1.06)^1 = \\
\textit{Deposit 4}\ \ 3000.00(1.06)^2 = \\
\textit{Deposit 3}\ \ 3000.00(1.06)^3 = 3000.00(1.06)\begin{bmatrix}(1.0)\\(1.06)\\(1.06)^2\\(1.06)^3\\(1.06)^4\end{bmatrix} = 3000.00(1.06)\begin{bmatrix}(1.0)\\(1.06)\\(1.1236)\\(1.191016)\\(1.262477)\end{bmatrix} \\
\textit{Deposit 2}\ \ 3000.00(1.06)^4 = \\
\textit{Deposit 1}\ \ 3000.00(1.06)^5 =
\end{array}
$$

$$
\begin{aligned}
&= 3000.00(1.06)(5.637093) \\
&= 16\,911.28(1.06) \\
&= \$17\,925.96
\end{aligned}
$$

*Note:* This example is the same as Example 11.2B except that the deposits are made at the beginning of each payment period rather than at the end. The answer to Example 11.2B was \$16 911.28. We could have obtained the answer to Example 13.1A simply by multiplying \$16 911.28 by 1.06. It appears that the future value of the annuity due can be obtained by multiplying the future value of the ordinary annuity by the factor $(1 + i)$.

The general notation for simple annuities due is the same as for ordinary simple annuities except that the accumulated value (future value) of the annuity due is represented by the symbol $FV_n(\text{due})$.

The formula for the future value of a simple annuity due is:

$$
\boxed{
\begin{aligned}
S_n(\text{due}) &= R(1 + i)\left[\frac{(1 + i)^n - 1}{i}\right] \\
&\text{restated as} \\
FV_n(\text{due}) &= PMT(1 + i)\left[\frac{(1 + i)^n - 1}{i}\right]
\end{aligned}
}
\qquad \text{Formula 13.1}
$$

*Note:* Formula 13.1, the future value of a simple annuity due, differs from Formula 11.1, the future value of an ordinary simple annuity, only by the factor $(1 + i)$.

$$
\begin{matrix}
\text{FUTURE VALUE OF} \\
\text{A SIMPLE ANNUITY DUE}
\end{matrix}
= (1 + i) \times
\begin{matrix}
\text{FUTURE VALUE OF THE} \\
\text{ORDINARY SIMPLE ANNUITY}
\end{matrix}
$$

The relationship between an annuity due and the corresponding ordinary annuity is graphically illustrated in the comparison of the line diagrams.

The two line graphs show the shift of the payments by one period. In an annuity due, every payment earns interest for one more period than in an ordinary annuity and this explains the factor $(1 + i)$.

**EXAMPLE 13.1B**

You deposit $100 at the beginning of each month for five years in an account paying 4.2% compounded monthly.

(i) What will the balance in your account be at the end of five years?
(ii) How much of the balance will you have contributed?
(iii) How much of the balance will be interest?

**SOLUTION**

(i) PMT = 100.00;   P/Y = 12;   C/Y = 12;   I/Y = 4.2;

$$i = \frac{4.2\%}{12} = 0.35\% = 0.0035; \quad n = 5(12) = 60$$

$$
\begin{aligned}
FV_n(\text{due}) &= 100.00(1.0035)\left(\frac{1.0035^{60} - 1}{0.0035}\right) \\
&= 100.00(1.0035)(66.635949) \\
&= 6663.5949(1.0035) \\
&= \$6686.92
\end{aligned}
$$

(ii) Your contribution is $(100.00)(60) = \$6000.00$.

(iii) The interest earned $= 6686.92 - 6000.00 = \$686.92$.

## POINTERS AND PITFALLS

To distinguish between problems dealing with ordinary annuities and annuities due, look for key words or phrases that signal one type of annuity or the other.

Ordinary annuities:
"payments (or deposits) made at the *end* of each (or every) ..."
"monthly payments, starting one month from today ..."
"interest payments"

Annuities due:
"payments (or deposits) made at the *beginning* of each (or every) ..."
"first payment is due on the date of sale (or signing)"
"payable in advance"
"monthly payments, starting today ..."
"lease or rent payments"

# B. Present value of a simple annuity due

**EXAMPLE 13.1C**

Find the present value of five payments of $3000 each made at the beginning of each of five consecutive years respectively if money is worth 6% compounded annually.

**SOLUTION**

As Figure 13.2 shows, the present value of the individual payments is obtained using Formula 9.1C, $PV = FV(1 + i)^{-n}$. The sum of the individual present values is easier to find when the common factor 3000.00 is taken out.

**FIGURE 13.2**    **Graphical Representation of Method and Data**

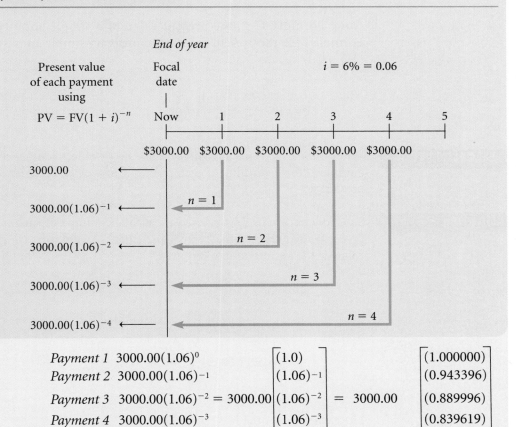

$$
\begin{array}{lll}
\textit{Payment 1} & 3000.00(1.06)^{0} & \\
\textit{Payment 2} & 3000.00(1.06)^{-1} & \\
\textit{Payment 3} & 3000.00(1.06)^{-2} = 3000.00 \\
\textit{Payment 4} & 3000.00(1.06)^{-3} & \\
\textit{Payment 5} & 3000.00(1.06)^{-4} &
\end{array}
\begin{bmatrix}
(1.0) \\
(1.06)^{-1} \\
(1.06)^{-2} \\
(1.06)^{-3} \\
(1.06)^{-4}
\end{bmatrix}
= 3000.00
\begin{bmatrix}
(1.000000) \\
(0.943396) \\
(0.889996) \\
(0.839619) \\
(0.792094)
\end{bmatrix}
$$

$$= 3000.00 \quad (4.465105)$$

$$= \$13\ 395.32$$

Example 13.1C is the same as Example 11.3B, except that the payments are made at the beginning of each payment period. The answer to Example 11.3B was $12 637.09. If this amount is multiplied by 1.06, the result is $13 395.32, the answer to Example 13.1C.

This result implies that we could have obtained the present value of the annuity due in Example 13.1C by multiplying the present value of the ordinary annuity in Example 11.3B by the factor 1.06, which is the factor $(1 + i)$.

The present value of an annuity due is represented by the symbol $PV_n(due)$. The formula for the present value of a simple annuity due is:

$$A_n(due) = R(1 + i)\left[\frac{1 - (1 + i)^{-n}}{i}\right]$$

restated as —————— Formula 13.2

$$PV_n(due) = PMT(1 + i)\left[\frac{1 - (1 + i)^{-n}}{i}\right]$$

*Note:* Formula 13.2, the present value of a simple annuity due, differs from Formula 11.2, the present value of an ordinary simple annuity, only by the factor $(1 + i)$.

$$\text{PRESENT VALUE OF A SIMPLE ANNUITY DUE} = (1 + i) \times \text{PRESENT VALUE OF THE ORDINARY SIMPLE ANNUITY}$$

**EXAMPLE 13.1D**   What is the cash value of a three-year lease of office facilities renting for $536.50 payable at the beginning of each month if money is worth 9% compounded monthly?

**SOLUTION**   Since the payments for the lease are at the beginning of each payment period, the problem involves an annuity due, and since we want the cash value, the present value of the annuity due is required.

$$PMT = 536.50; \quad i = \frac{9\%}{12} = 0.75\% = 0.0075; \quad n = 3(12) = 36$$

$$PV_n(due) = 536.50(1.0075)\left[\frac{1 - (1.0075)^{-36}}{0.0075}\right]$$

$$= 536.50(1.0075)(31.446805)$$

$$= 16\ 871.21(1.0075)$$

$$= \$16\ 997.74$$

The cash value of the lease is $16 997.74.

## C. Using preprogrammed financial calculators

The future value or the present value of an annuity due can easily be determined by using a preprogrammed financial calculator. One method is to begin by finding the corresponding value for an ordinary simple annuity and multiply it by $(1 + i)$. If you are using the Texas Instruments BAII Plus, set the calculator in "BGN" mode (since annuity due payments are made at the beginning of each payment period), then solve for the unknown variable the same way as you do for ordinary simple annuities. Using the Texas Instruments BAII Plus, follow this key sequence to set the calculator in "BGN" mode:

| *Key in* | *Press* | *Display shows* | |
|----------|---------|-----------------|---|
| 2nd | (BGN) | END *or* BGN | checks the mode |
| 2nd | (SET) | BGN | if previously in "**END**" mode. **BGN** will appear in the upper-right corner of the display. |
| | | *or* | |
| | | END | if previously in "**BGN**" mode. The display will be blank. Press 2nd (SET) again so that **BGN** appears in the display. |
| 2nd | (QUIT) | | returns to the standard calculation mode |

Refer to Appendix II for instruction for annuity due calculations if you are using the Sharp EL-733A or the Hewlett-Packard 10BII calculator.

---

**EXAMPLE 13.1E**

Payments of $425 are to be made at the beginning of each quarter for 10 years. If money is worth 6% compounded quarterly, determine

(i) the accumulated value of the payments;
(ii) the present value of the payments.

**SOLUTION**

(i) PMT = 425;   I/Y = 6;   P/Y, C/Y = 4;   $i = \dfrac{6\%}{4} = 1.5\%$;   $n = 40$

Using the Texas Instruments BAII Plus, ensure the calculator is in "BGN" mode, and then follow this key sequence to retrieve the *future value* of an annuity due.

(Set P/Y = 4) 0 PV 425 ± PMT 6.0 I/Y

40 N CPT FV 23409.81274

The accumulated value of the annuity due is $23 409.81.

(ii) Using the Texas Instruments BA II Plus, ensure the calculator is in "BGN" mode, and then follow this key sequence to retrieve the *present value* of an annuity due.

0 FV 425 ± PMT 6.0 I/Y 40 N CPT PV 12904.94772

The present value of the annuity due is $12 904.95.

---

**EXAMPLE 13.1F**

Frank deposited monthly receipts of $250 at the beginning of each month into a savings account paying 4.5% compounded monthly for four years. Frank made no further deposits after four years but left the money in the account.

(i) What will the balance be twelve full years after he made the first deposit?
(ii) How much in total was deposited?
(iii) How much interest will have been earned?

**SOLUTION**

This problem involves two time periods, which must be separated and calculated individually. The time periods are the four years when deposits are being made on a regular basis, and the remaining time period of $12 - 4 = 8$ years when no further deposits are being made but the balance is earning interest.

(i) First determine the balance at the end of four years. This problem involves finding the future value of a simple annuity due.

$$\text{PMT} = 250.00; \ \text{I/Y} = 4.5; \ \text{P/Y, C/Y} = 12; \ i = \frac{4.5\%}{12} = 0.375\%; \ n = 48$$

$$\text{FV}_n(\text{due}) = 250.00(1.00375)\left(\frac{1.00375^{48} - 1}{0.00375}\right)$$

$$= 250.00(1.00375)(52.483834)$$

$$= 13\ 120.96(1.00375)$$

$$= \$13\ 170.16$$

Now accumulate $13 170.16 for another eight years.

$$\text{PV} = 13\ 170.16; \quad i = 0.00375; \quad n = 8(12) = 96$$

$$\text{FV} = 13\ 170.16(1.00375)^{96} \underline{\hspace{2cm}} \text{substituting in Formula 9.1A}$$

$$= 13\ 170.16(1.432365)$$

$$= \$18\ 864.47$$

**Programmed Solution**

("BGN" mode) (Set P/Y = 12) 0 $\boxed{\text{PV}}$ 250 $\boxed{\pm}$ $\boxed{\text{PMT}}$

4.5 $\boxed{\text{I/Y}}$ 48 $\boxed{\text{N}}$ $\boxed{\text{CPT}}$ $\boxed{\text{FV}}$ $\boxed{\text{13170.16209}}$

13 170.16209 $\boxed{\pm}$ $\boxed{\text{PV}}$ 0 $\boxed{\text{PMT}}$ 4.5 $\boxed{\text{I/Y}}$

96 $\boxed{\text{N}}$ $\boxed{\text{CPT}}$ $\boxed{\text{FV}}$ $\boxed{\text{18864.47466}}$

The balance in the account after twelve years is $18 864.47.

(ii) The total deposited is $250.00(48) = \$12\ 000.00$.

(iii) Interest in the balance is $18\ 864.47 - 12\ 000.00 = \$6864.47$.

## D. Finding the periodic payment PMT of a simple annuity due

If the future value of an annuity $FV_n$(due), the number of conversion periods $n$, and the conversion rate $i$ are known, you can find the periodic payment PMT by substituting the given values in the future value Formula 13.1.

$$FV_n(\text{due}) = PMT(1 + i)\left[\frac{(1 + i)^n - 1}{i}\right]$$ ———— **Formula 13.1**

If the present value of an annuity $PV_n$(due), the number of conversion periods $n$, and the conversion rate $i$ are known, you can find the periodic payment PMT by substituting the given values in the present value Formula 13.2.

$$PV_n(\text{due}) = PMT(1 + i)\left[\frac{1 - (1 + i)^{-n}}{i}\right]$$ ———— **Formula 13.2**

When using a scientific calculator, you can find PMT by first rearranging the terms of the above formulas. Then substitute the three known values (FV(due) or PV(due), $n$, and $i$) into the appropriate rearranged formula and solve for PMT.

When using a preprogrammed financial calculator, you can find PMT by entering the five known values (FV(due) or PV(due), N, I/Y, P/Y, and C/Y) and pressing CPT PMT .

**EXAMPLE 13.1G**

What semi-annual payment must be made into a fund at the beginning of every six months to accumulate to $9600 in ten years at 7% compounded semi-annually?

**SOLUTION**

$FV_n(\text{due}) = 9600.00$; $i = \dfrac{7\%}{2} = 3.5\% = 0.035\%$; P/Y, C/Y = 2; I/Y = 7

$n = 10(2) = 20$

$$9600.00 = PMT(1.035)\left(\frac{1.035^{20} - 1}{0.035}\right)$$ ———— substituting in Formula 12.1

$9600.00 = PMT(1.035)(28.279682)$

$9600.00 = PMT(29.269471)$

$$PMT = \frac{9600.00}{29.269471}$$

$PMT = \$327.99$

**Programmed Solution**

("BGN" mode) 0 PV 9600 FV 7 I/Y 20 N CPT PMT -327.986799

The semi-annual payment is $327.99.

**EXAMPLE 13.1H**

What monthly rent payment at the beginning of each month for four years is required to fulfill a lease contract worth $7000 if money is worth 7.5% compounded monthly?

**SOLUTION**

$PV_n(\text{due}) = 7000.00$; $P/Y = 12$; $C/Y = 12$; $I/Y = 7.5$;

$$i = \frac{7.5\%}{12} = 0.625\% = 0.00625; \quad n = 4(12) = 48$$

$$7000.00 = PMT(1.00625)\left(\frac{1 - 1.00625^{-48}}{0.00625}\right) \text{ —— substituting in Formula 13.2}$$

$7000.00 = PMT(1.00625)(41.358371)$

$7000.00 = PMT(41.616861)$

$$PMT = \frac{7000.00}{41.616861}$$

$PMT = \$168.20$

**Programmed Solution**

("BGN" mode) (Set P/Y = 12; C/Y = 12) 0 [FV] 7000 [±] [PV]
7.5 [I/Y] 48 [N] [CPT] [PMT] [168.201057]

The monthly rent payment due at the beginning of each month is $168.20.

**EXAMPLE 13.1I**

How much will you have to deposit into an account at the beginning of every three months for twelve years if you want to have a balance of $100 000 twenty years from now and interest is 8% compounded quarterly?

**SOLUTION**

First, find the balance that you must have in the account at the end of the term of the annuity (after twelve years).

$FV = 100\,000.00$; $P/Y = 4$; $C/Y = 4$; $I/Y = 8$; $i = \frac{8\%}{4} = 2\% = 0.02$; $n = 8(4) = 32$

$PV = 100\,000.00(1.02)^{-32}$

$= 100\,000.00(0.530633)$

$= \$53\,063.33$

Next, find the quarterly payment needed at the beginning of each quarter to accumulate to $53 063.33.

$FV_n(\text{due}) = 53\,063.33$; $P/Y = 4$; $C/Y = 4$; $I/Y = 8$; $i = \frac{8\%}{4} = 0.02$; $n = 12(4) = 48$

$$53\,063.33 = PMT(1.02)\left(\frac{1.02^{48} - 1}{0.02}\right)$$

$$53\,063.33 = PMT(1.02)(79.353519)$$

$$53\,063.33 = PMT(80.940590)$$

$$PMT = \frac{53\,063.33}{80.940590}$$

$$PMT = 53\,063.33(0.012355)$$

$$PMT = \$\,655.58$$

**Programmed Solution**

(Set P/Y = 4; C/Y = 4) 0 [PMT] 100 000 [FV]

8 [I/Y] 32 [N] [CPT] [PV] [-53063.33035]

("BGN" mode) [±] 53 063.33035 [FV] 0 [PV]

8 [I/Y] 48 [N] [CPT] [PMT] [-655.583689]

The quarterly deposit at the beginning of each payment period is $655.58.

## E. Finding the term *n* of a simple annuity due

If the future value of an annuity $FV_n$(due), the periodic payment PMT, and the conversion rate *i* are known, you can find the term of the annuity *n* by substituting the given values in the future value Formula 13.1.

$$FV_n(\text{due}) = PMT(1 + i)\left[\frac{(1 + i)^n - 1}{i}\right] \qquad \text{Formula 13.1}$$

If the present value $PV_n$(due), the periodic payment PMT, and the conversion rate *i* are known, you can find the term of the annuity due *n* by substituting the given values in the present value Formula 13.2.

$$PV_n(\text{due}) = PMT(1 + i)\left[\frac{1 - (1 + i)^{-n}}{i}\right] \qquad \text{Formula 13.2}$$

When using a scientific calculator, you can find *n* by first rearranging the terms of the appropriate formula above. Then substitute the three known values (FV(due) or PV(due), PMT, and *i*) into the rearranged formula and solve for *n*.

When using a preprogrammed financial calculator, you can find *n* by entering the five known values (PV, PMT, I/Y, P/Y, and C/Y) and pressing [CPT] [N].

**EXAMPLE 13.1J**

Over what length of time will \$75 deposited at the beginning of each month grow to \$5000 at 4.5% compounded monthly?

**SOLUTION**

$FV_n(due) = 5000.00; \quad PMT = 75.00; \quad P/Y = 12; \quad C/Y = 12; \quad I/Y = 4.5;$

$i = \dfrac{4.5\%}{12} = 0.375\%; = 0.00375$

$$5000.00 = 75.00(1.00375)\left(\frac{1.00375^n - 1}{0.00375}\right) \quad \text{——— substituting in Formula 12.1}$$

$$5000.00 = 20\,075.00(1.00375^n - 1)$$

$$\frac{5000.00}{20\,075.00} = 1.00375^n - 1$$

$$0.249066 + 1 = 1.00375^n$$

$$n\ln 1.00375 = \ln 1.249066$$

$$n(0.003743) = 0.222396$$

$$n = \frac{0.222396}{0.003743}$$

$$n = 59.416748$$

As discussed in Example 11.5, $n$ should be rounded upward.

$$n = 60 \text{ (months)}$$

**Programmed Solution**

("BGN" mode)(Set P/Y = 12; C/Y = 12) 0 [PV] 5000 [FV]

75 [±] [PMT] 4.5 [I/Y] [CPT] [N] 59.416748

It will take 60 months or five years to accumulate \$5000.

**EXAMPLE 13.1K**

Surrey Credit Union intends to accumulate a building fund of \$150 000 by depositing \$4125 at the beginning of every three months at 7% compounded quarterly. How long will it take for the fund to reach the desired amount?

**SOLUTION**

$FV_n(due) = 150\,00.00; \quad PMT = 4125.00; \quad P/Y = 4; \quad C/Y = 4; \quad I/Y = 7;$

$i = \dfrac{7\%}{4} = 1.75\%$

**Programmed Solution**

("BGN" mode) (Set P/Y = 4; C/Y = 4) 150 000 [FV]

4125 [±] [PMT] 7 [I/Y] [CPT] [N] 28.000210

It will take 28 quarters or seven years to build up the fund.

**EXAMPLE 13.1L**

For how long can you withdraw $480 at the beginning of every three months from a fund of $9000 if interest is 10% compounded quarterly?

**SOLUTION**

$PV_n(\text{due}) = 9000.00;\quad PMT = 480.00;\quad P/Y = 4;\quad C/Y = 4;\quad I/Y = 10;$

$i = \dfrac{10\%}{4} = 2.5\% = 0.025$

$$9000.00 = 480.00(1.025)\frac{1 - 1.025^{-n}}{0.025} \quad\text{—— substituting in Formula 13.2}$$

$9000.00 = 19\,680.00(1 - 1.025^{-n})$

$\dfrac{9000.00}{19\,680.00} = 1 - 1.025^{-n}$

$0.457317 = 1 - 1.025^{-n}$

$1.025^{-n} = 1 - 0.457317$

$1.025^{-n} = 0.542683$

$-n \ln 1.025 = \ln 0.542683$

$-n(0.024693) = -0.611230$

$n = \dfrac{0.611230}{0.024693}$

$n = 24.753561$

$n = 25 \text{ (quarters)}$

**Programmed Solution**

(Set P/Y = 4; C/Y = 4) ("BGN" mode) 9000 $\boxed{\pm}$ $\boxed{\text{PV}}$

0 $\boxed{\text{FV}}$ 480 $\boxed{\text{PMT}}$ 10 $\boxed{\text{I/Y}}$ $\boxed{\text{CPT}}$ $\boxed{\text{N}}$ $\boxed{24.753560}$

Withdrawals of $480 can be made for 25 quarters or six years and three months. (The last withdrawal will be less than $480.)

**EXAMPLE 13.1M**

A lease contract valued at $7800 is to be fulfilled by rental payments of $180 due at the beginning of each month. If money is worth 9% compounded monthly, what should the term of the lease be?

**SOLUTION**

$PV_n(\text{due}) = 7800.00;\quad PMT = 180.00;\quad P/Y = 12;\quad C/Y = 12;\quad I/Y = 9;$

$i = \dfrac{9\%}{12} = 0.75\%$

**Programmed Solution**

("BGN" mode) (Set P/Y = 12; C/Y = 12) 0 $\boxed{\text{FV}}$ 7800 $\boxed{\pm}$ $\boxed{\text{PV}}$

180 $\boxed{\text{PMT}}$ 9 $\boxed{\text{I/Y}}$ $\boxed{\text{CPT}}$ $\boxed{\text{N}}$ $\boxed{52.123125}$

The term of the lease should be 53 months, or four years and five months.

## F. Finding the periodic rate of interest of a simple annuity due

Preprogrammed financial calculators are especially helpful when solving for the conversion rate $i$. Determining $i$ without a financial calculator is extremely time-consuming. However, it *can* be done by hand, as illustrated in Appendix II on the CD-ROM.

When the future value or present value, the periodic payment PMT, and the term $n$ of an annuity due are known, the periodic rate of interest $i$ can be found by entering the five known values into a preprogrammed financial calculator. (Remember, if both PV and PMT are non-zero, enter PV *only* as a negative amount.) For simple annuities due, retrieve the answer by being in "BGN" mode and pressing CPT I/Y . This is the nominal annual rate of interest.

---

**EXAMPLE 13.1N**

Compute the nominal annual rate of interest at which $100 deposited at the beginning of each month for ten years will amount to $15 000.

**SOLUTION**

$FV_n$(due) = 15 000; PMT = 100.00; P/Y = 12; C/Y = 12; $n$ = 120; $m$ = 12

("BGN" mode) (Set P/Y = 12; C/Y = 12) 0 PV 15 000 FV

100 ± PMT 120 N CPT I/Y 4.282801

         ↑
Allow several seconds
for the computation.

The nominal annual rate of interest is 4.28% compounded monthly.
The monthly conversion rate is 4.282801/12 = 0.356900%.

---

**EXAMPLE 13.1O**

A lease agreement valued at $7500 requires payment of $450 at the beginning of every quarter for five years. What is the nominal annual rate of interest charged?

**SOLUTION**

$PV_n$(due) = 7500.00; PMT = 450.00; P/Y = 4; C/Y = 4; $n$ = 20; $m$ = 4

("BGN" mode) (Set P/Y = 4; C/Y = 4) 0 FV 7500 ± PV

450.00 PMT 20 N CPT I/Y 8.032647

         ↑
Allow several seconds
for the computation.

The nominal annual rate of interest is 8.03% compounded quarterly.
The quarterly compounding rate is 8.032647/4 = 2.008162%.

---

## EXERCISE 13.1

If you choose, you can use Excel's *Present Value (PV)* function or *Future Value (FV)* function to answer the questions indicated below. Refer to **PV** and **FV** on the Spreadsheet Template Disk to learn how to use these Excel functions.

**A.** Find the future value and the present value of each of the following six simple annuities due.

| | Periodic Payment | Payment Interval | Term | Interest Rate | Conversion Period |
|---|---|---|---|---|---|
| 1. | $3000 | 3 months | 8 years | 8% | quarterly |
| 2. | 750 | 1 month | 5 years | 7.2 | monthly |
| 3. | 2000 | 6 months | 12 years | 5.6 | semi-annually |
| 4. | 450 | 3 months | 15 years | 4.4 | quarterly |
| 5. | 65 | 1 month | 20 years | 9 | monthly |
| 6. | 160 | 1 month | 15 years | 6 | monthly |

  **B.** Find the periodic payment for each of the following four simple annuities due.

| | Future Value | Present Value | Payment Period | Term | Interest Rate | Conversion Period |
|---|---|---|---|---|---|---|
| 1. | $20 000 | | 3 months | 15 years | 6% | quarterly |
| 2. | | $12 000 | 1 year | 8 years | 7 | annually |
| 3. | | $18 500 | 6 months | 12 years | 3 | semi-annually |
| 4. | 9 400 | | 1 month | 5 years | 12 | monthly |

  **C.** Find the length of the term for each of the following four simple annuities due.

| | Future Value | Present Value | Periodic Payment | Payment Period | Interest Rate | Conversion Period |
|---|---|---|---|---|---|---|
| 1. | $ 5 300 | | $ 35 | 1 month | 6% | monthly |
| 2. | | $8 400 | 440 | 3 months | 7 | quarterly |
| 3. | | 6 450 | 1 120 | 1 year | 10 | annually |
| 4. | 15 400 | | 396 | 6 months | 5 | semi-annually |

  **D.** Compute the nominal annual rate of interest for each of the following four simple annuities due.

| | Future Value | Present Value | Periodic Rent | Payment Interval | Term | Compounding Period |
|---|---|---|---|---|---|---|
| 1. | $70 000 | | $1 014.73 | 1 year | 25 years | annually |
| 2. | | $42 000 | 528.00 | 1 month | 10 years | monthly |
| 3. | | 28 700 | 2 015.00 | 6 months | 15 years | semi-annually |
| 4. | 36 000 | | 584.10 | 3 months | 12 years | quarterly |

  **E.** Answer each of the following questions.

**1.** Find the accumulated value of an annuity due of $300 payable at the beginning of every month for seven years at 6% compounded monthly.

*Reference Example 13.1A*

**2.** Determine the accumulated value after twelve years of deposits of $360 made at the beginning of every three months and earning interest at 7% compounded quarterly.

3. Until he retires sixteen years from now, Mr. Lait plans to deposit $300 at the beginning of every three months in an account paying interest at 5% compounded quarterly.
   (a) What will be the balance in his account when he retires?
   (b) How much of the balance will be interest?

4. Joanna contributes $750 at the beginning of every six months into an RRSP paying interest at 8% compounded semi-annually.
   (a) How much will her RRSP deposits amount to in twenty years?
   (b) How much of the amount will be interest?

5. Find the present value of payments of $2500 made at the beginning of every six months for ten years if money is worth 9.5% compounded semi-annually.

   Reference Example 13.1C

6. What is the discounted value of deposits of $240 made at the beginning of every three months for seven years if money is worth 8.8% compounded quarterly?

7. A washer-dryer combination can be purchased from a department store by making monthly credit card payments of $52.50 for two-and-a-half years. The first payment is due on the date of sale and interest is 21% compounded monthly.
   (a) What is the purchase price?
   (b) How much will be paid in installments?
   (c) How much is the cost of financing?

8. Diane Wallace bought a living-room suite on credit, signing an installment contract with a finance company that requires monthly payments of $62.25 for three years. The first payment is made on the date of signing and interest is 24% compounded monthly.
   (a) What was the cash price?
   (b) How much will Diane pay in total?
   (c) How much of what she pays will be interest?

9. The monthly premium on a three-year insurance policy is $64 payable in advance. What is the cash value at the beginning of the policy if money is worth 4.8% compounded monthly?

10. The monthly rent payment on office space is $535 payable in advance. What equivalent yearly payment made in advance would satisfy the lease if interest is 6.6% compounded monthly?

11. Claude made semi-annually deposits of $3100 at the beginning of a six-month period into a fund earning 6.8% compounded semi-annually for nine years. No further deposits were made.
    (a) How much will be in the account fifteen years after the first deposit?
    (b) How much in total was deposited?
    (c) How much interest will have been earned? Reference Example 13.1F

12. For Carly's education, her grandmother deposited $30 at the beginning of every month for seven years. Interest was earned at 4.85% compounded monthly.
    (a) How much will be in the account eighteen years after the first deposit?
    (b) How much in total was deposited?
    (c) How much interest will have been earned?

13. How much does a depositor have to save at the beginning of every three months for nine years to accumulate $35 000 if interest is 8% compounded quarterly?

Reference Example 13.1G

14. If Gary accumulated $5700 in his savings account over five years, how much did he deposit at the beginning of every month if interest is 4.32% compounded monthly?

15. Elspeth McNab purchased a boat valued at $12 500 on the installment plan requiring equal monthly payments for four years. If the first payment is due on the date of purchase and interest is 7.5% compounded monthly, what is the size of the monthly payment?

Reference Example 13.1H

16. Payments on a seven-year lease valued at $12 200 are to be made at the beginning of each month during the last five years of the lease. If interest is 9% compounded monthly, what is the size of the monthly payments?

17. Julia deposited $1500 in an RRSP at the beginning of every six months for twenty years. The money earned interest at 6.25% compounded semi-annually. After twenty years, she converted the RRSP into an RRIF from which she wants to withdraw equal amounts at the beginning of each month for fifteen years. If interest on the RRIF is 6.6% compounded monthly, how much does she receive each month?

Reference Example 13.1I

18. Mr. Clark wants to receive payments of $900 at the beginning of every three months for twenty years starting on the date of his retirement. If he retires in twenty-five years, how much must he deposit in an account at the beginning of every three months if interest on the account is 5.25% compounded quarterly?

19. Tom is saving $600 at the beginning of each month. How soon can he retire if he wants to have a retirement fund of $120 000 and interest is 5.4% compounded monthly?

Reference Example 13.1J

20. Ali deposits $450 at the beginning of every three months. He wants to build up his account so that he can withdraw $1000 every three months starting three months after the last deposit. If he wants to make the withdrawals for fifteen years and interest is 10% compounded quarterly, for how long must Ali make the quarterly deposits?

21. If you save $75 at the beginning of every month for ten years, for how long can you withdraw $260 at the beginning of each month starting ten years from now, assuming that interest is 6% compounded monthly?

22. Quarterly payments of $1445 are to be made at the beginning of every three months on a lease valued at $25 000. What should the term of the lease be if money is worth 8% compounded quarterly?

23. What nominal annual rate of interest was paid if contributions of $250 made into an RRSP at the beginning of every three months amounted to $14 559 after ten years?

Reference Example 13.1N

24. An insurance policy provides a benefit of $250 000 twenty years from now. Alternatively, the policy pays $4220 at the beginning of each year for twenty years. What is the effective annual rate of interest paid?

25. A vacation property valued at $25 000 was bought for fifteen payments of $2200 due at the beginning of every six months. What nominal annual rate of interest was charged?

26. A vehicle can purchased by paying $27 000 now, or it can be leased by paying $725 per month for the next four years, with the first payment due on the day of signing the lease. What nominal annual rate of interest charged on the lease?

# 13.2 GENERAL ANNUITIES DUE

## A. Future value of a general annuity due

As with a simple annuity due, the future value of a **general annuity due** is greater than the future value of the corresponding ordinary general annuity by the interest on it for one payment period.

Since the interest on a general annuity for one payment period is $(1 + i)^c$, or $(1 + p)$,

$$\text{PRESENT VALUE OF A GENERAL ANNUITY DUE} = (1 + p) \times \text{PRESENT VALUE OF THE CORRESPONDING ORDINARY GENERAL ANNUITY}$$

Thus, for the future value of a general annuity due use Formula 13.3:

$$S_{nc}(\text{due}) = R(1 + p)\left[\frac{(1 + p)^n - 1}{p}\right]$$

restated as

$$FV_{nc}(\text{due}) = PMT(1 + p)\left[\frac{(1 + p)^n - 1}{p}\right] \quad \text{—— Formula 13.3}$$

where $p = (1 + i)^c - 1$

**EXAMPLE 13.2A**

What is the accumulated value after five years of payments of $20 000 made at the beginning of each year if interest is 7% compounded quarterly?

**SOLUTION**

$PMT = 20\ 000.00; \quad n = 5; \quad c = 4; \quad P/Y = 1; \quad C/Y = 4; \quad I/Y = 7$

$i = \dfrac{7\%}{4} = 1.75\% = 0.0175$

The effective annual rate of interest

$p = 1.0175^4 - 1 = 1.071859 - 1 = 0.071859 = 7.1859\%$

$FV_{nc}(\text{due}) = 20\ 000.00(1.071859)\left(\dfrac{1.071859^5 - 1}{0.071859}\right)$ —— substituting in Formula 13.3

$\quad = 20\ 000.00(1.071859)(5.772109)$
$\quad = 20\ 000.00(6.186888)$
$\quad = \$123\ 737.75$

**Programmed Solution**

("BGN" mode) (Set P/Y = 1; C/Y = 4) 7 $\boxed{\text{I/Y}}$ 0 $\boxed{\text{PV}}$

20 000 $\boxed{\pm}$ $\boxed{\text{PMT}}$ 5 $\boxed{\text{N}}$ $\boxed{\text{CPT}}$ $\boxed{\text{FV}}$ $\boxed{123737.7535}$

The accumulated value after five years is $123 737.75.

## B. Present value of a general annuity due

For a general annuity due, the present value is greater than the present value of the corresponding ordinary general annuity by the interest on it for one payment period.

$$\begin{array}{c}\text{THE PRESENT VALUE OF A} \\ \text{GENERAL ANNUITY DUE}\end{array} = (1 + p) \times \begin{array}{c}\text{THE PRESENT VALUE OF THE} \\ \text{CORRESPONDING ORDINARY GENERAL ANNUITY}\end{array}$$

Thus, for the present value of a general annuity due use Formula 13.4. Using the effective rate of interest per payment period,

$$A_{nc}(\text{due}) = R(1 + p)\left[\frac{1 - (1 + p)^{-n}}{p}\right]$$

restated as

$$PV_{nc}(\text{due}) = PMT(1 + p)\left[\frac{1 - (1 + p)^{-n}}{p}\right]$$

——— **Formula 13.4**

where $p = (1 + i)^c - 1$

**EXAMPLE 13.2B**

A three-year lease requires payments of $1600 at the beginning of every three months. If money is worth 9.0% compounded monthly, what is the cash value of the lease?

**SOLUTION**

$PMT = 1600.00$; $n = 3(4) = 12$; $P/Y = 4$; $C/Y = 12$; $c = \dfrac{12}{4} = 3$; $I/Y = 9$;

$i = \dfrac{9.0\%}{12} = 0.75\% = 0.0075$

The effective quarterly rate of interest

$p = 1.0075^3 - 1 = 1.022669 - 1 = 0.022669 = 2.2669\%$

$PV_{nc}\text{ (due)} = 1600.00(1.022669)\left(\dfrac{1 - 1.022669^{-12}}{0.022669}\right)$ ——— substituting in Formula 13.4

$\qquad\quad = 1600.00(1.022669)(10.404043)$

$\qquad\quad = 1600.00(10.639894)$

$\qquad\quad = \$17\ 023.83$

**Programmed Solution**

("BGN" mode)(Set P/Y = 4; C/Y = 12) 9 [ I/Y ] 0 [ FV ]

1600.00 [ ± ] [ PMT ] 12 [ N ] [ CPT ] [ PV ] [ 17023.83049 ]

The cash value of the lease is $17 023.83.

## C. Finding the periodic payment PMT of a general annuity due

If the future value of an annuity $FV_{nc}$(due), the number of conversion periods $n$, and the conversion rate $i$ are known, you can find the periodic payment PMT by substituting the given values in the future value formula.

$$FV_{nc}(\text{due}) = PMT(1 + p)\left[\frac{(1 + p)^n - 1}{p}\right]$$

$$\text{where } p = (1 + i)^c - 1$$

—— **Formula 13.3**

If the present value of an annuity $PV_{nc}$(due), the number of conversion periods $n$, and the conversion rate $i$ are known, you can find the periodic payment PMT by substituting the given values in the present value formula.

$$PV_{nc}(\text{due}) = PMT(1 + p)\left[\frac{1 - (1 + p)^{-n}}{p}\right]$$

$$\text{where } p = (1 + i)^c - 1$$

—— **Formula 13.4**

When using a scientific calculator, you can find PMT by first rearranging the terms of the appropriate formulas above. Then substitute the three known values ($FV_{nc}$(due), $PV_{nc}$(due), $n$, and $i$) into the rearranged formula and solve for PMT.

When using a preprogrammed financial calculator, you can find PMT by entering the five known values ($FV_{nc}$(due) or $PV_{nc}$(due), N, I/Y, P/Y, and C/Y) and pressing [ CPT ] [ PMT ].

**EXAMPLE 13.2C**

What deposit made at the beginning of each month will accumulate to $18 000 at 5% compounded quarterly at the end of eight years?

**SOLUTION**

$FV_{nc}(\text{due}) = 18\ 000.00$; $n = 8(12) = 96$; P/Y = 12; C/Y = 4; $c = \dfrac{4}{12} = \dfrac{1}{3}$

$I/Y = 5$; $i = \dfrac{5\%}{4} = 1.25\% = 0.0125\%$

The effective monthly rate of interest

$$p = 1.0125^{\frac{1}{3}} - 1 = 1.004149 - 1 = 0.004149 = 0.4149\%$$

$$18\ 000.00 = PMT(1.004149)\left(\frac{1.004149^{96} - 1}{0.004149}\right) \quad\text{—— substituting in Formula 13.3}$$

$$18\ 000.00 = PMT(1.004149)(117.638106)$$
$$18\ 000.00 = PMT(118.126236)$$
$$PMT = \frac{18\ 000.00}{118.126236}$$
$$PMT = \$152.38$$

**Programmed Solution**

("BGN" mode) (Set P/Y = 12; C/Y = 4) 5 [ I/Y ] 0 [ PV ]

18 000 [ FV ] 96 [ N ] [ CPT ] [ PMT ] [ −152.379359 ]

The monthly deposit is $152.38.

---

**EXAMPLE 13.2D**

What monthly payment must be made at the beginning of each month on a five-year lease valued at $100 000 if interest is 10% compounded semi-annually?

**SOLUTION**

$$PV_{nc}(due) = 100\ 000.00;\ n = 5(12) = 60;\ P/Y = 12;\ C/Y = 2;\ c = \frac{2}{12} = \frac{1}{6};$$
$$I/Y = 10;\ i = \frac{10\%}{2} = 5\% = 0.05$$

The effective monthly rate of interest

$$p = 1.05^{\frac{1}{6}} - 1 = 1.008165 - 1 = 0.008165 = 0.8165\%$$

$$10\ 000.00 = PMT(1.008165)\left(\frac{1 - 1.008165^{-60}}{0.008165}\right) \quad\begin{array}{l}\text{substituting in}\\\text{Formula 13.4}\end{array}$$

$$100\ 000.00 = PMT(1.008165)(47.286470)$$
$$100\ 000.00 = PMT(47.672557)$$
$$PMT = \frac{100\ 000.00}{47.672557}$$
$$PMT = \$2097.64$$

**Programmed Solution**

("BGN" mode) (Set P/Y = 12; C/Y = 2) 10 [ I/Y ] 0 [ FV ]

100 000 [ ± ] [ PV ] 60 [ N ] [ CPT ] [ PMT ] [ 2097.642904 ]

The monthly payment due at the beginning of each month is $2097.64.

## D. Finding the term *n* of a general annuity due

If the future value of an annuity $FV_{nc}(\text{due})$, the periodic payment PMT, and the conversion rate $i$ are known, you can find the term of the annuity $n$ by substituting the given values in the future value Formula 13.3.

$$FV_{nc}(\text{due}) = PMT(1 + p)\left[\frac{(1 + p)^n - 1}{p}\right]$$

where $p = (1 + i)^c - 1$

—— **Formula 13.3**

If the present value $PV_{nc}(\text{due})$, the periodic payment PMT, and the conversion rate $i$ are known, you can find the term of the annuity $n$ by substituting the given values in the present value Formula 13.4.

$$PV_{nc}(\text{due}) = PMT(1 + p)\left[\frac{1 - (1 + p)^{-n}}{p}\right]$$

where $p = (1 + i)^c - 1$

—— **Formula 13.4**

When using a scientific calculator, you can find $n$ by first rearranging the terms of the appropriate formula. Then substitute the three known values ($FV_{nc}(\text{due})$ or $PV_{nc}(\text{due})$, PMT, and $i$) into the rearranged formula and solve for $n$.

When using a preprogrammed financial calculator, you can find $n$ by entering the five known values ($FV_{nc}(\text{due})$ or $PV_{nc}(\text{due})$, PMT, I/Y, P/Y, and C/Y) and pressing CPT N.

---

**EXAMPLE 13.2E**

Ted Davis wants to accumulate $140 000 in an RRSP by making annual contributions of $5500 at the beginning of each year. If interest on the RRSP is 11% compounded quarterly, for how long will Ted have to make contributions?

**SOLUTION**

$FV_{nc}(\text{due}) = 140\ 000.00$;   PMT $= 5500.00$;   P/Y $= 1$;   C/Y $= 4$;   $c = 4$;

I/Y $= 11$;   $i = \dfrac{11\%}{4} = 2.75\% = 0.0275$

The effective annual rate of interest

$p = 1.0275^4 - 1 = 1.114621 - 1 = 0.114621 = 11.4621\%$

$$140\ 000.000 = 5500.00(1.114621)\left(\frac{1.114621^n - 1}{0.114621}\right) \quad \text{—— using Formula 13.3}$$

$140\ 000.00 = 53\ 484.118(1.114621^n - 1)$

$2.617600 = 1.114621^n - 1$

$1.114621^n = 3.617600$

$n \ln 1.114621 = \ln 3.617600$

$$n(0.108515) = 1.285811$$

$$n = \frac{1.285811}{0.108515}$$

$$n = 11.849188$$

$$n = 12 \text{ years (approximately)}$$

**Programmed Solution**

("BGN" mode) (Set P/Y = 1; C/Y = 4) 11 [ I/Y ] 0 [ PV ]

5500 [ ± ] [ PMT ] 140 000 [ FV ] [ CPT ] [ N ] [ 11.849188 ]

Ted will have to contribute for about twelve years.

---

**EXAMPLE 13.2F**

Ted Davis, having reached his goal of a $140 000 balance in his RRSP, immediately converts it into an RRIF and withdraws from it $1650 at the beginning of each month. If interest continues at 5.75% compounded quarterly, for how long can he make withdrawals?

**SOLUTION**

$PV_{nc}(\text{due}) = 140\ 000.00$;  $PMT = 1650.00$;  $P/Y = 12$;  $C/Y = 4$;  $c = \dfrac{4}{12} = \dfrac{1}{3}$;

$I/Y = 5.75$;  $i = \dfrac{5.75\%}{4} = 1.4375\% = 0.014375$

The effective monthly rate of interest

$$p = 1.014375^{\frac{1}{3}} - 1 = 1.004769 - 1 = 0.004769 = 0.4769\%$$

$$140\ 000.00 = 1650.00(1.004769)\left(\frac{1 - 1.004769^{-n}}{0.004769)}\right) \quad \text{— using Formula 13.4}$$

$$140\ 000.00 = 347\ 642.59(1 - 1.004769^{-n})$$

$$0.402712 = 1 - 1.004769^{-n}$$

$$1.004769^{-n} = 0.597288$$

$$-n \ln 1.004769 = \ln 0.597288$$

$$-n(0.004758) = -0.515357$$

$$n = 108.32388$$

$$n = 109 \text{ months (approximately)}$$

**Programmed Solution**

("BGN" mode) (Set P/Y = 12; C/Y = 4) 5.75 [ I/Y ] 0 [ FV ]

140 000 [ ± ] [ PV ] 1650 [ PMT ] [ CPT ] [ N ] [ 108.323882 ]

Ted will be able to make withdrawals for 109 months, or nine years and one month.

## E. Finding the rate of interest of a general annuity due

When the future value or present value, the periodic payment PMT, and the term $n$ of a general annuity due are known, you can find the nominal interest rate by entering the given values into a preprogrammed calculator. Retrieve the value of I/Y by being in "BGN" mode and pressing [ CPT ] [ I/Y ] .

| | |
|---|---|
| **EXAMPLE 13.2G** | Compute the nominal annual rate of interest compounded monthly at which $500 deposited at the beginning of every three months for ten years will amount to $30 000. |
| **SOLUTION** | $FV_{nc}(due) = 30\,000.00;$ PMT $= 500.00;$ $n = 40;$ P/Y $= 4;$ C/Y $= 12;$ |

$$c = \frac{12}{4} = 3$$

**Programmed Solution**
("BGN" mode) (Set P/Y = 4; C/Y = 12) 0 [ PV ] 30 000 [ FV ]

500 [ ± ] [ PMT ] 40 [ N ] [ CPT ] [ I/Y ] [ 7.484516 ]

The nominal annual rate is 7.48% compounded monthly.

## EXERCISE 13.2

**EXCEL NOTES**

If you choose, you can use Excel's *Present Value (PV)* function or *Future Value (FV)* function to answer the questions indicated below. Refer to **PV** and **FV** on the Spreadsheet Template Disk to learn how to use these Excel functions.

**A.** For each of the following four annuities due, determine the unknown value represented by the question mark.

| | Future Value $FV_{nc}(due)$ | Present Value $PV_{nc}(due)$ | Periodic Payment PMT | Payment Interval | Term | Nominal Rate of Interest | Conversion Period |
|---|---|---|---|---|---|---|---|
| **1.** | ? | | $1500 | 6 months | 10 years | 5% | quarterly |
| **2.** | ? | | 175 | 1 month | 7 years | 7 | semi-annually |
| **3.** | | ? | 650 | 3 months | 6 years | 12 | monthly |
| **4.** | | ? | 93 | 1 month | 4 years | 4 | quarterly |

**B.** Find the periodic payment for each of the following four annuities due.

| | Future Value | Present Value | Payment Period | Term | Interest Rate | Conversion Period |
|---|---|---|---|---|---|---|
| **1.** | $16 500 | | 1 year | 10 years | 4% | quarterly |
| **2.** | 9 200 | | 3 months | 5 years | 5 | semi-annually |
| **3.** | | $10 000 | 3 months | 3 years | 6 | monthly |
| **4.** | | 24 300 | 1 month | 20 years | 9 | semi-annually |

**C.** Find the length of the term for each of the following four annuities due.

| | Future Value | Present Value | Periodic Payment | Payment Period | Interest Rate | Conversion Period |
|---|---|---|---|---|---|---|
| 1. | $32 000 | | $450 | 6 months | 7.5% | monthly |
| 2. | 7 500 | | 150 | 3 months | 11 | annually |
| 3. | | $12 500 | 860 | 3 months | 9 | monthly |
| 4. | | 45 000 | 540 | 1 month | 4 | semi-annually |

**D.** For each of the following four annuities due, determine the nominal annual rate of interest.

| | Future Value | Present Value | Periodic Payment | Payment Interval | Term | Conversion Period |
|---|---|---|---|---|---|---|
| 1. | $ 6 400 | | $200 | 6 months | 9 years | monthly |
| 2. | 25 000 | | 790 | 1 year | 15 years | quarterly |
| 3. | | $ 7 500 | 420 | 3 months | 5 years | monthly |
| 4. | | 60 000 | 450 | 1 month | 25 years | semi-annually |

**E.** Answer each of the following questions.

1. Bomac Steel sets aside $5000 at the beginning of every six months in a fund to replace equipment. If interest is 6% compounded quarterly, how much will be in the fund after five years?
Reference Example 13.2A

2. Jamie Dean contributes $125 at the beginning of each month into an RRSP paying interest at 6.5% compounded semi-annually. What will be the accumulated balance in the RRSP at the end of 25 years?

3. What is the cash value of a lease requiring payments of $750 at the beginning of each month for three years if interest is 8% compounded quarterly?
Reference Example 13.2B

4. Gerald and Marysia bought a property by making semi-annual payments of $2500 for seven years. If the first payment is due on the date of purchase and interest is 9% compounded quarterly, what is the purchase price of the property?

5. How much would you have to pay into an account at the beginning of every six months to accumulate $10 000 in eight years if interest is 7% compounded quarterly?
Reference Example 13.2C

6. Teachers' Credit Union entered a lease contract valued at $5400. The contract provides for payments at the beginning of each month for three years. If interest is 5.5% compounded quarterly, what is the size of the monthly payment?

7. Sarah Ling has saved $85 000. If she decides to withdraw $3000 at the beginning of every three months and interest is 6.125% compounded annually, for how long can she make withdrawals?
Reference Example 13.2F

8. For how long must contributions of $1600 be made at the beginning of each year to accumulate to $96 000 at 10% compounded quarterly?

9. What is the nominal annual rate of interest compounded annually on a lease valued at $21 600 if payments of $680 are made at the beginning of each month for three years?
Reference Example 13.2G

10. An insurance policy provides for a lump-sum benefit of $50 000 fifteen years from now. Alternatively, payments of $1700 may be received at the beginning of each of the next fifteen years. What is the effective annual rate of interest if interest is compounded quarterly?

>> BUSINESS MATH NEWS BOX

### Pay Off the Mortgage, or Top Up the RRSP?

The Vuongs have been happily married for more than a year. Now Danielle and her husband Vu own a bungalow in Toronto, and like many Canadian first-time homeowners, the Vuongs borrowed from their RRSPs for the down payment.

In fact, they each borrowed the personal maximum of $20 000 allowed under the federal government's Home Buyers Plan, which means they have an interest-free loan for up to 17 years.

On the not-so-bright side: the Vuongs have no registered retirement savings left.

Now they're faced with a dilemma—pay off the zero-interest RRSP loan as soon as they can, or use their spare cash to chip away at their $265 000 mortgage.

The answer to their big question is to focus on several goals at once.

The Vuongs are ahead of many couples—they have no consumer debt, and they're already paying their mortgage biweekly to get rid of it faster. But how do they work toward all their goals when there is only a limited amount of funds to do it all?

Once the $1700 monthly mortgage bill and other costs are paid, Danielle figures they have about $700 left over, though she admits "We have never added things up."

They spend their money on vacations, lindy hop dancing, and repairs and renovations on the house such as the chimney, a grounded electrical system, and air conditioning. They own their car outright, and earn a combined $120 000 annual salary, of which Danielle brings in one-quarter but has multiple tax write-offs for her business.

The Vuongs should consider developing a financial plan that factors in monthly payments of about $500, said Tom Zaks, an investment adviser at RBC Dominion Securities Inc. That money should build back their RRSPs and build an emergency fund of about three months' gross salary, he added.

*Source:* Theresa Ebden, "Pay Off the Mortgage, or Top Up the RRSP?," *The Globe and Mail*, October 9, 2006, p. B.10. Reprinted with permission of the author.

### QUESTIONS

1. Calculate the monthly payments required to pay off each of the $20 000 RRSP loans over a 17-year period.

2. If the family pays off the $265 000 mortgage by paying $1700 per month, calculate the mortgage rate. Assume the amortization period is over 25 years.

3. Given that the family earns a combined annual salary of $120 000 and their average tax rate is 30%, calculate the amount the family will have remaining after paying off the mortgage and the RRSP loan.

## 13.3 ORDINARY DEFERRED ANNUITIES

### A. Computation of an ordinary simple deferred annuity

A **deferred annuity** is one in which the first payment is made at a time *later* than the end of the first payment interval. The time period from the time referred to as "now" to the starting point of the term of the annuity is called the **period of deferment.** The number of compounding periods in the period of deferment is designated by the letter symbol $d$. The future value of a deferred ordinary simple annuity (designated by the symbol $FV_n(\text{defer})$) is the accumulated value of the periodic payments at the end of the term of the annuity.

**EXAMPLE 13.3A**

Deposits of $500 are due to be made at the end of each year for ten years. If the deposits are deferred for four years and interest is 6% compounded annually, what is the accumulated value of the deferred annuity?

**SOLUTION**

Since the deposits are not made during the first four years, there is no balance, and no interest is earned. During the following ten years, deposits are made, the balance increases, and interest is earned.

**FIGURE 13.3**    **Graphical Representation of Method and Data**

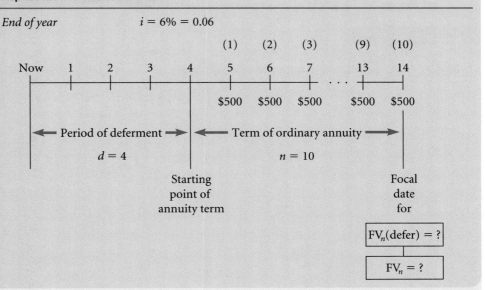

$$PMT = 500.00; P/Y = 1; C/Y = 1; I/Y = 6; i = 6\% = 0.06; n = 10; d = 4$$

$$FV_n(\text{defer}) = FV_n = 500.00\left(\frac{1.06^{10} - 1}{0.06}\right) \text{——— using Formula 11.1}$$

$$= 500.00(13.180795)$$

$$= \$6590.40$$

**Programmed Solution**

("END" mode) (Set P/Y = 1; C/Y = 1) 0 [ PV ] 500 [ ± ] [ PMT ]

10 [ N ] 6 [ I/Y ] [ CPT ] [ FV ] [ 6590.397471 ]

*Note:* The period of deferment does *not* affect the solution to the problem of finding the future value of a deferred annuity: $FV_n(\text{defer}) = FV_n$. Therefore, the problem of finding the future value of a deferred annuity is identical to the problem of finding the future value of an annuity. No further consideration is given in this text to the problem of finding the future value of a deferred annuity.

The present value of a deferred annuity is the discounted value of the periodic payment at the beginning of the period of deferment.

The present value of a deferred simple annuity is designated by the symbol $PV_n$ (defer).

The present value of a deferred general annuity is designated by the symbol $PV_{nc}$(defer).

---

**EXAMPLE 13.3B**  Payments of $500 are due at the end of each year for ten years. If the annuity is deferred for four years and interest is 6% compounded annually, determine the present value of the deferred annuity.

**SOLUTION**

**FIGURE 13.4**  **Graphical Representation of Method and Data**

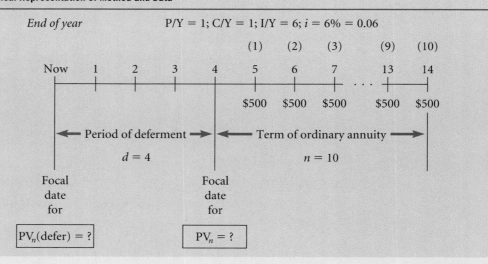

The problem of finding the present value of a deferred annuity can be divided into two smaller problems. We have used this approach in solving Example 11.3F in Chapter 11. We use it again in this problem to find the present value of the deferred annuity.

First, find the present value of the ordinary annuity (focal date at the beginning of the term of the annuity).

$$PV_n = 500.00 \left( \frac{1 - 1.06^{10}}{0.06)} \right) \quad \text{------ using Formula 11.2}$$

$$= 500.00(7.360087)$$

$$= \$3680.04$$

Second, find the present value of $PV_n$ at the focal date "now."

$$PV_n(\text{defer}) = PV = 3680.04(1.06^{-4}) \quad \text{------ using Formula 9.1C}$$

$$= 3680.04(0.792094)$$

$$= \$2914.94$$

**Programmed Solution**

(Set P/Y = 1; C/Y = 1) 0 [ FV ] 500 [ ± ] [ PMT ]

6 [ I/Y ] 10 [ N ] [ CPT ] [ PV ] [ 3680.043526 ]

0 [ PMT ] 3680.043526 [ FV ] 6 [ I/Y ] 4 [ N ] [ CPT ] [ PV ] [ −2914.939157 ]

You can find the periodic payment PMT for deferred annuities by first determining the future value of the known present value at the end of the period of deferment. Then substitute in the appropriate annuity formula.

---

**EXAMPLE 13.3C**

Find the size of the payment required at the end of every three months to repay a five-year loan of $25 000 if the payments are deferred for two years and interest is 6% compounded quarterly.

**SOLUTION**

The payments form a deferred ordinary annuity

$PV_n(\text{defer}) = 25\ 000.00;\ P/Y = 4;\ C/Y = 4;\ I/Y = 6;\ i = \dfrac{6\%}{4} = 1.5\% = 0.015;$

$n = 5(4) = 20;\ d = 2(4) = 8$

Value of $25 000.00 at the end of the period of deferment

$\begin{aligned} FV &= 25\ 000.00(1.015)^8 &&\text{—— using Formula 9.1A} \\ &= 25\ 000.00(1.126493) \\ &= \$28\ 162.32 \end{aligned}$

$28\ 162.32 = PMT\left(\dfrac{1 - 1.015^{-20}}{0.015}\right)$ —— subtituting in Formula 11.2

$28\ 162.32 = (17.168639)PMT$

$PMT = \dfrac{28\ 162.32}{17.168639}$

$PMT = \$1640.34$

**Programmed Solution**

(Set P/Y = 4; C/Y = 4) [ 2nd ] (CLR TVM) 25 000 [ ± ] [ PV ]

6 [ I/Y ] 8 [ N ] [ CPT ] [ FV ] [ 28162.31466 ]

28162.31466 [ ± ] [ PV ] 0 [ FV ] 6 [ I/Y ] 20 [ N ] [ CPT ] [ PMT ] [ −1640.334742 ]

The size of the required payment is $1640.33.

You can find the term for deferred ordinary annuities by the same approach used to determine the periodic payment PMT.

**EXAMPLE 13.3D**

For how long can you pay $500 at the end of each month out of a fund of $10 000, deposited today at 10.5% compounded monthly, if the payments are deferred for nine years?

**SOLUTION**

The payments form a deferred ordinary annuity.

$PV_n(\text{defer}) = 10\ 000.00;\ PMT = 500.00;\ P/Y = 12;\ C/Y = 12;\ I/Y = 10.5;$

$i = \dfrac{10.5\%}{12} = 0.875\% = 0.00875;\ d = 9(12) = 108$

The value of the $10 000.00 at the end of the period of deferment,

$$\begin{aligned}
FV &= 10\ 000.00(1.00875)^{108} \\
&= 10\ 000.00(2.562260) \\
&= 25\ 622.60
\end{aligned}$$

$$25\ 622.60 = 500.00\left(\frac{1 - 1.00875^{-n}}{0.00875}\right)$$

$$25\ 622.60 = 57\ 142.857(1 - 1.00875^{-n})$$

$$\frac{25\ 622.60}{57\ 142.857} = 1 - 1.00875^{-n}$$

$$0.448400 = 1 - 1.00875^{-n}$$

$$1.00875^{-n} = 0.551605$$

$$-n \ln 1.00875 = \ln 0.551605$$

$$-n(0.008712) = -0.594924$$

$$n = \frac{0.594924}{0.008712}$$

$$n = 68.288334$$

$$n = 69 \text{ (months)}$$

**Programmed Solution**

(Set P/Y = 12; C/Y = 12) 0 $\boxed{\text{PMT}}$ 10 000 $\boxed{\pm}$ $\boxed{\text{PV}}$

10.5 $\boxed{\text{I/Y}}$ 108 $\boxed{\text{N}}$ $\boxed{\text{CPT}}$ $\boxed{\text{FV}}$ $\boxed{25622.59753}$

$\boxed{\pm}$ 25 622.59753 $\boxed{\text{PV}}$ 0 $\boxed{\text{FV}}$ 10.5 $\boxed{\text{I/Y}}$

500 $\boxed{\text{PMT}}$ $\boxed{\text{CPT}}$ $\boxed{\text{N}}$ $\boxed{68.288332}$

Payments can be made for 69 months, or five years and nine months.

**EXAMPLE 13.3E**

Mr. Dhaliwal wants to receive payments of $800 at the end of each month for ten years after his retirement in seven years. If he invests $50 000 now to earn 6% compounded monthly until he retires, what monthly compounded nominal rate of interest must he earn after he retires?

**SOLUTION**

First, the accumulated value of the investment at retirement, after the first seven years, must be determined. The period of deferment is 7 years.

$PV_n = 50\,000.00$; $PMT = 0$; $P/Y = 12$; $C/Y = 12$; $i = \dfrac{6\%}{12} = 0.5\% = 0.005$;

$d = 7(12) = 84$

$FV_n = 50\,000.00(1.005^{84})$

$\quad\quad = 50\,000(1.520370)$

$\quad\quad = \$76\,018.48$

Next, for the period of ten years after retirement, the monthly payments form an ordinary annuity.

$PV_n = 76018.48$;  $PMT = 800.00$;  $P/Y = 12$;  $C/Y = 12$;  $n = 10(12) = 120$

**Programmed Solution**

(Set P/Y = 12; C/Y = 12) 50 000.00 ⎡ ± ⎤  ⎡ PV ⎤ 0 ⎡ PMT ⎤ 6 ⎡ I/Y ⎤

84 ⎡ N ⎤ ⎡ CPT ⎤ ⎡ FV ⎤  ⎡ 76018.4818 ⎤

76 018.4818 ⎡ ± ⎤ ⎡ PV ⎤ 0 ⎡ FV ⎤ 800 ⎡ PMT ⎤

120 ⎡ N ⎤ ⎡ CPT ⎤ ⎡ I/Y ⎤  ⎡ 4.830216 ⎤

Mr. Dhaliwal's investments must earn 4.83% compounded monthly.

## B. Computation of an ordinary general deferred annuity

The same principles apply to an ordinary general deferred annuity as apply to an ordinary simple deferred annuity.

**EXAMPLE 13.3F**

Payments of $1000 are due at the end of each year for five years. If the payments are deferred for three years and interest is 10% compounded quarterly, what is the present value of the deferred payments?

**SOLUTION**

**STEP 1**

Find the present value of the ordinary general annuity.

$PMT = 1000.00$; $n = 5$; $P/Y = 1$; $C/Y = 4$; $c = 4$; $I/Y = 10$;

$i = \dfrac{10\%}{4} = 2.5\% = 0.025$

The effective annual rate of interest

$p = 1.025^4 - 1 = 1.103813 - 1 = 0.103813 = 10.3813\%$

$$PV_{nc} = 1000.00\left(\frac{1 - 1.103813^{-5}}{0.103813}\right)\text{———— substituting in Formula 12.3}$$

$\quad\quad = 1000.00(3.754149)$

$\quad\quad = \$3754.15$

**Programmed Solution**

(Set P/Y = 1; C/Y = 4) 1000 ⎡ ± ⎤ ⎡ PMT ⎤ 0 ⎡ FV ⎤ 10 ⎡ I/Y ⎤

5 ⎡ N ⎤ ⎡ CPT ⎤ ⎡ 3754.148977 ⎤

STEP 2 | Find the present value of $PV_{nc}$ at the beginning of the period of deferment.
FV = 3754.15 is the present value of the general annuity $PV_{nc}$;
$d$ = 3 is the number of deferred payment intervals;
$p$ = 10.38129% is the effective rate of interest per payment interval.

$PV_{nc}$(defer) = PV = $3754.15(1.103813^{-3})$ ——————— substituting in Formula 9.1C
$= 3754.15(0.743556)$
$= \$2791.42$

**Programmed Solution**

3754.15 [FV] 10 [I/Y] 0 [PMT] 3 [N] [CPT] [PV] [−2791.420326]

The present value of the deferred payments is $2791.42.

---

EXAMPLE 13.3G | Mr. Kovacs deposited a retirement bonus of $31 500 in an income averaging annuity paying $375 at the end of each month. If payments are deferred for nine months and interest is 6% compounded quarterly, for what period of time will Mr. Kovacs receive annuity payments?

SOLUTION | $PV_{nc}$ (defer) = 31 500.00; PMT = 375.00; $d$ = 9; P/Y = 12; C/Y = 4;

$c = \dfrac{4}{12} = \dfrac{1}{3};$ I/Y = 6; $i = \dfrac{6\%}{4} = 1.5\% = 0.015$

The effective monthly rate of interest

$p = 1.015^{\frac{1}{3}} - 1 = 1.004975 - 1 = 0.004975 = 0.4975\%$

First find the accumulated value at the end of the period of deferment

$FV = 31\ 500.00(1.004975)^{9}$
$= 31\ 500.00(1.045678)$
$= 32\ 938.87$

**Programmed Solution**

(Set P/Y = 12; C/Y = 4) 6 [I/Y] 0 [PMT]

31 500 [±] [PV] 9 [N] [CPT] [FV] [32938.86881]

Then find the number of payments for an ordinary annuity with a present value of $32 938.87.

$32\ 938.87 = 375.00\left(\dfrac{1 - 1.004975^{-n}}{0.004975)}\right).$

$32\ 938.87 = 75\ 373.854(1 - 1.004975^{-n})$

$0.437007 = 1 - 1.004975^{-n}$

$1.00497^{-n} = 0.562993$

$-n \ln 1.00497 = \ln 0.562993$

$-n(0.004963) = -0.574487$

$$n = \frac{0.574487}{0.004963}$$
$$n = 115.75639$$
$$n = 116 \text{ months}$$

### Programmed Solution

32 938.869 | ± | | PV | 0 | FV | 6 | I/Y | 375 | PMT | | CPT | | N | | 115.757250 |

Mr. Kovacs will receive payments for 116 months, or nine years and eight months.

---

**EXAMPLE 13.3H**

A contract that has a cash value of \$36 000 requires payments at the end of every three months for six years. If the payments are deferred for three years and interest is 9% compounded semi-annually, what is the size of the quarterly payments?

**SOLUTION**

$\text{PV}_{nc}(\text{defer}) = 36\ 000.00$; $n = 6(4) = 24$; $d = 3(4) = 12$; $\text{P/Y} = 4$; $\text{C/Y} = 2$;

$c = \dfrac{2}{4} = 0.5$; $\text{I/Y} = 9$; $i = \dfrac{9\%}{2} = 4.5\% = 0.045$

The effective quarterly rate of interest
$$p = 1.045^{0.5} - 1 = 1.022252 - 1 = 0.022252 = 2.2252\%$$

First determine the accumulated value of the deposit at the end of the period of deferment.

$\text{FV} = 36\ 000.00(1.022252)^{12}$ ———————— substituting in Formula 9.1A
$= 36\ 000.00(1.302260)$
$= \$46\ 881.36$

### Programmed Solution

(Set P/Y = 4; C/Y = 2) 9 | I/Y | 0 | PMT | 36 000 | ± | | PV |

12 | N | | CPT | | FV | | 46881.36449 |

Now determine the periodic payment for the ordinary general annuity whose present value is \$46 881.36.

$$46\ 881.36 = \text{PMT} \left( \frac{1 - 1.022252^{-24}}{0.022252)} \right) \text{ — substituting in Formula 12.3}$$
$$46\ 881.36 = \text{PMT}(18.440075)$$
$$\text{PMT} = \frac{46\ 881.36}{18.440075}$$
$$\text{PMT} = \$2542.36$$

### Programmed Solution

46 881.36 | ± | | PV | 0 | FV | 9 | I/Y | 24 | N | | CPT | | PMT | | 2542.363174 |

The required quarterly payment is \$2542.36.

## EXERCISE 13.3

If you choose, you can use Excel's **Present Value (PV)** function to answer the questions indicated below. Refer to **PV** on the Spreadsheet Template Disk to learn how to use this Excel function.

  **A.** Find the present value of each of the following five ordinary deferred annuities.

| | Periodic Payment | Made At: | Payment Period | Period of Deferment | Term | Interest Rate | Conversion Period |
|---|---|---|---|---|---|---|---|
| 1. | $ 45.00 | end | 1 month | 5 years | 7 years | 12% | monthly |
| 2. | 125.00 | end | 6 months | 8 years | 15 years | 7 | semi-annually |
| 3. | 2125.00 | end | 1 month | 12 years | 20 years | 10.5 | monthly |
| 4. | 720.00 | end | 3 months | 4 years | 10 years | 12 | monthly |
| 5. | 1500.00 | end | 1 month | 2 years | 3 years | 5 | semi-annually |

**B.** Answer each of the following questions.

1. Calvin Jones bought his neighbour's farm for $10 000 down and payments of $5000 at the end of every three months for ten years. If the payments are deferred for two years and interest is 8% compounded quarterly, what was the purchase price of the farm? Reference Example 13.3B

2. Mrs. Bell expects to retire in seven years and would like to receive $800 at the end of each month for ten years following the date of her retirement. How much must Mrs. Bell deposit today in an account paying 7.5% compounded semi-annually to receive the monthly payments?

3. The Omega Venture Group needs to borrow to finance a project. Repayment of the loan involves payments of $8500 at the end of every three months for eight years. No payments are to be made during the development period of three years. Interest is 9% compounded quarterly.
   (a) How much should the Group borrow?
   (b) What amount will be repaid?
   (c) How much of that amount will be interest?

4. What sum of money invested now will provide payments of $1200 at the end of every three months for six years if the payments are deferred for nine years and interest is 10% compounded quarterly?

5. An annuity with a cash value of $14 500 earns 7% compounded semi-annually. End-of-period semi-annual payments are deferred for seven years, and then continue for ten years. How much is the amount of each payment? Reference Example 13.3C

6. A deposit of $20 000 is made for a twenty-year term. After the term expires, equal withdrawals are to be made for twelve years at the end of every six months. What is the size of the semi-annual withdrawal if interest is 4.75% compounded semi-annually?

7. Mr. Talbot received a bonus of $18 000, which he deposited in an RRSP. He intends to leave the money for fourteen years, then transfer the balance into an RRIF and make equal withdrawals at the end of every six months for twenty years. If interest is 6.5% compounded semi-annually, what will be the size of each withdrawal?

8. Josie won $8000 in an essay-writing contest. The money was deposited into a savings account earning 4.2% compounded monthly. She intends to leave the money for five-and-a-half years, then withdraw amounts at the end of each month for the next four years while she studies to become an entrepreneur. What will be the size of each withdrawal?

9. An annuity with a cash value of $8800 pays $325 at the end of every month. If the annuity earns 6% compounded monthly, and payments begin three years from now, how long will the payments last? Reference Example 13.3D

10. A deposit of $4000 is made today for a five-year period. For how long can $500 be withdrawn from the account at the end of every three months starting three months after the end of the five-year term if interest is 4% compounded quarterly?

11. For how long can $1000 be withdrawn at the end of each month from an account containing $16 000, if the withdrawals are deferred for six years and interest is 7.2% compounded monthly?

12. Greg borrowed $6500 at 6.4% compounded monthly to help finance his education. He contracted to repay the loan in monthly payments of $300 each. If the payments are due at the end of each month and the payments are deferred for four years, for how long will Greg have to make monthly payments?

13. Samantha wants to be able to withdraw $500 at the end of each month for two years while she travels, starting three years from now. If she invests $10 000 now to earn 4.68% compounded monthly until she begins to travel, what monthly compounded nominal rate of interest must she earn after she starts to travel? Reference Example 13.3E

14. Paul is in the process of purchasing a new sound system for his car. The cash price is $1500, or he can sign a contract to "buy now and pay later." During the first year, the loan charges interest at 12.4% compounded monthly. The terms of the contract state that he would start making payments at the end of the month that is twelve months from now, paying $114 per month for eighteen months to fulfill the contract.
    (a) What monthly compounded nominal rate of interest would he be paying during the time he would be making payments?
    (b) How much extra would Paul be paying to "buy now and pay later?"

15. Thomas is planning to withdraw $8000 from a savings account at the end of each quarter for four years. If the payments are deferred for five years and interest is 5.34% compounded semi-annually, what amount has to be invested now into the savings account? Reference Example 13.3F

16. Asa has invested money from the settlement of an insurance claim. She plans to withdraw $600 from her savings account at the end of each month for four years. If the payments are deferred for two years and interest is 6% compounded quarterly, what was the amount of the insurance settlement?

17. Arianne borrowed $6200 to buy a vehicle to drive to school. She plans to study for three years, and then start her career using her education. Interest is charged on the loan at 7.64% compounded annually. If she starts making month-end payments of $230 when she begins working, how many payments will she have to make? Reference Example 13.3G

18. Jean inherited $25 000, where the terms of the inheritance state that she is to receive $1500 at the end of each quarter, starting in three years, until the money is completely withdrawn. If the money is placed in a savings account earning 2.75% compounded monthly, how long will the inheritance last?

19. Amir invested $12 000 in a three-year term investment earning 4.48% compounded semi-annually. He then invested the money in an investment earning 3.82% compounded semi-annually. How many quarterly $1000 withdrawals can he make?

20. On the day of his daughter's birth, Mr. Dornan deposited $2000 in a trust fund with his credit union at 5% compounded quarterly. Following her eighteenth birthday, the daughter is to receive equal payments at the end of each month for four years while she is at college. If interest is to be 6% compounded monthly after the daughter's eighteenth birthday, how much will she receive every month?

21. An annuity purchased for $9000 makes month-end payments for seven years and earns interest at 5% quarterly. If payments are deferred for three years, how much is each payment?  Reference Example 13.3H

22. Ed Ainsley borrowed $10 000 from his uncle to finance his postgraduate studies. The loan agreement calls for equal payments at the end of each month for ten years. The payments are deferred for four years and interest is 8% compounded semi-annually. What is the size of the monthly payments?

# 13.4 DEFERRED ANNUITIES DUE

## A. Computation of a simple deferred annuity due

The same principles apply to a simple deferred annuity due as apply to a simple annuity due.

**EXAMPLE 13.4A**

Mei Willis would like to receive annuity payments of $2000 at the beginning of each quarter for seven years. The annuity is to start five years from now and interest is 5% compounded quarterly.

  (i) How much must Mei invest today?
 (ii) How much will Mei receive from the annuity?
(iii) How much of what she receives will be interest?

**SOLUTION**

(i) First, find the present value of the annuity due (the focal point is five years from now).

(i) PMT = 2000.00; P/Y = 4; C/Y = 4; I/Y = 5; $i = \dfrac{5\%}{4} = 1.25\% = 0.0125$;

$n = 7(4) = 28$

$$PV_n(\text{due}) = 2000.00(1.0125)\left[\frac{1 - 1.0125^{-28}}{1.0125}\right]$$

$$= 2000.00(1.0125)(23.502518)$$

$$= 47\ 005.035(1.0125)$$

$$= \$47\ 592.60$$

Second, determine the present value of $47 592.60 (the focal point is "now").

FV = 47 592.60;   $i = 1.25\%$;   $n = 5(4) = 20$

$$PV = 47\ 592.60(1.0125)^{-20}$$
$$= 47\ 592.60(0.780009)$$
$$= \$37\ 122.63$$

**Programmed Solution**

("BGN" mode) (Set P/Y = 4; C/Y = 4) 0 [ FV ] 2000 [ ± ] [ PMT ]

5 [ I/Y ] 28 [ N ] [ CPT ] [ PV ] [ 47592.5985 ]

47 592.5985 [ FV ] 0 [ PMT ] 5 [ I/Y ] 20 [ N ] [ CPT ] [ PV ] [ –37122.63367 ]

Mei will have to invest $37 122.63.

(ii)  Mei will receive 28(2000.00) = $56 000.00.

(iii) Interest will be 56 000.00 − 37 122.63 = $18 877.37.

---

**EXAMPLE 13.4B**

$2000 is to be withdrawn from a fund at the beginning of every three months for twelve years starting ten years from now. If interest is 10% compounded quarterly, what must be the balance in the fund today to permit the withdrawals?

**SOLUTION**

The withdrawals form an annuity due.

PMT = 2000.00;   P/Y = 4;   C/Y = 4;   I/Y = 10;   $i = \dfrac{10\%}{4} = 2.5\% = 0.025$;

$n = 12(4) = 48$

The period of deferment is 10 years, so $d = (10)(4) = 40$.

$$PV_n(due) = 2000.00(1.025)\left[\frac{1 - (1.025)^{-48}}{0.025}\right]$$

$$= 2000(1.025)(27.773154)$$

$$= 56\ 934.97$$

$$PV_n(defer) = 56\ 934.97(1.025)^{-40}$$

$$= 56\ 934.97(0.372431)$$

$$= 21\ 204.33$$

**Programmed Solution**

("BGN" mode) (Set P/Y = 4; C/Y = 4) 0 [ FV ] 2000 [ ± ] [ PMT ]

10 [ I/Y ] 48 [ N ] [ CPT ] [ PV ] [ 56934.9651 ]

56 934.9651 [ FV ] 0 [ PMT ] 10 [ I/Y ] 40 [ N ] [ CPT ] [ PV ] [ –21204.32456 ]

The balance in the fund today must be $21 204.33.

**EXAMPLE 13.4C**

What payment can be made at the beginning of each month for six years if $5000 is invested today at 12% compounded monthly and the payments are deferred for ten years?

**SOLUTION**

The payments form a deferred annuity due.

$PV_n(\text{defer}) = 5000.00$; $P/Y = 12$; $C/Y = 12$; $I/Y = 12$; $i = \dfrac{12\%}{12} = 1\% = 0.01$;

$n = 6(12) = 72$; $d = 10(12) = 120$

Value of the $5000 at the end of the period of deferment,

$$FV = 5000.00(1.01)^{120}$$
$$= 5000.00(3.300387)$$
$$= \$16\,501.94$$

$$16\,501.94 = PMT(1.01)\left(\frac{(1 - 1.01^{-72})}{0.01}\right) \quad\text{—— substituting in Formula 13.2}$$

$$16\,501.94 = PMT(1.01)(51.150392)$$
$$16\,501.94 = (51.661896)\,PMT$$

$$PMT = \frac{16\,501.94}{51.661896}$$
$$PMT = \$319.42$$

**Programmed Solution**

(Set P/Y = 12; C/Y = 12) 0 [PMT] 5000 [±] [PV]

12 [I/Y] 120 [N] [CPT] [FV] [16501.93447]

("BGN" mode) 16 501.93447 [±] [PV] 0 [FV]

12 [I/Y] 72 [N] [CPT] [PMT] [319.421778]

The monthly payment is $319.42.

**EXAMPLE 13.4D**

What payment can be received at the beginning of each month for fifteen years if $10 000 is deposited in a fund ten years before the first payment is made and interest is 6% compounded monthly?

**SOLUTION**

First, find the accumulated value of the initial deposit at the beginning of the term of the annuity due ten years after the deposit.

$PV = 10\,000.00$; $P/Y = 12$; $C/Y = 12$; $I/Y = 6$; $i = \dfrac{6\%}{12} = 0.5\% = 0.005$;

$n = 10(12) = 120$

$$FV = 10\,000(1.005)^{120}$$
$$= 10\,000.00(1.819397)$$
$$= \$18\,193.97$$

Now determine the monthly withdrawal that can be made at the beginning of each month from the initial balance of $18 193.97.

$PV_n(\text{due}) = 18\ 193.87; \quad i = 0.5\%; \quad n = 15(12) = 180$

$$18\ 193.97 = PMT(1.005)\left[\frac{1 - (1.005)^{-180}}{0.005}\right]$$

$$18\ 193.97 = PMT(1.005)(118.503515)$$

$$PMT = \frac{18\ 193.97}{119.096032}$$

$$PMT = \$152.77$$

### Programmed Solution

(Set P/Y = 12; C/Y =12) 0 | PMT | 10 000 | ± | | PV |

6 | I/Y | 120 | N | | CPT | | FV | | 18193.96734 |

("BGN" mode) 18 193.96734 | ± | | PV | 0 | FV |

6 | I/Y | 180 | N | | CPT | | PMT | | 152.767200 |

A payment of $152.77 can be made at the beginning of each month.

---

**EXAMPLE 13.4E**

A scholarship of $2000 per year is to be paid at the beginning of each year from a scholarship fund of $15 000 invested at 7% compounded annually. How long will the scholarship be paid if payments are deferred for five years?

**SOLUTION**

The annual payments form a deferred annuity due.

$PV_n(\text{defer}) = 15\ 000.00; \quad PMT = 2000.00; \quad P/Y = 1; \quad C/Y = 1; \quad I/Y = 7;$

$i = 7\% = 0.07; \quad d = 5$

The value of the $15 000 at the end of the period of deferment,

$FV = 15\ 000.00(1.07)^5$

$\quad\ \ = 15\ 000.00(1.402552)$

$\quad\ \ = 21\ 038.28$

$$21\ 038.28 = 2000.00(1.07)\left(\frac{1 - 1.07^{-n}}{0.07}\right)$$

$$21\ 038.28 = 30\ 571.43(1 - 1.07^{-n})$$

$$0.688168 = 1 - 1.07^{-n}$$

$$1.07^{-n} = 0.311832$$

$$-n \ln 1.07 = \ln 0.311832$$

$$-0.067659n = -1.165291$$

$$n = \frac{1.165291}{0.067659}$$

$$n = 17.223$$

$$n = 18 \text{ years (approximately)}$$

**Programmed Solution**

(Set P/Y = 1; C/Y = 1) 0 PMT 15 000 ± PV

7 I/Y 5 N CPT FV 21038.27596

("BGN" mode) 21 038.27596 ± PV 0 FV

7 I/Y 2000 PMT CPT N 17.223081

The scholarship fund will provide 17 payments of $2000 and a final payment of less than $2000.

## B. Computation of a general deferred annuity due

The same principles apply to a general deferred annuity due as apply to a simple annuity due.

---

**EXAMPLE 13.4F**

Tom Casey wants to withdraw $925 at the beginning of each quarter for twelve years. If the withdrawals are to begin ten years from now and interest is 4.5% compounded monthly, how much must Tom deposit today to be able to make the withdrawals?

**SOLUTION**

$PMT = 925.00;$ $\quad n = 12(4) = 48;$ $\quad d = 10(4) = 40;$ $\quad P/Y = 4;$ $\quad C/Y = 12;$

$I/Y = 4.5;$ $\quad c = \dfrac{12}{4} = 3;$ $\quad i = \dfrac{4.5\%}{12} = 0.375\% = 0.00375$

The effective quarterly rate of interest

$p = 1.00375^3 - 1 = 1.011292 - 1 = 0.011292 = 1.1292\%$

**STEP 1** Find the present value of the general annuity due.

$$PV_{nc}(\text{due}) = 925.00(1.011292)\left(\frac{1 - 1.011292^{-48}}{0.011292}\right) \text{———substituting in Formula 13.4}$$

$$= 925.00(1.011292)(36.898160)$$
$$= \$34\ 516.21$$

**Programmed Solution**

(Set P/Y = 4; C/Y = 12) ("BGN" mode) 4.5 I/Y 0 FV

925 ± PMT 48 N CPT PV 34516.21131

STEP 2

Find the present value of $PV_{nc}$(due) at the beginning of the period of deferment.

FV = 34 516.21 is the present value of the general annuity $PV_{nc}$(due)
$d = 40$ is the number of deferred payment intervals
$p = 1.1292\%$ is the effective rate of interest per payment interval

$$PV_{nc}(\text{defer}) = PV = 34\ 516.21(1.011292)^{-40} \quad\text{—— substituting in Formula 9.1C}$$
$$= 34\ 516.21(0.638165)$$
$$= \$22\ 027.04$$

**Programmed Solution**

34 516.21131 [ FV ]  4.5 [ I/Y ]  0 [ PMT ]  40 [ N ]  [ CPT ]  [ PV ]  -22027.03920

Tom must deposit \$22 027.04 to make the withdrawals. (A small difference in the results is due to rounding.)

**EXAMPLE 13.4G**

A lease contract that has a cash value of \$64 000 requires payments at the beginning of each month for seven years. If the payments are deferred for two years and interest is 8% compounded quarterly, what is the size of the monthly payment?

**SOLUTION**

$PV_{nc}(\text{defer}) = 64\ 000.00;\quad n = 7(12) = 84;\quad P/Y = 12;\quad C/Y = 4;$

$d = 2(12) = 24;\quad c = \dfrac{4}{12} = \dfrac{1}{3};\quad I/Y = 8;\quad i = \dfrac{8\%}{4} = 2\% = 0.02$

The effective monthly rate of interest
$P = 1.02^{\frac{1}{3}} - 1 = 1.006623 - 1 = 0.6623\%$

First determine the accumulated value of the cash value at the end of the period of deferment.

$$FV = 64\ 000.00(1.006623)^{24}$$
$$= 64\ 000.00(1.171659)$$
$$= \$74\ 986.20$$

**Programmed Solution**

(Set P/Y = 12; C/Y = 4) 8 [ I/Y ]  0 [ PMT ]

64 000 [ ± ]  [ PV ]  24 [ N ]  [ CPT ]  [ FV ]  74986.20038

Now determine the periodic payment for the general annuity due whose present value is \$74 986.20.

$$74\ 986.20 = PMT(1.006623)\left(\frac{1 - 1.006623^{-84}}{0.006623}\right)$$

$$74\ 986.20 = PMT(1.006623)(64.267570)$$

$$74\ 986.20 = PMT(64.693195)$$

$$PMT = \$1159.10$$

**Programmed Solution**

("BGN" mode) 74 986.20 [ ± ] [ PV ] 0 [ FV ]

8 [ I/Y ] 84 [ N ] [ CPT ] [ PMT ] [ 1159.104917 ]

The monthly payment is $1159.10.

---

**EXAMPLE 13.4H**

By age 65, Janice Berstein had accumulated $120 000 in an RRSP by making yearly contributions over a period of years. At age 69, she converted the existing balance into an RRIF from which she started to withdraw $2000 per month. If the first withdrawal was on the date of conversion and interest on the account is 6.5% compounded quarterly, for how long will Janice Berstein receive annuity payments?

**SOLUTION**

$PV_{nc}$ (defer) = 120 000.00;   PMT = 2000.00;   $d = 4(12) = 48$

$P/Y = 12$; $C/Y = 4$; $c = \dfrac{4}{12} = \dfrac{1}{3}$; $I/Y = 6.5$; $i = \dfrac{6.5\%}{4} = 1.625 = 0.01625$

The effective monthly rate of interest

$p = 1.01625^{\frac{1}{3}} - 1 = 1.005388 - 1 = 0.005388 = 0.5388\%$

Since payments are at the beginning of each month, the problem involves a deferred general annuity due.

First find the accumulated value at the end of the period of deferment.

$FV = 120\ 000.00(1.005388)^{48}$
$= 120\ 000.00(1.294222)$
$= \$155\ 306.70$

**Programmed Solution**

(Set P/Y = 12; C/Y = 4) 6.5 [ I/Y ] 0 [ PMT ]

120 000 [ ± ] [ PV ] 48 [ N ] [ CPT ] [ FV ] [ 155306.6971 ]

Then find the number of payments for an annuity due with a present value of $155 306.70.

$155\ 306.78 = 2000.00(1.005388)\left(\dfrac{1 - 1.005388^{-n}}{0.0053888}\right)$

$155\ 306.78 = 373\ 222.81(1 - 1.005388^{-n})$

$0.416124 = 1 - 1.005388^{-n}$

$1.005388^{-n} = 0.583876$

$-n \ln 1.005388 = \ln 0.583876$

$-n(0.005373) = -0.538066$

$n = 100.141$

$n = 101 \text{ months}$

**Programmed Solution**

("BGN" mode)  155 306.6971 [ ± ] [ PV ] 0 [ FV ]

6.5 [ I/Y ] 2000 [ PMT ] [ CPT ] [ N ] [ 100.139798 ]

Janice Berstein will receive payments for 101 months, or eight years and five months.

## EXERCISE 13.4

If you choose, you can use Excel's **Present Value (PV)** function to answer the questions indicated below. Refer to **PV** on the Spreadsheet Template Disk to learn how to use this Excel function.

Find the present value of each of the following five deferred annuities due.

| | Periodic Payment | Made At: | Payment Period | Period of Deferment | Term | Interest Rate | Conversion Period |
|---|---|---|---|---|---|---|---|
| **1.** | $850 | beginning | 1 year | 3 years | 10 years | 7.5% | annually |
| **2.** | 720 | beginning | 3 months | 6 years | 12 years | 4 | quarterly |
| **3.** | 85 | beginning | 1 month | 20 years | 15 years | 6 | monthly |
| **4.** | 145 | beginning | 6 months | 3 years | 5 years | 8 | quarterly |
| **5.** | 225 | beginning | 3 months | 6 years | 8 years | 9 | annually |

Answer each of the following questions.

**1.** Dana Kenyon intends to retire in twelve years and would like to receive $2400 every six months for fifteen years starting on the date of her retirement. How much must Dana deposit in an account today if interest is 6.5% compounded semi-annually?  *Reference Example 13.4A*

**2.** Arlene and Mario Dumont want to set up a fund to finance their daughter's university education. They want to be able to withdraw $400 from the fund at the beginning of each month for four years. Their daughter enters university in seven-and-a-half years and interest is 6% compounded monthly.

   **(a)** How much must the Dumonts deposit in the fund today?
   **(b)** What will be the amount of the total withdrawals?
   **(c)** How much of the amount withdrawn will be interest?

**3.** Edmonton Pizza borrowed money to redesign their restaurants. Payments of $1600 would be made at the beginning of each month for two years, starting in eighteen months. Interest on the loan is 7.12% compounded monthly.

   **(a)** How much must the company borrow today?
   **(b)** What will be the amount of the total payments?
   **(c)** How much of the amount paid will be interest?

**4.** An investment in a lease offers returns of $2500 per month due at the beginning of each month for five years. What investment is justified if the returns are deferred for two years and the interest required is 12% compounded monthly?

5. From his savings account, Samuel planned to withdraw amounts at the beginning of every three months for five years starting three years from now. If he started with $7200, and the account earned 9% compounded quarterly, what is the amount of each withdrawal? Reference Example 13.4C

6. To finance the development of a new product, a company borrowed $50 000 at 7% compounded quarterly. If the loan is to be repaid in equal quarterly payments over seven years and the first payment is due three years after the date of the loan, what is the size of the quarterly payment?

7. Mike borrowed $14 000 at 6.5% compounded semi-annually. If the loan is to be repaid in equal semi-annual payments over three years and the first payment is due four years after the date of the loan, what is the size of the semi-annual payment?

8. Matt's Machine Shop purchased a computer to use in tuning engines. To finance the purchase, the company borrowed $12 000 at 8% compounded monthly. To repay the loan, equal monthly payments are made over five years, with the first payment due one year after the date of the loan. What is the size of each monthly payment?

9. An RRIF with a beginning balance of $21 000 earns interest at 10% compounded quarterly. If withdrawals of $3485 are made at the beginning of every three months, starting eight years from now, how long will the RRIF last? Reference Example 13.4E

10. Mrs. Woo paid $24 000 into a retirement fund paying interest at 11% compounded semi-annually. If she retires in seventeen years, for how long can Mrs. Woo withdraw $10 000 from the fund at the beginning of every six months? Assume that the first withdrawal is on the date of retirement.

11. A lease valued at $32 000 requires payments of $4000 every three months. If the first payment is due three years after the lease was signed and interest is 12% compounded quarterly, what is the term of the lease?

12. For his business, Nicholas leased equipment valued at $23 000. The terms of the lease required payments of $1800 every month. If the first payment is due nine months after the lease was signed and interest is 11% compounded monthly, what is the term of the lease?

13. The sale of a property provides for payments of $2000 due at the beginning of every three months for five years. If the payments are deferred for two years and interest is 9% compounded monthly, what is the cash value of the property? Reference Example 13.4F

14. Annuity payments of $735 due at the beginning of every month for three years are deferred for two years. If interest is 6% compounded quarterly, how much must be invested today?

15. An annuity pays $6000 at the beginning of every year for twelve years. If the payments are deferred for seven years and interest is 4.38% compounded monthly, what is the cash value of the property?

16. The proceeds of a property sale were invested for six years, then transferred into an annuity paying $4000 at the beginning of every month for twenty

years. If interest is 4.88% compounded quarterly, how much was received from the property sale?

17. Sarah has just inherited a $12 650 annuity from her grandmother. The annuity earns interest at 6% quarterly and makes payments at the beginning of every six months for four years. If the payments begin in two years, what is the amount of each payment? Reference Example 13.4G

18. Dr. Young bought $18 000 worth of equipment from Medical Supply Company. The purchase agreement requires equal payments every six months for eight years. If the first payment is due two years after the date of purchase and interest is 7% compounded quarterly, what is the size of the payments?

19. A business borrows $250 000 to finance an expansion. The loan agreement requires equal payments every three months for nine years. If the first payment is due two years after the date of purchase and interest is 8.3% compounded monthly, what is the size of the payments?

20. Tina purchases a new computer by financing it on the "no payment until next year" plan. The cash price of the computer is $1384. The financing agreement requires equal payments every month for two years. If the first payment is due one year after the date of purchase and interest is 29.6% compounded annually, what is the size of the payments?

21. Mrs. McCarthy has paid a single premium of $22 750 for an annuity, with the understanding that she will receive $385 at the beginning of each month. How long will the annuity last if it earns 5% compounded semi-annually, and the first payment period starts one year from now? Reference Example 13.4H

22. Bhupinder, who has just had his fifty-fifth birthday, invested $3740 on that day for his retirement. The investment earns 8% compounded monthly. For how long will he be able to withdraw $1100 at the beginning of each year, starting on his sixty-fifth birthday?

23. A property development agreement valued at $45 000 requires annual lease payments of $15 000. The first payment is due five years after the date of the agreement and interest is 11% compounded semi-annually. For how long will payments be made?

24. A retirement bonus of $23 600 is invested in an annuity deferred for twelve years. The annuity provides payments of $4000 due at the beginning of every six months. If interest is 10% compounded annually, for how long will annuity payments be made?

# 13.5 PERPETUITIES

## A. Basic concepts

A **perpetuity** is an annuity in which the periodic payments begin on a fixed date and continue indefinitely. Interest payments on permanently invested sums of money are prime examples of perpetuities. Dividends on preferred shares fall into this category assuming that the issuing corporation has an indefinite life. Scholarships paid perpetually from an endowment fit the definition of perpetuity.

Since there is no end to the term, it is *not* possible to determine the future value of a perpetuity. However, the present value of a perpetuity *is* a definite value. This section deals with the present value of simple perpetuities.

## B. Present value of ordinary perpetuities

We will use the following symbols when dealing with perpetuities:

$A$ = the present value of the perpetuity;
$R$ = the periodic rent (or perpetuity payment);
$i$ = the rate of interest per conversion period;
$p$ = the effective rate of interest per payment period.

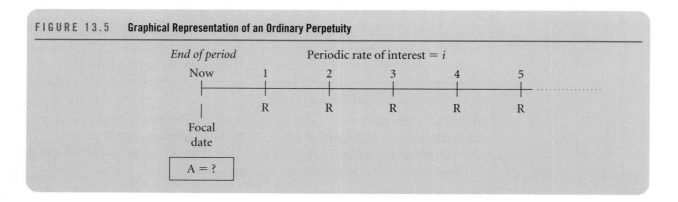

FIGURE 13.5    Graphical Representation of an Ordinary Perpetuity

The **perpetuity payment** R is the interest earned by the present value of the perpetuity in one interest period.

When N is determined, the present value of an ordinary simple annuity was calculated using the formula

$$PV_n = PMT\left[\frac{1 - (1 + i)^{-n}}{i}\right]$$

As N in the formula increases and approaches infinity, the factor $(1 + i)^{-n}$ approaches 0.

Thus, the formula for finding the present value of an ordinary simple perpetuity is:

$$A = \frac{R}{i}$$

restated as ——————— Formula 13.5

$$PV = \frac{PMT}{i}$$

Remember that the $i$ represents the periodic interest rate, calculated as the nominal interest rate divided by the number of conversion periods per year. That is, in the terms of the financial calculator, this represents the I/Y divided by the C/Y.

For an ordinary general perpetuity, the payment R (or PMT) is the interest earned by the present value of the perpetuity in one payment interval. That is,

R = $p$A or PMT = $p$PV

Thus, the formula for finding the present value of an ordinary general perpetuity is:

$$A = \frac{R}{p}$$

restated as

$$PV = \frac{PMT}{p}$$

where $p = (1 + i)^c - 1$

———————————————— Formula 13.6

where

$p$ = the effective rate of interest per payment interval;
$c$ = the number of conversion periods per payment period.

---

**EXAMPLE 13.5A**

What sum of money invested today at 10% compounded annually will provide a scholarship of $1500 at the end of every year?

**SOLUTION**

PMT = 1500.00;  $i$ = 10% = 0.10

$$PV = \frac{1500.00}{0.10} = \$15\,000.00$$ ———————— substituting in Formula 13.5

---

**EXAMPLE 13.5B**

The maintenance cost for Northern Railroad of a crossing with a provincial highway is $2000 at the end of each month. Proposed construction of an overpass would eliminate the monthly maintenance cost. If money is worth 12% compounded monthly, how much should Northern be willing to contribute toward the cost of construction?

**SOLUTION**

The monthly maintenance expense payments form an *ordinary simple perpetuity*.

$$PMT = 2000.00; \quad i = \frac{12\%}{12} = 0.01$$

$$PV = \frac{2000.00}{0.01} = \$200\,000.00$$

Northern should be willing to contribute $200 000 toward construction.

**EXAMPLE 13.5C**

What sum of money invested today at 8% compounded quarterly will provide for payments of $2500 to be paid at the end of each year indefinitely?

**SOLUTION**

Since the payments are to continue indefinitely, the payments form a perpetuity. Furthermore, since the payments are made at the end of each payment interval and the interest conversion period is not the same length as the payment interval, the problem involves an *ordinary general perpetuity*.

$$\text{PMT} = 2500.00; \quad c = 4; \quad i = \frac{8\%}{4} = 2\% = 0.02$$

The effective annual rate of interest
$$p = 1.02^4 - 1 = 1.082432 - 1 = 0.082432 = 8.2432\%$$

$$\text{PV} = \frac{2500.00}{0.082432} = \$30\ 327.95 \underline{\qquad\qquad} \text{substituting in Formula 13.6}$$

The required sum of money is $30 327.95.

**EXAMPLE 13.5D**

A will gives an endowment of $50 000 to a university with the provision that a scholarship be paid at the end of each year indefinitely. If the money is invested at 11% compounded annually, how much is the annual scholarship?

**SOLUTION**

$$\text{PV} = 50\ 000.00; \quad i = 11\% = 0.11$$

By rearranging the terms of Formula 13.5, we get the equation $\text{PMT} = \text{PV}i$.

$$\text{PMT} = \text{PV}i = 50\ 000.00(0.11) = \$5500.00$$

The annual scholarship is $5500.

**EXAMPLE 13.5E**

The alumni of Peel College collected $32 000 to provide a fund for ongoing bursaries. If the money is invested at 7% compounded annually, what is the size of the bursary that can be paid every six months?

**SOLUTION**

$$\text{PV} = 32\ 000.00; \quad c = \frac{1}{2}; \quad i = 7\% = 0.07$$

The effective semi-annual rate of interest

$$p = 1.07^{0.5} - 1 = 1.034408 - 1 = 0.034408 = 3.4408\%$$

By rearranging the terms of Formula 13.6, we get the equation $\text{PMT} = p\text{PV}$.

$$\text{PMT} = p\text{PV} = 0.034408(32\ 000.00) = \$1101.06$$

The size of the bursary is $1101.06.

## C. Present value of perpetuities due

A perpetuity due differs from an ordinary perpetuity only in that the first payment is made at the focal date. Therefore, a simple perpetuity due may be treated as consisting of an immediate payment R followed by an ordinary perpetuity. The formula for finding the present value of a simple perpetuity due is:

$$A(due) = R + \frac{R}{i}$$

restated as ———————————— Formula 13.7

$$PV(due) = PMT + \frac{PMT}{i}$$

A general perpetuity due can also be treated as consisting of an immediate payment R followed by an ordinary general perpetuity. Using the symbol A(due) for the present value, the formula for finding the present value of a general perpetuity due is:

$$A(due) = R + \frac{R}{p}$$

restated as ———————————— Formula 13.8

$$PV(due) = PMT + \frac{PMT}{p}$$

where $p = (1 + i)^c - 1$

**EXAMPLE 13.5F**

A tract of land is leased in perpetuity at $1250 due at the beginning of each month. If money is worth 7.5% compounded monthly, what is the present value of the lease?

**SOLUTION**

PMT = 1250.00; $i = \dfrac{7.5\%}{12} = 0.625\% = 0.00625$

$PV = 1250.00 + \dfrac{1250.00}{0.00625}$ ———————————— substituting in Formula 13.7

$= 1250.00 + 200\,000.00$

$= \$201\,250.00$

**EXAMPLE 13.5G**

What is the present value of perpetuity payments of $750 made at the beginning of each month if interest is 8.5% compounded semi-annually?

**SOLUTION**

PMT = 750.00; $c = \dfrac{2}{12} = \dfrac{1}{6}$; $i = \dfrac{8.5\%}{2} = 4.25\% = 0.0425$

The effective semi-annual rate of interest

$p = 1.0425^{\frac{1}{6}} - 1 = 1.006961 - 1 = 0.006961 = 0.6961\%$

$PV(due) = 750.00 + \dfrac{750.00}{0.006961} = \$108\,491.59$ ——— substituting in Formula 13.8

The present value of the perpetuity is $108 491.59.

**EXAMPLE 13.5H**

How much money must be invested today in a fund earning 5.5% compounded annually to pay annual scholarships of $2000 starting

    (i) one year from now?
    (ii) immediately?
    (iii) four years from now?

**SOLUTION**

$\text{PMT} = 2000.00; \quad i = 5.5\% = 0.055$

  (i) The annual scholarship payments form an ordinary perpetuity.
$$\text{PV} = \frac{2000.00}{0.055} = \$36\,363.64$$
The required sum of money is $36 363.64.

  (ii) The annual scholarship payments form a perpetuity due.
$$\text{PV} = 2000.00 + \frac{2000.00}{0.055}$$
$$= 2000.00 + 36\,363.64$$
$$= \$38\,363.64$$

The required sum of money is $38 363.64.

  (iii) The annual scholarship payments form an ordinary perpetuity deferred for three years. The first payment is at the end of the fourth year.
$$\text{PV(defer)} = \text{PV}(1.055^{-3})$$
$$= 36\,363.64(0.851614)$$
$$= \$30\,967.77$$
The required sum of money is $30 967.77.

**EXAMPLE 13.5I**

What sum of money invested today in a fund earning 6.6% compounded monthly will provide perpetuity payments of $395 every three months starting

    (i) immediately?
    (ii) three months from now?
    (iii) one year from now?

**SOLUTION**

$\text{PMT} = 395.00; \quad c = \dfrac{12}{4} = 3; \quad i = \dfrac{6.6\%}{12} = 0.55\% = 0.0055$

The effective quarterly rate of interest

$$p = 1.0055^3 - 1 = 1.016591 - 1 = 0.016591 = 1.6591\%$$

  (i) Because the perpetuity payments are at the beginning of each payment interval, they form a *perpetuity due*.
$$\text{PV(due)} = 395.00 + \frac{395.00}{0.016591} = 395.00 + 23\,808.23 = \$24\,203.23$$
The required sum of money is $24 203.23.

(ii) Since the first payment is three months from now, the perpetuity payments form an *ordinary perpetuity*.

$$PV = \frac{395.00}{0.016591} = \$23\ 808.23$$

The required sum of money is \$23 808.23.

(iii) If you consider that the payments are deferred for one year, they form a *deferred perpetuity due*.

$$
\begin{aligned}
PV(\text{defer}) &= PV(\text{due}) \times (1.0055)^{-12} \\
&= 24\ 203.23(0.936300) \\
&= \$22\ 661.49
\end{aligned}
$$

The required sum of money is \$22 661.49.

### Perpetuities Using a BAII Plus

Perpetuities can be treated like any other annuity on the BAII Plus. While technically there are two missing variables, present value and payments can be calculated using arbitrary values for time and future value. The suggested values to use are a time of 300 years when calculating the value of N and 0 for the future value. Using these values will allow the BAII Plus to mimic perpetuity and allow you to calculate perpetuity values the same way as you would any other annuity.

The process would be:

1. Set the calculator to beginning or end.
2. Set P/Y and C/Y.
3. Input the variables you know.
4. Compute the variable you want to know (present value or payments).

*Note:* When you are using this method, the answer may be marginally different from the formula due to rounding.

## EXERCISE 13.5

 **A.** Find the present value of each of the following eight perpetuities.

| | Perpetuity Payment | Made At: | Payment Interval | Interest Rate | Conversion Period |
|---|---|---|---|---|---|
| 1. | $1250 | end | 3 months | 6.8% | quarterly |
| 2. | 3420 | end | 1 year | 8.3 | annually |
| 3. | 5600 | end | 6 months | 12 | monthly |
| 4. | 380 | end | 3 months | 8 | semi-annually |
| 5. | 985 | beginning | 6 months | 4.5 | semi-annually |
| 6. | 125 | beginning | 1 month | 5.25 | monthly |
| 7. | 2150 | beginning | 3 months | 9 | monthly |
| 8. | 7250 | beginning | 1 month | 10 | quarterly |

**B.** Answer each of the following questions.

1. The Xorex Company pays a dividend of $4.25 every three months per pre-ferred share. What is the expected market price per share if money is worth 8% compounded semi-annually? Reference Example 13.5A

2. Transcontinental Pipelines is considering a technical process that is expected to reduce annual maintenance costs by $85 000. What is the maximum amount of money that could be invested in the process to be economically fea-sible if interest is 7% compounded quarterly?

3. What is the size of the scholarship that can be paid at the end of every six months from a fund of $25 000 if interest is 6.75% compounded quarterly? Reference Example 13.5D

4. Alain Rich wants to set up a scholarship fund for his alma mater. The annual scholarship payment is to be $2500 with the first such payment due four years after his deposit into the fund. If the fund pays 7.25% compounded annually, how much must Mr. Rich deposit?

5. A rental property provides a monthly income of $1150 due at the beginning of every month. What is the cash value of the property if money is worth 6.6% compounded monthly?

6. A rental property provides a net income of $4200 at the beginning of every three months. What is the cash value of the property if money is worth 9% compounded monthly?

7. Municipal Hydro offers to acquire a right-of-way from a property owner who receives annual lease payments of $2225 due in advance. What is a fair offer if money is worth 5.5% compounded quarterly? Reference Example 13.5F

8. The faculty of Eastern College collected $1400 for the purpose of setting up a memorial fund from which an annual award is to be made to a qualifying stu-dent. If the money is invested at 7% compounded annually and the first annual award payment is to be made five years after the money was deposited, what is the size of the annual award payment?

9. Barbara Katzman bought an income property for $28 000 three years ago. She has held the property for the three years without renting it. If she rents the property out now, what should be the size of the monthly rent payment due in advance if money is worth 6% compounded monthly?

10. What monthly lease payment due in advance should be charged for a tract of land valued at $35 000 if the agreed interest is 8.5% compounded semi-annually?

## Review Exercise

1. Find the future value and the present value of semi-annual payments of $540 for seven-and-a-half years if interest is 9.0% compounded semi-annually and the payments are made

   (a) at the end of every six months;

   (b) at the beginning of every six months.

2. Determine the future value and the present value of monthly payments of $50 each for eight years at 6% compounded monthly if

   (a) the payments form an annuity due;

   (b) the payments form an ordinary annuity.

3. Robert Deed deposited $100 in a trust account on the day of his son's birth and every three months thereafter. If interest paid is 7% compounded quarterly, what will the balance in the trust account be before the deposit is made on the son's twenty-first birthday?

4. Jim Wong makes deposits of $225 at the beginning of every three months. Interest earned by the deposits is 3% compounded quarterly.

   (a) What will the balance in Jim's account be after eight years?

   (b) How much of the balance will Jim have contributed?

   (c) How much of the balance is interest?

5. Home entertainment equipment can be purchased by making monthly payments of $82 for three-and-a-half years. The first payment is due at the time of purchase and the financing cost is 16.5% compounded monthly.

   (a) What is the purchase price?

   (b) How much will be paid in installments?

   (c) How much is the cost of financing?

6. How long will it take to build up a fund of $10 000 by saving $300 at the beginning of every six months at 4.5% compounded semi-annually?

7. How long will it take to accumulate $18 000 at 6% compounded monthly if $125 is deposited in an account at the beginning of every month?

8. For how long must $1000 be deposited at the beginning of every year to accumulate to $180 000 twelve years after the end of the year in which the last deposit was made if interest is 7.5% compounded annually?

9. Kelly Farms bought a tractor priced at $10 500 on February 1. Kelly agreed to make monthly payments of $475 beginning December 1 of the same year. For how long will Kelly Farms have to make these payments if interest is 10.5% compounded monthly?

10. Okanagan Vineyards borrowed $75 000 on a five-year promissory note. It agreed to make payments of $6000 every three months starting on the date of maturity. If interest is 8.5% compounded quarterly, for how long will the company have to make the payments?

11. At what nominal annual rate of interest compounded semi-annually will $1700 deposited at the beginning of every six months accumulate to $40 000 in nine years?

12. What is the effective annual rate of interest charged on a four-year lease valued at $9600 if payments of $235 are made at the beginning of each month for the four years?

13. Suppose you would like to have $10 000 in your savings account and interest is 8% compounded quarterly. How much must you deposit every three months for five years if the deposits are made

   (a) at the end of each quarter?

   (b) at the beginning of each quarter?

14. Equal sums of money are withdrawn monthly from a fund of $20 000 for fifteen years. If interest is 9% compounded monthly, what is the size of each withdrawal

   (a) if the withdrawal is made at the beginning of each month?

   (b) if the withdrawal is made at the end of each month?

15. Mrs. Bean contributes $450 at the beginning of every three months to an RRSP. Interest on the account is 6% compounded quarterly.

    (a) What will the balance in the account be after seven years?

    (b) How much of the balance will be interest?

    (c) If Mrs. Bean converts the balance after seven years into an RRIF paying 5% compounded quarterly and makes equal quarterly withdrawals for twelve years starting three months after the conversion into the RRIF, what is the size of the quarterly withdrawal?

    (d) What is the combined interest earned by the RRSP and the RRIF?

16. Art will receive monthly payments of $850 from a trust account starting on the date of his retirement and continuing for twenty years. Interest is 10.5% compounded monthly.

    (a) What is the balance in the trust account on the date of Art's retirement?

    (b) How much interest will be included in the payments Art receives?

    (c) If Art made equal monthly deposits at the beginning of each month for fifteen years before his retirement, how much did he deposit each month?

17. Alicia Sisko invested a retirement bonus of $12 500 in an RRSP paying 5.95% compounded semi-annually for ten years. At the end of ten years, she rolled the RRSP balance over into an RRIF paying $500 at the beginning of each month starting with the date of rollover. If interest on the RRIF is 5.94% compounded monthly, for how long will Alicia receive monthly payments?

18. Mrs. Ball deposits $550 at the beginning of every three months. Starting three months after the last deposit, she intends to withdraw $3500 every three months for fourteen years. If interest is 8% compounded quarterly, for how long must Mrs. Ball make deposits?

19. Terry saves $50 at the beginning of each month for sixteen years. Beginning one month after his last deposit, he intends to withdraw $375 per month. If interest is 6% compounded monthly, for how long can Terry make withdrawals?

20. Payments of $375 made every three months are accumulated at 3.75% compounded monthly. What is their amount after eight years if the payments are made

    (a) at the end of every three months?

    (b) at the beginning of every three months?

21. What is the accumulated value after twelve years of monthly deposits of $145 earning interest at 5% compounded semi-annually if the deposits are made

    (a) at the end of each month?

    (b) at the beginning of each month?

22. If you save $25 at the beginning of each month and interest is 4% compounded quarterly, how much will you accumulate in thirty years?

23. A property was purchased for quarterly payments of $1350 for ten years. If the first payment was made on the date of purchase and interest is 5.5% compounded annually, what was the purchase price of the property?

24. How much must be deposited into an account to accumulate to $32 000 at 7% compounded semi-annually

    (a) at the beginning of each month for twenty years?

    (b) at the end of each year for fifteen years?

25. Kelly Associates are the makers of a ten-year $75 000 promissory note bearing interest at 8% compounded semi-annually. To pay off the note on its due date, the company is making payments at the beginning of every three months into a fund paying 7.5% compounded monthly. What is the size of the quarterly payments?

26. A church congregation has raised $37 625 for future outreach work. If the money is invested

in a fund paying 7% compounded quarterly, what annual payment can be made for ten years from the fund to its mission if the first payment is to be made four years from the date of investment in the fund?

27. What sum of money can be withdrawn from a fund of $16 750 invested at 6.5% compounded semi-annually

   (a) at the end of every three months for twelve years?

   (b) at the beginning of each year for twenty years?

   (c) at the end of each month for fifteen years but deferred for ten years?

   (d) at the beginning of every three months for twelve years but deferred for twenty years?

   (e) at the end of each month in perpetuity?

   (f) at the beginning of each year in perpetuity?

28. In what period of time will payments of $450 accumulate to $20 000 at 6% compounded monthly if made

   (a) at the end of every three months?

   (b) at the beginning of every six months?

29. Over what period of time will RRSP contributions of $1350 made at the beginning of each year amount to $125 000 if interest is 7% compounded quarterly?

30. A lease contract valued at $50 000 requires semi-annual payments of $5200. If the first payment is due at the date of signing the contract and interest is 9% compounded monthly, what is the term of the lease?

31. A debt of $20 000 is repaid by making payments of $3500. If interest is 9% compounded monthly, for how long will payments have to be made

   (a) at the end of every six months?

   (b) at the beginning of each year?

   (c) at the end of every three months with payments deferred for five years?

   (d) at the beginning of every six months with payments deferred for three years?

32. What is the nominal rate of interest compounded quarterly at which payments of $400 made at the beginning of every six months accumulate to $8400 in eight years?

33. A contract is signed requiring payments of $750 at the end of every three months for eight years.

   (a) How much is the cash value of the contract if money is worth 10.5% compounded quarterly?

   (b) If the first three payments are missed, how much would have to be paid after one year to bring the contract up to date?

   (c) If, because of the missed payments, the contract has to be paid out at the end of one year, how much money is needed?

   (d) How much of the total interest paid is due to the missed payments?

34. Anne received $45 000 from her mother's estate. She wants to set aside part of her inheritance for her retirement nine years from now. At that time she would like to receive a pension supplement of $600 at the end of each month for twenty-five years. If the first payment is due one month after her retirement and interest is 6.5% compounded monthly, how much must Anne set aside?

35. Frank invested a retirement bonus of $15 000 in an income averaging annuity paying 6% compounded monthly. He withdraws the money in equal monthly amounts over five years. If the first withdrawal is made nine months after the deposit, what is the size of each withdrawal?

36. Aaron deposited $900 every six months for twenty years into a fund paying 5.5% compounded semi-annually. Five years after the last deposit he converted the existing balance in the fund into an ordinary annuity paying him equal monthly payments for fifteen years. If interest on the annuity is 6% compounded monthly, what is the size of the monthly payment he will receive?

37. Sally contributed $500 every six months for fourteen years into an RRSP earning interest at 6.5%

compounded semi-annually. Seven years after the last contribution, Sally converted the RRSP into an RRIF that is to pay her equal quarterly amounts for sixteen years. If the first payment is due three months after the conversion into the RRIF and interest on the RRIF is 7% compounded quarterly, how much will Sally receive every three months?

38. Wendy deposited $500 into an RRSP every three months for twenty-five years. Upon her retirement she converted the RRSP balance into an RRIF that is to pay her equal quarterly amounts for twenty years. If the first payment is due three months after her retirement and interest is 9% compounded quarterly, how much will Wendy receive every three months?

39. Ty received a separation payment of $25 000 at age thirty-five. He invested that sum of money at 5.5% compounded semi-annually until he was sixty-five. At that time he converted the existing balance into an ordinary annuity paying $6000 every three months with interest at 6% compounded quarterly. For how long will the annuity run?

40. Mr. Maxwell intends to retire in ten years and wishes to receive $4800 every three months for twenty years starting on the date of his retirement. How much must he deposit now to receive the quarterly payments from an account paying 6% compounded quarterly?

41. Tomac Swim Club bought electronic timing equipment on a contract requiring monthly payments of $725 for three years beginning eighteen months after the date of purchase. What was the cash value of the equipment if interest is 7.5% compounded monthly?

42. What sum of money invested today in a retirement fund will permit withdrawals of $800 at the end of each month for twenty years if interest is 5.75% compounded semi-annually and the payments are deferred for fifteen years?

43. A lease requires semi-annual payments of $6000 for five years. If the first payment is due in four years and interest is 9% compounded monthly, what is the cash value of the lease?

44. A debt of $40 000 is to be repaid in installments due at the end of each month for seven years. If the payments are deferred for three years and interest is 7% compounded quarterly, what is the size of the monthly payments?

45. Redden Ogilvie bought his parents' farm for $200 000. The transfer agreement requires Redden to make quarterly payments for twenty years. If the first payment is due in five years and the rate of interest is 10% compounded annually, what is the size of the quarterly payments?

46. An annuity provides payments of $4500 at the end of every three months. The annuity is bought for $33 500 and payments are deferred for twelve years. If interest is 12% compounded monthly, for how long will payments be received?

47. A retirement bonus of $25 000 is invested in an income-averaging annuity paying $1400 every three months. If the interest is 11.5% compounded semi-annually and the first payment is due in one year, for how long will payments be received?

48. $8000 was invested at a fixed rate of 5.95% compounded semi-annually for seven years. After seven years, the fund was converted into an ordinary annuity paying $450 per month. If interest on the annuity was 6.6% compounded monthly, what was the term of the annuity?

49. What single cash payment made now is equivalent to payments of $3500 every six months at 8% compounded quarterly if the payments are made

(a) at the end of every six months for fifteen years?

(b) at the beginning of every six months for ten years?

(c) at the end of every six months for eight years but deferred for four years?

(d) at the beginning of every six months for nine years but deferred for three years?

**(e)** at the end of every six months in perpetuity?

**(f)** at the beginning of every six months in perpetuity?

**50.** What is the principal invested at 4.75% compounded semi-annually from which monthly withdrawals of $240 can be made

**(a)** at the end of each month for twenty-five years?

**(b)** at the beginning of each month for fifteen years?

**(c)** at the end of each month for twenty years but deferred for ten years?

**(d)** at the beginning of each month for fifteen years but deferred for twelve years?

**(e)** at the end of each month in perpetuity?

**(f)** at the beginning of each month in perpetuity?

**51.** An income property is estimated to net $1750 per month continually. If money is worth 6.6% compounded monthly, what is the cash price of the property?

**52.** Preferred shares of Western Oil paying a quarterly dividend are to be offered at $55.65 per share. If money is worth 9% compounded semi-annually, what is the minimum quarterly dividend to make investment in such shares economically feasible?

**53.** The semi-annual dividend per preferred share issued by InterCity Trust is $7.50. If comparable investments yield 14% compounded quarterly, what should be the selling price of these shares?

**54.** Western Pipelines pays $8000 at the beginning of each year for using a tract of land. What should the company offer the property owner as a purchase price if interest is 9.5% compounded annually?

**55.** A fund to provide an annual scholarship of $4000 is to be set up. If the first payment is due in three years and interest is 11% compounded quarterly, what sum of money must be deposited in the scholarship fund today?

## Self-Test

**1.** Payments of $1080 are made into a fund at the beginning of every three months for eleven years. If the fund earns interest at 9.5% compounded quarterly, how much will the balance in the fund be after eleven years?

**2.** Find the present value of payments of $960 made at the beginning of every month for seven years if money is worth 6% compounded monthly.

**3.** Tim bought a boat valued at $10 104 on the installment plan. He made equal semi-annual payments for five years. If the first payment is due on the date of purchase and interest is 10.5% compounded semi-annually, what is the size of the semi-annual payments?

**4.** Sara Eng wants to withdraw $3000 at the beginning of every three months for thirty years starting at the date of her retirement. If she retires in twenty years and interest is 10% compounded quarterly, how much must Ms. Eng deposit into an account every month for the next twenty years starting now?

**5.** J.J. deposited $1680 at the beginning of every six months for eight years into a fund paying 5.5% compounded semi-annually. Fifteen years after the first deposit, he converted the existing balance into an annuity paying him equal monthly payments for twenty years. If the payments are made at the end of each month and interest is 6% compounded monthly, what is the size of the monthly payments?

6. The amount of $57 426 is invested at 6% compounded monthly for six years. After the initial six-year period, the balance in the fund is converted into an annuity due paying $3600 every three months. If interest on the annuity is 5.9% compounded quarterly, what is the term of the annuity in months?

7. What is the nominal annual rate of interest charged on a lease valued at $3840 if payments of $200 are made at the beginning of every three months for six years?

8. Deposits of $1400 made at the beginning of every three months amount to $40 000 after six years. What is the effective annual rate of interest earned by the deposits if interest is compounded quarterly?

9. A lease requires monthly payments of $950 due in advance. If interest is 12% compounded quarterly and the term of the lease is five years, what is the cash value of the lease?

10. Sally Smedley and Roberto Jones bought their neighbour's farm for $30 000 down and payments of $6000 at the end of every six months for six years. What is the purchase price of the farm if the semi-annual payments are deferred for four years and interest is 8.5% compounded semi-annually?

11. Eden would like to receive $3000 at the end of every six months for seven years after her retirement. If she retires ten years from now and interest is 6.5% compounded semi-annually, how much must she deposit into an account every six months starting now?

12. Ken acquired his sister's share of their business by agreeing to make payments of $4000 at the end of each year for twelve years. If the payments are deferred for three years and money is worth 5% compounded quarterly, what is the cash value of the sister's share of the business?

13. The amount of $46 200 is invested at 9.5% compounded quarterly for four years. After four years the balance in the fund is converted into an annuity. If interest on the annuity is 6.5% compounded semi-annually and payments are made at the end of every six months for seven years, what is the size of the payments?

14. What sum of money must be deposited in a trust fund to provide a scholarship of $960 payable at the end of each month if interest is 7.5% compounded monthly?

15. A bank pays a quarterly dividend of $0.75 per share. If comparable investments yield 13.5% compounded monthly, what is the sales value of the shares?

16. Western Pipelines pays $480 at the beginning of every half-year for using a tract of land. What should the company offer the property owner as a purchase price if interest is 11% compounded semi-annually?

17. Carla plans to invest in a property that after three years will yield $1200 at the end of each month indefinitely. How much should Carla be willing to pay if an alternative investment yields 9% compounded monthly?

18. Mr. Smart wants to set up an annual scholarship of $3000. If the first payment is to be made in five years and interest is 7.0% compounded annually, how much must Mr. Smart pay into the scholarship fund?

## Challenge Problems

1. A regular deposit of $100 is made at the beginning of each year for twenty years. Simple interest is calculated at $i$ % per year for the twenty years. At the end of the twenty-year period, the total interest in the account is $840. Suppose that interest of $i$ % compounded annually had been paid instead. How much interest would have been in the account at the end of the twenty years?

2. Herman has agreed to repay a debt by using the following repayment schedule. Starting today, he will make $100 payments at the beginning of each month for the next two-and-a-half years. He will then pay nothing for the next two years. Finally, after four-and-a-half years, he will make $200 payments at the beginning of each month for one year, which will pay off his debt completely. For the first four-and-a-half years, the interest on the debt is 9% compounded monthly. For the final year, the interest is lowered to 8.5% compounded monthly. Find the size of Herman's debt. Round your answer to the nearest dollar.

# Case Study 13.1 Planning for College

» Victor and Jasmine Gonzalez were discussing how to plan for their three young sons' university education. Stephen turned twelve years old in April, Jack turned nine in January, and Danny turned seven in March. Although university was still a long way off for the boys, Victor and Jasmine wanted to ensure enough funds were available for their studies.

Victor and Jasmine decided to provide each son with a monthly allowance that would cover tuition and some living expenses. Because they were uncertain about the boys' finding summer jobs in the future, Victor and Jasmine decided their sons would receive the allowance at the beginning of each month for four years. The parents also assumed that the costs of education would continue to increase.

Stephen would receive an allowance of $1000 per month starting September 1 of the year he turns eighteen.

Jack would receive an allowance that is 8% more than Stephen's allowance. He would also receive it at the beginning of September 1 of the year he turns eighteen.

Danny would receive an allowance that is 10% more than Jack's at the beginning of September of the year he turns eighteen.

Victor and Jasmine visited their local bank manager to fund the investment that would compensate the boys' allowances for university. The bank manager suggested an investment paying interest of 5.5% compounded monthly from now until the three boys had each completed their four years of education. Victor and Jasmine thought this sounded reasonable. So on June 1, a week after talking with the bank manager, they deposited the sum of money necessary to finance their sons' postsecondary educations.

### QUESTIONS

1. How much allowance will each of the boys receive per month based on their parents' assumptions of price increases?

2. **a.** How much money must Victor and Jasmine invest for each son on June 1 in order to provide them the desired allowance?
   **b.** Create a timeline of events for each of the sons.
   **c.** What is the total amount invested on June 1?

## Case Study 13.2 Setting Up Scholarships

» King's Cross University College recently launched a fundraising campaign for three new student bursaries. The Student Awards Committee of the college has been working with three community organizations to create and fund these bursaries: Friends of Education, Environmental Betterment Foundation, and Community Service Club. These organizations are all convinced that the best way to fund the bursaries is to make one large donation to the college. The donation would be invested so that it would grow over time, and regular, annual bursaries would be paid out indefinitely.

Friends of Education has agreed to donate a sum of money on September 1 that would allow its annual bursary of $1900 to be awarded immediately on September 1, and has agreed to allow the college to choose the best local student to receive its bursary every year.

Environmental Betterment Foundation would like to earn some interest on its September 1 donation before awarding its first bursary on December 1, three months later. The Foundation has agreed to award one bursary of $2100 per year. It will choose the recipient from all applications received.

Community Service Club will make its donation on September 1, but it wants to award its bursary of $1000 per year starting September 1 next year. This will give the club time to develop the criteria used to choose the recipient of the bursary.

### QUESTIONS

1. What sum of money must Friends of Education invest on September 1 if its donation is expected to earn 7.2% compounded semi-annually?

2. What sum of money must Environmental Betterment Foundation invest on September 1 if its donation is expected to earn 7.5% compounded quarterly?

3. What sum of money must Community Service Club invest on September 1 this year if its donation is expected to earn 6.6% compounded monthly?

## SUMMARY OF FORMULAS

**Formula 13.1**

$$S_n(\text{due}) = R(1 + i)\left[\frac{(1 + i)^n - 1}{i}\right]$$

restated as

$$FV_n(\text{due}) = PMT(1 + i)\left[\frac{(1 + i)^n - 1}{i}\right]$$

Finding the future value of a simple annuity due

**Formula 13.2**

$$A_n(\text{due}) = R(1 + i)\left[\frac{1 - (1 + i)^{-n}}{i}\right]$$

restated as

$$PV_n(\text{due}) = PMT(1 + i)\left[\frac{1 - (1 + i)^{-n}}{i}\right]$$

Finding the present value of a simple annuity due

**Formula 13.3**

$$S_{nc}(\text{due}) = R(1 + p)\left[\frac{(1 + p)^n - 1}{p}\right]$$

restated as

$$FV_{nc}(\text{due}) = PMT(1 + p)\left[\frac{(1 + p)^n - 1}{p}\right]$$

Finding the future value of a general annuity due using the effective rate of interest per payment period

where $p = (1 + i)^c - 1$

**Formula 13.4**

$$A_{nc}(\text{due}) = R(1 + p)\left[\frac{1 - (1 + p)^{-n}}{p}\right]$$

restated as

$$PV_{nc}(\text{due}) = PMT(1 + p)\left[\frac{1 - (1 + p)^{-n}}{p}\right]$$

Finding the present value of a general annuity due using the effective rate of interest per payment period

where $p = (1 + i)^c - 1$

**Formula 13.5**

$$A = \frac{R}{i}$$

restated as

$$PV = \frac{PMT}{i}$$

Finding the present value of an ordinary simple perpetuity

**Formula 13.6**

$$A = \frac{R}{p}$$

restated as

$$PV = \frac{PMT}{p}$$

Finding the present value of an ordinary general perpetuity

where $p = (1 + i)^c - 1$

Formual 13.7

$$A(due) = R + \frac{R}{i}$$

restated as

$$PV(due) = PMT + \frac{PMT}{i}$$  **Finding the present value of a simple perpetuity due**

Formual 13.8

$$A(due) = R + \frac{R}{p}$$

restated as

$$PV(due) = PMT + \frac{PMT}{p}$$  **Finding the present value of a general perpetuity due**

where $p = (1 + i)^c - 1$

## GLOSSARY

**Annuity due**   an annuity in which the periodic payments are made at the beginning of each payment interval *(p. 508)*

**Deferred annuity**   an annuity in which the first payment is made at a time later than the end of the first payment interval *(p. 532)*

**General annuity due**   a general annuity in which the payments are made at the beginning of each payment interval *(p. 524)*

**Period of deferment**   the period from the time referred to as "now" to the starting point of the term of the annuity *(p. 532)*

**Perpetuity**   an annuity in which the periodic payments begin at a fixed date and continue indefinitely *(p. 551)*

**Perpetuity payment**   the interest earned by the present value of the perpetuity in one interest period *(p. 552)*

## USEFUL INTERNET SITES

www.tdcanadatrust.com/mutualfunds/edu_planning.jsp
**RESPs**   Visit the Toronto-Dominion Bank's financial planning centre to read general information and FAQs about RESPs (Registered Education Savings Plans) and the products that TD Bank offers.

www.smartmoney.com
**SmartMoney.com**   SmartMoney has daily stock and mutual fund recommendations, hourly market updates, personal finance investing research tools and advice, and up-to-the-minute stock and mutual fund quotes and charts.

www.forbes.com
*Forbes* **Magazine**   This site provides access to articles on current financial business issues, as well as tools for mutual funds, stocks, and personal finances.

# 14 Amortization of Loans, Including Residential Mortgages

## OBJECTIVES

**Upon completing this chapter, you will be able to do the following:**

1. Perform computations associated with amortization of debts involving simple annuities, including the size of the periodic payments, outstanding balance, interest due, and principal repaid, and construct complete or partial amortization schedules.

2. Perform computations associated with the amortization of debts involving general annuities, and construct complete or partial amortization schedules.

3. Find the size of the final payment when all payments except the final payment are equal in size.

4. Compute the effective interest rate for fixed-rate residential mortgages.

5. Compute the periodic payments for fixed-rate mortgages and for demand mortgages.

6. Distinguish between regular mortgage payments and rounded mortgage payments.

7. Create statements for various types of residential mortgages.

When budgeting for the future, businesses often consider various loan terms. If you know the interest rate, you might want to calculate what the loan will cost over various time periods. You can do this by using the formulas for annuities that you are already very familiar with. By knowing the size of your equal loan payments, you can make an informed decision about which loan terms to arrange.

One of the largest loans most of us will ever have is a mortgage on a house or a condominium. Given the payment amounts, we can calculate the amount of each payment that goes toward principal and the amount that goes toward interest. This information can help us decide what we can afford to buy and how quickly we can pay off the mortgage.

## INTRODUCTION

Amortization of loans refers to the repayment of interest-bearing debts by a series of payments, usually equal in size, made at equal intervals of time. The periodic payments, when equal in size, form an annuity whose present value is equivalent to the original loan principal. Mortgages and many consumer loans are repaid by this method. An amortization schedule shows the allocation of each payment to first cover the interest due and then reduce the principal.

# 14.1 AMORTIZATION INVOLVING SIMPLE ANNUITIES

## A. Finding the periodic payment

What is **amortization**? An interest-bearing debt is *amortized* if both principal and interest are repaid by a series of equal payments made at equal intervals of time.

The basic problem in amortizing a debt is finding the size of the periodic payment. If the payment interval and the interest conversion period are equal in length, the problem involves finding the periodic payment for a simple annuity. Since debts are generally repaid by making payments at the end of the payment interval, the method and formula for ordinary simple annuities apply.

$$PV_n = PMT\left[\frac{1 - (1 + i)^{-n}}{i}\right]$$ ————Formula 11.2

**EXAMPLE 14.1A**  A debt of $5000 with interest at 9% compounded annually is to be repaid by equal payments at the end of each year for six years. What is the size of the annual payments?

**SOLUTION**

**FIGURE 14.1**  **Graphical Representation of Method and Data**

As Figure 14.1 shows, the equal annual payments (designated by PMT) form an ordinary simple annuity in which

$PV_n = 5000.00$;  $n = 6$;  $P/Y = 1$;  $C/Y = 1$;  $I/Y = 9$;  $i = 9\% = 0.09$

Using "now" as the focal date, you can find the value of the annual payment PMT using Formula 11.2.

$$5000.00 = PMT\left(\frac{1 - 1.09^{-6}}{0.09}\right) \qquad \text{using Formula 11.2}$$

$$5000.00 = PMT(4.485919)$$

$$PMT = \$1114.60$$

**Programmed Solution**

("END" mode) (Set P/Y = 1; C/Y = 1) 0 [ FV ] 5000 [ ± ] [ PV ] 9 [ I/Y ]

6 [ N ] [ CPT ] [ PMT ] [ 1114.598916 ]

The annual payment is $1114.60.

---

**EXAMPLE 14.1B**

A loan of $8000 made at 6% compounded monthly is amortized over five years by making equal monthly payments.

   (i) What is the size of the monthly payment?

  (ii) What is the total amount paid to amortize the loan?

 (iii) What is the cost of financing?

**SOLUTION**

(i) $PV_n = 8000.00;$    $n = 5(12) = 60;$    P/Y = 12;    C/Y = 12;    I/Y = 6;

$$i = \frac{6\%}{12} = 0.5\%$$

$$8000.00 = PMT\left(\frac{1 - 1.005^{-60}}{0.005}\right) \qquad \text{using Formula 11.2}$$

$$8000.00 = PMT(51.725561)$$

$$PMT = \$154.66$$

**Programmed Solution**

("END" mode) (Set P/Y = 12; C/Y = 12) 0 [ FV ] 8000 [ ± ] [ PV ] 6 [ I/Y ]

60 [ N ] [ CPT ] [ PMT ] [ 154.662412 ]

   (i) The monthly payment is $154.66.

  (ii) The total amount paid is 60(154.66) = $9279.60.

 (iii) The cost of financing is 9279.60 − 8000.00 = $1279.60.

## B. Amortization schedules

As previously discussed in Section 8.6, **amortization schedules** show in detail how a debt is repaid. Such schedules normally show the payment number (or payment date), the amount paid, the interest paid, the principal repaid, and the outstanding debt balance.

### 1. Amortization Schedule When All Payments Are Equal (Blended Payments)

When all payments are equal, you must first determine the size of the periodic payment, as shown in Examples 14.1A and 14.1B, then construct the amortization schedule.

**EXAMPLE 14.1C**

A debt of $5000 is amortized by making equal payments at the end of every three months for two years. If interest is 8% compounded quarterly, construct an amortization schedule, as in Example 14.1C.

**SOLUTION**

**STEP 1**

Determine the size of the quarterly payments.

$PV_n = 5000.00$; $n = 4(2) = 8$; $P/Y = 4$; $C/Y = 4$; $I/Y = 8$; $i = \dfrac{8\%}{4} = 2.0\%$

$$5000.00 = PMT\left(\frac{1 - 1.02^{-8}}{0.02}\right)$$

$$5000.00 = PMT(7.325481)$$

$$PMT = \$682.55$$

**Programmed Solution**

("END" mode) (Set P/Y = 4; C/Y = 4) 0 [ FV ] 5000 [ ± ] [ PV ] 8 [ I/Y ]

8 [ N ] [ CPT ] [ PMT ] [ 682.548996 ]

**STEP 2**

Construct the amortization schedule as shown below.

| Payment Number | Amount Paid | Interest Paid $i = 0.02$ | Principal Repaid | Outstanding Principal Balance |
|---|---|---|---|---|
| 0 | | | | 5000.00 |
| 1 | 682.55 | 100.00 | 582.55 | 4417.45 |
| 2 | 682.55 | 88.35 | 594.20 | 3823.25 |
| 3 | 682.55 | 76.47 | 606.08 | 3217.17 |
| 4 | 682.55 | 64.34 | 618.21 | 2598.96 |
| 5 | 682.55 | 51.98 | 630.57 | 1968.39 |
| 6 | 682.55 | 39.37 | 643.18 | 1325.21 |
| 7 | 682.55 | 26.50 | 656.05 | 669.16 |
| 8 | 682.54 | 13.38 | 669.16 | 0.00 |
| TOTAL | 5460.39 | 460.39 | 5000.00 | |

*Explanations regarding the construction of the amortization schedule*

1. Payment 0 is used to introduce the initial balance of the loan.
2. The interest included in the first payment is the periodic interest rate $i$ multiplied by the period's beginning balance, $0.02 \times 5000.00 = \$100.00$. Since the amount paid is $682.55, the amount available for repayment of principal is

682.55 − 100.00 = \$582.55. The outstanding principal balance after the first payment is 5000.00 − 582.55 = \$4417.45.

3. The interest included in the second payment is 0.02 × 4417.45 = \$88.35. Since the amount paid is \$682.55, the amount available for repayment of principal is 682.55 − 88.35 = \$594.20. The outstanding principal is 4417.45 − 594.20 = \$3823.25.

4. Computation of interest, principal repaid, and outstanding balance for Payments 3 to 7 are made in a similar manner.

5. The last payment of \$682.54 is slightly different from the other payments as a result of rounding in the amount paid or the interest paid. To allow for such rounding errors, the last payment is computed by adding the interest due in the last payment (0.02 × 669.16 = \$13.38) to the outstanding balance: 669.16 + 13.38 = \$682.54.

6. The three totals provide useful information and can be used as a check on the accuracy of the schedule.
   (a) The total principal repaid must equal the original outstanding balance;
   (b) The total amount paid is the periodic payment times the number of such payments plus/minus any adjustment in the last payment:
   682.55 × 8 − 0.01 = 5460.40 − 0.01 = \$5460.39;
   (c) The total interest paid is the difference between the amount paid and the original principal, 5460.39 − 5000.00 = \$460.39.

### Programmed Solution

The amortization schedule can also be built by using the Amortization function within the preprogrammed financial calculator. Using the Texas Instruments BAII Plus, follow these steps:

1. Enter all of the information within the TVM function and compute the payment, PMT, as above.

2. Press **2nd** **AMORT** to start the function.

3. On the calculator display, P1 refers to the number of the first period of the range to be specified. For example, to obtain data for periods 2 through 5, P1 would be entered as "2." Remember to press the **Enter** key to enter new data.

4. Press the down arrow **↓** to move to the next cell. P2 refers to the number of the last period of the range to be specified. For example, to obtain data for periods 2 through 5, P2 would be entered as "5." Note that, to obtain information for just one period, both P1 and P2 must be entered, as the same number. For example, to obtain data for period 1, both P1 and P2 must be entered as "1," specifying "from" period 1 and "to" period 1.

5. Press the down arrow **↓** to move to the next cell. BAL is automatically calculated as the loan balance at the end of the period specified in P2. In the amortization schedule above, when period 1 is specified, the BAL calculated is −4417.45. The outstanding balance appears as a negative number because the PV was entered as a negative number.

6. Press the down arrow [↓] to move to the next cell. PRN is automatically calculated as the portion of the principal that was repaid. In the amortization schedule on page 572, the PRN is calculated as 582.55.

7. Press the down arrow [↓] to move to the next cell. INT is automatically calculated as the portion of the period's payment that was interest on the loan. In the amortization schedule on page 572, the INT is calculated as 100.00.

With each method described, the results may be slightly different due to when and where rounding takes place.

## 2. Amortization Schedule When All Payments Except the Final Payment are Equal

When the size of the periodic payment is determined by agreement, usually because it is a convenient round figure rather than a computed blended payment, the size of the final payment will probably be different from the preceding agreed-upon payments. This final payment is obtained in the amortization schedule by adding the interest due on the outstanding balance to the outstanding balance.

This type of loan repayment schedule has been illustrated and explained in Section 8.6. The following example is included for review.

**EXAMPLE 14.1D**

Bronco Repairs borrowed $15 000 from National Credit Union at 10% compounded quarterly. The loan agreement requires payment of $2500 at the end of every three months. Construct an amortization schedule.

**SOLUTION**

$$i = \frac{10\%}{4} = 2.5\% = 0.025$$

| Payment Number | Amount Paid | Interest Paid $i = 0.025$ | Principal Repaid | Outstanding Principal Balance |
|---|---|---|---|---|
| 0 | | | | 15 000.00 |
| 1 | 2 500.00 | 375.00 | 2 125.00 | 12 875.00 |
| 2 | 2 500.00 | 321.88 | 2 178.12 | 10 696.88 |
| 3 | 2 500.00 | 267.42 | 2 232.58 | 8 464.30 |
| 4 | 2 500.00 | 211.61 | 2 288.39 | 6 175.91 |
| 5 | 2 500.00 | 154.40 | 2 345.60 | 3 830.31 |
| 6 | 2 500.00 | 95.76 | 2 404.24 | 1 426.07 |
| 7 | 1 461.72 | 35.65 | 1 426.07 | 0.00 |
| TOTAL | 16 461.72 | 1461.72 | 15 000.00 | |

*Note:* After Payment 6, the outstanding principal is less than the agreed-upon payment. When this happens, the final payment will be the outstanding balance plus the interest due on the outstanding balance.

$1426.07 + (1426.07 \times 0.025) = 1426.07 + 35.65 = \$1461.72$

## C. Finding the outstanding principal balance

For various reasons, such as early partial repayment or early full repayment or refinancing, either the borrower or the lender needs to know the outstanding balance at a certain time. This can be done by checking the amortization schedule, if available, or by direct mathematical computation. This computation is also useful for checking the accuracy of the schedule as it is developed.

### 1. Finding the Outstanding Principal When All Payments Are Equal

**EXAMPLE 14.1E**

For Example 14.1C, compute the outstanding balance just after the third payment has been made.

**SOLUTION**

The loan history showing the quarterly payments of $682.55 can be represented on a time diagram as shown in Figure 14.2.

**FIGURE 14.2    Graphical Representation of Loan Payments**

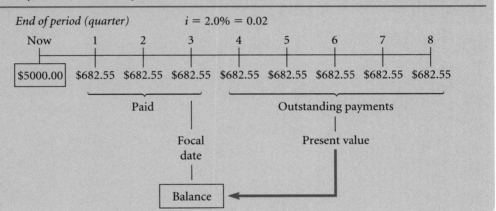

In the same way in which the original loan balance of $5000 equals the present value of the number of payments that are necessary to amortize the loan, the outstanding balance at the end of any payment interval just after a payment has been made is the present value of the remaining outstanding payments.

$$\begin{array}{c} \text{OUTSTANDING} \\ \text{BALANCE} \end{array} = \begin{array}{c} \text{PRESENT VALUE OF THE} \\ \text{OUTSTANDING PAYMENTS} \end{array}$$

To answer this problem, use Formula 11.2. Since three of the eight payments have been made, five payments remain outstanding.

$$\text{PMT} = 682.55; \quad n = 5; \quad \text{P/Y} = 4; \quad \text{I/Y} = 8; \quad i = 2.0\% = 0.02$$

$$\text{PV}_3 = 682.55\left(\frac{1 - 1.02^{-5}}{0.02}\right) \qquad \text{using Formula 11.2}$$

$$= 682.55(4.713460)$$

$$= \$3217.17$$

**Programmed Solution**

("END" mode) (Set P/Y = 4; C/Y = 4) 0 [ FV ] 682.55 [ ± ] [ PMT ] 8 [ I/Y ]

5 [ N ] [ CPT ] [ PV ] [ 3217.171788 ]

The outstanding balance after the third payment is $3217.17.

*Note:* Any minor difference in the amortization schedule is due to rounding.

**EXAMPLE 14.1F**

You borrow $7500 from a finance company at 13.5% compounded monthly with the agreement to make monthly payments. If the loan is amortized over five years, what is the loan balance after two years?

**SOLUTION**

First determine the size of the monthly payment.

$PV_n = 7500.00$;   $n = 5(12) = 60$;   P/Y = 12;   C/Y = 12;   I/Y = 13.5;

$$i = \frac{13.5\%}{12} = 1.125\% = 0.01125$$

$$7500.00 = PMT\left(\frac{1 - 1.01125^{-60}}{0.01125}\right)$$

$$7500.00 = PMT(43.459657)$$

$$PMT = \$172.57$$

**Programmed Solution**

("END" mode) (Set P/Y = 12; C/Y = 12) 0 [ FV ] 7500 [ ± ] [ PV ] 13.5 [ I/Y ]

60 [ N ] [ CPT ] [ PMT ] [ 172.573845 ]

Now determine the balance after two years.

After two years, 24 of the 60 payments have been made; 36 payments remain outstanding.

$PMT = 172.57$;   $n = 36$;   $i = 1.125\%$

$$PV_{24} = 172.57\left(\frac{1 - 1.01125^{-36}}{0.01125}\right)$$

$$= 172.57(29.467851)$$

$$= \$5085.27$$

**Programmed Solution**

("END" mode) (Set P/Y = 12; C/Y = 12) 172.57 [ ± ] [ PMT ] 0 [ FV ]

13.5 [ I/Y ] 36 [ N ] [ CPT ] [ PV ] [ 5085.267094 ]

The outstanding balance after two years is $5085.27.

The method used in Examples 14.1E and 14.1F is called the **prospective method** of finding the outstanding balance, because it considers the future prospects of the debt—the payments that remain outstanding.

Alternatively, the outstanding balance can be found by the **retrospective method**, which considers the payments that have been made. This method finds the outstanding balance by deducting the accumulated value of the payments that have been made from the accumulated value of the original debt.

$$\text{OUTSTANDING BALANCE} = \begin{array}{l} \text{ACCUMULATED VALUE OF THE ORIGINAL DEBT} - \\ \text{ACCUMULATED VALUE OF THE PAYMENTS MADE} \end{array}$$

*For Example 14.1E*
The accumulated value of the original debt at the end of three payment intervals

$$\text{FV} = 5000.00(1.02^3) \qquad \text{——————} \qquad \text{using Formula 9.1A}$$
$$= 5000.00(1.061208)$$
$$= 5306.04$$

The accumulated value of the payments made

$$\text{FV}_3 = 682.55\left(\frac{1.02^3 - 1}{0.02}\right)$$
$$= 682.55(3.060400)$$
$$= \$2088.88$$

**Programmed Solution**

("END" mode) (Set P/Y = 4; C/Y = 4) [ 2nd ] (CLR TVM) 5000 [ ± ] [ PV ]

8 [ I/Y ] 3 [ N ] [ CPT ] [ FV ] [ 5306.04 ]

0 [ PV ] 682.55 [ ± ] [ PMT ] 8 [ I/Y ] 3 [ N ] [ CPT ] [ FV ] [ 2088.87602 ]

The outstanding balance is 5306.04 − 2088.88 = \$3217.16.

*For Example 14.1F*
The accumulated value of the debt after two years (24 payments)

$$\text{FV} = 7500.00(1.01125^{24})$$
$$= 7500.00(1.307991)$$
$$= \$9809.93$$

The accumulated value of the 24 payments made

$$\text{FV}_{24} = 172.57\left(\frac{1.01125^{24} - 1}{0.01125}\right)$$
$$= 172.57(27.376998)$$
$$= \$4724.45$$

**Programmed Solution**

("END" mode) (Set P/Y = 12; C/Y = 12) [2nd] (CLR TVM) 7500 [ ± ] [ PV ]

13.5 [ I/Y ] 24 [ N ] [ CPT ] [ FV ] [9809.934198]

0 [ PV ] 172.57 [ ± ] [ PMT ] 13.5 [ I/Y ] 24 [ N ] [ CPT ] [ FV ] [4724.448528]

The outstanding balance is 9809.93 − 4724.45 = $5085.48.

*Note:* The different balances produced by the two methods—$5085.48 versus $5085.27—are a result of rounding in the payment.

Because the prospective method is more direct, it is preferred when finding the outstanding balance of loans repaid by installments that are all equal.

### 2. Finding the Outstanding Balance When All Payments Except the Final Payment are Equal

When the last payment is different from the other payments, the retrospective method for finding the outstanding balance is preferable.

**EXAMPLE 14.1G**

For Example 14.1D, compute the outstanding balance after four payments.

**SOLUTION**

The accumulated value of the original debt after four payments

$$FV = 15\,000.00(1.025^4)$$
$$= 15\,000.00(1.103813)$$
$$= \$16\,557.19$$

The accumulated value of the four payments

$$FV = 2500.00\left(\frac{1.025^4 - 1}{0.025}\right)$$
$$= 2500.00(4.152516)$$
$$= \$10\,381.29$$

**Programmed Solution**

("END" mode) (Set P/Y = 4; C/Y = 4) [2nd] (CLR TVM) 15 000 [ ± ] [ PV ] 10

[ I/Y ] 4 [ N ] [ CPT ] [ FV ] [16557.19336]

0 [ PV ] 2500 [ ± ] [ PMT ] 10 [ I/Y ] 4 [ N ] [ CPT ] [ FV ] [10381.28906]

The outstanding balance is 16 557.19 − 10 381.29 = $6175.90.

**EXAMPLE 14.1H**

A debt of $25 000 with interest at 11% compounded semi-annually is amortized by making payments of $2000 at the end of every six months. Determine the outstanding balance after five years.

$$PV_n = PV = 25000.00; P/Y = 2; C/Y = 2; I/Y = 11; i = \frac{11\%}{2} = 5.5\% = 0.055$$

The accumulated value of the original principal after five years

$$FV = 25\,000.00(1.055^{10})$$
$$= 25\,000.00(1.708145)$$
$$= \$42\,703.61$$

The accumulated value of the first ten payments

$$FV_{10} = 2000.00\left(\frac{1.055^{10} - 1}{0.055}\right)$$

$$= 2000.00(12.875354)$$
$$= \$25\,750.71$$

### Programmed Solution

("END" mode) (Set P/Y = 2; C/Y = 2) [2nd] (CLR TVM) 25 000 [±] [PV] 11 [I/Y] 10 [N] [CPT] [FV] 42703.61146

0 [PV] 2000 [±] [PMT] 11 [I/Y] 10 [N] [CPT] [FV] 25750.70758

The outstanding balance after five years is 42 703.61 − 25 750.71 = \$16 952.90.

## D. Finding the interest paid and the principal repaid; constructing partial amortization schedules

Apart from computing the outstanding balance at any one time, all the other information contained in an amortization schedule, such as interest paid and principal repaid, can also be computed.

For Example 14.1C, compute

(i) the interest paid in the fifth payment period;
(ii) the principal repaid in the fifth payment period.

(i) The interest due for any given payment period is based on the outstanding balance at the beginning of the period. This balance is the same as the outstanding balance at the end of the previous payment period.

To find the interest paid by the fifth payment, we need to know the outstanding balance after the fourth payment.

$$PV_4 = 682.55\left(\frac{1 - 1.02^{-4}}{0.02}\right)$$

$$= 682.55(3.807729)$$
$$= \$2598.97$$

**Programmed Solution**

("END" mode) (Set P/Y = 4; C/Y = 4) 0 [ FV ] 682.55 [ ± ] [ PMT ] 8 [ I/Y ]

4 [ N ] [ CPT ] [ PV ] [ 2598.965223 ]

Interest for Payment Period 5 is 2598.97(0.02) = \$51.98.

(ii) Principal repaid = Amount paid − Interest paid
= 682.55 − 51.98
= \$630.57

You can use Excel's ***Cumulative Interest Paid Between Two Periods (CUMIPMT)*** *and **Cumulative Principal Paid Between Two Periods (CUMPRINC)*** functions to answer questions like these. Refer to **CUMIPMT** and **CUMPRINC** on the Spreadsheet Template Disk to learn how to use these Excel functions.

**EXAMPLE 14.1J**

Jackie Kim borrowed \$6000 from her trust company at 9% compounded monthly. She was to repay the loan with monthly payments over five years.

(i) What is the interest included in the 20th payment?

(ii) What is the principal repaid in the 36th payment period?

(iii) Construct a partial amortization schedule showing the details of the first three payments, the 20th payment, the 36th payment, and the last three payments, and determine the totals of amount paid, interest paid, and principal repaid.

**SOLUTION**

$PV_n = 6000.00$;   $n = 5(12) = 60$;   P/Y = 12;   C/Y = 12;   I/Y = 9;

$i = \dfrac{9\%}{12} = 0.75\% = 0.0075$

$$6000.00 = PMT\left(\frac{1-1.0075^{-60}}{0.0075}\right)$$

$6000.00 = PMT(48.173374)$
$PMT = \$124.55$

**Programmed Solution**

("END" mode) (Set P/Y = 12; C/Y = 12) 0 [ FV ] 6000 [ ± ] [ PV ] 9 [ I/Y ]

60 [ N ] [ CPT ] [ PMT ] [ 124.550131 ]

(i) The outstanding balance after the 19th payment

$$PV_{19} = 124.55\left(\frac{1-1.0075^{-41}}{0.0075}\right)$$

$$= 124.55(35.183064)$$
$$= \$4382.05$$

**Programmed Solution**

0 `FV` 124.55 `±` `PMT` 9 `I/Y` 41 `N` `CPT` `PV` `4382.050802`

The interest included in the 20th payment is $4382.05(0.0075) = \$32.87$.

(ii) The outstanding balance after the 35th payment

$$PV_{35} = 124.55\left(\frac{1-1.0075^{-25}}{0.0075}\right)$$

$$= 124.55(22.718755)$$
$$= \$2829.62$$

**Programmed Solution**

0 `FV` 124.55 `±` `PMT` 9 `I/Y` 25 `N` `CPT` `PV` `2829.620994`

The interest included in Payment 36 is $2829.62(0.0075) = \$21.22$.
The principal repaid by Payment 36 is $124.55 - 21.22 = \$103.33$.

(iii) We can develop the first three payments of the amortization schedule in the usual way. To show the details of the 20th payment, we need to know the outstanding balance after 19 payments (computed in part (i)). For the 36th payment, we need to know the outstanding balance after 35 payments (computed in part (ii)). Since there are 60 payments, the last three payments are Payments 58, 59, and 60. To show the details of these payments, we must determine the outstanding balance after Payment 57.

$$PV_{57} = 124.55\left(\frac{1-1.0075^{-3}}{0.0075}\right)$$

$$= 124.55(2.955556)$$
$$= \$368.11$$

**Programmed Solution**

0 `FV` 124.55 `±` `PMT` 9 `I/Y` 3 `N` `CPT` `PV` `368.114529`

*Partial amortization schedule*

| Payment Number | Amount Paid | Interest Paid $i = 0.0075$ | Principal Repaid | Outstanding Principal Balance |
|---|---|---|---|---|
| 0 | | | | 6000.00 |
| 1 | 124.55 | 45.00 | 79.55 | 5920.45 |
| 2 | 124.55 | 44.40 | 80.15 | 5840.30 |
| 3 | 124.55 | 43.80 | 80.75 | 5759.55 |
| • | • | • | • | • |
| • | • | • | • | • |

*(continued)*

| Payment Number | Amount Paid | Interest Paid $i = 0.0075$ | Principal Repaid | Outstanding Principal Balance |
|---|---|---|---|---|
| 19 | • | • | • | 4382.05 |
| 20 | 124.55 | 32.87 | 91.68 | 4290.37 |
| • | • | • | • | • |
| • | • | • | • | • |
| 35 | • | • | • | 2829.62 |
| 36 | 124.55 | 21.22 | 103.33 | 2726.29 |
| • | • | • | • | • |
| • | • | • | • | • |
| 57 | • | • | • | 368.11 |
| 58 | 124.55 | 2.76 | 121.79 | 246.32 |
| 59 | 124.55 | 1.85 | 122.70 | 123.62 |
| 60 | 124.55 | 0.93 | 123.62 | 0.00 |
| TOTAL | 7473.00 | 1473.00 | 6000.00 | |

*Note:* The total principal repaid must be $6000; the total amount paid is $124.55(60) = \$7473$; the total interest paid is $7473 - 6000 = \$1473$.

**EXAMPLE 14.1K**

The Erin Construction Company borrowed $75 000 at 14% compounded quarterly to buy construction equipment. Payments of $3500 are to be made at the end of every three months.

(i) Determine the principal repaid in the 16th payment.
(ii) Construct a partial amortization schedule showing the details of the first three payments, the 16th payment, the last three payments, and the totals.

**SOLUTION**

(i) Since the quarterly payments are not computed blended payments, the last payment will probably be different from the preceding equal payments. Use the retrospective method for finding the outstanding balance.

$PV = 75\ 000.00; \quad PMT = 3500.00; \quad P/Y = 4; \quad C/Y = 4; \quad I/Y = 14;$

$i = \dfrac{14\%}{4} = 3.5\% = 0.035$

The accumulated value of the original principal after the 15th payment

$FV = 75\ 000.00(1.035^{15})$
$= 75\ 000.00(1.675349)$
$= \$125\ 651.16$

**Programmed Solution**

("END" mode) (Set P/Y = 4; C/Y = 4) [2nd] (CLR TVM) 75 000 [±] [PV] 14 [I/Y] 15 [N] [CPT] [FV] [125651.1623]

The accumulated value of the first 15 payments

$$FV_{15} = 3500.00\left(\frac{1.035^{15} - 1}{0.035}\right)$$

$$= 3500.00(19.295681)$$
$$= \$67\ 534.88$$

### Programmed Solution

0 [ PV ] 3500 [ ± ] [ PMT ] 14 [ I/Y ] 15 [ N ] [ CPT ] [ FV ] [ 67534.88308 ]

The outstanding principal after the 15th payment
$$= 125\ 651.16 - 67\ 534.88$$
$$= \$58\ 116.28$$

The interest included in the 16th payment is $58\ 116.28(0.035) = \$2034.07$. The principal repaid by the 16th payment is $3500.00 - 2034.07 = \$1465.93$.

(ii) To show details of the last three payments, we need to know the number of payments required to amortize the loan principal.

$$PV_n = 75\ 000.00; \quad PMT = 3500.00; \quad i = 3.5\%$$

$$75\ 000.00 = 3500.00\left(\frac{1 - 1.035^{-n}}{0.035}\right)$$

$$0.75 = 1 - 1.035^{-n}$$
$$1.035^{-n} = 0.25$$
$$-n \ln 1.035 = \ln 0.25$$
$$-n(0.034401) = -1.386294$$
$$n = 40.297584$$

### Programmed Solution

0 [ FV ] 75 000 [ ± ] [ PV ] 3500 [ PMT ] 14 [ I/Y ] [ CPT ] [ N ] [ 40.2975834 ]

Forty-one payments (40 payments of $3500.00 each plus a final payment) are required. This means the amortization schedule should show details of Payments 39, 40, and 41. To do so, we need to know the outstanding balance after 38 payments.

The accumulated value of the original loan principal after 38 payments

$$FV = 75\ 000.00(1.035^{38})$$
$$= 75\ 000.00(3.696011)$$
$$= \$277\ 200.85$$

### Programmed Solution

[ 2nd ] (CLR TVM) 75 000 [ ± ] [ PV ] 14 [ I/Y ] 38 [ N ] [ CPT ] [ FV ]

[ 277200.8486 ]

The accumulated value of the first 38 payments

$$FV_{38} = 3500.00\left(\frac{1.035^{38} - 1}{0.035}\right)$$

$$= 3500.00(77.028895)$$
$$= \$269\ 601.13$$

**Programmed Solution**

0 [ PV ] 3500 [ ± ] [ PMT ] 14 [ I/Y ] 38 [ N ] [ CPT ] [ FV ] [ 269601.1315 ]

The outstanding balance after the 38th payment
$$= 277\ 200.85 - 269\ 601.13$$
$$= \$7599.72$$

*Partial amortization schedule*

| Payment Number | Amount Paid | Interest Paid $i = 0.035$ | Principal Repaid | Outstanding Principal Balance |
|---|---|---|---|---|
| 0 | | | | 75 000.00 |
| 1 | 3 500.00 | 2 625.00 | 875.00 | 74 125.00 |
| 2 | 3 500.00 | 2 594.38 | 905.62 | 73 219.38 |
| 3 | 3 500.00 | 2 562.68 | 937.32 | 72 282.06 |
| • | • | • | • | • |
| • | • | • | • | • |
| • | • | • | • | • |
| 15 | • | • | • | 58 116.28 |
| 16 | 3 500.00 | 2 034.07 | 1 465.93 | 56 650.35 |
| • | • | • | • | • |
| • | • | • | • | • |
| • | • | • | • | • |
| 38 | • | • | • | 7 599.72 |
| 39 | 3 500.00 | 265.99 | 3 234.01 | 4 365.71 |
| 40 | 3 500.00 | 152.80 | 3 347.20 | 1 018.51 |
| 41 | 1 054.16 | 35.65 | 1 018.51 | 0.00 |
| TOTAL | 141 054.16 | 66 054.16 | 75 000.00 | |

# E. Computer application—amortization schedule

The amortization schedule in Example 14.1C displays the manual calculations for the repayment of $5000 with quarterly payments and interest at 8% compounded quarterly. Microsoft Excel and other spreadsheet programs can be used to create a file that will immediately display the results of a change in the principal, interest rate, or amount paid.

Following are general instructions for creating a file to calculate the amortization schedule in Example 14.1C. The formulas in the spreadsheet file were created using Excel; however, most spreadsheet software works in a similar manner.

This exercise assumes a basic understanding of spreadsheet applications, but an individual who has no previous experience with spreadsheets will be able to complete it.

**STEP 1**    Enter the labels shown in Figure 14.3 in row 1 and in column A.

**FIGURE 14.3**

Workbook 1

| | A | B | C | D | E | F |
|---|---|---|---|---|---|---|
| **1** | Payment Number | Amount Paid | Interest Paid | Principal Repaid | Outstanding Principal Balance | |
| **2** | 0 | | | | 5000.00 | 682.55 |
| **3** | 1 | = $F$2 | = $F$4*E2 | = B3−C3 | = E2−D3 | |
| **4** | 2 | = $F$2 | = $F$4*E3 | = B4−C4 | = E3−D4 | = 0.08/4 |
| **5** | 3 | = $F$2 | = $F$4*E4 | = B5−C5 | = E4−D5 | |
| **6** | 4 | = $F$2 | = $F$4*E5 | = B6−C6 | = E5−D6 | |
| **7** | 5 | = $F$2 | = $F$4*E6 | = B7−C7 | = E6−D7 | |
| **8** | 6 | = $F$2 | = $F$4*E7 | = B8−C8 | = E7−D8 | |
| **9** | 7 | = $F$2 | = $F$4*E8 | = B9−C9 | = E8−D9 | |
| **10** | 8 | = C10+D10 | = $F$4*E9 | = E9 | = E9−D10 | |
| **11** | Totals | = SUM(B3:B10) | = SUM(C3:C10) | = SUM(D3:D10) | | |

**STEP 2**    Enter the principal in cell E2. Do not type in the dollar sign or a comma.

**STEP 3**    Enter only the formulas shown in cells B3, C3, D3, and E3. Make sure that the formula entry includes the dollar ($) signs as shown in the figure.

**STEP 4**    The formulas that were entered in Step 3 can be copied through the remaining cells.
(a)  Select and Copy the formulas in cells B3, C3, D3, and E3.
(b)  Select cells B4 to E9 and Paste.
(c)  The formulas are now active in all the cells.

Alternatively, to copy formulas in Excel you can use the Fill handle, dragging it down the desired range through consecutive cells.

**STEP 5**    Enter the formulas shown in cells B10, C10, D10, and E10.

**STEP 6**    Enter the formula shown in cell B11, and then use Copy and Paste to enter the formulas in cells C11 and D11.

**STEP 7**    To ensure readability of the spreadsheet, format the numbers to display with two decimal places, and widen the columns to display the full labels.
This spreadsheet can now be used to reflect changes in aspects of the loan and create a new amortization schedule. Use cell E2 for new principal amounts and cell F4 for new interest rates.

## EXERCISE 14.1

If you choose, you can use Excel's **CUMIPMT, CUMPRINC, NPER, PMT,** or **PV** functions or **Template4** to answer the questions indicated below. Refer to the Spreadsheet Template Disk to find **Template4** or to learn how to use these Excel functions.

   **A.** For each of the following four debts amortized by equal payments made at the end of each payment interval, compute (a) the size of the periodic payments; (b) the outstanding principal at the time indicated; (c) the interest paid; and (d) the principal repaid by the payment following the time indicated for finding the outstanding principal.

|   | Debt Principal | Repayment Period | Payment Interval | Interest Rate | Conversion Period | Outstanding Principal Required After: |
|---|---|---|---|---|---|---|
| 1. | $12 000 | 8 years | 3 months | 10% | quarterly | 20th payment |
| 2. | 8 000 | 5 years | 1 month | 12 | monthly | 30th payment |
| 3. | 15 000 | 10 years | 6 months | 8 | semi-annually | 15th payment |
| 4. | 9 600 | 7 years | 3 months | 6 | quarterly | 12th payment |

   **B.** For each of the following four debts repaid by periodic payments as shown, compute (a) the number of payments required to amortize the debts; (b) the outstanding principal at the time indicated.

|   | Debt Principal | Debt Payment | Payment Interval | Interest Rate | Conversion Period | Outstanding Principal Required After: |
|---|---|---|---|---|---|---|
| 1. | $12 000 | $ 750 | 3 months | 8% | quarterly | 16th payment |
| 2. | 7 800 | 175 | 1 month | 12 | monthly | 24th payment |
| 3. | 21 000 | 2000 | 6 months | 9 | semi-annually | 10th payment |
| 4. | 15 000 | 800 | 3 months | 6 | quarterly | 12th payment |

   Answer each of the following questions.

1. Mr. and Mrs. Good purchased a ski chalet for $36 000. They paid $4000 down and agreed to make equal payments at the end of every three months for fifteen years. Interest is 8% compounded quarterly. Reference Example 14.1B
   (a) What size payment are the Goods making every three months?
   (b) How much will they owe after ten years?
   (c) How much will they have paid in total after fifteen years?
   (d) How much interest will they pay in total?

2. A contractor's price for a new building was $96 000. Slade Inc., the buyers of the building, paid $12 000 down and financed the balance by making equal

payments at the end of every six months for twelve years. Interest is 12% compounded semi-annually.
(a) What is the size of the semi-annual payment?
(b) How much will Slade Inc. owe after eight years?
(c) What is the total cost of the building for Slade Inc.?
(d) What is the total interest included in the payments?

3. Sam's Auto Repairs Inc. borrowed $5500 to be repaid by end-of-month payments over four years. Interest on the loan is 9% compounded monthly.
(a) What is the size of the periodic payment?
(b) What is the outstanding principal after the thirteenth payment?
(c) What is the interest paid in the fourteenth payment?
(d) How much principal is repaid in the fourteenth payment?
Reference Example 14.1H

4. To start their business, Ming and Ling borrowed $24 000 to be repaid by semi-annual payments over twelve years. Interest on the loan is 7% compounded semi-annually.
(a) What is the size of the periodic payment?
(b) What is the outstanding principal after the seventh payment?
(c) What is the interest paid in the eighth payment?
(d) How much principal is repaid in the eighth payment?

5. A loan of $10 000 with interest at 10% compounded annually is to be amortized by equal payments at the end of each year for seven years. Find the size of the annual payments and construct an amortization schedule showing the total paid and the cost of financing.

6. A loan of $8000 is repaid by equal payments made at the end of every three months for two years. If interest is 7% compounded quarterly, find the size of the quarterly payments and construct an amortization schedule showing the total paid and the total cost of the loan.

7. Hansco borrowed $9200 paying interest at 13% compounded annually. If the loan is repaid by payments of $2000 made at the end of each year, construct an amortization schedule showing the total paid and the total interest paid.

8. Pinto Brothers are repaying a loan of $14 500 by making payments of $2600 at the end of every six months. If interest is 7% compounded semi-annually, construct an amortization schedule showing the total paid and the total cost of the loan.

9. For Question 5, calculate the interest included in the fourth payment. Verify your answer by checking the amortization schedule.

10. For Question 6, calculate the principal repaid in the fifth payment period. Verify your answer by checking the amortization schedule.

11. For Question 7, calculate the principal repaid in the fourth payment period. Verify your answer by checking the amortization schedule.

12. For Question 8, calculate the interest included in the fifth payment. Verify your answer by checking the amortization schedule.

13. Apex Corporation borrowed $85 000 at 8% compounded quarterly for eight years to buy a warehouse. Equal payments are made at the end of every three months.

   (a) Determine the size of the quarterly payments.
   (b) Compute the interest included in the 16th payment.
   (c) Determine the principal repaid in the 20th payment period.
   (d) Construct a partial amortization schedule showing details of the first three payments, the last three payments, and totals.     Reference Example 14.1J

14. Mr. Brabham borrowed $7500 at 15% compounded monthly. He agreed to repay the loan in equal monthly payments over five years.

   (a) What is the size of the monthly payment?
   (b) How much of the 25th payment is interest?
   (c) What is the principal repaid in the 40th payment period?
   (d) Prepare a partial amortization schedule showing details of the first three payments, the last three payments, and totals.

15. Thornhill Equipment Co. borrowed $24 000 at 11% compounded semi-annually. It is to repay the loan by payments of $2500 at the end of every six months.

   (a) How many payments are required to repay the loan?
   (b) How much of the sixth payment is interest?
   (c) How much of the principal will be repaid in the tenth payment period?
   (d) Construct a partial amortization schedule showing details of the first three payments, the last three payments, and totals.

16. Locust Inc. owes $16 000 to be repaid by monthly payments of $475. Interest is 6% compounded monthly.

   (a) How many payments will Locust Inc. have to make?
   (b) How much interest is included in the 18th payment?
   (c) How much of the principal will be repaid in the 30th payment period?
   (d) Construct a partial amortization schedule showing details of the first three payments, the last three payments, and totals.

# 14.2 AMORTIZATION INVOLVING GENERAL ANNUITIES

## A. Finding the periodic payment and constructing amortization schedules

If the length of the payment interval is different from the length of the interest conversion period, the equal debt payments form a general annuity. The amortization of such debts involves the same principles and methods discussed in Section 14.1 except that general annuity formulas are applicable. Provided that the payments are made at the end of the payment intervals, use Formula 12.5.

$$PV_{nc} = PMT\left[\frac{1 - (1 + p)^{-n}}{p}\right]$$

where $p = (1 + i)^c - 1$

——————Formula 12.5

**EXAMPLE 14.2A**

A debt of $30 000 with interest at 12% compounded quarterly is to be repaid by equal payments at the end of each year for seven years.

(i) Compute the size of the yearly payments.
(ii) Construct an amortization schedule.

**SOLUTION**

(i) $PV_{nc} = 30\ 000.00$; $n = 7$; $P/Y = 1$; $C/Y = 4$; $c = 4$; $I/Y = 12$;

$$i = \frac{12\%}{4} = 3\% = 0.03$$

$$p = 1.03^4 - 1 = 1.125509 - 1 = 0.125509 = 12.5509\%$$

$$30\ 000.00 = PMT\left(\frac{1 - 1.125509^{-7}}{0.125509}\right)$$

$$30\ 000.00 = PMT(4.485127)$$

$$PMT = \$6688.77$$

**Programmed Solution**

("END" mode) (Set P/Y = 1; C/Y = 4) 0 [FV] 30 000 [±] [PV] 12 [I/Y]

7 [N] [CPT] [PMT] 6688.77031

(ii) *Amortization schedule*

| Payment Number | Amount Paid | Interest Paid $p = 0.125509$ | Principal Repaid | Outstanding Principal Balance |
|---|---|---|---|---|
| 0 | | | | 30 000.00 |
| 1 | 6 688.77 | 3 765.26 | 2 923.51 | 27 076.49 |
| 2 | 6 688.77 | 3 398.34 | 3 290.43 | 23 786.06 |
| 3 | 6 688.77 | 2 985.36 | 3 703.41 | 20 082.65 |
| 4 | 6 688.77 | 2 520.55 | 4 168.22 | 15 914.43 |
| 5 | 6 688.77 | 1 997.40 | 4 691.37 | 11 223.06 |
| 6 | 6 688.77 | 1 408.59 | 5 280.18 | 5 942.88 |
| 7 | 6 688.76 | 745.88 | 5 942.88 | 0.00 |
| TOTAL | 46 821.38 | 16 821.38 | 30 000.00 | |

# B. Finding the outstanding principal

### 1. Finding the Outstanding Principal When All Payments Are Equal

When all payments are equal, the prospective method used in Section 14.1 is the more direct method when finding the outstanding principal at any point during the repayment of the loan.

| EXAMPLE 14.2B | For Example 14.2A, compute the outstanding balance after three payments. |
|---|---|

| SOLUTION | The outstanding balance after three payments is the present value of the remaining four payments. |
|---|---|

$$\text{PMT} = 6688.77; \quad n = 4; \quad c = 4; \quad i = 3\%; \quad p = 12.5509\%$$

$$\text{PV}_{nc} = 6688.77\left(\frac{1 - 1.125509^{-4}}{0.125509}\right)$$

$$= 6688.77(3.002443)$$

$$= \$20\,082.65$$

**Programmed Solution**

("END" mode) (Set P/Y = 1; C/Y = 4) 0 [FV] 6688.77 [±] [PMT] 12 [I/Y]

4 [N] [CPT] [PV] [20082.65134]

The outstanding balance after three payments is \$20 082.65.

| EXAMPLE 14.2C | A \$25 000 mortgage amortized by monthly payments over twenty years is renewable after five years. |
|---|---|

    (i) If interest is 6.5% compounded semi-annually, what is the outstanding balance at the end of the five-year term?

   (ii) If the mortgage is renewed for a further three-year term at 6% compounded semi-annually, what is the size of the new monthly payment?

  (iii) What is the payout figure at the end of the three-year term?

| SOLUTION | (i) $\text{PV}_{nc} = 25\,000.00; \quad n = 20(12) = 240; \quad \text{P/Y} = 12; \quad \text{C/Y} = 2; \quad \text{I/Y} = 6.5;$ |
|---|---|

$$c = \frac{2}{12} = \frac{1}{6}; \quad i = \frac{6.5\%}{2} = 3.25\% = 0.0325;$$

$$p = 1.0325^{\frac{1}{6}} - 1 = 1.005345 - 1 = 0.005345 = 0.5345$$

$$25\,000.00 = \text{PMT}\left[\frac{1 - (1.005345)^{-240}}{0.005345}\right]$$

$$25\,000.00 = \text{PMT}(135.043813)$$

$$\text{PMT} = \$185.13$$

The number of outstanding payments after five years is 15(12)=180.

$$\text{PV}_{nc} = 185.13\left[\frac{1 - (1.005345)^{-180}}{0.005345}\right]$$

$$= 185.13(115.424194)$$

$$= \$21\,368.48$$

**Programmed Solution**

("END" mode) (Set P/Y = 12; C/Y = 2) 0 [FV] 25 000 [±] [PV]

6.5 [I/Y] 240 [N] [CPT] [PMT] [185.125104]

0 [FV] 185.13 [±] [PMT] 6.5 [I/Y] 180 [N] [CPT] [PV] [21368.48105]

The outstanding balance after five years is $21 368.48.

(ii) After the five-year term is up, the outstanding balance of $21 368.48 is to be amortized over the remaining fifteen years.

$PV_{nc} = 21\ 368.48$;  $n = 15(12) = 180$;  P/Y = 12;  C/Y = 2;  I/Y = 6;

$$c = \frac{1}{6}; \quad i = \frac{8\%}{2} = 4\% = 0.04;$$

$$p = 1.03^{\frac{1}{6}} - 1 = 1.004939 - 1 = 0.004939 = 0.4939\%$$

$$21\ 368.48 = PMT\left[\frac{1 - (1.004939)^{-180}}{0.004939}\right]$$

$$21\ 368.48 = PMT(119.064232)$$

$$PMT = \$179.47$$

**Programmed Solution**

("END" mode) (Set P/Y = 12; C/Y = 2) 0 [FV] 21 368.48 [±] [PV]

6 [I/Y] 180 [N] [CPT] [PMT] [179.470187]

The monthly payment for the three-year term will be $179.47.

(iii) At the end of the three-year term, the number of outstanding payments is 144.

$$PV_{nc} = 179.47\left[\frac{1 - (1.004939)^{-144}}{0.004939}\right]$$

$$= 179.47(102.876118)$$

$$= \$18\ 463.18$$

**Programmed Solution**

("END" mode) (Set P/Y = 12; C/Y = 2) 0 [FV] 179.47 [±] [PMT] 6 [I/Y]

144 [N] [CPT] [PV] [18463.17693]

The outstanding balance at the end of the three-year term will be $18 463.18.

## 2. Finding the Outstanding Balance When All Payments Except the Final Payment Are Equal

When the final payment is different from the preceding payments, use the retrospective method for finding the outstanding balance. Since this method requires finding the future value of an ordinary general annuity, Formula 12.2 applies.

$$FV_{nc} = PMT\left[\frac{(1 + p)^n - 1}{p}\right] \quad \text{where } p = (1 + i)^c - 1 \quad \text{—— Formula 12.2}$$

**EXAMPLE 14.2D**

A loan of $12 000 with interest at 12% compounded monthly and amortized by payments of $700 at the end of every three months is repaid in full after three years. What is the payout figure just after the last regular payment?

**SOLUTION**

Accumulate the value of the original principal after three years.

$$PV = 12\,000.00; \quad n = 3(12) = 36; \quad i = \frac{12\%}{12} = 1\% = 0.01$$

$$
\begin{aligned}
FV &= 12\,000.00(1.01^{36}) \\
&= 12\,000.00(1.430769) \\
&= \$17\,169.23
\end{aligned}
$$

**Programmed Solution**

("END" mode) (Set P/Y = 12; C/Y = 12) [2nd] (CLR TVM) 12 000 [±] [PV]

12 [I/Y] 36 [N] [CPT] [FV] [17169.2254]

Accumulate the value of the twelve payments made.

$$PMT = 700.00; \quad n = 3(4) = 12; \quad P/Y = 4; \quad C/Y = 12; \quad I/Y = 12; \quad c = \frac{12}{4} = 3;$$

$$i = 1\%$$

$$p = 1.01^3 - 1 = 1.030301 - 1 = 0.030301 = 3.0301\%$$

$$
\begin{aligned}
FV_{nc} &= 700.00\left(\frac{1.030301^{12} - 1}{0.030301}\right) \\
&= 700.00(14.216322) \\
&= \$9951.43
\end{aligned}
$$

**Programmed Solution**

("END" mode) (Set P/Y = 4; C/Y = 12) 0 [PV] 700 [±] [PMT] 12 [I/Y]

12 [N] [CPT] [FV] [9951.425646]

The outstanding balance after three years is 17 169.23 − 9951.43 = $7217.80. The payout figure after three years is $7217.80.

**Alternative Programmed Solution**

(Set P/Y = 4; C/Y = 12) 12 000 [±] [PV] 700 [PMT] 12 [I/Y]

12 [N] [CPT] [FV] [7217.799757]

## C. Finding the interest paid and the principal repaid; constructing partial amortization schedules

**EXAMPLE 14.2E**

Mr. and Mrs. Poh took out a $40 000, 25-year mortgage renewable after five years. The mortgage bears interest at 9.5% compounded semi-annually and is amortized by equal monthly payments.

   (i) What is the interest included in the 13th payment?
  (ii) How much of the principal is repaid by the 13th payment?
 (iii) What is the total interest cost during the first year?
  (iv) What is the total interest cost during the fifth year?
   (v) What will be the total interest paid by the Pohs during the initial five-year term?

**SOLUTION**

(i)  First find the size of the monthly payment.

$$PV_{nc} = 40\ 000.00; \quad n = 300; \quad P/Y = 12; \quad C/Y = 2; \quad I/Y = 9.5;$$

$$c = \frac{1}{6}; \quad i = 4.75\%$$

$$p = 1.0475^{\frac{1}{6}} - 1 = 1.007764 - 1 = 0.007764 = 0.7764\%$$

$$40\ 000.00 = PMT\left(\frac{1 - 1.007764^{-300}}{0.007764}\right)$$

$$40\ 000.00 = PMT(116.140291)$$
$$PMT = \$344.41$$

**Programmed Solution**

("END" mode) (Set P/Y = 12; C/Y = 2) 0 [FV] 40 000 [±] [PV]

9.5 [I/Y] 300 [N] [CPT] [PMT] [344.411053]

Now find the outstanding balance after one year.

PMT = 344.41; $p = 0.7764\%$

The number of outstanding payments after one year $n = 288$.

$$PV_{nc} = PMT\left(\frac{1 - 1.007764^{-288}}{0.007764}\right)$$

$$= 344.41(114.90953)$$
$$= \$39\ 576.05$$

**Programmed Solution**

0 [ FV ] 344.41 [ ± ] [ PMT ] 9.5 [ I/Y ] 288 [ N ] [ CPT ] [ PV ] [ 39576.05454 ]

The resulting difference in the present value amount is due to rounding of the payment.

The interest in the 13th payment is 39 576.05(0.007764) = $307.28.

(ii) The principal repaid in the 13th payment is 344.41 − 307.28 = $37.13.

(iii) The total amount paid during the first year is 344.41(12) = $4132.92
The total principal repaid is 40 000.00 − 39 576.05      =   423.95
The total cost of interest for the first year      = $3708.97

(iv) After four years, $n = 300 - 48 = 252$.

$$PV_{nc} = 344.41\left(\frac{1 - 1.007764^{-252}}{0.007764}\right)$$

$$= 344.41(110.45204)$$

$$= \$38\ 040.79$$

**Programmed Solution**

("END" mode) (Set P/Y = 12; C/Y = 2) 0 [ FV ] 344.41 [ ± ] [ PMT ]

9.5 [ I/Y ] 252 [ N ] [ CPT ] [ PV ] [ 38040.84291 ]

After five years, $n = 300 - 60 = 240$.

$$PV_{nc} = 344.41\left(\frac{1 - 1.007764^{-240}}{0.007764}\right)$$

$$= 344.41(108.66827)$$

$$= \$37\ 426.44$$

**Programmed Solution**

("END" mode) (Set P/Y = 12; C/Y = 2) 0 [ FV ] 344.41 [ ± ] [ PMT ]

9.5 [ I/Y ] 240 [ N ] [ CPT ] [ PV ] [ 37426.49132 ]

The total amount paid during the fifth year is 344.41(12)      =   $4132.92
The total principal repaid in Year 5 is 38 040.84 − 37 426.49  =     614.35
The total cost of interest in Year 5      =   $3518.57

(v) The total amount paid during the first five years is 344.41(60) = $20 664.60
The total principal repaid is 40 000.00 − 37 426.49      =   2 573.51
The total cost of interest for the first five years      = $18 091.09

**EXAMPLE 14.2F**

Confederated Venture Company financed a project by borrowing $120 000 at 7% compounded annually and is repaying the loan at the rate of $7000 due at the end of every three months.

(i) Compute the interest paid and the principal repaid by the tenth payment.
(ii) Construct a partial amortization schedule showing the first three payments, the tenth payment, the last three payments, and the totals.

**SOLUTION**

(i) Accumulate the value of the original loan after nine payments.

$$PV = 120\ 000.00; \quad n = 9; \quad P/Y = 4; \quad C/Y = 1; \quad I/Y = 7; \quad c = \frac{1}{4} = 0.25;$$

$$i = 7\% = 0.07;$$

$$p = 1.07^{0.25} - 1 = 1.017059 - 1 = 0.017059 = 1.7059\%$$

$$FV = 120\ 000.00(1.017059^9)$$
$$= 120\ 000.00(1.16443)$$
$$= \$139\ 731.61$$

**Programmed Solution**

("END" mode) (Set P/Y = 4; C/Y = 1) [2nd] (CLR TVM) 120 000 [±]

[PV] 7 [I/Y] 9 [N] [CPT] [FV] [139731.6366]

Accumulate the value of the first nine payments.

$$PMT = 7000.00; \quad n = 9$$

$$FV_{nc} = 7000.00\left(\frac{1.017059^9 - 1}{0.017059}\right)$$
$$= 7000.00(9.639186)$$
$$= \$67\ 474.30$$

**Programmed Solution**

("END" mode) (Set P/Y = 4; C/Y = 1) 0 [PV] 7000 [±] [PMT] 7 [I/Y]

9 [N] [CPT] [FV] [67474.30606]

The outstanding balance after nine payments is 139 731.64 − 67 474.31 = $72 257.33.

The interest included in the tenth payment is 72 257.33(0.017059) = $1232.60.

The principal repaid by the tenth payment is 7000.00 − 1232.60 = $5767.40.

(ii) To show the details of the last three payments, we need to know the number of payments required to amoritize the loan.

$$PV_{nc} = 120\ 000.00; \quad PMT = 7000.00; \quad p = 1.7059\%$$

$$120\ 000.00 = 7000.00\left(\frac{1 - 1.017059^{-n}}{0.017059}\right)$$

$$0.292432 = 1 - 1.017059^{-n}$$
$$1.017059^{-n} = 0.707568$$
$$-n\ln 1.017059 = \ln 0.707568$$
$$-n(0.016915) = -0.345921$$
$$n = 20.450975 \text{ (There may be a difference due to rounding.)}$$

### Programmed Solution

("END" mode) (Set P/Y = 4; C/Y = 1) 0 [FV] 120 000 [±] [PV]

7000 [PMT] 7 [I/Y] [CPT] [N] [20.450975]

Twenty-one payments (20 payments of $7000 plus a final payment) are required. This means the amortization schedule needs to show details of Payments 19, 20, and 21. To do so, we need to know the outstanding balance after 18 payments. Accumulate the value of the original principal after 18 payments.

$$FV = 120\ 000.00(1.017059^{18})$$
$$= 120\ 000.00(1.355898)$$
$$= \$162\ 707.75$$

### Programmed Solution

("END" mode) (Set P/Y = 4; C/Y = 1) [2nd] (CLR TVM) 120 000 [±]

[PV] 7 [I/Y] 18 [N] [CPT] [FV] [162707.7523]

Accumulate the value of the first 18 payments.

$$FV_{nc} = 7000.00\left(\frac{1.017059^{18} - 1}{0.017059}\right)$$
$$= 7000.00(20.863348)$$
$$= \$146\ 4043.43$$

### Programmed Solution

("END" mode) (Set P/Y = 4; C/Y = 1) 0 [PV] 7000 [±] [PMT]

7 [I/Y] 18 [N] [CPT] [FV] [146043.4329]

The outstanding balance after 18 payments is 162 707.75 − 146 043.43 = $16 664.32.

*Partial amortization schedule*

| Payment Number | Amount Paid | Interest Paid $p = 0.017059$ | Principal Repaid | Outstanding Principal Balance |
|---|---|---|---|---|
| 0 | | | | 120 000.00 |
| 1 | 7 000.00 | 2 047.02 | 4 952.98 | 115 047.02 |
| 2 | 7 000.00 | 1 962.53 | 5 037.47 | 110 009.55 |
| 3 | 7 000.00 | 1 876.60 | 5 123.40 | 104 886.15 |
| • | • | • | • | • |
| • | • | • | • | • |
| 9 | • | • | • | 72 257.33 |
| 10 | 7 000.00 | 1 232.60 | 5 767.40 | 66 489.93 |
| • | • | • | • | • |
| • | • | • | • | • |
| • | • | • | • | • |
| 18 | • | • | • | 16 664.32 |
| 19 | 7 000.00 | 284.27 | 6 715.73 | 9 948.59 |
| 20 | 7 000.00 | 169.71 | 6 830.29 | 3 118.30 |
| 21 | 3 171.49 | 53.19 | 3 118.30 | 0.00 |
| TOTAL | 143 171.49 | 23 171.49 | 120 000.00 | |

As an alternative, use the calculator's Amortization function. Instructions on its use are available on the CD-ROM accompanying this book.

## D. Computer application—Amortization schedule

 As shown in Section 14.1E, amortization schedules can be created using spreadsheet programs like Excel. Refer to Section 14.1E for instructions for creating amortization schedules in spreadsheets. Using those instructions and the formulas shown in Figure 14.4 below, you can create the amortization schedule for the debt in Example 14.2A.

**FIGURE 14.4**

| | A | B | C | D | E | F |
|---|---|---|---|---|---|---|
| 1 | Payment Number | Amount Paid | Interest Paid | Principal Repaid | Outstanding Principal Balance | |
| 2 | 0 | | | | 30000.00 | 6688.77 |
| 3 | 1 | = $F$2 | = $F$4*E2 | = B3−C3 | = E2−D3 | |
| 4 | 2 | = $F$2 | = $F$4*E3 | = B4−C4 | = E3−D4 | 0.1255088 |
| 5 | 3 | = $F$2 | = $F$4*E4 | = B5−C5 | = E4−D5 | |
| 6 | 4 | = $F$2 | = $F$4*E5 | = B6−C6 | = E5−D6 | |
| 7 | 5 | = $F$2 | = $F$4*E6 | = B7−C7 | = E6−D7 | |
| 8 | 6 | = $F$2 | = $F$4*E7 | = B8−C8 | = E7−D8 | |
| 9 | 7 | = C9+D9 | = $F$4*E8 | = E8 | = E8−D9 | |
| 10 | Totals | = SUM(B3:B9) | = SUM(C3:C9) | = SUM(D3:D9) | | |

Workbook 1

## EXERCISE 14.2

If you choose, you can use Excel's **CUMIPMT, CUMPRINC, EFFECT, NPER, PMT,** or **PV** functions or **Template4** to answer the questions indicated below. Refer to the Spreadsheet Template Disk to find **Template4** or to learn how to use these Excel functions.

  **A.** For each of the following four loans amortized by equal payments made at the end of each payment interval, compute: (a) the size of the periodic payments; (b) the outstanding principal at the time indicated; (c) the interest paid; and (d) the principal repaid by the payment following the time indicated for finding the outstanding principal.

| | Debt Principal | Repayment Period | Payment Interval | Interest Rate | Conversion Period | Outstanding Principal Required After: |
|---|---|---|---|---|---|---|
| 1. | $36 000 | 20 years | 6 months | 8% | quarterly | 25th payment |
| 2. | 15 000 | 10 years | 3 months | 12 | monthly | 15th payment |
| 3. | 8 500 | 5 years | 1 month | 6 | semi-annually | 30th payment |
| 4. | 9 600 | 7 years | 3 months | 9 | semi-annually | 10th payment |

  **B.** For each of the following four loans repaid by periodic payments as indicated, compute: (a) the number of payments required to amortize the debts; and (b) the outstanding principal at the time indicated.

| | Debt Principal | Debt Repayment | Payment Interval | Interest Rate | Conversion Period | Outstanding Principal Required After: |
|---|---|---|---|---|---|---|
| 1. | $ 6 000 | $ 400 | 3 months | 6% | monthly | 10th payment |
| 2. | 8 400 | 1200 | 6 months | 10 | quarterly | 5th payment |
| 3. | 23 500 | 1800 | 3 months | 7 | annually | 14th payment |
| 4. | 18 200 | 430 | 1 month | 8 | semi-annually | 48th payment |

 **C.** Answer each of the following questions.

1. A debt of $45 000 is repaid over fifteen years with semi-annual payments. Interest is 9% compounded monthly.
   (a) What is the size of the periodic payments?
   (b) What is the outstanding principal after the eleventh payment?
   (c) What is the interest paid in the twelfth payment?
   (d) How much principal is repaid in the twelfth payment?   *Reference Example 14.2E*

2. A debt of $60 000 is repaid over twenty-five years with monthly payments. Interest is 7% compounded semi-annually.
   (a) What is the size of the periodic payments?
   (b) What is the outstanding principal after the 119th payment?
   (c) What is the interest paid in the 120th payment?
   (d) How much principal is repaid in the 120th payment?

**3.** A $36 000 mortgage amortized by monthly payments over twenty-five years is renewable after three years.
   **(a)** If interest is 7% compounded semi-annually, what is the size of each monthly payment?
   **(b)** What is the mortgage balance at the end of the three-year term?
   **(c)** How much interest will have been paid during the first three years?
   **(d)** If the mortgage is renewed for a further three-year term at 9% compounded semi-annually, what will be the size of the monthly payments for the renewal period?

**4.** Fink and Associates bought a property valued at $80 000 for $15 000 down and a mortgage amortized over fifteen years. The firm makes equal payments due at the end of every three months. Interest on the mortgage is 6.5% compounded annually and the mortgage is renewable after five years.
   **(a)** What is the size of each quarterly payment?
   **(b)** What is the outstanding principal at the end of the five-year term?
   **(c)** What is the cost of the mortgage for the first five years?
   **(d)** If the mortgage is renewed for a further five years at 9% compounded semi-annually, what will be the size of each quarterly payment?

**5.** A loan of $10 000 with interest at 10% compounded quarterly is repaid by payments of $950 made at the end of every six months.
   **(a)** How many payments will be required to amortize the loan?
   **(b)** If the loan is repaid in full after six years, what is the payout figure?
   **(c)** If paid out, what is the total cost of the loan?

**6.** The owner of the Blue Goose Motel borrowed $12 500 at 12% compounded semi-annually and agreed to repay the loan by making payments of $700 at the end of every three months.
   **(a)** How many payments will be needed to repay the loan?
   **(b)** How much will be owed at the end of five years?
   **(c)** How much of the payments made at the end of five years will be interest?

**7.** A loan of $16 000 with interest at 9% compounded quarterly is repaid in seven years by equal payments made at the end of each year. Find the size of the annual payments and construct an amortization schedule showing the total paid and the total interest.                    Reference Example 14.2E

**8.** A debt of $12 500 with interest at 7% compounded semi-annually is repaid by payments of $1900 made at the end of every three months. Construct an amortization schedule showing the total paid and the total cost of the debt.

**9.** For Question 7, calculate the interest included in the fifth payment period. Verify your answer by checking the amortization schedule.

**10.** For Question 8, compute the principal repaid in the sixth payment period. Verify your answer by checking the amortization schedule.

11. A $40 000 mortgage amortized by monthly payments over 25 years is renewable after five years.
    (a) If interest is 8.5% compounded semi-annually, what is the size of each monthly payment?
    (b) Find the total interest paid during the first year.
    (c) Compute the interest included in the 48th payment.
    (d) If the mortgage is renewed after five years at 10.5% compounded semi-annually, what is the size of the monthly payment for the renewal period?
    (e) Construct a partial amortization schedule showing details of the first three payments for each of the two five-year terms.

12. A debt of $32 000 is repaid by payments of $2950 made at the end of every six months. Interest is 12% compounded quarterly.
    (a) What is the number of payments needed to retire the debt?
    (b) What is the cost of the debt for the first five years?
    (c) What is the interest paid in the tenth payment period?
    (d) Construct a partial amortization schedule showing details of the first three payments, the last three payments, and totals.

# 14.3 FINDING THE SIZE OF THE FINAL PAYMENT

## A. Three methods for computing the final payment

When all payments except the final payment are equal, three methods are available to compute the size of the final payment.

**METHOD 1** Compute the value of the term $n$ and determine the present value of the outstanding fractional payment. If the final payment is made at the end of the payment interval, add interest for one payment interval to the present value.

**METHOD 2** Use the retrospective method to compute the outstanding principal after the last of the equal payments. If the final payment is made at the end of the payment interval, add to the outstanding principal the interest for one payment interval.

**METHOD 3** Assume all payments to be equal, compute the overpayment, and subtract the overpayment from the size of the equal payments. This method must not be used when the payments are made at the beginning of the payment interval.

**EXAMPLE 14.3A** For Example 14.1D, compute the size of the final payment using each of the three methods. Compare the results with the size of the payment shown in the amortization schedule.

**SOLUTION**

**METHOD 1** $PV = 15\,000.00$; $PMT = 2500.00$; $P/Y = 4$; $C/Y = 4$; $I/Y = 10$; $i = 2.5\%$

$$15\,000.00 = 2500.00\left(\frac{1 - 1.025^{-n}}{0.025}\right)$$

$$6.00 = \frac{1 - 1.025^{-n}}{0.025}$$

$$0.15 = 1 - 1.025^{-n}$$

$$1.025^{-n} = 0.85$$

$$-n \ln 1.025 = \ln 0.85$$

$$-n(0.024693) = -0.162519$$

$$n = 6.581684$$

**Programmed Solution**

("END" mode) (Set P/Y = 4; C/Y = 4) 0 | FV | 15 000 | ± | | PV | 2500 | PMT |

10 | I/Y | | CPT | | N | | 6.581682 |

$$PMT = 2500.00; \quad i = 2.5\%; \quad n = 0.581684$$

$$PV_n = 2500.00\left(\frac{1 - 1.025^{-0.581684}}{0.025}\right)$$

$$= 2500.00(0.570426)$$

$$= \$1426.06$$

**Programmed Solution**

0 | FV | 2500 | ± | | PMT | 10 | I/Y | 0.581684 | N | | CPT | | PV | | 1426.058892 |

Interest for one interval is $1426.06(0.025) = \$35.65$.
Final payment is $1426.06 + 35.65 = \$1461.71$.

**METHOD 2**   Compute the value of $n$ as done in Method 1.
Since $n = 6.581684$, the number of equal payments is 6.
The accumulated value of the original principal after six payments

$$FV = 15\,000.00(1.025^6)$$

$$= 15\,000.00(1.159693)$$

$$= \$17\,395.40$$

**Programmed Solution**

("END" mode) (Set P/Y = 4; C/Y = 4) | 2nd | (CLR TVM) 15 000 | ± | | PV |

10 | I/Y | 6 | N | | CPT | | FV | | 17395.40127 |

The accumulated value of the first six payments

$$FV_6 = 2500.00\left(\frac{1.025^6 - 1}{0.025}\right)$$

$$= 2500.00(6.387737)$$

$$= \$15\,969.34$$

**Programmed Solution**

0 [PV] 2500 [±] [PMT] 10 [I/Y] 6 [N] [CPT] [FV] [15969.34182]

The outstanding balance after six payments is 17 395.40 − 15 969.34 = $1426.06.
The final payment = outstanding balance + interest for one period
$$= \text{the accumulated value of \$1426.06 for one year}$$
$$= 1426.06(1.025)$$
$$= \$1461.71$$

**METHOD 3** Compute the value of $n$ as done in Method 1.
Since $n = 6.581684$, the number of assumed full payments is 7.
The accumulated value of the original principal after seven payments

$$\text{FV} = 15\,000.00(1.025^7)$$
$$= 15\,000.00(1.188686)$$
$$= \$17\,830.29$$

**Programmed Solution**

("END" mode) (Set P/Y = 4; C/Y = 4) [2nd] (CLR TVM) 15 000 [±] [PV]

10 [I/Y] 7 [N] [CPT] [FV] [17830.28631]

The accumulated value of seven payments

$$\text{FV}_7 = 2500.00\left(\frac{1.025^7 - 1}{0.025}\right)$$
$$= 2500.00(7.547430)$$
$$= \$18\,868.58$$

**Programmed Solution**

0 [PV] 2500 [±] [PMT] 10 [I/Y] 7 [N] [CPT] [FV] [18868.57537]

Since the accumulated value of seven payments is greater than the accumulated value of the original principal, there is an overpayment.

18 868.58 − 17 830.29 = $1038.29

The size of the final payment is 2500.00 − 1038.29 = $1461.71.

*Note:*

1. For all three methods, you must determine the term $n$ using the methods shown in Chapters 11 and 12.

2. When using a scientific calculator, Method 1 is preferable, because it is the most direct method. It is the method used in Subsection B below.

## POINTERS AND PITFALLS

When dealing with loan repayment problems in which the size of the final payment must be determined, once $n$ has been calculated, the size of the final payment *cannot* be calculated by simply multiplying the periodic pay (PMT) by the decimal portion of $n$ (i.e., the non-integral part of $n$). For example, if you had done it *incorrectly*, the final rent payment in Example 14.3A would have shown as $0.586488 \times \$2500.00 = \$1454.21$ Using the *correct* method, the value for the size of the final rent payment in Example 14.3A, Method 1 is $1461.71. The difference is due to interest on the outstanding balance of the loan for the final payment period.

## B. Applications

**EXAMPLE 14.3B**

On his retirement, Art received a bonus of $8000 from his employer. Taking advantage of the existing tax legislation, he invested his money in an annuity that provides for payments of $1200 at the end of every six months. If interest is 6.25% compounded semi-annually, determine the size of the final payment. (See Chapter 11, Example 11.5D.)

**SOLUTION**

To start, the number of payments must be determined.

$PV_n = 8000.00;$   $PMT = 1200.00;$   $P/Y = 2;$   $C/Y = 2;$   $I/Y = 6.25;$

$$i = \frac{6.25\%}{2} = 3.125\%$$

$$8000.00 = 1200.00\left(\frac{1 - 1.03125^{-n}}{0.03125}\right)$$

$$0.208333 = 1 - 1.03125^{-n}$$

$$1.03125^{-n} = 0.791667$$

$$-n \ln 1.03125 = \ln 0.791667$$

$$-n(0.030772) = -0.233615$$

$$n = 7.59188 \text{ (half-year periods)}$$

The annuity will be in existence for four years. Art will receive seven payments of $1200.00 and final payment that will be less than $1200.00

$PMT = 1200.00;$   $i = 3.125\%;$   $n = 0.59188$

$$PV_n = 1200.00\left(\frac{1 - 1.03125^{-0.59188}}{0.03125}\right)$$

$$= 1200.00(0.577545)$$

$$= \$693.05$$

The final step is to determine the interest for that final period, and add it to the beginning-of-period balance to determine the final payment.

The final payment including the interest for one payment interval is 693.06(1.03125) = \$714.72.

**Programmed Solution**

("END" mode) (Set P/Y = 2; C/Y = 2) 0 FV 8000 ± PV 1200 PMT
6.25 I/Y CPT N 7.591884

0 FV 1200 ± PMT 6.25 I/Y 0.591884 N

CPT PV 693.057863

---

**EXAMPLE 14.3C**

A lease contract valued at \$7800 is to be fulfilled by payments of \$180 due at the beginning of each month. If money is worth 9% compounded monthly, determine the size of the final lease payment. (See Chapter 13, Example 13.1O.)

**SOLUTION**

$PV_n$(due) = 7800.00; PMT = 180.00; P/Y = 12; C/Y = 12; I/Y = 9;

$i = \dfrac{9\%}{12} = 0.75\%$

$n = 52.123125$ (see solution to Example 13.1O)

Present value of the final payment

PMT = 180.00; $i = 0.75\%$; $n = 0.123125$

$$PV_n(\text{due}) = 180.00(1.0075)\left(\frac{1 - 1.0075^{-0.123125}}{0.0075}\right) \quad \text{Formula 12.2}$$

$$= 180.00(1.0075)(0.122609)$$
$$= 180.00(0.123529)$$
$$= \$22.24$$

**Programmed Solution**

("BGN" mode) (Set P/Y = 12; C/Y = 12) 0 FV 180 PMT 9 I/Y 7800 ±
PV CPT N 52.123125

("BGN" mode) 0 FV 180 ± PMT 9 I/Y 0.123125 N

CPT PV 22.235252

Since the payment is made at the beginning of the last payment interval, no interest is added. The final payment is \$22.24.

**EXAMPLE 14.3D**

Payments of $500 deferred for nine years are received at the end of each month from a fund of $10 000 deposited at 10.5% compounded monthly. Determine the size of the final payment. (See Chapter 13, Example 13.3E.)

**SOLUTION**

$PV_n(\text{defer}) = 10\ 000.00$; $PMT = 500.00$; $d = 9(12) = 108$; $P/Y = 12$; $C/Y = 12$;

$I/Y = 10.5$;   $i = \dfrac{10.5\%}{12} = 0.875\%$

$n = 68.288334$ (see solution to Example 13.3E)

Present value of the final payment

$PMT = 500.00$;   $i = 0.875\%$;   $n = 0.288334$

$$PV_n = 500.00\left(\frac{1 - 1.00875^{-0.288334}}{0.00875}\right)$$

$$= 500.00(0.286720)$$

$$= \$143.36$$

**Programmed Solution**

("END" mode) (Set P/Y = 12; C/Y = 12) 0 [ FV ] 500 [ ± ] [ PMT ] 10.5 [ I/Y ]

0.288334 [ N ] [ CPT ] [ PV ] [ 143.359793 ]

The size of the final payment is $143.36(1.00875) = \$144.61$.

**EXAMPLE 14.3E**

A business valued at $96 000 is purchased for a down payment of 25% and payments of $4000.00 at the end of every three months. If interest is 9% compounded monthly, what is the size of the final payment? (See Chapter 12, Example 12.4B.)

**SOLUTION**

$PV_{nc} = 96\ 000.00(0.75) = 72\ 000.00$;   $PMT = 4000.00$;   $P/Y = 4$;   $C/Y = 12$;

$I/Y = 9$; $c = \dfrac{12}{4} = 3$; $i = \dfrac{9\%}{12} = 0.75\% = 0.0075$; $p = 1.0075^3 - 1 = 2.2669\%$;

$n = 23.390585$ (see solution to Example 12.4B)

Present value of the final payment

$PMT = 4000.00$;   $p = 2.2669\%$;   $n = 0.390585$

$$PV_n = 4000.00\left(\frac{1 - 1.022669^{-0.390585}}{0.022669}\right)$$

$$= 4000.00(0.384538)$$

$$= \$1538.15$$

**Programmed Solution**

("END" mode) (Set P/Y = 4; C/Y = 12) 0 [ FV ] 4000 [ ± ] [ PMT ]

9 [ I/Y ] 0.390585 [ N ] [ CPT ] [ PV ] [ 1538.151278 ]

The final payment is $1538.15(1.022669) = \$1573.02$.

**EXAMPLE 14.3F**

Ted Davis, having reached his goal of a $140 000 balance in his RRSP, converts it into an RRIF and withdraws from it $1650 at the beginning of each month. If interest is 5.75% compounded quarterly, what is the size of the final withdrawal? (See Chapter 13, Example 13.2G.)

**SOLUTION**

$PV_{nc} = 140\,000.00;$   $PMT = 1650.00;$   $P/Y = 12;$   $C/Y = 4;$   $I/Y = 5.75;$

$$c = \frac{4}{12} = \frac{1}{3}; \quad i = \frac{5.75\%}{4} = 1.4375\% = 0.014375;$$

$$p = 1.014375^{\frac{1}{3}} - 1 = 1.004769 - 1 = 0.4769\%$$

$n = 108.32388$ (see solution to Example 13.2G)

Present value of final payment

$PMT = 1650.00;$   $p = 0.47689\%;$   $n = 0.32388$

$$PV_n = 1650.00(1.004769)\left(\frac{1 - 1.004769^{-0.32395}}{0.004769}\right)$$

$$= 1650.00(1.004769)(0.322861)$$

$$= 1650.00(0.324401)$$

$$= \$535.26$$

**Programmed Solution**

("BGN" mode) (Set P/Y = 12; C/Y = 4) 0 $\boxed{PV}$ 1650 $\boxed{\pm}$ $\boxed{PMT}$ 5.75 $\boxed{I/Y}$

0.32388 $\boxed{N}$ $\boxed{CPT}$ $\boxed{PV}$ $\boxed{535.261739}$

Since the payment is at the beginning of the last payment interval, it is $535.26.

## EXERCISE 14.3

If you choose, you can use Excel's **NPER** or **PV** function to answer the questions indicated below. Refer to the Spreadsheet Template Disk to learn how to use these Excel functions.

**A.** For each of the following six loans, compute the size of the final payment.

|   | Principal | Periodic Payment | Payment Interval | Payment Made At: | Interest Rate | Conversion Period |
|---|---|---|---|---|---|---|
| **1.** | $17 500 | $1100 | 3 months | end | 9% | quarterly |
| **2.** | 7 800 | 775 | 6 months | beginning | 7 | semi-annually |
| **3.** | 9 300 | 580 | 3 months | beginning | 7 | quarterly |
| **4.** | 15 400 | 1600 | 6 months | end | 8 | quarterly |
| **5.** | 29 500 | 1650 | 3 months | end | 9 | monthly |
| **6.** | 17 300 | 425 | 1 month | beginning | 6 | quarterly |

**B.** Answer each of the following questions.

1. A loan of $7200 is repaid by payments of $360 at the end of every three months. Interest is 11% compounded quarterly.
   **(a)** How many payments are required to repay the debt?
   **(b)** What is the size of the final payment?  Reference Example 14.3B

2. Seanna O'Brien receives pension payments of $3200 at the end of every six months from a retirement fund of $50 000. The fund earns 7% compounded semi-annually.
   **(a)** How many payments will Seanna receive?
   **(b)** What is the size of the final pension payment?

3. A loan of $35 000 is repaid by payments of $925 at the end of every month. Interest is 12% compounded monthly.
   **(a)** How many payments are required to repay the debt?
   **(b)** What is the size of the final payment?

4. An annuity with a cash value of $10 500 pays $900 at the beginning of every three months. The investment earns 11% semi-annually.
   **(a)** How many payments will be paid?
   **(b)** What is the size of the final annuity payment?

5. Payments of $1200 are made out of a fund of $25 000 at the end of every three months. If interest is 6% compounded monthly, what is the size of the final payment?

6. A debt of $30 000 is repaid in monthly installments of $550. If interest is 8% compounded quarterly, what is the size of the final payment?

7. A lease valued at $20 000 requires payments of $1000 every three months due in advance. If money is worth 7% compounded quarterly, what is the size of the final lease payment?  Reference Example 14.3C

8. Eduardo Martinez has saved $125 000. If he withdraws $1250 at the beginning of every month and interest is 10.5% compounded monthly, what is the size of the last withdrawal?

9. Equipment priced at $42 000 was purchased on a contract requiring payments of $5000 at the beginning of every six months. If interest is 9% compounded quarterly, what is the size of the final payment?

10. Noreen Leung has agreed to purchase her partner's share in the business by making payments of $1100 every three months. The agreed transfer value is $16 500 and interest is 10% compounded annually. If the first payment is due at the date of the agreement, what is the size of the final payment?

11. David Jones has paid $16 000 for a retirement annuity from which he will receive $1375 at the end of every three months. The payments are deferred for ten years and interest is 10% compounded quarterly.
    **(a)** How many payments will David receive?
    **(b)** What is the size of the final payment?

**(c)** How much will David receive in total?

**(d)** How much of what he receives will be interest? Reference Example 14.3D

12. A contract valued at $27 500 requires payments of $6000 every six months. The first payment is due in four years and interest is 11% compounded semi-annually.

**(a)** How many payments are required?

**(b)** What is the size of the last payment?

**(c)** How much will be paid in total?

**(d)** How much of what is paid is interest?

# 14.4 RESIDENTIAL MORTGAGES IN CANADA

## A. Basic concepts and definitions

A **residential mortgage** is a claim to a residential property given by a borrower to a lender as security for the repayment of a loan. It is often the largest amount of money ever borrowed by an individual. The borrower is called the **mortgagor**; the lender is called the **mortgagee**. The **mortgage contract** spells out the obligations of the borrower and the rights of the lender, including the lender's rights in case of default in payment by the borrower. If the borrower is unable to make the mortgage payments, the lender ultimately has the right to dispose of the property under *power of sale* provisions.

To secure legal claim against a residential property, the lender must register the mortgage against the property at the provincial government's land titles office. A **first mortgage** is the first legal claim against a residential property if the mortgage payments cannot be made and the property must be sold. **Equity** in a property is the difference between the property's market value and the total debts, or mortgages, registered against the property. It is possible to have a **second mortgage** on a residential property that is backed by equity in the property, even if there is a first mortgage already registered against the property. If the borrower defaults on the mortgage payments and the property must be sold, the first mortgagee gets paid before the second mortgagee. For this reason, second mortgages are considered riskier investments than first mortgages. They command higher interest rates than first mortgages to compensate for this risk. Home improvement loans, home equity loans, or home equity lines of credit (HELOCs) are often secured by second mortgages. It is even possible to obtain *third mortgages* against residential properties. Third mortgages rank behind first and second mortgages. Thus, they command even higher interest rates.

Financial institutions offer two types of mortgages—fixed-rate mortgages and demand (or variable-rate) mortgages. A **fixed-rate mortgage** is a mortgage for which the rate of interest is fixed for a specific period of time. A **demand** (or **variable-rate**) **mortgage** is a mortgage for which the rate of interest changes as money market conditions change. The interest rate change is usually related to the change in a bank's prime lending rate. Both types of mortgage are usually repaid by equal payments that blend principal and interest. Payments are often required to be made monthly, but some lenders are more flexible and allow semi-monthly, bi-weekly, and even weekly payments.

For all types of mortgages, the amortization period is a part of the mortgage agreement. The amortization period is used to calculate the amount of the blended payments. The most common amortization period is twenty-five years for fixed-rate mortgages and twenty years for demand mortgages. Other amortization periods, such as thirty, fifteen, or ten years, may be used at the discretion of the lender or the borrower.

The *term* of the mortgage specifies the period of time for which the interest rate is fixed. By definition, only fixed-rate mortgages have terms. The term ranges from six months to five years. Longer terms, such as seven and ten years, are becoming available more frequently.

For fixed-rate mortgages, Canadian law dictates that interest must be calculated semi-annually or annually, not in advance. In this context, "not in advance" means that interest is calculated at the end of each six-month or twelve-month period, not at the beginning. It is Canadian practice to calculate fixed-rate mortgage interest semi-annually, not in advance.

Fixed-rate mortgages can be either open or closed. Closed mortgages restrict the borrower's ability to increase payments, make lump-sum payments, change the term of the mortgage, or transfer the mortgage to another lender without penalty. Most closed mortgages contain some prepayment privileges. For example, some mortgages allow a lump-sum payment each year of up to 10% or 15% of the original mortgage principal, usually on the anniversary date of the mortgage. Some lenders permit increases in the periodic payments up to 10% or 15% once each calendar year. Changes in the term or transfers are usually subject to prohibitive penalties.

Open mortgages allow prepayment or repayment of the mortgage at any time without penalty. They are available from most lenders for terms of up to two years. However, interest rates on open mortgages are significantly higher than interest rates on closed mortgages. For a six-month term, the usual charge (i.e., the premium) for an open mortgage is an interest rate at least 0.5% (i.e., 50 basis points) higher than for a closed mortgage. For one-year and two-year terms, the interest rate is usually at least 1.0% (i.e., 100 basis points) higher.

As we stated above, a demand (or variable-rate) mortgage is a mortgage for which the rate of interest changes over time. Interest is calculated on a daily basis. Therefore, demand mortgages are not subject to the legal restriction of compounding semi-annually, not in advance. Demand mortgages also do not have a fixed term, because the interest rate may fluctuate.

## B. CMHC mortgages

Fixed-rate mortgages and demand mortgages are usually available from financial institutions for up to 75% of the value of a property (calculated as the lesser of the purchase price and the appraised value of a property). This means the borrower needs to have at least a 25% down payment for the purchase of a residential property or at least 25% equity in a property. To borrow beyond the 75% level, the mortgage must be insured by the Canada Mortgage and Housing Corporation (CMHC).

**Canada Mortgage and Housing Corporation (CMHC)** is the corporation of the federal government that administers the National Housing Act (NHA) and provides mortgage insurance to lenders. CMHC acts as the insurer for the lender in the event that the borrower defaults on the mortgage payments. Anyone buying a home as a principal residence can qualify as an eligible borrower under certain conditions.

CMHC borrowers must qualify to determine how much they can pay by meeting the two affordability rules:

- First affordability rule: monthly housing costs as a percentage of the gross household monthly income. The maximum **Gross Debt Service (GDS) ratio,** including heating costs, is 32%. (The GDS ratio is the percent of your gross annual income required to cover housing costs such as mortgage payments, property taxes, and heating costs.)

- Second affordability rule: monthly debt load as a percentage of the gross monthly income. The maximum **Total Debt Service (TDS) ratio** is 40%. (The TDS ratio is the percent of your gross annual income required to cover housing costs *and* all other debts and obligations, such as a car loan or lease.)

Although the usual amortization period is twenty-five years, extended amortization periods have recently been introduced, such as thirty and thirty-five years, to further facilitate home ownership.

There is no maximum on the amount of the mortgage loan available, but if the mortgage is insured by CMHC, home buyers may borrow up to 95% of the purchase price. The borrower must pay the insurance premium to CMHC as a single lump-sum or as an amount added to the mortgage payment.

CMHC insurance premiums depend on the ratio determined when the amount of the financing required is compared to the maximum home price. For example, a home buyer purchasing a $200 000 home with a $40 000 or 20% down payment needs to borrow $160 000 or 80% of the maximum home price.

The current insurance premiums are as follows:

| | |
|---|---|
| Up to and including 65% | 0.50% of loan amount |
| Up to and including 75% | 0.65% of loan amount |
| Up to and including 80% | 1.00% of loan amount |
| Up to and including 85% | 1.75% of loan amount |
| Up to and including 90% | 2.00% of loan amount |
| Between 90.01 and 95% | 2.75% of loan amount |

**EXAMPLE 14.4A** The Wongs want to purchase a home in Vancouver with a CMHC-approved mortgage. They have qualified under the affordability rules, and the house that they have chosen is valued at $450 000. They have saved enough to meet the 5% down payment rule, and will have to pay mortgage loan insurance at 2.75% of the mortgage balance. According to the CMHC terms and conditions, determine the maximum initial mortgage balance if the Wongs want the insurance premium added to the maximum allowable loan balance.

**SOLUTION**

The maximum CMHC loan balance = 95% of $450 000 = $427 500;

the insurance premium = 2.75% of $427 500 = $11 756.25;

the maximum initial mortgage balance = $427 500.00 + $11 756.25 = $439 256.25.

## C. Computing the effective rate of interest for fixed-rate mortgages

For residential mortgages, Canadian legislation requires the rate of interest charged by the lender to be calculated annually or semi-annually, not in advance. The fixed rates advertised, posted, or quoted by lenders are usually nominal annual rates. To meet the legislated requirements, the applicable nominal annual rate of interest must be converted into the equivalent effective rate of interest per payment period.

This is done as explained in Section 12.1A by using Formula 12.1.

$$p = (1 + i)^c - 1$$

where $p$ = the effective rate of interest per payment period

where $i$ = the rate per conversion period

$$c = \frac{\text{THE NUMBER OF INTEREST CONVERSION PERIODS PER YEAR}}{\text{THE NUMBER OF PAYMENT PERIODS PER YEAR}}$$

Note that when using the BAII Plus financial calculator, this means that the $c$ in the formula above can be derived by dividing the C/Y by the P/Y.

The prevailing practice is semi-annual compounding and monthly payment for most mortgages. For most mortgages (with semi-annual compounding and monthly payment),

$$c = \frac{2 \text{ (compounding periods per year)}}{12 \text{ (payments per year)}} = \frac{1}{6}$$

**EXAMPLE 14.4B**

Suppose a financial institution posted the interest rates for closed mortgages shown below. The interest is compounded semi-annually and the mortgages require monthly payments.

| Term | Interest Rate |
|------|---------------|
| 6 months | 5.25% |
| 1 year | 5.50% |
| 2 years | 6.50% |
| 3 years | 7.00% |
| 4 years | 7.25% |
| 5 years | 7.50% |

Compute the effective rate of interest per payment period for each term.

**SOLUTION**

$$c = \frac{1}{6}; \quad p = (1 + i)^{\frac{1}{6}} - 1$$

For the six-month term, $i = \dfrac{5.25\%}{2} = 2.625\% = 0.02625$

$$p = (1 + 0.02625)^{\frac{1}{6}} - 1$$
$$= 1.004328 - 1$$
$$= 1.004328, \text{ or } 0.4328\%$$

For the one year term, $i = \dfrac{5.50\%}{2} = 2.75\% = 0.0275$

$$p = (1.0275)^{\frac{1}{6}} - 1 = 0.004532 = 0.4532\%$$

You can obtain the effective rates using a preprogrammed financial calculator by using the function keys as follows:

("END" mode) (Set P/Y = 1; C/Y = 1) [ 2nd ] (CLR TVM) 1 [ ± ] [ PV ]

$$\frac{1}{6} = 0.166667 \; [ \; \textbf{N} \; ] \quad \text{(enter applicable interest rate)}$$

[ **I/Y** ] [ **CPT** ] [ **FV** ]   | Display Shows $(1 + p)$ |

For the two-year term, $i = 3.25\% = 0.0325$; $p = (1.0325^{\frac{1}{6}}) - 1 = 0.005345 = 0.5345\%$

[ 2nd ] (CLR TVM) 1 [ ± ] [ PV ] 0.166667 [ N ]

3.25 [ **I/Y** ] [ **CPT** ] [ **FV** ]  [ 1.005345 ]

$p = 0.5345\%$

(Note that if you perform these calculations in succession, you do not have to key in PV and N each time.)

For the three-year term, $i = 3.5\% = 0.035$; $p = (1.035^{\frac{1}{6}}) - 1$
$$= 0.00575 = 0.575\%$$

[ 2nd ] (CLR TVM) 1 [ ± ] [ PV ] 0.166667 [ N ]

3.5 [ **I/Y** ] [ **CPT** ] [ **FV** ]  [ 1.005750 ]

$p = 0.5750\%$

For the four-year term, $i = 3.625\% = 0.03625$; $p = (1.03625^{\frac{1}{6}}) - 1$
$$= 0.00592 = 0.5952\%$$

[ 2nd ] (CLR TVM) 1 [ ± ] [ PV ] 0.166667 [ N ]

3.625 [ **I/Y** ] [ **CPT** ] [ **FV** ]  [ 1.005952 ]

$p = 0.5952\%$

For the five-year term, $i = 3.75\% = 0.0375$; $p = (1.0375^{\frac{1}{6}}) - 1$
$= 0.00615 = 0.6155\%$

2nd (CLR TVM) 1 ± PV 0.166667 N

3.75 I/Y CPT FV 1.006155

$p = 0.6155\%$

## D. Computing mortgage payments and balances

Blended residential mortgage payments are ordinary general annuities. Therefore, Formula 12.3 applies.

$$PV_{nc} = PMT\left[\frac{1 - (1 + p)^{-n}}{p}\right], \text{ where } p = (1 + i)^c - 1 \quad\text{———Formula 11.5}$$

The periodic payment PMT is calculated using the method shown in Section 12.3.

**EXAMPLE 14.4C**

A mortgage for $120 000 is amortized over 25 years. Interest is 7.5% p.a., compounded semi-annually, for a five-year term and payments are monthly.

(i) Compute the monthly payment.
(ii) Compute the balance at the end of the five-year term.
(iii) Compute the monthly payment if the mortgage is renewed for a four-year term at 7.0% compounded semi-annually.

**SOLUTION**

(i) When computing the monthly payment, $n$ is the total number of payments in the amortization period. The term for which the rate of interest is fixed (in this case, five years) does *not* enter into this calculation.

$PV_{nc} = 120\ 000.00$; $\quad n = 12(25) = 300$; $\quad P/Y = 12$; $\quad C/Y = 2$;

$I/Y = 7.5$; $\quad i = \dfrac{7.5\%}{2} = 3.75\%$; $\quad c = \dfrac{1}{6}$

We must first compute the effective monthly rate of interest.

$p = (1.0375)^{\frac{1}{6}} - 1 = 1.006155 - 1 = 0.006155 = 0.06155\%$

$$120\ 000.00 = PMT\left(\frac{1 - (1.006155)^{-300}}{0.006155}\right) \quad\text{——— using Formula 12.3}$$

$120\ 000.00 = PMT\ (136.695138)$

$PMT = \$877.87$

**Programmed Solution**

("END" mode) (Set P/Y = 12; C/Y = 2) 0 FV 120 000 ± PV 7.5 I/Y

300 N CPT PMT 877.865900

The monthly payment for the original five-year term is $877.87.

(ii) The balance at the end of the five-year term is the present value of the outstanding payments. After five years, 60 of the required 300 payments have been made; 240 payments remain outstanding. Note that the payment has been rounded to the nearest cent.

$$PMT = 877.87; \quad n = 240; \quad p = 0.6155\%$$

$$PV_{nc} = 877.87\left(\frac{1 - (1.006155)^{-240}}{0.006155}\right) \quad \text{——using Formula 11.5}$$

$$= 877.87(125.218804)$$

$$= \$109\ 925.83$$

**Programmed Solution**

0 | FV | 877.87 | ± | PMT | 240 | N | 7.5 | I/Y | CPT | PV | 109925.8315

The mortgage balance at the end of the first five-year term is $109 925.83.

(iii) For the renewed term, the starting principal is the balance at the end of the five-year term. The amortization period is the number of years remaining after the initial term. We must recalculate $p$ for the new interest rate.

$$PV_{nc} = 109\ 925.83; \quad n = 12(20) = 240; \quad I/Y = 7; \quad i = 3.5\%$$

$$p = (1.035)^{\frac{1}{6}} - 1 = 1.00575 - 1 = 0.00575 = 0.575\%$$

$$109\ 925.83 = PMT\left(\frac{1 - (1.00575)^{-240}}{0.00575}\right)$$

$$109\ 925.83 = PMT(129.986504)$$

$$PMT = \$845.67$$

**Programmed Solution**

0 | FV | 109 925.83 | ± | PV | 7 | I/Y

240 | N | CPT | PMT | 845.671102

The monthly payment for the renewed four-year term is $845.67.

## E. Rounded payments

Mortgage payments are sometimes rounded up to an exact cent or dollar value (such as to the next cent, the next dollar, or the next ten dollars). The payment calculation of $845.671102 might be rounded up to $845.68 or $850 or even $900. Rounded payments up to a higher value will result in a lower balance at the end of the term. In the final renewal term, rounding will affect the size of the final payment.

**EXAMPLE 14.4D**

A mortgage balance of \$17 321.50 is renewed for the remaining amortization period of three years at 8% compounded semi-annually.

(i) Compute the size of the monthly payments.
(ii) Determine the size of the last payment if the payments computed in part (i) have been rounded up to the next cent.
(iii) Determine the size of the last payment if the payments computed in part (i) have been rounded up to the next ten dollars.

**SOLUTION**

(i) $PV_{nc} = 17\ 321.50$; $n = 12(3) = 36$; $P/Y = 12$; $C/Y = 2$; $I/Y = 8$;

$i = 4\%$; $c = \dfrac{1}{6}$

$p = (1.04)^{\frac{1}{6}} - 1 = 1.006558 - 1 = 0.6558\%$

$17\ 321.50 = PMT\left(\dfrac{1 - (1.006558)^{-36}}{0.006558}\right)$

$17\ 321.05 = PMT\,(31.973037)$

$PMT = \$541.75$

**Programmed Solution**

("END" mode) (Set P/Y = 12; C/Y = 2) 0 [ FV ] 17 321.50 [ ± ] [ PV ] 8 [ I/Y ]

36 [ N ] [ CPT ] [ PMT ] [ 541.75335 ]

The monthly payment is \$541.75.

(ii) If payments are rounded up to \$541.76, the last payment will be less than a full payment. To calculate the size of the last payment we need to determine the number of payments of \$541.76 that are required to amortize the loan balance.

$PV_{nc} = 17\ 321.50$; $PMT = 541.76$; $p = 0.6558\%$

$17\ 321.50 = 541.76\left(\dfrac{1 - (1.006558)^{-n}}{0.006558}\right)$

$0.209683 = 1 - 1.006558^{-n}$

$1.006558^{-n} = 0.790317$

$-n(\ln 1.006558) = \ln 0.790317$

$-n(0.006537) = -0.235321$

$n = 35.999502$

**Programmed Solution**

0 [ FV ] 17 321.50 [ ± ] [ PV ] 8 [ I/Y ]

541.76 [ PMT ] [ CPT ] [ N ] [ 35.999502 ]

There will be 35 payments of \$541.76 and a final payment smaller than \$541.76. We need to determine the balance after the 35th payment.

$$PMT = 541.76; \quad n = 0.999502; \quad p = 0.6558\%$$

$$PV_{nc} = 541.76\left(\frac{1 - (1.006558)^{-0.999502}}{0.006558}\right)$$

$$= 541.76(0.992991)$$

$$= \$537.96$$

### Programmed Solution

$$0 \; \boxed{FV} \quad 541.76 \; \boxed{\pm} \quad \boxed{PMT} \; 8 \; \boxed{I/Y} \quad 0.999502 \; \boxed{N}$$

$$\boxed{CPT} \; \boxed{PV} \quad \boxed{537.963017}$$

The final payment includes interest on the balance of \$537.96.
Final payment = 537.96(1.006558) = \$541.49.

(iii) If payments are rounded to \$550, the last payment will be less than \$550. To calculate the size of the last payment we need to determine the number of payments of \$550 that are required to amortize the loan balance.

$$PV_{nc} = 17\ 321.50; \quad PMT = 550.00; \quad p = 0.6558\%$$

$$17\ 321.50 = 550.00\left(\frac{1 - (1.006558)^{-n}}{0.006558}\right)$$

$$0.206541 = 1 - 1.006558^{-n}$$

$$1.006558^{-n} = 0.793459$$

$$-n(\ln 1.006558) = \ln 0.793459$$

$$-n(0.006537) = -0.231354$$

$$n = 35.392625$$

### Programmed Solution

$$0 \; \boxed{FV} \quad 17\ 321.50 \; \boxed{\pm} \quad \boxed{PV} \; 8 \; \boxed{I/Y} \quad 550 \; \boxed{PMT} \; \boxed{CPT} \; \boxed{N} \quad \boxed{35.392625}$$

There will be 35 payments of \$550 and a final payment smaller than \$550. We need to determine the balance after the 35th payment.

$$PMT = 550.00; \quad n = 0.392625; \quad p = 0.6558\%$$

$$PV_{nc} = 550.00\left(\frac{1 - (1.006558)^{-0.392625}}{0.006558}\right)$$

$$= 550.00(0.390842)$$

$$= \$214.96$$

**Programmed Solution**

0 [ FV ] 550.00 [ ± ] [ PMT ] 8 [ I/Y ] 0.392625 [ N ]

[ CPT ] [ PV ] [ 214.963019 ]

The final payment includes interest on the balance of $214.96.
Final payment = 214.96(1.006558) = $216.37.

## ≫ BUSINESS MATH NEWS BOX

### How to Have a Million-Dollar Baby

If you're about to experience the miracle of birth in your household, consider doing this—get your spouse and all the grandparents together in one room and shake out everybody's pockets and purses to come up with $7000. That's a stretch, I know—but if you can find $7000 and put it in a non-registered investment when your new child is born, your baby will retire a millionaire.

Sounds like smoke and mirrors, doesn't it? Well, it is magic of a sort—the magic of compounding.

Albert Einstein, who knew a lot about math, is reported to have claimed that compounding was the greatest mathematical discovery of all time. And it certainly is true that compounding is a basic investing strategy—a concept that, when used correctly, can make an investor wealthy. Interest can be very interesting—and financially fantastic!

There are two ways to earn interest on money:

• Simple interest is a rate of interest applied only to principal (the amount of money originally invested). Any interest earned does not become part of the principal.

• Compound interest is interest earned on interest. It is calculated not only on the principal investment, but also on the interest that has been generated. This is the key to the magic of compounding because, over time, the interest on interest (also known as accumulated reinvested interest) adds tremendously to investment growth.

The key to success—start early and stay invested. The key to compounding is time. The longer you leave your investment alone, the more powerful the effect of compound interest. And the earlier you start your investment, the more you make from compound interest.

*Source:* "How to have a million-dollar baby," Investors Group Financial Services Inc. *The Guardian*, Charlottetown, P.E.I., August 20, 2005, p.B7. This column, written and published by Investors Group Financial Services Inc. (in Quebec – a Financial Services Firm), presents general information only and is not a solicitation to buy or sell any investments. For more information on this topic please contact your Investors Group Consultant.

### QUESTIONS

1. If you invested $7000 in a plan for sixty-five years, what is the rate of return required to reach the $1 000 000 benchmark? Assume interest is compounded annually.

2. **a.** Assume $1000 was initially invested at birth to age twenty-five years at a rate of 2.9% compounded quarterly. From age 26 to 65 years, what monthly payments are required to reach the $1 000 000 benchmark? Assume a 6.6% interest compounded semi-annually.

   **b.** Calculate the effects of monthly payments made at the beginning of the month versus the end of the month on this calculation.

## F. Mortgage statement

Currently, when financial institutions record monthly mortgage payments, they calculate interest for the exact number of days that have elapsed since the last payment. This is done by multiplying the effective monthly rate of interest by 12 to convert it into a simple annual rate of interest. The annual rate is then multiplied by the number of days expressed as a fraction of 365.

For example, $p = 0.6558\%$ becomes the simple annual interest rate $12(0.6558\%) = 7.86984\%$.

This approach takes into account that the number of days elapsed between payments fluctuates depending on the number of days in a particular month. It also allows for fluctuations in receiving payments, and permits semi-monthly, bi-weekly, or weekly payments for mortgages requiring contractual monthly payments.

**EXAMPLE 14.4E**

A credit union member made the contractual mortgage payment of $725 on May 31, leaving a mortgage loan balance of $75 411.79. The effective monthly fixed rate was 0.5345%. The member made the contractual payments on June 28, July 31, August 30, September 30, October 29, November 28, and December 30. The credit union agreed to convert the fixed-rate mortgage to a demand mortgage on October 29 at 5.25% compounded annually. This rate was changed to 4.75% on December 2. Determine the mortgage balance on December 30.

**SOLUTION**

The monthly effective rate $p = 0.5345\%$ is equivalent to the simple annual rate $12(0.5345\%) = 6.4136\%$.

| Payment Date | Number of Days | Amount Paid | Interest Paid | Principal | Balance Repaid |
|---|---|---|---|---|---|
| May 31 | rate is 6.4136% | | | | 75 411.79 |
| June 28 | 28 | 725.00 | 371.03 | 353.97 | 75 057.82 |
| July 31 | 33 | 725.00 | 435.23 | 289.77 | 74 768.05 |
| August 30 | 30 | 725.00 | 394.14 | 330.86 | 74 437.19 |
| September 30 | 31 | 725.00 | 405.47 | 319.53 | 74 117.66 |
| October 29 | 29 | 725.00 | 377.69 | 347.31 | 73 770.35 |
| October 29 | rate becomes 5.25% | | | | |
| November 28 | 30 | 725.00 | 318.32 | 406.68 | 73 363.67 |
| December 2 | rate becomes 4.75% | | | | |
| December 30 | 32 | 725.00 | 309.54* | 415.46 | 72 948.21 |

*__Note:__ Interest calculation for December is

| | |
|---|---|
| 4 days at 5.25% on $73 363.67 | $ 42.21 |
| 28 days at 4.75% on $73 363.67 | 267.33 |
| TOTAL | $309.54 |

**EXAMPLE 14.4F**

A mortgage of $55 000 closed on April 12, amortized over 15 years at 8.50% compounded semi-annually for a five-year term. It requires contractual monthly payments rounded up to the nearest $10. The lender agreed to accept bi-weekly payments of half the contractual monthly amount starting April 24. The mortgagor's second June payment was three days late.

   (i) Determine the size of the contractual monthly payment.
  (ii) Produce a mortgage statement to June 30.
 (iii) Compute the accrued interest on June 30.

**SOLUTION**

(i) $PV_{nc} = 55\,000.00; \quad n = 12(15) = 180; \quad i = 4.25; \quad c = \dfrac{1}{6}$

$$p = (1.0425)^{\frac{1}{6}} - 1 = 1.006961 - 1 = 0.006961\%$$

$$55\,000.00 = PMT\left(\frac{1 - 1.006961^{-180}}{0.006961}\right)$$

$$55\,000.00 = PMT(102.44)$$

$$PMT = \$536.89$$

The contractual monthly payment is $540.

 (ii) The bi-weekly payment is $270.
     The annual rate of interest is $12(0.6961) = 8.3533\%$.

| Payment Date | Number of Days | Amount Paid | Interest Paid | Principal | Balance Repaid |
|---|---|---|---|---|---|
| April 12 | | | | | 55 000.00 |
| April 24 | 12 | 270.00 | 151.05 | 118.95 | 54 881.05 |
| May 8 | 14 | 270.00 | 175.84 | 94.16 | 54 786.89 |
| May 22 | 14 | 270.00 | 175.54 | 94.46 | 54 692.43 |
| June 5 | 14 | 270.00 | 175.24 | 94.76 | 54 597.67 |
| June 22 | 17 | 270.00 | 212.42 | 57.58 | 54 540.09 |

The mortgage balance on June 30 is $54 540.09.

(iii) On June 30 interest has accrued for 8 days.

$$\text{The amount of accrued interest} = 54\,540.09(0.083533)\left(\frac{8}{365}\right) = \$99.86.$$

## EXERCISE 14.4

If you choose, you can use Excel's **NPER, PMT, PV,** or **RATE** functions or **Template4** to answer the questions indicated below. Refer to the Spreadsheet Template Disk to find **Template4** or to learn how to use these Excel functions.

**A.** Answer each of the following questions.

1. A $90 000 mortgage is to be amortized by making monthly payments for 25 years. Interest is 8.5% compounded semi-annually for a five-year term.
   (a) Compute the size of the monthly payment.
   (b) Determine the balance at the end of the five-year term.
   (c) If the mortgage is renewed for a three-year term at 7% compounded semi-annually, what is the size of the monthly payment for the renewal term? *Reference Example 14.4C*

2. A demand (variable-rate) mortgage of $150 000 is amortized over 20 years by equal monthly payments. After 18 months the original interest rate of 6% p.a. was raised to 6.6% p.a. Two years after the mortgage was taken out, it was renewed at the request of the mortgagor at a fixed rate of 7.5% compounded semi-annually for a four-year term.
   (a) Calculate the mortgage balance after 18 months.
   (b) Compute the size of the new monthly payment at the 6.6% rate of interest.
   (c) Determine the mortgage balance at the end of the four-year term.

3. A $40 000 mortgage is to be repaid over a ten-year period by monthly payments rounded up to the next-higher $50. Interest is 9% compounded semi-annually.
   (a) Determine the number of rounded payments required to repay the mortgage.
   (b) Determine the size of the last payment.
   (c) Calculate the amount of interest saved by rounding the payments up to the next-higher $50. *Reference Example 14.4D*

4. A mortgage balance of $23 960 is to be repaid over a seven-year term by equal monthly payments at 11% compounded semi-annually. At the request of the mortgagor, the monthly payments were set at $440.
   (a) How many payments will the mortgagor have to make?
   (b) What is the size of the last payment?
   (c) Determine the difference between the total actual amount paid and the total amount required to amortize the mortgage by the contractual monthly payments.

5. A mortgage of $80 000 is amortized over 15 years by monthly payments of $826.58. What is the nominal annual rate of interest compounded semi-annually?

6. At what nominal annual rate of interest will a $195 000 demand (variable-rate) mortgage be amortized by monthly payments of $1606.87 over 20 years?

7. Interest for the initial four-year term of a $105 000 mortgage is 7.25% compounded semi-annually. The mortgage is to be repaid by equal monthly payments over 20 years. The mortgage contract permits lump-sum payments at each anniversary date up to 10% of the original principal.
   (a) What is the balance at the end of the four-year term if a lump-sum payment of $7000 is made at the end of the third year?

**(b)** How many more payments will be required after the four-year term if there is no change in the interest rate?
   **(c)** What is the difference in the cost of the mortgage if no lump-sum payment is made?

8. The Berezins agreed to monthly payments rounded up to the nearest $100 on a mortgage of $36 000 amortized over ten years. Interest for the first five years was 8.75% compounded semi-annually. After 30 months, as permitted by the mortgage agreement, the Berezins increased the rounded monthly payment by 10%.
   **(a)** Determine the mortgage balance at the end of the five-year term.
   **(b)** If the interest rate remains unchanged over the remaining term, how many more of the increased payments will amortize the mortgage balance?
   **(c)** How much did the Berezins save by exercising the increase-in-payment option?

9. A $40 000 mortgage taken out on June 1 is to be repaid by monthly payments rounded up to the nearest $10. The payments are due on the first day of each month starting July 1. The amortization period is 12 years and interest is 5.5% compounded semi-annually for a six-month term. Construct an amortization schedule for the six-month term. Reference Example 14.4E

10. For Question 9, produce the mortgage statement for the six-month term. Assume all payments have been made on time. Compare the balance to the balance in Question 9 and explain why there may be a difference.

11. For the mortgage in Question 9, develop a mortgage statement for the six-month term if semi-monthly payments equal to one-half of the monthly payment are made on the first day and the 16th day of each month. The first payment is due June 16. Compare the balance to the balances in Question 9 and Question 10. Explain why there are differences.

12. For the mortgage in Question 9, develop a mortgage statement for the six-month term if bi-weekly payments equal to one-half of the rounded monthly payments are made starting June 16. Compare the balance to the balances in Questions 9, 10, and 11. Explain why it differs significantly from the other three balances.

Go to MyMathLab at www.mathxl.com. You can practise many of this chapter's exercises as often as you want. The guided solutions help you find an answer step by step. You'll find a personalized study plan available to you too!

## Review Exercise

1. Sylvie Cardinal bought a business for $45 000. She made a down payment of $10 000 and agreed to repay the balance by equal payments at the end of every three months for eight years. Interest is 8% compounded quarterly.

   (a) What is the size of the quarterly payments?

   (b) What will be the total cost of financing?

   (c) How much will Sylvie owe after five years?

   (d) How much interest will be included in the 20th payment?

   (e) How much of the principal will be repaid by the 24th payment?

   (f) Construct a partial amortization schedule showing details of the first three payments, Payments 10, 11, 12, the last three payments, and totals.

2. Angelo Lemay borrowed $8000 from his credit union. He agreed to repay the loan by making equal monthly payments for five years. Interest is 9% compounded monthly.

   (a) What is the size of the monthly payments?

   (b) How much will the loan cost him?

   (c) How much will Angelo owe after eighteen months?

   (d) How much interest will he pay in his 36th payment?

   (e) How much of the principal will be repaid by the 48th payment?

   (f) Prepare a partial amortization schedule showing details of the first three payments, Payments 24, 25, 26, the last three payments, and totals.

3. Comfort Swim Limited borrowed $40 000 for replacement of equipment. The debt is repaid in installments of $2000 made at the end of every three months.

   (a) If interest is 7% compounded quarterly, how many payments are needed?

   (b) How much will Comfort Swim owe after two years?

   (c) How much of the 12th payment is interest?

   (d) How much of the principal will be repaid by the 20th payment?

   (e) Construct a partial amortization schedule showing details of the first three payments, the last three payments, and totals.

4. A $48 000 mortgage amortized by monthly payments over 35 years is renewable after five years. Interest is 9% compounded semi-annually.

   (a) What is the size of the monthly payments?

   (b) How much interest is paid during the first year?

   (c) How much of the principal is repaid during the first five-year term?

   (d) If the mortgage is renewed for a further five-year term at 8% compounded semi-annually, what will be the size of the monthly payments?

   (e) Construct a partial amortization schedule showing details of the first three payments for each of the two five-year terms, the last three payments for the second five-year term, and totals at the end of the second five-year term.

5. Pelican Recreational Services owes $27 500 secured by a collateral mortgage. The mortgage is amortized over fifteen years by equal payments made at the end of every three months and is renewable after three years.

   (a) If interest is 7% compounded annually, what is the size of the payments?

   (b) How much of the principal is repaid by the fourth payment?

   (c) What is the balance at the end of the three-year term?

   (d) If the mortgage is renewed for a further four years but amortized over eight years and interest is 7.5% compounded semi-annually, what is the size of the quarterly payments for the renewal period?

(e) Construct a partial amortization schedule showing details of the first three payments for each of the two terms, the last three payments in the four-year term, and totals at the end of the four-year term.

6. A debt of $17 500 is repaid by payments of $2850 made at the end of each year. Interest is 8% compounded semi-annually.

   (a) How many payments are needed to repay the debt?

   (b) What is the cost of the debt for the first three years?

   (c) What is the principal repaid in the fifth year?

   (d) Construct an amortization schedule showing details of the first three payments, the last three payments, and totals.

7. A debt of $25 000 is repaid by payments of $3500 made at the end of every six months. Interest is 11% compounded semi-annually.

   (a) How many payments are needed to repay the debt?

   (b) What is the size of the final payment?

8. Jane Evans receives payments of $900 at the beginning of each month from a pension fund of $72 500. Interest earned by the fund is 6.30% compounded monthly.

   (a) What is the number of payments Jane will receive?

   (b) What is the size of the final payment?

9. A lease agreement valued at $33 000 requires payment of $4300 every three months in advance. The payments are deferred for three years and money is worth 10% compounded quarterly.

   (a) How many lease payments are to be made under the contract?

   (b) What is the size of the final lease payment?

10. A contract worth $52 000 provides benefits of $20 000 at the end of each year. The benefits are deferred for ten years and interest is 11% compounded quarterly.

    (a) How many payments are to be made under the contract?

    (b) What is the size of the last benefit payment?

11. A mortgage for $135 000 is amortized over 25 years. Interest is 8.7% p.a., compounded semi-annually, for a five-year term and payments are monthly.

    (a) Compute the monthly payment.

    (b) Compute the balance at the end of the five-year term.

    (c) Compute the monthly payment if the mortgage is renewed for a three-year term at 7.8% compounded semi-annually.

12. A $180 000 mortgage is to be amortized by making monthly payments for 25 years. Interest is 7.9% compounded semi-annually for a four-year term.

    (a) Compute the size of the monthly payment.

    (b) Determine the balance at the end of the four-year term.

    (c) If the mortgage is renewed for a five-year term at 8.8% compounded semi-annually, what is the size of the monthly payment for the renewal term?

13. An $80 000 mortgage is to be repaid over a 10-year period by monthly payments rounded up to the next-higher $50. Interest is 8.5% compounded semi-annually.

    (a) What is the number of rounded payments required to repay the mortgage?

    (b) What is the size of the last payment?

    (c) How much interest was saved by rounding the payments up to the next-higher $50?

14. A $160 000 mortgage is to be repaid over a 20-year period by monthly payments rounded up to the next-higher $100. Interest is 9.2% compounded semi-annually.

    (a) Determine the number of rounded payments required to repay the mortgage.

    (b) Determine the size of the last payment.

(c) Calculate the amount of interest saved by rounding the payments up to the next-higher $100.

15. A debt of $6500 is repaid in equal monthly installments over four years. Interest is 9% compounded monthly.

(a) What is the size of the monthly payments?

(b) What will be the total cost of borrowing?

(c) What is the outstanding balance after one year?

(d) How much of the 30th payment is interest?

(e) Construct a partial amortization schedule showing details of the first three payments, the last three payments, and totals.

16. Milton Investments borrowed $32 000 at 11% compounded semi-annually. The loan is repaid by payments of $4500 due at the end of every six months.

(a) How many payments are needed?

(b) How much of the principal will be repaid by the fifth payment?

(c) Prepare a partial amortization schedule showing the details of the last three payments and totals.

17. A mortgage of $95 000 is amortized over 25 years by monthly payments of $748.06. What is the nominal annual rate of interest compounded semi-annually?

18. At what nominal annual rate of interest will a $135 000 mortgage be amortized by monthly payments of $1370.69 over 15 years?

19. A $28 000 mortgage is amortized by quarterly payments over twenty years. The mortgage is renewable after three years and interest is 6% compounded semi-annually.

(a) What is the size of the quarterly payments?

(b) How much interest will be paid during the first year?

(c) What is the balance at the end of the three-year term?

(d) If the mortgage is renewed for another three years at 7% compounded annually, what will be the size of the quarterly payments for the renewal period?

20. The Superior Tool Company is repaying a debt of $16 000 by payments of $1000 made at the end of every three months. Interest is 7.5% compounded monthly.

(a) How many payments are needed to repay the debt?

(b) What is the size of the final payment?

## Self-Test

1. A $9000 loan is repaid by equal monthly payments over five years. What is the outstanding balance after two years if interest is 12% compounded monthly?

2. A loan of $15 000 is repaid by quarterly payments of $700 each at 8% compounded quarterly. What is the principal repaid by the 25th payment?

3. A $50 000 mortgage is amortized by monthly payments over twenty years. If interest is 9% compounded semi-annually, how much interest will be paid during the first three years?

4. A debt of $24 000 is repaid by quarterly payments of $1100. If interest is 6% compounded quarterly, what is the size of the final payment?

**5.** A $190 000 mortgage is to be amortized by making monthly payments for 20 years. Interest is 6.5% compounded semi-annually for a three-year term.
   **(a)** Compute the size of the monthly payment.
   **(b)** Determine the balance at the end of the three-year term.
   **(c)** If the mortgage is renewed for a five-year term at 7.25% compounded semi-annually, what is the size of the monthly payment for the renewal term?

**6.** A $140 000 mortgage is to be repaid over a 15-year period by monthly payments rounded up to the next-higher $50. Interest is 8.25% compounded semi-annually.
   **(a)** Determine the number of rounded payments required to repay the mortgage.
   **(b)** Determine the size of the last payment.
   **(c)** Calculate the amount of interest saved by rounding the payments up to the next-higher $50.

**7.** A mortgage of $145 000 is amortized over 25 years by monthly payments of $1297. What is the nominal annual rate of interest compounded semi-annually?

**8.** A loan of $12 000 is amortized over ten years by equal monthly payments at 7.5% compounded monthly. Construct an amortization schedule showing details of the first three payments, the fortieth payment, the last three payments, and totals.

## Challenge Problems

**1.** A debt is amortized by monthly payments of $250. Interest is 8% compounded monthly. If the outstanding balance is $3225.68 just after a particular payment (say, the $x$th payment), what was the balance just after the previous payment (i.e., the $(x - 1)$th payment)?

**2.** Captain Sinclair has been posted to Cold Lake, Alberta. He prefers to purchase a condo rather than live on the base. He knows that in four years he will be posted overseas. The condo he wishes to purchase will require a mortgage of $130 000, and he has narrowed his choices to two lenders. Trust Company A is offering a five-year mortgage at 6.75% compounded semi-annually. This mortgage can be paid off at any time but there is a penalty clause in the agreement requiring two months' interest on the remaining principal. Trust Company B is offering a five-year mortgage for 7% compounded semi-annually. It can be paid off at any time without penalty. Both mortgages are amortized over 25 years and require monthly payments. Captain Sinclair will have to sell his condo in four years and pay off the mortgage at that time before moving overseas. Given that he expects to earn 3% compounded annually on his money over the next five years, which mortgage offer is cheaper? By how much is it cheaper?

# Case Study 14.1 Managing a Mortgage

» Malcolm and Shannon purchased their first apartment with a $180 000 mortgage. Their five-year mortgage had a 7.5% semi-annually compounded interest rate, and was amortized over 25 years. Payments were made monthly.

After three years, interest rates had fallen. Malcolm and Shannon considered that they should pay out the old mortgage (in spite of the interest penalties), and negotiate a new mortgage at the lower rate. They met with the loans officer at their bank, who laid out the options for them.

Interest on mortgages with a five-year term was 5.5% compounded semi-annually, the lowest rate in many years. The loans officer had informed Malcolm and Shannon that there is a penalty for renegotiating a mortgage early, before the end of the current term. According to their mortgage contract, the penalty for renegotiating the mortgage before the end of the five-year term is the greater of:

**A.** Three months' interest at the original rate of interest. (Banks generally calculate this as one month's interest on the mortgage principal remaining to be paid, multiplied by three.)

**B.** The interest differential over the remainder of the original term. (Banks generally calculate this as the difference between the interest the bank would have earned over the remainder of the original term at the original [higher] mortgage rate and at the renegotiated [lower] mortgage rate.)

The loans officer also explained that there are two options for paying the penalty amount: (1) you can pay the full amount of the penalty at the beginning of the new mortgage period or (2) the penalty amount can be added to the principal when the mortgage is renegotiated, allowing the penalty to be paid off over the term of the new mortgage.

Malcolm and Shannon agreed to look at their options before giving the loans officer their final decision.

## QUESTIONS

1. Suppose there was no penalty for refinancing the mortgage after three years. How much would Malcolm and Shannon save per month by refinancing their mortgage for a five-year term at the new rate?

2. Suppose the couple choose to refinance their mortgage for a five-year term at the new interest rate.
   (a) What is the amount of penalty A?
   (b) What is the amount of penalty B?
   (c) What penalty would Malcolm and Shannon have to pay in this situation?

3. If they pay the full amount of the penalty at the beginning of the new five-year term, what will Malcolm and Shannon's new monthly payment be?

4. If the penalty amount is added to the principal when the mortgage is renegotiated, what will the new monthly payment be?

# Case Study 14.2 Steering the Business

» On March 1, 2006, Sandra and her friend Francisco arranged a loan to purchase two used black limousines for $28 000 and $35 000 respectively, and launched their new business, Classy Limousine Services. The loan was for four years at 9.5% compounded semi-annually. Payments were made quarterly beginning on March 1, 2006.

Business was brisk, especially for weddings. To meet the demand, the partners bought a new stretch limousine on August 1, 2006 for $90 000. They arranged a five-year loan for this amount at 8.8% interest compounded monthly. Payments were made monthly beginning on August 1, 2006.

On September 1, 2006, the partners were given an opportunity to buy a black super-stretch limousine for $120 000. They arranged a two-year loan for this amount at 7.8% interest compounded monthly. The monthly payments began on September 1, 2006.

Business continued to increase. Sandra and Francisco discussed the need for a new parking garage and office space they could own instead of rent. When an industrial warehouse large enough to house their expanding fleet became available, they decided to purchase it. The $475 000 mortgage had an interest rate of 8.9% compounded semi-annually for a five-year term. It was amortized over 20 years, and the end-of-month mortgage payments began on March 1, 2007.

## QUESTIONS

1. What are the quarterly payments for the original loan obtained on March 1, 2005?

2. What are the monthly payments for the loan on the stretch limousine?

3. What are the monthly payments for the loan on the black super-stretch limousine?

4. (a) What are the monthly payments required for the mortgage on the warehouse?

   (b) What principal will remain to be paid at the end of the mortgage's five-year term?

## SUMMARY OF FORMULAS

No new formulas were introduced in this chapter. However, some of the formulas introduced in Chapters 9 to 12 have been used, namely Formulas 9.1A, 11.2, 11.5, 12.1, 12.2, 12.3, and 12.5.

## GLOSSARY

**Amortization**   repayment of both interest and principal of interest-bearing debts by a series of equal payments made at equal intervals of time *(p. 570)*

**Amortization schedule**   a schedule showing in detail how a debt is repaid *(p. 571)*

**Canada Mortgage and Housing Corporation (CMHC)**   the corporation of the federal government that administers the National Housing Act (NHA) and provides mortgage insurance to lenders *(p. 609)*

**Demand mortgage**    a mortgage for which the rate of interest changes as money market conditions change *(p. 608)*

**Equity**    the difference between the price for which a property could be sold and the total debts registered against the property *(p. 608)*

**First mortgage**    the first legal claim registered against a property; in the event of default by the borrower, first mortgagees are paid before all other claimants *(p. 608)*

**Fixed-rate mortgage**    a mortgage for which the rate of interest is fixed for a specific period of time; it can be open or closed *(p. 608)*

**Gross Debt Service (GDS) ratio**    the percent of gross annual income required to cover such housing costs as mortgage payments, property taxes, and heating costs *(p. 610)*

**Mortgage contract**    a document specifying the obligations of the borrowers and the rights of the lender *(p. 608)*

**Mortgagee**    the lender *(p. 608)*

**Mortgagor**    the borrower *(p. 608)*

**Prospective method**    a method for finding the outstanding debt balance that considers the payments that remain outstanding *(p. 577)*

**Residential mortgage**    a claim to a residential property given by a borrower to a lender as security for the repayment of a loan *(p. 608)*

**Retrospective method**    a method of finding the outstanding balance of a debt that considers the payments that have been made *(p. 577)*

**Second mortgage**    the second legal claim registered against a property; in the event of default by the borrower, second-mortgage holders are paid only after first-mortgage holders have been paid *(p. 608)*

**Total Debt Service (TDS) ratio**    the percent of gross annual income required to cover such housing costs as mortgage payments, property taxes, and heat, and all other debts and obligations *(p. 610)*

**Variable-rate mortgage**    *see* **Demand mortgage**

## USEFUL INTERNET SITES

www.cmhc-schl.gc.ca

**Canada Mortgage and Housing Corporation (CMHC)** As the Government of Canada's national housing agency, CMHC plays a major role in Canada's housing industry. CMHC develops new ways to finance home purchases.

www.tdcanadatrust.com

**Mortgage Calculator** Click on "Mortgages," then "How Much Can I Afford?" By entering values for the relevant variables in this tool on the TD Canada Trust site, you can calculate the payment, principal, or amortization period of a mortgage. You can also obtain mortgage rates and general mortgage information.

www.businessfinancemag.com

***Business Finance Magazine*** Presents information on business management and technology issues for accountants and finance professionals, controllers, chief financial officers, and treasurers.

# 15 Bond Valuation and Sinking Funds

## OBJECTIVES

**Upon completing this chapter, you will be able to do the following:**

1. Determine the purchase price of bonds, redeemable at par or otherwise, bought on or between interest dates.

2. Calculate the premium or discount on the purchase of a bond.

3. Construct bond schedules showing the amortization of premiums or accumulation of discounts.

4. Calculate the yield rate for bonds bought on the market by the method of averages.

5. Make sinking fund computations when payments form simple annuities, including the size of the periodic payments, accumulated balance, interest earned, and increase in the fund.

6. Construct complete or partial sinking fund schedules.

Many financial planners recommend bonds as a part of a balanced investment portfolio. Historically, bonds represent a less risky investment than stocks. Companies and governments issue bonds to raise large sums of money. To have the funds to pay for the bonds when they mature, companies often create a *sinking fund* by making regular equal investments from the outset of the bond issue. Both individuals and companies use annuity formulas to decide about possible investments in bonds and sinking funds.

## INTRODUCTION

Bonds are contracts used to borrow sizeable sums of money, usually from a large group of investors. The indenture, or contract, for most bonds provides for the repayment of the principal at a specified future date plus periodic payment of interest at a specified percent of the face value. Bonds are negotiable; that is, they can be freely bought and sold. The mathematical issues arising from the trading of bonds are the topic of this chapter.

# 15.1 PURCHASE PRICE OF BONDS

## A. Basic concepts and terminology

Corporations and governments use bonds to borrow money, usually from a large group of lenders (investors). To deal with the expected large number of investors, the borrower prints up written contracts, called *bonds* or *debentures*, in advance.

The printed bonds specify the terms of the contract including

(a) the **face value** (or **par value** or **denomination**), which is the amount owed to the holder of the bond when it matures, usually a multiple of $100 such as $100, $1000, $5000, $10 000, $25 000, $100 000;

(b) the **bond rate** (or **coupon rate** or **nominal rate**), which is the rate of interest paid, usually semi-annually, based on the face value of the bond;

(c) the **maturity date** (or **redemption date** or **due date**), which is the date on which the principal of the bond is to be repaid;

(d) the **principal** (or **redemption value** or **maturity value**), which is the money paid by the issuer to the bondholder at the date of surrender of the bonds.

Most bonds are **redeemable at par**; that is, they are redeemable at their *face* value. However, some bonds have a redemption feature either to make the bonds more attractive to the investor or because they are callable, that is, because they can be redeemed *before* maturity. In either case, the bonds will be **redeemable at a premium**, that is, at a price *greater* than their face price. The redemption value in such cases is stated as a percent of the face value. For example, the redemption value of a $5000 bond redeemable at 104 is 104% of $5000, or $5200.

Investors in bonds expect to receive periodic interest payments during the term of the bond from the date of issue to the date of maturity and they expect to receive the principal at the date of maturity. The bond rate is used to determine the periodic interest payments.

To facilitate the payment of interest, some bonds have dated interest **coupons** attached that can be cashed on or after the stated interest payment date at any bank. For example, a twenty-year, $1000.00 bond bearing interest at 10% payable semi-annually will have attached to it at the date of issue forty coupons of $50 each. Each coupon represents the semi-annual interest due on each of the forty interest payment dates.

The issuer may or may not offer security such as real estate, plant, or equipment as a guarantee for the repayment of the principal. Bonds for which no security is offered are called **debentures**.

Bonds are marketable and may be freely bought and sold. When investors acquire bonds, they buy two promises:

1. a promise to be paid the principal of the bond at maturity;
2. a promise to be paid the periodic interest payments according to the rate of interest and the terms stated on the bond.

Two basic problems arise for investors when buying bonds:

1. What should be the purchase price of a bond to provide the investor with a given rate of return?
2. What is the rate of interest that a bond will yield if purchased at a given price?

In this section we will deal with the first of these two problems.

## B. Purchase price of a bond bought on an interest date

**EXAMPLE 15.1A**

A $1000 bond bearing interest at 6% payable semi-annually is due in four years. If money is worth 7% compounded semi-annually, what is the value of the bond if purchased today?

**SOLUTION**

The buyer of the bond acquires two promises:

1. A promise of $1000 four years from now.

2. A promise of $30 interest due at the end of every six months. The annual interest is 6% and the periodic interest rate is 6%/2 = 3%. The interest amount paid is the periodic interest rate stated on the bond multiplied by the face value or maturity value of the bond. This interest will be paid semi-annually for four years, or eight times.

The two promises can be represented on a time graph as Figure 15.1 shows.

**FIGURE 15.1** Graphical Representation of Method and Data

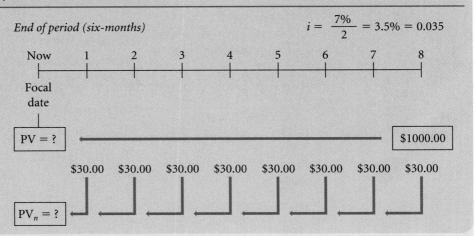

The focal date for evaluating the two promises is "now." The rate of interest to be used for the valuation at the focal date is the rate money is worth at that date. In this example, use the rate of 7% compounded semi-annually. The principal is the future value.

The value at the focal date of the principal of $1000 is its present value.

$$FV = 1000.00; \quad n = 4(2) = 8; \quad P/Y = 2; \quad C/Y = 2; \quad I/Y = 7; \quad i = \frac{7\%}{2} = 35\% = 0.035$$

$$PV = 1000.00(1.035)^{-8} \text{———————————————— using Formula 9.1C}$$
$$= 1000.00(0.759412)$$
$$= \$759.41$$

**Programmed Solution**

("END" mode) (Set P/Y = 2; C/Y = 2) [ 2nd ] (CLR TVM) 1000 [ FV ] 7 [ I/Y ]

8 [ N ] [ CPT ] [ PV ] [ −759.411556 ]

The value "now" of the semi-annual interest payments is the present value of an ordinary annuity.

$$PMT = \frac{6\% \text{ of } 1000.00}{2} = 30.00; \quad n = 8; \quad i = 3.5\%$$

$$PV_n = 30.00\left(\frac{1 - 1.035^{-8}}{0.035}\right) \text{————————— using Formula 11.2}$$
$$= 30.00(6.873956)$$
$$= \$206.22$$

**Programmed Solution**

0 [ FV ] 30 [ PMT ] 7 [ I/Y ] 8 [ N ] [ CPT ] [ PV ] [ −206.218666 ]

The purchase price of the bond is the sum of the present values of the two promises

$$= PV + PV_n$$

$$= 759.41 + 206.22 = \$965.63$$

$$\begin{array}{ccc} \text{THE PURCHASE PRICE OF} & & \text{THE PRESENT VALUE OF} \\ \text{A BOND BOUGHT ON} & = & \text{THE REDEMPTION PRICE} \\ \text{AN INTEREST PAYMENT DATE} & & \end{array} + \begin{array}{c} \text{THE PRESENT VALUE OF} \\ \text{THE INTEREST PAYMENTS} \end{array}$$

The two steps involved in using the above relationship can be combined.

$$\text{PURCHASE PRICE} = P + A_n$$

$$= S(1 + i)^{-n} + R\left[\frac{1 - (1 + i)^{-n}}{i}\right]$$

restated as ————— Formula 15.1

$$\text{PURCHASE PRICE} = PV + PV_n$$

$$= FV(1 + i)^{-n} + PMT\left[\frac{1 - (1 + i)^{-n}}{i}\right]$$

where FV = the principal of the bond;

PMT = the periodic interest payment (coupon);

$n$ = the number of outstanding interest payments (or compounding periods);

$i$ = the yield rate per payment interval.

*Note:* It is important to recognize that two rates of interest are used in determining the purchase price:

1. the bond rate determines the size of the periodic interest payments (coupons);

2. the **yield rate** is used to determine the present values of the two promises.

**EXAMPLE 15.1B**

A $5000 bond bearing interest at 6.5% payable semi-annually matures in ten years. If it is bought to yield 5.8% compounded semi-annually, what is the purchase price of the bond?

**SOLUTION**

PRESENT VALUE OF THE PRINCIPAL + PRESENT VALUE OF THE PRINCIPAL COUPONS

$$= \quad PV \quad + \quad PV_n$$

$$= \quad 5000.00(1.029^{-20}) \quad + \quad 162.50\left(\frac{1 - 1.029^{-20}}{0.029}\right)$$

$$= \quad 5000.00(0.564537) \quad + \quad 162.50(15.015961)$$

$$= \quad 2822.69 \quad + \quad 2440.09$$

$$= \quad \$5262.78$$

**Programmed Solution**

("END" mode) (Set P/Y = 2; C/Y = 2) [2nd] (CLR TVM) 5000 [FV] 5.8 [I/Y]

20 [N] [CPT] [PV] [−2822.685609]

0 [FV] 162.50 [PMT] 5.8 [I/Y] 20 [N] [CPT] [PV] [−2440.093714]

(These keystrokes can be eliminated, since they are still programmed in the calculator from the previous step.)

The purchase price is 2822.69 + 2440.09 = $5262.78.

*Note:* The calculator steps may be combined into one calculation by entering both the future value and the payment as positive numbers, then computing the present value. The present value will appear as a negative number.

**EXAMPLE 15.1C**

A municipality issues ten-year bonds in the amount of $1 000 000. Interest on the bonds is 10% payable annually. What is the issue price of the bonds if the bonds are sold to yield 11% compounded quarterly?

**SOLUTION**

The principal of the bonds FV = 1 000 000.00;
the annual interest payment PMT = 1 000 000.00(0.10) = $100 000.00.

Since the interest payment period (annual) is not equal in length to the yield rate conversion period (quarterly), the interest payments form an ordinary general annuity.

$$n = 10; \ P/Y = 1; \ C/Y = 4; \ c = \frac{4}{1} = 4; \ I/Y = 11; \ i = \frac{11\%}{4} = 2.75\% = 0.0275;$$

$$p = 1.0275^4 - 1 = 1.114621 - 1 = 0.114621 = 11.4621\%$$

The present value of the redemption price

$$\begin{aligned} PV &= 1\,000\,000.00(1.114621^{-10}) \\ &= 1\,000\,000.00(0.337852) \\ &= \$337\,852.22 \end{aligned}$$

The present value of the annual interest payments

$$PV_{nc} = 100\,000.00\left[\frac{(1 - 1.114621^{-10})}{0.114621}\right] \quad\text{——— using Formula 12.3}$$

$$\begin{aligned} &= 100\,000.00(5.776832) \\ &= \$577\,683.22 \end{aligned}$$

**Programmed Solution**

("END" mode) (Set P/Y = 1; C/Y = 4) [2nd] (CLR TVM) 1 000 000 [FV] 11

[I/Y] 10 [N] [CPT] [PV] -337852.2208

0 [FV] 100 000 [PMT] 11 [I/Y] 10 [N] [CPT] [PV] 577683.2174

The issue price is 337 852.22 + 577 683.22 = $915 535.44.

We can modify Formula 15.1 to allow for the general annuity case by using Formula 12.3.

$$\text{PURCHASE PRICE} = P + A_{nc} = S(1 + p)^{-n} + R\left[\frac{1 - (1 + p)^{-n}}{p}\right]$$

restated as

$$\text{PURCHASE PRICE} = PV + PV_{nc} = FV(1 + p)^{-n} + PMT\left[\frac{1 - (1 + p)^{-n}}{p}\right] \quad\text{——— Formula 15.2}$$

where $p = (1 + i)^c - 1$

## C. Purchase price of bonds between interest dates

Bonds are not just purchased and sold on interest payment dates. In practice, most bonds are traded between interest dates.

In such cases, we can compute the price of the bond on the date of purchase by first finding the purchase price on the interest date immediately preceding the date of purchase. The resulting value can then be accumulated using the future value formula for simple interest at the bond rate for the number of days elapsed between the interest payment date and the purchase date.

**EXAMPLE 15.1D**

A bond with a face value of $1000 bearing interest at 6% payable semi-annually matures on August 1, 2012. What is the purchase price of the bond on April 18, 2010 to yield 5.4% compounded semi-annually?

**SOLUTION**

**STEP 1** Find the purchase price on the preceding interest date.

The principal FV = $1000.00;

the semi-annual coupon PMT $= 1000.00 \left( \dfrac{0.06}{2} \right) = \$30.00.$

Since the maturity date is August 1, the semi-annual interest dates are February 1 and August 1. The interest date preceding the date of purchase is February 1, 2010. The time period from February 1, 2010 to the date of maturity is 2.5 years.

$n = 2.5(2) = 5; \ P/Y = 2; \ C/Y = 2; \ I/Y = 5.4; \ i = \dfrac{5.4\%}{2} = 2.7\% = 0.027$

The purchase price of the bond on February 1, 2010

$= 1000.00(1.027^{-5}) + 30.00 \left( \dfrac{1 - 1.027^{-5}}{0.027} \right)$

$= 1000.00(0.875282) + 30.00(4.619201)$

$= 875.28 + 138.58$

$= \$1013.86$

**Programmed Solution**

("END" mode) (Set P/Y = 2; C/Y = 2) [ 2nd ] (CLR TVM) 1000 [ FV ]

5.4 [ I/Y ] 5 [ N ] [ CPT ] [ PV ] [ −875.281566 ]

0 [ FV ] 30 [ PMT ] 5.4 [ I/Y ] 5 [ N ] [ CPT ] [ PV ] [ −138.576038 ]

The purchase price is 875.28 + 138.58 = $1013.86.

**STEP 2** Accumulate the interest on February 1, 2010 at simple interest based on the bond rate.

The number of days from February 1, 2010 to April 18, 2010 is 76; the number of days in the interest interval February 1, 2010 to August 1, 2010 is 181.

$PV = 1000.00; \quad r = i = 0.03; \quad t = \dfrac{76}{181}$

$Interest = 1000.00 \left[ 0.03 \left( \dfrac{76}{181} \right) \right] = \$12.60$

The purchase price of the bond on April 18, 2010 is $1013.86 + 12.60 = $1026.46.

The bonds are offered for sale at the **market price**. In the example above, the market price is $1013.86. The total purchase price of $1026.46 is called the **cash price** or purchase price. This price includes interest that has accrued from February 1, 2010 to April 18, 2010 but will not be paid until August 1, 2010.

CASH PRICE = MARKET PRICE + ACCRUED INTEREST

**EXAMPLE 15.1E**

A $5000 bond redeemable at par in seven years and four months bearing interest at 6.5% payable semi-annually is bought to yield 7.5% compounded semi-annually. Determine

(i) the market price;
(ii) the accrued interest;
(iii) the cash price.

**SOLUTION**

(i) The redemption price FV = $5000.00;

the semi-annual coupon PMT = $5000.00\left(\dfrac{0.065}{2}\right) = \$162.50$.

The interest date preceding the purchase date is 7.5 years before maturity.

$n = 7.5(2) = 15$; P/Y = 2; C/Y = 2; I/Y = 7.5; $i = \dfrac{7.5\%}{2} = 3.75\% = 0.0375$

The purchase price on the interest date preceding the date of purchase

$= 5000.00(1.0375^{-15}) + 162.50\left(\dfrac{1 - 1.0375^{-15}}{0.0375}\right)$

$= 5000.00(0.575676) + 162.50(11.315296)$
$= 2878.38 + 1838.74$
$= \$4717.12$

**Programmed Solution**

("END" mode) (Set P/Y = 2; C/Y = 2) $\boxed{\text{2nd}}$ (CLR TVM) 5000 $\boxed{\text{FV}}$

7.5 $\boxed{\text{I/Y}}$ 15 $\boxed{\text{N}}$ $\boxed{\text{CPT}}$ $\boxed{\text{PV}}$ $\boxed{-2878.381956}$

0 $\boxed{\text{FV}}$ 162.50 $\boxed{\text{PMT}}$ 7.5 $\boxed{\text{I/Y}}$ 15 $\boxed{\text{N}}$ $\boxed{\text{CPT}}$ $\boxed{\text{PV}}$ $\boxed{-1838.735638}$

The purchase price is 2878.38 + 1838.74 = $4717.12.

(ii) The accrued interest two months later

PV = 5000.00; $r = i = 0.0325$; $t = \dfrac{2}{6}$;

Interest $= 5000.00\left[0.0325\left(\dfrac{2}{6}\right)\right] = \$54.17$

(iii) The cash price two months later is $4717.12 + 54.17 = 4771.29.

## EXERCISE 15.1

**EXCEL NOTES**

Excel has a **Bond Purchase Price (PRICE)** function you can use to find the price per $100 face value of a security that pays periodic interest. If you choose, you can use this function to answer the questions in Part A and Part B below. Refer to **PRICE** on the Spreadsheet Template Disk to learn how to use this Excel function.

**A.** Determine the purchase price at the indicated time before maturity of each of the bonds redeemed at par shown in the table below.

| | Par Value | Bond Rate Payable Semi-annually | Time Before Maturity | Yield Rate | Conversion Period |
|---|---|---|---|---|---|
| 1. | $100 000 | 7% | 5.5 years | 7.5% | semi-annually |
| 2. | 5 000 | 8 | 12 years | 7 | semi-annually |
| 3. | 25 000 | 6 | 7 years | 7 | semi-annually |
| 4. | 1 000 | 8.5 | 12.5 years | 8 | semi-annually |
| 5. | 50 000 | 6.5 | 10 years | 6 | annually |
| 6. | 20 000 | 7.5 | 6.5 years | 8 | quarterly |
| 7. | 8 000 | 8 | 18.5 years | 9 | monthly |
| 8. | 3 000 | 6 | 20 years | 8 | quarterly |

 Excel has a number of functions you can choose to answer the questions in Part B below: ***Days Since Last Interest Date (COUPDAYBS), Total Number of Days in the Coupon Period (COUPDAYS),*** and ***Total Number of Remaining Coupon Periods (COUPNUM)***. Refer to **COUPDAYBS, COUPDAYS,** and **COUPNUM** on the Spreadsheet Template Disk to learn how to use these Excel functions.

 **B.** Answer each of the following questions.

1. A $500 bond matures on March 1, 2014. Interest is 6% payable semi-annually. Find the purchase price of the bond on September 1, 2008 to yield 7.5% compounded semi-annually.  Reference Example 15.1A

2. A $25 000, 10% bond is purchased twelve years before maturity to yield 7% compounded semi-annually. If the bond interest is payable semi-annually, what is the purchase price of the bond?

3. A $15 000, 7.5% bond is purchased six years and six months before maturity to yield 8% semi-annually. If the bond interest is payable semi-annually, what is the purchase price of the bond?

4. A $5000, 6% bond is purchased thirteen years before maturity to yield 6.5% semi-annually. If the bond interest is payable semi-annually, what is the purchase price of the bond?

5. A $10 000, 9% bond is purchased nine years and six months before maturity to yield 8.5% semi-annually. If the bond interest is payable semi-annually, what is the purchase price of the bond?

6. A $2000, 5.5% bond is purchased six years before maturity to yield 7.5% semi-annually. If the bond interest is payable semi-annually, what is the purchase price of the bond?

7. A 25-year bond issue of $5 000 000 and bearing interest at 7.25% payable annually is sold to yield 8.5% compounded semi-annually. What is the issue price of the bonds?

8. A $100 000 bond bearing interest at 6.75% payable semi-annually is bought eight years before maturity to yield 7.35% compounded annually. If the bond is redeemable at par, what is the purchase price?

9. Bonds with a maturity value of $40 000 in 7.5 years bearing interest at 8% payable quarterly are sold to yield 6.8% compounded semi-annually. Determine the purchase price of the bonds.

10. Six $1000 bonds with 7.4% coupons payable semi-annually are bought to yield 6.3% compounded monthly. If the bonds mature in eight years, what is the purchase price?

11. A $1000, 9% bond is purchased 8.5 years before maturity to yield 6.5% compounded semi-annually. If the bond interest is payable semi-annually, what is the purchase price of the bond?

12. A $100 000 bond is redeemable at par in fifteen years. If interest on the bond is 7.5% payable semi-annually, what is the purchase price to yield 8% compounded semi-annually?

13. A $25 000, 10% bond redeemable at par on December 1, 2021 is purchased on September 25, 2010 to yield 7.6% compounded semi-annually. Bond interest is payable semi-annually.
   (a) What is the quoted price of the bond?
   (b) What is the accrued interest?
   (c) What is the cash price?

Reference Example 15.1D

14. A $100 000 bond redeemable at par on October 1, 2030 is purchased on January 15, 2009. Interest is 5.9% payable semi-annually and the yield is 9% compounded semi-annually.
   (a) What is the quoted price of the bond?
   (b) What is the accrued interest?
   (c) What is the cash price?

# 15.2 PREMIUM AND DISCOUNT

## A. Basic concepts—bond rate versus yield (or market) rate

A comparison of the redemption values with the purchase prices obtained in Examples 15.1A to 15.1E (see Table 15.1) shows that the purchase price is sometimes less than and sometimes more than the principal.

Table 15.1 Comparison of Redemption Values with Purchase Prices for Examples 15.1A to 15.1E

| Example | Principal Value FV | Purchase Price PP | Comparison of FV and PP | Premium or Discount | Amount of Premium or Discount | Bond Rate $b$ | Yield Rate $i$ | $b$ Versus $i$ |
|---------|--------------------|--------------------|--------------------------|---------------------|-------------------------------|---------------|----------------|----------------|
| 15.1A | $ 1 000 | $ 965.63 | FV > PP | discount | $ 34.37 | 3% | 3.5% | $b < i$ |
| 15.1B | 5 000 | 5 262.78 | PP > FV | premium | 262.78 | 3.25 | 2.9 | $b > i$ |
| 15.1C | 1 000 000 | 915 535.44 | FV > PP | discount | 84 464.56 | 10 | 11.46 | $b < i$ |
| 15.1D | 1 000 | 1 013.86 | PP > FV | premium | 13.86 | 3 | 2.7 | $b > i$ |
| 15.1E | 5 000 | 4 717.12 | FV > PP | discount | 282.88 | 3.25 | 3.75 | $b < i$ |

If the purchase price of a bond is greater than the principal, the bond is said to be bought at a premium and the difference between the purchase price and the principal is called the **premium**.

PREMIUM = PURCHASE PRICE − PRINCIPAL
where purchase price > principal

If the purchase price of a bond is less than the principal, the bond is said to be bought at a discount and the difference between the principal and the purchase price is called the **discount**.

DISCOUNT = PRINCIPAL − PURCHASE PRICE
where principal > purchase price

An examination of the size of the bond rate $b$ relative to the size of the market rate $i$ shows that this relationship determines whether there is a premium or discount.

The bond rate (or coupon rate) stated on the bond is the percent of the *face* value of the bond that will be paid at the end of each interest period to the bondholder. This rate is established at the time of issue of the bonds and remains the same throughout the term of the bond.

On the other hand, the rate at which lenders are willing to provide money fluctuates in response to economic conditions. The combination of factors at work in the capital market at any given time in conjunction with the perceived risk associated with a particular bond determines the yield rate (or market rate) for a bond and thus the price at which a bond will be bought or sold.

The bond rate and the market rate are usually *not* equal. However, if the two rates happen to be equal, then bonds that are redeemable at par will sell at their face value. If the bond rate is *less* than the market rate, the bond will sell at a price less than the face value, that is, at a *discount*. If the bond rate is *greater* than the market rate, the bond will sell at a price above its face value, that is, at a *premium*.

Conversely, if a bond is redeemable at par (i.e., at 100), purchasers will realize the bond rate if they pay 100. They will realize less than the bond rate if they buy at a premium and more than the bond rate if they buy at a discount.

At any time, one of three possible situations exists for any given bond:

**(1)** Bond rate = Market rate ($b = i$)     The bond sells at *par*.
**(2)** Bond rate < Market rate ($b < i$)     The bond sells at a *discount*.
**(3)** Bond rate > Market rate ($b > i$)     The bond sells at a *premium*.

---

**EXAMPLE 15.2A**     A $10 000 bond is redeemable at par and bears interest at 10% compounded semi-annually.

(i) What is the purchase price ten years before maturity if the market rate compounded semi-annually is
(a) 10%;     (b) 12%;     (c) 8%?

(ii) What is the purchase price five years before maturity if the market rate compounded semi-annually is
(a) 10%;     (b) 12%;     (c) 8%?

(i) FV = 10 000.00; PMT = 10 000.00(0.05) = 500.00; $n = 10(2) = 20$; $b = 5\%$

(a) $i = \dfrac{10\%}{2} = 5\% = 0.05$; $(b = i)$

Purchase price $= 10\,000.00(1.05^{-20}) + 500.00\left(\dfrac{1 - 1.05^{-20}}{0.05}\right)$

$= 10\,000.00(0.376889) + 500.00(12.46221)$
$= 3768.89 + 6231.11$
$= \$10\,000.00$

**Programmed Solution**

("END" mode) (Set P/Y = 2; C/Y = 2) [2nd] (CLR TVM) 10 000 [FV]

10 [I/Y] 20 [N] [CPT] [PV] [−3768.894829]

0 [FV] 500 [PMT] 10 [I/Y] 20 [N] [CPT] [PV] [−6231.105171]

The purchase price is 3768.89 + 6231.11 = \$10 000.00.
The bond sells at par.

(b) $i = \dfrac{12\%}{2} = 6\% = 0.06$; $(b < i)$

Purchase price $= 10\,000.00(1.06^{-20}) + 500.00\left(\dfrac{1 - 1.06^{-20}}{0.06}\right)$

$= 10\,000.00(0.311805) + 500.00(11.469921)$
$= 3118.05 + 5734.96$
$= \$8853.01$

**Programmed Solution**

("END" mode) (Set P/Y = 2; C/Y = 2) [2nd] (CLR TVM) 10 000 [FV]

12 [I/Y] 20 [N] [CPT] [PV] [−3118.047269]

0 [FV] 500 [PMT] 12 [I/Y] 20 [N] [CPT] [PV] [−5734.960609]

The purchase price is 3118.05 + 5734.96 = \$8853.01.
The bond sells below par.
The discount is 10 000.00 − 8853.01 = \$1146.99.

(c) $i = \dfrac{8\%}{2} = 4\% = 0.04; \quad (b > i)$

Purchase price $= 10\ 000.00(1.04^{-20}) + 500.00\left(\dfrac{1 - 1.04^{-20}}{0.04}\right)$

$\qquad = 10\ 000.00(0.456387) + 500.00(13.590326)$
$\qquad = 4563.87 + 6795.16$
$\qquad = \$11\ 359.03$

### Programmed Solution

("END" mode) (Set P/Y = 2; C/Y = 2) [2nd] (CLR TVM) 10 000 [FV]

$\qquad$ 8 [I/Y] 20 [N] [CPT] [PV] [-4563.869462]

0 [FV] 500 [PMT] 8 [I/Y] 20 [N] [CPT] [PV] [-6795.163172]

The purchase price $4563.87 + 6795.16 = \$11\ 359.03$.
The bond sells above par.
The premium $11\ 359.03 - 10\ 000.00 = \$1359.03$.

(ii) FV = 10 000.00;  PMT = 500.00;  $n = 5(2) = 10$;  $b = 5\%$

$\quad$ (a) $i = 5\% \ (b = i)$

Purchase price $= 10\ 000.00(1.05^{-10}) + 500.00\left(\dfrac{1 - 1.05^{-10}}{0.05}\right)$

$\qquad = 6139.13 + 3860.87$
$\qquad = \$10\ 000.00$

### Programmed Solution

("END" mode) (Set P/Y = 2; C/Y = 2) [2nd] (CLR TVM) 10 000 [FV]

$\qquad$ 10 [I/Y] 10 [N] [CPT] [PV] [-6139.132535]

0 [FV] 500 [PMT] 10 [I/Y] 10 [N] [CPT] [PV] [-3860.867465]

The purchase price is $6139.13 + 3860.87 = \$10\ 000.00$.
The bond sells at par.

$\quad$ (b) $i = 6\%; \ (b < i)$

Purchase price $= 10\ 000.00(1.06^{-10}) + 500.00\left(\dfrac{1 - 1.06^{-10}}{0.06}\right)$

$\qquad = 5583.95 + 3680.04$
$\qquad = \$9263.99$

**Programmed Solution**

("END" mode) (Set P/Y = 2; C/Y = 2) [2nd] (CLR TVM) 10 000 [FV]

12 [I/Y] 10 [N] [CPT] [PV] [-5583.947769]

0 [FV] 500 [PMT] 12 [I/Y] 10 [N] [CPT] [PV] [-3680.043526]

The purchase price is 5583.95 + 3680.04 = $9263.99.

The bond sells below par.

The discount is 10 000.00 − 9263.99 = $736.01. It is smaller than in part (i) because the time to maturity is shorter.

(c) $i = 4\%$;   $(b > i)$

Purchase price $= 10\,000.00(1.04^{-10}) + 500.00\left(\dfrac{1 - 1.04^{-10}}{0.04}\right)$

$$= 6755.64 + 4055.45$$
$$= \$10\,811.09$$

**Programmed Solution**

("END" mode) (Set P/Y = 2; C/Y = 2) [2nd] (CLR TVM) 10 000 [FV]

8 [I/Y] 10 [N] [CPT] [PV] [-6755.641688]

0 [FV] 500 [PMT] 8 [I/Y] 10 [N] [CPT] [PV] [-4055.44789]

The purchase price is 6755.64 + 4055.45 = $10 811.09.

The bond sells above par.

The premium is 10 811.09 − 10 000.00 = $811.09. It is smaller than in part (i) because the time to maturity is shorter.

## B. Direct method of computing the premium or discount— alternative method for finding the purchase price

**EXAMPLE 15.2B**

A $5000, 7% bond with semi-annual interest coupons is bought six years before maturity to yield 5.6% compounded semi-annually. Determine the premium or discount.

**SOLUTION**

$FV = 5000.00$;   $P/Y = 2$;   $C/Y = 2$;   $I/Y = 5.6$;   $b = \dfrac{7\%}{2} = 3.5\% = 0.035$;

$PMT = 5000.00(0.035) = 175.00$;   $i = \dfrac{5.6\%}{2} = 2.8\% = 0.028$;   $n = 6(2) = 12$

Since $b > i$, the bond will sell at a premium.

Purchase price $= 5000.00(1.028^{-12}) + 175.00\left(\dfrac{1 - 1.028^{-12}}{0.028}\right)$

$$= 5000.00(0.717931) + 175.00(10.073898)$$
$$= 3589.65 + 1762.93$$
$$= \$5352.58$$

**Programmed Solution**

("END" mode) (Set P/Y = 2; C/Y = 2) [2nd] (CLR TVM) 5000 [FV] 5.6 [I/Y]

12 [N] [CPT] [PV] [−3589.65432]

0 [FV] 175 [PMT] 5.6 [I/Y] 12 [N] [CPT] [PV] [−1762.932101]

The purchase price is 3589.66 + 1762.93 = \$5352.59.

The premium is 5352.59 − 5000.00 = \$352.59.

While you can always determine the premium by the basic method using Formula 15.1, it is more convenient to determine the premium directly by considering the relationship between the bond rate $b$ and the yield rate $i$.

As previously discussed, a premium results when $b > i$. When this is the case, the premium is paid because the periodic interest payments received exceed the periodic interest required according to the yield rate.

*In Example 15.2B*

| | |
|---|---|
| The semi-annual interest payment | $5000.00(0.035) = \$175.00$ |
| The required semi-annual interest based on the yield rate | $5000.00(0.028) = \underline{\phantom{0}140.00}$ |
| The excess of the actual interest received over the required interest to make the yield rate | $= \underline{\$\phantom{0}35.00}$ |

This excess is received at the end of every payment interval; thus it forms an ordinary annuity whose present value can be computed at the yield rate $i$.

PMT (the excess interest) = 35.00; $i = 2.8\%$; $n = 12$

$$PV_n = 35.00\left(\frac{1 - 1.028^{-12}}{0.028}\right)$$

$$= 35.00(10.073898)$$

$$= \$352.59$$

**Programmed Solution**

("END" mode) (Set P/Y = 2; C/Y = 2) 0 [FV] 35 [PMT] 5.6 [I/Y]

12 [N] [CPT] [PV] [−352.58642]

The premium is \$352.59.

The purchase price is 5000.00 + 352.59 = \$5352.59.

The premium is the present value of the ordinary annuity formed by the excess of the actual bond interest over the required interest based on the yield rate. We can obtain the purchase price by adding the premium to the principal.

$$\text{PREMIUM} = (\text{PERIODIC BOND INTEREST} - \text{REQUIRED INTEREST}) \left[ \frac{1 - (1 + i)^{-n}}{i} \right]$$

$$= (\text{FACE VALUE} \times b - \text{REDEMPTION PRICE} \times i) \left[ \frac{1 - (1 + i)^{-n}}{i} \right]$$

**EXAMPLE 15.2C**

A $5000, 6% bond with semi-annual interest coupons is bought six years before maturity to yield 8% compounded semi-annually. Determine the premium or discount.

**SOLUTION**

$FV = 5000.00; \quad P/Y = 2; \quad C/Y = 2; \quad b = \dfrac{6\%}{2} = 3\% = 0.03;$

$PMT = 5000.00(0.03) = 150.00; \quad I/Y = 8; \quad i = \dfrac{8\%}{2} = 4\% = 0.04;$

$n = 6(2) = 12$

Since $b < i$, the bond will sell at a discount.

$$\text{Purchase price} = 5000.00(1.04^{-12}) + 150.00 \left( \frac{1 - 1.04^{-12}}{0.04} \right)$$
$$= 5000.00(0.624597) + 150.00(9.385074)$$
$$= 3122.99 + 1407.76$$
$$= \$4530.75$$

**Programmed Solution**

("END" mode) (Set P/Y = 2; C/Y = 2) [ **2nd** ] (CLR TVM) 5000 [ **FV** ]

8 [ **I/Y** ] 12 [ **N** ] [ **CPT** ] [ **PV** ] [ -3122.985248 ]

0 [ **FV** ] 150 [ **PMT** ] 8 [ **I/Y** ] 12 [ **N** ] [ **CPT** ] [ **PV** ] [ -1407.761064 ]

The purchase price is 3122.99 + 1407.76 = $4530.75.

The discount is 5000.00 − 4530.75 = $469.25.

As in the case of a premium, while you can always determine the discount by the basic method using Formula 15.1, it is more convenient to determine the discount directly.

When $b < i$, a discount results. The discount on a bond is received because the periodic interest payments are less than the periodic interest required to earn the yield rate.

*In Example 15.2C*

| | |
|---|---|
| The semi-annual interest payment | 5000.00(0.03) = $150.00 |
| The required semi-annual interest based on the yield rate | 5000.00(0.04) = 200.00 |
| The shortage of the actual interest received compared to the required interest based on the yield rate | = $ 50.00 |

This shortage occurs at the end of every interest payment interval; it forms an ordinary annuity whose present value can be computed at the yield rate $i$.

$$\text{PMT} = 50.00; \quad i = 4\%; \quad n = 12$$

$$\text{PV}_n = 50.00\left(\frac{1 - 1.04^{-12}}{0.04}\right)$$

$$= 50.00(9.385074)$$

$$= \$469.25$$

**Programmed Solution**

("END" mode) (Set P/Y = 2; C/Y = 2) 0 $\boxed{\text{FV}}$ 50 $\boxed{\text{PMT}}$ 8 $\boxed{\text{I/Y}}$

12 $\boxed{\text{N}}$ $\boxed{\text{CPT}}$ $\boxed{\text{PV}}$ $\boxed{-469.253686}$

The discount is \$469.25.

The purchase price is $5000.00 - 469.25 = \$4530.75$.

The discount is the present value of the ordinary annuity formed by the shortage of the actual bond interest received as compared to the required interest based on the yield rate. We can obtain the purchase price by subtracting the discount from the principal.

$$\text{DISCOUNT} = (\text{REQUIRED INTEREST} - \text{PERIODIC BOND INTEREST})\left[\frac{1 - (1 + i)^{-n}}{i}\right]$$

$$= -(\text{PERIODIC BOND INTEREST} - \text{REQUIRED INTEREST})\left[\frac{1 - (1 + i)^{-n}}{i}\right]$$

$$= -(\text{FACE VALUE} \times b - \text{REDEMPTION PRICE} \times i)\left[\frac{1 - (1 + i)^{-n}}{i}\right]$$

Since in both cases the difference between the periodic bond interest and the required interest is involved, the premium or discount on the purchase of a bond can be obtained using the same relationship.

$$\begin{array}{l}\text{PREMIUM} \\ \text{or} \\ \text{DISCOUNT}\end{array} = (b \times \text{FACE VALUE} - i \times \text{REDEMPTION PRICE})\left[\frac{1 - (1 + i)^{-n}}{i}\right] \quad\text{——— Formula 15.3}$$

**EXAMPLE 15.2D**

A \$1000, 8.5% bond with semi-annual interest coupons redeemable at par in fifteen years is bought to yield 7% compounded semi-annually. Determine

(i) the premium or discount;

(ii) the purchase price.

**SOLUTION**

(i) FV = 1000.00; P/Y = 2; C/Y = 2; $b = \dfrac{8.5\%}{2} = 4.25\% = 0.0425$;

PMT $= 1000.00(0.0425) = 42.50$; I/Y = 7; $i = \dfrac{7\%}{2} = 3.5\% = 0.035$;

$n = 15(2) = 30$

Since $b > i$, the bond will sell at a premium.

The required interest based on the yield rate is $1000.00(0.035) = 35.00$; the excess interest is $42.50 - 35.00 = 7.50$.

The premium is $7.50\left(\dfrac{1 - 1.035^{-30}}{0.035}\right) = 7.50(18.392045) = \$137.94$.

**Programmed Solution**

("END" mode) (Set P/Y = 2; C/Y = 2) 0 [ FV ] 7.50 [ PMT ] 7 [ I/Y ]

30 [ N ] [ CPT ] [ PV ] [ −137.940341 ]

(ii) The purchase price is $1000.00 + 137.94 = \$1137.94$.

---

**EXAMPLE 15.2E**

A $50 000, 7.2% bond with quarterly interest coupons redeemable at par in ten years is purchased to yield 8% compounded quarterly.

(i) What is the premium or discount?

(ii) What is the purchase price?

**SOLUTION**

(i) FV = 50 000.00;  P/Y = 4;  C/Y = 4;  $b = \dfrac{7.2\%}{4} = 1.8\% = 0.018$;

$n = 10(4) = 40$;  I/Y = 8;  $i = \dfrac{8\%}{4} = 2\% = 0.02$

Since $b < i$, the bond will sell at a discount.

Discount $= (0.018 \times 50\,000.00 - 0.02 \times 50\,000.00)\left(\dfrac{1 - 1.02^{-40}}{0.02}\right)$

⎣——————— using Formula 15.3

$= (900.00 - 1000.00)(27.355479)$

$= (-100.00)(27.355479)$

$= -\$2735.55$ ——————— the negative sign indicates a discount

**Programmed Solution**

("END" mode)

First compute PMT $= (0.018 \times 50\,000) - (0.02 \times 50\,000) = -100.00$

(Set P/Y = 4; C/Y = 4) 0 [ FV ] 100 [ PMT ] 8 [ I/Y ] 40

[ N ] [ CPT ] [ PV ] [ −2735.547924 ]

(ii) The purchase price is $50\,000.00 - 2735.55 = \$47\,264.45$.

## EXERCISE 15.2

If you choose, you can use these Excel functions to answer the questions indicated below: *Bond Purchase Price (PRICE), Days Since Last Interest Date (COUPDAYBS), Total Number of Days in the Coupon Period (COUPDAYS),* and *Total Number of Remaining Coupon Periods (COUPNUM).* Refer to **PRICE, COUPDAYBS, COUPDAYS,** and **COUPNUM** on the Spreadsheet Template Disk to learn how to use these Excel functions.

**A.** For each of the six bonds redeemed at par in the table below, use Formula 15.3 to determine
(a) the premium or discount;
(b) the purchase price.

| | Par Value | Bond Rate Payable Semi-annually | Time Before Maturity | Yield Rate Compounded Semi-annually |
|---|---|---|---|---|
| **1.** | $25 000 | 6% | 10 years | 9% |
| **2.** | 5 000 | 8.5 | 8 years | 7 |
| **3.** | 10 000 | 9 | 15 years | 11 |
| **4.** | 7 000 | 9 | 5 years | 8.5 |

**B.** Answer each of the following questions.

1. A $100 000, 8% bond redeemable at par with quarterly coupons is purchased to yield 6.5% compounded quarterly. Find the premium or discount and the purchase price if the bond is purchased
   (a) fifteen years before maturity;
   (b) five years before maturity. Reference Example 15.2A

2. A $5000, 7.5% bond redeemable at par with semi-annual coupons is purchased to yield 6% compounded semi-annually. What is the premium or discount and the purchase price if the bond is bought
   (a) ten years before maturity?
   (b) six years before maturity?

3. A $25 000, 9% bond redeemable at par with interest payable annually is bought six years before maturity. Determine the premium or discount and the purchase price if the bond is purchased to yield
   (a) 13.5% compounded annually;
   (b) 6% compounded annually.

4. A $1000, 8% bond redeemable at par in seven years bears coupons payable annually. Compute the premium or discount and the purchase price if the yield, compounded annually, is
   (a) 6.5%;
   (b) 7.5%;
   (c) 8.5%.

5. A $5 000 000 issue of ten-year bonds redeemable at par offers 7.25% coupons payable semi-annually. What is the issue price of the bonds to yield 8.4% compounded monthly? Reference Example 15.2D

6. A $3000 issue of nine-year bonds redeemable at par offers 7.5% coupons paid semi-annually. What is the issue price of the bonds to yield 10.5% semi-annually?

7. Twenty $5000 bonds redeemable at par bearing 8.4% coupons payable quarterly are sold eight years before maturity to yield 8.0% compounded annually. What is the purchase price of the bonds?

8. Sixty $1000 bonds redeemable at par bearing 7% coupons payable semi-annually are sold seven years before maturity to yield 9.5% compounded semi-annually. What is the purchase price of the bonds?

## ≫ BUSINESS MATH NEWS BOX

### Making It Last—Stretching Your Retirement Savings

Your retirement is here at last, and all those years of saving are over. The question now is, how much can you spend?

The answer hinges on how your resources match up against your ambitions. Begin by deciding on the lifestyle you would like. Will you travel? Take up gardening or another, more expensive, hobby? Perhaps you plan to downsize to a smaller home. Do you foresee major debts such as home renovation or medical bills? And do you plan on spending most of your hard-earned money, or will you save some of it for your heirs?

Write down all the expenses involved in the retirement you would like, including monthly payments on your mortgage and any other debts. No item should escape notice, including clothing, entertainment, and drug and dental expenses, if not covered by a pension plan. It may help to track your expenses for a few months, says Prime. "Carry a little book, and every time you spend something, write it down."

Now the big question: how much can you withdraw from your savings each year without reducing the value of your portfolio? Many retirees blithely assume that they will be able to draw out 10% or more a year of their assets—$50 000 a year, say, on a $500 000 portfolio.

Not so. A high withdrawal rate can quickly run down your savings if the stock market goes down and stays down for two or three years. Most studies show that you should count on withdrawing no more than 4% of your assets each year if you want your money to last through a typical 30-year retirement. More aggressive withdrawal strategies may approach 5%, but 6% is pushing it.

*Source:* Susanne Ruder, "Making It Last," *MoneySense* 7(6) (December 2005/January 2006), p. S34.

### QUESTIONS

1. Calculate the number of years a $500 000 investment would last given a $50 000-per-year withdrawal. Assume interest on the investment averages 4.5% per annum, compounded monthly.

2. If you desired to withdraw from this $500 000 plan on a monthly basis, what amount could be withdrawn in order to satisfy a 30-year retirement? Assume a 4.5% interest compounded monthly.

3. You wish to live comfortably with an annual retirement income of $60 000 per year for 30 years. What monthly payments are required to develop this retirement plan over a 25-year period using a 3.8% interest rate compounded quarterly?

4. Given an initial investment of $75 000 and a retirement plan goal of $740 000 in 25 years, calculate the quarterly contributions required at 4.2% compounded quarterly.

# 15.3 BOND SCHEDULES

## A. Amortization of premium

If a bond is purchased for more than the principal, the resulting premium is not recovered when the bond is redeemed at maturity, so it becomes a capital *loss*. To avoid the capital loss at maturity, the premium is written down or expensed gradually over the period from the date of purchase to the maturity date. The writing down of the premium gradually reduces the bond's book value until it equals the principal at the date of maturity.

The process of writing down the premium is called **amortization of the premium**. The most direct method of amortizing a premium assigns the difference between the interest received (coupon) and the interest required according to the yield rate to write down the premium. The details of writing down the premium are often shown in a tabulation referred to as a *schedule of amortization of premium*.

**EXAMPLE 15.3A**   A $1000, 12% bond redeemable at par matures in three years. The coupons are payable semi-annually and the bond is bought to yield 10% compounded semi-annually.

(i) Compute the purchase price.

(ii) Construct a schedule of amortization of premium.

**SOLUTION**   (i) $FV = 1000.00$;   $n = 3(2) = 6$;   $P/Y = 2$;   $C/Y = 2$;

$$b = \frac{12\%}{2} = 6\% = 0.06; \quad I/Y = 10; \quad i = \frac{10\%}{2} = 5\% = 0.05$$

Since $b > i$, the bond sells at a premium.

$$\text{Premium} = (0.06 \times 1000.00) - (0.05 \times 1000.00)\left(\frac{1 - 1.05^{-6}}{0.05}\right)$$
$$= (60.00 - 50.00)(5.075692)$$
$$= (10.00)(5.075692)$$
$$= \$50.76$$

**Programmed Solution**

$PMT = (0.06 \times 1000.00) - (0.05 \times 1000.00) = 10.00$

("END" mode)

(Set P/Y = 2; C/Y = 2) 0 [FV] 10 [PMT] 10 [I/Y]

6 [N] [CPT] [PV] [−50.756921]

The purchase price is $1000.00 + 50.76 = \$1050.76$.

### (ii) *Schedule of amortization of premium*

| End of Interest Payment Interval | Bond Interest Recevied (Coupon) $b = 6\%$ | Interest on Book Value at Yield Rate $i = 5\%$ | Amount of Premium Amortized | Book Value of Bond | Remaining Premium |
|---|---|---|---|---|---|
| 0 | | | | 1050.76 | 50.76 |
| 1 | 60.00 | 52.54 | 7.46 | 1043.30 | 43.30 |
| 2 | 60.00 | 52.17 | 7.83 | 1035.47 | 35.47 |
| 3 | 60.00 | 51.77 | 8.23 | 1027.24 | 27.24 |
| 4 | 60.00 | 51.36 | 8.64 | 1018.60 | 18.60 |
| 5 | 60.00 | 50.93 | 9.07 | 1009.53 | 9.53 |
| 6 | 60.00 | 50.47 | 9.53 | 1000.00 | 0.00 |
| TOTAL | 360.00 | 309.24 | 50.76 | | |

*Explanations of schedule*

1. The original book value shown is the purchase price of $1050.76.

2. At the end of the first interest payment interval, the interest received (coupon) is 1000.00(0.06) = $60.00; the interest required according to the yield rate is 1050.76(0.05) = $52.54; the difference 60.00 − 52.54 = 7.46 is used to write down the premium to $43.30 and reduces the book value from $1050.76 to $1043.30.

3. The coupon at the end of the second interest payment interval is again $60. The interest required according to the yield rate is 1043.30(0.05) = $52.17; the difference 60.00 − 52.17 = 7.83 reduces the premium to $35.47 and the book value of the bond to $1035.47.

4. Continue in a similar manner until the maturity date when the principal is reached. If a rounding error becomes apparent at the end of the final interest payment interval, adjust the final interest on the book value at the yield rate to make the premium zero and to obtain the exact principal as the book value.

5. The totals provide useful accounting information showing the total interest received ($360) and the net income realized ($309.24).

## B. Accumulation of discount

If a bond is bought at less than the principal, there will be a gain at the time of redemption equal to the amount of discount. It is generally accepted accounting practice that this gain does not accrue in total to the accounting period in which the bond is redeemed. Instead, some of the gain accrues to each of the accounting periods from the date of purchase to the date of redemption.

To adhere to this practice, the discount is decreased gradually so that the book value of the bond increases gradually until, at the date of redemption, the discount is reduced to zero while the book value equals the principal. The process of reducing the discount so as to increase the book value is called **accumulation of discount**.

In the case of discount, the interest required according to the yield rate is greater than the actual interest received (the coupon). Similar to amortization of a premium, the most direct method of accumulating a discount assigns the difference between the interest required by the yield rate and the coupon to reduce the discount. The details of decreasing the discount while increasing the book value of a bond are often shown in a tabulation called a *schedule of accumulation of discount.*

**EXAMPLE 15.3B**

A $10 000 bond, redeemable at par in four years with 5.5% coupons payable semi-annually, is bought to yield 7% compounded semi-annually.

(i) Determine the discount and the purchase price.

(ii) Construct a schedule of accumulation of discount.

**SOLUTION**

(i) FV = 10 000.00;  $n = 4(2) = 8$;  P/Y = 2;  C/Y = 2;

$b = \dfrac{5.5\%}{2} = 2.75\% = 0.0275$;  I/Y = 7;  $i = \dfrac{7\%}{2} = 3.5\% = 0.035$

Since $b < i$, the bond sells at a discount.

Discount $= (0.0275 \times 10\ 000.00) - (0.035 \times 10\ 000.00)\left(\dfrac{1 - 1.035^{-8}}{0.035}\right)$

$= (275.00 - 350.00)(6.873956)$

$= (-75.00)(6.873956)$

$= -\$515.55$

**Programmed Solution**

PMT $= (0.0275 \times 10\ 000) - (0.035 \times 10\ 000) = 275.00$

("END" mode)

(Set P/Y = 2; C/Y = 2) 0 [FV] 75 [PMT] 7 [I/Y]

8 [N] [CPT] [PV] [−515.546665]

The purchase price is 10 000.00 − 515.55 = $9484.45.

(ii) *Schedule of accumulation of discount*

| End of Interest Payment Interval | Coupon $b = 2.75\%$ | Interest on Book Value at Yield Rate $i = 3.5\%$ | Amount of Discount Accumulated | Book Value of Bond | Remaining Discount |
|---|---|---|---|---|---|
| 0 | | | | 9484.55 | 515.55 |
| 1 | 275.00 | 331.96 | 56.96 | 9541.41 | 458.59 |
| 2 | 275.00 | 333.95 | 58.95 | 9600.36 | 399.64 |
| 3 | 275.00 | 336.01 | 61.01 | 9661.37 | 338.63 |
| 4 | 275.00 | 338.15 | 63.15 | 9724.52 | 275.48 |
| 5 | 275.00 | 340.36 | 65.36 | 9789.88 | 210.12 |
| 6 | 275.00 | 342.65 | 67.65 | 9857.53 | 142.47 |
| 7 | 275.00 | 345.01 | 70.01 | 9927.54 | 72.46 |
| 8 | 275.00 | 347.46 | 72.46 | 10 000.00 | 0.00 |
| TOTAL | 2200.00 | 2715.55 | 515.55 | | |

*Explanations of schedule*

1. The original book value shown is the purchase price of $9484.55.
2. At the end of the first interest payment interval, the coupon is 10 000.00(0.0275) = $275; the interest required according to the yield rate is 9484.55(0.035) = $331.96; the difference used to reduce the discount and to increase the book value is 331.96 − 275.00 = $56.96; the book value is 9484.55 + 56.96 = $9541.41; and the remaining discount is 515.55 − 56.96 = $458.59.
3. The coupon at the end of the second interest payment interval is again $275; the interest required on the book value is 9541.41(0.035) = $333.95; the difference is 333.95 − 275.00 = $58.95; the book value is 9541.41 + 58.95 = $9600.36; and the remaining discount is 458.59 − 58.95 = $399.64.
4. Continue in a similar manner until the maturity date when the principal is reached. If a rounding error becomes apparent at the end of the final interest payment interval, adjust the final interest on the book value at the yield rate to make the remaining discount equal to zero and obtain the exact principal as the book value.
5. The totals provide useful accounting information showing the total interest received ($2200) and the net income realized ($2715.55).

## C. Book value of a bond—finding the gain or loss on the sale of a bond

**EXAMPLE 15.3C**

A $10 000, 8% bond redeemable at par with semi-annual coupons was purchased fifteen years before maturity to yield 6% compounded semi-annually. The bond was sold three years later at 101.25. Find the gain or loss on the sale of the bond.

**SOLUTION**

The market quotation of 101.25 indicates that the bond was sold at 101.25% of its face value. The proceeds from the sale of the bond are 10 000.00(1.0125) = $10 125. To find the gain or loss on the sale of the bond, we need to know the book value of the bond at the date of sale. This we can do by determining the original purchase price, constructing a bond schedule, and reading the book value at the time of sale from the schedule.

$$FV = 10\,000.00; \quad n = 15(2) = 30$$

$$P/Y = 2; \quad C/Y = 2; \quad I/Y = 6; \quad b = \frac{8\%}{2} = 4\% = 0.04; \quad i = \frac{6\%}{2} = 3\% = 0.03$$

Since $b > i$, the bond was bought at a premium.

$$\text{Premium} = (0.04 \times 10\,000.00) - (0.03 \times 10\,000.00)\left(\frac{1 - 1.03^{-30}}{0.03}\right)$$
$$= (400.00 - 300.00)(19.600441)$$
$$= (100.00)(19.600441)$$
$$= \$1960.04$$

## Programmed Solution

$PMT = (0.04 \times 10\ 000) - (0.03 \times 10\ 000) = 100.00$

("END" mode)

(Set P/Y = 2; C/Y = 2) 0 [FV] 100 [PMT] 6 [I/Y] 30 [N]

[CPT] [PV] [−1960.044135]

The purchase price is 10 000.00 + 1960.04 = $11 960.04.

### Schedule of amortization of premium

| End of Interest Payment Interval | Coupon $b = 4\%$ | Interest on Book Value at Yield Rate $i = 3\%$ | Amount of Premium Amortized | Book Value of Bond | Remaining Premium |
|---|---|---|---|---|---|
| 0 | | | | 11 960.04 | 1960.04 |
| 1 | 400.00 | 358.80 | 41.20 | 11 918.84 | 1918.84 |
| 2 | 400.00 | 357.57 | 42.43 | 11 876.41 | 1876.41 |
| 3 | 400.00 | 356.29 | 43.71 | 11 832.70 | 1832.70 |
| 4 | 400.00 | 354.98 | 45.02 | 11 787.68 | 1787.68 |
| 5 | 400.00 | 353.63 | 46.37 | 11 741.31 | 1741.31 |
| 6 | 400.00 | 352.24 | 47.76 | 11 693.55 | 1693.55 |
| | etc. | | | | |

The book value after three years (six semi-annual periods) is $11 693.55. Since the book value is greater than the proceeds, the loss on the sale of the bond is 11 693.55 − 10 125.00 = $1568.55.

We can solve this problem more quickly by computing the book value directly. The book value of a bond at a given time is the purchase price of the bond on that date. We can determine the book value of a bond without constructing a bond schedule by using Formula 15.1 or 15.3. This approach can also be used to verify book values in a bond schedule.

$FV = 10\ 000.00$; $n = (15 - 3)(2) = 24$; $b = 4\%$; $i = 3\%$

$Premium = (0.04 \times 10\ 000.00) - (0.03 \times 10\ 000.00)\left(\dfrac{1 - 1.03^{-24}}{0.03}\right)$

$= (100.00)(16.935542) = \$1693.55$

## Programmed Solution

$PMT = (0.04 \times 10\ 000) - (0.03 \times 10\ 000) = 100.00$

("END" mode)

(Set P/Y = 2; C/Y = 2) 0 [FV] 100 [PMT] 6 [I/Y]

24 [N] [CPT] [PV] [−1693.554212]

The purchase price is 10 000.00 + 1693.55 = $11 693.55.
The loss on the sale is 11 693.55 − 10 125.00 = $1568.55.

## EXERCISE 15.3

If you choose, you can use these Excel functions to answer the questions indicated below: *Bond Purchase Price (PRICE), Days Since Last Interest Date (COUPDAYBS), Total Number of Days in the Coupon Period (COUPDAYS),* and *Total Number of Remaining Coupon Periods (COUPNUM).* Refer to **PRICE, COUPDAYBS, COUPDAYS,** and **COUPNUM** on the Spreadsheet Template Disk to learn how to use these Excel functions.

  **A.**

For each of the following bonds, compute the premium or discount and the purchase price, and construct the appropriate bond schedule.

1. A $5000, 6% bond redeemable at par in three-and-a-half years with semi-annual coupons is purchased to yield 6.5% compounded semi-annually.                    Reference Example 15.3B

2. A $25 000 bond with interest at 12.5% payable quarterly redeemable at par is bought two years before maturity to yield 11% compounded quarterly.

3. A $1000, 12% bond with semi-annual coupons redeemable at par on September 1, 2011 is bought on March 1, 2008 to yield 10% compounded semi-annually.

4. A $10 000, 7.75% bond with annual coupons redeemable at par in seven years is bought to yield 7.25% compounded annually.

**B.** Find the gain or loss on the sale of each of the following bonds without constructing a bond schedule.

1. A $25 000, 10.5% bond redeemable at par with semi-annual coupons bought ten years before maturity to yield 12% compounded semi-annually is sold four years before maturity at 99.25.                    Reference Example 15.3C

2. Four $5000, 8.5% bonds with interest payable semi-annually redeemable at par were bought twenty years before maturity to yield 7.5% compounded semi-annually. The bonds were sold three years later at 103.625.

3. A $5000 bond with 8% interest payable semi-annually redeemable at par on June 1, 2019 was bought on December 1, 2005 to yield 9% compounded semi-annually. The bond was sold on September 22, 2009 at 101.375.

4. Three $10 000, 10.5% bonds with quarterly coupons redeemable at par on August 1, 2015 were bought on May 1, 2001 to yield 12% compounded quarterly. The bonds were sold on January 16, 2009 at 93.5.

# 15.4 FINDING THE YIELD RATE

## A. Quoted price of a bond—buying bonds on the market

Bonds are usually bought or sold through a bond exchange where agents trade bonds on behalf of their clients. To allow for the different denominations, bonds are offered at a market price stated as a percent of their face value.

It is understood that, if the bond is bought between interest dates, such a quoted price does not include any accrued interest. As explained in Section 15.1, the seller of a bond is entitled to the interest earned by the bond to the date of sale and the interest is added to the quoted price to obtain the cash price.

**EXAMPLE 15.4A**

A $5000, 8% bond with semi-annual coupons payable April 1 and October 1 is purchased on August 25 at 104.75. What is the cash price of the bond?

**SOLUTION**

The quoted price is 5000.00(1.0475) = $5237.50.
The time period April 1 to August 25 contains 146 days; the number of days in the interest payment interval April 1 to October 1 is 183.

$$PV = 5000.00; \quad r = i = \frac{8\%}{2} = 4\% = 0.04; \quad t = \frac{146}{183}$$

The accrued interest is $5000.00(0.04)\left(\dfrac{146}{183}\right) = \$159.56.$

The cash price is 5237.50 + 159.56 = $5397.06.

## B. Finding the yield rate—the average investment method

When bonds are bought on the market, the yield rate is not directly available; it needs to be determined. The simplest method in use is the so-called **method of averages**, which gives a reasonable approximation of the yield rate as the ratio of the average income per interest payment interval to the average book value.

$$\text{APPROXIMATE VALUE OF } i = \frac{\text{AVERAGE INCOME PER INTEREST PAYMENT INTERVAL}}{\text{AVERAGE BOOK VALUE}}$$

where

$$\text{AVERAGE BOOK VALUE} = \frac{1}{2}(\text{QUOTED PRICE} + \text{REDEMPTION PRICE})$$

and

$$\begin{aligned} \text{AVERAGE INCOME} \\ \text{PER INTEREST} \\ \text{PAYMENT INTERVAL} \end{aligned} = \frac{\text{TOTAL INTEREST PAYMENTS} \begin{array}{l} - \text{ PREMIUM} \\ + \text{ DISCOUNT} \end{array}}{\text{NUMBER OF INTEREST PAYMENT INTERVALS}}$$

———— Formula 15.4

**EXAMPLE 15.4B**

A $25 000, 7.5% bond with semi-annual coupons redeemable at par in ten years is purchased at 103.5. What is the approximate yield rate?

**SOLUTION**

The quoted price (initial book value) is 25 000.00(1.035) = $25 875.00; the principal is $25 000.00.

The average book value is $\dfrac{1}{2}$(25 875.00 + 25 000.00) = $25 437.50.

The semi-annual interest payment is $25\,000.00\left(\dfrac{0.075}{2}\right) = \$937.50;$

the number of interest payments to maturity is $10(2) = 20$;
the total interest payments are $20(937.50) = \$18\,750.00$;
the premium is $25\,875.00 - 25\,000.00 = \$875.00$.

$$\text{Average income per interest payment interval} = \frac{18\,750.00 - 875.00}{20} = \$893.75$$

$$\text{Approximate value of } i = \frac{893.75}{25\,437.50} = 0.035135 = 3.51\%$$

The yield rate is $2(3.51) = 7.02\%$.

---

**EXAMPLE 15.4C**

Eight $1000, 6% bonds with semi-annual coupons redeemable at par in seventeen years are purchased at 97.375. What is the approximate yield rate?

**SOLUTION**

The quoted price is $8000.00(0.97375) = \$7790.00$;
the principal is $8000.00;

$$\text{the average book value is } \frac{(7790.00 + 8000.00)}{2} = \$7895.00.$$

$$\text{The semi-annual interest payment is } 8000.00\left(\frac{0.06}{2}\right) = \$240.00;$$

the number of interest payments to maturity is $17(2) = 34$;
the total interest payments are $34(240.00) = \$8160.00$;
the bond discount is $8000.00 - 7790.00 = \$210.00$.

$$\text{Average income per interest payment interval} = \frac{(8160.00 + 210.00)}{34} = \$246.18$$

$$\text{The approximate value of } i \text{ is } \frac{246.18}{7895.00} = 0.031182 = 3.12\%.$$

The approximate yield rate is $2(3.12\%) = 6.24\%$.

---

**EXAMPLE 15.4D**

A $5000, 10% bond with semi-annual coupons redeemable at par on July 15, 2018 is quoted on December 2, 2006 at 103.75. What is the approximate yield rate?

**SOLUTION**

To find the approximate yield rate for a bond purchased between interest dates, assume that the price was quoted on the nearest interest date. Since the interest dates are January 15 and July 15, the nearest interest date is January 15, 2007, which is 11.5 years before maturity.

The quoted price is $5000.00(1.0375) = \$5187.50$;
the redemption price is $5000.00;

$$\text{the average book value is } \frac{(5187.50 + 5000.00)}{2} = \$5093.75.$$

$$\text{The semi-annual interest is } 5000.00\left(\frac{0.10}{2}\right) = \$250.00;$$

the number of interest payments to maturity is $11.5(2) = 23$;
the total interest payments are $23(250.00) = \$5750.00$;
the premium is $5187.50 - 5000.00 = \$187.50$.

$$\text{The average income per interest payment interval} = \frac{(5750.00 - 187.50)}{23}$$

$$= \$241.85$$

$$\text{The approximate value of } i \text{ is } \frac{241.85}{5093.75} = 0.047480 = 4.75\%.$$

The approximate yield rate is $2(4.75\%) = 9.50\%$.

## C. Finding the accurate yield rate by trial and error

 A method of trial and error similar to the one used to find the nominal rate of interest may be used to obtain as precise an approximation to the yield rate as desired. The method is illustrated in Appendix B on the CD-ROM to this book.

### EXERCISE 15.4

Use the method of averages to find the approximate yield rate for each of the six bonds shown in the table below. All are redeemed at par.

| | Face Value | Bond Rate Payable Semi-annually | Time Before Maturity | Market Quotation |
|---|---|---|---|---|
| 1. | $10 000 | 6% | 15 years | 101.375 |
| 2. | 5 000 | 10.5 | 7 years | 94.75 |
| 3. | 25 000 | 7.5 | 10 years | 97.125 |
| 4. | 1 000 | 8.5 | 8 years | 101 |
| 5. | 50 000 | 9 | 5 years, 4 months | 98.875 |
| 6. | 20 000 | 7 | 9 years, 8 months | 109.25 |

# 15.5 SINKING FUNDS

## A. Finding the size of the periodic payment

**Sinking funds** are interest-bearing accounts into which payments are made at periodic intervals to provide a desired sum of money at a specified future time. Such funds usually involve large sums of money used by both the private and the public sector to repay loans, redeem bonds, finance future capital acquisitions, provide for the replacement of depreciable plant and equipment, and recover investments in depletable natural resources.

The basic problem in dealing with sinking funds is to determine the *size of the periodic payments* that will accumulate to a known future amount. These payments form an annuity in which the accumulated value is known.

Depending on whether the periodic payments are made at the end or at the beginning of each payment period, the annuity formed is an ordinary annuity or an annuity due. Depending on whether or not the payment interval is equal in length to the interest conversion period, the annuity formed is a simple annuity or a general annuity. However, since sinking funds are normally set up so that the payment interval and the interest conversion period are equal in length, only the simple annuity cases are considered in this text.

(a) For sinking funds with payments at the beginning of each payment interval,

$$FV_n = PMT\left[\frac{(1 + i)^n - 1}{i}\right] \text{——————— Formula 11.1}$$

(b) For sinking funds with payments at the beginning of each payment interval,

$$FV_n(\text{due}) = PMT(1 + i)\left[\frac{(1 + i)^n - 1}{i}\right] \text{——————— Formula 13.1}$$

---

**EXAMPLE 15.5A**

Western Oil plans to create a sinking fund of $20 000 by making equal deposits at the end of every six months for four years. Interest is 6% compounded semi-annually.

(i) What is the size of the semi-annual deposit into the fund?

(ii) What is the total amount deposited into the fund?

(iii) How much of the fund will be interest?

**SOLUTION**

(i) $FV_n = 20\ 000.00$; P/Y = 2; C/Y = 2; $n = 4(2) = 8$; I/Y = 6; $i = \dfrac{6\%}{2} = 3\%$

$$20\ 000.00 = PMT\left(\frac{1.03^8 - 1}{0.03}\right)$$

$$20\ 000.00 = PMT(8.892336)$$

$$PMT = \$2249.13$$

**Programmed Solution**

("END" mode)

(Set P/Y = 2; C/Y = 2) 0 [ PV ] 20 000 [ FV ] 6 [ I/Y ]

8 [ N ] [ CPT ] [ PMT ] [ -2249.127777 ]

The size of the semi-annual payment is $2249.13.

(ii) The total deposited into the sinking fund is 8(2249.13) = $17 993.04.

(iii) The amount of interest in the fund is 20 000.00 − 17 993.04 = $2006.96.

---

**EXAMPLE 15.5B**

Ace Machinery wants to provide for replacement of equipment seven years from now estimated to cost $60 000.00. To do so, the company set up a sinking fund into which it will pay equal sums of money at the beginning of each of the next seven years. Interest paid by the fund is 11.5% compounded annually.

(i) What is the size of the annual payment into the fund?

(ii) What is the total paid into the fund by Ace Machinery?

(iii) How much of the fund will be interest?

**SOLUTION**

(i) $FV_n(due) = 60\,000.00$; $P/Y = 1$; $C/Y = 1$; $I/Y = 11.5$; $n = 7$; $i = 11.5\%$

$$60\,000.00 = PMT(1.115)\left(\frac{1.115^7 - 1}{0.115}\right)$$

$$60\,000.00 = PMT(1.115)(9.934922)$$
$$PMT = \$5416.42$$

**Programmed Solution**

("BGN" mode)
(Set P/Y = 1; C/Y = 1) 0 [PV] 60 000 [FV] 11.5 [I/Y]

7 [N] [CPT] [PMT] [-5416.415057]

The size of the annual payment is $5416.42.

(ii) The total paid into the fund by Ace Machinery will be
7(5416.42) = \$37\,914.94.

(iii) The interest earned by the fund will be 60 000.00 − 37 914.94 = \$22 085.06.

## B. Constructing sinking fund schedules

The details of a sinking fund can be presented in the form of a schedule. Sinking fund schedules normally show the payment number (or payment date), the periodic payment into the fund, the interest earned by the fund, the increase in the fund, and the accumulated balance.

**EXAMPLE 15.5C**

Construct a sinking fund schedule for Example 15.5A.

**SOLUTION**

$PMT = 2249.13$; $n = 8$; $i = 3\% = 0.03$

*Sinking fund schedule*

| Payment Interval Number | Periodic Payment | Interest for Payment Interval $i = 0.03$ | Increase in Fund | Balance in Fund at End of Payment Interval |
|---|---|---|---|---|
| 0 | | | | 0.00 |
| 1 | 2 249.13 | 0.00 | 2 249.13 | 2 249.13 |
| 2 | 2 249.13 | 67.47 | 2 316.60 | 4 565.73 |
| 3 | 2 249.13 | 136.97 | 2 386.10 | 6 951.83 |
| 4 | 2 249.13 | 208.55 | 2 457.68 | 9 409.51 |
| 5 | 2 249.13 | 282.29 | 2 531.42 | 11 940.93 |
| 6 | 2 249.13 | 358.23 | 2 607.36 | 14 548.29 |
| 7 | 2 249.13 | 436.45 | 2 685.58 | 17 233.87 |
| 8 | 2 249.13 | 517.02 | 2 766.15 | 20 000.02 |
| TOTAL | 17 993.04 | 2006.98 | 20 000.02 | |

*Explanations regarding the construction of the sinking fund schedule*

1. The payment number 0 is used to introduce the beginning balance.

2. The first deposit is made at the end of the first payment interval. The interest earned by the fund during the first payment interval is $0, the increase in the fund is $2249.13, and the balance is $2249.13.

3. The second deposit is added at the end of the second payment interval. The interest for the interval is 0.03(2249.13) = $67.47. The increase in the fund is 2249.13 + 67.47 = $2316.60, and the new balance in the fund is 2249.13 + 2316.60 = $4565.73.

4. The third deposit is made at the end of the third payment interval. The interest for the interval is 0.03(4565.73) = $136.97, the increase in the fund is 2249.13 + 136.97 = $2386.10, and the new balance in the fund is 2386.10 + 4565.73 = $6951.83.

5. Calculations for the remaining payment intervals are made in a similar manner.

6. The final balance in the sinking fund will probably be slightly different from the expected value. This difference is a result of rounding. The balance may be left as shown ($20 000.02) or the exact balance of $20 000.00 may be obtained by adjusting the last payment to $2249.11.

7. The three totals shown are useful and should be obtained for each schedule. The total increase in the fund must be the same as the final balance. The total periodic payments are 8(2249.13) = 17 993.04. The total interest is the difference: 20 000.02 − 17 993.04 = $2006.98.

**EXAMPLE 15.5D**

Construct a sinking fund schedule for Example 15.5B (an annuity due with payments at the beginning of each payment interval).

**SOLUTION**

PMT = 5416.42 (made at the beginning);   $n = 7$;   $i = 11.5\% = 0.115$

*Sinking fund schedule*

| Payment Interval Number | Periodic Payment | Interest for Payment Interval $i = 0.115$ | Increase in Fund | Balance in Fund at End of Payment Interval |
|---|---|---|---|---|
| 0 | | | | 0.00 |
| 1 | 5 416.42 | 622.89 | 6 039.31 | 6 039.31 |
| 2 | 5 416.42 | 1 317.41 | 6 733.83 | 12 773.14 |
| 3 | 5 416.42 | 2 091.80 | 7 508.22 | 20 281.36 |
| 4 | 5 416.42 | 2 955.24 | 8 371.66 | 28 653.02 |
| 5 | 5 416.42 | 3 917.99 | 9 334.41 | 37 987.43 |
| 6 | 5 416.42 | 4 991.44 | 10 407.86 | 48 395.29 |
| 7 | 5 416.42 | 6 188.35 | 11 604.77 | 60 000.06 |
| TOTAL | 37 914.94 | 22 085.12 | 60 000.06 | |

*Explanations regarding the construction of the sinking fund schedule*

1. The starting balance is $0.

2. The first deposit is made at the beginning of the first payment interval and the interest earned by the fund during the first payment interval is $0.115(5416.42) = \$622.89$. The increase in the fund is $5416.42 + 622.89 = \$6039.31$ and the balance is $6039.31.

3. The second deposit is made at the beginning of the second payment interval, the interest earned is $0.115(6039.31 + 5416.42) = \$1317.41$, the increase is $5416.42 + 1317.41 = \$6733.83$, and the balance is $6039.31 + 6733.83 = \$12\,773.14$.

4. The third deposit is made at the beginning of the third payment interval, the interest earned is $0.115(12\,773.14 + 5416.42) = \$2091.80$, the increase is $5416.42 + 2091.80 = \$7508.22$, and the balance is $12\,773.14 + 7508.22 = \$20\,281.36$.

5. Calculations for the remaining payment intervals are made in a similar manner. Be careful to add the deposit to the previous balance when computing the interest earned.

6. The final balance of $60\,000.06 is slightly different from the expected balance of $60\,000.00 due to rounding. The exact balance may be obtained by adjusting the last payment to $5416.36.

7. The total increase in the fund must equal the final balance of $60\,000.06. The total periodic payments are $7(5416.42) = \$37\,914.94$. The total interest is $60\,000.06 - 37\,914.94 = \$22\,085.12$.

## C. Finding the accumulated balance and interest earned or increase in a sinking fund for a payment interval; constructing partial sinking fund schedules

**EXAMPLE 15.5E**

For Examples 15.5A and 15.5B, compute

(i) the accumulated value in the fund at the end of the third payment interval;

(ii) the interest earned by the fund in the fifth payment interval;

(iii) the increase in the fund in the fifth interval.

**SOLUTION**

(i) The balance in a sinking fund at any time is the accumulated value of the payments made into the fund.
*For Example 15.5A* (when payments are made at the end of each payment interval)

$$PMT = 2249.13; \quad n = 3; \quad i = 3\%$$

$$FV_n = 2249.13\left(\frac{1.03^3 - 1}{0.03}\right)$$
$$= 2249.13(3.0909)$$
$$= \$6951.83 \quad\text{——————— see sinking fund schedule, Example 15.5C}$$

**Programmed Solution**

("END" mode)

(Set P/Y = 2; C/Y = 2) 0 [PV] 2249.13 [±] [PMT] 6 [I/Y]

3 [N] [CPT] [FV] [6951.835917]

*For Example 15.5B* (when payments are made at the beginning of each payment interval)

PMT = 5416.42;   $n = 3$;   $i = 11.5\%$

$$FV_n(due) = 5416.42(1.115)\left(\frac{1.115^3 - 1}{0.115}\right)$$
$$= 5416.42(1.115)(3.358225)$$
$$= \$20\,281.36 \quad\text{——— see sinking fund schedule, Example 15.5D}$$

**Programmed Solution**

("BGN" mode)

(Set P/Y = 1; C/Y = 1) 0 [PV] 5416.42 [±] [PMT]

11.5 [I/Y] 3 [N] [CPT] [FV] [20281.35612]

(ii) The interest earned during any given payment interval is based on the balance in the fund at the beginning of the interval. This figure is the same as the balance at the end of the previous payment interval.

*For Example 15.5A*
The balance at the end of the fourth payment interval

$$FV_4 = 2249.13\left(\frac{1.03^4 - 1}{0.03}\right)$$
$$= 2249.13(4.183627)$$
$$= \$9409.52$$

**Programmed Solution**

("END" mode)

(Set P/Y = 2; C/Y = 2) 0 [PV] 2249.13 [±] [PMT]

6 [I/Y] 4 [N] [CPT] [FV] [9409.520995]

The interest earned by the fund in the fifth payment interval is
0.03(9409.52) = \$282.29.

*For Example 15.5B*
The balance in the fund at the end of the fourth payment interval

$$FV_4 = 5416.42(1.115)\left(\frac{1.115^4 - 1}{0.115}\right)$$
$$= 5416.42(1.115)(4.744421)$$
$$= \$28\ 653.02$$

**Programmed Solution**

("BGN" mode)

(Set P/Y = 1; C/Y = 1) 0 [ PV ] 5416.42 [ ± ] [ PMT ]

11.5 [ I/Y ] 4 [ N ] [ CPT ] [ FV ] [ 28653.02037 ]

The interest earned by the fund in the fifth payment interval is
0.115(28 653.02 + 5416.42) = 0.115(34 069.44) = \$3917.99.

(iii) The increase in the sinking fund in any given payment interval is the interest earned by the fund during the payment interval plus the periodic payment.

*For Example 15.5A*
The increase in the fund during the fifth payment interval is
282.29 + 2249.13 = \$2531.42.

*For Example 15.5B*
The increase in the fund during the fifth payment interval is
3917.99 + 5416.42 = \$9334.41.

---

**EXAMPLE 15.5F**

The board of directors of National Credit Union decided to establish a building fund of \$130 000 by making equal deposits into a sinking fund at the end of every three months for seven years. Interest is 12% compounded quarterly.

   (i) Compute the increase in the fund during the twelfth payment interval.

   (ii) Construct a partial sinking fund schedule showing details of the first three deposits, the twelfth deposit, the last three deposits, and totals.

**SOLUTION**

Size of the quarterly deposit:

$$FV_n = 130\ 000.00; \quad P/Y = 4; \quad C/Y = 4; \quad I/Y = 12$$
$$n = 7(4) = 28; \quad i = \frac{12\%}{4} = 3\%$$
$$130\ 000.00 = PMT\left(\frac{1.03^{28} - 1}{0.03}\right)$$
$$130\ 000.00 = PMT(42.930922)$$
$$PMT = \$3028.12$$

**Programmed Solution**

("END" mode)

(Set P/Y = 4; C/Y = 4) 0 [ PV ] 130 000 [ FV ] 12 [ I/Y ]

28 [ N ] [ CPT ] [ PMT ] [ -3028.120347 ]

(i) Balance in the fund at the end of the eleventh payment interval

$$FV_n = 3028.12\left(\frac{1.03^{11} - 1}{0.03}\right)$$
$$= 3028.12(12.807796)$$
$$= \$38\,783.54$$

**Programmed Solution**

("END" mode)

(Set P/Y = 4; C/Y = 4) 0 [ PV ] 3028.12 [ ± ] [ PMT ]

12 [ I/Y ] 11 [ N ] [ CPT ] [ FV ] [ 38783.54229 ]

The interest earned by the fund during the twelfth payment interval is 0.03(38 783.54) = \$1163.51.

The increase in the fund during the twelfth payment interval is 1163.51 + 3028.12 = \$4191.63.

(ii) The last three payments are Payments 26, 27, and 28. To show details of these, we must know the accumulated value after 25 payment intervals.

$$FV_{25} = 3028.12\left(\frac{1.03^{25} - 1}{0.03}\right) = 3028.12(36.459264) = \$110\,403.03$$

**Programmed Solution**

("END" mode)

(Set P/Y = 4; C/Y = 4) 0 [ PV ] 3028.12 [ ± ] [ PMT ]

12 [ I/Y ] 25 [ N ] [ CPT ] [ FV ] [ 110403.0275 ]

*Partial sinking fund schedule*

| Payment Interval Number | Periodic Payment Made at End | Interest for Payment Interval $i = 0.03$ | Increase in Fund | Balance in Fund at End of Payment Interval |
|---|---|---|---|---|
| 0 | | | | 0.00 |
| 1 | 3 028.12 | 0.00 | 3 028.12 | 3 028.12 |
| 2 | 3 028.12 | 90.84 | 3 118.96 | 6 147.08 |
| 3 | 3 028.12 | 184.41 | 3 212.53 | 9 359.61 |
| • | • | • | • | • |
| • | • | • | • | • |

| Payment Interval Number | Periodic Payment Made at End | Interest for Payment Interval $i = 0.03$ | Increase in Fund | Balance in Fund at End of Payment Interval |
|---|---|---|---|---|
| 11 | • | • | • | 38 783.54 |
| 12 | 3 028.12 | 1 163.51 | 4 191.63 | 42 975.17 |
| • | • | • | • | • |
| • | • | • | • | • |
| 25 | • | • | • | 110 403.03 |
| 26 | 3 028.12 | 3 312.09 | 6 340.21 | 116 743.24 |
| 27 | 3 028.12 | 3 502.30 | 6 530.42 | 123 273.66 |
| 28 | 3 028.12 | 3 698.21 | 6 726.33 | 129 999.99 |
| TOTAL | 84 787.36 | 45 212.63 | 129 999.99 | |

**EXAMPLE 15.5G**

Laurin and Company want to build up a fund of $75 000 by making payments of $2000 at the beginning of every six months into a sinking fund earning 11% compounded semi-annually. Construct a partial sinking fund schedule showing details of the first three payments, the last three payments, and totals.

**SOLUTION**

To show details of the last three payments, we need to know the number of payments.

$FV_n(due) = 75\ 000.00;$ PMT = 2000.00; P/Y = 2; C/Y = 2; I/Y = 11;
$i = \dfrac{11\%}{2} = 5.5\%$

$$75\ 000.00 = 2000.00(1.055)\left(\frac{1.055^n - 1}{0.055}\right)$$

$$1.055^n = 2.954976$$
$$n \ln 1.055 = \ln 2.954976$$
$$n\,(0.053541) = 1.0834906$$
$$n = 20.236741$$

**Programmed Solution**

("BGN" mode)

(Set P/Y = 2; C/Y = 2) 0 [ PV ] 75 000 [ FV ] 2000 [ ± ] [ PMT ]

11 [ I/Y ] [ CPT ] [ N ] [ 20.236741 ]

Twenty-one payments are needed. The last three payments are Payments 19, 20, and 21. The balance in the fund at the end of the 18th payment interval

$$FV_{18}(due) = 2000.\,00(1.055)\left(\frac{1.055^{18} - 1}{0.055}\right)$$
$$= 2000.00(1.055)(29.481205)$$
$$= \$62\ 205.34$$

**Programmed Solution**

("BGN" mode)

(Set P/Y = 2; C/Y = 2) 0 [ PV ] 2000 [ ± ] [ PMT ]

11 [ I/Y ] 18 [ N ] [ CPT ] [ FV ] [ 62 205.3422 ]

*Partial sinking fund schedule*

| Payment Interval Number | Periodic Payment Made at Beginning | Interest for Payment Interval $i = 0.055$ | Increase in Fund | Balance in Fund at End of Payment Interval |
|---|---|---|---|---|
| 0 | | | | 0.00 |
| 1 | 2 000.00 | 110.00 | 2 110.00 | 2 110.00 |
| 2 | 2 000.00 | 226.05 | 2 226.05 | 4 336.05 |
| 3 | 2 000.00 | 348.48 | 2 348.48 | 6 684.53 |
| • | • | • | • | • |
| • | • | • | • | • |
| 18 | • | • | • | 62 205.34 |
| 19 | 2 000.00 | 3 531.29 | 5 531.29 | 67 736.63 |
| 20 | 2 000.00 | 3 835.51 | 5 835.51 | 73 572.14 |
| 21 | 1 427.86 | 0.00 | 1 427.86 | 75 000.00 |
| TOTAL | 41 427.86 | 33 572.14 | 75 000.00 | |

*Note:* The desired balance in the sinking fund will be reached at the beginning of the 21st payment interval by depositing $1427.86.

## D. Computer application—sinking fund schedule

The schedule in Example 15.5C displays the manual calculations for a sinking fund with an interest rate of 3% and eight periodic payments. Microsoft Excel and other spreadsheet programs can be used to create a file that will immediately display the results of a change in the interest rate, the increase in the fund, and the accumulated balance.

The following steps are general instructions for creating a file to calculate the sinking fund schedule in Example 15.5C. The formulas in the spreadsheet file were created using Excel; however, most spreadsheet software works similarly.

Although this exercise assumes a basic understanding of spreadsheet applications, someone without previous experience with spreadsheets will be able to complete it.

**STEP 1**   Enter the labels shown in Figure 15.2 in row 1 and in column A.

**STEP 2**   Enter the numbers shown in cells E2, F2, and F4. Do not type in a dollar sign or a comma.

**STEP 3**   Enter only the formulas shown in cells B3, C3, D3, and E3. Make sure that the formula entry includes the dollar ($) sign as shown in the figure.

**STEP 4**    The formulas entered in Step 3 can be copied through the remaining cells.
   (a) Select and Copy the formulas in cells B3, C3, D3, and E3.
   (b) Select cells B4 to B10 and then Paste.
   (c) The formulas are now active in all the cells.

**STEP 5**    Enter the formula shown in cell B11, and then use Copy and Paste to enter the formula in cells C11 and D11.

**STEP 6**    To ensure readability of the spreadsheet, format the numbers to display in two decimal places, and widen the columns to display the full labels. This spreadsheet can now be used to reflect changes in aspects of the sinking fund and create a new schedule. Use cell F2 for new payment amounts and cell F4 for new interest rates.

**Figure 15.2**

|  | A | B | C | D | E | F |
|---|---|---|---|---|---|---|
| 1 | Payment Interval | Periodic Payment | Interest | Increase in Fund | Balance at End | |
| 2 | 0 | | | | 0 | 2249.13 |
| 3 | 1 | = $F$2 | = $F$4*E2 | = B3+C3 | = E2+D3 | |
| 4 | 2 | = $F$2 | = $F$4*E3 | = B4+C4 | = E3+D4 | = 0.03 |
| 5 | 3 | = $F$2 | = $F$4*E4 | = B5+C5 | = E4+D5 | |
| 6 | 4 | = $F$2 | = $F$4*E5 | = B6+C6 | = E5+D6 | |
| 7 | 5 | = $F$2 | = $F$4*E6 | = B7+C7 | = E6+D7 | |
| 8 | 6 | = $F$2 | = $F$4*E7 | = B8+C8 | = E7+D8 | |
| 9 | 7 | = $F$2 | = $F$4*E8 | = B9+C9 | = E8+D9 | |
| 10 | 8 | = $F$2 | = $F$4*E9 | = B10+C10 | = E9+D10 | |
| 11 | Totals | = SUM(B3:B10) | = SUM(C3:C10) | = SUM(D3:D10) | | |

Workbook 1

# E. Debt retirement by the sinking fund method

When a sinking fund is created to retire a debt, the debt principal is repaid in total at the due date from the proceeds of the sinking fund while interest on the principal is paid periodically. The payments into the sinking fund are usually made at the same time as the interest payments are made. The sum of the two payments (debt interest payment plus payment into the sinking fund) is called the **periodic cost of the debt**. The difference between the debt principal and the sinking fund balance at any point is called the **book value of the debt**.

## POINTERS AND PITFALLS

When a debt is retired by the sinking fund method, the borrower is, in effect, paying two separate annuities. Sinking fund installments are made to the fund's trustee, while periodic interest payments are made to the lender. Because of these two payment streams, two interest rates must be quoted in questions involving sinking fund debt retirement. One rate determines the *interest revenue* generated by the sinking fund, and the other rate determines the *interest penalty* paid by the borrower to the lender.

**EXAMPLE 15.5H**

The City Board of Education borrowed $750 000 for twenty years at 13% compounded annually to finance construction of Hillview Elementary School. The board created a sinking fund to repay the debt at the end of twenty years. Equal payments are made into the sinking fund at the end of each year and interest earned by the fund is 10.5% compounded annually. Rounding all computations to the nearest dollar,

(i) determine the annual cost of the debt;

(ii) compute the book value of the debt at the end of ten years;

(iii) construct a partial sinking fund schedule showing the book value of the debt, the three first payments, the three last payments, and the totals.

**SOLUTION**

(i) The annual interest cost on the principal:

$PV = 750\,000$;  $P/Y = 1$;  $C/Y = 1$;  $I/Y = 13$;  $i = 13\% = 0.13$;
$I = 750\,000(0.13) = \$97\,500$

The annual payment into the sinking fund

$FV_n = 750\,000$;  $n = 20$;  $I/Y = 10.5$;  $i = 10.5\%$

$$750\,000 = PMT\left(\frac{1.105^{20} - 1}{0.105}\right)$$

$750\,000 = PMT(60.630808)$
   $PMT = \$12\,369.95$

**Programmed Solution**

("END" mode)

(Set P/Y = 1; C/Y = 1) 0 [ PV ] 750 000 [ FV ] 10.5 [ I/Y ]

20 [ N ] [ CPT ] [ PMT ] [ −12369.94895 ]

The annual cost of the debt is 97 500 + 12 370 = $109 870.

(ii) The balance in the sinking fund after the tenth payment

$$FV_{10} = 12\,370\left(\frac{1.105^{10} - 1}{0.105}\right)$$

$= 12\,370(16.324579)$
$= \$201\,935$

**Programmed Solution**

("END" mode)

(Set P/Y = 1; C/Y = 1) 0 [ PV ] 12 370 [ ± ] [ PMT ] 10.5 [ I/Y ]

10 [ N ] [ CPT ] [ FV ] [ 201935.0483 ]

The book value of the debt at the end of the tenth year is
750 000 − 201 935 = $548 065.

(iii) The last three payments are Payments 18, 19, and 20. The balance in the sinking fund at the end of Year 17

$$FV_{17} = 12\,370\left(\frac{1.105^{17} - 1}{0.105}\right) = 12\,370(42.47213) = \$525\,380$$

**Programmed Solution**

("END" mode)

(Set P/Y = 1; C/Y = 1) 0 $\boxed{\text{PV}}$ 12 370 $\boxed{\pm}$ $\boxed{\text{PMT}}$

10.5 $\boxed{\text{I/Y}}$ 17 $\boxed{\text{N}}$ $\boxed{\text{CPT}}$ $\boxed{\text{FV}}$ $\boxed{525380.2441}$

*Partial sinking fund schedule*

| Payment Interval Number | Periodic Payment Made at End | Interest for Payment Interval i = 0.105 | Increase in Fund | Balance in Fund at End of Payment Interval | Book Value of Debt |
|---|---|---|---|---|---|
| 0 | | | | 0 | 750 000 |
| 1 | 12 370 | 0 | 12 370 | 12 370 | 737 630 |
| 2 | 12 370 | 1 299 | 13 669 | 26 039 | 723 961 |
| 3 | 12 370 | 2 734 | 15 104 | 41 143 | 708 857 |
| • | • | • | • | • | • |
| • | • | • | • | • | • |
| 17 | • | • | • | 525 380 | 224 620 |
| 18 | 12 370 | 55 165 | 67 535 | 592 915 | 157 085 |
| 19 | 12 370 | 62 256 | 74 626 | 667 541 | 82 459 |
| 20 | 12 367 | 70 092 | 82 459 | 750 000 | 0 |
| TOTAL | 247 397 | 502 603 | 750 000 | | |

*Note:* The last payment has been adjusted to create a fund of exactly $750 000.

# EXERCISE 15.5

If you choose, you can use Excel's *Periodic Payment Size (PMT)* functions to answer the questions indicated below. Refer to **PMT** on the Spreadsheet Template Disk to learn how to use these Excel functions.

**A.** For each of the four sinking funds listed in the table below, compute (a) the size of the periodic payment; (b) the accumulated balance at the time indicated.

| Amount of Sinking Fund | Payment Interval | Payments Made At: | Term | Interest Rate | Conversion Period | Accumulated Balance Required After: |
|---|---|---|---|---|---|---|
| **1.** $15 000 | 6 months | end | 10 years | 6% | semi-annually | 10th payment |
| **2.** 9 600 | 1 month | end | 8 years | 12 | monthly | 36th payment |
| **3.** 8 400 | 1 month | beginning | 15 years | 9 | monthly | 96th payment |
| **4.** 21 000 | 3 months | beginning | 20 years | 8 | quarterly | 28th payment |

 **B.** Each of the four debts listed in the table below is retired by the sinking fund method. Interest payments on the debt are made at the end of each payment interval and the payments into the sinking fund are made at the same time. Determine

**(a)** the size of the periodic interest expense of the debt;
**(b)** the size of the periodic payment into the sinking fund;
**(c)** the periodic cost of the debt;
**(d)** the book value of the debt at the time indicated.

| Debt Principal | Term of Debt | Payment Interval | Interest Rate On Debt | Interest Rate On Fund | Conversion Period | Book Value Required After: |
|---|---|---|---|---|---|---|
| **1.** $20 000 | 10 years | 3 months | 10% | 12% | quarterly | 6 years |
| **2.** 14 500 | 8 years | 6 months | 7 | 8.5 | semi-annually | 5 years |
| **3.** 10 000 | 5 years | 1 month | 7.5 | 6.0 | monthly | 4 years |
| **4.** 40 000 | 15 years | 3 months | 8.0 | 7.0 | quarterly | 10 years |

 **C.** Answer each of the following questions.

**1.** Hein Engineering expects to expand its plant facilities in six years at an estimated cost of $75 000. To provide for the expansion, a sinking fund has been established into which equal payments are made at the end of every three months. Interest is 5% compounded quarterly.
 **(a)** What is the size of the quarterly payments?
 **(b)** How much of the maturity value will be payments?
 **(c)** How much interest will the fund contain?

**2.** To redeem a $100 000 promissory note due in ten years, Cobblestone Enterprises has set up a sinking fund earning 7.5% compounded semi-annually. Equal deposits are made at the beginning of every six months.
 **(a)** What is the size of the semi-annual deposits?
 **(b)** How much of the maturity value of the fund is deposits?
 **(c)** How much is interest?

**3.** Equal deposits are made into a sinking fund at the end of each year for seven years. Interest is 5.5% compounded annually and the maturity value of the fund is $20 000. Find the size of the annual deposits and construct a sinking fund schedule showing totals.

**4.** A sinking fund amounting to $15 000 is to be created by making payments at the beginning of every six months for four years. Interest earned by the fund is

12.5% compounded semi-annually. Determine the size of the semi-annual payments and prepare a sinking fund schedule showing totals.

5. For Question 3, calculate the increase in the fund for the fourth year. Verify your answer by checking the sinking fund schedule.

6. For Question 4, compute the interest earned during the fifth payment interval. Verify your answer by checking the sinking fund schedule.

7. HY Industries Ltd. plans to replace a warehouse in twelve years at an anticipated cost of $45 000. To pay for the replacement, a sinking fund has been established into which equal payments are made at the end of every quarter. Interest is 10% compounded quarterly.
   (a) What is the size of the quarterly payments?
   (b) What is the accumulated balance just after the sixteenth payment?

8. To provide for expansion, Champlain Company has established a sinking fund earning 7% semi-annually. The fund is anticipated to reach a balance of $72 000 in fifteen years. Payments are made at the beginning of every six months.
   (a) What is the size of the semi-annual payment?
   (b) What is the accumulated balance at the end of the twentieth payment period?

9. Winooski Lamp Co. has borrowed $95 000 for capital expansion. The company must pay the interest on the loan at the end of every six months and make equal payments at the time of the interest payments into a sinking fund until the loan is retired in twenty years. Interest on the loan is 9% compounded semi-annually and interest on the sinking fund is 7% compounded semi-annually. (Round all answers to the nearest dollar.)
   (a) Determine the size of the periodic interest expense of the debt.
   (b) Determine the size of the periodic payment into the sinking fund.
   (c) What is the periodic cost of the debt?
   (d) What is the book value of the debt after fifteen years?

10. The City of Chatham has borrowed $80 000 to expand a community centre. The city must pay the interest on the loan at the end of every month and make equal payments at the time of the interest payments into a sinking fund until the loan is retired in twelve years. Interest on the loan is 6% compounded monthly and interest on the sinking fund is 7.5% compounded monthly. (Round all answers to the nearest dollar.)
   (a) Determine the size of the periodic interest expense of the debt.
   (b) Determine the size of the periodic payment into the sinking fund.
   (c) What is the periodic cost of the debt?
   (d) What is the book value of the debt after eight years?

11. Kirk, Klein & Co. requires $100 000 fifteen years from now to retire a debt. A sinking fund is established into which equal payments are made at the end of every month. Interest is 7.5% compounded monthly.
   (a) What is the size of the monthly payment?
   (b) What is the balance in the sinking fund after five years?

(c) How much interest will be earned by the fund in the 100th payment interval?

(d) By how much will the fund increase during the 150th payment interval?

(e) Construct a partial sinking fund schedule showing details of the first three payments, the last three payments, and totals.

12. The Town of Keewatin issued debentures worth $120 000 maturing in ten years to finance construction of water and sewer facilities. To redeem the debentures, the town council decided to make equal deposits into a sinking fund at the beginning of every three months. Interest earned by the sinking fund is 6% compounded quarterly.

(a) What is the size of the quarterly payment into the sinking fund?

(b) What is the balance in the fund after six years?

(c) How much interest is earned by the fund in the 28th payment interval?

(d) By how much will the fund increase in the 33rd payment interval?

(e) Prepare a partial sinking fund schedule showing details of the first three payments, the last three payments, and totals.

13. The Township of Langley borrowed $300 000 for road improvements. The debt agreement requires that the township pay the interest on the loan at the end of each year and make equal deposits at the time of the interest payments into a sinking fund until the loan is retired in twenty years. Interest on the loan is 8.25% compounded annually and interest earned by the sinking fund is 5.5% compounded annually. (Round all answers to the nearest dollar.)

(a) What is the annual interest expense?

(b) What is the size of the annual deposit into the sinking fund?

(c) What is the total annual cost of the debt?

(d) How much is the increase in the sinking fund in the tenth year?

(e) What is the book value of the debt after fifteen years?

(f) Construct a partial sinking fund schedule showing details, including the book value of the debt, for the first three years, the last three years, and totals.

14. Ontario Credit Union borrowed $225 000 at 13% compounded semi-annually from League Central to build an office complex. The loan agreement requires payment of interest at the end of every six months. In addition, the credit union is to make equal payments into a sinking fund so that the principal can be retired in total after fifteen years. Interest earned by the fund is 11% compounded semi-annually. (Round all answers to the nearest dollar.)

(a) What is the semi-annual interest payment on the debt?

(b) What is the size of the semi-annual deposits into the sinking fund?

(c) What is the total annual cost of the debt?

(d) What is the interest earned by the fund in the 20th payment interval?

(e) What is the book value of the debt after twelve years?

(f) Prepare a partial sinking fund schedule showing details, including the book value of the debt, for the first three years, the last three years, and totals.

## Review Exercise

1. A $5000, 11.5% bond with interest payable semi-annually is redeemable at par in twelve years. What is the purchase price to yield

   (a) 10.5% compounded semi-annually?

   (b) 13% compounded semi-annually?

2. A $10 000, 6% bond with semi-annual coupons is redeemable at par. What is the purchase price to yield 7.5% compounded semi-annually

   (a) nine years before maturity?

   (b) fifteen years before maturity?

3. A $25 000, 9% bond with interest payable quarterly is redeemable at par in six years. What is the purchase price to yield 8.25% compounded annually?

4. A $1000, 9.5% bond with semi-annual coupons redeemable at par on March 1, 2018 was purchased on September 19, 2009 to yield 7% compounded semi-annually. What was the purchase price?

5. Four $5000, 7% bonds with semi-annual coupons are bought seven years before maturity to yield 6% compounded semi-annually. Find the premium or discount and the purchase price if the bonds are redeemable at par.

6. Nine $1000, 8% bonds with interest payable semi-annually and redeemable at par are purchased ten years before maturity. Find the premium or discount and the purchase price if the bonds are bought to yield

   (a) 6%;

   (b) 8%;

   (c) 10%.

7. A $100 000, 5% bond with interest payable semi-annually redeemable at par on July 15, 2020 was purchased on April 18, 2009 to yield 7% compounded semi-annually. Determine

   (a) the premium or discount;

   (b) the purchase price;

   (c) the cash price.

8. Four $10 000 bonds bearing interest at 6% payable quarterly and redeemable at par on September 1, 2022 were purchased on January 23, 2010 to yield 5% compounded quarterly. Determine

   (a) the premium or discount;

   (b) the purchase price;

   (c) the cash price.

9. A $5000, 8% bond with semi-annual coupons redeemable at par in ten years is purchased to yield 10% compounded semi-annually. What is the purchase price?

10. A $1000 bond bearing interest at 8% payable semi-annually redeemable at par on February 1, 2017 was purchased on October 12, 2010 to yield 7% compounded semi-annually. Determine the purchase price.

11. A $50 000, 11% bond with semi-annual coupons redeemable at par on April 15, 2015 was purchased on June 25, 2008 at 92.375. What was the approximate yield rate?

12. A $1000, 8.5% bond with interest payable annually is purchased six years before maturity to yield 10.5% compounded annually. Compute the premium or discount and the purchase price and construct the appropriate bond schedule.

13. A $5000, 12.25% bond with interest payable annually redeemable at par in seven years is purchased to yield 13.5% compounded annually. Find the premium or discount and the purchase price and construct the appropriate bond schedule.

14. Three $25 000, 11% bonds with semi-annual coupons redeemable at par were bought eight years before maturity to yield 12% compounded semi-annually. Determine the gain or loss if the bonds are sold at 89.375 five years later.

15. A $10 000 bond with 5% interest payable quarterly redeemable at par on November 15, 2020 was bought on July 2, 2004 to yield 9%

compounded quarterly. If the bond was sold at 92.75 on September 10, 2010, what was the gain or loss on the sale?

16. A $25 000, 9.5% bond with semi-annual coupons redeemable at par is bought sixteen years before maturity at 78.25. What was the approximate yield rate?

17. A $10 000, 7.5% bond with quarterly coupons redeemable at par on October 15, 2021 was purchased on May 5, 2009 at 98.75. What is the approximate yield rate?

18. What is the approximate yield realized if the bond in Question 17 was sold on August 7, 2014 at 92?

19. A 6.5% bond of $50 000 with interest payable quarterly is to be redeemable at par in twelve years.

   (a) What is the purchase price to yield 8% compounded quarterly?

   (b) What is the book value after nine years?

   (c) What is the gain or loss if the bond is sold nine years after the date of purchase at 99.625?

20. A $5000, 14.5% bond with semi-annual coupons redeemable at par on August 1, 2022 was purchased on March 5, 2011 at 95.5. What was the approximate yield rate?

21. To provide for the purchase of heavy construction equipment estimated to cost $110 000, Valmar Construction is paying equal sums of money at the end of every six months for five years into a sinking fund earning 7.5% compounded semi-annually.

   (a) What is the size of the semi-annual payment into the sinking fund?

   (b) Compute the balance in the fund after the third payment.

   (c) Compute the amount of interest earned during the sixth payment interval.

   (d) Construct a sinking fund schedule showing totals. Check your answers to parts (b) and (c) with the values in the schedule.

22. Alpha Corporation is depositing equal sums of money at the beginning of every three months into a sinking fund to redeem a $65 000 promissory note due eight years from now. Interest earned by the fund is 12% compounded quarterly.

   (a) Determine the size of the quarterly payments into the sinking fund.

   (b) Compute the balance in the fund after three years.

   (c) Compute the increase in the fund during the 24th payment interval.

   (d) Construct a partial sinking fund schedule showing details of the first three deposits, the last three deposits, and totals.

23. The municipality of Kirkfield borrowed $100 000 to build a recreation centre. The debt principal is to be repaid in eight years and interest at 13.75% compounded annually is to be paid annually. To provide for the retirement of the debt, the municipal council set up a sinking fund into which equal payments are made at the time of the annual interest payments. Interest earned by the fund is 11.5% compounded annually.

   (a) What is the annual interest payment?

   (b) What is the size of the annual payment into the sinking fund?

   (c) What is the total annual cost of the debt?

   (d) Compute the book value of the debt after three years.

   (e) Compute the interest earned by the fund in Year 6.

   (f) Construct a sinking fund schedule showing the book value of the debt and totals. Verify your computations in parts (d) and (e) against the schedule.

24. The Harrow Board of Education financed the acquisition of a building site through a $300 000 long-term promissory note due in fifteen years. Interest on the promissory note is 9.25% compounded semi-annually and is payable at the end of every six months. To provide for the redemption of the note, the board agreed to make equal payments at the

end of every six months into a sinking fund paying 8% compounded semi-annually. (Round all answers to the nearest dollar.)

(a) What is the semi-annual interest payment?

(b) What is the size of the semi-annual payment into the sinking fund?

(c) What is the annual cost of the debt?

(d) Compute the book value of the debt after five years.

(e) Compute the increase in the sinking fund in the 20th payment interval.

(f) Construct a partial sinking fund schedule showing details, including the book value of the debt, for the first three years, the last three years, and totals.

25. Northern Flying Service is preparing to buy  an aircraft estimated to cost $60 000 by making equal payments at the end of every three months into a sinking fund for five years. Interest earned by the fund is 8% compounded quarterly.

(a) What is the size of the quarterly payment made to the sinking fund?

(b) How much of the maturity value of the fund will be interest?

(c) What is the accumulated value of the fund after two years?

(d) How much interest will the fund earn in the 15th payment interval?

26. A sinking fund of $10 000 is to be created by equal annual payments at the beginning of

each year for seven years. Interest earned by the fund is 7.5% compounded annually.

(a) Compute the annual deposit into the fund.

(b) Construct a sinking fund schedule showing totals.

27. Joe Ngosa bought a retirement fund for $15 000. Beginning twenty-five years from the date of purchase, he will receive payments of $17 500 at the beginning of every six months. Interest earned by the fund is 12% compounded semi-annually.

(a) How many payments will Joe receive?

(b) What is the size of the last payment?

28. The town of Kildare bought firefighting equipment for $96 000. The financing agreement provides for annual interest payments and equal payments into a sinking fund for ten years. After ten years the proceeds of the sinking fund will be used to retire the principal. Interest on the debt is 14.5% compounded annually and interest earned by the sinking fund is 13% compounded annually.

(a) What is the annual interest payment?

(b) What is the size of the annual payment into the sinking fund?

(c) What is the total annual cost of the debt?

(d) What is the book value of the debt after four years?

(e) Construct a partial sinking fund schedule showing details, including the book value of the debt, for the last three years and totals.

## Self-Test

1. A $10 000, 10% bond with quarterly coupons redeemable at par in fifteen years is purchased to yield 11% compounded quarterly. Determine the purchase price of the bond.

2. What is the purchase price of a $1000, 7.5% bond with semi-annual coupons redeemable at par in ten years if the bond is bought to yield 6% compounded semi-annually?

3. A $5000, 8% bond with semi-annual coupons redeemable at par is bought six years before maturity to yield 6.5% compounded semi-annually. Determine the premium or discount.

4. A $20 000, 10% bond with semi-annual coupons redeemable at par March 1, 2017 was purchased on November 15, 2010 to yield 9% compounded semi-annually. What was the purchase price of the bond?

5. A $5000, 7% bond with semi-annual coupons redeemable at par on December 15, 2020 was purchased on November 9, 2009 to yield 8.5% compounded semi-annually. Determine the cash price.

6. A $5000, 11.5% bond with semi-annual coupons redeemable at par is bought four years before maturity to yield 13% compounded semi-annually. Construct a bond schedule.

7. A $100 000, 13% bond with semi-annual interest payments redeemable at par on July 15, 2018 is bought on September 10, 2011 at 102.625. What was the approximate yield rate?

8. A $25 000, 6% bond with semi-annual coupons redeemable at par in twenty years is purchased to yield 8% compounded semi-annually. Determine the gain or loss if the bond is sold seven years after the date of purchase at 98.25.

9. A $10 000, 12% bond with semi-annual coupons redeemable at par on December 1, 2020 was purchased on July 20, 2009 at 93.875. Compute the approximate yield rate.

10. Cottingham Pies made semi-annual payments into a sinking fund for ten years. If the fund had a balance of $100 000 after ten years and interest is 11% compounded semi-annually, what was the accumulated balance in the fund after seven years?

11. A fund of $165 000 is to be accumulated in six years by making equal payments at the beginning of each month. If interest is 7.5% compounded monthly, how much interest is earned by the fund in the 20th payment interval?

12. Gillian Armes invested $10 000 in an income fund at 13% compounded semi-annually for twenty years. After twenty years, she is to receive semi-annual payments of $10 000 at the end of every six-month period until the fund is exhausted. What is the size of the final payment?

13. A company financed a plant expansion of $750 000 at 9% compounded annually. The financing agreement requires annual payments of interest and the funding of the debt through equal annual payments for fifteen years into a sinking fund earning 7% compounded annually. What is the book value of the debt after five years?

14. Annual sinking fund payments made at the beginning of every year for six years earning 11.5% compounded annually amount to $25 000 at the end of six years. Construct a sinking fund schedule showing totals.

## Challenge Problems

1. A $2000 bond with annual coupons is redeemable at par in five years. If the first coupon is $400, and subsequent annual coupons are worth 75% of the previous year's coupon, find the purchase price of the bond that would yield an interest rate of 10% compounded annually.

2. An issue of bonds, redeemable at par in $n$ years, is to bear coupons at 9% compounded semi-annually. An investor offers to buy the entire issue at a premium of 15%. At the same time, the investor advises that if the coupon rate were raised to 10% compounded semi-annually, he would offer to buy the whole issue at a premium of 25%. At what yield rate compounded semi-annually are these two offers equivalent?

# Case Study 15.1 Investing in Bonds

» Isabella recently attended a personal financial planning seminar, whereby the speaker discussed that bonds should be a component of a balanced investment portfolio. Currently, Isabella's RRSP contains mutual funds and a guaranteed investment certificate (GIC), but no bonds. She has decided to invest up to $6000 of her RRSP funds in bonds and has narrowed her choices to three.

- Bond A is a $1000, 4.3% bond with semi-annual coupons redeemable in six years. Isabella can purchase up to six of these bonds at 98.45.

- Bond B is a $1000, 5.4% bond with semi-annual coupons redeemable in seven years. She can purchase up to six of these bonds at 102.10.

- Bond C is a $1000, 6.2% bond with semi-annual coupons redeemable in eight years. Isabella can purchase up to four of these bonds at 103.85.

### QUESTIONS

1. Suppose Isabella wants to invest in only one bond. Use the average investment method to answer the following questions.
   (a) What is the approximate yield of Bond A?
   (b) What is the approximate yield of Bond B?
   (c) What is the approximate yield of Bond C?
   (d) Assume Isabella is willing to hold the bond she chooses until it matures. Which bond has the highest yield?

2. Suppose Isabella decides to buy two $1000 denominations of Bond A. Bond A's semi-annual coupons are payable on January 1 and July 1. Suppose Isabella purchases these bonds on March 27.
   (a) What is the accrued interest on these two bonds up to the date of Isabella's purchase?
   (b) What is Isabella's cash price for these two bonds?

3. Suppose Isabella decides to buy three $1000 denominations of Bond B on April 17. Bond B's semi-annual coupons are payable on February 1 and August 1.
   (a) What is the accrued interest on these two bonds up to the date of Isabella's purchase?
   (b) What is Isabella's cash price for these two bonds?

# Case Study 15.2 Raising Capital Through Bonds

» ScanSoft Development Company is developing a new process to manufacture optical discs. The development costs were higher than expected, so ScanSoft required an immediate cash inflow of $5 200 000. To raise the required capital, the company decided to issue bonds. Since ScanSoft had no expertise in issuing and selling bonds, the company decided to work with an investment dealer. The investment dealer bought the company's entire bond issue at a discount, and then sold the bonds to the public at face value or the current market value. To ensure it would raise the $5 200 000 it required, ScanSoft issued 5400 bonds with a face value of $1000 each on January 20, 2005. Interest is paid semi-annually on July 20 and January 20, beginning July 20, 2005. The bonds pay interest at 5.5% compounded semi-annually.

ScanSoft directors realize that when the bonds mature on January 20, 2025, there must be $5 200 000 available to repay the bondholders. To have enough money on hand to meet this obligation, the directors set up a sinking fund using a specially designated savings account. The company earns interest of 3.2% compounded semi-annually on this sinking fund account. The directors began making semi-annual payments to the sinking fund on July 20, 2005.

ScanSoft Development Company issued the bonds, sold them all to the investment dealer, and used the money raised to continue its research and development.

## QUESTIONS

1. How much would an investor have to pay for one of these bonds to earn 6.6% compounded semi-annually?

2. (a) What is the size of the sinking fund payment?
   (b) What will be the total amount deposited into the sinking fund account?
   (c) How much of the sinking fund will be interest?

3. Suppose ScanSoft discovers on January 20, 2015 that it can earn 4.8% interest compounded semi-annually on its sinking fund account.
   (a) What is the balance in the sinking fund after the January 20, 2015 sinking fund payment?
   (b) What is the new sinking fund payment if the fund begins to earn 4.8% on January 21, 2015?
   (c) What will be the total amount deposited into the sinking fund account over the life of the bonds?
   (d) How much of the sinking fund will then be interest?

# SUMMARY OF FORMULAS

**Formula 15.1**

$$PP = FV(1 + i)^{-n} + PMT\left[\frac{1 - (1 + i)^{-n}}{i}\right]$$

Basic formula for finding the purchase price of a bond when the interest payment interval and the yield rate conversion period are equal

**Formula 15.2**

$$PP = FV(1 + p)^{-n} + PMT\left[\frac{1 - (1 + p)^{-n}}{p}\right]$$

where $p = (1 + i)^c - 1$

Basic formula for finding the purchase price of a bond when the interest payment interval and the yield rate conversion period are different

**Formula 15.3**

Direct formula for finding the premium or discount of a bond (a negative answer indicates a discount)

$$\begin{aligned}\text{PREMIUM OR DISCOUNT}\\= (b \times \text{FACE VALUE} - i \times \text{REDEMPTION PRICE})\end{aligned}\left[\frac{1 - (1 + i)^{-n}}{i}\right]$$

**Formula 15.4**

Basic formula for finding the yield rate using the method of averages

$$\text{APPROXIMATE VALUE OF } i = \frac{\text{AVERAGE INCOME PER INTEREST PAYMENT INTERVAL}}{\text{AVERAGE BOOK VALUE}}$$

where

$$\text{AVERAGE BOOK VALUE} = \frac{1}{2}(\text{QUOTED PRICE} + \text{REDEMPTION PRICE})$$

and

$$\begin{aligned}\text{AVERAGE INCOME}\\\text{PER INTEREST}\\\text{PAYMENT INTERVAL}\end{aligned} = \frac{\text{TOTAL INTEREST PAYMENTS} \begin{array}{l}- \text{ PREMIUM}\\+ \text{ DISCOUNT}\end{array}}{\text{NUMBER OF INTEREST PAYMENT INTERVALS}}$$

In addition, Formulas 9.1C, 11.1, 11.2, 12.3, and 13.1 were used in this chapter.

# GLOSSARY

**Accumulation of discount**  the process of reducing a bond discount (*p. 650*)

**Amortization of the premium**  the process of writing down a bond premium (*p. 649*)

**Bond rate**  the rate of interest paid by a bond, stated as a percent of the face value (*p. 630*)

**Book value of a debt**  the difference at any time between the debt principal and the associated sinking fund balance (*p. 667*)

**Cash price**  the total purchase price of a bond (including any accrued interest) (*p. 635*)

**Coupon**  a voucher attached to a bond to facilitate the collection of interest by the bondholder (*p. 630*)

**Coupon rate**  *see* **Bond rate**

**Debentures**  bonds for which no security is offered (*p. 630*)

**Denomination**  *see* **Face value**

**Discount**  the difference between the purchase price of a bond and its principal when the purchase price is less than the principal (*p. 639*)

**Due date**  *see* **Redemption date**

**Face value**  the amount owed by the issuer of the bond to the bondholder (*p. 630*)

**Market price**  *see* **Quoted price**

**Maturity date**  *see* **Redemption date**

**Maturity value**  *see* **Redemption value**

**Method of averages**  a method for finding the approximate yield rate (*p. 655*)

Nominal rate    *see* **Bond rate**

Par value    *see* **Face value**

Periodic cost of a debt    the sum of the interest paid and the payment into the sinking fund when a debt is retired by the sinking fund method *(p. 667)*

Premium    the difference between the purchase price of a bond and its principal when the purchase price is greater than the principal *(p. 639)*

Principal value    *see* **Redemption value**

Quoted price    the net price (without accrued interest) at which a bond is offered for sale *(p. 635)*

Redeemable at a premium    bonds whose principal is greater than the face value *(p. 630)*

Redeemable at par    bonds that are redeemed at their face value *(p. 630)*

Redemption date    the date at which the bond principal is repaid *(p. 630)*

Redemption value    the amount that the issuer of the bond pays to the bondholder upon surrender of the bond on or after the date of maturity *(p. 630)*

Sinking fund    a fund into which payments are made to provide a specific sum of money at a future time; usually set up for the purpose of meeting some future obligation *(p. 657)*

Yield rate    the rate of interest that an investor earns on his or her investment in a bond *(p. 633)*

## USEFUL INTERNET SITES

www.cis-pec.gc.ca

**Canada Investment and Savings**    (CIS) CIS is a special operating agency of the Department of Finance that markets and manages savings and investment products for Canadians. This Website provides information on products, including Canada Savings Bonds and Canada Premium Bonds.

www.bankofcanada.ca/en

**Bond Market Rates**    Click on "Rates and Statistics." The current Government of Canada bond yields and marketable bond average yields are found at this site. The site also provides links to selected historical interest rates.

www.carswell.com

**The Payroll Community**    This site, hosted by Carswell publishers, provides information about payroll, FAQs, new products, payroll publications, and links to relevant sites.

www.benefitscanada.com

*Benefits Canada*    This magazine deals with employee benefits and pension investments.

# 16 Investment Decision Applications

## OBJECTIVES

**Upon completing this chapter, you will be able to do the following:**

1. Determine the discounted value of cash flows and choose between alternative investments on the basis of the discounted cash flow criterion.

2. Determine the net present value of a capital investment project and infer from the net present value whether a project is feasible or not.

3. Compute the rate of return on investment.

Choices among different investment opportunities must be made often by both individuals and companies. Whether one is deciding between buying and leasing a car or how to increase plant capacity, an understanding of the time value of money is critical. When comparing different ways of achieving the same goal, we should always examine cash flows at the same point in the time—usually at the beginning when a decision must be made. Only then can we know whether it is better to buy or lease that car, or to expand the plant now or to wait.

## INTRODUCTION

When making investment decisions, all decision makers must consider the comparative effects of alternative courses of action on the cash flows of a business or of an individual. Since cash flow analysis needs to take into account the time value of money (interest), present value concepts are useful.

When only cash inflows are considered, the value of the discounted cash flows is helpful in guiding management toward a rational decision. If outlays as well as inflows are considered, the net present value concept is applicable in evaluating projects.

The net present value method indicates whether or not a project will yield a specified rate of return. To be a worthwhile investment, the rate of return on a capital project must be attractive or meet a desired minimum target. Required rates of return tend to be high to be attractive. Knowing the actual rate of return provides useful information to the decision maker. It may be computed using the net present value concept.

# 16.1 DISCOUNTED CASH FLOW

## A. Evaluation of capital expenditures—basic concepts

Projects expected to generate benefits over a period of time longer than one year are called capital investment projects, and they result in capital expenditures. The benefits resulting from these projects may be in either monetary or non-monetary form. The methods of analysis considered in this chapter will deal only with investment projects generating cash flows in monetary form.

While capital expenditures normally result in the acquisition of assets, the primary purpose of investing in capital expenditures is to acquire a future stream of benefits in the form of an inflow of cash. When an investment is being considered, analysis of the anticipated future cash flows aids in the decision to acquire or replace assets, and whether to buy or lease them.

The analysis generally uses the technique of discounted cash flow. This technique involves estimating all anticipated future cash flows flowing from an investment or project, projecting an interest rate, and calculating the present value of these cash flows. It is important that the present value be calculated, not the future value, due to the need to make a decision on the investment in the beginning, or in the present, before cash or other resources are invested. The decision to be made might involve determining whether to invest in a project, or choosing which project to invest in.

In some situations, the cash flows estimated may not be certain, or there may be other, non-financial concerns. The analysis techniques considered in this text are concerned only with the amount and the timing of cash receipts and cash payments under the assumption that the amount and timing of the cash flow are certain.

From the mathematical point of view, the major issue in evaluating capital expenditure projects is the time value of money. This value prevents direct comparison of cash received and cash payments made at different times. The concept of present value, as introduced in Chapter 9 and subsequent chapters, provides the vehicle for making sums of money received or paid at different times comparable at a given time.

## B. Discounted cash flow

**Discounted cash flow** is the present value of all cash payments. When using the discounting technique to evaluate alternatives, two fundamental principles serve as decision criteria:

1. *The bird-in-the-hand principle.* Given that all other factors are equal, earlier benefits are preferable to later benefits.
2. *The the-bigger-the-better principle.* Given that all other factors are equal, bigger benefits are preferable to smaller benefits.

**EXAMPLE 16.1A**

Suppose you are offered a choice of receiving $1000 today or receiving $1000 three years from now. What is the preferred choice?

**SOLUTION**

Accepting the bird-in-the-hand principle, you should prefer to receive $1000 today rather than three years from now. The rationale is that $1000 can be invested to earn interest and will accumulate in three years to a sum of money greater than $1000. Stated another way, the present value of $1000 to be received in three years is less than $1000 today.

**EXAMPLE 16.1B**

Consider a choice of $2000 today or $3221 five years from now. Which alternative is preferable?

**SOLUTION**

No definite answer is possible without considering interest. A rational choice must consider the time value of money; that is, we need to know the rate of interest. Once a rate of interest is established, we can make the proper choice by considering the present value of the two sums of money and applying the principle of the-bigger-the-better.

If you choose "now" as the focal date, three outcomes are possible.

1. The present value of $3221 is greater than $2000. In this case, the preferred choice is $3221 five years from now.

2. The present value of $3221 is less than $2000. In this case, the preferred choice is $2000 now.

3. The present value of $3221 equals $2000. In this case, either choice is equally acceptable.

(a) *Suppose the rate of interest is 8%.*
$FV = 3221.00; \quad i = 8\% = 0.08; \quad n = 5$
$PV = 3221.00(1.08^{-5}) = 3221.00(0.680583) = \$2192.16$
Since at 8% the discounted value of $3221 is greater than $2000, the preferred choice at 8% is $3221 five years from now.

(b) *Suppose the rate of interest is 12%.*
FV = 3221.00;   $i$ = 12% = 0.12;   $n$ = 5
PV = 3221.00$(1.12^{-5})$ = 3221.00(0.567427) = \$1827.68
Since at 12% the discounted value is less than \$2000, the preferred choice is \$2000 now.

(c) *Suppose the rate of interest is 10%.*
FV = 3221.00;   $i$ = 10% = 0.10;   $n$ = 5
PV = 3221.00$(1.10^{-5})$ = 3221.00(0.620921) = \$1999.99
Since at 10% the discounted value is equal to \$2000, the two choices are equally acceptable.

**Programmed Solution**

("END" mode)

(Set P/Y = 1; C/Y = 1)

(a)  2nd  (CLR TVM) 3221  FV  8  I/Y  5  N  CPT  PV  −2192.158478

(b)  2nd  (CLR TVM) 3221  FV  12  I/Y  5  N  CPT  PV  −1827.681902

(c)  2nd  (CLR TVM) 3221  FV  10  I/Y  5  N  CPT  PV  −1999.987582

**EXAMPLE 16.1C**

Two investment alternatives are available. Alternative A yields a return of \$6000 in two years and \$10 000 in five years. Alternative B yields a return of \$7000 now and \$7000 in seven years. Which alternative is preferable if money is worth

(i) 11%?     (ii) 15%?

**SOLUTION**

To determine which alternative is preferable, we need to compute the present value of each alternative and choose the alternative with the higher present value.

Since the decision is to be made immediately, choose a focal point of "now."

(i) For $i$ = 11%

**Alternative A**
The present value of Alternative A is the sum of the present values of \$6000 in two years and \$10 000 in five years.

Present value of \$6000 in two years
= 6000$(1.11^{-2})$ = 6000(0.811622)        =        \$ 4 870
Present value of \$10 000 in five years
= 10 000$(1.11^{-5})$ = 10 000(0.593451)        =        5 935
The present value of Alternative A        =        \$10 805

**Alternative B**
The present value of Alternative B is the sum of the present values of $7000 now and $7000 in seven years.

| | | |
|---|---|---|
| Present value of $7000 now | = | $ 7 000 |
| Present value of $7000 in seven years $= 7000(1.11^{-7}) = 7000(0.481658)$ | = | 3 372 |
| The present value of Alternative B | = | $10 372 |

**Programmed Solution**

**Alternative A**

("END" mode)

(Set P/Y = 1; C/Y = 1)

$\boxed{\text{2nd}}$ (CLR TVM) 6000 $\boxed{\text{FV}}$ 11 $\boxed{\text{I/Y}}$ 2 $\boxed{\text{N}}$ $\boxed{\text{CPT}}$ $\boxed{\text{PV}}$ $\boxed{-4869.734599}$

$\boxed{\text{2nd}}$ (CLR TVM) 10 000 $\boxed{\text{FV}}$ 11 $\boxed{\text{I/Y}}$ 5 $\boxed{\text{N}}$ $\boxed{\text{CPT}}$ $\boxed{\text{PV}}$ $\boxed{-5934.513281}$

$4870 + $5935 = $10 805

**Alternative B**

$\boxed{\text{2nd}}$ (CLR TVM) 7000 $\boxed{\text{FV}}$ 11 $\boxed{\text{I/Y}}$ 7 $\boxed{\text{N}}$ $\boxed{\text{CPT}}$ $\boxed{\text{PV}}$ $\boxed{-3371.608876}$

$3372 + $7000 = $10 372

Since at 11% the present value of Alternative A is greater than the present value of Alternative B, Alternative A is preferable.

(ii) For $i = 15\%$

**Alternative A**

| | | |
|---|---|---|
| Present value of $6000 in two years $= 6000(1.15^{-2}) = 6000(0.756144)$ | = | $4537 |
| Present value of $10 000 in five years $= 10 000(1.15^{-5}) = 10 000(0.497177)$ | = | 4972 |
| The present value of Alternative A | = | $9509 |

**Alternative B**

| | | |
|---|---|---|
| Present value of $7000 now | = | $7000 |
| Present value of $7000 in seven years $= 7000(1.15^{-7}) = 7000(0.375937)$ | = | 2632 |
| The present value of Alternative B | = | $9632 |

**Programmed Solution**

**Alternative A**

("END" mode)

(Set P/Y = 1; C/Y = 1)

| 2nd | (CLR TVM) 6000 | FV | 15 | I/Y | 2 | N | CPT | PV | -4536.862004 |

| 2nd | (CLR TVM) 10 000 | FV | 15 | I/Y | 5 | N | CPT | PV | -4971.767353 |

$4537 + $4972 = $9509

**Alternative B**

| 2nd | (CLR TVM) 7000 | FV | 15 | I/Y | 7 | N | CPT | PV | -2631.559279 |

$2632 + $7000 = $9632

Since at 15% the present value of Alternative B is greater than the present value of Alternative A, Alternative B is preferable.

*Note:* Applying present value techniques to capital investment problems usually involves estimates. For this reason, dollar amounts in the preceding example and all following examples may be rounded to the nearest dollar. We suggest that you do the same when working on problems of this nature.

**EXAMPLE 16.1D**

An insurance company offers to settle a claim either by making a payment of $50 000 immediately or by making payments of $8000 at the end of each year for ten years. What offer is preferable if interest is 8% compounded annually?

**SOLUTION**

Present value of $8000 at the end of each year for ten years is the present value of an ordinary annuity in which PMT = 8000, $n = 10$, and $i = 8\%$.

$$PV_n = 8000\left(\frac{1 - 1.08^{-10}}{0.08}\right) = 8000(6.710081) = \$53\ 681$$

**Programmed Solution**

("END" mode)

(Set P/Y = 1; C/Y = 1)

| 0 | FV | 8000 | PMT | 10 | N | 8 | I/Y | CPT | PV | -53680.65119 |

Since the immediate payment is smaller than the present value of the annual payments of $8000, the annual payments of $8000 are preferable.

**EXAMPLE 16.1E**

National Credit Union needs to decide whether to buy a high-speed scanner for $6000 and enter a service contract requiring the payment of $45 at the end of every three months for five years, or to enter a five-year lease requiring the payment of $435 at the beginning of every three months. If leased, the scanner can be bought after five years for $600. At 9% compounded quarterly, should the credit union buy or lease?

**SOLUTION**

To make a rational decision, the credit union should compare the present value of the cash outlays if buying the scanner with the present value of the cash outlays if leasing the scanner.

**Present value of the decision to buy**

Present value of cash payment for the scanner $\qquad$ = $\qquad$ $6000

Present value of the service contract involves an ordinary annuity in which PMT = 45, $n$ = 20, P/Y = 4; C/Y = 4; I/Y = 9; $i$ = 2.25%

$$= 45\left(\frac{1 - 1.0225^{-20}}{0.0225}\right) = 45(15.963712) \qquad = \qquad 718$$

Present value of decision to buy $\qquad$ = $\qquad$ $\underline{\$6718}$

**Present value of the decision to lease**

Present value of the quarterly lease payments involves an annuity due: PMT = 435, $n$ = 20, $i$ = 2.25%

$$= 435(1.0225)\left(\frac{1 - 1.0225^{-20}}{0.0225}\right) = 435(1.0225)(15.963712) \qquad = \qquad \$7100$$

Present value of purchase price after five years
$= 600(1.0225^{-20}) = 600(0.640816) \qquad = \qquad 384$

Present value of decision to lease $\qquad$ = $\qquad$ $\underline{\$7484}$

## Programmed Solution

**Present value of the decision to buy**

Present value of cash payment for the scanner $\qquad$ = $\qquad$ $6000

Present value of the service contract

("END" mode)

(Set P/Y = 4; C/Y = 4)

$\boxed{0 \ \fbox{FV} \ 45 \ \fbox{PMT} \ 20 \ \fbox{N} \ 9 \ \fbox{I/Y} \ \fbox{CPT} \ \fbox{PV} \ -718.367057}$

Present value of decision to buy is $6000 + 718 = $6718.

**Present value of the decision to lease**

Present value of the quarterly lease payments:

("BGN" mode)

$\boxed{0 \ \fbox{FV} \ 435 \ \fbox{PMT} \ 20 \ \fbox{N} \ 9 \ \fbox{I/Y} \ \fbox{CPT} \ \fbox{PV} \ -7100.459716}$

Present value of purchase price after five years:

$\boxed{0 \ \fbox{PMT} \ 600 \ \fbox{FV} \ 20 \ \fbox{N} \ 9 \ \fbox{I/Y} \ \fbox{CPT} \ \fbox{PV} \ -384.489883}$

Present value of the decision to lease is $7100 + 384 = $7484.

In the case of costs, the selection criterion follows the principle of the-*smaller-the-better*. Since the present value of the decision to buy is smaller than the present value of the decision to lease, the credit union should buy the scanner.

**EXAMPLE 16.1F**

Hans Machine Service needs a brake machine. The machine can be purchased for $4600 and after five years will have a salvage value of $490, or the machine can be leased for five years by making monthly payments of $111 at the beginning of each month. If money is worth 10% compounded annually, should Hans Machine Service buy or lease?

**SOLUTION**

**Alternative 1: Buy machine**

| | | |
|---|---|---|
| Present value of cash price | = | $4600 |
| Less: Present value of salvage value | | |
| $= 490(1.10^{-5}) = 490(0.620921)$ | = | 304 |
| Present value of decision to buy | = | $4296 |

**Alternative 2: Lease machine**

The monthly lease payments form a general annuity due in which

$$\text{PMT} = 111; \quad \text{P/Y} = 12; \quad \text{C/Y} = 1; \quad \text{I/Y} = 10; \quad c = \frac{1}{12}; \quad n = 60; \quad i = 10\%;$$

$$p = 1.10^{\frac{1}{12}} - 1 = 1.007974 - 1 = 0.7974\%$$

Present value of the monthly lease payments

$$= 111(1.007974)\left(\frac{1 - 1.007974^{-60}}{0.007974}\right)$$

$$= 111(1.007974)(47.538500)$$

$$= \$5319$$

The present value of the decision to lease is $5319.

**Programmed Solution**

**Alternative 1: Buy machine**

| | | |
|---|---|---|
| Present value of cash price | = | $4600 |
| Less: Present value of salvage value | | |

("END" mode)

(Set P/Y = 12; C/Y = 1)

2nd (CLR TVM) 490 FV 60 N 10 I/Y CPT PV −304.251448

Present value of decision to buy is $4600 − 304 = $4296.

**Alternative 2: Lease machine**

Present value of the monthly lease payments

("BGN" mode) (Set P/Y = 12; C/Y = 1) 0 FV 111 PMT

60 N 10 I/Y CPT PV −5318.851263

Since the present value of the decision to buy is smaller than the present value of the decision to lease, Hans Machine Service should buy the machine.

## EXERCISE 16.1

You can use Excel's Net Present Value (NPV) function to answer the questions below. Refer to **NPV** on the Spreadsheet Template Disk to learn how to use this function.

**A.** For each of the following, compute the present value of each alternative and determine the preferred alternative according to the discounted cash flow criterion.

1. The D Company must make a choice between two investment alternatives. Alternative 1 will return the company $20 000 at the end of three years and $60 000 at the end of six years. Alternative 2 will return the company $13 000 at the end of each of the next six years. The D Company normally expects to earn a rate of return of 12% on funds invested.

2. The B Company has a policy of requiring a rate of return on investment of 16%. Two investment alternatives are available but the company may choose only one. Alternative 1 offers a return of $50 000 after four years, $40 000 after seven years, and $30 000 after ten years. Alternative 2 will return the company $750 at the end of each month for ten years.

3. An obligation can be settled by making a payment of $10 000 now and a final payment of $20 000 in five years. Alternatively, the obligation can be settled by payments of $1500 at the end of every three months for five years. Interest is 10% compounded quarterly.

4. An unavoidable cost may be met by outlays of $10 000 now and $2000 at the end of every six months for seven years or by making monthly payments of $500 in advance for seven years. Interest is 7% compounded annually.

5. A company must purchase new equipment costing $2000. The company can pay cash on the basis of the purchase price or make payments of $108 at the end of each month for 24 months. Interest is 7.8% compounded monthly. Should the company purchase the new equipment with cash or make payments on the installment plan?

6. For less than a dollar a day, Jerri can join a fitness club. She would have to pay $24.99 at the end of each month for 30 months, or she can pay a lump sum of $549 at the beginning. Interest is 16.2% compounded monthly. Should Jerri pay a lump sum or use the monthly payment feature?

**B.** Answer each of the following questions.

1. A contract offers $25 000 immediately and $50 000 in five years or $10 000 at the end of each year for ten years. If money is worth 6%, which offer is preferable?

2. A professional sports contract offers $400 000 per year paid at the end of each of six years or $100 000 paid now, $200 000 paid at the end of each of the second and third years, and $800 000 paid at the end of each of the last three years. If money is worth 7.3%, which offer is preferable?

3. Bruce and Carol want to sell their business. They have received two offers. If they accept Offer A, they will receive $15 000 immediately and $20 000 in three years. If they accept Offer B, they will receive $3000 now and $3000 at the end of every six months for six years. If interest is 10%, which offer is preferable?

4. When Peter decided to sell his farm, he received two offers. If he accepts the first offer, he would receive $250 000 now, $750 000 one year from now, and $500 000 two years from now. If he accepts the second offer, he would receive $600 000 now, $300 000 one year from now, and $600 000 two years from now. If money is worth 9.8%, which offer should he accept?

5. A warehouse can be purchased for $90 000. After twenty years the property will have a residual value of $30 000. Alternatively, the warehouse can be leased for twenty years at an annual rent of $10 000 payable in advance. If money is worth 8%, should the warehouse be purchased or leased?

6. A car costs $9500. Alternatively, the car can be leased for three years by making payments of $240 at the beginning of each month and can be bought at the end of the lease for $4750. If interest is 9% compounded semi-annually, which alternative is preferable?

# 16.2 NET PRESENT VALUE METHOD

## A. Introductory examples

**EXAMPLE 16.2A**

Net cash inflows from two ventures are as follows:

| End of Year: | 1 | 2 | 3 | 4 | 5 | Total |
|---|---|---|---|---|---|---|
| Venture A | 12 000 | 14 400 | 17 280 | 20 736 | 24 883 | 89 299 |
| Venture B | 17 000 | 17 000 | 17 000 | 17 000 | 17 000 | 85 000 |

Which venture is preferable if the required yield is 20%?

**SOLUTION**

**Present value of Venture A**

$$= 12\ 000(1.20^{-1}) + 14\ 400(1.20^{-2}) + 17\ 280(1.20^{-3})$$
$$+ 20\ 736(1.20^{-4}) + 24\ 883(1.20^{-5})$$
$$= 12\ 000(0.833333) + 14\ 400(0.694444) + 17\ 280(0.578704)$$
$$+ 20\ 736(0.482253) + 24\ 883(0.401878)$$
$$= 10\ 000 + 10\ 000 + 10\ 000 + 10\ 000 + 10\ 000$$
$$= \$50\ 000$$

**Present value of Venture B**

$$= 17\ 000\left(\frac{1 - 1.20^{-5}}{0.20}\right) = 17\ 000(2.990612) = \$50\ 840$$

**Programmed Solution**

**Present value of Venture A**

("END" mode)

(Set P/Y = 1; C/Y = 1)

| 2nd | (CLR TVM) 12 000 | FV | 20 | I/Y | 1 | N | CPT | PV | −10000 |

| 2nd | (CLR TVM) 14 400 | FV | 20 | I/Y | 2 | N | CPT | PV | −10000 |

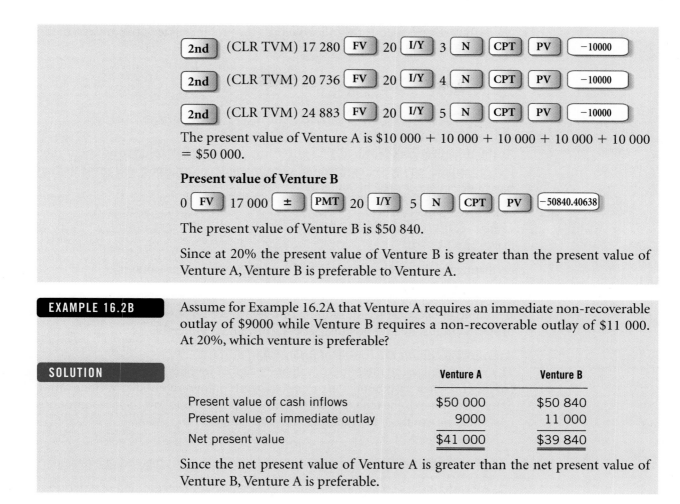

The present value of Venture A is $10 000 + 10 000 + 10 000 + 10 000 + 10 000 = $50 000.

**Present value of Venture B**

The present value of Venture B is $50 840.

Since at 20% the present value of Venture B is greater than the present value of Venture A, Venture B is preferable to Venture A.

**EXAMPLE 16.2B**

Assume for Example 16.2A that Venture A requires an immediate non-recoverable outlay of $9000 while Venture B requires a non-recoverable outlay of $11 000. At 20%, which venture is preferable?

**SOLUTION**

| | Venture A | Venture B |
|---|---|---|
| Present value of cash inflows | $50 000 | $50 840 |
| Present value of immediate outlay | 9000 | 11 000 |
| Net present value | $41 000 | $39 840 |

Since the net present value of Venture A is greater than the net present value of Venture B, Venture A is preferable.

## B. The net present value concept

When the present value of the cash outlays is subtracted from the present value of cash inflows, the resulting difference is called the **net present value**. In Example 16.2A, Venture B was preferable, where only the cash inflows were considered. In Example 16.2B, the present value of the outlays as well as the present value of the cash inflows resulted in the net present value being calculated. This approach is necessary when the cash outlays are different.

$$\text{NET PRESENT VALUE} \atop (\text{NPV}) = {\text{PRESENT VALUE} \atop \text{OF INFLOWS}} - {\text{PRESENT VALUE} \atop \text{OF OUTLAYS}}$$  ———— Formula 16.1

Since the net present value involves the difference between the present value of the inflows and the present value of the outlays, three outcomes are possible:

1. If the present value of the inflows is greater than the present value of the outlays, then the net present value is greater than zero.

2. If the present value of the inflows is smaller than the present value of the outlays, then the net present value is smaller than zero.

3. If the present value of the inflows equals the present value of the outlays, then the net present value is zero.

$$PV_{IN} > PV_{OUT} \longrightarrow NPV > 0 \text{ (positive)}$$
$$PV_{IN} = PV_{OUT} \longrightarrow NPV = 0$$
$$PV_{IN} < PV_{OUT} \longrightarrow NPV < 0 \text{ (negative)}$$

### *Criterion rule*

At the organization's required rate of return, accept those capital investment projects that have a positive or zero net present value and reject those projects that have a negative net present value.

For a given rate of return:
ACCEPT if NPV > 0 or NPV = 0;
REJECT if NPV < 0.

To distinguish between a negative and a positive net present value, use

$$NPV = PV_{IN} - PV_{OUT}.$$

If a company is considering more than one project but can choose only one, the project with the greatest positive net present value is preferable.

### *Assumptions about the timing of inflows and outlays*

The net present value method of evaluating capital investment projects is particularly useful when cash outlays are made and cash inflows received at various times. Since the timing of the cash flows is of prime importance, follow these assumptions regarding the timing of cash inflows and cash outlays.

Unless otherwise stated:

1. All cash inflows (benefits) are assumed to be received at the end of a period.

2. All cash outlays (costs) are assumed to be made at the beginning of a period.

## C. Applications

**EXAMPLE 16.2C**

A company is offered a contract promising annual net returns of $36 000 for seven years. If it accepts the contract, the company must spend $150 000 immediately to expand its plant. After seven years, no further benefits are available from the contract and the plant expansion undertaken will have no residual value. Should the company accept the contract if the required rate of return is

(i) 12%?   (ii) 18%?   (iii) 15%?

**SOLUTION**

The net inflows and outlays can be represented on a time graph.

*End of period (year)*

| Now | 1 | 2 | 3 | 4 | 5 | 6 | 7 |

<150 000>  36 000   36 000   36 000   36 000   36 000   36 000   36 000

*Note:* Cash outlays (costs) are identified in such diagrams by a minus sign or by using accounting brackets.

(i) For $i = 12\%$

Since we assume the annual net returns (benefits) are received at the end of a period unless otherwise stated, they form an ordinary annuity in which

$$\text{PMT} = 36\,000; \quad n = 7; \quad i = 12\%$$

$$\text{PV}_{\text{IN}} = 36\,000\left(\frac{1 - 1.12^{-7}}{0.12}\right) = 36\,000(4.563756) \quad = \quad \$164\,295$$

$$\text{PV}_{\text{OUT}} = \text{Present value of } 150\,000 \text{ now} \qquad\qquad = \quad \underline{150\,000}$$
$$\text{The net present value (NPV)} = 164\,295 - 150\,000 \quad = \quad \underline{\$\ 14\,295}$$

Since at 12% the net present value is greater than zero, the contract should be accepted. The fact that the net present value at 12% is positive means that the contract offers a return on investment of more than 12%.

(ii) For $i = 18\%$

$$\text{PV}_{\text{IN}} = 36\,000\left(\frac{1 - 1.18^{-7}}{0.18}\right) = 36\,000(3.811528) \quad = \quad \$137\,215$$

$$\text{PV}_{\text{OUT}} \qquad\qquad\qquad\qquad\qquad\qquad\qquad = \quad \underline{150\,000}$$
$$\text{NPV} = 137\,215 - 150\,000 \qquad\qquad\qquad = \quad -\underline{\$\ 12\,785}$$

Since at 18% the net present value is less than zero, the contract should not be accepted. The contract does not offer the required rate of return on investment of 18%.

(iii) For $i = 15\%$

$$\text{PV}_{\text{IN}} = 36\,000\left(\frac{1 - 1.15^{-7}}{0.15}\right) = 36\,000(4.16042) \quad = \quad \$149\,775$$

$$\text{PV}_{\text{OUT}} \qquad\qquad\qquad\qquad\qquad\qquad\qquad = \quad \underline{150\,000}$$
$$\text{NPV} = 149\,775 - 150\,000 \qquad\qquad\qquad = \quad -\underline{\$\qquad 225}$$

The net present value is slightly negative, which means that the net present value method does not provide a clear signal as to whether to accept or reject the contract. The rate of return offered by the contract is almost 15%.

### Programmed Solution

(i) For $i = 12\%$
("END" mode)

$\text{PV}_{\text{IN}}$: (Set P/Y = 1; C/Y = 1) 0 [ FV ] 36 000 [ PMT ] 7 [ N ]

12 [ I/Y ] [ CPT ] [ PV ] $\boxed{-164295.2354}$

$\text{PV}_{\text{OUT}} = \text{Present value of } 150\,000 \text{ now} = \$150\,000$
The net present value (NPV) = $\$164\,295 - 150\,000 = \$14\,295$.

(ii) For $i = 18\%$
("END" mode)

$\text{PV}_{\text{IN}}$: (Set P/Y = 1; C/Y = 1) 0 [ FV ] 36 000 [ PMT ] 7 [ N ]

18 [ I/Y ] [ CPT ] [ PV ] $\boxed{-137214.9934}$

$$PV_{OUT} = \$150\ 000$$
$$NPV = 137\ 215 - 150\ 000 = -\$12\ 785$$

(iii) For $i = 15\%$

("END" mode)

PV$_{IN}$: (Set P/Y = 1; C/Y = 1) 0 [ FV ] 36 000 [ PMT ] 7 [ N ]

15 [ I/Y ] [ CPT ] [ PV ] $-149775.1104$

$$PV_{OUT} = \$150\ 000$$
$$NPV = \$149\ 775 - 150\ 000 = -\$225$$

**EXAMPLE 16.2D**

A project requires an initial investment of $80 000 with a residual value of $15 000 after six years. It is estimated to yield annual net returns of $21 000 for six years. Should the project be undertaken at 16%?

**SOLUTION**

The cash flows are represented in the diagram below.

*End of period(year)*          $i = 16\%$

| | Now | 1 | 2 | 3 | 4 | 5 | 6 |
|---|---|---|---|---|---|---|---|
| *Out* | <80> | | | | | | 15 |
| *In* | | 21 | 21 | 21 | 21 | 21 | 21 |

**Note:** The residual value of $15 000 is considered to be a reduction in outlays. Its present value should be subtracted from the present value of other outlays.

$$PV_{IN} = 21\ 000\left(\frac{1 - 1.16^{-6}}{0.16}\right) = 21\ 000(3.684736) \qquad = \qquad \$77\ 379$$

$$PV_{OUT} = 80\ 000 - 15\ 000(1.16^{-6})$$
$$= 80\ 000 - 15\ 000(0.410422) = 80\ 000 - 6157 \qquad = \qquad 73\ 843$$
$$= \text{Net present value (NPV)} \qquad\qquad\qquad = \qquad \underline{\underline{\$\ 3\ 536}}$$

**Programmed Solution**

("END" mode)

PV$_{IN}$: (Set P/Y = 1; C/Y = 1) 0 [ FV ] 21 000 [ PMT ] 6 [ N ]

16 [ I/Y ] [ CPT ] [ PV ] $-77379.45407$

PV$_{OUT}$: 0 [ PMT ] 15 000 [ FV ] 6 [ N ] 16 [ I/Y ] [ CPT ] [ PV ] $-6156.63382$

NPV = $77 379 − (80 000 − 6157) = $3536

Since the net present value is positive (the present value of the benefits is greater than the present value of the costs), the rate of return on the investment is greater than 16%. The project should be undertaken.

**EXAMPLE 16.2E**

The UBA Corporation is considering developing a new product. If undertaken, the project requires the outlay of $100 000 per year for three years. Net returns beginning in Year 4 are estimated at $65 000 per year for twelve years. The residual value of the outlays after fifteen years is $30 000. If the corporation requires a return on investment of 14%, should it develop the new product?

**SOLUTION**

The net returns, due at the end of Year 4 to Year 15 respectively, form an ordinary annuity deferred for *three* years in which PMT = 65 000, $n = 12$, $d = 3$, $i = 14\%$.

$$PV_{IN} = 65\,000\left(\frac{1 - 1.14^{-12}}{0.14}\right)(1.14^{-3})$$

$$= 65\,000(5.660292)(0.674972)$$
$$= \$248\,335$$

The outlays, assumed to be made at the beginning of each year, form an annuity due in which PMT = 100 000, $n = 3$, $i = 14\%$.

$$PV_{OUT} = 100\,000(1.14)\left(\frac{1 - 1.14^{-3}}{0.14}\right) - 30\,000(1.14^{-15})$$

$$= 100\,000(1.14)(2.321632) - 30\,000(0.140096)$$
$$= 264\,666 - 4203$$
$$= \$260\,463$$
$$NPV = 248\,335 - 260\,463 = <\$12\,128>$$

**Programmed Solution**

("END" mode)

$PV_{IN}$: (Set P/Y = 1; C/Y = 1) 0 **FV** 65 000 **PMT** 12 **N**

14 **I/Y** **CPT** **PV** [−367918.9882]

0 **PMT** 367 919 **FV** 3 **N** 14 **I/Y** **CPT** **PV** [−248334.853]

("BGN" mode)

$PV_{OUT}$: 0 **FV** 100 000 **PMT** 3 **N** 14 **I/Y** **CPT** **PV** [−264666.0511]

0 **PMT** 30 000 **FV** 15 **N** 14 **I/Y** **CPT** **PV** [−4202.894462]

$NPV = \$248\,335 - (264\,666 - 4203) = -\$12\,128$

Since the net present value is negative, the investment does not offer a 14% return. The corporation should not develop the product.

**EXAMPLE 16.2F**

A feasibility study concerning a contemplated venture yielded the following estimates:

> Initial cost outlay: $1 300 000;
> further outlays in Years 2 to 5: $225 000 per year;
> residual value after 20 years: $625 000;
> net returns: Years 5 to 10: $600 000 per year;
>                     Years 11 to 20: $500 000 per year.

Should the venture be undertaken if the required return on investment is 15%?

**SOLUTION**

$$PV_{IN} = 600\,000\left(\frac{1 - 1.15^{-6}}{0.15}\right)(1.15^{-4}) + 500\,000\left(\frac{1 - 1.15^{-10}}{0.15}\right)(1.15^{-10})$$

$$= 600\,000(3.784483)(0.571753) + 500\,000(5.018769)(0.247185)$$
$$= \$1\,298\,274 + 620\,281$$
$$= \$1\,918\,555$$

$$PV_{OUT} = 1\,300\,000 + 225\,000\left(\frac{1 - 1.15^{-4}}{0.15}\right) - 625\,000(1.15^{-20})$$

$$= 1\,300\,000 + 225\,000(2.854978) - 625\,000(0.061100)$$
$$= \$1\,300\,0000 + 642\,370 - 38\,188$$
$$= \$1\,904\,182$$
$$NPV = 1\,918\,555 - 1\,904\,182 = \$14\,373$$

**Programmed Solution**

("END" mode)

$PV_{IN}$: (Set P/Y = 1; C/Y = 1)

0 [FV] 600 000 [PMT] 15 [I/Y] 6 [N] [CPT] [PV] −2270689.616

0 [PMT] 2 270 689 [FV] 15 [I/Y] 4 [N] [CPT] [PV] −1298273.805

0 [FV] 500 000 [PMT] 15 [I/Y] 10 [N] [CPT] [PV] −2509384.313

0 [PMT] 2 509 384 [FV] 15 [I/Y] 10 [N] [CPT] [PV] −620281.3466

$PV_{IN}$ = $1 298 274 + 620 281 = $1 918 555

$PV_{OUT}$ 0 [FV] 225 000 [PMT] 15 [I/Y] 4 [N] [CPT] [PV] −642370.1316

0 [PMT] 625 000 [FV] 15 [I/Y] 20 [N] [CPT] [PV] −38187.67434

$$PV_{OUT} = \$1\ 300\ 000 + 642\ 370 - 38\ 188 = \$1\ 904\ 182$$
$$NPV = \$1\ 918\ 555 - 1\ 904\ 182 = \$14\ 373$$

Since the net present value is positive, the rate of return on investment is greater than 15%. The venture should be undertaken.

Net present value can be determined by using a preprogrammed financial calculator.

## EXERCISE 16.2

If you choose, you can use Excel's **_Net Present Value (NPV)_** function to answer the questions in Part A and Part B below. Refer to **NPV** on the Spreadsheet Template Disk to learn how to use this Excel function.

**A.** For each of the following six investment choices, compute the net present value. Determine which investment should be accepted or rejected according to the net present value criterion.

1. A contract is estimated to yield net returns of $3500 quarterly for seven years. To secure the contract, an immediate outlay of $50 000 and a further outlay of $30 000 three years from now are required. Interest is 12% compounded quarterly.

2. Replacing old equipment at an immediate cost of $50 000 and an additional outlay of $30 000 six years from now will result in savings of $3000 per quarter for twelve years. The required rate of return is 10% compounded annually.

3. A business has two investment choices. Alternative 1 requires an immediate outlay of $2000 and offers a return of $7000 after seven years. Alternative 2 requires an immediate outlay of $1800 in return for which $250 will be received at the end of every six months for the next seven years. The required rate of return on investment is 17% compounded semi-annually.

4. Suppose you are offered two investment alternatives. If you choose Alternative 1, you will have to make an immediate outlay of $9000. In return, you will receive $500 at the end of every three months for the next ten years. If you choose Alternative 2, you will have to make an outlay of $4000 now and $5000 in two years. In return, you will receive $30 000 ten years from now. Interest is 12% compounded semi-annually.

5. You have two investment alternatives. Alternative 1 requires an immediate outlay of $8000. In return, you will receive $900 at the end of every quarter for the next three years. Alternative 2 requires an immediate outlay of $2000, and an outlay of $1000 in two years. In return, you will receive $300 at the end of every quarter for the next three years. Interest is 7% compounded quarterly. Which alternative would you choose? Why?

6. Your old car costs you $300 per month in gas and repairs. If you replace it, you could sell the old car immediately for $2000. To buy a new car that would last five years, you need to pay out $10 000 immediately. Gas and repairs would cost you only $120 per month on the new car. Interest is 9% compounded monthly. Should you buy a new car? Why?

**B.** Answer each of the following questions.

1. Teck Engineering normally expects a rate of return of 12% on investments. Two projects are available but only one can be chosen. Project A requires an immediate investment of $4000. In return, a revenue payment of $4000 will be received in four years and a payment of $9000 in nine years. Project B requires an investment of $4000 now and another $2000 in three years. In return, revenue payments will be received in the amount of $1500 per year for nine years. Which project is preferable?

2. The owner of a business is presented with two alternative projects. The first project involves the investment of $5000 now. In return the business will receive a payment of $8000 in four years and a payment of $8000 in ten years. The second project involves an investment of $5000 now and another $5000 three years from now. The returns will be semi-annual payments of $950 for ten years. Which project is preferable if the required rate of return is 14% compounded annually?

3. Northern Track is developing a special vehicle for Arctic exploration. The development requires investments of $60 000, $50 000, and $40 000 for the next three years respectively. Net returns beginning in Year 4 are expected to be $33 000 per year for twelve years. If the company requires a rate of return of 14%, compute the net present value of the project and determine whether the company should undertake the project.

4. The Kellog Company has to make a decision about expanding its production facilities. Research indicates that the desired expansion would require an immediate outlay of $60 000 and an outlay of a further $60 000 in five years. Net returns are estimated to be $15 000 per year for the first five years and $10 000 per year for the following ten years. Find the net present value of the project. Should the expansion project be undertaken if the required rate of return is 12%?

5. Agate Marketing Inc. intends to distribute a new product. It is expected to produce net returns of $15 000 per year for the first four years and $10 000 per year for the following three years. The facilities required to distribute the product will cost $36 000 with a disposal value of $9000 after seven years. The facilities will require a major facelift costing $10 000 each after three and after five years respectively. If Agate requires a return on investment of 20%, should the company distribute the new product?

6. A company is considering a project that will require a cost outlay of $15 000 per year for four years. At the end of the project the salvage value will be $10 000. The project will yield returns of $60 000 in Year 4 and $20 000 in Year 5. There are no returns after Year 5. Alternative investments are available that will yield a return of 16%. Should the company undertake the project?

**7.** Demand for a product manufactured by Eagle Manufacturing is expected to be 15 000 units per year during the next ten years. The net return per unit is $2. The manufacturing process requires the purchase of a machine costing $140 000. The machine has an economic life of ten years and a salvage value of $20 000 after ten years. Major overhauls of the machine require outlays of $20 000 after four years and $40 000 after seven years. Should Eagle invest in the machine if it requires a return of 12% on its investments?

 **8.** Magnum Electronics Company expects a demand of 20 000 units per year for a special purpose component during the next six years. Net return per unit is $4. To produce the component, Magnum must buy a machine costing $250 000 with a life of six years and a salvage value of $40 000 after six years. The company estimates that repair costs will be $20 000 per year during Years 2 to 6. If Magnum requires a return on investment of 18%, should it market the component?

## >> BUSINESS MATH NEWS BOX

### General Motors Planning Its Comeback

Corvette! Cadillac! Buick! These words remind most people of performance and luxury automobiles made by automobile giant General Motors. Founded in 1908, GM prides itself on being the world's largest automobile maker. However, this distinction may not last much longer.

To say GM's Chief Executive Officer Rick Wagoner has been busy is an understatement. He has been closing production facilities, selling $17 billion worth of assets, and reorganizing the company ever since GM posted a massive $10.6 billion loss.

Changing consumer preference has transformed the automobile industry; buyers focus on quality and price, and are no longer concerned with brand loyalty when purchasing their next vehicle. With fierce competition from Japanese manufacturer Toyota and Korean automaker Hyundai, GM has seen its market share peak at 51% in 1962 and fall to 24.7% in August 2006.

To entice buyers, GM and other domestic automobile manufacturers such as Ford and DaimlerChrysler offered extremely generous incentives such as zero-interest loans and additional price cuts. Although these enticements may have increased GM's total sales, the cost of selling some of the vehicles was equal to or greater than the selling price of the vehicle. This marketing strategy has changed the way investors look at General Motors. GM is a public company trading its shares on the New York Stock Exchange. Over the past 10 years, the company's shares have declined significantly. In addition, GM's bond rating has deteriorated to "junk bond" status. This decline in credit rating means that investors require GM to pay a higher rate of interest because of the risk associated with borrowing money. GM's debt is rated B by Standard & Poor's and Caa1 by Moody's.

*Sources:* Mark Pittman and Aparajita Saha-Bubna. Bloomberg News. "GM May Sell First Bonds Since 2004 as Debt Rallies." September 11, 2006. (New York); *Bonds Online* website. Downloaded February 13, 2007. www.bondsonline.com/asp/research/bondratings.asp; *Wikipedia—The Free Encyclopedia* website. Downloaded February 13, 2007. http://en.wikipedia.org/wiki/General_Motors_Corporation; CNW Group website, Auto Sales, Downloaded February 13, 2007. "GM's U.S. Divisions Deliver 301,317 Vehicles in October." www.newswire.ca/en/releases/archive/November2006/01/c7268.html.

**QUESTIONS:**

1. Calculate the average annual decline of GM's market share from 1962 to 2006.
2. Research Standard & Poor's and Moody's bond ratings. Focus your search on the Internet.
3. Examine the relationship between bond price and bond yield. Focus your search on the Internet.
4. GM sold 9.17 million vehicles in 2005. If the average discount provided to customers was $1500, calculate the potential revenue lost as a result of the discount.
5. The average selling price of a GM vehicle is $21 000. If GM offers a zero-interest loan on a 5-year monthly loan, determine the potential revenue lost per vehicle when compared to an interest rate of 6% compounded monthly.

# 16.3 FINDING THE RATE OF RETURN ON INVESTMENT

## A. Net present value, profitability index, rate of return

The **rate of return** on investment (R.O.I.) is widely used to measure the value of an investment. This rate of return is often referred to as the **internal rate of return** (I.R.R.). Since it takes interest into account, knowing the rate of return that results from a capital investment project provides useful information when evaluating a project.

The method of finding the rate of return that is explained and illustrated in this section uses the net present value concept introduced in Section 16.2. However, instead of being primarily concerned with a specific discount rate and with comparing the present value of the cash inflows and the present value of the cash outlays, this method is designed to determine the rate of return on the investment.

As explained in Section 16.2, three outcomes are possible when using Formula 16.1. These three outcomes indicate whether the rate of return is greater than, less than, or equal to the discount rate used in finding the net present value.

1. If the net present value is greater than zero (positive), then the rate of return is greater than the discount rate used to determine the net present value.

2. If the net present value is less than zero (negative), then the rate of return is less than the discount rate used.

3. If the net present value is equal to zero, then the rate of return is equal to the rate of discount used.

| If NPV $> 0$ (POSITIVE) | R.O.I. $> i$ |
| If NPV $< 0$ (NEGATIVE) | R.O.I. $< i$ |
| If NPV $= 0$ | R.O.I. $= i$ |

It follows, then, that the rate of return on investment (R.O.I.) is that rate of discount for which the NPV $= 0$, that is, for which $PV_{IN} = PV_{OUT}$.

The above definition of the rate of return and the relationship between the net present value, the rate of discount used to compute the net present value, and the rate of return are useful in developing a method of finding the rate of return.

However, before computing the rate of return, it is useful to consider a ratio known as the **profitability index** or **discounted benefit–cost ratio**. It is defined as the ratio that results when comparing the present value of the cash inflows with the present value of the cash outlays.

PROFITABILITY INDEX (or
DISCOUNTED BENEFIT-COST RATIO) $= \dfrac{PV_{IN}}{PV_{OUT}}$ ———————— Formula 16.2

Since a division is involved, three outcomes are possible when computing this ratio. Each of these outcomes gives an indication of the rate of return.

**1.** If the numerator ($PV_{IN}$) is greater than the denominator ($PV_{OUT}$), then the profitability index is greater than one, and the rate of return is greater than the discount rate used.

**2.** If the numerator ($PV_{IN}$) is less than the denominator ($PV_{OUT}$), then the profitability index is less than one, and the rate of return is less than the discount rate used.

**3.** If the numerator ($PV_{IN}$) is equal to the denominator ($PV_{OUT}$), then the profitability index is equal to one, and the rate of return equals the discount rate used.

The relationship between the present value of the inflows, the present value of the outlays, the net present value, the profitability index, and the rate of return at a given rate of discount $i$ is summarized below.

| $PV_{IN}$ Versus $PV_{OUT}$ | Net Present Value (NPV) | Profitability Index | Rate of Return (R.O.I.) |
|---|---|---|---|
| $PV_{IN} > PV_{OUT}$ | NPV > 0 | > 1 | > $i$ |
| $PV_{IN} = PV_{OUT}$ | NPV = 0 | = 1 | = $i$ |
| $PV_{IN} < PV_{OUT}$ | NPV < 0 | < 1 | < $i$ |

# B. Procedure for finding the rate of return by trial and error

From the relationships noted above, the rate of return on investment can be defined as the rate of discount for which the present value of the inflows (benefits) equals the present value of the outlays (costs). This definition implies that the rate of return is the rate of discount for which the net present value equals zero or for which the profitability index (benefit–cost ratio) equals 1. This conclusion permits us to determine the rate of return by trial and error.

**STEP 1**    Arbitrarily select a discount rate and compute the net present value at that rate.

**STEP 2**    From the outcome of Step 1, draw one of the three conclusions.

(a) If NPV $= 0$, infer that the R.O.I. $= i$.
(b) If NPV $> 0$, infer that the R.O.I. $> i$.
(c) If NPV $< 0$, infer that the R.O.I. $< i$.

**STEP 3**    (a) If, in Step 1, NPV $= 0$, then R.O.I. $= i$ and the problem is solved.
       (b) If, in Step 1, NPV $> 0$ (positive), then we know that R.O.I. $> i$. A second attempt is needed. This second try requires choosing a discount rate greater

than the rate used in Step 1 and computing the net present value using the higher rate.

   If the resulting net present value is still positive, choose a still higher rate of discount and compute the net present value for that rate. Repeat this procedure until the selected rate of discount yields a negative net present value.

(c) If, in Step 1, NPV $< 0$ (negative), then we know that R.O.I. $< i$. The second try requires choosing a discount rate less than the rate used in Step 1 and computing the net present value using the lower rate.

   If the resulting net present value is still negative, choose a still lower rate of discount and compute the net present value for that rate. Repeat this procedure until the selected rate of discount yields a positive net present value.

**STEP 4**   The basic aim of Step 3 is to find one rate of discount for which the net present value is positive and a second rate for which the net present value is negative. Once this has been accomplished, the rate of return must be a rate between the two rates used to generate a positive and a negative net present value.

   You can now obtain a reasonably accurate value of the rate of return by using linear interpolation. To ensure sufficient accuracy in the answer, we recommend that the two rates of discount used when interpolating be no more than two percentage points apart. The worked examples in this section have been solved using successive even rates of discounts when interpolating.

**STEP 5**   (Optional) You can check the accuracy of the method of interpolation when using an electronic calculator by computing the net present value. Use as the discount rate the rate of return determined in Step 4. Expect the rate in Step 4 to be slightly too high. You can obtain a still more precise answer by further trials.

## C. Selecting the rate of discount—using the profitability index

While the selection of a discount rate in Step 1 of the procedure is arbitrary, a sensible choice is one that is neither too high nor too low. Since the negative net present value immediately establishes a range between zero and the rate used, it is preferable to be on the high side. Choosing a rate of discount within the range 12% to 24% usually leads to quick solutions.

   While the initial choice of rate is a shot in the dark, the resulting knowledge about the size of the rate of return combined with the use of the profitability index should ensure the selection of a second rate that is fairly close to the actual rate of return.

   In making the second choice, use the profitability index.

**1.** Compute the index for the first rate chosen and convert the index into a percent.

**2.** Deduct 100% from the index and divide the difference by 4.

**3.** If the index is greater than 1, add the above result to obtain the rate that you should use for the second attempt. If, however, the index is smaller than 1, deduct the above result from the rate of discount initially used.

To illustrate, assume that the rate of discount initially selected is 16%. The resulting $PV_{IN}$ = 150 and the $PV_{OUT}$ = 120.

**1.** The profitability index is $\dfrac{150}{120}$ = 1.25 = 1.25%.

**2.** The difference (125% − 100%) divided by 4 = 6.25%.

**3.** Since the index is greater than 1, add 6.25% to the initial rate of 16%; the recommended choice is 22%.

Assume that the rate of discount initially selected is 20%. The resulting $PV_{IN}$ = 200 and the $PV_{OUT}$ = 250.

**1.** The profitability index is $\dfrac{200}{250}$ = 0.80 = 80%.

**2.** The difference (80% − 100%) divided by 4 = −5%.

**3.** Since the index is less than 1, subtract 5% from the initial rate of 20%; the recommended choice is 15%. (If, as in this text, you are using only even rates, try either 14% or 16%.)

## D. Using linear interpolation

The method of linear interpolation used in Step 4 of the suggested procedure is illustrated in Example 16.3A below.

**EXAMPLE 16.3A**

Assume that the net present value of a project is $420 at 14% and −$280 at 16%. Use linear interpolation to compute the rate of return correct to the nearest tenth of a percent.

**SOLUTION**

The data can be represented on a line diagram.

The line segment AB represents the distance between the two rates of discount that are associated with a positive and a negative net present value respectively.

At Point A,   where $i$ = 14%, the NPV = 420;
at Point B,   where $i$ = 16%, the NPV = −280;
at Point X,   where $i$ is unknown, the NPV = 0.

By definition, the rate of return is that rate of discount for which the net present value is zero. Since 0 is a number between 420 and −280, the NPV = 0 is located at a point on AB. This point is marked X.

We can obtain two useful ratios by considering the line segment from the two points of view shown in the diagram.

(i) In terms of the discount rate $i$,

AB = 2% —————————— 16% − 14%
AX = $d$% —————————— the unknown percent that must be added to 14% to obtain the rate of discount at which the NPV = 0

$$\frac{AX}{AB} = \frac{d\%}{2\%}$$

(ii) In terms of the net present value figures,

AB = 700 —————————— 420 + 280
AX = 420

$$\frac{AX}{AB} = \frac{420}{700}$$

Since the ratio AX:AB is written twice, we can derive a proportion statement.

$$\frac{d\%}{2\%} = \frac{420}{700}$$

$$d\% = \frac{420}{700} \times 2\%$$

$$d\% = 1.2\%$$

Therefore, the rate at which the net present value is equal to zero is 14% + 1.2% = 15.2%. The rate of return on investment is 15.2%.

## E. Computing the rate of return

**EXAMPLE 16.3B**

A project requires an initial outlay of $25 000. The estimated returns are $7000 per year for seven years. Compute the rate of return (correct to the nearest tenth of a percent).

**SOLUTION**

The cash flows (in thousands) are represented in the diagram below.
The inflows form an ordinary annuity since inflows are assumed to be received at the end of each year.

$$PV_{IN} = 7000\left[\frac{1 - (1 + i)^{-7}}{i}\right]$$

The outlays consist of an immediate payment.

$$PV_{OUT} = 25\ 000$$

To determine the rate of return, we will choose a rate of discount, compute the net present value, and try further rates until we find two successive even rates. For one, the NPV $> 0$ (positive) and, for the other, NPV $< 0$ (negative).

**STEP 1**    Try $i = 12\%$.

$$PV_{IN} = 7000\left(\frac{1 - 1.12^{-7}}{0.12}\right) = 7000(4.563757) \qquad\qquad = \qquad \$31\ 946$$

$$PV_{OUT} \qquad\qquad\qquad\qquad\qquad\qquad\qquad\qquad\qquad = \qquad 25\ 000$$
$$NPV\ at\ 12\% \qquad\qquad\qquad\qquad\qquad\qquad\qquad\qquad = \qquad \underline{\$\ 6\ 946}$$

Since the NPV $> 0$, R.O.I. $> 12\%$.

**STEP 2**    Compute the profitability index to estimate what rate should be used next.

$$INDEX = \frac{PV_{IN}}{PV_{OUT}} = \frac{31\ 946}{25\ 000} = 1.278 = 127.8\%$$

Since at $i = 12\%$, the profitability index is 27.8% more than 100%, the rate of discount should be increased by $\frac{27.8\%}{4} = 7\%$ approximately. To obtain another even rate, the increase should be either 6% or 8%. In line with the suggestion that it is better to go too high, increase the previous rate by 8% and try $i = 20\%$.

**STEP 3**    Try $i = 20\%$.

$$PV_{IN} = 7000\left(\frac{1 - 1.20^{-7}}{0.20}\right) = 7000(3.604592) \qquad\qquad = \qquad \$25\ 232$$

$$PV_{OUT} \qquad\qquad\qquad\qquad\qquad\qquad\qquad\qquad\qquad = \qquad 25\ 000$$
$$NPV\ at\ 20\% \qquad\qquad\qquad\qquad\qquad\qquad\qquad\qquad = \qquad \underline{\$\quad 232}$$

Since the NPV $> 0$, R.O.I. $> 20\%$.

**STEP 4**    Since the net present value is still positive, a rate higher than 20% is needed. The profitability index at 20% is $\frac{25\ 232}{25\ 000} = 1.009 = 100.9\%$. The index exceeds 100% by 0.9%; division by 4 suggests an increase of 0.2%. For interpolation, the recommended minimum increase or decrease is 2%. The next try should use $i = 22\%$.

**STEP 5**    Try $i = 22\%$.

$$PV_{IN} = 7000\left(\frac{1 - 1.22^{-7}}{0.22}\right) = 7000(3.415506) \qquad\qquad = \qquad \$23\ 909$$

$$PV_{OUT} \qquad\qquad\qquad\qquad\qquad\qquad\qquad\qquad\qquad = \qquad -\$25\ 000$$
$$NPV\ at\ 22\% \qquad\qquad\qquad\qquad\qquad\qquad\qquad\qquad = \qquad \underline{\underline{-\$\ 1\ 091}}$$

Since the NPV $< 0$, R.O.I. $< 22\%$.
Therefore, $20\% <$ R.O.I. $< 22\%$.

**STEP 6** Now that the rate of return has been located between two sufficiently close rates of discount, linear interpolation can be used as illustrated in Example 16.3A.

$$\frac{d}{2} = \frac{232}{232 + 1091}$$

$$d = \frac{232(2)}{1323} = 0.35$$

The rate of discount for which the NPV = 0 is approximately 20% + 0.35% = 20.35%. The rate of return is approximately 20.3%. (A more precisely computed value is 20.3382%.)

*Note:* Three attempts were needed to locate the R.O.I. between 20% and 22%. Three is the usual number of tries necessary. The minimum number is two attempts. Occasionally four attempts may be needed. To produce a more concise solution, organize the computation as shown below. Since estimates are involved, it is sufficient to use present value factors with only three decimal positions. In the following examples, all factors are rounded to three decimals.

| Present Value of Amounts in General Form | Attempts | | | | | |
|---|---|---|---|---|---|---|
| | $i = 12\%$ | | $i = 20\%$ | | $i = 22\%$ | |
| $PV_{IN}$ | Factor | $ | Factor | $ | Factor | $ |
| $7000\left[\dfrac{1 - (1 + i)^{-7}}{i}\right]$ | 4.563757 | 31 946 | 3.604592 | 25 232 | 3.415506 | 23 909 |
| $PV_{OUT}$ 25 000 now | | 25 000 | | 25 000 | | 25 000 |
| NPV | | 6 946 | | 232 | | <1 091> |

**Programmed Solution**

(Set P/Y = 1; C/Y = 1)

| Present Value of Amounts in General Form | Attempts | | | | | |
|---|---|---|---|---|---|---|
| | $i = 12\%$ | $i = 20\%$ | $i = 22\%$ | $i = 20.5\%$ | $i = 20.3\%$ | $i = 20.34\%$ |
| $PV_{IN}$ | 0 FV | 0 FV | 0 FV | 0 FV | 0 FV | 0 FV |
| $7000\left[\dfrac{1 - (1 + i)^{-7}}{i}\right]$ | −7000 PMT | −7000 PMT | −7000 PMT | −7000 PMT | −7000 PMT | −7000 PMT |
| | 7 N | 7 N | 7 N | 7 N | 7 N | 7 N |

| Present Value of Amounts in General Form | Attempts | | | | | |
|---|---|---|---|---|---|---|
| | *i* = 12% | *i* = 20% | *i* = 22% | *i* = 20.5% | *i* = 20.3% | *i* = 20.34% |
| | 12 I/Y CPT PV | 20 I/Y CPT PV | 22 I/Y CPT PV | 20.5 I/Y CPT PV | 20.3 I/Y CPT PV | 20.34 I/Y CPT PV |
| PV$_{IN}$ | 31 946 | 25 232 | 23 909 | 24 890 | 25 026 | 24 999 |
| PV$_{OUT}$ 25 000 now | 25 000 | 25 000 | 25 000 | 25 000 | 25 000 | 25 000 |
| NPV | 6946 | 232 | −1091 | −110 | 26 | −1 |
| R.O.I. | > 12% | > 20% | < 22% | < 20.5% | > 20.3% | = 20.34% |

**EXAMPLE 16.3C**

A venture that requires an immediate outlay of $320 000 and an outlay of $96 000 after five years has a residual value of $70 000 after ten years. Net returns are estimated to be $64 000 per year for ten years. Compute the rate of return.

**SOLUTION**

The cash flow is represented in the diagram below (in thousands).

*End of year*

| Now | 1 | 2 | 3 | 4 | 5 | 6 | 7 | 8 | 9 | 10 |

*Out* <320>                                    <96>                                70
*In*          64    64    64    64    64    64    64    64    64    64

The computations are organized in a chart; explanations regarding the computations follow.

| Present Value of Amounts in General Form | Attempts | | | | | |
|---|---|---|---|---|---|---|
| | $i = 20\%$ | | $i = 14\%$ | | $i = 12\%$ | |
| PV of benefits | Factor | $ | Factor | $ | Factor | $ |
| $64\,000\left[\dfrac{1-(1+i)^{-10}}{i}\right]$ | 4.192 | 268 288 | 5.216 | 333 824 | 5.650 | 361 600 |
| PV of costs:<br>320 000 now<br>$96\,000(1+i)^{-5}$<br>$\langle 70\,000(1+i)^{-10}\rangle$ | <br><br>0.402<br>0.162 | <br>320 000<br>38 592<br>\<11 340\> | <br><br>0.519<br>0.270 | <br>320 000<br>49 824<br>\<18 900\> | <br><br>0.567<br>0.322 | <br>320 000<br>54 432<br>\<22 540\> |
| TOTAL | | 347 252 | | 350 924 | | 351 892 |
| NPV | | \<78 964\> | | \<17 100\> | | 9 708 |

## *Explanations for computations*

**STEP 1**  Try $i = 20\%$.
Since NPV < 0,  R.O.I. < 20%

Index at 20% $= \dfrac{268\,288}{347\,252} = 0.773 = 77.3\%$

Reduction in rate $= \dfrac{22.7\%}{4} = 5.7\% \longrightarrow 6\%$

**STEP 2**  Try $i = 14\%$.
NPV < 0,  R.O.I. < 14%

Index $= \dfrac{333\,824}{350\,924} = 0.951 = 95.1\%$

Reduction in rate $= \dfrac{4.9\%}{4} = 1.2\% \longrightarrow 2\%$

**STEP 3**  Try $i = 12\%$
NPV > 0;  R.O.I. > 12%
12% < R.O.I. < 14%

**STEP 4**  $\dfrac{d}{2} = \dfrac{9708}{9708 + 17\,100} = \dfrac{9708}{26\,808} = 0.362131$

$d = 2(0.362131) = 0.724$

The rate of discount at which the net present value is zero is 12% + 0.72% = 12.72%. The rate of return is 12.7%.

## Programmed Solution

(Set P/Y = 1; C/Y = 1)

| Present Value of Amounts in General Form | Attempts | | | | |
|---|---|---|---|---|---|
| | $i = 20\%$ | $i = 14\%$ | $i = 12\%$ | $i = 12.7\%$ | $i = 12.68\%$ |
| PV of benefits $$64\,000\left[\frac{1-(1+i)^{-10}}{i}\right]$$ | 0 FV <br> −64 000 PMT <br><br> 10 N <br> 20 I/Y <br> CPT <br> PV | 0 FV <br> −64 000 PMT <br><br> 10 N <br> 14 I/Y <br> CPT <br> PV | 0 FV <br> −64 000 PMT <br><br> 10 N <br> 12 I/Y <br> CPT <br> PV | 0 FV <br> −64 000 PMT <br><br> 10 N <br> 12.7 I/Y <br> CPT <br> PV | 0 FV <br> −64 000 PMT <br><br> 10 N <br> 12.68 I/Y <br> CPT <br> PV |
| PV$_{IN}$ | 268 318 | 333 831 | 361 614 | 351 484 | 351 767 |
| PV of costs 320 000 now | 320 000 | 320 000 | 320 000 | 320 000 | 320 000 |
| $96\,000(1+i)^{-5}$ | 0 PMT <br> 96 000 FV <br> 5 N <br> 20 I/Y <br> CPT <br> PV | 0 PMT <br> 96 000 FV <br> 5 N <br> 14 I/Y <br> CPT <br> PV | 0 PMT <br> 96 000 FV <br> 5 N <br> 12 I/Y <br> CPT <br> PV | 0 PMT <br> 96 000 FV <br> 5 N <br> 12.7 I/Y <br> CPT <br> PV | 0 PMT <br> 96 000 FV <br> 5 N <br> 12.68 I/Y <br> CPT <br> PV |
| Outflow | −38 580 | −49 859 | −54 473 | −52 802 | −52 849 |
| $<70\,000(1+i)^{-10}>$ | 70 000 FV <br> 10 N <br> 20 I/Y <br> CPT <br> PV | 70 000 FV <br> 10 N <br> 14 I/Y <br> CPT <br> PV | 70 000 FV <br> 10 N <br> 12 I/Y <br> CPT <br> PV | 70 000 FV <br> 10 N <br> 12.7 I/Y <br> CPT <br> PV | 70 000 FV <br> 10 N <br> 12.68 I/Y <br> CPT <br> PV |
| <inflow> | <11 305> | <18 882> | <22 538> | <21 177> | <21 214> |
| PV$_{OUT}$ | 347 275 | 350 977 | 351 935 | 351 625 | 351 635 |
| NPV | <78 957> | <17 146> | 9 679 | <141> | 132 |
| R.O.I. | <20% | <14% | >12% | <12.7% | >12.68% |

**EXAMPLE 16.3D**

A project requires an immediate investment of $33 000 with a residual value of $7000 at the end of the project. It is expected to yield a net return of $7000 in Year 1, $8000 in Year 2, $11 000 per year for the following six years, and $9000 per year for the remaining four years. Find the rate of return.

**SOLUTION**

The cash flows for the project (in thousands) are represented in the diagram below.

End of year

| | Now | 1 | 2 | 3 | 4 | 5 | 6 | 7 | 8 | 9 | 10 | 11 | 12 |
|---|---|---|---|---|---|---|---|---|---|---|---|---|---|
| Out | <33> | | | | | | | | | | | | 7 |
| In | | 7 | 8 | 11 | 11 | 11 | 11 | 11 | 11 | 9 | 9 | 9 | 9 |

The computations are organized in the chart that follows.

| Present Value of Amounts in General Form | Attempts | | | | | |
|---|---|---|---|---|---|---|
| | $i = 20\%$ | | $i = 28\%$ | | $i = 26\%$ | |
| PV of returns | Factor | $ | Factor | $ | Factor | $ |
| $7000(1 + i)^{-1}$ | 0.833 | 5 831 | 0.781 | 5 467 | 0.794 | 5 558 |
| $8000(1 + i)^{-2}$ | 0.694 | 5 552 | 0.610 | 4 880 | 0.630 | 5 040 |
| $11\,000\left[\dfrac{1-(1+i)^{-6}}{i}\right]$ | 3.326 | | 2.759 | | 2.885 | |
| | × | 25 391 | × | 18 513 | × | 19 993 |
| $\times (1 + i)^{-2}$ | 0.694 | | 0.610 | | 0.630 | |
| $9000\left[\dfrac{1-(1+i)^{-4}}{i}\right]$ | 2.589 | | 2.241 | | 2.320 | |
| | × | 5 429 | × | 2 803 | × | 3 278 |
| $\times (1 + i)^{-8}$ | 0.233 | | 0.139 | | 0.157 | |
| TOTAL PV$_{IN}$ | | 42 203 | | 31 663 | | 33 869 |
| PV of costs 33 000 now | | 33 000 | | 33 000 | | 33 000 |
| $<7000(1 + i)^{-12}>$ | 0.112 | <784> | 0.052 | <364> | 0.062 | <434> |
| TOTAL PV$_{OUT}$ | | 32 216 | | 32 636 | | 32 566 |
| NPV | | 9 987 | | <973> | | 1 303 |

*Explanations for computations*

**STEP 1**   The present value of the returns consists of $7000 discounted for one year, $8000 discounted for two years, the present value of an ordinary annuity of six payments of $11 000 deferred for two years, and the present value of an ordinary annuity of four payments of $9000 deferred for eight years. The present value of the costs consists of the lump sum of $33 000 less the salvage value of $7000 discounted for twelve years.

**STEP 2**   The rate of discount chosen for the first attempt is 20%.
For $i = 20\%$, NPV $> 0$; R.O.I. $> 20\%$

$$\text{Index} = \frac{42\ 203}{32\ 216} = 1.310 = 131.0\%$$

$$\text{Increase in rate} = \frac{31.0}{4} = 7.75\% \text{ or } 8\%$$

**STEP 3**   For $i = 28\%$, NPV $< 0$; R.O.I $< 28\%$

$$\text{Index} = \frac{31\ 663}{32\ 636} = 0.970 = 97.0\%$$

$$\text{Decrease in rate} = \frac{3}{4} = 0.75\% \text{ or } 2\% \text{ (rounded up)}$$

**STEP 4**   For $i = 26\%$, NPV $> 0$; R.O.I. $> 26\%$
$26\% <$ R.O.I. $< 28\%$

**STEP 5**   $$d = \frac{1303}{1303 + 973} \times 2 = \frac{2606}{2276} = 1.14499$$

The rate of discount for which the net present value is zero is approximately $26\% + 1.14\% = 27.14\%$. The rate of return, correct to the nearest tenth of a percent, is 27.1%.

## POINTERS AND PITFALLS

Investors should always be aware of the fact that higher rates of return (yield) are accompanied typically by higher levels of investment risk. For the most daring investors, high-risk/high-yield investments include derivatives, commodities, precious metals, gemstones, collectible items, common stocks, and growth stocks. For investors more comfortable with moderate-risk/moderate-yield, investment choices include mutual funds, real estate, corporate bonds, and preferred stocks. Low-risk/low-yield options such as savings accounts, term deposits, guaranteed investment certificates (GICs), and Canada Savings Bonds (CSBs) are designed to appeal to the most conservative investors.

Internal rate of return can be determined by using a preprogrammed financial calculator.

## EXERCISE 16.3

If you choose, you can use Excel's *Internal Rate of Return (IRR)* function to answer the questions in Part B below. Refer to **IRR** on the Spreadsheet Template Disk to learn how to use this Excel function.

**A.** Use linear interpolation to find the approximate value of the rate of return for each of the projects below. State your answer correct to the nearest tenth of a percent.

| | Positive NPV at *i* | Negative NPV at *i* |
|---|---|---|
| **1.** | $2350 at 24% | −$1270 at 26% |
| **2.** | $850 at 8% | −$370 at 10% |
| **3.** | $135 at 20% | −$240 at 22% |
| **4.** | $56 at 16% | −$70 at 18% |

**B.** Find the rate of return for each of the six situations below (correct to the nearest tenth of a percent).

1. The proposed expansion of CIV Electronics' plant facilities requires the immediate outlay of $100 000. Expected net returns are

   Year 1: Nil          Year 2: $30 000          Year 3: $40 000
   Year 4: $60 000          Year 5: $50 000          Year 6: $20 000

2. The introduction of a new product requires an initial outlay of $60 000. The anticipated net returns from the marketing of the product are expected to be $12 000 per year for ten years.

3. Your firm is considering introducing a new product for which net returns are expected to be

   Year 1 to Year 3 inclusive:          $2000 per year
   Year 4 to Year 8 inclusive:          $5000 per year
   Year 9 to Year 12 inclusive:          $3000 per year

   The introduction of the product requires an immediate outlay of $15 000 for equipment estimated to have a salvage value of $2000 after twelve years.

4. A project requiring an immediate investment of $150 000 and a further outlay of $40 000 after four years has a residual value of $30 000 after nine years. The project yields a negative net return of $10 000 in Year 1, a zero net return in Year 2, $50 000 per year for the following four years, and $70 000 per year for the last three years.

5. You are thinking of starting a hot dog business that requires an initial investment of $16 000 and a major replacement of equipment after ten years amounting to $8000. From competitive experience, you expect to have a net loss of $2000 the first year, a net profit of $2000 the second year, and, for the remaining years of the first fifteen years of operations, net returns of $6000 per year. After fifteen years, the net returns will gradually decline and will be zero at the end of twenty-five years (assume returns of $3000 per year for that period).

After twenty-five years, your lease will expire. The salvage value of equipment at that time is expected to be just sufficient to cover the cost of closing the business.

 **6.** The Blue Sky Ski Resort plans to install a new chair lift. Construction is estimated to require an immediate outlay of $220 000. The life of the lift is estimated to be fifteen years with a salvage value of $80 000. Cost of clearing and grooming the new area is expected to be $30 000 for each of the first three years of operation. Net cash inflows from the lift are expected to be $40 000 for each of the first five years and $70 000 for each of the following ten years.

Go to MyMathLab at www.mathxl.com. You can practise many of this chapter's exercises as often as you want. The guided solutions help you find an answer step by step. You'll find a personalized study plan available to you too!

## Review Exercise

1. Wells Inc. has to choose between two investment alternatives. Alternative A will return the company $20 000 after three years, $60 000 after six years, and $40 000 after ten years. Alternative B will bring returns of $10 000 per year for ten years. If the company expects a return of 14% on investments, which alternative should it choose?

2. A piece of property may be acquired by making an immediate payment of $25 000 and payments of $37 500 and $50 000 three and five years from now respectively. Alternatively, the property may be purchased by making quarterly payments of $5150 in advance for five years. Which alternative is preferable if money is worth 15% compounded semi-annually?

3. An investor has two investment alternatives. If he chooses Alternative 1, he will have to make an immediate outlay of $7000 and will receive $500 every three months for the next nine years. If he chooses Alternative 2, he will have to make an immediate outlay of $6500 and will receive $26 000 after eight years. If interest is 12% compounded quarterly, which alternative should the investor choose on the basis of the net present value criterion?

4. Replacing old equipment at an immediate cost of $65 000 and $40 000 five years from now will result in a savings of $8000 semi-annually for ten years. At 14% compounded annually, should the old equipment be replaced?

5. A real estate development project requires annual outlays of $75 000 for eight years. Net cash inflows beginning in Year 9 are expected to be $250 000 per year for fifteen years. If the developer requires a rate of return of 18%, compute the net present value of the project.

6. A company is considering a project that will require a cost outlay of $30 000 per year for four years. At the end of the project, the company expects to salvage the physical assets for $30 000. The project is estimated to yield net returns of $60 000 in Year 4, $40 000 in Year 5,

and $20 000 for each of the following five years. Alternative investments are available yielding a rate of return of 14%. Compute the net present value of the project.

7. An investment requires an initial outlay of $45 000. Net returns are estimated to be $14 000 per year for eight years. Determine the rate of return.

8. A project requires an initial outlay of $10 000 and promises net returns of $2000 per year over a twelve-year period. If the project has a residual value of $4000 after twelve years, what is the rate of return?

9. Compute the rate of return for Question 5.

10. Compute the rate of return for Question 6.

11. Superior Jig Co. has developed a new jig for which it expects net returns as follows.

| | |
|---|---|
| Year 1: | $8 000 |
| Years 2 to 6 inclusive: | $12 000 per year |
| Years 7 to 10 inclusive: | $6 000 per year |

The initial investment of $36 000 has a residual value of $9000 after ten years. Compute the rate of return.

12. The owner of a sporting goods store is considering remodelling the store in order to carry a larger inventory. The cost of remodelling and additional inventory is $60 000. The expected increase in net profit is $8000 per year for the next four years and $10 000 each year for the following six years. After ten years, the owner plans to retire and sell the business. She expects to recover the additional $40 000 invested in inventory but not the $20 000 invested in remodelling. Compute the rate of return.

13. Outway Ventures evaluates potential investment projects at 20%. Two alternative projects are available. Project A will return the company $5800 per year for eight years. Project B will return the company $13 600 after one year, $17 000 after five years, and $20 400 after eight years. Which alternative should the company choose according to the discounted cash flow criterion?

**14.** Project A requires an immediate investment of $8000 and another $6000 in three years. Net returns are $4000 after two years, $12 000 after four years, and $8000 after six years. Project B requires an immediate investment of $4000, another $6000 after two years, and $4000 after four years. Net returns are $3400 per year for seven years. Determine the net present value at 10%. Which project is preferable according to the net present value criterion?

**15.** Net returns from an investment are estimated to be $13 000 per year for twelve years. The investment involves an immediate outlay of $50 000 and a further outlay of $30 000 after six years. The investments are estimated to have a residual value of $10 000 after twelve years. Find the net present value at 20%.

**16.** The introduction of a new product requires an immediate outlay of $45 000. Anticipated net returns from the marketing of the product are expected to be $12 500 per year for ten years. What is the rate of return on the investment (correct to the nearest tenth of a percent)?

**17.** Games Inc. has developed a new electronic game and compiled the following product information.

| | Production Cost | Promotion Cost | Sales Revenue |
|---|---|---|---|
| Year 1 | $32 000 | — | — |
| Year 2 | 32 000 | $64 000 | $ 64 000 |
| Year 3 | 32 000 | 96 000 | 256 000 |
| Year 4 | 32 000 | 32 000 | 128 000 |
| Year 5 | 32 000 | | 32 000 |

Should the product be marketed if the company requires a return of 16%?

**18.** Farmer Jones wants to convert his farm into a golf course. He asked you to determine his rate of return on the basis of the following estimates: development cost for each of the first three years, $80 000; construction of a clubhouse in Year 4, $240 000; upon his retirement in fifteen years, improvements in the property will yield him $200 000; net returns from the operation of the golf course will be nil for the first three years and $100 000 per year afterwards until his retirement.

# Self-Test

**1.** Opportunities Inc. requires a minimum rate of return of 15% on investment proposals. Two proposals are under consideration but only one may be chosen. Alternative A offers a net return of $2500 per year for twelve years. Alternative B offers a net return of $10 000 each year after four, eight, and twelve years respectively. Determine the preferred alternative according to the discounted cash flow criterion.

**2.** A natural resources development project requires an immediate outlay of $100 000 and $50 000 at the end of each year for four years. Net returns are nil for the first two years and $60 000 per year thereafter for fourteen years. What is the net present value of the project at 16%?

**3.** An investment of $100 000 yields annual net returns of $20 000 for ten years. If the residual value of the investment after ten years is $30 000, what is the rate of return on the investment (correct to the nearest tenth of a percent)?

**4.** A telephone system with a disposable value of $1200 after five years can be purchased for $6600. Alternatively, a leasing agreement is available that requires an immediate payment of $1500 plus payments of $100 at the beginning of each month for five years. If money is worth 12% compounded monthly, should the telephone system be leased or purchased?

5. A choice has to be made between two investment proposals. Proposal A requires an immediate outlay of $60 000 and a further outlay of $40 000 after three years. Net returns are $20 000 per year for ten years. The investment has no residual value after ten years. Proposal B requires outlays of $29 000 in each of the first four years. Net returns starting in Year 4 are $40 000 per year. The residual value of the investment after ten years is $50 000. Which proposal is preferable at 20%?

6. Introducing a new product requires an immediate investment in plant facilities of $180 000 with a disposal value of $45 000 after seven years. The facilities will require additional capital outlays of $50 000 each after three and five years respectively. Net returns on the investment are estimated to be $75 000 per year for each of the first four years and $50 000 per year for the remaining three years. Determine the rate of return on investment (correct to the nearest tenth of a percent).

## Challenge Problems

1. The owners of a vegetable processing plant can buy a new conveyor system for $85 000. They estimate they can save $17 000 per year on labour and maintenance costs. They can purchase the same conveyor system with an automatic loader for $114 000, and estimate they can save $22 000 per year with that system. If the owners expect both systems to last ten years and they require at least 14% return per year, should they buy the system with the automatic loader?

2. CheeseWorks owns four dairies in your province and has planned upgrades for all locations. The owners are considering four projects, each of which is independent of the other three projects. The details of each project—A, B, C, and D—are shown below.

| Project | Cost at Beginning of Year 1 | Year 1 | Year 2 | Year 3 | Year 4 | Year 5 |
|---------|-----------------------------|--------|--------|--------|--------|--------|
| | | \multicolumn{5}{c}{Revenues and Cost Savings at End of:} | | | | |
| A | 300 000 | 150 000 | 120 000 | 120 000 | 0 | 0 |
| B | 360 000 | 0 | 40 000 | 200 000 | 200 000 | 200 000 |
| C | 210 000 | 10 000 | 10 000 | 100 000 | 120 000 | 120 000 |
| D | 125 000 | 30 000 | 40 000 | 40 000 | 40 000 | 40 000 |

The owners of CheeseWorks have $700 000 to invest in these projects. They expect at least 12% return on all of their projects. In which projects should the owners of CheeseWorks invest to maximize the return on their investment?

# Case Study 16.1 To Lease or Not to Lease?

» To travel to her new job, Dharshana required a car. Reading the newspaper, she noticed an ad for an Acura TSX. It was just the vehicle she wanted.

The ad quoted both a cash purchase price of $37 500 and a monthly lease payment option. Since she did not have enough money to pay for a car, she would have to finance it from Honda by paying interest of 7.8% compounded monthly on the loan.

The lease option required payments of $594 a month for 48 months with a $1330 down payment or equivalent trade. Freight and air tax was included. Dharshana did not have a vehicle to offer as a trade-in. If the vehicle was leased, then after 48 months it could be purchased for $16 155. The lease was based on a finance interest rate of 3.8%. During the term of the lease, kilometres were limited to 24 000 per year, and an additional charge of $0.08 per kilometre for excess kilometres. The costs included freight, but excluded taxes, registration, licence, and dealer administration charges. Dharshana was particularly impressed with the "four-years or 100 000 kilometre" warranty on the engine and transmission. The manufacturer also offered 24-hour roadside assistance.

Dharshana must decide whether to buy or lease this car. She lives in a province with a 7% PST and 6% GST tax rate. She realizes that the costs of licence and insurance must be paid, but she will ignore these in her calculations.

## QUESTIONS

1. If Dharshana buys the car, what is the total purchase price, including taxes?

2. Since Dharshana has no down payment, she must finance the car if she purchases it.
   (a) Is it cheaper to borrow the money from the bank or to lease?
   (b) The bank is offering a vehicle loan rate of 8% compounded annually. Is it better to buy or to lease the car at this rate?

3. Suppose Dharshana has a $4000 down payment for this car.
   (a) What is the purchase price of the car if she pays cash for it? Assume the down payment is subtracted from the price of the car including tax.
   (b) If the monthly lease payment is $594, is it cheaper to lease or buy the car if Dharshana can get the special dealer rate of 3.8%?

# Case Study 16.2 Building a Business

» Advanced Manufacturing Ltd. has demolished an old warehouse to make room for additional manufacturing capacity. The company has decided to construct a new building, but must decide on how to proceed. There are two alternatives for the new building, both of which will create a building with an expected life of sixty years. The residual value is unknown but will be the same for either alternative.

Alternative A is to construct a new building that would have 210 000 square metres. Construction costs will initially total $2 800 000 at the start. Maintenance costs are expected to be $18 000 per year. The building will need to be repainted every ten years (starting in ten years) at an estimated cost of $15 000.

Alternative B is to construct the building in two stages: build 100 000 square metres now; and add 110 000 square metres in ten years. Construction costs for the first stage will be $1 900 000 at the start of the project. Construction costs for the second stage will be $1 000 000 when the addition is completed at the end of Year 10. Maintenance costs are expected to be $12 000 per year for the first ten years, then $21 000 per year after that. The building and the addition will have to be painted every ten years, beginning in Year 20, at an estimated cost of $15 000.

## QUESTIONS

1. Suppose the company's required rate of return is 12%.
   (a) What is the present value of Alternative A?
   (b) What is the present value of Alternative B?
   (c) Which alternative would you recommend on the basis of your discounted cash flow analysis?

2. Which alternative would you recommend if the company's required rate of return was 18%? Show all calculations.

3. Suppose the company could rent a portion of its building for $55 000 per year for the first ten years if it chose Alternative A.
   (a) If the company's required rate of return is 12%, what is the net present value of Alternative A?
   (b) On the basis of the new information, would you recommend Alternative A or Alternative B if the company's required rate of return is 18%?

# SUMMARY OF FORMULAS

**Formula 16.1**

$$\underset{\text{(NPV)}}{\text{NET PRESENT VALUE}} = \underset{\text{OF INFLOWS}}{\text{PRESENT VALUE}} - \underset{\text{OF OUTLAYS}}{\text{PRESENT VALUE}}$$

**Formula for finding the difference between the present value of cash inflows and the present value of cash outflows, known as the net present value**

**Formula 16.2**

$$\text{PROFITABILITY INDEX} = \frac{\text{PRESENT VALUE OF INFLOWS}}{\text{PRESENT VALUE OF OUTLAYS}} = \frac{PV_{IN}}{PV_{OUT}}$$

**Formula for finding the relationship by dividing the present value of cash inflows by the present value of cash outflows, known as the profitability index**

In addition, Formulas 9.1B, 9.1C, 11.2, 12.3, 13.2, and 13.4 were used in this chapter.

# GLOSSARY

**Discounted benefit–cost ratio**   *see* **Profitability index**

**Discounted cash flow**   the present value of cash payments *(p. 700)*

**Internal rate of return**   *see* **Rate of return**

**Net present value**   the difference between the present value of the inflows (benefits) and the present value of the outlays (costs) of a capital investment project *(p. 691)*

**Profitability index**   the ratio of the present value of the inflows (benefits) to the present value of the outlays (costs) of a capital investment project *(p. 700)*

**Rate of return**   the rate of discount for which the net present value of a capital investment project is equal to zero *(p. 700)*

# USEFUL INTERNET SITES

**www.tsx.com**
**TSX Group**   Visit this site for information on all the companies that are traded on the Toronto Stock Exchange (TSX).

**www.investorwords.com**
**InvestorWords.com**   A comprehensive financial glossary with definitions and related terms.

**http://finance.yahoo.com**
**Yahoo! Finance**   A full education site that also contains quotes, charts, historical analysis, and reports.

# II Instructions and Tips for Three Preprogrammed Financial Calculator Models

Different models of financial calculators vary in their operation and labelling of the function keys and face plate. This appendix provides you with instructions and tips for solving compound interest and annuity problems with these financial calculators: Texas Instruments BAII Plus, Sharp EL-733A, and Hewlett-Packard 10B. The specific operational details for each of these calculators are given using the following framework:

## A. Basic Operations

1. Turning the calculator on and off
2. Operating modes
3. Using the Second function
4. Clearing operations
5. Displaying numbers and display formats
6. Order of operations
7. Memory capacity and operations
8. Operating errors and calculator dysfunction

## B. Pre-Calculation Phase (Initial Set-up)

1. Setting to the financial mode, if required
2. Adjusting the calculator's interest key to match the text presentation, if required
3. Setting to the floating-decimal-point format, if required
4. Setting up order of operations, if required

## C. Calculation Phase

1. Clearing preprogrammed registers
2. Adjusting for annuities (beginning and end of period), if required
3. Entering data using cash flow sign conventions and correcting entry errors
4. Calculating the unknown variable

## D. Example Calculations

1. Compound interest
2. Annuities

### E. Checklist for Resolving Common Errors

Go to the section of this appendix that pertains to your calculator. You may want to flag those pages for easy future reference.

# II.1  TEXAS INSTRUMENTS BAII PLUS

## A. Basic operations

### 1. Turning the calculator on and off

The calculator is turned on by pressing ON/OFF . If the calculator was turned off using this key, the calculator returns in the standard-calculator mode. If the Automatic Power Down (APD) feature turned the calculator off, the calculator will return exactly as you left it—errors and all, if that was the case. The calculator can be turned off either by pressing ON/OFF again or by not pressing any key for approximately 10 minutes, which will activate the APD feature.

### 2. Operating modes

The calculator has two modes: the standard-calculation mode and the prompted-worksheet mode. In the standard-calculation mode, you can perform standard math operations and all of the financial calculations presented in this text. This is the default mode for your calculator. Refer to your calculator's *Guidebook* to learn more about the worksheet mode, since it is not addressed in this appendix.

### 3. Using the Second function

The primary function of a key is indicated by a symbol on its face. Second functions are marked on the face plate directly above the keys. To access the Second function of a key, press 2nd ("2nd" will appear in the upper-left corner of the display) and then press the key directly under the symbol on the face plate ("2nd" will then disappear from the display).

### 4. Clearing operations

→ clears one character at a time from the display, including decimal points.

CE/C clears an incorrect entry, an error condition, or an error message from the display.

2nd (QUIT) clears all pending operations in the standard-calculation mode and returns the display to 0.

CE/C CE/C clears any calculation you have started but not yet completed.

2nd (CLR TVM) sets the financial function registers to 0 and returns to standard-calculation mode.

### 5. Displaying numbers and display formats

The display shows entries and results up to 10 digits but internally stores numeric values to an accuracy of 13 digits. The default setting in the calculator is 2 decimal places. To change the number of fixed decimal places, press [2nd] (FORMAT) along with a number key for the decimal places desired. Then press [ENTER] to complete the installation. For a floating-decimal-point format, press [2nd] (FORMAT) [9] [ENTER]. Return to standard-calculation mode by pressing [2nd] (QUIT).

### 6. Order of operations

The default for the BAII Plus is Chn. To change to AOS, which will have the calculator do all mathematical calculations in the proper order according to the rules of mathematics, press [2nd] (FORMAT), arrow down four times, and with display on Chn press [2nd] [SET]. Press [2nd] (QUIT) to go back to the standard-calculation mode.

### 7. Memory capacity and operations

The calculator has ten memory addresses available, numbered 0 through 9. To store a displayed value in a memory address (0 through 9), press [STO] and a digit key [0] through [9]. To recall a value from memory and display it, press [RCL] and a digit key [0] through [9]. The numeric value is displayed but is also retained in that memory address.

To clear each memory address individually, store "0" in each selected memory. To clear all of the addresses at the same time, press [2nd] (MEM) [2nd] (CLR WORK).

Memory arithmetic allows you to perform a calculation with a stored value and then store the result with a single operation. You may add, subtract, multiply, divide, or apply an exponent to the value in the memory. Use this key sequence:

(number in display) [STO] [+] (or [−] or [×] or [÷] or [$x^{-1}$]) and a digit key [0] to [9] for the memory address.

### 8. Operating errors and calculator dysfunction

The calculator reports error conditions by displaying the message "Error n," where n is a number that corresponds to a particular error discussed in the calculator's *Guidebook* on pages 80–82. Errors 4, 5, 7, and 8 are the most common financial calculation errors. A list of possible solutions to calculator dysfunction is given on page 87 of the *Guidebook*. Generally, if you experience difficulties operating the calculator, press [2nd] (RESET) [ENTER] to clear the calculator, and repeat your calculations.

# B. Compound interest and annuity calculations

The BAII Plus calculator can be used for virtually all compound interest calculations using the third row of the calculator *after* the payment and interest schedules have been set up in the Second function area of the calculator. Each key represents one of the variables in the formula. The variables are:

- N—Represents time. The value is arrived at by taking the number of *years* involved in the transaction and multiplying it by the value set up in P/Y.
- I/Y—The stated or nominal yearly interest rate.
- PV—The amount of money one has at the beginning of the transaction.
- PMT—The amount of money paid on a regular basis.
- FV—The amount of money one has at the end of the transaction.

To perform compound interest or annuity calculations, the process will be to input the variables that are known and to compute the unknown variable.

For compound interest, the process will be:

1. Set up the payment and interest schedules in the Second function of the calculator. This is done by pressing [ 2nd ] (P/Y) and inputting the payment and interest schedules as prompted. Since the transaction will not have any payments, simply make the payment and interest schedules the same. For example, if there are no payments and interest is compounded quarterly, the process would be [ 2nd ] (P/Y), 4, [Enter] [ 2nd ] (QUIT). This will set up the proper schedules in both P/Y and C/Y and take you back to the calculator mode.

2. Clear out any old information with [ 2nd ] (CLR TVM).

3. Input the variables you know.

4. Compute the variable you need to find.

For annuity calculations, the process will be:

1. Set up the calculator for either an ordinary annuity (payments made at the end) or an annuity due (payments made at the beginning). This is done by hitting [ 2nd ] (BGN) and then setting up the display to END or BGN. [ 2nd ] (SET) will allow you to switch between the two options. [ 2nd ] (QUIT) will take you back to the calculcator. Note: if the calculator is in END mode, the display will be clear in the upper-right-hand corner of the display; if it is in BGN mode, the letters BGN will appear in the upper-right-hand corner.

2. Set up the payment and interest schedules in the Second function of the calculator. This is done by pressing [ 2nd ] (P/Y) and inputting the payment and interest schedules as prompted. For example, if the transaction had monthly payments with quarterly compounding, the process would be [ 2nd ] (P/Y) 12, [Enter], [ ↓ ], 4, [Enter], [ 2nd ] (QUIT). This would set up monthly payments with interest compounded quarterly.

3. Clear out the old information with [ 2nd ] (CLR TVM).

4. Input the variables you know.

5. Compute the variable you need to find.

## C. Calculation phase

**1, 2.** The steps required to perform calculations and an example calculation appear on pages 339–341 in Chapter 9. The steps required for annuities and sample annuity calculations appear on pages 477–478 in Chapter 12.

### 3. Entering data using cash flow sign conventions and correcting entry errors

Data can be entered in any order, but you *must* observe the cash flow sign conventions. For compound interest calculations, always enter PV as a negative number and all other values (N, I/Y, FV) as positive numbers. An error message will be displayed when calculating I/Y or N if both FV and PV are entered using the same sign. For annuity calculations, enter either PV or PMT as negative numbers and all other values (N, I/Y, FV) as positive numbers. When PV = 0, designate PMT as the negative number and all other values (N, I/Y, FV) as positive numbers. Failure to observe this sign convention will result in either an error message in the display when calculating I/Y values or an incorrect negative number when calculating values of N.

Data entry errors can be corrected one character at a time by using [ → ] or the entry, and error messages can be cleared from the display by using [ CE/C ]

### 4. Calculating the unknown variable

Press [ CPT ] and the financial key representing the unknown variable after all the known variable data are entered (including 0 for PV or FV if required). Successive calculations are possible because numerical values stored in the function key registers remain there until cleared or replaced. The value stored in any of the function key registers can be determined without altering its value by pressing [ RCL ] and the function key.

## D. Example calculations

### 1. Compound interest

See pages 339–341 in Chapter 9 for an example of a compound interest calculation using this calculator.

### 2. Annuities

See pages 478 and 481 in Chapter 11 for examples of annuity calculations using this calculator.

## E. Checklist for resolving common errors

**1.** Confirm that the P/Y and C/Y are properly set.
**2.** Confirm that the decimal place format is set to a floating decimal point.
**3.** If attempting annuity calculations, check to see that the calculator is in the appropriate payment mode ("END" or "BGN").
**4.** Clear all function key registers before entering your data.

**5.** Be sure to enter a numerical value, using the cash flow sign convention, for all known variables before solving for the unknown variable, even if one of the variables is 0.

# II.2 SHARP EL-733A BUSINESS/FINANCIAL CALCULATOR

## A. Basic operations

### 1. Turning the calculator on and off

[C·CE] turns the calculator on. [OFF] turns the calculator off. To conserve battery life, the calculator will turn itself off automatically 9 to 13 minutes after the last key operation.

### 2. Operating modes

The available operational modes are financial (FIN), statistical (STAT), and Normal (no message). The message FIN, STAT, or no message appears in the upper right corner of the display to indicate the current mode. Change the mode by pressing [2nd F] (MODE) until the desired mode is displayed.

### 3. Using the Second function

The primary function of a key is indicated by a symbol on the face of the key. Second functions are marked on the face plate directly above the keys. To access the Second function of a key, press [2nd F] ("2ndF" will appear in the upper-left corner of the display), and then press the key directly under the symbol on the face plate ("2ndF" will then disappear from the display).

### 4. Clearing operations

[2nd F] (CA) clears the numerical values and calculation commands including data for financial calculations. The contents of memory register storage are not affected.

[C·CE] [x→M] clears the memory.

[C·CE] clears the last entry.

[C·CE] [C·CE] clears the calculator of all data *except* the data for financial calculations.

[→] clears the last digit entered.

### 5. Displaying numbers and display formats

The display shows entries and results up to 10 digits. The default setting in the calculator is the floating decimal. To change the number of fixed decimal places, press [2nd F] (TAB) along with a number key for the decimal places desired. For a floating-decimal-point format, press [2nd F] (TAB) [•]. The number of decimal places is retained even when the power is turned off.

Various messages can appear in the display from time to time. Refer to page 73 of the *Operation Manual and Application Manual* for a complete list.

### 6. Memory capacity and operations

This calculator has one memory address. To store a displayed value in memory, press $\boxed{x \to M}$.

To clear the memory of values other than zero, press $\boxed{\text{C·CE}}$ $\boxed{x \to M}$.

To recall a value from memory and display it, press $\boxed{\text{RM}}$.

To add a displayed amount to the value in the memory, press $\boxed{\text{M+}}$. To subtract a displayed amount to the value in the memory, press $\boxed{\pm}$ $\boxed{\text{M+}}$.

### 7. Operating errors and calculator dysfunction

Operational errors are indicated by the symbol **E** in the lower-left corner of the display. See pages 74–77 of the *Operation Manual and Application Manual* for a complete description of errors and error conditions that may affect the operation and functioning of your calculator. The error symbol is cleared from the display by pressing $\boxed{\text{C·CE}}$.

## B. Pre-calculation phase

With the calculator on, set the financial mode by pressing $\boxed{\text{2nd F}}$ (MODE) until the FIN message appears in the upper-right corner of the display. The calculator requires no change to a register or mode in order to match the text presentation. To set the calculator to the floating-decimal-point format, press $\boxed{\text{2nd F}}$ (TAB) $\boxed{\bullet}$.

## C. Calculation phase

### 1. Clearing preprogrammed registers

$\boxed{\text{2nd F}}$ (CA) clears the preprogrammed registers of numerical values and sets them to 0 for financial calculations.

### 2. Adjusting for annuities (beginning and end of period)

The default mode for annuity calculations is "end of period." If "beginning of period" calculations are required, press $\boxed{\text{BGN}}$. "BGN" will appear in the upper-right corner of the display. To return to "end of period" mode, press $\boxed{\text{BGN}}$ again. "BGN" will disappear from the display.

### 3. Entering data using cash flow sign conventions and correcting entry errors

Data can be entered in any order but you must observe the cash flow sign conventions to avoid operational errors and incorrect answers. For compound interest calculations, *always* designate PV as a negative number and all other values (N, *i*, FV) as positive numbers. If you do not observe this sign convention when you enter data, your answer will be the same numerical value but the opposite sign of the answer in the text. An error message will be displayed when calculating *i* or N if both FV and PV are entered using the same sign. For annuity calculations, when FV = 0, designate PV as a negative number and all other values (N, *i*, PMT) as positive numbers. When PV = 0, designate PMT as the negative number and all other values (N, *i*, FV) as positive numbers. Failure to observe this sign convention will result in either an error message in the display when calculating *i* values or an incorrect negative number when calculating values of N.

### 4. Calculating the unknown variable

Press [ COMP ] and the financial key representing the unknown variable after all the known variable data are entered (including 0 for PV or FV if required). Successive calculations are possible because numerical values stored in the function key registers remain there until cleared or replaced. The value stored in any of the function key registers can be determined without altering its value by pressing [2nd F] (RCL) and the function key.

## D. Example calculations

### 1. Compound interest (Example 9.2A, page 337)

| Key in | Press | Display shows | |
|--------|-------|---------------|---|
| | [2nd F] (CA) | no change | clears all registers |
| 6000 | [ ± ] [ PV ] | −6000 | this enters the present value P (principal) with the correct sign convention |
| 2.5 | [ *i* ] | 2.5 | this enters the periodic interest rate *i* as a percent |
| 20 | [ N ] | 20 | this enters the number of compounding periods *n* |
| | [ COMP ] [ FV ] | 9831.698642 | this computes and displays the unknown future value S |

**2. Annuities** (Example 11.2D, pages 428–429)

| Key in | Press | Display shows | |
|--------|-------|---------------|---|
| 0 | PV | 0 | a precaution to avoid incorrect answers |
| 10 | ± PMT | −10 | this enters the periodic payment R |
| 0.5 | i | 0.5 | this enters the conversion rate *i* as a percent |
| 60 | N | 60 | this enters the number of payments *n* |
| | COMP FV | 697.7003051 | this computes the unknown future value $S_n$ |

## E. Checklist for resolving common errors

**1.** Check to see that your calculator is in the financial (FIN) mode.

**2.** Check to see that the calculator is in the appropriate payment mode (BGN or end mode).

**3.** Clear all registers before entering your data by pressing 2nd F (CA).

**4.** Be sure to enter values for all variables except the unknown variable, before solving for the unknown variable, even if one of the variables is 0.

**5.** Observe the cash flow sign conventions (discussed above) when entering the data to avoid unwanted negative signs, display errors, or incorrect answers.

# II.3 HEWLETT-PACKARD 10B II BUSINESS CALCULATOR

## A. Basic operations

### 1. Turning the calculator on and off

Turn the calculator on by pressing ON . Turn the calculator off by pressing the orange ▢ (SHIFT) OFF .

To conserve energy, the calculator turns itself off automatically approximately 10 minutes after you stop using it. The calculator has a continuous memory, so turning it off does not affect the information you have stored in the memory.

### 2. Operating modes

You can perform all of the financial calculations presented in this text as soon as you turn on the calculator. No mode adjustment is required for financial-, statistical-, or standard-mode calculations.

### 3. Using the SHIFT function

The primary function of a key is indicated by a symbol on the top face of the key. SHIFT functions are marked on the bottom face of the key. To access the SHIFT function of a key, press [ ▭ ] (SHIFT) ("SHIFT" will appear in the lower-left corner of the display), and then press the key with the symbol on the lower face of the key ("SHIFT" will then disappear from the display).

### 4. Clearing operations

[ ON ] [ N ] [ FV ] , all held down at the same time, clears all memory and resets all modes.

[ ▭ ] [ C ALL ] (CLEAR ALL) clears all memory, but does not reset the modes.

[ ← ] [ C ] clears the message and restores the original constants.

[ C ] clears the entered number to 0.

[ ← ] clears the last digit entered.

### 5. Displaying numbers and display formats

The display shows entries and results up to 12 digits. Brightness is controlled by holding down [ ON ] and then pressing [ + ] or [ − ] . The default setting is 2 decimal places. Regardless of the display format, each number entered is stored with a signed 12-digit number and a signed 3-digit exponent. To change the number of fixed decimal places, press [ ▭ ] [ DISP ] and a number key for the number of decimal places desired. For a floating decimal point, press [ ▭ ] [ DISP ] [ • ] . To temporarily view all 12 digits, press [ ▭ ] [ DISP ] and hold [ = ] .

Graphics in the display are used to indicate various settings, operating modes, error conditions, and calculator dysfunctions. Refer to the *Owner's Manual*, pages 137–138, for a complete list.

### 6. Memory capacity and operations

This calculator has 10 numbered registers available to store numbers, as well as a single storage register called the M register.

To store a number in the M register, press [ →M ] .

To recall a value from the M register and display it, press [ RM ] .

To add a displayed amount to the value in the M register, press [ M+ ] . To subtract a displayed amount to the value in the memory, press [ ± ] [ M+ ] .

To store a displayed value in a numbered memory register (numbered 0 to 9), press [ ▭ ] [ STO ] and a digit key [ 0 ] through [ 9 ] .

To recall a number from a numbered memory register, press [ RCL ] and the digit key for the memory register number.

### 7. Operating errors and calculator dysfunction

Operational errors are indicated by an error message appearing in the display. For a complete description of the error messages, refer to pages 137–138 of the *Owner's*

*Manual.* For calculator dysfunctions, refer to pages 121–122 of the *Owner's Manual.*

No additional adjustment is required to set the calculator to the financial mode. Begin calculations as soon as you turn on your calculator.

## B. Calculation phase

### 1. Clearing preprogrammed registers

[____] [C ALL] sets all key numerical registers to 0 and momentarily displays the P/YR value.

### 2. Adjusting for annuities (beginning and end of period)

The default mode for annuity calculations is "end of period." If "beginning of period" calculations are required, press [____] [BEG/END] . "BEGIN" will appear in the lower middle portion of the display. To return to "end of period" mode, press [____] [BEG/END] again. "BEGIN" will disappear from the display.

### 3. Entering data using cash flow sign conventions and correcting entry errors

Data can be entered in any order using the financial function keys. To confirm the values already in the registers or to validate your data entry, press [RCL] and the desired function key.

You must observe the cash flow sign conventions to avoid errors like "no solution" or incorrect answers when calculating N. For compound interest calculations, *always* enter PV as a negative number and the other variables as positive numbers. For annuity calculations, when FV = 0, enter PV as a negative number and all other values (N, I/YR, PMT) as positive numbers. However, when PV = 0, enter PMT as a negative number and all other values (N, I/YR, FV) as positive numbers. If you do not observe the sign convention, the numerical value you calculate will be identical to that of this text except when calculating N (your answer will be incorrect) or when calculating I/YR (an error message may appear in the display).

Data entry errors can be corrected character by character by pressing [←] or the entry can be cleared from the display by pressing [ C ] .

### 4. Calculating the unknown variable

Press the financial key representing the unknown variable after all the known variable data are entered (including 0 for PV or FV if required). Successive calculations are possible because numerical values stored in the function key registers remain there until cleared or replaced. The value stored in any of the function key registers can be determined without altering its value by pressing [RCL] and the function key.

# C. Example calculations

### 1. Compound interest (Example 9.2A, page 337)

| Key in | Press | Display shows | |
|---|---|---|---|
| | ▭ C ALL | 0 ———— | clears the function key registers and confirms the value in the P/YR register |
| 6000 | ± PV | −6000 ———— | this enters the present value P (principal) with the correct sign convention |
| 10 | I/YR | 10 ———— | this enters the periodic interest rate $i$ as a percent |
| 4 | ▭ P/YR | 4 | |
| 20 | N | 20 ———— | this enters the number of compounding periods $n$ |
| | FV | 9831.698642 ———— | this computes and displays the unknown future value S |

### 2. Annuities (Example 11.2D, pages 428–429)

| Key in | Press | Display shows | |
|---|---|---|---|
| 0 | PV | 0 ———— | a precaution to avoid incorrect answers |
| 10 | ± PMT | -10 ———— | this enters the periodic payment R |
| 6 | I/YR | 6 ———— | this enters the conversion rate $i$ as a percent |
| 12 | ▭ P/YR | 12 | |
| 60 | N | 60 ———— | this enters the number of payments $n$ |
| | FV | 697.700305 ———— | this computes the unknown future value $S_n$ |

## D. Checklist for resolving common errors

1. Confirm that P/YR is properly set.
2. Clear all registers before entering your data by pressing [ ⬜ ] [C ALL].
3. Check to see that the calculator is in the appropriate payment mode (BEGIN or END mode).
4. Be sure to enter values for all variables except the unknown variable, before solving for the unknown variable, even if one of the variables is 0.
5. Observe the cash flow sign conventions (discussed above) when entering the data to avoid unwanted negative signs, display errors, or incorrect answers.

# Answers to Odd-Numbered Problems, Review Exercises, and Self-Tests

## CHAPTER 5

### Exercise 5.1

**A.** 1. $11.07; $13.53
3. $33\frac{1}{3}$%; $25.65
5. 15%; $252.60
7. $133.36; $50.01
9. $134.96; $50.61

**B.** 1. $30.24; 32.5%
3. $137.89; 48.55%
5. $1583.33; 61%

**C.** 1. $78.25
3. 15.9%
5. $3200
7. $74.10
9. $4.26
11. (a) 38.75%
(b) 48.26%
13. (a) $318.67
(b) $280.33
(c) 46.8%
15. (a) $443.79
(b) $342.41
(c) 43.552%
17. 15%
19. 5%
21. $180.00
23. 15%
25. 8.7%

### Exercise 5.2

**A.** 1. $640.00
3. $776.11
5. $1136.80
7. $4581.50

**B.** 1. $582.00; $850.00
3. $564.50; $536.28
5. $810.00;
$810.00

**C.** 1. (a) May 23
(b) $2449.02
3. (a) $799.90
(b) $825.16
(c) $842.00

5. $2507.19
7. $2184.00
9. (a) September 10
(b) $5276.85
(c) $103.20
11. (a) $1164.00
(b) $733.54
(c) Amount
paid on
October 25
is $600.00.
13. (a) $1925.00
(b) $3400.00
15. (i) $1.96
(ii) 3.5%

### Exercise 5.3

**A.** 1. (a) $6.00
(b) $3.84
(c) $2.16
(d) 25%
(e) 20%
3. (a) $35.00
(b) $31.50
(c) $3.50
(d) $66\frac{2}{3}$%
(e) 40%
5. (a) $10.50
(b) $12.75
(c) ($2.25)
(d) $38\frac{8}{9}$%
(e) 28%

**B.** 1. $6.25; 25%;
20%
3. $102.40; 60%;
37.5%
5. $75.95; $21.70;
28.6%
7. 44.24; $22.12;
$33\frac{1}{3}$%
9. $78.10; $46.86;
150%
11. $111.30; $133.56;
20%

**C.** 1. $13.60
3. $3.00
5. $102.08
7. (a) 150%
(b) 60%
9. (a) $36.50
(b) $29.93
(c) 21.95%
11. (a) $1.65
(b) $66\frac{2}{3}$%
13. (a) $234.20
(b) 47.37%
15. (a) $140.00
(b) $66\frac{2}{3}$%
17. (a) $16.80
(b) 27.3%

### Exercise 5.4

**A.** 1. $51.00; $59.00;
($8.00)
3. $96.40; $30.65;
$7.91
5. $160.00; $19.20;
12%

**B.** 1. (a) $21.99
(b) $17.59
(c) $4.62
3. 20%
5. 16%
7. (a) $7.00
(b) 21.21%
9. (a) $17.79
(b) $25.44
(c) 12.28%
(d) 38.66%

### Exercise 5.5

**A.** 1. (a) $228.69
(b) 54%
3. (a) 40%
(b) ($8.00)
(c) 10.3%
(d) $9\frac{1}{3}$%
5. ($2.23)

7. (a) normal quality
= $14.85
seconds = $9.92
substandard = $6.60
(b) $957.00
(c) 34.5%
9. (a) $72.00
(b) $54.00
(c) 25%
11. ($6.50)
13. ($97.50)
15. ($82.50)

### Review Exercise

1. (a) $31.92
(b) $24.08
(c) $43%
3. 45.66%
5. 15%
7. $30.00
9. September 12;
$25 117.40
11. (a) $1940.00
(b) $2813.00
13. (a) $1645.00
(b) $1500.00
15. (a) $90.00
(b) $58.50
(c) 53.85%
(d) $74.88
(e) −$6.48
17. (a) $77.50
(b) 42.86%
19. $240.00
21. (a) −$0.60
(b) 26.98%
23. (a) −$13.20
(b) 25%
25. (a) $189.00
(b) 21.25%
(c) $133\frac{1}{3}$%
27. (a) $2152.40
(b) 69.43%
(c) 40.98%

## Self-Test

1. $295.77
3. 50.5%
5. $1635.04
7. $1450.00
9. $240.00
11. $348.36
13. 180%
15. 23.40%
17. −$660.45

## CHAPTER 7

### Exercise 7.1

A. 1. 0.035; 1.25
   3. 0.0825; $\frac{183}{365}$
B. 1. $1096.88
   3. $95.21
   5. $75.34
   7. $10.87
   9. $21.76
   11. $26.44
C. 1. $88.77
   3. $48.63

### Exercise 7.2

A. 1. $1224.00
   3. 10.75%
   5. 14 months
   7. 144 days
B. 1. $3296.00
   3. 9.5%
   5. 8.4%
   7. 11
   9. 126
   11. $876.00
   13. $400 000
   15. 9%
   17. 41

### Exercise 7.3

A. 1. $490.13
   3. $768.75
   5. $849.21
   7. $1298.00
B. 1. $2542.53
   3. $13 800.00
   5. $26 954.84
   7. $13 864.50

9. (a) $51 975
   (b) $51 943.53
   (c) 3.887%

### Exercise 7.4

A. 1. $266.00; $13.30
   3. $517.50; $547.17
   5. $2025.00; 292 days
B. 1. $1222.00
   3. $1704.60
   5. $644.00
   7. $6947.60
   9. $23 000.00

### Exercise 7.5

A. 1. $829.33
   3. $617.50
   5. $1103.37
   7. $856.47
   9. $777.81
   11. $1070.39
B. 1. $1156.80
   3. $2248.66
   5. $1722.00
   7. $519.48
   9. $569.45
   11. $421.97
   13. $811.93
   15. $1408.21
   17. $1599.35

### Review Exercise

1. (a) 172
   (b) 214
3. (a) $1160.00
   (b) $601.77
5. (a) $750.00
   (b) $5709.97
7. $3000.17
9. 8.25%
11. 196 days
13. $1601.89
15. $3200.00
17. $1736.47
19. $2664.00
21. $3404.32
23. $1614.74
25. $961.50
27. $1587.06

## Self-Test

1. $21.40
3. 6.5%
5. $6187.50
7. $4306.81
9. 359 days
11. $7432.80
13. $1163.85
15. $1799.23

## CHAPTER 8

### Exercise 8.1

A. 1. December 30, 2010
   3. $530.00
   5. 154 days
   7. $544.54
B. 1. (a) March 3, 2012
      (b) 155 days
      (c) $21.40
      (d) $861.40
   3. (a) April 3, 2008
      (b) 63 days
      (c) $14.02
      (d) $1264.02

### Exercise 8.2

A. 1. $631.24
   3. $837.19
   5. $856.35
   7. $10 413.71

### Exercise 8.3

A. 1. $500.00
B. 1. $1471.28
   3. $1615.56
C. 1. $99 054.15
   3. 2.73%
   5. (a) 2.72%
      (b) $99 636.18
      (c) 2.706%

### Exercise 8.4

A. 1. $37.50
   3. $22.50
   5. $307.56
B. 1. $3785.67
   3. $1825.63
   5. $178.66

### Exercise 8.5

A. 1. (a) $0.16
      (b) $4.16
      (c) $1.24
      (d) $10.00
      (e) −$956.34

### Exercise 8.6

A. 1. Totals are
      $1233.69;
      $33.69;
      $1200.00
   3. Totals are
      $922.36; $22.36;
      $900

### Review Exercise

1. (a) November 2
   (b) $35.62
   (c) $1635.62
3. $1500.00
5. $5125.75
7. $814.17
9. $1269.57
11. 6.1493%
13. $449.12
15. (a) $54.57; $62.49;
       $70.82; $69.86;
       $70.75
    (b) −$10 623.49

## Self-Test

1. $19.79
3. $1160.00
5. $1664.66
7. (a) $98 116.43
   (b) 3.680%
9. $340.26
11. Totals are $4070.41;
    $70.41; $4000.00

## CHAPTER 9

### Exercise 9.1

A. 1. 1; 0.12; 5
   3. 4; 0.01375; 36
   5. 2; 0.0575; 27
   7. 12; 0.0066667; 150
   9. 2; 0.06125; 9

**B.** **1.** 1.7623417
   **3.** 1.6349754
   **5.** 4.5244954
   **7.** 2.7092894
   **9.** 1.7074946
**C.** **1.** (a) 48
   (b) 2.5%
   (c) $1.025^{48}$
   (d) 3.2714896

## Exercise 9.2

**A.** **1.** $713.39
   **3.** $2233.21
   **5.** $5468.38
   **7.** $6639.51
   **9.** $662.02
   **11.** $4152.58
   **13.** $2052.74
**B.** **1.** $6884.47; $1884.47
   **3.** $1441.71
   **5.** (a) $199.26
   (b) $202.24
   (c) $203.81
   (d) $204.89
   **7.** (a) $148.59; $48.59
   (b) $220.80; 120.80
   (c) $487.54; 387.54
   **9.** $8712.50
   **11.** $761.75
   **13.** $17 116.96
   **15.** 162.81
   **17.** (a) Bank;
   $6968.27; $6914.09
   (b) $54.18
**C.** **1.** $2372.65
   **3.** $1452.79
   **5.** $3956.97
   **7.** $1102.13
   **9.** $1444.24
   **11.** $10 526.69

## Exercise 9.3

**A.** **1.** $574.37
   **3.** $371.86
   **5.** $409.16
   **7.** $500.24
   **9.** $749.91
   **11.** $4344.21

**B.** **1.** $1338.81; $261.19
   **3.** $762.84
   **5.** $3129.97
   **7.** $1398.85
   **9.** two payments;
   $4835.49
   **11.** two payments

## Exercise 9.4

**A.** **1.** $1767.71; $232.29
   **3.** $3981.87; $1018.13
   **5.** $2642.50; $557.50
   **7.** $1012.96; $671.00
   **9.** $2310.82; $720.62
   **11.** $2036.86;
   $540.42
   **13.** $1332.82;
   $261.78
**B.** **1.** $4589.47
   **3.** $1345.06
   **5.** $3800.24
   **7.** $1561.49
**C.** **1.** $8452.52
   **3.** $2346.36
   **5.** $3488.29
   **7.** $1074.71
   **9.** $1972.80
   **11.** $1492.15

## Exercise 9.5

**A.** **1.** $5983.40
   **3.** $2537.13
   **5.** $1673.49
   **7.** $641.36
**B.** **1.** $3426.73
   **3.** $2464.35
   **5.** $1536.03
   **7.** $987.93
**C.** **1.** (a) $2851.94
   (b) $3265.19
   (c) $4000.00
   (d) $5610.21
   **3.** $6805.31
   **5.** $655.02
   **7.** $2464.35
   **9.** $1955.51
   **11.** $1231.82
   **13.** (a) $646.41
   (b) $946.41

**15.** $3076.33
**17.** $987.93

## Review Exercise

**1.** (a) $1198.28
   (b) $1221.61
   (c) $1227.05
**3.** (a) $2890.09
   (b) $890.09
**5.** (a) $6144.45;
   $4344.45
   (b) $3305.27;
   $2055.27
**7.** $10 681.77
**9.** $11 102.50
**11.** $4194.33
**13.** $9791.31
**15.** $2830.68;
   $3190.63
**17.** $9294.85
**19.** $1035.70
**21.** $2838.62
**23.** $2079.94
**25.** $110 440.03
**27.** $26 048.42
**29.** (a) $2742.41
   (b) $2911.55
   (c) $3281.79
**31.** $4857.56
**33.** $1820.32
**35.** $3574.57

## Self-Test

**1.** $2129.97
**3.** 2.7118780
**5.** $6919.05
**7.** $14 711.80
**9.** $4504.29
**11.** $10 138.19
**13.** $2661.85
**15.** $848.88

# CHAPTER 10
## Exercise 10.1

**A.** **1.** (a) 13.4 years
   (b) 28 quarters
   (c) 117.8 months
   (d) 8 half-years

   (e) 37.313 quarters
   (f) 37.167 half-
   years
**B.** **1.** 9.329 years
   **3.** 17.501 years
   **5.** 5.622 years
   **7.** November 1, 2011
   **9.** 21 months
   **11.** 2 years, 298 days
   **13.** 3 years, 230 days

## Exercise 10.2

**A.** **1.** 4.5%
   **3.** 9.6%
   **5.** 9.778%
**B.** **1.** 9.237%
   **3.** (a) 10.402%
   (b) 7.585%
   **5.** 3.5%
   **7.** 4.771%

## Exercise 10.3

**A.** **1.** (a) 12.891%
   (b) 6.168%
   (c) 7.397%
   (d) 10.691%
   **3.** (a) 8.9%
   (b) 6.465%
   (c) 7.385%
   (d) 4.273%
**B.** **1.** 6.991%
   **3.** 4.656%
   **5.** 8.945%
   **7.** 6.2196%
   **9.** 7.385%
   **11.** (a) $714.57
   (b) $114.57
   (c) 3.5567%
   **13.** (a) $1831.40
   (b) $631.40
   (c) 4.3182%

## Review Exercise

**1.** 5.592%
**3.** 1 year, 231 days
**5.** 22.517085 half-
   years (11 years,
   95 days)

7. 6.03%

9. **(a)** 5.92%
   **(b)** 14.35%
   **(c)** 8.833%
   **(d)** 8.24%

11. **(a)** 4.59%
    **(b)** 5.96%

13. 8.44%

15. **(a)** 4.0%
    **(b)** 3.7852%
    **(c)** 3.5462%
    **(d)** 3.2989%

17. 1.831663 years
    (1 year, 304 days)

19. 1.5677878 years
    (1 year, 208 days)

21. 6.8287904 years
    (6 years, 303 days–
    2007-09-30)

## Self-Test

1. 10.50 half-years
   (63 months)

3. 5.535675%

5. 7.352%

7. 10.0%

9. 7.5%

## CHAPTER 11

### Exercise 11.1

**A.** 1. **(a)** annuity certain
     **(b)** annuity due
     **(c)** general annuity
   3. **(a)** perpetuity
     **(b)** deferred
         annuity
     **(c)** general annuity
   5. **(a)** annuity certain
     **(b)** deferred
         annuity due
     **(c)** simple annuity

### Exercise 11.2

**A.** 1. $54 193.60
   3. $59 185.19
   5. $17 915.08

**B.** 1. $13 045.68
   3. $32 434.02

5. **(a)** $8531.12
   **(b)** $4500.00
   **(c)** $4031.12

7. **(a)** $20090.19
   **(b)** $15 000.00
   **(c)** $5090.19

9. $62177.25

### Exercise 11.3

**A.** 1. $9515.19
   3. $30 941.11
   5. $10 544.91

**B.** 1. $6897.02
   3. **(a)** $9906.20
     **(b)** $2093.80
   5. **(a)** $2523.82
     **(b)** $372.06
   7. $12 710.96
   9. Joel, $280.28

### Exercise 11.4

**A.** 1. $821.39
   3. $1117.37
   5. $272.73
   7. $232.54
   9. $1653.70
   11. $317.49
   13. $229.33
   15. $62.61
   17. $8567.28
   19. $10 017.56
   21. $438.10

### Exercise 11.5

**A.** 1. 14.6023573 years
       (14 years,
       8 months)
   3. 93.0687373
       months (7 years,
       10 months)
   5. 15.5775778
       half-years (7 years,
       10 months)

7. 15.395937 semi-
   annual periods
   (7 years, 9 months)

9. 71.517450 months
   (6 years)

**B.** 1. 74.498331 months
       (6 years, 3 months)
   3. 22 deposits
   5. 45.648036 months
       (3 years, 10 months)
   7. 27.973645 months
       (2 years, 4 months)
   9. 47.999053 months
       (4 years)
   11. 12.384875 semi-
       annual periods
       (6.192437 years)
   13. 9 months

### Exercise 11.6

**A.** 1. 5.0%
   3. 9.0%
   5. 7.6%
   7. 11.37%

**B.** 1. 12.5%
   3. 3.04%
   5. 7.2%
   7. 9.50%
   9. 7.685%

### Review Exercise

1. **(a)** $26 734.60
   **(b)** $17 280.00
   **(c)** $9454.60

3. $722.62

5. 12.575297 years (12
   years, 7 months)

7. $411.57

9. $101 517.64

11. 10.524175
    half-years (5 years,
    4 months)

13. 7.25%

15. $34 031.63

17. 8.583884 half-
    years (9 semi-
    annual payments)

19. $16 102.46

## Self-Test

1. $35 786.08
3. 10.9%
5. 28.06 quarters
   (84 months)
7. $40 385.39
9. $3268.62

## CHAPTER 12

### Exercise 12.1

**A.** 1. $45 855.46
   3. $16 317.77
   5. $63 686.72
   7. $32 876.06

**B.** 1. $23 268.52
   3. $2326.66
   5. **(a)** $13 265.50
     **(b)** $3265.50
   7. $31 293.63
   9. $1592.095784

### Exercise 12.2

**A.** 1. $47 583.23
   3. $42 505.51
   5. $5106.97
   7. $34 627.97

**B.** 1. $10 041.88
   3. $31 736.57
   5. **(a)** $29 829.03
     **(b)** $5170.97
   7. $80 000.02
   9. $52 937.17
   11. $223.27

### Exercise 12.3

**A.** 1. $823.60
   3. $1121.26
   5. $273.20
   7. $1426.84
   9. $271.68

**B.** 1. $124.41
   3. $799.39
   5. $330.63
   7. $117.26
   9. $26.63

## Exercise 12.4

**A.** **1.** 14.51 years
(14 years, 6 months)
**3.** 92.97 months
(7 years, 9 months)
**5.** 15.64 semi-annual
periods (7 years,
10 months)
**7.** 15.43 half-years
(7 years, 9 months)
**9.** 71.57 months
(6 years)

**B.** **1.** 44.76 months
(3 years, 9 months)
**3.** 39.42 months
(3 years, 4 months)
**5.** 13 years,
7.3 months
**7.** 21.27 months
**9.** 40 deposits

## Exercise 12.5

**A.** **1.** 6.01%
**3.** 6.86%
**5.** 12.41%
**7.** 4.40%

**B.** **1.** 5.09%
**3.** 7.31%
**5.** 8.82%
**7.** 10.778%
**9.** 7.86%
**11.** 9.24%

## Exercise 12.6

**A.** **1.** (a) 1016.40
(b) 18 229.63
**3.** (a) 27 748.40
(b) 35 011.37
(c) 1413.54
(d) 7262.97

**B.** **1.** 17 790.55
**3.** 107 789.17

## Review Exercise

**1.** $13 509.62
**3.** $64 125.87
**5.** $75 962.59
**7.** (a) $101.81
(b) $1714.37

**9.** (a) 30.62 quarters
(7 years, 8 months)
(b) 27.84 semi-
annual periods (13
years, 11 months)
**11.** (a) 12.46 months
(6 years, 3 months)
(b) 23.24 months
(1 year, 11 months)
**13.** 16.33 quarters
(4 years, 1 month)
**15.** 8.30 quarters
(2 years, 1 month)
**17.** (a) $13 719.16
(b) $3951.16
(c) $382.25
(d) $8580.00
**19.** 96.82 months
(8 years, 1 month)
**21.** $160 296.97

## Self-Test

**1.** $55 246.47
**3.** 17.34 quarters
(4 years, 4 months)
**5.** $3003.81
**7.** 32 quarters
(8 years)
**9.** $13 355.86; $96.29
**11.** $302 131.40

## CHAPTER 13

## Exercise 13.1

**A.** **1.** $135 334.71;
$71 813.10
**3.** $69 033.69;
$35 581.67
**5.** $43 738.24
$7278.61

**B.** **1.** $204.80
**3.** $909.95

**C.** **1.** $n = 113$ months
(9 years, 5 months)
**3.** $n = 8$ years

**D.** **1.** nominal annual
rate = 7.125%
**3.** nominal annual
rate = 12.498%

**E.** **1.** $31 378.29
**3.** (a) $29 513.14
(b) $10 313.14
**5.** $33 338.44
**7.** (a) $1238.56
(b) $1575.00
(c) $336.44
**9.** $2150.38
**11.** (a) $77 820.42
(b) $55 800.00
(c) $22 020.42
**13.** $659.95
**15.** $300.36
**17.** $1046.16
**19.** 11 years, 11 months
**21.** 4 years, 4 months
**23.** 7.0%
**25.** 8.58%

## Exercise 13.2

**A.** **1.** $39 342.74
**3.** $11 304.97

**B.** **1.** $1316.98
**3.** $903.61

**C.** **1.** $n = 35$ half-years
(17.5 years)
**3.** $n = 18$ quarters
(4.5 years)

**D.** **1.** nominal annual
rate = 11.28%
**3.** nominal annual
rate = 4.89%

**E.** **1.** $59 113.10
**3.** $24 111.08
**5.** $459.47
**7.** $n = 37$ quarters
(9 years, 3 months)
**9.** nominal annual
rate = 9.18%

## Exercise 13.3

**A.** **1.** $1403.20
**3.** $3058.17
**5.** $45 376.41

**B.** **1.** $126 738.19
**3.** (a) −$147 329.91
(b) $272 000.00
(c) $124 670.09

**5.** $1651.45
**7.** $1984.62
**9.** $n = 36$ months
(3 years)
**11.** $n = 26.712$
months
**15.** $88 092.69
**17.** 37.78
**19.** $n = 14.75$
**21.** $147.55

## Exercise 13.4

**A.** **1.** $5048.75
**3.** $3058.17
**5.** $3135.48

**B.** **1.** $21831.32
**3.** (a) $32 277.80
(b) $38 400.00
(c) $6122.20
**5.** $576.10
**7.** $3259.68
**9.** 16 quarters (4 years)
**11.** 13.660591 quarters
**13.** $27 246.85
**15.** $42 162.27
**17.** $1972.34
**19.** $11 499.21
**21.** 71.862 months
(72 months)
**23.** $n = 6.861579$ years

## Exercise 13.5

**A.** **1.** $73 529.41
**3.** $91 027.01
**5.** $44 762.78
**7.** $96 992.34

**B.** **1.** $214.60
**3.** $850.87
**5.** $210 240.91
**7.** $41 854.67
**9.** $166.70

## Review Exercise

**1.** (a) $S_n$ = $11 223.39
$A_n$ = $5799.35
(b) $S_n$(due)
= $11 728.44
$A_n$(due)
= $6060.32

3. $19 153.93
5. (a) $2638.84
   (b) $3444.00
   (c) $805.16
7. $n = 109$ months
9. $n = 28$ months
11. nominal annual
    rate = 5.51%
13. (a) $411.57
    (b) $403.50
15. (a) $15 749.42
    (b) $3149.42
    (c) $432.91
    (d) $8179.68
17. $n = 51$ months
19. $n = 49$ months
21. (a) $28 435.38
    (b) $28 552.64
23. $42 092.99
25. $2736.49
27. (a) $503.87
    (b) $1437.96
    (c) −$275.12
    (d) $1782.29
    (e) $89.52
    (f) $1037.88
29. $n = 29$ years
31. (a) $n = 6.78$
    half-years
    (b) $n = 7.51$ years
    (c) $n = 10.111884$
    quarters
    (d) $n = 8.86133$
    half-years
33. (a) $16 102.46
    (b) $3120.21
    (c) $17 860.97
    (d) $120.21
35. $301.80
37. $910.15
39. $n = 26$ quarters
    (6 years,
    6 months)
41. $20 964.79
43. $34 543.54
45. $8908.36
47. $n = 28.605079$
    quarters

49. (a) $60 229.26
    (b) $49 312.99
    (c) $29 620.76
    (d) $36 229.73
    (e) $86 633.66
    (f) $90 133.66
51. $318 181.82
53. $105.30
55. $28 089.24

## Self-Test

1. $84 209.75
3. $1258.38
5. $357.34
7. Nominal Annual
   Rate = 8.185%
9. $43 246.07
11. $1170.69
13. $6056.04
15. $21.97
17. $122 263.84

## CHAPTER 14
### Exercise 14.1

A.  1. (a) $549.22
       (b) $5633.77
       (c) $140.84
       (d) $408.38
    3. (a) $1103.73
       (b) $4913.61
       (c) $196.54
       (d) $907.19

B.  1. (a) $n = 19.48$
          payments
       (b) $2493.97
    3. (a) $n = 14.53$
       (b) $8035.94

C.  1. (a) $920.57
       (b) $15 052.64
       (c) $59 234.20
       (d) $23 234.20
    3. (a) $136.87
       (b) $4199.54
       (c) $31.50
       (d) $105.37
    5. $2054.05; totals
       are $14 378.41;

$4378.41;
$10 000.00
7. totals are
   $14 943.16;
   $5743.16;
   $9200.00
9. $651.11
11. $1160.09
13. (a) $3621.90
    (b) $1035.27
    (c) $2799.85
    (d) $10 445.14;
    totals are
    $115 900.80;
    $30 900.80;
    $8500.00
15. (a) $n = 14.022508$
    (b) $957.79
    (c) $1910.53
    (d) $4664.98; totals
    are $35 057.75;
    $11 057.75;
    $24 000.00

### Exercise 14.2

A.  1. (a) $1829.69
       (b) $20 286.42
       (c) $819.57
       (d) $1010.12

(e)

*Partial Amortization Schedule*

| Payment number | Amount paid | Interest paid | Principal repaid | Outstanding principal |
|---|---|---|---|---|
| 0 | | | | 40 000.00 |
| 1 | 318.15 | 278.44 | 39.71 | 39 960.29 |
| 2 | 318.15 | 278.17 | 39.98 | 39 920.31 |
| 3 | 318.15 | 277.89 | 40.26 | 39 880.05 |
| ⋮ | ⋮ | ⋮ | ⋮ | ⋮ |
| ⋮ | ⋮ | ⋮ | ⋮ | ⋮ |
| 60 | ⋮ | ⋮ | ⋮ | 37 056.28 |
| 61 | 364.44 | 317.37 | 47.07 | 37 009.21 |
| 62 | 364.44 | 316.97 | 47.47 | 36 961.74 |
| 63 | 364.44 | 316.56 | 47.88 | 36 913.86 |
| ⋮ | ⋮ | ⋮ | ⋮ | ⋮ |

3. (a) $164.04
   (b) $4563.53
   (c) $22.54
   (d) $141.50
B.  1. (a) $n = 17.13$
       (b) $2685.85
    3. (a) $n = 14.894762$
       (b) $1584.96
C.  1. (a) $2790.38
       (b) $34 892.23
       (c) $1599.89
       (d) $1190.49
    3. (a) $252.15
       (b) $34 200.11
       (c) $7277.51
       (d) $294.24
    5. (a) $n = 15.413529$
       (b) $2911.17
       (c) $4311.17
    7. $3212.01; totals
       are $22 484.09;
       $6484.09;
       $16 000.00
    9. $752.68
    11. (a) $318.15
        (b) $3323.27
        (c) $263.14
        (d) $364.44

## Exercise 14.3

**A.** 1. $1006.24
   3. $348.26
   5. $306.39

**B.** 1. (a) $n = 29.434057$
      (b) $157.46
   3. (a) $n = 47.779687$
      (b) $722.00
   5. $234.53
   7. $301.45
   9. $1152.87
   11. (a) $n = 61.523813$
       (b) $724.48
       (c) $84 599.48
       (d) $68 599.48

## Exercise 14.4

**A.** 1. (a) $715.83
      (b) $83 375.45
      (c) $641.41
   3. (a) $503.15
      rounded to $550.00;
      $n = 104.522813$
      months
      (b) $288.05
      (c) $2889.95
   5. nominal annual
      rate compounded
      semi-annually
      = 9.50%
   7. (a) $86 514.51
      (b) $n = 165.56125$
      months
      (c) $54 269.19
   9. $380.00; balance
      $38 794.01
   11. Balance December 1
       = $38 795.58

## Review Exercise

   1. (a) $1491.37
      (b) $12 723.84
      (c) $15 771.75
      (d) $338.49
      (e) $1247.91
      (f) $4300.94; totals
          are $47 723.84; $12
          723.84; $35 000.00

3. (a) $n = 24.830989$
   (b) $28 940.29
   (c) $426.66
   (d) $1807.58
   (e) $5477.40; totals
       are $49 664.41;
       $9664.41; 40 000.00
5. (a) $735.80
   (b) $280.57
   (c) $23 981.92
   (d) $1000.88
   (e) $15 900.11;
       totals are
       $24 843.68;
       $11 087.74;
       $13 755.94
7. (a) $n = 9.3198366$
   (b) $1139.88
9. (a) $n = 11.744464$
   (b) $3211.27
11. (a) $1091.28
    (b) $125 324.69
    (c) $1023.15
13. (a) $n = 117.33202$
    months
    (b) $332.79
    (c) $118 274.40;
        $117 332.79;
        $941.61
15. (a) $161.75
    (b) $1264.00
    (c) $5086.52
    (d) $21.41
    (e) $478.06; totals
        are $7764.00;
        $1264.00;
        $6500.00
17. 8.38%
19. (a) $601.20
    (b) $1651.04
    (c) $25 598.05
    (d) $638.94

## Self-Test

1. $6027.52
3. $12 866.98
5. (a) $1406.95
   (b) $174 506.12

(c) $1479.66
7. 10.0%

# CHAPTER 15

## Exercise 15.1

**A.** 1. $97 780.05
   3. $23 634.93
   5. $52 193.61
   7. $7173.32

**B.** 1. $466.70
   3. $14 625.54
   5. $10 321.48
   7. $4 278 801.75
   9. $42 940.38
   11. $1161.31
   13. (a) $29 546.64
       (b) $792.35
       (c) $30 338.99
   15. $5450.07

*Schedule of Accumulation of Discount*

| Payment interval | coupon $b = 3\%$ | Interest on book $i = 3.25\%$ | Discount accumulated | Book value | Discount balance |
|---|---|---|---|---|---|
| 0 | | | | 4922.85 | 77.15 |
| 1 | 150.00 | 159.99 | 9.99 | 4932.84 | 67.16 |
| 2 | 150.00 | 160.32 | 10.32 | 4943.16 | 56.84 |
| 3 | 150.00 | 160.65 | 10.65 | 4953.81 | 46.19 |
| 4 | 150.00 | 161.00 | 11.00 | 4964.81 | 35.19 |
| 5 | 150.00 | 161.36 | 11.36 | 4976.17 | 23.83 |
| 6 | 150.00 | 161.73 | 11.73 | 4987.90 | 12.10 |
| 7 | 150.00 | 162.10 | 12.10 | 5000.00 | — |
| Total | 1050.00 | 1127.15 | 77.15 | | |

3. 57.86; 1057.86

*Schedule of Amortization of Premium*

| Payment interval | Coupon $b = 6\%$ | Interest on book $i = 5\%$ | Premium amortized | Book value | Premium balance |
|---|---|---|---|---|---|
| 0 | | | | 1057.86 | 57.86 |
| 1 | 60.00 | 52.89 | 7.11 | 1050.75 | 50.75 |
| 2 | 60.00 | 52.54 | 7.46 | 1043.29 | 43.29 |
| 3 | 60.00 | 52.16 | 7.84 | 1035.45 | 35.45 |
| 4 | 60.00 | 51.77 | 8.23 | 1027.22 | 27.22 |
| 5 | 60.00 | 51.36 | 8.64 | 1018.58 | 18.58 |
| 6 | 60.00 | 50.93 | 9.07 | 1009.51 | 9.51 |
| 7 | 60.00 | 50.49 | 9.51 | 1000.00 | — |
| Total | 420.00 | 362.14 | 57.86 | | |

## Exercise 15.2

**A.** 1. (a) $4877.98
      (b) $20 122.02
   3. (a) $1453.37
      (b) $8546.63

**B.** 1. (a) $14 304.00;
          $114 304.00
      (b) $6359.60;
          $106 359.60
   3. (a) $–4435.32;
          $20 564.68
      (b) $3687.99;
          $28 687.99
   5. $4 569 384.48
   7. $103 723.59

## Exercise 15.3

**A.** 1. –$77.15;
          $4922.85

**B.** 1. $976.84
3. $387.55

## Exercise 15.4

1. 5.868%
3. 7.9%
5. 9.26%

## Exercise 15.5

**A.** 1. (a) $558.24
(b) $6399.60
3. (a) $22.03
(b) $3104.14

**B.** 1. (a) $500.00
(b) $265.25
(c) $765.25
(d) $10 868.38
3. (a) $62.50
(b) $143.33
(c) $205.83
(d) $2246.16

**C.** 1. (a) $2699.00
(b) $64 776.00
(c) $10 224.00
3. $2419.29; totals
are $16 935.03;
$3064.99;
$20 000.02
5. $2840.83
7. (a) $495.27
(b) $9598.44
9. (a) $4275.00
(b) $1124.00
(c) $5399.00
(d) $36 976.00
11. (a) $302.01
(b) $21 903.91
(c) $257.62
(d) $764.19
(e) $97 252.61;
totals are
$54 361.80;
$45 637.43;
$99 999.23
13. (a) $24 750.00
(b) $8604.00
(c) $33 354.00
(d) $13 931.00

(e) $107 196.00
(f) $232 277.00;
totals are
$172 073.00;
$127 921.00;
$300 000.00

## Review Exercise

1. (a) $5336.73
(b) $4550.35
3. $26 174.35
5. $1129.61;
$21 129.61
7. (a) $15 620.41
(b) $84 379.59
(c) $85 664.12
9. $4527.64
11. (a) $12.56%
13. $272.16;
$4727.84
15. gain of
$1899.18
17. $7.65%
19. (a) $44 248.79
(b) $48 017.12
(c) $1795.38
21. (a) $9268.75
(b) $28 862.02
(c) $1873.21
(d) Totals are
$92 687.50;
$17 312.54;
$110 000.04
23. (a) $13 750.00
(b) $8279.90
(c) $22 029.90
(d) $72 194.23
(e) $5989.29
(f) Totals are
$66 239.23;
$33 760.77;
$100 000.00
25. (a) $2469.40
(b) $10 612.00
(c) $21 194.78
(d) $788.92
27. (a) $n = 38.468063$
(b) $8318.12

## Self-Test

1. $9269.44
3. $367.77 (premium)
5. $4596.98
7. 12.46%
9. 12.94%
11. $240.24
13. $603 102.20

# CHAPTER 16

## Exercise 16.1

**A.** 1. Alternative 2;
PV $44 634;
$53 448
3. Alternative 1;
PV $22 205;
$23 384
5. Alternative 1
PV $2000;
$2392.76

**B.** 1. Alternative 2;
PV $62 363;
$73 601
3. Offer A; PV
$30 026; $29 769
5. Buy; Cost of
buying = $83 564;
leasing = $106 036

## Exercise 16.2

**A.** 1. Reject; NPV is
−$5367
3. Alternative 1; NPV
$234; $203
5. Alternative 1; NPV
$1666; $352

**B.** 1. Project B; NPV
$2568; $1787
3. No; NPV is
−$8561
5. Yes; NPV $5696
7. Yes; NPV $5142

## Exercise 16.3

**A.** 1. 25.3%
3. 20.7%

**B.** 1. at 18%, NPV
= $6102; at 20%
NPV = −$292;
R.O.I. = 19.9%
3. at 18%, NPV
= $1286; at 20%,
NPV = −$104;
R.O.I. = 19.9%
5. at 22%, NPV
= $148; at 24%,
NPV = −$1538;
R.O.I. = 22.2%

## Review Exercise

1. Alternative B;
PV $51 624;
$52 161
3. Alternative 1;
NPV $3916; $3597
5. −$22 226
7. at 26%, NPV
= $370; at 28%,
NPV = −$1939;
R.O.I. = 26.3%
9. at 16%, NPV
= $47 272; at 18%,
NPV = −$22 226;
R.O.I = 17.4%
11. at 24%, NVP
= $2035; at 26%,
NVP = −$184;
R.O.I = 25.8%
13. Project B; PV
$22 256, $22 909
15. −$1215
17. Yes; NPV = $28 940

## Self-Test

1. Alternative A; PV
$13 552; $10 856
3. at 16%, NPV =
$3466; at 18%,
NPV =−$4386;
R.O.I. = 16.9%
5. Proposal B; NPV
$701; $1427

# Index

## A

accumulated balance, 661–666
accumulated value of one dollar per
  period, 428
accumulation factor, 332
  *see also* compounding factor
accumulation of discount, 650–652
acquisition of assets, 682
affordability rules, 610
amortization
  finding size of final payment, 600–606
  general annuities. *See* amortization
    involving general annuities
  generally, 570
  meaning of, 570
  residential mortgages. *See* residential
    mortgages
  simple annuities. *See* amortization
    involving simple annuities
amortization involving general annuities
  finding interest paid, 593–597
  finding outstanding principal,
    589–592
  finding periodic payment, 588–589
  finding principal repaid, 593–597
  outstanding balance when all payments
    are equal, 589–591
  outstanding balance when all payments
    except final payment are equal,
    591–592
  partial amortization schedules,
    593–597
amortization involving simple annuities
  finding interest paid, 579–585
  finding outstanding principal balance,
    575–579
  finding principal repaid, 579–585
  outstanding principal balance when all
    payments are equal, 575–578
  outstanding principal balance when all
    payments except final payment are
    equal, 578–579
  periodic payment, 570–571
  prospective method, 577
  retrospective method, 577
amortization of the premium, 649–650
amortization schedule
  *see also* loan repayment schedules
  computer application, 584–585, 597
  described, 571
  general annuities, 588–589
  partial amortization schedules, 579–585,
    593–597
  simple annuities, 571–574
  when all payments are equal (blended
    payments), 572–574
  when all payments except final payment
    are equal, 574
amount, 295
  *see also* future value
amount of loan, 331
annual rent, 423
annuities certain, 423

annuities due
  deferred annuities due, 542–551
  defined, 508
  described, 424
  financial calculator, 512–514
  general annuities due. *See* general
    annuities due
  *versus* ordinary annuities, 510
annuity
  annual rent, 423
  annuities certain, 423
  annuity due. *See* annuities due
  basic concepts, 423
  compounding factor for annuities, 428
  constant-growth annuities, 494–499
  contingent annuities, 423
  deferred annuity. *See* deferred annuity
  defined, 423
  described, 423
  future value of an annuity, 427
  general annuity, 424, 588–597
  geometric progression, 428
  investment period, determination of, 457
  loan repayment, determination of, 457
  ordinary annuity, 424
  ordinary general annuities. *See* ordinary
    general annuities
  ordinary simple annuity. *See* ordinary
    simple annuity
  payment interval, 423
  payment period, 423
  periodic rent, 423
  perpetuity. *See* perpetuity
  simple annuity, 424, 570–585
  term of an annuity, 423
  types of, 423–425
Apple Computer Inc., 272
applications
  *see also* basic applications
  discounting negotiable financial
    instruments at compound interest,
    357–363
  investment decision applications. *See*
    investment decision applications
  simple interest applications. *See* simple
    interest applications
average investment method, 655–657

## B

bigger-the-better principle, 683
Bills of Exchange Act, 295
bird-in-the-hand principle, 683
blended payments, 283
blended residential mortgage payments,
  613–614
bond exchange, 654
bond market, 491, 699
bond rate, 630, 638–642
bond schedules
  accumulation of discount, 650–652
  amortization of premium, 649–650
  book value of a bond, 652–653

bonds
  alternative method for finding purchase
    price, 642–646
  average investment method, 655–657
  basic concepts and terminology,
    630–631
  bond rate, 630, 638–642
  book value, 652–653
  buying bonds, 631
  buying bonds on the market, 654–655
  coupon rate, 630
  coupons, 630
  debentures, 630
  denomination, 630
  described, 630
  direct method of computing premium
    or discount, 642–646
  discount, 638–648
  due date, 630
  face value, 630, 639
  gain or loss on sale of bond, 652–653
  market rate, 638–642
  maturity date, 630
  maturity value, 630
  method of averages, 655–657
  nominal rate, 630
  par value, 630
  premium, 638–648
  principal, 630
  purchase price of bond bought on an
    interest date, 631–634
  purchase price of bonds between interest
    dates, 634–636
  quoted price of a bond, 654–655
  redeemable at a premium, 630
  redeemable at par, 630
  redemption date, 630
  redemption value, 630
  trial and error method, 657
  yield rate, 633, 638–642, 654–657
book value of a bond, 652–653
book value of the debt, 667

## C

calculator. *See* financial calculator; scientific
  calculator; TI BAII Plus; specific
  computations
Canada Mortgage and Housing Corporation
  (CMHC), 609–610
capital expenditures, 682–683
capital investment projects, 682
case studies
  building a business, 718
  business of borrowing, 324
  choosing a credit card, 419–420
  comparing car loans, 420
  cost of financing pay now or pay later,
    290–291
  debt consolidation, 324–325
  fiscal fitness, 504
  getting the picture, 466–467
  investing in bonds, 677–678